ELECTRONIC COMMERCE

Electronic Commerce
A Managerial Perspective

Efraim Turban
ßCity University of Hong Kong

Jae Lee
Korea Advanced Institute of Science and Technology

David King
Comshare Inc.

H. Michael Chung
California State University, Long Beach

Prentice Hall, Upper Saddle River, NJ 07458

VP/Editorial Director: Jim Boyd
Editor-in-Chief: Mickey Cox
Acquisitions Editor: David Alexander
Managing Editor: Lucinda Gatch
Editorial Assistant: Lori Cerreto
Senior Marketing Manager: Kris King
Production Coordinator: Kelly Warsak
Permissions Coordinator: Monica Stipanov
Director of Production: Michael Weinstein
Production Manager: Gail Steier de Acevedo
Manufacturing Buyer: Natacha St. Hill Moore
Senior Manufacturing and Prepress Manager: Vincent Scelta
Cover Design: Joan O'Conner
Cover Illustration: John Bleck/Showcase Stock
Full Service Composition: UG / GGS Information Services, Inc.

Library of Congress Cataloging-in-Publication Data

Electronic commerce : a managerial perspective / Efraim Turban …
[et al.].
     p. cm.
   Includes index.
   ISBN 0-13-975285-4
   1. Electronic commerce.   2. Electronic commerce—Management.
3. Information technology—Management.   4. Business
enterprises—Computer networks.   I. Turban, Efraim.
   HF5548.32   .E34   1999
   658' .05—dc21

                                                        99-22245
                                                        CIP

Reprinted with corrections December, 1999.

Prentice-Hall International (UK) Limited, London
Prentice-Hall of Australia Pty. Limited, Sydney
Prentice-Hall Canada, Inc., Toronto
Prentice-Hall Hispanoamericana, S.A., Mexico
Prentice-Hall of India Private Limited, New Delhi
Prentice-Hall of Japan, Inc., Tokyo
Prentice-Hall (Singapore) Pte Ltd.
Editora Prentice-Hall do Brasil, Ltda., Rio de Janeiro

Printed in the United States of America

10 9 8 7 6 5 4 3 2

To all those eager to learn
about electronic commerce

Brief Contents

Contents

Preface

As we enter the second millennium we experience one of the most important changes in our lives—the move to an Internet-based society. Almost everything will be changed at home, in school, at work, in the government—even in our leisure activities. Some changes are already here and they are spreading around the globe. Others are just beginning. One of the most significant changes is in the manner we conduct business especially in how we manage the marketplace and commerce.

Electronic commerce (EC) describes the manner in which transactions take place over networks, mostly the Internet. It is the process of electronically buying and selling goods, services, and information. Certain EC applications, such as buying and selling stocks or books on the Internet, areß growing at a rate of several hundred percent every year. Electronic commerce could have an impact on a significant portion of the world, on businesses, professions, and, of course, on people.

However, the impact of EC is not just the creation of Web-based corporations. It is the building of a new industrial order. Vice President Albert Gore Jr. put it this way:

> We are on the verge of a revolution that is just as profound as the change in the economy that came with the industrial revolution. Soon electronic networks will allow people to transcend the barriers of time and distance and take advantage of global markets and business opportunities not even imaginable today, opening up a new world of economic possibility and progress.

Such a revolution brings a myriad of opportunities as well as risks. Bill Gates is aware of that, as Microsoft is continually developing Internet and EC products and services. Yet, Gates said that Microsoft is always two years away from failure, that somewhere out there is a competitor, unborn and unknown, who will render your business model obsolete. Bill Gates knows that competition today is not among products, but among business models. He knows that irrelevancy is a bigger risk than inefficiency. What is true for Microsoft is true for just about every other company. The hottest and most dangerous new business models out there are on the Web.

The purpose of this book is to describe what EC is; how it is being conducted and managed; and its major opportunities, limitations, issues, and risks. Electronic commerce is an interdisciplinary topic and, therefore, it should be of interest to managers and professional people in any functional area of the business world.

In addition, people in government, education, health services, and more could benefit from learning about EC. This book is structured around the notion that EC applications, such as home banking or electronic fund transfers, require certain technological infrastructures and other support mechanisms. The applications are divided into business-to-consumers, business-to-business, and intrabusiness. The infrastructure is in the areas of hardware, networks, and software. The support services range from secured payment systems to communication standards and legal issues.

This book is one of the first texts entirely dedicated to EC. It is written by experienced authors who share academic as well as real-world experiences. It is a comprehensive text that can be used in a one-semester course, or it can supplement a text on Internet fundamentals, on MIS, or on marketing.

Features of the book

Several features are unique to this book. They include:

- *Managerial Orientation*
  Electronic commerce can be approached from two major aspects: technological and managerial. This text uses the second approach. Most of the presentations are about EC applications and implementation and are geared toward functional and general managers. However, we do recognize the importance of the technology; therefore, we present the essentials of EC infrastructure in chapter 11. We also provide some more detailed technology material in the appendices at the end of the book.

- *Interdisciplinary Approach*
  Electronic commerce is interdisciplinary and we illustrate this throughout the book. Major related disciplines are Accounting, Finance, Information Systems, Marketing, Management, and Human Resources Management. In addition, some nonbusiness disciplines are related, especially Computer Science, Engineering, Psychology, Political Science, and the Legal field. Finally, Economics plays a major role in the understanding of EC.

- *Real-World Orientation*
  Extensive, vivid examples from large corporations, small businesses, and government and not-for-profit agencies make concepts come alive by showing students the capabilities of EC, its cost and justification, and some of the innovative ways real corporations are using EC in their operations.

- *Solid Theoretical Background*
  Throughout the book we present the theoretical foundations necessary for understanding EC, ranging from consumer behavior to economic theory of competition. Furthermore, we provide extensive references, Web site addresses, and many exercises to supplement the theoretical presentations.

- *Most Current*
  The book presents the most current topics of EC, as evidenced by the many 1998 and 1999 citations. Topics such as extranets, organizational knowledge bases, Web-based supply chain systems, and EC economics are presented both from the theoretical point of view and from the application side.

- *Economic Justification*
  Information technology is mature enough to stand the difficult test of economic justification, a topic ignored by most textbooks. It is our position that investment in EC must be scrutinized like any other investment, despite the difficulties of measuring technology benefits.

- *Integrated Systems*
  In contrast with other books that highlight isolated Internet-based systems, we emphasize those systems that support the enterprise and supply chain management. Interorganizational systems are particularly highlighted, including the latest innovations in global EC and in Electronic Data Interchange (EDI).

- *Global Perspective*
  The importance of global competition, partnerships, and trading is rapidly increasing. Electronic commerce facilitates export and import, managing multinational companies, and trading electronically around the globe. International examples are provided throughout the book.

- *Comprehensiveness and Ease of Reading*
  All major topics of EC are covered. Furthermore, the book is user friendly, easy to understand and follow, and full of interesting real-world examples and "war stories" that keep the reader's interest at a high level.

Organization of the book

The book is divided into five parts composed of 12 chapters with three technology appendices supplementing them.

PART I—INTRODUCTION

In this part we provide an overview of the entire book as well as the fundamentals of EC and some of its terminology (chapter 1).

PART II—APPLICATIONS

In this part we describe EC applications in six chapters. Chapters 2 and 3 are dedicated mostly to business-to-consumer commerce (chapter 2 deals with retailing, chapter 3 with Internet consumers and market research). Chapter 4 deals with EC advertisement, which is mostly related to business-to-consumer. In chapter 5 we present EC in service industries. These can be for individual consumers, for businesses or for both. Chapters 7 and 8 deal with various aspects of business-to-business and intrabusiness EC.

PART III—SUPPORTING ELECTRONIC COMMERCE

To support EC one needs various infrastructures and mechanisms, most importantly the payments (chapter 8), which are more relevant to business-to-consumer activities. Corporate strategy toward EC, especially planning, justification, and implementation, are treated in chapter 9. The last chapter in this part, chapter 10, deals with issues of public policy, privacy, legal issues, and ethics.

PART IV—TECHNOLOGICAL INFRASTRUCTURE

The technological infrastructure is covered in chapter 11, with details presented in Appendices A–C.

PART V—ADVANCED EC TOPICS

The book concludes in chapter 12 with a glance at the economics of EC as well as at several other issues, such as global EC, small businesses and EC, and EC research. This chapter also provides an overview of future EC directions.

Learning aids

We developed a number of learning aids including:

- *Chapter Outline*
  The detailed outlines in the Contents at the beginning of the book provide a quick indication of the major topics covered.

- *Learning Objectives*
  Learning objectives at the beginning of each chapter help students focus their efforts and alert them to the important concepts to be discussed.

- *Opening Vignettes*
  Each chapter opens with a *real-world* example that illustrates the importance of EC to modern corporations. These cases were carefully chosen to call attention to the major topics covered in the chapters.

- *Managerial Issues*
  The final section of every chapter explores some of the special concerns managers face as they adapt to doing business in cyberspace.

- *Key Terms*
  All boldface terms introduced within the chapter appear in a list at the end of the chapter and are defined in the glossary at the end of the book.

- *Chapter Summary*
  The chapter summary is linked to the learning objectives introduced at the beginning of each chapter.

- *End-of-Chapter Exercises*
  Different types of questions measure students' comprehension and their ability to apply knowledge. Questions for Review ask students to summarize the concepts introduced. Discussion Questions are intended to promote class discussion and develop critical thinking skills. Exercises are challenging assignments that require students to apply what they have learned. The Group Assignments are class projects designed to foster teamwork.

- *Internet Exercises*
  About 100 hands-on exercises send students to interesting Web sites to conduct research, investigate an application, or learn about state-of-the-art *technology.*

- *Application Cases*
  In-text cases highlight real-world problems encountered by corporations as they develop and implement EC.

- *Real-World Cases*
  Each chapter ends with a somewhat more in-depth real-world case. Case questions follow.

Supplementary materials

The following material is available to support this book:

- *Instructor's Manual with Test Item File* (Test Bank)
  This manual includes answers to all review and discussion questions, exercises, and case questions. The printed Test Item File includes multiple-

choice questions for each chapter. An electronic version of the Test Item File is available in the form of the Windows PH Test Manager.

- *PowerPoint Lecture Notes*
  An extensive set of Microsoft PowerPoint lecture notes, oriented toward text learning objectives, is available for each chapter. Lecture Notes can be downloaded from the text's Web site at www.prenhall.com/turban.

- *Web Site*
  The book is supported by a Companion Web site that includes:
  a. A password-protected faculty area where instructors can download the PowerPoint Lecture Notes and the Instructor's Manual.
  b. URLs for all the major topics in the book with links to other sources.
  c. Links to a large number of case studies, including customer success stories and academically oriented cases.
  d. Links to many EC vendors' sites.
  e. Supplemental material for each chapter.
  f. Several case studies, some with teaching notes

Acknowledgments

Many individuals helped us create this text. Faculty feedback was solicited via reviews and through a focus group. We are grateful to the following faculty for their contributions.

David Ambrosini
Cabrillo College

Deborah Ballou
University of Notre Dame

Martin Barriff
Illinois Institute of Technology

Joseph Brooks
University of Hawaii

John Bugado
National University

Christer Carlsson
Abo Akademi University

Jack Cook
State University of New York at Geneseo

Larry Corman
Fort Lewis College

Mary Culnan
Georgetown University

Ted Ferretti
Northeastern University

Jeffrey Johnson
Utah State University

Morgan Jones
University of North Carolina

Douglas Kline
Sam Houston State University

Byungtae Lee
University of Illinois at Chicago

Michael McLeod
East Carolina University

Susan McNamara
Northeastern University

Bud Mishra
New York University

William Nance
San Jose State University

Linda Salchenberger
Loyola University of Chicago

George Schell
University of North Carolina at Wilmington

J. P. Shim
Missisippi State University

Kan Sugandh
DeVry Institute of Technology

Linda Volonino
Canisius College

Pirkko Walden–Abo Akademi
University, Finland

James Zemanek
East Carolina University

Many students at California State University, Long Beach; City University of Hong Kong; and Korea Advanced Institute of Science and Technology (KAIST) participated in this project in many ways. Some helped us to find materials while others provided feedback. There are too many to name, but thanks goes to all of you.

Several individuals helped us with the administrative work. Special mention goes to Judy Lang of Eastern Illinois University, who helped in typing and editing; to Flavia Chung Yan from City University of Hong Kong, who created the lecture notes in *PowerPoint*; and to Duan Ning Zhou from City University of Hong Kong, who assisted in organizing the chapters. We thank all of them for the dedication and the superb performance shown throughout the project.

We also recognize the various organizations and corporations that provided us with permission to reproduce material.

Finally, thanks goes to the Prentice Hall team who helped us from the inception of the project under the leadership of David Alexander. The dedicated staff include Keith Kryszczun, Lucinda Gatch, Lori Cerreto, Kelly Warsak, and Gail Steier.

CHAPTER 1

Foundations of Electronic Commerce

Learning Objectives

Upon completion of this chapter, the reader will be able to:

- Define electronic commerce (EC) and describe its various categories.

- Distinguish between electronic markets and interorganizational systems.

- Describe the benefits of EC to organizations, consumers, and society.

- Describe the limitations of EC.

- Describe and discuss the framework of EC and its major components.

- Understand the forces that drive the widespread use of EC.

- Describe and discuss the changes that will be caused by EC.

- Discuss some major managerial issues regarding EC.

1.1 Intel Corp. and Happy Puppy

THE CASE OF INTEL CORP.[1]

The Problem

Intel Corp., the world's largest producer of chips (ICs), sells its products to thousands of manufacturers. Most of its business is in the PC market, in which companies such as Dell Computers use only Intel's chips ("Intel Inside" logo). However, other manufacturers use either or also the competitors' chips. In the ICs market the competition is intense. Intel creates customized catalogs and sends them to its potential customers together with information on product availability. Until summer 1998 it was all done on paper, making the distribution process slow, expensive, and frequently not up to date.

---

[1]Source: Compiled from *InternetWeek* (November 23, 1998), pp. 1, 98.

The Solution

Companies such as Cisco Systems and Dell Computers started to use the Web to do their business in 1995 and 1996 on a small scale; they were slowly pushing for large-scale adoption. In contrast, Intel did not rush into doing business electronically. However, in summer 1998, when Intel launched its online business, it did so instantly. Intel disclosed that sales on its EC site had gone from zero to $1 billion per month—all in the first month of operation. It took Cisco Systems (chapter 6) more than a year to achieve this! Why is this so?

Electronic commerce in 1998 was much more mature than in 1995 and 1996, and Intel created a much more comprehensive system. Intel approached EC as a "new way of doing business," and, therefore, management decided to do something big so their customers would know that they were serious. Incidentally, the $1 billion per month exceeds the EC sales volume of all companies during 1995 in the United States.

The site is a self-service extranet, called E-Business Program, which is focused on procurement and customer support for a range of products, including microprocessors, motherboards, embedded chips, chipsets, and flash memory. In 1998, it reached several hundred small and midsize business customers worldwide, who entered orders manually using browsers. Access to the site is restricted to authorized business partners.

Placing orders is only part of what Intel offers. The site also features self-service order tracking and a library of product documentation and road maps that replace the work of customer service representatives who previously sent information manually to customers.

Intel specifically targeted the small and midsize customers because they had previously communicated with Intel largely by phone and fax, whereas larger companies typically were connected to Intel on **electronic data interchange** (EDI) networks. The site does not offer an automated way to funnel data into customers' business applications, but it is integrated with Intel's own back office. Eleven of Intel's larger customers were connected in fall 1998 to another system called Supply Line Management, which lets Intel link to customer plants across the Internet to track part consumption.

The Results

Intel officials said they would begin measuring cost savings in 1999 and noted that the company has been able to eliminate 45,000 faxes per quarter to Taiwan alone. The customers are using the site on a consistent basis.

Intermediaries who distribute Intel components said they are not threatened by Intel's EC push. Earle Zucht, senior vice president for semiconductor marketing at Wyle Electronics, said his company still offers value in selling smaller quantities. "I don't think Intel's strategy is to touch 100,000 customers a day," Zucht said. "Someone has to stock and sell by ones and twos; someone has to pull them and pack them the way the customer asks for them."

THE CASE OF HAPPY PUPPY

The Problem

Making a reasonable profit from creating electronic games can be a difficult task, especially for independent game writers. The games go through several marketing channels, each taking a share of the profits, leaving very little to the creators. Happy Puppy's founders had this experience until they decided to use the Internet to sell their games directly to consumers. Within a year the firm became a success story.

The Solution

Established in 1995, the site is a pioneer EC marketer. This is how the Internet works for Happy Puppy: Demonstration software of computer games, written by both the company's founders and other companies, are placed on the company's Web site (http:www.happypuppy.net) as shareware, demos, or freeware. Game-related downloads are also available. Customers can download the demos and try them free of cost. If customers like a game, they can purchase its full version. The site also includes a weekly newsletter, bulletin board, and chat room.

The Happy Puppy Web site is well known. Several million copies of games are downloaded every month. It is referred to by more than 10,000 links available in other Web sites. The company's employees search EC bulletin boards and newsgroups for queries or discussions related to electronic games. When they find a relevant item, they send e-mail to the parties involved or post a note on the bulletin board referencing Happy Puppy's Web site.

The Results

Happy Puppy's owners make money not only from selling their own and others' games but also from selling ads to other companies on their popular Web site. In addition, they allow customers to download demo software only after completing a questionnaire. The results are analyzed and sold to electronic game manufacturers. Because the site is visited by more than 4 million users a month, it has become a popular place for developers, game companies, job seekers, and many others to advertise.

1.2   Definitions and Content of the Field

The two opening vignettes illustrate a new way of conducting business[2]: electronically, using networks and the Internet. These are examples of *electronic commerce* (EC), in which business transactions take place via telecommunications networks. The Happy Puppy case illustrated a *business-to-consumer* (B2C) (customer) transaction, whereas Intel's case dealt with *business-to-business* (B2B) transactions.

The opening vignettes, and especially Intel's case, point to some issues that involve implementation of EC. These issues are discussed in subsequent chapters. For example:

- How to deal with the introduction of a new way of doing business (chapter 9)
- Selling to individual customers (chapters 2 and 3) versus to corporations (chapters 6 and 7)
- The economic impacts, especially on competition (chapter 12)
- The extranet as a B2B infrastructure (chapter 7)
- The role of the intermediaries (chapters 2, 5, 12)
- The interaction of EC and supply chain management (chapters 6, 7, 9)
- Improving customer service (chapter 3)
- The differences between EDI and the extranet (chapter 7)
- Advertisement on popular sites (chapter 4)

Electronic commerce could become a significant global economic element in the next century (Clinton and Gore 1997). The infrastructure for EC is *networked computing,* which is emerging as the standard computing environment in business, home, and government. Networked computing connects several computers and other electronic devices by telecommunication networks. This allows users to access informa-

---

[2]In this book, a reference to a "business" means either a private or a public organization.

APPLICATION CASE 1.1

Egghead Becomes a Virtual Software Company

Egghead Software was a successful retailer, selling PC software in North America. The company grew 20 percent in a year, until 1995, when sales reached a peak of $434 million. Since then, however, sales declined about 10 percent per year, and the losses grew to $40 million in 1997. The company closed its unprofitable stores, but due to competition from large companies such as CompUSA and Best Buy, losses continued to increase. In 1997, the company started to sell on the Internet on three Web sites and also to operate a telephone mail-order system. However, closing stores did not help much. By February 1998, the mounting losses forced the company to close all its stores. The company changed its name to Egghead.com and concentrated on EC. Within a week its stock price jumped 60 percent. By late 1998 the company's revenues increased significantly when the company started to sell nonsoftware products and conduct auctions online. Its stock price climbed 300 percent.

Source: Condensed from *Infoworld* (February 9, 1998) p. 53, and *Internet World* (March 9, 1998), p. 78.

---

tion stored in several places and to communicate and collaborate with others from their desktop computers. Although some people still use a stand-alone computer exclusively, the vast majority of people use computers connected to a global networked environment known as the **Internet**, or its counterpart within organizations, called an **intranet**. An intranet is a corporate network that functions with Internet technologies, such as browsers, using Internet protocols. Another computer environment is an **extranet**, a network that links the intranets of business partners over the Internet (chapter 7).

This new breed of computing is helping large numbers of organizations, private and public, in manufacturing, agriculture, and services, not only to excel but also frequently to survive. An interesting example is Egghead Software (Application Case 1.1).

Why are companies resorting to EC? The reason is simple. *Information technology* (IT) in general and EC in particular have become the major facilitators of business activities in the world today (Tapscott and Caston 1993, Mankin 1996, and Gill 1996). Electronic commerce is also a catalyst of fundamental changes in the structure, operations, and management of organizations (Dertouzos 1997).

DEFINITIONS

Electronic commerce is an emerging concept that describes the process of buying and selling or exchanging of products, services, and information via computer networks including the Internet. Kalakota and Whinston (1997) define EC from these perspectives:

- From a **communications perspective**, EC is the delivery of information, products/services, or payments over telephone lines, computer networks, or any other electronic means.
- From a **business process perspective**, EC is the application of technology toward the automation of business transactions and work flow.
- From a **service perspective**, EC is a tool that addresses the desire of firms, consumers, and management to cut service costs while improving the quality of goods and increasing the speed of service delivery.
- From an **online perspective**, EC provides the capability of buying and selling products and information on the Internet and other online services.

The term *commerce* is viewed by some as transactions conducted between business partners. Therefore, the term *electronic commerce* seems to be fairly narrow to some people. Thus, many use the term **e-business.** It refers to a broader definition of EC, not just buying and selling but also servicing customers and collaborating with business partners, and conducting electronic transactions within an organization. According to Lou Gerstner, IBM's CEO: "E-business is all about cycle time, speed, globalization, enhanced productivity, reaching new customers and sharing knowledge across institutions for competitive advantage."

In this book we use the term *electronic commerce* in its broadest scope, which is basically equivalent to e-business.

Pure versus Partial EC

Electronic commerce can take many forms depending on the degree of digitization of the product (service) sold, the process, and the delivery agent (or intermediary). Choi et. al (1997) created a model that explains the possible configurations of these three dimensions (Figure 1.1). A product can be physical or digital, an agent can be physical or digital, and the process can be physical or digital. These create eight cubes, each of which has three dimensions. In traditional commerce all dimensions are physical (lower left cube), and in pure EC all dimensions are digital (upper right cube). All other cubes include a mix of digital and physical dimensions. If there is at least one digital dimension we will consider the situation EC (but not a pure one). For example, buying a book from Amazon is not pure, because the book is delivered by FedEx. However, buying software from Egghead is pure EC because the delivery, payment, and agent are digital.

Electronic commerce uses several technologies ranging from EDI to e-mail. For example, buying food from a vending machine using a *smart card* can also be viewed as EC.

FIGURE 1.1 The Dimensions of Electronic Commerce.

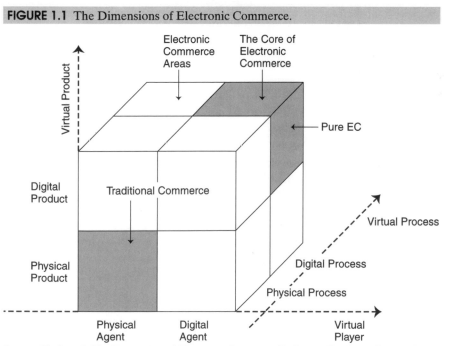

Source: Choi et al, *The Economics of Electronic Commerce* (Indianapolis: Macmillan Technical Publications, 1997), p. 18.

THE EC FIELD

The Framework of EC

Many people think EC is just having a Web site, but EC is much more than that. There are dozens of applications of EC such as home banking, shopping in online stores and malls, buying stocks, finding a job, conducting an auction, and collaborating electronically on research and development projects. To execute these applications, it is necessary to have supporting information and organizational infrastructure and systems. Figure 1.2 shows that the EC applications are supported by infrastructures (chapter 11), and their implementation is dependent on four major areas (shown as supporting pillars): people, public policy, technical standards and protocols, and other organizations. The EC management coordinates the applications, infrastructures, and pillars.

Figure 1.2 can be viewed as a framework for understanding the relationships among the EC components and for conducting research in the field (Zwass 1996). In

FIGURE 1.2 A Framework for Electronic Commerce.

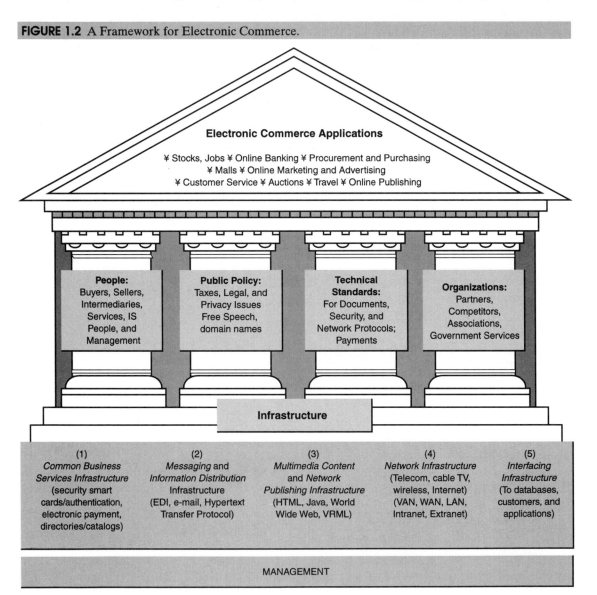

Electronic Commerce Applications

¥ Stocks, Jobs ¥ Online Banking ¥ Procurement and Purchasing
¥ Malls ¥ Online Marketing and Advertising
¥ Customer Service ¥ Auctions ¥ Travel ¥ Online Publishing

| **People:** Buyers, Sellers, Intermediaries, Services, IS People, and Management | **Public Policy:** Taxes, Legal, and Privacy Issues Free Speech, domain names | **Technical Standards:** For Documents, Security, and Network Protocols; Payments | **Organizations:** Partners, Competitors, Associations, Government Services |

Infrastructure

| (1) *Common Business Services Infrastructure* (security smart cards/authentication, electronic payment, directories/catalogs) | (2) *Messaging and Information Distribution Infrastructure* (EDI, e-mail, Hypertext Transfer Protocol) | (3) *Multimedia Content and Network Publishing Infrastructure* (HTML, Java, World Wide Web, VRML) | (4) *Network Infrastructure* (Telecom, cable TV, wireless, Internet) (VAN, WAN, LAN, Intranet, Extranet) | (5) *Interfacing Infrastructure* (To databases, customers, and applications) |

MANAGEMENT

Source: Turban et al. 1999.

this book we will provide details on the applications, infrastructures, issues of the pillars, and management considerations. Less attention is devoted to the fast-changing infrastructure.

CLASSIFICATION OF EC APPLICATIONS

Applications of EC are divided into 3 categories
1. Buying and selling goods & services. These are usually referred to as **electronic markets**.
2. Facilitating inter and intra-organization flow of information, communication and collaboration. These are sometimes referred to as **interorganizational systems.**
3. Providing **customer service**.

ELECTRONIC MARKETS

A *market* is a network of interactions and relationships where information, products, services, and payments are exchanged. When the marketplace is electronic, the business center is not a physical building but rather a network-based location where business interactions occur (Figure 1.3). As can be seen in the figure, the electronic market is the place where shoppers and sellers meet. The market handles all the necessary

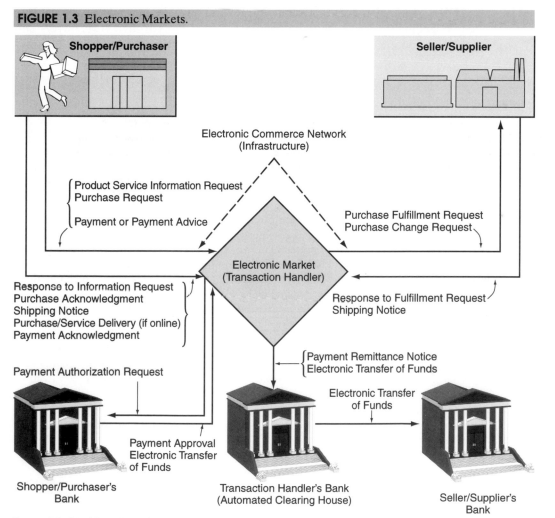

FIGURE 1.3 Electronic Markets.

Source: Modified from Senn (1996), p. 19.

transactions, including the transfer of money between banks. Details about this process will be provided in chapters 2, 8, and 11.

In electronic markets, the principal participants—transaction handlers, buyers, brokers, and sellers, are not only at different locations but seldom even know one another. The means of interconnection varies among parties and can change from event to event, even between the same parties.

INTERORGANIZATIONAL INFORMATION SYSTEMS AND ELECTRONIC MARKETS

An **IOS** involves information flow among two or more organizations. Its major objective is efficient transaction processing, such as transmitting orders, bills, and payments using EDI or extranets.[3] All relationships are predetermined; there is no negotiation, just execution. In contrast, in **electronic markets**, sellers and buyers negotiate, submit bids, agree on an order, and finish the execution on- or offline. The distinction between the two is shown in Table 1.1. Interorganizational systems are used exclusively for B2B applications, whereas electronic markets exist in both the B2B and B2C cases.

INTERORGANIZATIONAL INFORMATION SYSTEMS

Scope

An IOS is a unified system encompassing several business partners. A typical IOS will include a company and its suppliers and/or customers. Through IOS, buyers and sellers arrange routine business transactions. Information is exchanged over commu-

TABLE 1.1 Distinctive Features of Interorganizational Systems and Electronic Markets

Interorganizational Systems	*Electronic Markets*
Customer/supplier relationship is determined in advance with the anticipation it will be an ongoing relationship based on multiple transactions.	Two types of relationships may exist: • Customer/seller linkage is established at time of transactions and may be for one transaction only (i.e., purchase transaction). • Customer/seller purchase agreement is established whereby the seller agrees to deliver services or products to customer for a defined period of time (i.e., a subscription transaction).
Interorganizational systems may be built around private or publicly accessible networks.	Electronic markets are typically built around publicly accessible networks.
When outside communications companies are involved, they are typically value-added carriers (VANs).	When outside communications companies are involved, they are typically online service providers (which function as market makers).
Advance arrangements result in agreements on the nature and format of business documents that will be exchanged and payments.	Sellers determine, in conjunction with the market maker, which business transactions they will provide.
Advance arrangements are made so both parties know which communication networks will be integral to the system.	Customers and sellers independently determine which communication networks they will use in participating in the electronic market. The network used may vary from transaction to transaction.
Joint guidelines and expectations of each party are formulated so each knows how the system is to be used and when transactions will be submitted and received by each business partner.	No joint guidelines are drawn in advance.

Source: Senn (1996), p. 17.

[3]This discussion is based on Senn (1996). The term *electronic markets*, though it defines a portion of EC, is sometimes used interchangeably with EC.

nications networks using prearranged formats, so there is no need for telephone calls, paper documents, or business correspondence. In the past, IOSs were delivered on proprietary communication links. Now, however, many IOSs are moving to the Internet, mainly through extranets.

Types of Interorganizational Systems

The term *IOS* describes a variety of business activities, some of which are used in non-EC-related activities. The most prominent types of interorganizational systems are as follows:

- Electronic data interchange (EDI), which provides secured B2B connection over **value-added networks** (VANs) (chapter 6).
- Extranets, which provide secured B2B connection over the Internet (chapter 7).
- Electronic funds transfer (chapter 8).
- Electronic forms (chapter 6).
- Integrated messaging—delivery of e-mail and fax documents through a single electronic transmission system that can combine EDI, e-mail, and electronic forms (chapters 6 and 11).
- Shared databases—information stored in repositories is shared between trading partners and is accessible to all. Such databases are often used to reduce elapsed time in communicating information between parties as well as arranging cooperative activities. The sharing is mainly done over extranets (chapter 7).
- **Supply chain management**—cooperation between a company and its suppli-

---

APPLICATION CASE 1.2

Wal-Mart Uses IOSs

Being the world's largest retailer (more than $110 billion sales in 1999) does not guarantee success. Stiff competition drove very large retailers, such as Montgomery Ward, to file for bankruptcy. Wal-Mart is well aware of the need to innovate, use IT, and quickly respond to market fluctuations. To deal with today's business pressures, organizations recognized the need to integrate their internal systems. By doing so, production, marketing, finance, and other functional areas can coordinate their efforts to provide cost-effective products or services. Moreover, integrated operations are critical for providing superb customer service. Therefore, Wal-Mart embarked on using computers, networks, and specialized software to integrate its internal operations. However, such integration is not sufficient. To excel, Wal-Mart recognized the need to integrate its efforts with that of its suppliers and customers. Integrated networks and computing are changing worldwide

patterns of commerce. Wal-Mart, for example, provides each of its major suppliers with a monthly profit-and-loss statement for each of the goods received from that supplier.

One of the major reasons for the integration was the difficulty with the demand forecast, which is a key for inventory management and delivery scheduling. Usually, the retailer makes its forecast, the supplier makes its forecast, and the difference is systematic inefficiency: excess inventory, out-of-stock products, lost opportunity, and competitive disadvantage. The major retailers, under Wal-Mart leadership, created an initiative called Collaborative Forecasting and Replenishment (CFAR) to help retailers and their suppliers to collaborate on a *single*, short-term forecast and then freeze it, moving it from the realm of wishes to reality of work orders. Because the retailers and the suppliers are committed to the forecast, it becomes a plan that enables

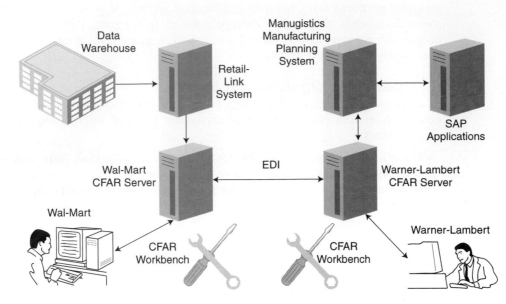

In a pilot project, Wal-Mart has linked up with one of it's key suppliers—Warner-Lambert, manufacturer of consumer products like Listerine—by using the Collaborative Forecasting and Replenishing (CFAR) standard. Through CFAR workbenches (spreadsheet-like documents with ample space for collaborative comments), Wal-Mart buyers and Warner-Lambert planners are able to jointly develop product forecasts.

much lower fluctuations and inventories. Also, out-of-stock situations, a major reason why customers leave stores, is reduced drastically. Finally, the retailers can offer a marketing plan because they no longer fear the suppliers' reactions.

A schematic view of a pilot project of CFAR that links Wal-Mart with a major supplier (Warner-Lambert) is shown in the above figure.

The process starts from a 30-terabyte (in 1998) data warehouse, which is designed for CFAR. The Retail Link System extracts the data relevant to Warner-Lambert products (such as Listerine) sales. The data are then stored in the CFAR server. Wal-Mart buying agents use a spreadsheet (CFAR Workbench) to make a pre-

liminary forecast. Copy of this forecast appears on Warner-Lambert's CFAR server, so Warner-Lambert's planners can add comments and suggested revisions. This is viewed by Wal-Mart planners. After a few iterations, an agreed-upon forecast is made for each product. This is used as a guide for the manufacturing planning at Warner-Lambert (using SAP applications) and the inventory management at Wal-Mart.

The communication between Wal-Mart and Warner-Lambert is done by EDI. The same system is used with other Wal-Mart suppliers.

Source: Condensed from C. B. Darling and J. W. Semich: "Extreme Integration," *Datamation* (November 1996). Also see *Business Week* (Oct 21, 1998), p. 140.

ers and/or customers regarding demand forecasting, inventory management, and orders fulfillment can reduce inventories, speed shipments, and enable just-in-time manufacturing. An example of such an EC system is provided in Application Case 1.2.

CLASSIFICATION OF THE EC FIELD BY THE NATURE OF THE TRANSACTIONS

A common classification of EC is by the nature of transaction. The following types are distinguished:

APPLICATION CASE 1.3

HBO Uses the Intranet to Boost Sales Efforts

Home Box Office (HBO), a cable television movie network, used more than 200 salespeople working directly with local cable operators in 10 geographic regions to develop marketing programs. These salespeople needed multimedia material such as graphics, sound bits, and video clips, which change constantly. The solution was found in the corporate intranet. With a single visit to the company's internal Web site, salespeople can download ready-to-use art that can be transformed into billboards, incorporated into four-color brochures, or integrated into custom mailings. They can also download ready-made radio commercials and video clips that can be converted into television ads. Previously, the company mailed videocassettes and other promotional material, frequently using expensive overnight mail. Now, the company can save time and money. Salespeople can show customers how an advertising campaign, which was designed only hours earlier, will work. The company has also published on the intranet a video tour of its New York headquarters to acquaint new salespeople with the company. Other training material is also available. Finally, a voice recognition system allows users to retrieve information from the intranet. This application increased productivity and provides better customer service.

Source: Based on S. V. Haar, "HBO Uses the Intranet to Boost Sales Efforts," *Interactive Week* (March 26, 1996), p. 40.

- **Business-to-business (B2B).** Most of EC today is of this type. It includes the IOS transactions described earlier and electronic market transactions between organizations.
- **Business-to-consumer (B2C).** These are retailing transactions with individual shoppers. The typical shopper at Amazon.com is a consumer, or customer.
- **Consumer-to-consumer (C2C).** In this category consumer sells directly to consumers. Examples are individuals selling in classified ads (e.g., www.classified2000.com) and selling residential property, cars, and so on. Advertising personal services on the Internet and selling knowledge and expertise is another example of C2C. Several auction sites allow individuals to put items up for auctions. Finally, many individuals are using intranets and other organizational internal networks to advertise items for sale or services.
- **Consumer-to-business (C2B).** This category includes individuals who sell products or services to organizations, as well as individuals who seek sellers, interact with them, and conclude a transaction.
- **Nonbusiness EC.** An increased number of nonbusiness institutions such as academic institutions, not-for-profit organizations, religious organizations, social organizations, and government agencies are using various types of EC to reduce their expenses (e.g., improve purchasing) or to improve their operations and customer service. (Note that in the previous categories one can usually replace the word *business* with *organization*.)
- **Intrabusiness (organizational) EC.** In this category we include all internal organizational activities, usually performed on intranets, that involve exchange of goods, services, or information. Activities can range from selling corporate products to employees to online training and cost-reduction activities. These will be described in chapter 7. Also see Application Case 1.3.

Notice that what we described as IOSs is a part of B2B. Electronic markets, on the other hand, can be associated with either B2B or with B2C.

FIGURE 1.4 How Does an Electronic Market Work?

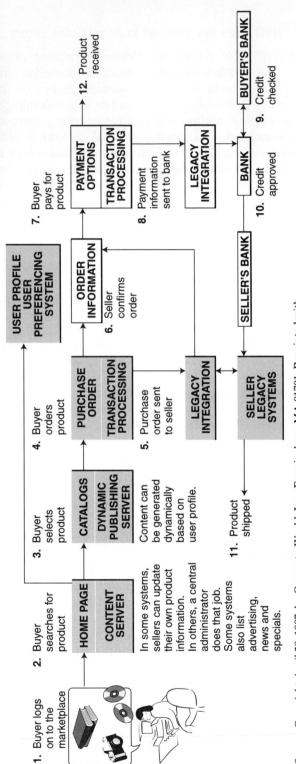

1. Buyer logs on to the marketplace

2. Buyer searches for product

3. Buyer selects product

4. Buyer orders product

5. Purchase order sent to seller

6. Seller confirms order

7. Buyer pays for product

8. Payment information sent to bank

9. Credit checked

10. Credit approved

11. Product shipped

12. Product received

HOME PAGE
CONTENT SERVER

In some systems, sellers can update their own product information. In others, a central administrator does that job. Some systems also list advertising, news and specials.

CATALOGS
DYNAMIC PUBLISHING SERVER

Content can be generated dynamically based on user profile.

USER PROFILE USER PREFERENCING SYSTEM

PURCHASE ORDER
TRANSACTION PROCESSING

ORDER INFORMATION

PAYMENT OPTIONS
TRANSACTION PROCESSING

LEGACY INTEGRATION

SELLER LEGACY SYSTEMS

LEGACY INTEGRATION

BANK

SELLER'S BANK

BUYER'S BANK

Source: Copyright April 28, 1997, by ComputerWorld, Inc., Farmingham, MA 01701. Reprinted with permission from *ComputerWorld.*

THE ELECTRONIC MARKETING PROCESS

For a trade to occur between a buyer and seller, a certain process must occur. This process may involve the steps shown in Figure 1.4. Obviously, if the buyer is an organization or a repeat customer, some of the steps may be changed or eliminated. Later, we deal with the major steps of this process, as well as with the specific products and services of electronic markets.

A BRIEF HISTORY OF EC

Electronic commerce applications started in the early 1970s, with such innovations as **electronic fund transfers** (EFT). However, the extent of the applications was limited to large corporations, financial institutions, and a few daring small businesses. Then came EDI, which expanded from financial transactions to other transaction processing and enlarged the participating companies from financial institutions to manufacturers, retailers, services, and so on. Many other applications followed, ranging from stock trading to travel reservation systems. Such systems were described as *telecommunication applications* and their strategic value was widely recognized. With the commercialization of the Internet in the early 1990s and its rapid growth to millions of potential customers, the term *electronic commerce* was coined, and EC applications expanded rapidly. One reason for the rapid expansion of the technology was the development of networks, protocols, software, and specifications. The other reason was the increase in competition and other business pressures, described in section 1.4. From 1995 to 1999 we have witnessed many innovative applications ranging from advertisement to auctions and virtual reality experiences. Almost every medium- and large-sized organization in the United States already has a Web site. Many are very extensive; for example, in 1999 General Motors Corporation (www.gm.com) offered 18,000 pages of information that included 98,000 links to its products, services, and dealers.

INTERDISCIPLINARY NATURE OF EC

Electronic commerce, being a new field, is just developing its theoretical or scientific foundations. It is clear that EC is based on several disciplines. The major disciplines of EC with some samples of the issues with which they are concerned follow:

- *Marketing.* Many issues of marketing offline are relevant to online EC— for example, cost benefits of advertisements and advertisement strategies. Other issues are unique to EC, ranging from online marketing strategy to interactive kiosks.
- *Computer sciences.* Many of the issues listed in the infrastructure box of Figure 1.2, such as languages, multimedia, and networks, fall into the discipline of computer sciences. Intelligent agents play a major role in EC as well.
- *Consumer behavior and psychology.* Consumer behavior is the key to the success of B2C trade, but so is the behavior of the sellers. The relationship between cultures and consumer attitude in electronic market is an example of a research issue in the field.
- *Finance.* The financial markets and banks are one of the major participants in EC. Also, financing arrangements are part of many online transactions. Issues such as using the Internet as a substitute for a stock exchange and fraud in online stock transactions are a sample of the many topics of the field.
- *Economics.* Electronic commerce is influenced by economic forces and has a major impact on world and country economies. Also, theories of micro and

macronomics need to be considered in EC planning, as well as the economic impacts of EC on firms.

- *Management information systems (MIS).* The information systems department is usually responsible for the deployment of EC. This discipline covers issues ranging from systems analysis to system integration, not to mention planning, implementation, security, and payment systems, among others.
- *Accounting and auditing.* The back-office operations of electronic transactions are similar to other transactions in some respects, but different in others. For example, auditing electronic transactions presents a challenge for the accounting profession; so does the development of methodologies for cost-benefit justification.
- *Management.* Electronic commerce efforts need to be managed properly, and because of the interdisciplinary nature of EC, its management may require new approaches and theories.
- *Business law and ethics.* Legal and ethical issues are extremely important in EC, especially in a global market. A large number of legislative bills are pending, and many ethical issues are interrelated with legal ones, such as privacy and intellectual property.
- *Others.* Several other disciplines are involved in various aspects of EC to a lesser extent—for example, linguistics (translation in international trades), robotics and sensory systems, operations research/management science, statistics, and public policy and administration. Also, EC is of interest to engineering, health care, communication, and entertainment publishing. In this book we cover various disciplines' involvement in EC.

THE FUTURE OF EC

In 1996, Forrester Research Institute (www.forrester.com) predicted that B2C would be a $6.6 billion business in 2000, up from $518 million in 1996. Then they revised the figure to $20 billion, and the prediction keeps growing. In 1997, about $10 billion worth of B2B transactions were conducted over the Internet. Predictions on the total size of EC vary. For 2002, total online shopping and B2B transactions are estimated to be in the range of $500 billion to $3 trillion. Some EC applications, such as auctions and online stock trading, are growing at a rate of 15 percent to 25 percent per month, and the number of Internet users worldwide is predicted to reach 750 million by 2008. As many as 50 percent of Internet users are predicted to be online shoppers. One indication of the prospect of EC is the price of EC-related stocks on the Internet. For example, on November 12, 1998, the price of a share of AcTel surged from $2 to $31 in one day (more than 1,250 percent) after AcTel developed a high-speed Internet connection. A day later, the shares of the Internet community Theglobe.com soared on their first day of trade by 606 percent. Further discussion of the future of EC is provided in chapter 12.

Most EC companies, such as Amazon.com, are not making a profit. They are expanding operations and generating sales growth. It is believed that by 2002 most of the major EC companies will start to generate sizable profits. Is EC just another buzzword or is it real? We believe that it is real because of its potential benefits.

1.3 Benefits and Limitations

THE BENEFITS OF EC

Few innovations in human history encompass as many potential benefits as EC does. The global nature of the technology, low cost, opportunity to reach hundreds of millions of people (projected within 10 years), interactive nature, variety of possibilities, and resourcefulness and rapid growth of the supporting infrastructures (especially the Web) result in many potential benefits to organizations, individuals, and society. These benefits are just starting to materialize, but they will increase significantly as EC expands. It is not surprising that some maintain that the EC revolution is just "as profound as the change that came with the industrial revolution" (Clinton and Gore 1997).

Benefits to Organizations

The benefits to organizations are as follows:

- Electronic commerce expands the marketplace to national and international markets. With minimal capital outlay, a company can easily and quickly locate more customers, the best suppliers, and the most suitable business partners worldwide. For example, in 1997, Boeing Corporation reported a savings of 20 percent after a request for a proposal to manufacture a subsystem was posted on the Internet. A small vendor in Hungary answered the request and won the electronic bid. Not only was the subsystem cheaper, but it was delivered quickly.
- Electronic commerce decreases the cost of creating, processing, distributing, storing, and retrieving paper-based information. For example, by introducing an electronic procurement system, companies can cut the purchasing administrative costs by as much as 85 percent. Another example is benefit payments. For the U.S. federal government, the cost of issuing a paper check is 43¢. The cost of electronic payment is 2¢.
- Ability for creating highly specialized businesses. For example, dog toys which can be purchased only in pet shops or department and discounte stores in the physical world, are sold now in a specialized www.dogtoys.com (also see www.cattoys.com).
- Electronic commerce allows reduced inventories and overhead by facilitating "pull"-type supply chain management. In a pull-type system the process starts from customer orders and uses just-in-time manufacturing.
- The pull-type processing enables expensive customization of products and services which provides competitive advantage to its implementers. A classic example is Dell Computer Corp., whose case will be described later.
- Electronic commerce reduces the time between the outlay of capital and the receipt of products and services.
- Electronic commerce initiates business processes reengineering projects. By changing processes, productivity of salespeople, knowledge workers, and administrators can increase by 100 percent or more.
- Electronic commerce lowers telecommunications cost—the Internet is much cheaper than VANs.
- Other benefits include improved image, improved customer service, newfound business partners, simplified processes, compressed cycle and delivery time, increased productivity, eliminating paper, expediting access to information, reduced transportation costs, and increased flexibility.

Benefits to Consumers

The benefits of EC to consumers are as follows:

- Electronic commerce enables customers to shop or do other transactions 24 hours a day, all year round, from almost any location.
- Electronic commerce provides customers with more choices; they can select from many vendors and from more products.

- Electronic commerce frequently provides customers with less expensive products and services by allowing them to shop in many places and conduct quick comparisons.
- In some cases, especially with digitized products, EC allows quick delivery.
- Customers can receive relevant and detailed information in seconds, rather than days or weeks.
- Electronic commerce makes it possible to participate in virtual auctions.
- Electronic commerce allows customers to interact with other customers in *electronic communities* and exchange ideas as well as compare experiences.
- Electronic commerce facilitates competition, which results in substantial discounts.

Benefits to Society

The benefits of EC to society are as follows:

- Electronic commerce enables more individuals to work at home and to do less traveling for shopping, resulting in less traffic on the roads and lower air pollution.
- Electronic commerce allows some merchandise to be sold at lower prices, so less affluent people can buy more and increase their standard of living.
- Electronic commerce enables people in Third World countries and rural areas to enjoy products and services that otherwise are not available to them. This includes opportunities to learn professions and earn college degrees.
- Electronic commerce facilitates delivery of public services, such as health care, education, and distribution of government social services at a reduced cost and/or improved quality. Health-care services, for example, can reach patients in rural areas.

THE LIMITATIONS OF EC

The limitations of EC can be grouped into technical and nontechnical categories; most of them are discussed elsewhere in this book, as indicated in parenthesis.

Technical Limitations of EC

The technical limitations of EC are as follows:

- There is a lack of system security, reliability, standards, and some communication protocols (chapters 8, 11).
- There is insufficient telecommunication bandwidth (chapter 11).
- The software development tools are still evolving and changing rapidly (chapter 11).
- It is difficult to integrate the Internet and EC software with some existing applications and databases (chapter 11).
- Vendors may need special Web servers and other infrastructures, in addition to the network servers (chapter 11).
- Some EC software might not fit with some hardware, or may be incompatible with some operating systems or other components.

As time passes, these limitations will lessen or be overcome; appropriate planning can minimize their impact.

Nontechnical Limitations

Of the many nontechnical limitations that slow the spread of EC, the following are the major ones, according to a survey conducted by *InternetWeek* (1998).

- ***Cost and justification***   (34.8 percent of the respondents). The cost of developing EC in-house can be very high, and mistakes due to lack of experience may result in delays. There are many opportunities for outsourcing, but where and how to do it is not a simple issue (chapter 9). Furthermore, to justify the system one must deal with some intangible benefits (such as improved customer service and the value of advertisement), which are difficult to quantify (see chapters 4 and 9 for discussion).

- *Security and privacy*   (17.2 percent). These issues are especially important in the B2C area, especially security issues which are perceived to be more serious than they really are when appropriate encryption is used. (chapters 8 and 11). Privacy measures are constantly improved (chapter 10). Yet, the customers perceive these issues as very important, and, the EC industry has a very long and difficult task of convincing customers that online transactions and privacy are, in fact, very secure.

- *Lack of trust and user resistance*   (4.4 percent). Customers do not trust an unknown faceless seller (sometimes they do not trust even known ones), paperless transactions, and electronic money. So switching from physical to virtual stores may be difficult (see chapter 3 for discussion).

- *Other limiting factors*   Lack of touch and feel online. Some customers like to touch items such as clothes and like to know exactly what they are buying (see chapter 3 for discussion).
  - Many legal issues are as yet unresolved, and government regulations and standards are not refined enough for many circumstances (chapter 10).
  - Electronic commerce, as a discipline, is still evolving and changing rapidly. Many people are looking for a stable area before they enter into it.
  - There are not enough support services. For example, copyright clearance centers for EC transactions do not exist, and high-quality evaluators, or qualified EC tax experts, are rare.
  - In most applications there are not yet enough sellers and buyers for profitable EC operations.
  - Electronic commerce could result in a breakdown of human relationships (chapter 10).
  - Accessibility to the Internet is still expensive and/or inconvenient for many potential customers. (With Web TV, cell telephone access, kiosks, and constant media attention, the critical mass will eventually develop.)

Despite these limitations, rapid progress in EC is taking place. For example, the number of people in the United States who buy and sell stocks electronically increased from 300,000 at the beginning of 1996 to about 10 million in fall 1999. As experience accumulates and technology improves, the ratio of EC benefits to costs will increase, resulting in a greater rate of EC adoption.

The potential benefits may not be convincing enough reasons to start EC activities. Much more compelling are the business drivers that may *force* companies to engage in EC, such as the case of Egghead Software.

1.4 The Driving Forces of Electronic Commerce

To understand why EC is becoming so popular, it is worthwhile to examine today's business environment, the pressures it creates on organizations, the responses used by organizations, and the potential role of EC.

THE NEW WORLD OF BUSINESS

Market, economical, societal, and technological factors are creating a highly competitive business environment in which customers are the focal point. Furthermore, these factors can change quickly, sometimes in an unpredictable manner (Knoke 1996). Therefore, companies need to react frequently and quickly to both the problems and the opportunities resulting from this new business environment (Drucker 1999). Because the pace of change and the degree of uncertainty in tomorrow's competitive environment are expected to accelerate, organizations will be operating under increasing pressures to produce more and faster, using fewer resources.

Boyett and Boyett (1995) emphasize this dramatic change and describe it with a set of **business pressures** or **drivers**. They maintain that in order to succeed (or even to survive) in this dynamic world, companies must take not only traditional actions such as lowering cost and closing unprofitable facilities (as in the case of Egghead Software) but also innovative activities such as customizing products, creating new products, or providing superb customer service. We refer to the traditional and the innovative activities, some of which are interrelated, as *critical response activities.* They can be performed in some or all of the processes of the organization, from the daily routine processing of payroll and order entry to strategic activities such as the acquisition of a company. They can also occur in what is known as the *extended supply chain,* namely in the process of interaction among a company and its suppliers, customers, and other partners, such as in the cases of Intel and Wal-Mart. A response can be a reaction to a pressure already in existence, or it can be an initiative that will defend an organization against future pressures. It can also be an activity that exploits an opportunity created by changing conditions. Many response activities can be greatly facilitated by EC. In some cases EC is the only solution to these business pressures (Tapscott et al 1998 and Callon 1996).

The relationship among business pressures, organizational responses, and EC is shown in Figure 1.5, which illustrates a model of the new world of business. The business drivers create pressures on organizations. Organizations respond with activities

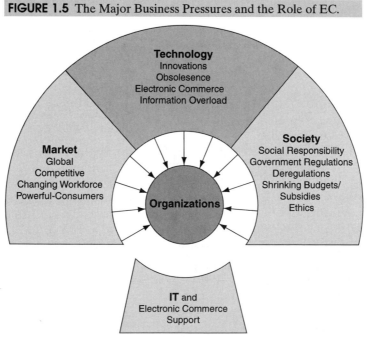

FIGURE 1.5 The Major Business Pressures and the Role of EC.

Source: Turban et al. (1999).

TABLE 1.2 Major Business Pressures	
Category	
Market and economic pressures	Strong competition
	Global economy
	Regional trade agreeements (e.g., NAFTA)
	Extremely low labor cost in some countries
	Frequent and significant changes in markets
	Increased power of consumers
Societal and environmental pressures	Changing nature of workforce
	Government deregulations
	Shrinking government subsidies
	Increased importance of ethical and legal issues
	Increased social responsibility of organizations
	Rapid political changes
Technological pressures	Rapid technological obsolescence
	Increased innovations and new technologies
	Information overload
	Rapid decline in technology cost versus performance ratio

supported by IT in general and EC in particular. Now, let's examine the components of the model in more detail.

BUSINESS PRESSURES

To understand the role of EC in today's organizations, it is useful to review the major business environmental factors that create pressures on organizations. The business environment refers to the social, economic, legal, technological, and political actions that affect business activities. In this book, the business pressures are divided into the following categories: market, societal, and technological. These are summarized in Table 1.2.

ORGANIZATIONAL RESPONSES

To help you understand the impact of the business pressures on organizations, we will use a classic management framework originally developed by Levitt, later modified by Scott-Morton (Scott-Morton and Allen 1994), and further modified by the authors, to reflect the role of IT in general and EC in particular. The framework is depicted in Figure 1.6 (page 20).

Organizations are composed of five major components, one of which is IT (including EC)—and they are surrounded by an environment that also includes EC. The five components are in a stable condition, called equilibrium, as long as no significant change occurs in the environment or in any of the components. However, as soon as a significant change occurs, the system becomes unstable, and then it is necessary to adjust some or all of the internal parts. As you can see in the figure, the internal components are interrelated. For example, a significant change in an organization's strategy may create a change in the corporate structure. Similarly, the introduction of EC, either in the environment (e.g., by a competitor) or the initiation of EC in the company itself, creates a change. Unstable organizations may be unable to excel or even survive; therefore, organizations need to engage in critical response activities.

However, traditional response activities may not work in todays environment, so many old solutions need to be modified, supplemented, or eliminated, as in the case of

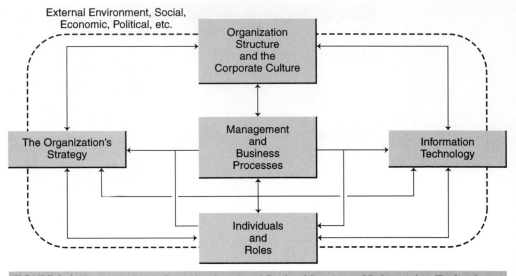

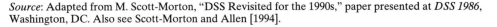

FIGURE 1.6 Framework for Organizational and Societal Impacts of Information Technology.

Source: Adapted from M. Scott-Morton, "DSS Revisited for the 1990s," paper presented at *DSS 1986*, Washington, DC. Also see Scott-Morton and Allen [1994].

Egghead Software. Organizations can also take proactive measures to create a change in the marketplace. Such activities include exploiting opportunities created by the external drivers. The major critical response activities are summarized in Figure 1.7 (page 21).

Organizations' major responses are divided here into five categories: strategic systems for competitive advantage, continuous improvement efforts, business process reengineering (BPR), business alliances, and EC. Several responses can be interrelated; they can be found in more than one category. Electronic commerce can also facilitate the other categories as will be shown later. The four categories are described in the following sections.

Strategic Systems

Strategic systems (Callon 1996) provide organizations with strategic advantages, thus enabling them to increase their market share, better negotiate with their suppliers, or prevent competitors from entering into their territory. There is a variety of EC-supported strategic systems. An example is FedEx's overnight delivery system and the company's ability to track the status of every individual package anywhere in the system. Most of FedEx's competitors have already mimicked the system. So, FedEx moved the system to the Internet. However, the competitors quickly followed, and now FedEx is introducing new activities (see Application Case 1.4 on p. 22).

Continuous Improvement Efforts

Many companies continuously conduct innovative programs in an attempt to improve their productivity and quality. Examples of such programs are provided in Table 1.3 (page 23). For example, Dell Computer takes its orders electronically and immediately moves them via Enterprise Resources Planning software (from SAP Corp.), into the just-in-time assembly operation. Intel is tracking its products' consumption in 11 of its largest customers, using its extranets, almost in real time, and determining production schedules and deliveries accordingly. However, continuous improvement programs may not be adequate in all occasions all the times. Strong

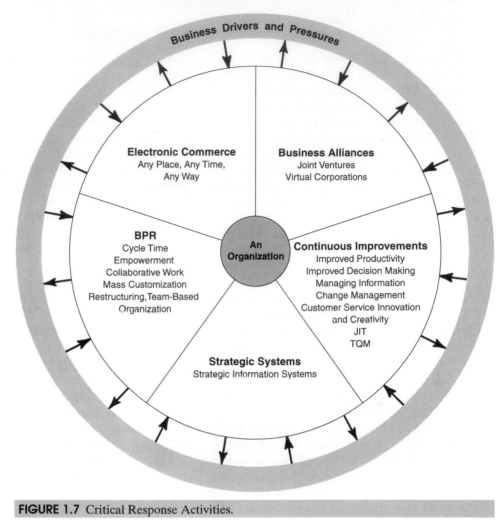

FIGURE 1.7 Critical Response Activities.

Source: Turban et al. (1999).

business pressures may require a radical change. Such an effort is referred to as **business process reengineering** (BPR).

BUSINESS PROCESS REENGINEERING

Business process reengineering refers to a major innovation in the organization's structure and the way it conducts the business. Technological, human, and organizational dimensions of a firm may all be changed in BPR (Hammer and Champy 1993). More than 70 percent of all large U.S. companies claim to be doing reengineering of some sort.

Information technology and especially EC play a major role in BPR. For example, EDI facilitates rapid paperless transactions that enable companies to reduce some departments by as much as 80 percent (Ford Case in Hammer and Champy 1993). Electronic commerce provides flexibility in manufacturing, permits faster delivery to customers and supports rapid and paperless transactions among suppliers, manufacturers, and retailers.

The major areas in which EC supports BPR are as follows:

* ***Reducing cycle time and time to market.***   Reducing the business process

FedEx's Web Shopping/Shipping Service

FedEx created a B2B service called Virtual Order, which integrates the Web catalogs of companies and the ordering from these catalogs with fulfillment and delivery using FedEx's own trucks and planes (see the attached figure). This move by FedEx marks the first stage of FedEx moving its whole logistics and order processing to the Internet. It also marks a new stage for EC on the Internet because service companies like FedEx can offer services to companies that do not want to deal directly with transactions over the Internet. The companies can just subcontract those services out.

Virtual Order works like this: FedEx hosts the Web pages for the companies that want to put catalogs on the Internet. If the selling company doesn't have a catalog or Web page set up, FedEx provides the necessary software to create the on-line catalog for the selling company. These Web pages run on FedEx servers, but they are exclusively the selling company's branded site. Customer orders are taken 24 hours a day, seven days a week. When an order comes through, all of the applicable charges are calculated and are sent to the buyer, to the selling company's server, and the information is linked to the selling company's database for real-time inventory management. FedEx offers a secure server, so both the selling company and its customers can be assured of a safe, secure transaction. The order then is routed to the selling company's product warehouse, where FedEx packages and ships the product. Alternatively, FedEx can manage the inventory of the product on its own premises, usually in Memphis, the hub of its planes. As with any other FedEx shipping, both the customer and the selling company can track the shipment. FedEx also provides a 24-hour Web-based technical support line for Virtual Order merchants. Finally, FedEx offers other services, such as confirmation, invoicing, and after-sales service for returns and repairs. The idea for Virtual Order came to FedEx when it set up a similar process for Insight Direct, a computer equipment and supplies distributor. During the first year of this venture, Insight Direct was shipping more than 1,000 orders per month over the Internet using FedEx technology.

Along with the services offered with Virtual Order, FedEx launched a marketing alliance program. The program is designed to help companies boost their business sales by offering points to the companies using the Virtual Order system. The selling company obtains these points through the Virtual Order system by directly selling products. The reward points can be redeemed for prizes offered by FedEx.

Source: Compiled from www.fedex.com/virtualorder/ (November 1997).

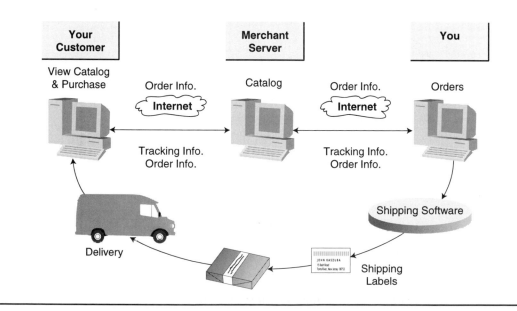

TABLE 1.3 Continuous Improvement Efforts	
Area/Subject	*Description*
Productivity improvement	Increasing output to input ratio
Just-in-time	A comprehensive production and inventory control program
Total quality management (TQM)	Corporate-wide effort to improve quality
Improved decision making	Making better and more timely decisions
Managing information and knowledge	Proper storage, retrieval, and use of information
Innovation and creativity	Encouraging innovation and using creative thinking
Change management	Introducing and properly managing change
Customer service	Planning and providing superb customer service

time (cycle time) is extremely important for increasing productivity and competitiveness (Wetherbe 1996). Similarly, reducing the time from the inception of an idea until its implementation—time to market—is important because those who can be first on the market with a product, or who can provide customers with a service faster than competitors, enjoy a distinct competitive advantage. Extranet-based applications can be used to expedite the various steps in the process of product or service development, testing, and implementation. An example of **cycle time reduction** in bringing new drugs to the market is shown in Application Case 1.5, on page 24.

- ***Empowerment of employees and collaborative work.*** Giving employees the authority to act and make decisions on their own is a strategy used by many organizations as part of their BPR. **Empowerment** is related to the concept of self-directed teams (Mankin et al. 1996 and Lipnack and Stamps 1997). Management delegates authority to teams who can execute the work faster and with fewer delays. Information technology allows the *decentralization* of decision making and authority but simultaneously supports a centralized control. For example, the Internet and intranets enable empowered employees to access data, information, and knowledge they need for making quick decisions. Networked expert systems can give advice to team members whenever human experts are not available. As a matter of fact, selling knowledge on the Internet is becoming an important EC activity.

- ***Knowledge management.*** Employees can access organizational know-how via their company's intranet. Some knowledge bases are open to the public for a fee over the Internet, generating income (for example, see www.knowledgespace.com).

- ***Customer-focused approach.*** Companies are becoming increasingly customer oriented. In other words, they must pay more attention to customers and their preferences and reengineer themselves to meet consumer demands. This can be done in part by changing manufacturing processes from mass production to mass customization (Pine and Gilmore 1997). In mass production, a company produces a large quantity of identical items. In mass customization, items are produced in a large quantity but are customized to fit the desires of each customer. Electronic commerce is an ideal facilitator of mass customization.

- ***Business alliances.*** Many companies realize that alliances with other companies, even competitors, can be beneficial. For example, General Motors, Ford, and Chrysler created an extranet with their suppliers (chapter 7). There are several types of alliances, such as sharing resources, establishing permanent

APPLICATION CASE 1.5

The Internet and the Intranet Shorten Time to Market of New Drugs

THE PROBLEM

The Federal Drug Administration (FDA) must be extremely careful in approving new drugs. However, there is public pressure on the FDA to approve new drugs quickly, especially for cancer and HIV. The problem is that to assure quality, the FDA requires companies to conduct extensive research and clinical testing. The development programs of such research and testing cover 300,000 to 500,000 pages of documentation for each drug. The subsequent results and analysis are reported on 100,000 to 200,000 additional pages. These pages are reviewed by the FDA prior to approval of new drugs. Manual processing of this information significantly slows the work of the FDA, so the total process takes 6 to 10 years.

THE SOLUTION

Computer-Aided Drug Application Systems (from Research Data Corporation of New Jersey) is a software program that uses a network-distributed document-processing system. The pharmaceutical company scans all its related documents into a database. The documents are indexed, and full-text search and retrieval software is attached to the system. Using keywords, corporate employees can search the database via their company's Intranet. The database is also accessible, via the Internet, to FDA employees, who no longer have to spend hours looking for a specific piece of data. (It takes only six to eight seconds to access an image in the database.) Any viewed information can be processed or printed at the user's desktop computer. The system not only helps the FDA but also the companies' researchers, who can have any required information at their fingertips. Remote corporate and business-partner users can also access the system. The overall results: The time to market of a new drug is reduced by up to a year. (Each week saved can be translated into the saving of many lives and can also yield up to $1 million profit.) The system also reduces the time it takes to patent a new drug.

An interesting example is the case of ISIS pharmaceutical. ISIS developed an extranet-based system similar to the one described here. The company uses a CD-ROM to submit the reports to the FDA and open its Intranet to FDA personnel. This alone could save 6 to 12 months from the average 15-month review time. A month of preparation time of an FDA report is saved with the electronic submission. To cut time further, SmithKline Beecham Corporation is using electronic publishing and hypertext links to enable quick navigation.

Source: Condensed from *IMC Journal* (May/June 1993), pp. 23, 25. ISIS story is published in *INCTechnology* (No. 3, 1997), pp. 48+. Also see www.openmarket.com/products/folio/smithkline.htm.1999.

supplier-company relationships, and creating joint research efforts. One of the most interesting types is the temporary joint venture, in which companies form a special organization for a specific, limited-time mission. This is an example of a **virtual corporation**, which could be a common business organization in the future. A more permanent type of business alliance that links manufacturers, suppliers, and finance corporations is known as *keiretsu* (a Japanese term meaning a permanent business alliance). Similarly, supply chain management is facilitated by extranets (chapter 7 and the Wal-Mart case here). This and other types of alliances can be heavily supported by EC technologies ranging from EDI to electronic transmission of maps and drawings.

1.5 Impact of EC: Everything Will Be Changed

The field of EC is relatively new; as such, little statistical data or empirical research is

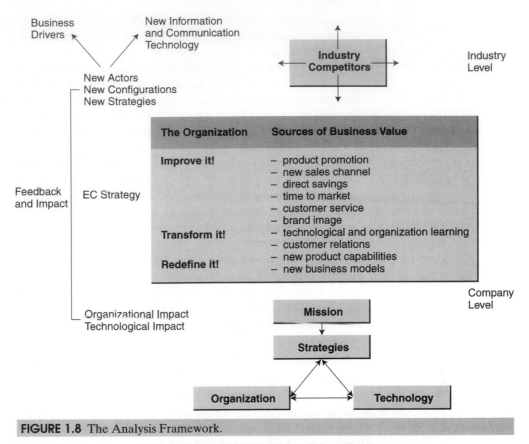

FIGURE 1.8 The Analysis Framework.

Source: Block and Segev (1998). Reproduced with permission of the authors.

available. Therefore, the discussion in this section is based primarily on experts' opinions, logic, and some actual data. The discussion here is also based in part on the work of Bloch and Segev (1998), who approached the impact of EC from a value-added point of view. Their model (shown in Figure 1.8) divides the impact of EC into three major categories: EC *improves* direct marketing, EC *transforms* organizations, and EC *redefines* organizations.

IMPROVING DIRECT MARKETING

Traditional direct marketing is done by mail order (catalogs) and telephone (telemarketing). In 1998, $75 billion in sales were estimated in the United States. In 1998, direct marketing via computers (B2C) reached about $2 billion in the United States. This figure is small, but it grew more than 1,000 percent in less than four years. Bloch et al. (1996) suggest the following EC impacts:

- **Product promotion.** Electronic commerce enhances promotion of products and services through direct, information-rich, and interactive contact with customers.
- **New sales channels.** Electronic commerce creates a new distribution channel for existing products, thanks to its direct reach of customers and the bidirectional nature of communication.
- **Direct savings.** The cost of delivering information to customers over the Internet results in substantial savings to senders (when compared with non-

electronic delivery or delivery via VAN systems). Major savings are also realized in delivering digitized products (such as music and software) versus physical delivery.

- **Reduced cycle time.** The delivery of digitized products and services can be reduced to seconds. Also, the administrative work related to physical delivery, especially across international borders, can be reduced significantly, cutting the cycle time by more than 90 percent. One example is TradeNet in Singapore, which reduces the administrative time of port-related transactions from days to minutes.

- **Customer service.** Customer service can be greatly enhanced by enabling customers to find detailed information online (for example, FedEx allows customers to trace the status of their packages). Also, intelligent agents can answer standard e-mail questions in seconds. Finally, human experts' services can be expedited using help-desk software, for example.

- **Brand or corporate image.** On the Web, newcomers can establish corporate images very quickly. What Amazon.com did in three years took traditional companies generations to achieve. Corporate image means *trust*, which is necessary for direct sales. Traditional companies such as Intel, Disney, Wal-Mart, Dell, and Cisco use their Web activities to affirm their corporate identity and brand image.

OTHER MARKETING-RELATED IMPACTS

Customization

Electronic commerce provides for **customization** of products and services, in contrast to buying in a store or ordering from a television, which is usually limited to standard products. Dell Computers Inc. is a success story of customization. Today, you can configure not only computers but also cars, jewelry, gifts, and hundreds of other products and services (travel and insurance, for example). If properly done, one can achieve mass customization that provides a competitive advantage as well as increases the overall demand for certain products and services.

Advertisement

With direct marketing and customization comes a one-to-one or direct advertisement, which is much more effective than mass advertisement. This creates a fundamental change in the manner in which advertisement is conducted not only for online trades but also for products and services that are ordered and shipped in traditional ways. As is discussed in chapter 4, the entire concept of advertisement is going through a fundamental change due to EC.

Ordering Systems

Taking orders from customers can drastically be improved if it is done online and fewer mistakes are made. When taken electronically, orders can be quickly routed to the appropriate order-processing site. This saves time and reduces expenses so salespeople have more time to sell. Also, customers can compute the cost of their orders, saving time for all parties involved.

Markets

Traditional markets are being changed by EC. The physical market disappears as does the need to deliver the goods to the marketplace. In a **marketspace,** which is an

TABLE 1.4 A Marketing Shift from Marketplace to Marketspace

Shift from	*To*	*Sources*
Mass marketing and advertisement	Target, one-to-one interactive marketing and advertisement	Martin (1996), Mougayar (1998)
Mass production (standard products, services)	Mass customization	Pine and Gilmore (1997) Pine (1993)
Monologue	Dialogue	Komenar (1997)
Paper catalog	Electronic catalogs	Kosiur (1997)
One-to-many communication model	Many-to-many	Hoffman and Novak (1996)
Supply-side thinking	Demand-side thinking	Raport and Sviokla (1995) Martin (1996)
Customer as a target	Customer as a partner	Komenar (1997)
Segmentation	Communities	Hagel and Armstrong (1997)
Physical products and services	Digital products and services	Block et al (1996)
Branding, megabrand	Communication, diversify	Martin (1996)
Intermediation	Disintermediation, new intermediation	Mougayar (1998), Komenar (1997)

Source: Modified from Kiani (1998).

electronic market, goods are delivered directly to buyers when purchasing is completed making markets much more efficient. Traditional markets can be very inefficient, as is shown in chapters 7 and 12.

For those products that are digitally based—software, music, and information—the changes will be dramatic. Already, small but powerful software packages are delivered over the Internet. This fundamentally affects packaging and greatly reduces the need for historical distribution models.

New selling models such as shareware, freeware, and pay-as-you-use, are emerging to maximize the potential of the Internet. Although these models have emerged in particular sectors, such as software and publishing industries, they will eventually pervade other sectors. New forms of marketing will also emerge, such as Web-based advertising, linked advertising, direct e-mail, and an increased emphasis on relationship (interactive) marketing.

Many other activities can improve sales, as we will see throughout the text. For example, customer's convenience is greatly enhanced (any place, any time), availability of products and services is much greater (e.g., 10 million books in Amazon.com's catalog), and cheaper products are offered (e.g., Book-A-Million discounts books online up to 50 percent).

All these provide EC with a competitive advantage over the traditional direct sales methods. Furthermore, because the competitive advantage is so large, EC is likely to replace many nondirect marketing channels. Some people predict the "fall of the shopping malls," and many retail stores and brokers of services (stocks, real estate, and insurance) are labeled by some as "soon to be endangered species."

As is discussed throughout the book, the role of marketing channels, wholesalers, retailers, intermediaries, and storefronts may be dramatically changed by EC. A summary of these changes is provided in Table 1.4 together with appropriate references.

TRANSFORMING ORGANIZATIONS
Technology and Organizational Learning

Rapid progress in EC will force companies to adapt quickly to the new technology and offer them an opportunity to experiment with new products, services, and processes. Companies will have to immediately learn the new technologies (why did it take Barnes & Noble two years to move online?). Learning may be followed by strategic and structural changes. These changes may transform the way in which business is done, such as in the case of Egghead Software described earlier.

Bloch et al. (1996) believe that if this assertion is true, it will have a large and durable impact on the strategies of most organizations. Therefore, it is critical that these organizations quickly become familiar with the technology. The learning curve of mastering such technologies and understanding their power to reshape customer relationships is steep and cannot be achieved overnight. It is often an iterative process, requiring organizations to try new offerings and rearrange them according to customer feedback.

In a similar fashion, new technologies require new organizational approaches. For instance, the structure of the organizational unit dealing with EC might have to be different from the conventional sales and marketing departments. To be more flexible and responsive to the market, new processes must be put in place. For instance, to deal with the authorization of publishing corporate information on the Internet. This type of corporate change must be planned and managed. Before getting it right, organizations might have to struggle with different experiments.

Changing Nature of Work

The nature of work and employment will be transformed in the Digital Age; it is already happening before our eyes. Driven by increased competition in the global marketplace, firms are reducing the number of employees down to a core of essential staff and outsourcing whatever work they can to countries where wages are significantly less expensive. The upheaval brought on by these changes is creating new opportunities and new risks and forcing us into new ways of thinking about jobs, careers, and salaries.

The Digital Age workers will have to become very flexible. Few of them will have truly secure jobs in the traditional sense, and all of them will have to be willing and able to constantly learn, adapt, make decisions, and stand by them. They will as likely work from home as in an office.

The Digital Age company will have to prize its workers as its most valuable asset. It will have to constantly nurture and empower them and provide them with every means possible to expand their knowledge and skill base.

REDEFINING ORGANIZATIONS
New Product Capabilities

Electronic commerce allows for new products to be created and/or for existing products to be customized in innovative ways. Such changes may redefine organizations' missions and the manner in which they operate. Electronic commerce also allows suppliers to gather personalized data on customers. Building customer profiles, as is described in chapter 3, as well as collecting data on certain groups of customers, can be used as a source of information for improving products or designing new ones.

Mass customization, as described earlier, enables manufacturers to create specific products for each customer, based on his or her exact needs. For example, Motorola gathers customer needs for a pager or a cellular phone, transmits them electronically to the manufacturing plant where they are manufactured, along with the customer's specifications (like color and features), and then sends the product to the customer within a day. Dell Computers, JCPenney, and Levi's use the same approach. Using the Web, customers can design or configure products for themselves. For example, customers can design their T-shirts, furniture, cars, jewelry, and even a Swatch watch. Using mass customization methods, this is done at a retail-like price or only slightly higher.

New Business Models

These changes affect not only individual companies and their products but entire industries. This will lead to the use of new business models, based on the wide availability of information and its direct distribution to consumers. One such model is the new kinds of intermediaries, such as in the case of Chemdex, extranet creator for the biochemistry market, which is described in chapter 12; other new business models are described in chapters 2–7. As a matter of fact, we have seen many new businesses that provide Web services ranging from banner exchanges to product comparisons. Also, traditional intermediaries redefine their role in order to survive, as shown in chapter 5 (Application Case 5.1).

IMPACTS ON MANUFACTURING

Electronic commerce, as is shown later, is changing manufacturing systems from mass production to demand-driven and possibly customized, just-in-time manufacturing. Furthermore, the production systems are integrated with finance, marketing, and other functional systems, as well as with business partners and customers, as illustrated in Intel's case. Using Web-based ERP systems (supported by software such as SAP R/3), orders that are taken from customers can be directed to designers (who use computer-aided design) and/or to the production floor, within seconds. Production cycle time is cut by 50 percent or more in many cases, especially when production is done in a different country from where the designers and engineers are located.

Companies like IBM, General Motors, General Electric, and Boeing are assembling products for which the components are manufactured in many locations. Sub-assemblers gather materials and parts from their vendors, and they may use one or more tiers of manufacturers. Communication, collaboration, and coordination become critical in such multitier systems. Using electronic bidding, assemblers get sub-assemblies 15 percent to 20 percent cheaper than before and 80 percent faster (e.g., GE case in chapter 6). Furthermore, such systems are flexible and adaptable, allowing for fast changes with minimum cost. Also, costly inventories that are part of mass production systems can be minimized.

IMPACT ON FINANCE AND ACCOUNTING

Electronic commerce requires special finance and accounting systems. Most notable are the payment systems. Traditional payment systems are ineffective or inefficient for electronic trade. The use of the new payment systems such as electronic cash is complicated because it involves legal issues and agreements on international standards. Nevertheless, electronic cash is certain to come soon, and it will change the manner in which payments are being made.

In many ways, electronic cash, which can be backed by currency or other assets, represents the biggest revolution in currency since gold replaced cowry shells. Its diversity and pluralism is perfectly suited to the Internet. It could change consumers' financial lives and shake the foundations of financial systems and even governments. Payment systems involve security issues, interinstitutional transfer of funds, and much more (chapter 8).

Executing an electronic order triggers an action in what we call the **back office**. Back-office transactions include buyer's credit checks, product availability checks, confirmation, movements in accounts payable and receivable, billing, and much more. These activities must be efficient and fast so the electronic trade will not be slowed down. An example is trading stocks online. In most cases orders are executed in less than three seconds and the trader can find a confirmation online immediately. Speaking of online trading, it is interesting to note that today individual investors have substantial free information at their fingertips. This information cost users tens of thousands of dollars just three years ago. With commissions of less than $10 per trade, many individuals are taking their money from mutual funds and trying to trade on their own. **Day trading** is becoming a big success for some.

Several EC activities are fairly complex, involving an intermediary, EC software company, paying and receiving banks, and so on. Payments of commissions to all parties, for every transaction, are part of such systems, and they need to be planned for and made secure.

HUMAN RESOURCE MANAGEMENT, TRAINING, AND EDUCATION

Electronic commerce, as shown in chapter 5, is changing the manner in which people are recruited, evaluated, promoted, and developed. The intranets play a major role in this transformation (chapter 7). Training and education will be different. Distance learning online is exploding, providing opportunities that never existed before. Companies are cutting training costs by 50 percent and more, and virtual courses, programs, and universities are mushrooming.

New distance learning systems can offer two-way video, on-the-fly interaction, and application sharing. Such systems provide for interactive remote instruction systems, which link sites over a high-speed intranet. For example, at Old Dominion University in Virginia, Telechnet systems use broadcast satellite technology with terrestrial audio feedback from students and e-mail to connect the main campus to 23 community colleges as well as government and industrial sites. More than 3,400 students were enrolled in the 1998 spring semester. City University of Hong Kong is teaching an interactive MBA program on the Internet and interactive television as of 1999 (chapter 5). At the same time, corporations are finding that distance learning may be a ticket to survival because changing environments, new technologies, and continuously changing procedures make it necessary for employees to be trained and retrained constantly.

1.6   Putting It All Together

Companies today are using the Internet, intranets, and extranets in an integrated manner to conduct various EC activities, as shown in Figure 1.9.

The hypothetical company Toys Inc. has an intranet for conducting all its internal communication, collaboration, and dissemination of information and accessing databases. The company uses an extranet (on the upper left of Figure 1.9) to cooperate with its large business partners (e.g., suppliers, distributors, noncorporate retail stores, liquidators). In addition, the company is connected to the toy industry extranet (upper right of Figure 1.9) which includes other manufacturers, professional associations, and large suppliers.

The company may be networked to additional extranets. For example, some major corporations may allow Toys Inc. to connect to their intranet, via their own extranets. Toys Inc. is also connected with its banks and other financial institutions (loan providers, stock issuers) over a highly secured EDI that runs on a VAN. The company is also using the VAN-based EDI with some of its largest suppliers and other business partners. An

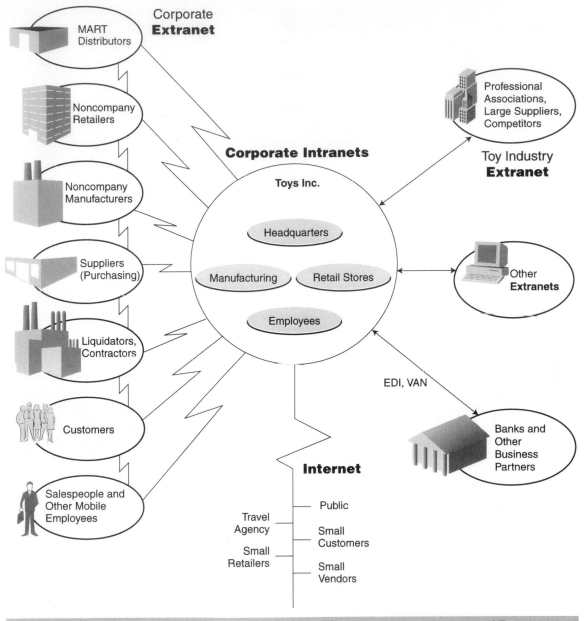

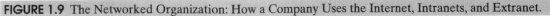

FIGURE 1.9 The Networked Organization: How a Company Uses the Internet, Intranets, and Extranet.

Internet-based EDI is used with smaller business partners that are not on the corporate EDI or extranet. The company communicates with others on the regular Internet.

Many companies are moving toward a similar network configuration. Today, it is almost impossible to do business without being connected through an EDI, extranets, and the Internet to the business partners.

The remaining chapters of the book are divided into four parts that are related to the scope of EC, as illustrated in Figure 1.9. The applications are presented in part II and are organized into six chapters. Chapter 2 deals with retailing on the Net, and chapter 3 covers the related topic of consumer behavior and market research. Chapter 4 deals with In-ternet-based advertisement. In addition to retailing, B2C includes many services, ranging

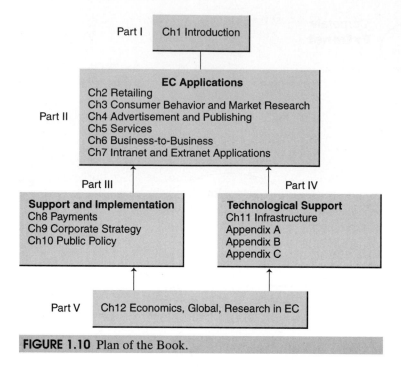

FIGURE 1.10 Plan of the Book.

from travel to home banking, as described in chapter 5. Some of these services are available in B2B transactions, which are the subject of chapters 6 and 7. All EC applications are supported by payments, corporate and public policies (chapters 8 through 10), and by the technological infrastructure (chapter 11 and appendices A, B, and C). Chapter 12 concludes the book by presenting the issue of EC economics, global EC, and research opportunities in EC. The relationship among the various chapters is shown in Figure 1.10.

1.7 Managerial Issues

Many managerial issues are related to EC. They can be discovered throughout the book. Some introductory issues follow:

1. **Is it real?** The first question that comes to the mind of those not involved in EC is "Is it real?" We do believe that the answer is definitely "yes." Just ask anyone who has experienced home banking, online stock purchasing, or buying a book from Amazon. An interesting tip was given by Randy Mott, Wal-Mart's CIO: "Start EC as soon as possible; it is too dangerous to wait".

2. **How to evaluate the magnitude of the business pressures.** The best approach is to solicit the expertise of research institutions, such as GartnerGroup or Forrester Research, which specialize in EC. Often, by the time you determine what is going on it may be too late. The big certified public accounting companies may be of help. (Price Waterhouse and Andersen Consulting provide considerable EC information on their Web site.) Management especially needs to know what is going on in its industry.

3. **What should be my company's strategy toward EC?** There are three basic strategies: lead, wait, or experiment. This issue is revisited in chapter 9 together with related issues such as cost-benefit of EC, integration of EC into the business, what aspect of EC to outsource, and how to handle resistance to change.

4. **What is the best way to learn EC?** Start with this book. It provides a comprehensive treatment of the EC field and points to many support resources. It has a supportive Web page with many links to major EC resources. You may be astonished to learn how much information already exists on EC (try a search on EC at www.Yahoo.com). It is not a bad idea to create a task force dedicated to EC in your organization.

5. **What ethical issues exist?** Organizations must deal with ethical issues of their employees, customers, and suppliers. This may be difficult because what is ethical in one company or country may be unethical in another. Ethical issues are very important because they can damage the image of an organization as well as destroy the morale of its employees. The use of EC raises many ethical issues, ranging from the surveillance of e-mail to the potential invasion of privacy of millions of customers whose data are stored in private and public databases. Because EC is new and rapidly changing, there is little experience or agreement on how to deal with EC-related ethical issues.

Summary

The compilation of this chapter helps you in attaining the following learning objectives:

1. **Define EC and describe its categories.** Electronic commerce involves conducting transactions electronically. Its major categories are B2B, B2C, and intraorganization transactions.

2. **Electronic markets and interorganizations systems.** Electronic markets involve selling and buying of products and services in a competitive marketplace. These can be B2C or B2B. Interorganizational information systems (IOS) refer to flow of standard transactions', information between business partners, such as placing orders, billing or paying.

3. **Benefits to organizations, consumers, and society.** There are many benefits for all. They are substantial and they cannot be ignored. Therefore, EC is real and not a fad.

4. **Limitations of EC.** The many limitations of EC can be categorized as technological and nontechnological. With passage of time the importance of the technological limitations diminish, because issues such as capacity, security, and accessibility continually improve due to technological innovations. The nontechnical limitations also diminish with time, but some of them, especially the behavioral ones, may be strong in particular organizations.

5. **The framework of EC.** The applications of EC, and there are many of them, are based on infrastructures and supported by people, public policies, technical standards, and organizations—all bonded by management.

6. **The driving forces of EC.** Market (economics), technological, and societal pressures force organizations to respond. Traditional responses may not be sufficient due to the magnitude of the pressures and the frequent changes involved. Therefore, organizations frequently must use innovations and reengineer their operations. In many cases, EC is the major facilitator of organizational responses.

7. **The changes brought by EC.** Everything will be changed, starting with marketing theories and practices and concluding with product innovation and supply chain management.

8. **Managerial issues of EC.** Management would like to know if EC is real, how to assess the business pressures, what EC strategy to use, and how to learn about EC. This book should clarify these issues.

Keywords

- Back office (for EC)
- Business process reengineering (BPR)
- Business drivers
- Cycle time reduction
- Customization
- Day trading
- E-business

- Electronic commerce (EC)
- Electronic data interchange (EDI)
- Electronic markets
- Empowerment
- Extranets
- Internet
- Interorganizational information

- systems (IOS)
- Intranets
- Marketspace
- Supply chain management
- Value-added networks
- Virtual corporations

Questions for Review

1. Define EC and e-business.
2. List the organizational, consumer, and societal benefits of EC.
3. List the major technological and nontechnological limitations of EC.
4. List the market, technological, and societal drivers (pressures).
5. List the major activities taken by organizations to deal with the business pressures.
6. Define *intranet* and *extranet*.
7. Describe the major components of the EC framework (Figure 1.2).
8. Define one-to-one marketing.
9. List the major activities of BPR.
10. List the major impacts of EC on direct marketing.
11. Define a *virtual corporation*.

Questions for Discussion

1. Distinguish between IOS and electronic markets. Describe the major characteristics of each.
2. Carefully examine the nontechnological limitations of EC. Which of them are company-dependent and which are generic?
3. What, in your opinion, motivated Intel and Happy Puppy to engage in EC?
4. What are the benefits to Intel's customers?
5. Why is it said that EC is a catalyst of fundamental changes in organizations?
6. What drove HBO to EC? Why?
7. It is said that EC facilitates supply chain management. Why?
8. Explain how EC can reduce cycle time, improve empowerment of employees, and support enhancements of teams.
9. How can EC facilitate customization of products and services?
10. Why is buying with a smart card from a vending machine considered EC?
11. Why is Wal-Mart joining its competitors in the CFAR project?
12. Compare EC with mail order from paper catalogs and television.
13. What are the advantages of customization and how is it supported by EC?
14. Why is distance learning considered EC?
15. Examine all the EC applications presented in this chapter. Which of them can be classified as electronic markets and which as IOS? Also distinguish which are B2B, which are B2C, and which are intraorganizational?
16. Read Clinton and Gore's paper. Why do they emphasize the importance of global EC?
17. Why in a specialized store for dog toys feasible on the internet but not in the physical market place?

Internet Exercises

1. Chevron Corporation's Web site for children (www.chevroncars.com) was selected as the "most innovative site in 1998." Visit the site and try to determine why.

2. Find recent information on Amazon.com and its battle with Barnes & Noble.
   a. Enter Amazon's site and print a list of current books on EC.
   b. Find a review of one of these books.
   c. Review the services you can get from Amazon and describe all the benefits you can receive.
   d. Enter Barnes & Noble's Web site (www.bn.com). Compare the two sites.
   e. You can find Amazon's logo on many popular sites, but not Barnes & Noble's. Such advertisement is very expensive, and as a result Amazon does not have any profit. Is this strategy logical? Why or why not?
3. Find information on the progress of the CFAR project.
4. Enter www.fedex.com (you will need to go to the "U.S. operations"), and find information about recent EC projects that are related to logistics and supply chain management.
5. Enter www.musicmaker.com and create a CD. Then enter www.iprint.com and create your own business card. Finally, enter www.ford.com and configure a car. What are the advantages of such activities? The disadvantages?

R E A L   W O R L D   C A S E

Grocery supermarket keeps it fresh: Woolworths of Australia

Perishable goods such as fruit, vegetables, meat and milk are significant in any retail marketplace. Innovative start-up companies like Peapod (US), and Greengrocer.com (Australia) have found new ways to satisfy customers.

How is a well-established major player to respond? With huge investments in bricks-and-mortar stores, Woolworths of Australia found itself dealing with just this question. The grocery market in Australia is dominated by three major players: Coles-Myers, Woolworths and Franklins. Between them they control some 80% of the marketplace. Franklins, which is Hong Kong-owned, takes a low-cost minimum service approach ahd the others, both Australian-owned, provide a full range of products, including fresh foods and prepared meals.

Woolworths' initial approach was to set up a standard web site offering a limited range of goods, but excluding perishable items. This was trailed in areas near major supermarkets. They felt that they had to respond to the newly emerging approaches from entrepreneurs. If those organizations were allowed to take over a sizeable segment of the market, it could be difficult to recover it.

It was not long before management realized that this was not an attractive approach. Woolworths' staff had to walk the aisles, fill the baskets, pack the goods and deliver them. For an organization that had optimized its supply chain in order to cut costs, here was a sudden explsion in costs. When gross margins are only 10% and net margins around 4%, it is very easy to become unprofitible.

Furthermore, Woolworths has established its place in public perceptions as 'the fresh food people' with fruit and vegetables, freshly-baked bread, meat and prepared meals being promoted heavily. If home shopping ignores these, Woolworths is avoiding its strengths.

Woolworths' Homeshop, the second generation home shopping site (www.woolworths.com.au), is designed with freshness in mind and all the fresh food is available for delivery. Deliveries are arranged from major regional supermarkets, rather than from every local store. There is a A$50 minimum order, 7.5% surcharge for home delivery, as well as a A$6 delivery charge. This helps in recovering the additional costs, but an average order around A$200 still returns little profit.

New users can only register if deliveries are possible to their postal address. On first use of the system, the customer is guided to find the products that they want with suggestions from the list of best-selling items. Alternatively the customer can browse for items by category or search by keyword. Items are accumulated in the 'shopping trolley' (cart). The first order can form a master list for future orders, as can subsequent orders.

When the customer has selected the required items, they select 'checkout' where the total value is computed and the customer confirms delivery is required. Payment is made only at time of delivery is required. Payment is made only at time of delivery using a mobile (cellular) electronic funds transfer (EFTPOS) terminal, and either a credit card or a debit card. In this way, precise charges can be made based on weight of meat or fish, as well as allowing for out-of-stock items.

The customer has to set the delivery time and day, and will bear an additional charge if they are not at home to accept the delivery.

Additional services that are available include dietary advice, recipes and recording of preferred food items. At the present, these do not link directly into the shopping trolley.

CASE QUESTIONS

1. Visit the Woolworths Homeshop site and find new activities not mentioned above.

2. Who would be the target customers for this site?
3. How easy is it to order regularly used items from this site? One-off items? Suggest improvements to the design.
4. How does this service disrupt the previously highly-tuned supply chain?
5. Compare the advantages and disadvantages of the EFTPOS payment mechanism used with the more usual 'credit card at time of order'.
6. Should the newer start-ups such as greengrocer.com and peapod be threatened by this service? How about the traditional local grocery stores, such as Dewsons Wembley (www.dewsons.com.au)?

References

N. Adam and Y. Yesha, *Electronic Commerce: Current Research Issues and Applications* (New York: Springer, 1996).

M. Block and A. Segev, "Leveraging Electronic Commerce for Competitive Advantage: A Business Value Framework" Proceedings of the 9th International Conference on EDI-IOS (Bled, Slovenia: June, 1996).

J. H. Boyett, and J. T. Boyett, *Beyond Workplace 2000: Essential Strategies for the New American Corporation* (New York: Dutton, 1995).

J. D. Callon, *Competitive Advantage Through Information Technology* (New York: McGraw-Hill, 1996).

W. J. Clinton and A. Gore Jr., "A Framework for Global Electronic Commerce," (July 1997) http://www.iitf.nist.gov/eleccomm/ecomm.htm.

M. Dertouzos, *What Will Be: How the New World of Information Will Change Our Lives* (San Francisco: Harper Edge, 1997).

P. D. Drucker, *Managing Challenges for the 21st Century* (New York: Harper Business, 1999).

"Electronic Commerce on the Internet," *Communications of the ACM* (special issue, June 1996).

B. Gates, *Business @ the Speed of Thought,* (New York: Warner Books, 1999).

K. S. Gill, ed., *Information Society* (London: Springer Publishing Co., 1996).

J. Hagel, and A. Armstrong, *Net Gain: Expanding Markets Through Virtual Communities* (Boston: Harvard Business Press, 1997).

M. Hammer and J. Champy, *Reengineering the Corporation* (New York: Harper Business, 1993).

M. Hills, *Intranet Business Strategy* (New York: Wiley Computer Publishing, 1996).

Internet Week (August 31, 1998).

D. S. Janal, *101 Businesses You Can Start on the Internet* (New York: Van Nostrand Reinhold, 1995).

R. Kalakota and A. B. Whinston, *Electronic Commerce: A Manager's Guide* (Reading, MA: Addison-Wesley, 1997).

R. Kalakota and A. B. Whinston, *Frontiers of Electronic Commerce* (Reading, MA: Addison-Wesley, 1996).

R. M. Kanter, *World Class: Thriving Locally in the Global Economy* (New York: Simon and Schuster, 1995).

R. Kiani, "Marketing Opportunities in the Digital World," *Internet Research: Electronic Networking Applications & Policy* vol. 8, #2, 1998.

W. Knoke, *Bold New World: The Essential Road Map to the 21st Century* (New York: Rodensha America, 1996).

M. Komenar, *Electronic Marketing* (New York: John Wiley & Sons, 1997).

D. R. Kosiur, *Understanding Electronic Commerce* (Seattle: Microsoft Press, 1997).

J. Lipnack and J. Stamps, *Virtual Teams—Reaching Across Space, Time and Organizations with Technology* (New York: John Wiley & Sons, 1997).

J. McGonagle Jr., and C. Vella, *The Internet Age of Competitive Intelligence* (Quorum Books, 1999).

D. Mankin, *The Digital Economy* (New York: McGraw-Hill, 1996).

W. Mougayar, *Opening Digital Markets: Advanced Strategies for Internet Driven Commerce,* (New York: McGraw-Hill, 1998).

C. Martin, *The Digital Estate: Strategies for Competing, Surveying, and Thriving in an Internetworked World* (New York: McGraw-Hill, 1997).

J. Martin, *Cybercorp: The New Business Revolution* (New York: Amacom, American Management Association, 1996).

J. Naisbitt, *Global Paradox* (London: N. Breadly, 1994).

N. Negroponte, *Being Digital* (New York: Knopf, 1995).

Net.Genesis Corporation, *Build a World Wide Web Commerce Center* (New York: John Wiley & Sons, 1996).

J. B. Pine II, *Mass Customization* (Boston: Harvard Business School Press, 1993).

B. J. Pine II, and J. Gilmore, "The Four Faces of Mass Customization," *Harvard Business Review* (Jan./Feb. 1997).

M. Scott-Morton and T. J. Allen, eds., *Information Technology and the Corporation of the 1990's* (New York: Oxford University Press, 1994).

J. A. Senn, "Capitalization on Electronic Commerce," *Information Systems Management* (Summer 1996).

J. H. Shonk, *Team-Based Organizations* (Homewood, IL: Business One Irwin, 1992).

T. M. Siebel and M. S. Malone, *Virtual Selling* (New York: The Free Press, 1996).

D. Tapscott et al., eds., *Blueprint to the Digital Economy: Wealth Creation in the Era of E-Business* (New York: McGraw-Hill, 1998).

D. Tapscott and A. Caston, *Paradigm Shift: The New Promise of Information Technology* (New York: McGraw-Hill, 1993).

E. Turban et al., *Information Technology for Management,* 2^d ed. (New York: John Wiley & Sons. 1999).

T. Vassos, *Strategic Internet Marketing* (Indianapolis: Que Pub. Co., 1996).

J. C. Wetherbe, *The World on Time* (Santa Monica, CA: Knowledge Exchange, 1996).

V. Zwass, "Electronic Commerce: Structures and Issues," *International Journal of Electronic Commerce* (Fall 1996).

CHAPTER **2**

Retailing in Electronic Commerce

Learning Objectives

Upon completion of this chapter, the reader will be able to:

- Define the factors that determine the business models of electronic marketing.
- Identify the critical success factors of direct marketing.
- Design the desirable relationship within the direct marketing setting.
- Analyze the critical success factors of electronic brokers.
- Identify the typical products that sell well in the electronic market.
- Observe the reactive strategy of traditional department stores.
- Discuss whether EC should always target the global market.
- Identify the consumer's shopping procedure on the Internet.
- Discuss the types of comparison-shopping aids.
- Describe the impact of EC on disintermediation and reintermediation in retailing.

2.1 Amazon's Competitive Structure

Competition selling books online is growing rapidly, with companies aiming at niche markets (such as old books, technical books, children's books, and price comparison). The global cyber book market is expected to grow to $1.1 billion by 2000. Consider the famous cyber-bookstore Amazon at www.amazon.com. In this chapter, let us investigate the competition structure of the cyber book market by comparing the strength and weakness of Amazon with its competitors. For this purpose, Barnes & Noble is selected as a key competitor.

Amazon is the largest cyber-bookstore in the world, with 50 percent of the cyber book market share. Amazon was opened in July 1995, and it sold $15.7 million in 1996. Its sales climbed to $600 million in 1998, with an astonishing monthly (not annual) growth rate of 34 percent. Amazon listed more than 10 million titles in its electronic catalog in spring 2000, although it actually keeps an inventory of only few thousand high-selling titles in its own warehouse. The other ordered titles are forwarded to the wholesaler Ingram, and FedEx delivers the merchandise to customers. In 1996, Amazon's annual turnover rate of its own inventory was 42, in contrast to 2.1 for Barnes & Noble, who sold books at physical stores. According to our survey performed during summer 1998, both Amazon.com and barnesandnoble.com sold books approximately 14.2 percent cheaper than what traditional bookstores charge. In spite of its loss of $27 million in 1997, Amazon's stock value has risen significantly, hitting $200 per share in January 1999.

Amazon carries 23 categories of books that can be found by clicking "Browse books by subject" (visit Amazon's home page). To assist in finding books, Amazon provides not only a subject directory but also a keyword search engine, as most large electronic shopping malls do. In addition, Amazon provides information about bestsellers, related books for contextual selling, and critiques about many books in the "Hot This Week" corner. It takes about 3 to 7 business days to deliver in the United States, and 4 to 10 weeks abroad. Customers pay the shipping; for the standard U.S. domestic shipments, the charge is $3.00 per shipment plus $0.95 per book. After gaining a reputation as the cyber-bookstore, Amazon expanded its offerings to music, video, gifts, and auction.

The largest retail bookstore chain, Barnes & Noble (www.barnesandnoble.com), started a counterattack in cyberspace in 1997 with the cooperation of Lycos search engine, and it has quickly reached 15 percent of cyber book market share. The strength of Barnes & Noble is its high profit margin of 36 percent (Amazon's margin is 22 percent). In contrast with Amazon's losses, Barnes & Noble had $51 million in profits in 1997—when you combine traditional store and the cyber-bookstore's earnings. Recently, barnesandnoble.com opened an online bookstore for the business market. Barnes & Noble has also acquired Ingram.

Managerial concern in this situation is who can be the most competitive eventually? Is the cooperating model of Amazon and Ingram more effective than the cyber book-retailing channel barnesandnoble.com (www.bn.com) with the traditional nationwide bookstore network? New competitors to both Amazon and Barnes & Noble are BestBookBuys.com, which compares the prices of 18 competitive cyber-bookstores including Amazon and Barnes & Noble (see Application Box 2.2 on p. 56), and Buy.com, which sells books at the lowest price (see the Real World Case at the end of this chapter). What can be the critical success factors for winning the market? See Internet Exercise 5.

2.2 Overview of Electronic Marketing Structure

The opening vignette has demonstrated a competitive structure of electronic retailers. The goal of this chapter is to understand the competitive structures of the electronic market from various angles. As indicated in chapter 1, electronic marketing can be classified as **consumer-oriented** (B2C) and **business-oriented electronic marketing** (B2B). This chapter focuses on consumer-oriented marketing over the Internet. Consumer-oriented electronic marketing is also growing offline, mainly using smart cards, although it is still experimental. There are many common features between consumer-oriented and business-oriented marketing. For instance, the cyber-bookstore Amazon can be used not only by a private consumer but also by a business's acquisition department. Indeed, Amazon's chief rival, Barnes & Noble, has opened a special division that caters only to business customers. Wal-Mart Online sells to both individuals and businesses (via their Sam's Club). Dell sells their computers to both consumers and businesses. Under the seller-centered electronic mall architecture, there are only minor difference in dealing with individual consumers and businesses.

However, with the high volume of transaction and large amount payments, business purchases do need more precise record keeping, trackability, accountability, and formal contracts. The distinctive features of business-oriented electronic marketing are covered in chapter 6, and we focus on consumer-oriented electronic marketing in this chapter. The common features to both consumer-oriented and business-oriented electronic marketing are mainly covered here.

By using the Internet, manufacturers can directly contact customers without using intermediaries. The manufacturer's **direct marketing** can be realized as long as they sell established brands and their home site is well known, as is the case with Dell Computer. Later we will describe how Dell was able to succeed and why other PC makers were not able to duplicate their success.

If a manufacturer's site does not have high visibility, just opening a home page and passively waiting for customers' access may not contribute greatly to sales. Therefore, it is necessary for companies to heavily advertise their Web sites' address. Any cost-effective advertisement method can be employed for this purpose. One example is to link the site to well known electronic directories, and most manufacturers use the directory service of intermediaries. These intermediary sites are called **electronic shopping malls** (or **e-malls**). We can observe two types of electronic shopping malls: **electronic distributors** and **electronic brokers** (e-broker). If the e-mall takes responsibility for order fulfillment, it is an electronic distributor—for example, Amazon and JCPenney Online. In contrast, electronic brokers only help the search process—for example, Choice Mall. The actual order is forwarded to a manufacturer or distributor.

At least during the initial EC stage, established distributors like department stores and discount stores were not the major players in electronic retailing. The traditional distributors used their home pages and electronic catalogs to attract customers to the physical stores, although large distributors like Wal-Mart and JCPenney take orders over the Internet as well. Therefore, we need to study the competition structure of electronic distributors, brokers, and online department stores.

Initially, the main concern for electronic marketing involved securing technologies necessary to implement Internet-based marketing, such as powerful search capability and secure electronic payment. However, today the main concern of management is shifting to how to utilize the opportunity of Internet-based marketing to enhance competitiveness in harmony with existing marketing channels. So we need to examine the use of the coneptually new electronic business models.

Another aspect of electronic marketing is whether it is more effective to use the Internet for **global** or **regional marketing.** To illustrate this we will study later Peapod, which delivers groceries to busy workers in certain urban areas.

In this chapter, we will first explore the criteria of determining business models of electronic marketing. This is described in section 2.4, together with the typical business models. By studying these typical business models, readers will be able to associate an appropriate business model for a particular company. It is also important to understand how to design effective electronic marketing systems. For this purpose, we investigate the customers' purchasing procedure and review the available aids that support the procedure. Those issues are described in sections 2.10 and 2.11.

2.3 Forecast of the B2C Electronic Markets

Before we proceed to the business models, let us review the forecasts about the electronic markets. During the Christmas season in 1998, the U.S. sales volume over the Internet amounted to $5 billion. This is four times the sales volume during the same period in 1997 and more than double the forecast. In this embryonic stage of EC, it is very difficult to predict the sales volume. Nevertheless, it is useful to refer to the forecast to glimpse the experts' opinions.

According to the Organization for Economic Cooperation and Development (OECD) report, many research institutions have attempted to forecast the B2C electronic market size as shown in Table 2.1 (OECD 1997). We notice a large variance in the forecasts with a mean value of $134,906 million. We can explain the high variation in forecasts due to lack of historical data. But even past data (1997) are reported differently. One explanation is the existence of different definitions of what EC is, depending upon the purpose of study. Large figures may include the investment cost in the Internet infrastructure, whereas small figures include merely the pure transactions conducted via the Internet.

Another issue is the kinds of items sold (and those that may be sold in the future) on the Internet. According to the amalgamated report based on various surveys (OECD 1997), the major items sold are apparel, gifts and flowers, books, food and drinks, and computers. However, bigger market items (at least $1 billion each in 2000) are expected to be digitized goods and services such as software, music, video subscriptions, online games, and consumer finance and insurance. These markets are described in the remainder of this chapter as well as in chapters 3 and 5. According to a report in *The Wall Street Journal* (Anders 1998), the expected order of sales volume in 2002 is: travel, PC hardware, books, grocery, apparel and accessories, software, ticketing, music, and specialty gifts, as listed in Table 2.2.

Another useful source of electronic market surveys is the Graphics, Visualization, & Usability (GVU) Center at Georgia Institute of Technology (www.cc.gatech.edu/gvu/user_surveys). A summary of the tenth survey conducted in October 1998 by market segments and by the size of amount purchased is found in Table 2.3. The order of items purchased online are software, books, hardware, music, travel, video, and so forth.

TABLE 2.1 Forecast of B2C Electronic Market Size		
Forecasting Institutions	*1997*	*2000*
IDC	1,000	117,000
VSAComm	48	3,500
VeriFone	350	65,000
Actif Media	436	46,000
Killen & Assoc.		775,000
Yankee	850	144,000
Jupiter	45	580
E-land	450	10,000
EU		228,000
USA	200	
EITO	363	200,000
AEA/AU	200	45,000
Hambrecht & Quest	1,170	23,200
Forrester	518	6,579
mean value	469	134,906
median value	399	46,000

Source: Compiled from OECD (1997 Unit: Millions of U.S. Dollars).

TABLE 2.2	Online Sales by Category (in Millions of U.S. Dollars)	
	1997	*2002*
Travel	$911	$11,699
PC hardware	986	6,434
Grocery	63	3,529
Software	85	2,379
Books	152	3,661
Apparel and accessories	103	2,844
Ticketing	52	1,810
Specialty gifts	100	1,357
Music	37	1,591
Videos	15	575
Toys	2	555
Consumer electronics	15	792
Health and beauty	2	1,183
Other	485	2,689

Source: Compiled from Anders (1998).

TABLE 2.3	Items Purchased Online (Number of Respondents: 645)		
Order	*Items*	*Percentage of Responses*	*Count of Responses*
1	Software	58.0	374
2	Books	52.6	339
3	Hardware	48.5	313
4	Music	41.4	267
5	Travel	30.2	195
6	Video	15.6	102
7	Magazines	14.9	96
8	Electronics	14.0	90
9	Apparel	13.6	88
10	Flowers	13.3	86
11	Banking	12.1	78
12	Investements	11.8	76
13	Concerts	9.9	64
14	Quotes	9.1	59
15	Recreation	5.3	34
16	Autos	4.3	28
17	Generic	2.5	16
18	Insurance	2.5	16
19	Wine	2.3	15
20	Real Estate	2.0	13
21	Jewelry	1.6	10
22	Brand	1.2	8
23	Legal	1.1	7
24	Metals	0.8	5
	Others	12.2	79

Source: Compiled from GVU Center's 10th WWW User Survey 1998.

Within the same product category, the items that meet the following characteristics are expected to sell more:

1. Items with high brand recognition.
2. Hard goods that can be transformed to digitized goods, like books, music, and videos.
3. Items with a security guarantee given by highly reliable or known vendors.
4. Relatively cheap items.
5. Repetitively purchasing items such as groceries.
6. Commodities with standard specifications.
7. Items whose operating procedure can be more effectively demonstrated by video.
8. Packaged items that are well known to customers and that cannot be opened even in a traditional store.

Retailers have to offer satisfactory merchandise, service, promotion, and convenience. Online retail stores, however, should additionally support the fast checkout and ease of navigation throughout the electronic store (Lohse and Spiller 1998).

2.4 Business Models of Electronic Marketing

In this chapter, we explore the major issues related to electronic marketing to consumers. Our discussion began with examination of a competitive structure of online retailers in selling books. To establish the **business models of electronic marketing** to consumers, let us define the important perspectives that compose the electronic business (e-business) models. These perspectives and business models can also be applied to the B2B EC that is described in chapter 6.

DIRECT MARKETING VERSUS INDIRECT MARKETING

Direct marketing means that manufacturers advertise and distribute their own products to customers via the Internet-based electronic store (or other telemarketing media) without intervention of any intermediaries. Dell Computer belongs to this category. On the other hand, **indirect marketing** means the products are distributed through third-party intermediaries such as e-malls.

Manufacturers may sell their own products on the Internet if their electronic stores have high visibility. However, if the direct visibility of the company and brand is too low or managing an independent server is not economically justifiable, which can be the case with small companies, the items may be better displayed in the well-known third-party e-malls.

FULL CYBERMARKETING VERSUS PARTIAL CYBERMARKETING

Full cybermarketing (or **pure cybermarketing**) means the companies like Amazon sell their products and services only through the Internet, whereas **partial cybermarketing** means the companies like Barnes & Noble sell not only through the Internet but also through traditional physical stores. Full cybermarketing companies are new ones born in the e-business era, whereas partial cybermarketing is a reactive response of existing companies who have done business through the physical distribution channels.

ELECTRONIC DISTRIBUTOR VERSUS ELECTRONIC BROKER

Among electronic intermediaries, let us distinguish the *electronic distributors* from *electronic brokers* depending upon whether an electronic intermediary is responsible for order fulfillment and guarantee. Electronic brokers only introduce suppliers who deal with the items that the customers are looking for.

Electronic stores like eToy, Amazon and Wal-Mart Online belong to the category of electronic distributors, whereas the Choice Mall (www.choicemall.com), BestBook-Buys.com and Compare.net belong to the category of electronic brokers. The directory sites like Yahoo can also be regarded as playing the role of electronic brokers. The payments may be collected either by the brokers or by the suppliers depending upon the contract between brokers and suppliers.

ELECTRONIC STORE VERSUS ELECTRONIC SHOPPING MALL

It is not easy to define the difference between an **electronic store (e-store)** and an **electronic shopping mall (e-mall).** In the physical world, a shopping mall is a collection of stores, and the stores in the mall are independent distributors. In this sense, the role of electronic directory broker along with the associated e-stores matches with that of electronic mall. However, many online department stores, call their sites electronic shopping malls instead of electronic stores. The term *electronic shopping mall* is sometimes used as a wide umbrella term of electronic shops and stores as well as malls.

Nevertheless, we need to adopt a default definition to clarify the concept. In this chapter, we will adopt the "number of independent stores" as the default criterion of distinguishing the e-mall from the e-store. Thus, we define an **electronic store** as an electronic distributor whose dealing items are handled by a single store. An *electronic shopping mall* is an electronic distributor or broker whose dealing items are handled by more than a single electronic store.

GENERALIZED E-MALLS/STORES VERSUS SPECIALIZED E-MALLS/STORES

The **generalized e-malls/stores** deal with various categories of items, so the supply items is very wide. Online department stores belong to this category. On the other hand, the **specialized e-malls/stores** focus on only special types of items. The cyberbookstores like Amazon belong to the specialized e-mall, and Dell, which focuses on its own computer products, belongs to the specialized e-store.

PROACTIVE VERSUS REACTIVE STRATEGIC POSTURE TOWARD CYBERMARKETING

Proactive strategic posture toward cybermarketing means that a company's main distribution channel is the Internet, and internal activities such as inventory and operations management are focused to capitalize on the benefit of cybermarketing. In contrast, a **reactive strategic posture toward cybermarketing** means that the traditional physical distribution channels continues to be the main ones even though the company has opened an online distribution channel. So the traditional internal management style and activities are left unchanged.

For instance, Dell has taken a proactive strategic posture in adopting the cybermarketing channel, contacting the customers directly, and making the manufacturing system flexible for mass customization. However, some other PC makers have only reactively turned to cybermarketing as an additional distribution channel, without changing the traditional way of distribution and manufacturing. Most newly created pure cybermarketing companies take the proactive strategic posture, whereas most partial cybermarketing companies take the reactive strategic posture. Two key questions a company will face are which strategic posture is more competitive in the long run, and how will a company transform toward a more effective strategic posture with a given initial condition.

GLOBAL VERSUS REGIONAL MARKETING

Even though the Internet is connected to the entire world, some products and services cannot be provided globally. For instance, perishable items like groceries cannot be delivered long distances. Peapod (www.peapod.com), a grocery delivery service based in Evanston, Illinois, belongs to this category. Delivery costs can limit the range of service to a certain region; legal boundaries limit range of service, as in the case of banking and insurance; and language can also limit business range. So management must decide the geographical range of business considering these factors.

SALES VERSUS CUSTOMER SERVICE

The Web sites of some companies are used mainly or solely for customer service. All major computer hardware and software companies provide customer service sites, which can enhance customer satisfaction while reducing the cost of maintaining call center personnel. Intel, for example, used its site until 1998 primarily for customer service. Some companies use two sites: one for sales and one for service.

Using the eight business models of EC, readers can analyze the current business model of a company and establish an appropriate business model for the future. Planning the transformation of the current situation to the targeted business model is a major managerial concern. In the following sections, we study cases with the perspective of business models.

2.5 Direct Marketing

As an example of a proactive and full direct marketing model, let us investigate the case of Dell Computer Corporation. The readers need to understand how Dell can sell close to $15 million per day (1999) on the Internet, while other computer makers cannot easily duplicate Dell's success. Because Dell sells its products to both consumers and business, this case can also be used for B2B EC in chapter 6. Next, as a contrasting example of reactive and partial direct marketing, we examine the Ford case.

PROACTIVE AND FULL DIRECT MARKETING: THE DELL COMPUTER CASE
Founding Spirit of Dell: Telemarketing

Headquartered in Round Rock, Texas, Dell Computer Corporation was founded in 1984 when Michael Dell pioneered the idea of selling custom-built computers through the mail directly to customers. **Telemarketing** has been the major business strategy since the birth of the company. Therefore, with the emergence of the Internet, it was natural to consider using it as a direct marketing channel. The results were astonishing. By 1998, Dell had become the largest manufacturer and marketer of business PCs in the world, and in 1999 the first for the entire PC market. It has been growing the fastest among all major computer systems makers worldwide. Dell sells computers in more than 170 countries. (See Dell, 1999).

Astonishingly High Growth and Return

Net revenue of Dell for fiscal year 1998 had increased to $18.2 billion, a 48 percent rise from 1997 and four times the industry rate. Net income had risen 82 percent, and the return on invested capital was 186 percent for the year. The stock price had risen more than 1,000 percent during the past two and a half years and recorded the largest share-price gain in the industry. What could make these records possible? The Internet? This is partially true (see Dell, 1999). It is important, however, to observe the factors behind its Internet-based home page.

Revenue via the Internet

In July 1996, Dell launched Internet-based online sales and services at www.dell.com. In Fall 1999, Dell sold $15 million per day through the Internet, and Internet sales have reached about 27 percent of total revenue. In the near future, Dell expects to see 50 percent of its sales over the Internet.

Dell's Products on the Internet

Dell sells all the items it produces on the Internet: desktops, workstations, notebooks, network servers and storage devices, software, and add-ons (e.g., zip drive, printer, Microsoft Plus! 98). Those items are also sold by telephone, fax, and mail, implying that the call center service can complement the Internet home page. Service, support, and introduction to the company are also prepared on the home page.

Dell's Critical Success Factors

Dell's success story is very impressive, so competitors must have a desire to imitate Dell's strategy. But why is it so hard to copy? We can observe six reasons:

- *Advanced Web applications.*   Dell was the first Web-based computer seller and has the best connection, from the end consumers all the way back through the supply chain. Dell uses the Web thoroughly and creatively. Dell allows business buyers to download Premier Pages, which enable customers to configure what information their employees can see, and even which employees can see it (Thurm 1998).
- *Price competitiveness owing to mass customization.*   Direct marketing to small consumers as well as corporate buyers means the manufacturing system should be adaptive to the small orders in a *make-to-order* fashion. To keep the price competitive without longer delivery time, efficient procurement of small numbers of parts from vendors, flexible manufacturing systems, and economical distribution to customers are a must.

    Recall that Dell Computer was born with the spirit of telemarketing, and the Internet is just another excellent medium of contacting distant customers interactively. There was no need for Dell to change business strategy to adopt Internet commerce. However, for other companies, this may not be the case. Changing the business strategy fundamentally may be very difficult, expensive, and time-consuming.
- *Database marketing and customer intimacy.*   Dell's direct relationship with all of its customers makes one-to-one database marketing possible. Dell can learn about its customers by watching how they use the Web site. For this purpose, the database, as well as the tools for data mining such as statistical analysis, inductive learning, and neural network modeling, are used to classify customer segments. This is essential for focusing on and deepening the personalized relationship. This can be used for advertisement and customer services as well.
- *Global reach and value-added services at a single contact point.*   Dell has more than 10,000 service providers around the world who provide technology planning and acquisition, system deployment, network, and product maintenance. The Internet can provide an efficient single point of contact

for these services backed by corporate-level accountability for their products and services. The Internet makes it easier and reduces costs for customers to do business with Dell. Because the customers spend their own time to obtain the service from the Internet, which required human agents in the call center previously; the Internet also reduces Dell's cost. The Internet can be used effectively to enhance relationships with suppliers as well as customers.

- *High reliability and reputation.* If the products do not have high reliability, customers will hesitate to order the items without a trial. Dell was well prepared in this regard. Dell's products OptiPlex and Dell Dimension Desktop computer, have garnered an unprecedented 174 awards for performance, reliability, and service. Dell's customers do not worry about the reliability of the Dell brand.

- *Delivery support.* An inherent disadvantage of telemarketing is the relatively longer lead time needed for delivery. To overcome this deficiency, Dell provides the estimated delivery time as well as online order tracking information for each order. When the product inventory and/or parts are available, Dell can deliver a simple configuration in 2–3 days, average in 5 days, and complex in 7–10 days. However, if the parts are not readily available, the lead time is estimated and the customer is informed.

We have seen how Dell became successful, and why it is not easy for other manufacturers to duplicate the success. Nevertheless, no major manufacturers can neglect the opportunity of direct marketing. Managerial concern is the degree of strategic change. In this process, the ultimate measure will be the economics of EC. Is the benefit of EC bigger than its implementation cost?

Major benefits include increased revenue, enhanced consumer goodwill owing to the online service and support, and reduced operating costs for distribution and purchasing. Benefits will be relative to the initial business position of each company and its possibility of changing business structure toward telemarketing and make-to-order systems.

Basic costs of implementing EC include home page system development and maintenance, server and network acquisition and operation, merchandising, order fulfillment, collection of payment, and optional call center operation. However, a more fundamental cost can be incurred when management commits to change the way of doing business, such as changing the major distribution channels and manufacturing systems. For a comprehensive discussion on the economics of EC, see chapter 12.

REACTIVE AND PARTIAL DIRECT MARKETING: FORD CASE

In contrast with proactive and full direct marketers, who fully commit to direct marketing, other companies, which we call reactive and partial direct marketers, sell their products mainly through traditional channels like dealers, department stores, discount stores, and franchises; however, they also open online factory outlets on the Internet. Most computer makers belong to this category. We foresee that all major manufacturers will adopt either a proactive or reactive direct marketing strategy in the near future.

In this section, we investigate the Ford case as an example of reactive and partial direct marketing. Ford, like other automakers, could not switch its distribution channel to the Internet overnight. So it opened its e-store as an additional distribution channel.

Ford Case

The benefit of ordering online is bypassing dealers, thereby reducing the selling price and/or increasing profit. However, automakers cannot completely eliminate dealers because many customers do not have access to the Internet or do not want to shop online. Under such a circumstance, including dealers as partners is an optimal arrangement because orders that are received directly by the automakers cannot be physically fulfilled without the cooperation of dealers. An order received can then be assigned to the nearest dealer that has the desired car in its inventory. For such co-operation, dealers' inventories should be shared by automakers through a common network like the ANX extranet (chapter 7). Internet Exercise 4 provides practice in online car configuration, which is described next.

Ford's Reactive Direct Marketing Model

Ford implemented a variation of the reactive direct marketing (refer to www.ford. com). To order a new car online, you need to select the brand, body style, option pack-age, exterior paint color, and interior upholstery. Then the Online Shopping System provides you with a Vehicle Summary, including a suggested retail price. You can change options to accommodate your budget and finalize the configuration. Next, you decide whether to lease or buy with the aid of the Payment Calculator System. Ford searches for a nearby dealer and sends the Vehicle Summary to the dealer. The dealer will contact you with a price and availability of the vehicle you configured. Here you have a chance to negotiate.

In the current procedure, the information about which dealer keeps inventory that meets the required configuration is not available to the buyer. In this sense, the current system is a semiautomatic support. In the future, the buyer will have such information as well as an estimated time for preparing a customized car not available in stock.

Ford also supports a Preowned Showroom (www.fordpreowned.com). To buy a used car online, you need to enter the zip code and search the inventory. By entering your personal information, you can reserve your vehicle and select a dealership for test drive and delivery. The rest of the process is the same as the current purchasing procedure.

In both of these Ford business models, we can see that the dealers are not targeted for elimination but are partners who are cooperating in a new sales procedure as a result of the Internet. It is reported that only 2 percent of 15 million new vehicle sales and 33 million used vehicle sales were consummated over the Internet in 1997. But it is predicted that 25 percent of all car sales in the United States in 2000 will be initiated online.

Some car manufacturers, like Toyota and Daewoo, are considering the possibility of eliminating the dealers and offering all service, including financing, on the Internet. They will also consider coming to your home for the test drive. For more on selling automobiles on the Internet, see www. autodytel.com and Application Case 2.1.

2.6   Online Customer Service

Online customer service is provided in conjunction with online sales, as can be seen in Dell's site. Customer service online is also provided to products that are sold offline. From the serving company's point of view, there is no difference whether the customers are consumers or businesses. The Service and Support home page of Hewlett Packard (www.hp.com) offers software support, hardware support, services, consulting and outsourcing, customer education, and technology financing. It is reported that

---

APPLICATION CASE 2.1

Automobile Sales Online

GM's Web site, BuyPower, Chrysler's Web site, Get a Quote, and Ford's Web site take orders to sell cars. Manufacturers envision the Web sites as tools to fend off competition from savvy retailers such as AutoNation, a nationwide dealership chain. Many dealers fear that the Internet could one day force them out of business or reduce them to mere order takers. Fifty percent of dealers see the Internet as a threat, and only 10 percent see Internet-based sales as a positive development. Automakers have tried to calm the dealers' fears, arguing that the Web sites are really developed for dealers because the taken orders will be eventually connected to the dealers. Some dealers are proactive. For instance, Ira Motor Group is set to roll out a series of on-site kiosks at its nine dealerships. The kiosks let customers not only browse inventory without walking onto the lot but also pick out a car and its option, apply for credit with multiple lenders, and get approval, all without talking to a salesperson (Fontana 1998). Ira Motor Group found positive reaction from customers and expects the kiosks to become more popular.

Third-party online showrooms have also opened. For instance, Microsoft's CarPoint is a challenging distribution system. CarPoint, Auto-By-Tel, and Autovantage are equipped with agents. A question is how will these distribution systems compete with each other, and what will be the role of dealers in the long run? Can dealers be eliminated completely? Under what circumstances would this happen, and when would it not? See also Team Exercise 1.

---

65 percent of customers' technical support inquiries are handled over the Web. It is also reported that Cisco has saved $500 million in supporting costs owing to a $20 million investment for Internet-based customer service systems.

To support the configuration of sophisticated products, Web-based expert systems combined with motion pictures and virtual reality will be employed in the next-generation EC platforms. In the meantime, a call center equipped with computer telephone integration (CTI) can be synergistically adopted with electronic marketing (see chapter 3). By using CTI technology, the same screen that a customer sees can be automatically displayed to the human agent (and vice versa) who responds to the customer's call while watching the online data about the customer (Moon et al. 1998).

2.7 Electronic Intermediaries

Now let us explore the business models of intermediating retailers. Again, the retailers can be classified as pure and partial electronic intermediaries depending upon the level of commitment to the electronic retailing business.

Pure e-mall implies that the company's retailing business exists only on the Internet, so the company has a full commitment to electronic retailing. In contrast, a company with a *partial e-mall strategy* regards the e-mall as one of distribution business. For a comprehensive list of e-malls, visit a cyber-mall directory site (www.cybermall.com). This site shows the list of premium malls, specialty malls, regional malls, shopper's resources, and hot stores. Volunteering malls can link to this site free of charge.

The pure e-malls can be classified into two categories: *electronic distributors* or *electronic brokers* (e-brokers). As briefly defined in section 2.4, an electronic distributor takes full responsibility for fulfilling orders and collecting payment. In contrast, an electronic broker just assists the search for the appropriate product and its vendors. So a broker does not need to execute the order fulfillment, guarantee, and payment collection. Brokers may receive commissions from vendors to whom the orders are channeled.

The expertise that e-brokers need involves computer and network technology, security, and search capability. Therefore, the scope of covering items tends to be very broad. Also, e-brokers can link many e-stores worldwide. For example, the www.shopnow.com includes more than 30,000 stores, linking many companies worldwide. In contrast, the expertise that electronic distributors need is merchandising, quality assurance, and customer service. Therefore, electronic distributors usually deal with items much smaller in scope, covering specialized categories of products in which the e-store can keep a competitive advantage. For instance, Amazon specializes in books, CDNow in music, 1-800-Flowers.com in flowers, and Virtual Vineyard in wines. In this section, let us analyze the effectiveness of generalized and specialized e-malls.

GENERALIZED E-BROKERS

Open Market (www.openmarket.com), Internet Mall (www.internet-mall.com), and iMall (www.imall.com) are typical examples of e-brokers. In November 1996, more than 47,000 electronic shops worldwide registered with Open Market, hoping to generate orders through Open Market's directory service. Electronic brokers must provide a directory, keyword search engine, message encryption, optional Web site hosting service, and a common platform of electronic payments in order to attract electronic shops. Many technology-driven companies jumped into this kind of business in the early stage of EC.

There are no precise statistics on how many orders are received through these brokers. However, we have observed an unfortunate phenomenon. Open Market's registration has not increased significantly since 1996, and the company closed their brokerage service. Several other broker-type malls went out of business in 1998. This makes us believe that sales volume through these brokers was not sufficient. It is important to explore why this happened.

Recently, comparison aids using software agents are emerging as a new breed of brokers. For instance, the site Compare.net compares the selected items from multiple perspectives (see section 2.11 for the comparison aids). The directory and search sites also perform the role of broker. For instance, the Y!Auction corner of Yahoo, and Excite, practically support the process of seeking items in need. Now, let us consider the factors that are necessary to make the e-broker business successful.

Screening for Assurance

Obviously the most critical success factor of B2C EC is consumer behavior in cyberspace. Will consumers order unknown brands? Will they even explore the site of an unknown company? It seems that without advance knowledge and assurance, few customers are willing to seek the unfamiliar brand of an unfamiliar company, especially in a foreign country. In this sense, providing a wide range of options by itself is not sufficient. Customers need a way to assess the quality and reliability of brands and companies, as the established department stores do. But this was not the expertise of technology-intensive brokering companies. See chapter 3 for more on customer behavior.

Competing Electronic Channels

Another point is that e-brokers are not the only electronic channel of finding items in need. For instance, to buy a book, will customers visit Amazon, Barnes & Noble, or Shopnow? To buy a Dell Computer, will customers visit Dell's site or the Choice Mall or JCPenney Online? If the URLs of the sites that deal with personal computers are not known, will customers consult Yahoo, Alta Vista, or the Shopnow? If the Shopnow is not the choice in the answer to these questions—which seems the case at the moment—e-brokers like the Shopnow should provide some differentiated attraction. Otherwise, the role of e-broker may diminish further.

Nevertheless, the directory capability of generalized malls is useful for customers in searching for new suppliers and retailers. Typical sites for this purpose include www.aol.com, www.shopper.com, www.virtualemporium.com, and www.yahoo.com.

SPECIALIZED ELECTRONIC DISTRIBUTORS

Some specialized electronic distributors that sell one or a few groups of products are very successful. Typically, successful specialty stores sell books, CDs, flowers, consumer electronic products, computer hardware and software, automobiles, and clothing. In addition, there are successful online services such as online stock trade brokers, travel agents, and online banks as described in chapter 5. Let us review some successful cases in the following sections.

Cyber Bookstores

As described in the opening case, Amazon competes with Barnes & Noble, which has an advertisement linkage on the search engine site Lycos Inc. Although there are more competitors in the book market, it is useful to compare these two business models. Recall the following factors that will determine long-term competitiveness in cyber-bookstores: scope of titles, price competitiveness, provision of not only book sales but also information about books, relationship marketing support with the registered customer community, a reliable recommendation center, many categories of books (e.g., technical books, childrens' books), and so forth. Another challenge comes for a software agent for seeking the lowest price, as in BestBookBuys.com (see Application Case 2.2) and Buy.com (see Real World Case) do. We also need to consider the impact of electronic publishing on the cyber book retailing business with a long-term perspective.

Other factors that we should not neglect are language and cultural barriers. For example, neither Amazon nor Barnes & Noble carry Korean books, so the popular bookstores in Korea can go online without any competition from these English sites.

Cyber CD Stores

Columbia House (www.columbia.house), Music Boulevard (www.n2k.com), CD Universe (www.cduniverse.com), and CDNow (www.cdnow.com) are the most successful (in 1999) CD dealers in cyberspace. CDNow earned a $6 million profit in 1996. Columbia House and Music Boulevard had 3.1 million and 2.3 million visits respectively during October 1998. These sites usually provide online sample music service. But the following business models challenge these specialized CD vendors:

- Competing online vendors, such as N_2k(www.n2k.com, which is merging with CDNow), and K-Tel(www.ktel.com)
- Cyber-bookstores: Amazon sells CDs, too
- Traditional CD distributors' online sites:
  Allegro Corporation (www.teleport.com/~allegro)
  Multicultural Media (www.multiculturalmedia.com)
- CD manufacturers' online sites:
  BMG Entertainment (www.bmg.com)
  Sony (www.music.sony.com)
  Polygram (www.polygram.com)
  EMI (www.emiclassics.com)

A major, managerial concern is how the electronic CD stores can survive in such a competitive environment.

Digitized Products and Services Stores

Software, games, CDs, and videos are usually sold in the same sites, but www.intraware.com, www.egghead.com (up to 1999), and www.softwarebuyline.com are dedicated mainly to software sales. Even though they sell most software via diskettes at the moment, they will mainly be distributing through the Internet in the future. The sites www.hotwired.com and www.real.com are examples of real audio-augmented sites. With the advent of MP3 (Motion Picture Expert Group, Layer 3) technology, quality music can be directly delivered over the Internet, so CDs may no longer have a monopoly on storing and distributing music. Vendors will have to consider which business model will be the most competitive in the long run. It is interesting to note that Egghead merged with onsale, adding auctions to its business model.

Cyber Flower Shops

As a case of a specialized electronic store, let us review 1-800-Flowers. The company is the world's largest florist with sales of $300 million in 1997 and an average 40 percent compound growth rate during 1995–1997. The company handled 9 million orders per year through 1-800-Flowers stores, a toll-free telephone number, and their interactive Internet service. To meet the demand, 150 shops are company owned or franchised, and 2,500 shops are in business partnership. Internet-based sales through www.1800flowers.com contributed approximately 13 percent of overall sales in 1999. In this case, the traditional toll-free order-receiving model is well aligned with the business model of the e-store.

2.8   Reactive Electronic Department Stores

Popular department stores and discount stores worldwide have opened reactive online department stores on the Internet. In the beginning stage, the sites were used just for advertisement, to attract customers to physical stores. But now, many of the sites receive orders and payments online. In contrast to the pure and proactive electronic stores like Amazon, let us classify the strategy of established department stores like JCPenney and Wal-Mart as **partial and reactive electronic department stores.** The JCPenney case demonstrates this business model.

THE JCPENNEY CASE

The well-known department store JCPenney is positioned to serve consumers in nearly 1,200 physical stores, through catalog offerings, and over the Internet. In 1998, the company completed an extensive database marketing study about shopping patterns of 90 million U.S. households. JCPenney has in early 1999 begun to mine these data to identify areas of opportunity in market segments that have the highest potential for future sales.

Internet-based revenue amounts to less than or 2 percent of $30.5 billion total sales in 1997. The total revenues were realized as follows: department stores, 52 percent; catalog, 13 percent; drugstores, 32 percent; and insurance, 3 percent.

To complement sales in physical department stores, JCPenney opened the nation's largest paper catalog operation. Catalog shopping is viewed as an area of growing opportunity, particularly for the aging population, which places increasing emphasis on convenience.

Catalog desks are located in virtually all domestic JCPenney stores, in a number of drugstores, and in stand-alone catalog stores—a total of 1,902 locations. Catalog orders are handled through the country's largest privately owned telecommunications network and six Catalog Fulfillment Centers. Now the business is expanding, using the Internet and EC.

About 400 million printed catalogs were distributed in 1997, in conjunction with the electronic catalog on the Internet. The electronic catalog is a natural extension of printed catalogs, making JCPenney one of the pioneering department stores that has opened an online shopping service. Because updating prices and adding new items to the electronic catalogs are convenient and inexpensive, the electronic catalog can overcome the limitation of paper catalogs without incurring extra distribution costs. For further discussion about electronic catalogs, see chapter 4.

ELECTRONIC DEPARTMENT STORES WORLDWIDE

Wal-Mart offered more than 80,000 items on the Internet in 1998. Most leading department stores worldwide—like Marks & Spencer in the United Kingdom, La Redoute in France, Jusco in Japan, Nordstrom and Macys in the United States, and Lotte and Hyundai Department Stores in Korea—have online shopping sites on the Internet.

A common strategic question to these reactive electronic department stores is "What are the value-added benefits to customers: Reduced price? Reduced shopping time? Offering products that cannot be found in the physical store? Or just convenience of shopping anytime from any place?" If there are no significant benefits, and the consumers have to visit the stores physically to pick up the merchandise, such reactive electronic department stores may not attract shoppers. Nevertheless, department stores today must offer electronic service on the Internet as a supplementary channel of advertisement, even though the actual online sales may be very low. However, it is predicted that in 1999, 39 percent of all U.S. major retailers will have an online selling website.

2.9 Regional Shopping Service

Even though the Internet can reach the entire world, the feasible service may be limited if the items are perishable, the service network is geographically limited, and delivery cost is significant and increases rapidly with distance. As a model of regional shopping service, let us observe the characteristics of Peapod Inc. (See Internet Exercise 1 and chapter 3 for a discussion of Netgrocer, a national distributor of online non-perishable items. See also the red word case of Chapter 1).

Peapod Case

Peapod Inc. is the leading Internet supermarket, providing consumers with broad product choices and local delivery services. In 1998, the company provided such services in seven metropolitan markets in the United States and served more than 103,000 members. Based in Evanston, Illinois, Peapod was founded in 1989 as a telephone- and catalog-based service provider. Its business motto is a "smart shopping aid for busy people for 25,000 grocery and drugstore items."

The site www.peapod.com provides pictures, nutritional content, past purchase records and food recipe to encourage repetitive purchase. Busy shoppers order online, and a nearby partner supermarket packs the ordered items and delivers within 90 minutes or at an appointed time. Express delivery within 30 minutes can be requested for an extra fee. The handling and delivery service is $6.95 plus 5 percent of the purchased amount. Unlike other e-malls and e-stores, there is a $4.95-per-month membership fee. Despite the extra fees, the customer retention rate is greater than 80 percent. The major merit is saving time. The users are middle- and upper-class people, some of whom are single parents, and all of whom are very busy, or home bound.

2.10 Procedure for Internet Shopping: The Consumer's Perspective

To understand the procedure of electronic shopping, let us examine the purchasing steps with illustrative cases. One factor that we must pay attention to is that the number of storefronts on the Internet is sveral millions. How can customers find what they need? To answer this question, it is first necessary to examine the purchasing procedure on the Internet from the consumer's point of view. Consumers' mercantile activities can be classified into seven steps, all of which need to be satisfied to keep customers:

1. Preliminary requirement determination
2. Search for the available items that can meet the requirement
3. Compare (possibly with negotiation) the candidate items with multiple perspectives: specification, price, delivery date, and other terms or conditions
4. Place an order
5. Pay the bill
6. Receive the delivered items and inspect them
7. Contact the vendor to get after-service and support, or to return if disappointed

To find the best quality and price, consumers need to visit many potential e-malls to compare multiple alternatives. On the other hand, each vendor tries to hold the customers at its own site. So many of the e-malls tend to request membership registration, offering their own shopping cart. If an e-mall can provide all comparable alternatives, the customer can find the best selection by comparing the alternatives within the mall. However, this is not the case in most shopping. Visiting many sites sitting in front of a computer is a very time-consuming task. It is not a trivial matter to compare the items in different sites. So customers need a systematic supporting tool like software agents for this purpose. For a comprehensive review of agents, refer to appendix C.

Let us illustrate each step with examples of Tom's purchasing a personal computer and Judy's purchasing a book. Observe the contrast of the two cases carefully.

PRELIMINARY REQUIREMENT DETERMINATION

Suppose Tom wants to buy a personal computer with which to access the Internet, but he also needs a word processor and spreadsheet software. If the price is reasonable, he may buy a notebook computer with the options of high-quality multimedia and wireless connectability. He also needs a color printer. In this example, we can see that the need may not be fixed in the beginning stage, because the price and function are negotiable in Tom's mind.

Next, suppose Judy wants to give the book *Monica's Story* by Andrew Morton to her friend. In this case, Judy's requirement is clearly known and fixed. This means Tom needs more comparison between functionality and price than Judy does.

SEARCH FOR AVAILABLE ITEMS

Tom may want to visit several online department stores, discount stores, auction sites, and factory outlets; Judy may access either Amazon or Barnes & Noble. Suppose Tom already knows that online JCPenney, Wal-Mart, and Dell Computer sell personal computers, and he also wants to survey stores that are not known to him yet. How can he find other stores that sell similar computers at lower prices? Tom can start by consulting one of the search engines listed in the Netscape home pages like Yahoo,

BestBookBuys.com Finds the Best Price

Best Book Buys has won the 1998 "Coolest Book Site of the Year" Award at the fourth annual Cool Site of the Year Awards in New York City, beating out Amazon, Barnes & Noble, Borders, and Audio Book Club.

The Best Book Buys search engine searches 18 electronic bookstores including Amazon and Barnes & Noble. Agents collect these data and display them in a comparison table. Try to find a book through BestBookBuys.com. Find out the prices of the book at Amazon and Barnes &

Noble. Does Amazon or Barnes & Noble offer the cheapest price? Will you still order from Amazon or Barnes & Noble? What is the expected behavior of overall book buyers?

Will Amazon allow the visit of agents for price comparison? If the lowest price is not the most attractive aspect of a certain cyber-bookstore, what should be a differentiated benefit to offer to the customers?

Reference site: biz.yahoo.com/bw/990222/ca_best_we_1.html.

Excite, Hot Bot, AltaVista, and so on. But such a search can be lengthy and unproductive at times. In addition, Tom has to compare the alternatives, considering functions and price. So the search itself is not the final step of product selection.

On the other hand, all that Judy seeks is the bookstore that sells the book at the lowest price because the book is the same no matter where one buys it. Judy may visit Amazon. She may also consult BestBookBuys.com (Application Case 2.2) to compare the prices in 18 bookstores, and she could check the price of Buy.com, whose strategy is selling books at the lowest price.

COMPARE THE CANDIDATE ITEMS WITH MULTIPLE PERSPECTIVES

Tom noticed that many e-malls tried to keep him as an eternal customer, asking him to register and provide personal data. This bothers him very much. But let us assume that Tom is very patient. He believes that entering personal information one time in a first visit to a site is better than physically visiting each store for every shopping experience for the rest of his lifetime. However, Tom has to search for each e-mall using its own directory and/or keyword search engine. Each e-mall asks him to put products into a shopping cart or bag, as shown in Figure 2.1. He believes that the electronic shopping system with a shopping cart at each e-mall is very ineffective for comparison. This is particularly true for B2B EC, in which comparisons are a must. To help Tom, the e-broker Compare.net searches for the products that meet the requirements and display the comparison table in terms of specification and price. Upon selection after this comparison process, Compare.net links you to the e-store, which actually takes the order. For aids to comparison shopping, see section 2.11.

In contrast, Judy does not hesitate to put the book into the shopping bag because she does not need to compare functionalities, and she selected the lowest price.

PLACE AN ORDER

Suppose Tom has selected a PC from JCPenney. Tom can then place the items in the shopping cart and click the checkout button to order. Judy can of course order her book in a similar way at a cyber-bookstore like Amazon.

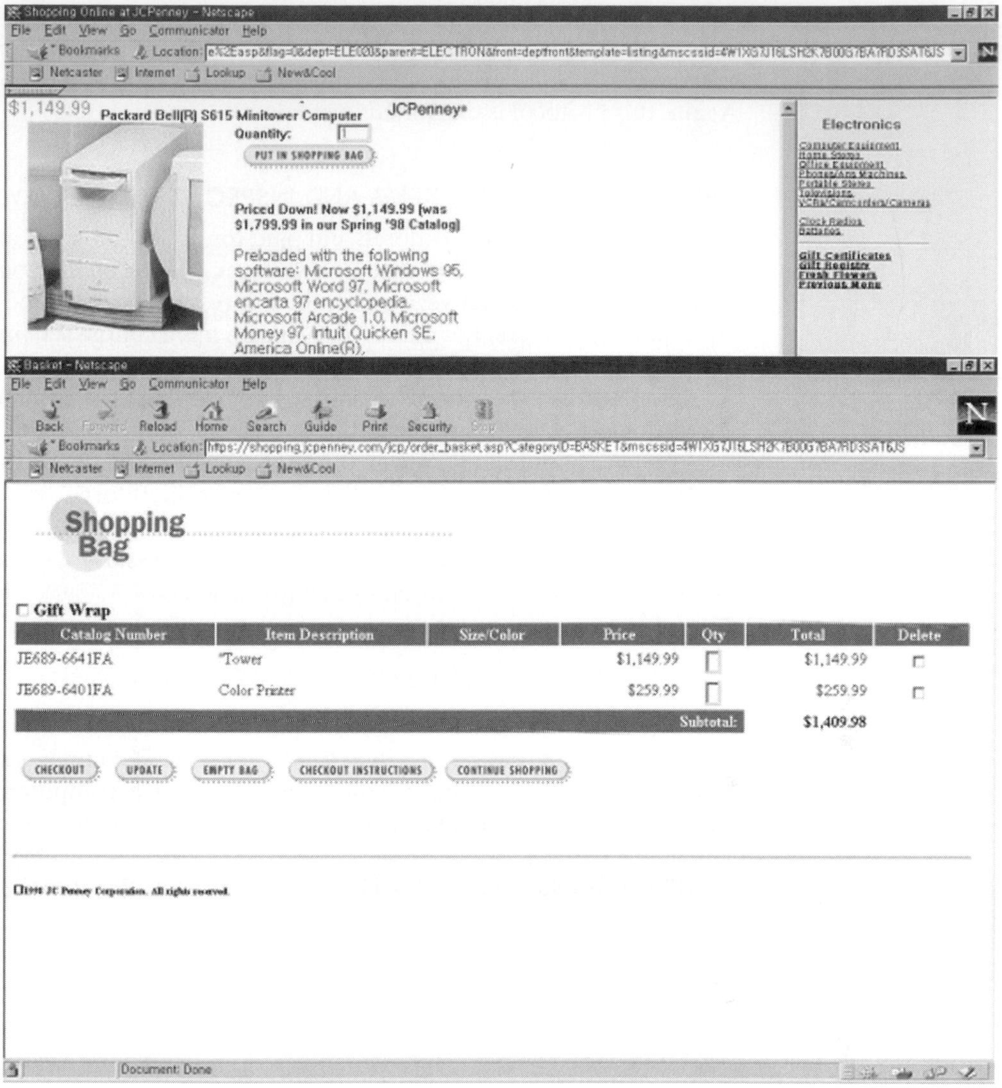

FIGURE 2.1 Place the Selected Items in the Shopping Bag.

PAY FOR THE GOODS

Now both Tom and Judy have to pay for the merchandise they purchased. To pay with a credit card, buyers select a card type and key-in the name of the card, card number, and expiration date, much as when shopping over the phone. The locked key in the bottom left-hand of the browser implies the current message will be encrypted by the Secure Socket Layer (SSL) protocol. (Chapter 8 explains these payment and security schemes.) Can Tom feel safe with the SSL encryption? He thinks so. However, he recalls that he has shown the card and allowed service providers to duplicate the information on the plastic card many times at restaurants and supermarkets. Tom may fear that his personal information can be abused whether he types the information on the Internet or not.

To prevent faked authenticity, a safer method that involves high-level encryption and certification on a smart card is needed. These are implemented in a protocol called SET (Secure Electronic Transaction), which the EC community is pursuing. Again, this protocol is explained in chapter 8.

RECEIVE THE DELIVERED ITEMS AND INSPECT THEIR QUALITY

As the selected items are ordered and paid for, the vendor will arrange the delivery. In this example, JCPenney may use its own truck, whereas Amazon will ask FedEx to deliver. To identify the delivery point, the address should be filled out. Delivery charges differ among vendors. For example, Amazon has a charge scheme depending upon the delivery location, shipping time, and number of books.

Suppose Judy wants to read only several chapters from the book, so she decides to order an electronic version from the publisher. Then, the digitized book will be delivered over the Internet. Software that has been distributed on diskettes or on CD-ROMs will be encouraged to be delivered over the Internet as well, because the delivery time takes only seconds and the tax may be waived. This electronic delivery of digitized goods can really automate the entire process of EC—order, payment, and delivery without any intervention of human agents.

CONTACT THE VENDOR TO GET AFTER-SERVICE AND SUPPORT, OR RETURN THE GOODS IF DISAPPOINTED

If Tom needs support in installing the system, the JCPenney service department may provide it. In contrast, his neighbor, who bought a computer from Dell, consulted Dell's service corner on Dell's home page and found there may be no need for a physical visit.

This procedure illustrates how to purchase on the Internet from the customer's point of view. This procedure also illustrates how storefronts and e-malls should be designed so that they can optimally meet the customer's needs.

2.11   Aiding Comparison Shopping

In steps 2 and 3 in the previous section, we learn that EC aids search and comparison. This is a consumer's dream but a merchant's nightmare. The Internet empowers consumers with more information than they could possibly get by cruising the shopping malls by car. The capability of searching for goods on hundreds of Web sites in seconds puts unprecedented pressure on Web retailers to beat their competitors' prices. Many retailers worry that comparison shopping will set off a vicious pricing war in cyberspace and force them to slice profit margins to razor-thin levels (Quick 1998). Infact, the price war has already begun (Application Case 2.2).

Now let us investigate the ways EC aids comparison shopping, which we can classify into five categories. They are described in the following sections.

SEARCH OF HYPERTEXT FILES BY AGENTS

Early commercial sites were developed in hypertext files (appendices A and B). The major concern at this stage is the collection of distributed HTML (Hypertext Markup Language) files and the interpretation of natural-language-like descriptions.

An early experimental agent, BargainFinder (bf.cstar.ac.com/bf), belongs to this category. Suppose a customer has asked BargainFinder for a CD of Selena's "Dreaming of You." The agent responds with the list price and vendor's name along with shipping cost. This can be useful information to customers, but the agent should have spent significant effort to interpret the files if they are not. Because of this and other limitation (see Chapter 3), BargainFinder and similar agents could not proceed beyond the experimental stage.

Another issue not treated sufficiently at this stage is that customers may want to search for not only price but also other features. For example, high-quality brand owners would not be interested in searching for the minimum priced items, neglecting all other aspects of products—functionality, reliability, guarantee, and so on. Coming soon from MIT labs are the agents that will deal with multicriteria comparison.

SEARCH IN A WEB-BASED DATABASE: HUMAN AND SOFTWARE AGENTS SHARING INFORMATION

Because of the difficulty of processing orders using hypertext files, electronic catalogs were built using a Dynamic Web-based DBMS (DataBase Management System). In this architecture, HTML is regarded as another kind of report-writing language. The price and specification could be retrieved from the database via query languages for software agents. In addition, a formatted hypertext file can be generated dynamically upon the request of a URL (Uniform Resource Locator). In this manner, human and software agents can share the electronic catalog stored in the database.

Several software agents are available for this purpose, they are listed in Table 2.4. For example, the agents Jango, Junglee, MySimon, CompareNet, Shopfido, Uvision, and Comparisonshopping can find products and compare their prices (Internet Exercise 3). Several search engines specialize in certain products. For example, Auto-by-tel, Autovantage, and Carpoint help you to shop for cars. Netbuyer helps with the purchase of computers and communication. The agent in www.atyouroffice.com helps you with office supplies. In addition, agents such as Firefly, Empirical, and Webdoggie have the capability of learning about customers' preferences. There are many other services that can help you to shop. For example, www.100hot.com will list the 100 hot Web sites in many categories.

A group of commercialized middleware can be used to help the development of electronic catalog, ordering, and payment management. These tools are awkwardly called *merchant*. Typical tools in the market are Oracle's ICS (1999), IBM's NetCommerce (1999a,b), Microsoft's SiteServer (1999a,b), Intershop (1999), and Open Market (1999). These tools are only equipped with the search engines, leaving the comparison to the customer. However, owing to the capability of query language in DBMS, the customer's inquiry can be flexibly expressed in a menu-driven dialogue, as illustrated in Figure 2.2 (Compare.net [www.compare.net]).

COMPARABLE ITEM RETRIEVAL AND TABULAR COMPARISON

Compare.net also supports the retrieval of comparable items. Definition of the term *comparable* can vary from system to system, but the concept is useful. The similarity measure adopted in case-based reasoning (Kolodner 1993) can be applied for this purpose. Interesting items can be picked up and asked for the tabular comparison as illustrated in Figure 2.3 (page 63). By providing such a display, multiple-criteria comparisons can become more effectively supported. In this example, two notebook models

TABLE 2.4 Survey of Key Agent Applications and Technology

Agent Classification	Product	Description	URL
Learning Agents	Firefly	Helps users find music that they are likely to enjoy. It uses information gathered from others, similar to the users' in tastes and opinions, to suggest new music.	www.firefly.com
	Empirical	Surveys users' reading interests and then uses machine learning to find new Web pages and news articles using neural-network-based collaborative filtering technology.	www.empirical.com
	Webdoggie	Attempts to mitigate the impact of information overload. Either on demand or periodically, the system recommends Web documents based on user-expressed preferences (e.g., interesting, boring, and so on).	webhound.www.media.mit .edu/projects/webhound
Comparison Shopping Agents	Jango	Adapted to Excite's shopping guide.	www.jango.com
	Junglee	Construct a lot of shopping guides such as Yahoo, Visa, Compaq, Hot Bot, and so on.	www.junglee.com
	MySimon	Using VLA (Virtual Learning Agent) technology, Simon can shop at merchants in hundreds of product categories on the Web. Simon shops with real-time interface for the best price.	www.mysimon.com
	CompareNet	An interactive buyer's guide that educates shoppers and allows them to make direct comparisons between brands and products.	www.compare.net
	Shopfido	Centralized database query site built by Continuum Software Inc.	www.shopfido.com
	Uvision	Provides shopping guide by linking to other sites.	www.shopper.com
	Comparison shopping	Front door service.	www.comparisonshopping .com
AI/Logic-Supported Approaches	Personalogic	AOL's shopping decision guide.	www.aol.personalogic.com
	Analog Device	Online catalog sales using Case Based Reasoning (WEBSELL Project).	wwwagr.informatik.uni-kl.de/,lsa/CBR/www cbrindex.html
Computer-Related Shopping Guide	Netbuyer	Supplies sales and marketing solutions to technology companies, by delivering actionable, fact-based information on computer and communications industry trends, product developments, and buyer activity.	www.netbuyer.com
Car-Related Shopping Guide	Auto-By-Tel	A low-cost, no-haggle car-buying system of choice for leading search engines and online programs such as Excite, Netscape's NetCenter, Lycos, and AT&T WorldNet Services.	www.autobytel.com
	Autovantage	Provides the Web's premier savings site for great deals on auto, travel, shopping, dining, and other services.	www.cendant.com/ctg/cgi-bin/AutoVantage
	Carpoint	Makes the auto site a one-stop shopping place for searching and purchasing automobiles.	carpoint.msn.com
Microsoft-Related Agent Technology	Agentmart	Introduces and reviews Microsoft's agent. Provides agent infospace and agent directory. First Web site on animated conversational characters such as Genie, Merlin, and so on.	www.argolink.com (www.agentmart.com)
Agent Technology-Related Software	Agentsoft	Automates much of what users do for Web browsing and searching. Developed using script style (LiveAgent Pro Ver 1.1).	www.agentsoft.com

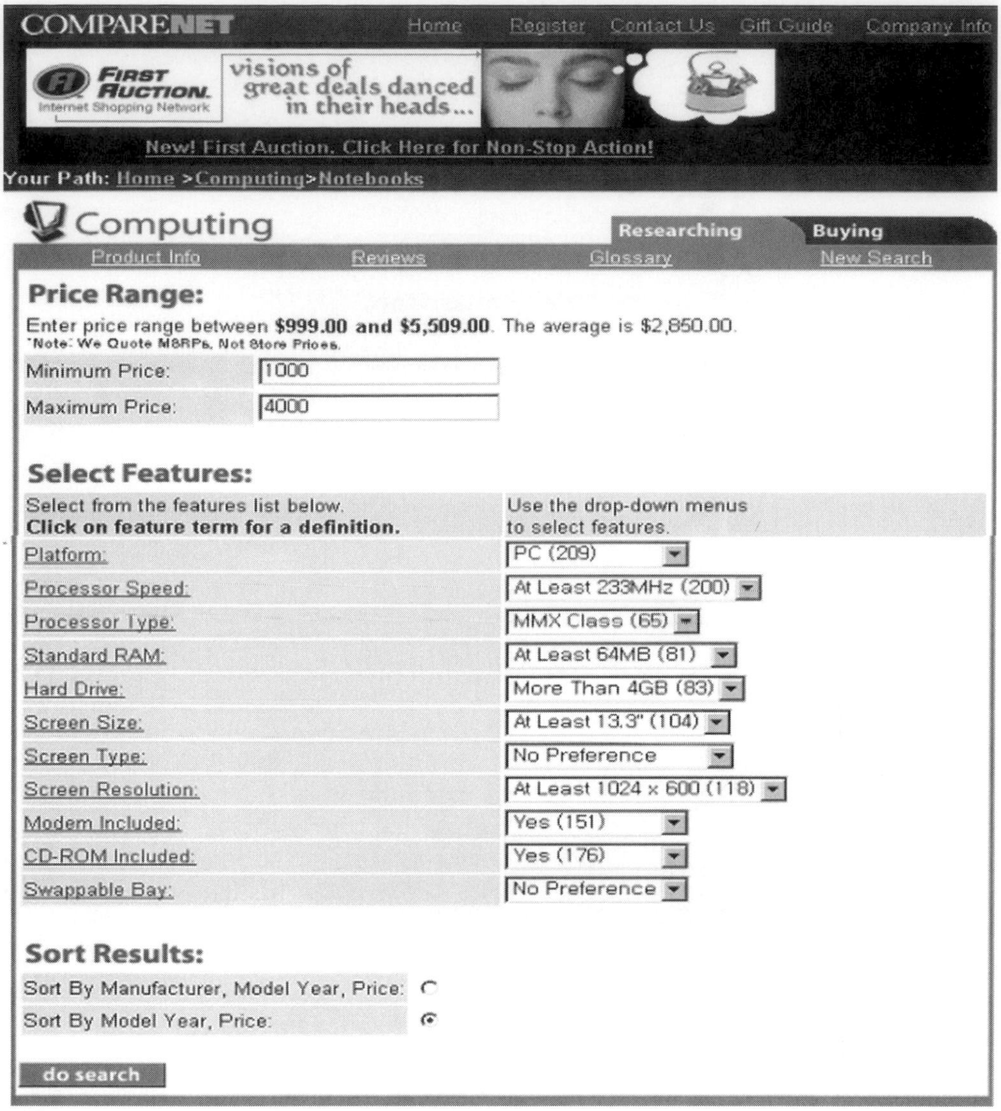

FIGURE 2.2 Specification of Customer's Requirement.

are compared using 30 different aspects. A tabular comparison is also supported by BestBookBuys.com for the comparison of book prices.

COMPARISON OF MULTIPLE ITEMS FROM MULTIPLE MALLS

The comparison capability in Compare.net is very appealing. However, Compare.net cannot keep the list of tentatively selected items in the shopping bag. Therefore, the bag itself may be stored in either the server of a third party like Compare.net or the customer's computer, as illustrated in Figure 2.4 (Song and Lee 1998). By using the customer's personalized shopping bag, the customer can tentatively pick whatever is interesting during the search stage. The nonselected items can be erased from the shopping bag. The finally selected items from multiple malls can be ordered by a

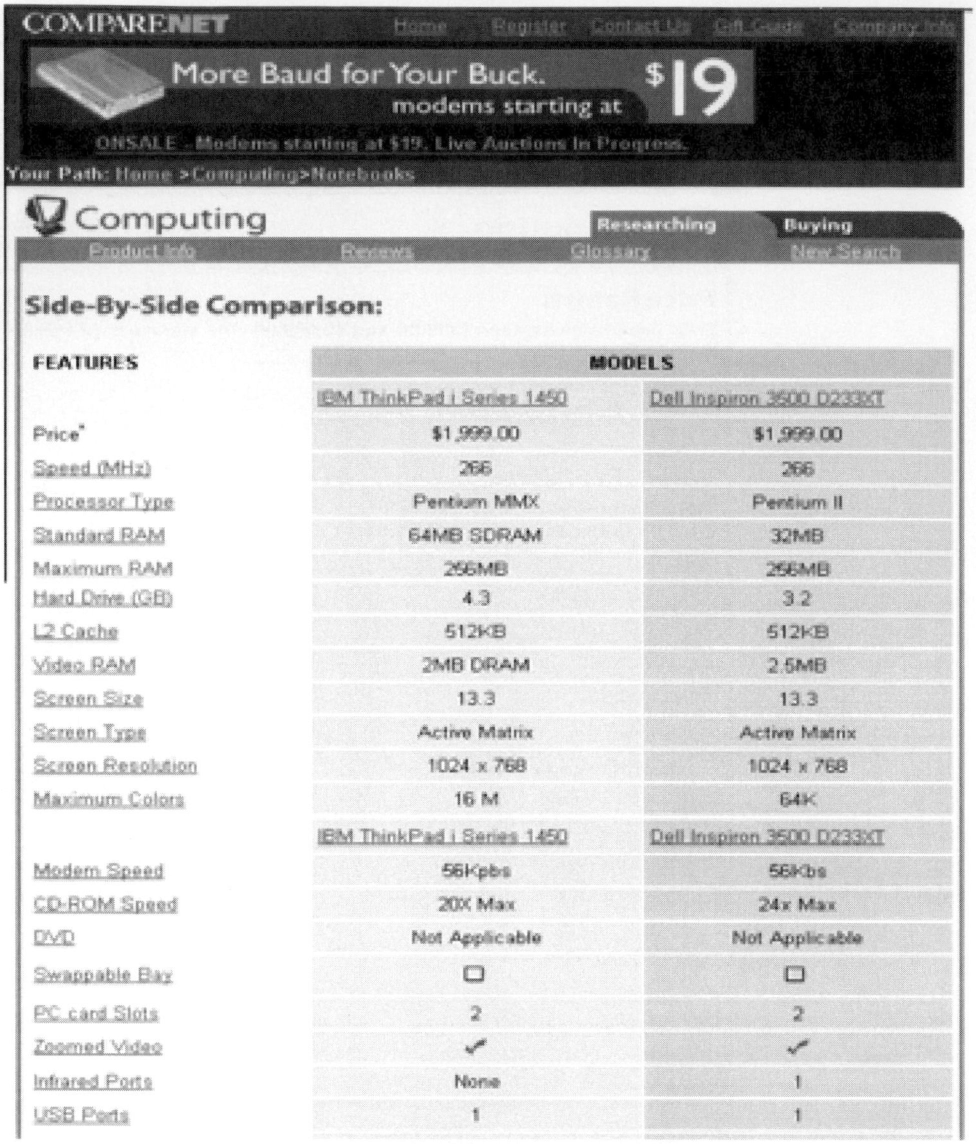

FEATURES	MODELS	
	IBM ThinkPad i Series 1450	Dell Inspiron 3500 D233XT
Price*	$1,999.00	$1,999.00
Speed (MHz)	266	266
Processor Type	Pentium MMX	Pentium II
Standard RAM	64MB SDRAM	32MB
Maximum RAM	256MB	256MB
Hard Drive (GB)	4.3	3.2
L2 Cache	512KB	512KB
Video RAM	2MB DRAM	2.5MB
Screen Size	13.3	13.3
Screen Type	Active Matrix	Active Matrix
Screen Resolution	1024 x 768	1024 x 768
Maximum Colors	16 M	64K
	IBM ThinkPad i Series 1450	Dell Inspiron 3500 D233XT
Modem Speed	56Kpbs	56Kbs
CD-ROM Speed	20X Max	24x Max
DVD	Not Applicable	Not Applicable
Swappable Bay	☐	☐
PC card Slots	2	2
Zoomed Video	✓	✓
Infrared Ports	None	1
USB Ports	1	1

FIGURE 2.3 Side-by-Side Tabular Comparison.

click. This capability is particularly important for corporate buyers. The information in the shopping bag can be easily integrated with the buyer's information system.

COMPARISON AS MULTIPLE-CRITERIA DECISION MAKING

The first step of comparison depends on search, but the next step needs to support the elimination of dominated options, and the negotiation between conflicting criteria in terms of price, specification, and delivery time. This decision process is not structured, so the notion of decision support systems needs to be taken into consideration.

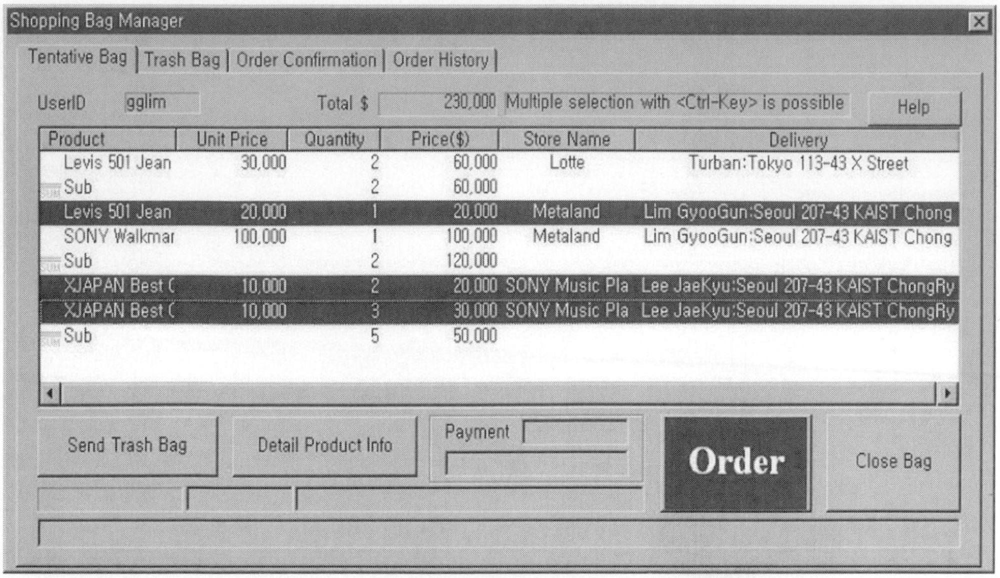

FIGURE 2.4 Electronic Shopping Bag in Customer's PC.

2.12 The Impact of EC on Traditional Retailing Systems

Let us review the impact of EC on traditional retailing systems based on the business models discussed in this chapter. A key impact is disintermediation of traditional distribution channels and electronic reintermediation.

DISINTERMEDIATION AND REINTERMEDIATION

By using the Internet, manufacturers can sell directly to customers and provide customer support online. In this sense, the traditional intermediaries are eliminated. Let us call this phenomenon **disintermediation.** However, new electronic intermediaries— e-malls and product selection agents—are emerging instead. Occurrence of a new breed of electronic intermediaries is called **reintermediation.**

In response to this change, traditional intermediaries like department stores are joining the bandwagon of the new opportunity but still keeping their traditional way of doing business. However, the traditional distribution business can never be the same again, because it has to provide something that the electronic intermediaries cannot provide. On the other hand, some manufacturers like automakers still need to cooperate with dealers in a different way (see the Ford case earlier in the chapter). These phenomena are another evolution toward reintermediation rather than disintermediation.

Now let us elaborate the notion of disintermediation and reintermediation further. *Disintermediation* is a new term that refers to the removal of organizations or business process layers responsible for certain intermediary steps in a given value chain. In the traditional distribution channel, there are intermediating layers, such as wholesaler, distributor, and retailer, between the manufacturer and consumer as depicted in Figure 2.5. In Japan, there sometimes exist 10 layers, which add a 500 percent markup. Owing to the presence of the Internet as a marketing and product selection vehicle, customers are beginning to question the value offered by the distribution

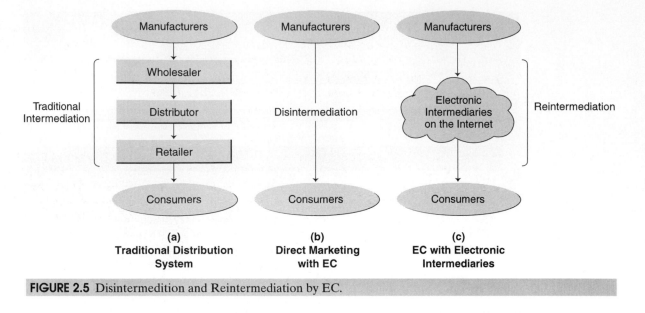

FIGURE 2.5 Disintermedition and Reintermediation by EC.

channels, when they can theoretically obtain the same products directly from the manufacturer. If manufacturers are able to connect directly with consumers and shorten the traditional distribution chain they used to depend on, it is theoretically possible to get rid of the inefficiencies of the current structure.

A logical alternative to disintermediation is reintermediation, which actually points to the shifting or transfer of the intermediary function, rather than the complete elimination of it (this phenomenon is discussed in the service sector in chapter 5). In the EC era, the intermediaries such as e-malls, directory and search engine services, and comparison-shopping agents can create the role of reintermediation. These new intermediaries replace the role of traditional intermediary layers. Another reintermediation can emerge by differentiating the service of traditional intermediaries from online intermediation. This can be realized, for instance, by offering entertainment during shopping and by upgrading the shopping as pleasant as hobby. In summary, customers have more choices of alternative intermediaries.

IMPACT ON MANUFACTURERS' DISTRIBUTION STRATEGY

In addition to disintermediation and reintermediation, an interesting emergence of manufacturers' distribution strategies is the following:

1. **Manufacturer's monopolistic Internet-based distribution.** Levi's does not allow anyone else to sell the Levi's product on the Internet. This is possible because Levi's has such a name value, and customers like to have a single contact point in cyberspace. (In late 1999, Levi's changed its policy).
2. **Coexistence with the dealers.** This is the case in car distribution. Automakers need to keep the traditional dealers as test-drive servers even though they sell on the Internet.
3. **Regionally mixed strategy.** In a certain region a particular company may sell on the Internet, while in another region it sells through the traditional retailer. For instance, Nike sells on the Internet but only in the United States. Nike provides physical retailing stores abroad. The policy depends upon the maturity of Internet-based customer groups.

4. **Mass customization for make-to-order.** Manufacturers have to be adaptive to the customized orders of ultimate consumers. This means the manufacturer should be ready for mass customization.
5. **Powerful suppliers.** According to *Fortune*, Aug. 16, 1999, Home Depot sent a letter to its major suppliers (e.g. www.whirlpool.com), reminding them that Home Depot has the right not to carry their products if they will sell online, directly to customers.

2.13   Managerial Issues

1. In section 2.4 we examined eight criteria that determine the business models of electronic marketing. The combination of these criteria can construct various business models depending upon the initial position of each individual company. Typical cases of key business models are examined throughout this book.
2. A new opportunity is available to pure direct marketing manufacturers and pure cyber-retailers. New business models have diminished the role of traditional intermediaries. From an electronic intermediary's point of view, its management should decide whether to commit to being a generalized directory service or to retail specialized items.
3. However, the emergence of pure cyber-marketing companies has irritated traditional distributors. Traditional manufacturers have had to decide whether they want to transform to a full commitment to direct marketing, restructuring the current manufacturing and distribution system; or regard the electronic storefront merely as an additional channel of distribution. A similar strategic question applies to traditional retailers.
4. A critical question to traditional manufacturers and retailers is how to transform their business posture incorporating the benefits of electronic marketing with existing distribution channels to satisfy customers most effectively at the minimum operating cost. Management also has to investigate starting a completely new business to cultivate the future opportunity of EC.

Summary

The compilation of this chapter helps you in attaining the following learning objectives:

1. **Factors that determine the business models of electronic marketing.** Direct versus indirect marketing, full versus partial cybermarketing, electronic distributor versus electronic broker, e-store versus e-mall, generalized versus specialized e-mall, proactive versus reactive strategic posture, global versus regional marketing, and sales versus customer support.
2. **Critical success factors of proactive and full direct marketing: Dell case.** Advanced Web design, price competitiveness, mass customization, database marketing and customer intimacy, global reach, customer's single contact point, high reliability of products, and delivery-tracking service.
3. **Relationship with dealers in reactive and partial direct marketing strategy: Ford case.** Ford does not eliminate dealers because Ford alone cannot keep the inventory for a wide geographical area and cannot arrange the test drives (yet). So it keeps partnership with dealers even though the orders are received over the Internet. Ford can only partially sell through the Internet.

4. **Critical success factors of generalized electronic brokers.** Scope of covering area, effectiveness of search engine, screening capability for quality assurance, and capability of aiding comparison.

5. **Typical products that succeed by using specialized electronic distributors.** Books, software, hardware, CDs, videos, travel reservations, electronics, apparel, banking, stock brokerage, and flowers.

6. **Strategy of traditional department stores.** Partial and reactive electronic intermediary.

7. **Reasons for regional business with the Internet.** Perishable goods, high delivery cost, range of after-service, and legal boundaries.

8. **Consumer's shopping procedure on the Internet: seven steps.** Preliminary requirement determination, search for available items that can meet the requirement, compare (possibly with negotiation) the candidate items with multiple perspectives, place order, pay, receive the delivered items and inspect the quality, and contact the vendor to get after-service support, or a return.

9. **Five types of aiding comparison shopping.** Search on hypertext files, search on the databases, tabular comparison, comparison of multiple items from multiple malls, comparison as multiple-criteria decision making.

10. **Impact of EC on disintermediation and reintermediation in retailing.** EC disintermediates the role of traditional distribution channels by allowing the customers to bypass the channels. In contrast, reintermediation occurs in electronic form through search aids and differentiated service of traditional intermediaries.

- Business-to-business (B2B) electronic marketing
- Business-to-consumer (B2C) electronic marketing
- Business models of electronic marketing
- Direct marketing
- Disintermediation
- Electronic broker (e-broker)

- Electronic distributor
- Electronic shopping mall (e-mall)
- Electronic store (e-store)
- Full cybermarketing
- Generalized electronic store/broker
- Global marketing
- Indirect marketing
- Online customer service

- Partial cybermarketing
- Proactive strategic posture
- Pure cybermarketing
- Reactive strategic posture
- Reintermediation
- Regional marketing
- Specialized electronic store
- Telemarketing

Keywords

Questions for Review

1. What is the current and prospective size of the electronic market? Describe in terms of B2C versus B2B electronic market.
2. What are the success factors of Amazon, and what are the threats to Amazon?
3. Describe the process of Internet shopping. List all the major steps.
4. What is direct marketing?
5. What is the difference between full and partial cybermarketing?
6. What is the difference between an electronic distributor and an e-broker?
7. What is the difference between proactive and reactive strategic postures?
8. Is Internet commerce always global? When does it become regional?
9. List the critical success factors of Dell.
10. Describe the strategic posture of Ford.
11. How did online customer service benefit Hewlett Packard?
12. Which business model was more successful: generalized e-brokers or specialized e-stores? Show a case from each model.

13. What is the strategic posture of department stores?
14. What is the strategic posture of 1-800-Flowers?
15. Describe a successful regional marketing model.

Questions for Discussion

1. Who are the competitors of Amazon, and what are the opportunities and threats to Amazon? (Look at small competitirs in niche markets!)
2. Why are books such a natural target of EC?
3. Discuss the major business models of online retailing.
4. Why is it that other PC makers cannot easily duplicate the success of Dell?
5. Why is selling flowers online (shipping them to friends or relatives) such a success? Compare 1-800-Flowers with Virtual Flowers and comment on the differences.
6. What are the alternative channels of finding the desired items besides the Web site on the Internet? Is the Internet the most convenient way of finding what you want? Discuss both a book and a personal computer you want to buy.
7. Why do customers like Web-based purchases? Is it because of more options or because of low prices? Discuss, using books and personal computers as examples.
8. To implement direct marketing for car sales, how should automakers arrange the ordered specification? How should the dealers' inventory and the automakers' inventory and manufacturing scheduling be coordinated to meet a specific order with a due date?
9. How can a manufacturer ensure the delivery date of small orders to consumers? (e.g. check how this is done by Microsoft).
10. Which way will you find the item you need: your own bookmark, search engines, a specialized electronic shopping mall, or an electronic directory broker? Why? Discuss, using books and personal computers. Also discuss with an item of your own interest.
11. How does the quality assurance of the e-mall work in ordering an unknown brand?
12. In what way is the Web-based bookstore better than a traditional bookstore?
13. Why are established department stores usually not aggressive and not successful in the electronic market?
14. It is claimed that generalized e-brokers do not win over specialized e-malls. Do you agree? Why and why not?

Internet Exercises

1. Enter the sites www.peapod.com and www.netgrocer.com. Compare the services offered by the two companies and evaluate their chances for success. If you had money to invest in only one of the two companies, in which one would you invest and why?
2. Paper coupons are a big business, and now you can get them on the Internet. Visit the sites www.hotcoupons.com and www.supermarkets.com, and find one more site. Compare the offerings in the three sites; also speculate on how electronic coupons can be integrated with electronic supermarkets such as peapod.com.
3. There are many search engines for finding products and comparing prices. How effective are they? Try the following engines: www.jango.com, www.compare.com, www.comparisonshopping.net, and www.agentsoft.com. Try to find a winter coat, a vacuum cleaner, a plain paper fax machine, and a four-seat airplane. Summarize your experiences. Comment on the strong and weak points of such search engines.
4. Almost all car manufacturers allow you to configure your car online. Enter www.toyota.com and www.ford.com and configure a car of your choice. After you decide what you want, examine the payment options and your monthly payments. Luxury car lovers may try www.bmw.com.
5. Investigate the book online industry. Trace the latest strategic moves of Amazon.com and www.bn.com. Also, identify other specialty online book vendors.

List all the features that you think attract many shoppers to a virtual bookstore.

6. Investigate the high-volume items that are being retailed on the Internet. Some examples are as follows:

   Toys (www.etoy.com and www.toysrus.com)

   Software (www.eggheads.com, www.softwarebuyline.com)

   Movies (www.real.com)

   CDs (www.CDNow.com)

   Find more best-selling categories.

   What are the common attributes for these successful retailers?

7. Review the annual internet shopping studies at www.ey.com/industry/consumer/internetshopping/overview.asp

   Observe changes over time

Team Exercises

1. Investigate the topic of cars online. Assign each member one of the following categories:

   1. Advertise, provide information, and configure only
   2. Buy new cars
   3. Buy used cars (Auction: www.aucnet.com)
   4. Buy used cars by dealers (www.manheim.com)
   5. Buy antique cars and collector-type 1913
   6. Internet intermediary such as www.autobytel.com and www.priceline.com
   7. Car auctions at www.autoweb.com, at www.autobytell.com and at www.manheim.com

   Prepare a report that will show all the common and unique elements of car buying.

2. Assign each member to one of the following teams. Let each of them report a business plan to be competitive during the next five years.

   1. Amazon.com (refer to the opening vignette)
   2. Barnesandnoble.com (refer to the opening vignette)
   3. BestBookBuys.com (refer to Application Case 2.1)
   4. Buy.com (refer to the Real World Case at the end of this chapter)
   5. An electronic book publisher (e.g., McGraw-Hill. Prentice Hall)

   Let each member present the strategy, and let the other students grade each presentation.

REAL WORLD CASE

Lowest Price on Earth: Buy.com

If Scott Blum succeeds, we all may be able to buy products at the manufacturers' prices or even lower on the Internet. His company, Buy.com, is selling products at the "lowest prices on earth." The company is committed to being the price leader—even if this means losing money on every sale. Its intelligent agents search competitors' sites to make sure Buy.com has the lowest prices on the Web. Random checking showed that they indeed sell 10 percent to 30 percent lower than others on computer products. They are continously expanding to other products. Starting in November 1998, with sales of 15 million per month and increasing to 19 million in December 1998, the company could easily break Compaq's first-year sales record of $111 million, making it the fastest growing company in U.S. history. However, true success is reflected in profits, not sales generated by losses. The company believes that when volume picks up, advertisers will pay large amounts for their banners to be on Buy.com's site.

Here are some strategies used by the company to support their plans:

1. The company purchased more than 2,000 domain names that start with "buy."
2. Buy.com offers 30,000 different products for sale or lease. When an order comes in, Buy.com automatically transfers the order to Ingram Micro, which then packages and ships the order to the customer.
3. The profit margin is 0 percent to 2 percent. Relying on a slim margin to gain a

market share is a risky strategy. However, the company expects to make money from ads on its site and from its "buy" stores (see the following item).
4. The customized "buy" stores are online retail sites devoted to selling a particular company's product. There are brand names such as BuyNokia.

Two interesting economic implications are related to this case.

First of all, if Buy.com succeeds, we will have proof that it is possible to build a brand completely on price. Selection, customer service, and user experience all matter, of course, but on the Web it is very simple for a consumer to experience these things on one site and close his or her transaction with the low-price leader. Several Web sites offer extraordinary amounts of research on expensive brand-name products such as computers and cameras, but their prices are not extraordinary.

Second, Buy.com's success could change the very way wholesalers and distributors conceptualize their businesses. Sure, extreme discounting by one reseller raises the eyebrows of a distributor's other customers. But most distributors will accept this discomfort rather than lose sales created by that reseller. The virtual reseller may lose money, but the distributor still receives its standard margin. Even manufacturers do not seem to mind having their products used as a loss leader—provided it is the reseller that takes the bath. ■

CASE QUESTIONS

1. What are the similarities and differences between Buy.com and online stockbrokers who charge minimal transaction fees?
2. In what ways will the business of distributors such as Ingram Micro be changed?
3. What is the logic for creating a customized "buy" site? Why does a company such as

Nokia needs Buy.com?
4. In what way can Buy.com use a domain name such as www.10percentoffamazon.com to its advantage?
5. Softbank, a major Japanese technology investment group, which is known for correctly investing in start-ups such as

Yahoo and E*Trade, spent $20 million to buy 10.5 percent of Buy.com. What could have attracted Softbank, which is known as a careful investor, to a company that is taking such a great risk?

References

C. Allen, D. Kania, and B. Yaeckel, *Internet World Guide to One-to-One Marketing (Internet World Series)* (New York: John Wiley & Sons, 1998).

G. Anders, "Click and Buy: Why and Where Internet Commerce Is Succeeding," *The Wall Street Journal* (December 7, 1998): R4.

Dell Computer Corporation, *Annual Report*, 1998. www.dell.com.

M. Dell, *Direct From Dell: Strategy that Revvolutionized an Industry*: (New York: Harper Business, 1999)

R. B. Doorenbos, O. Etzioni, and D. S. Weld, "A Scalable Comparison Shopping Agent for the World Wide Web," *1st International Conference on Autonomous Agents*, 1997.

Electronic Industries Association, *Electronic Market Data Book 1998* (Marina del Ray, California, Electronic Industries Association, 1998).

J. Fontana, "Dealer Cuts Costs with Web Kiosks," *InternetWeek*, (March 2, 1998). www.techweb.com.

M. Friedfertig, and G. West, *The Electronic Day Trader* (New York: McGraw-Hill, 1998).

M. R. Genesereth, A. M. Keller, and O. Duschka, "Infomaster: An Information Integration System," *Proceedings of 1997 ACM SIGMOD Conference* (Tucson, Arizona: May 1997), 539–542.

R. E. Gielgun, *1 Business, 2 Approaches: How to Succeed in Internet Business by Employing Real-World Strategies* (Brooklyn, NY, 1998).

Graphics, Visualization, and Usability (GVU) Center in Georgia Institute of Technology, *10th Survey*, 1998. www.cc.gatech.edu/gvu/user_surveys.

S. Hedberg, "Agents for Sale: First Wave of Intelligent Agents Go Commercial," *IEEE Expert* (December 1996): 16–19.

IBM, Net.Commerce *White Paper*, 1999b. www.software.ibm.com/commerce/net.commerce/lit.html.

Intershop *White Paper*, 1999. www.intershop.com/products.

B. Jamison, J. Gold, and W. Jamison, *Electronic Selling: Twenty-Three Steps to E-Selling Profits* (New York: McGraw-Hill, 1997).

R. Kalakota, and A. B. Whinston, *Electronic Commerce: A Manager's Guide* (Reading, MA: Addison-Wesley, 1997).

R. Kalakota and A. B. Whinston, *Frontiers of Electronic Commerce* (Reading, MA: Addison-Wesley, 1996).

R. Kalakota and A. B. Whinston, eds., *Readings in Electronic Commerce* (Reading, MA: Addison-Wesley, 1997).

M. D. Kare-Silver, *E-Shock: The Electronic Shopping Revolution: Strategies for Retailers and Manufacturers* (New York: AMACOM, 1999).

J. Kolodner, *Case-Based Reasoning* (San Francisco: Morgan Kaufmann Publishers, 1993).

M. Komenar, *Electronic Marketing* (New York: John Wiley & Sons, 1997).

J. K. Lee, Y. U. Song, and J. W. Lee, "A Comparison Shopping Architecture over Multiple Malls: The Meta-Malls Architecture," *Proceedings of the International Conference on Electronic Commerce* (Seoul, Korea 1998): 149–154.

D. Leebaert, *The Future of the Electronic Marketplace* (Boston: MIT Press, 1998).

G. L. Lohse, and P. Spiller, "Electronic Shopping," *Communication of ACM*, 41 (July 7, 1998): 81–87.

P. Maes, R. Guttman and A. Moukas, "Agents that Buy and Sell: Transforming Commerce as We Know It," *Communications of the ACM* (March 1999): 56–62.

Microsoft, Site Server 3.0, www.microsoft.com/siteserver/commerce/1999a.

Microsoft, Site Server 3.0 Datasheet, www.microsoft.com/backoffice/siteserver/commerce/30/gen/ssdatac.htm, 1999b.

B. K. Moon, J. K. Lee, and K. J. Lee, "A Next Generation Multimedia Call Center on the Internet: IMC," *Proceedings of the International Conference on Electronic Commerce* (1998), 92–97.

National Retail Federation Series, *The Electronic Retailing Market*, (New York: John Wiley & Sons, 1996).

M. Nemzow, *Building Cyberstores: Installation, Transaction Processing, and Management* (New York: McGraw-Hill, Inc., 1997).

D. O'Leary, "AI and Navigation on the Internet and Intranet," *IEEE Expert* (April 1996): 8–10.

C. O'Malley, "Junglee Fever On the Web," *Time* (December 14, 1998): 33.

OECD, "Measuring Electronic Commerce," Paris (September 18–19): 1997.

OECD, "Gateways to the Global Market: Consumers and Electronic Commerce," 1998.

Open Market's *White Paper*, 1999. www.openmarket.com/wp/icp.cfm.

Oracle, ICS *White Paper*, 1999. ntsolutions.oracle.com/products/ics/html/ics_wp.htm.

Personalogic's *White Paper*, 1999. www.pesonalogic.com.

R. Quick, "The Attack of the Robots: Comparison-Shopping Technology Is Here—Whether Retailers Like It or Not," *The Wall Street Journal* (December 7, 1998): R14.

R. Raisglid, W. Mikulak, and C. Turner, *Buying and Leasing Cars on the Internet* (Renaissance Books, 1998).

A. Rajaraman and P. Norvig, "Virtual DataBase Technology: Transforming the Internet into a Database," *IEEE Internet Computing*, (July–August 1998): 55–58.

L. M. Ross, *businessplan.com: How to Write a Web Woven Strategic Business Plan (psi business library)*. (Grants Pass, Oregon: Psi Research—Oasis Press, 1998).

S. Thurm, "Leading the PC Pack: Why Does Dell Stand Out?" *The Wall Street Journal* (December 7, 1998): R27.

G. W. Treese and L. C. Stewart, *Designing Systems for Internet Commerce* (Reading, MA: Addison-Wesley, 1998).

E. Turban, E. McLean, and J. Wetherbe, *Information Technology for Management*, 2^d ed. (New York: John Wiley & Sons, 1999).

I. Vollrath, W. Wilke, and R. Gergmann, "Case Based Reasoning Support for Online Catalog Sales," *IEEE Internet Computing* (July–August 1998): 47–54.

CHAPTER **3**

Internet Consumers and Market Research

Learning Objectives

Upon completion of this chapter, the reader will be able to:

■ Describe the essentials of consumer behavior.

■ Describe the characteristics of Internet surfers and EC purchasers.

■ Understand the process of consumer purchasing decision making.

■ Describe the way companies are building relationships with customers.

■ Explain the implementation of customer service.

■ Describe consumer market research in EC.

■ Understand the role of intelligent agents in consumer applications.

■ Describe the organizational buyer behavior model.

3.1   Building Customer Relationships: Ritchey's bikes online

Ritchey Design Inc., of Redwood City, California, is a relatively small ($15-million per year) designer and manufacturer of mountain-bike components. The company sells its products to distributors and/or retailers, who sell them to individual consumers. The company opened a Web site in 1995, (http://www.ritcheylogic.com), but like so many companies' Web sites, Ritchey's was more a status symbol than a business tool. Most of the site's visitors came to get the dirt on Team Ritchey, the company's world-class mountain-bike team, or to find out where Ritchey products were sold. But that's where the site's usefulness ended. It didn't give customers all the information they wanted or allow the company to gain insight into those customers.

Getting marketing and customer information had become one of the company's biggest problems. The company was getting information from informal conversations with distributors and retailers, but formal market research was too expensive for the small company.

In late 1995 Philip Ellinwood, Ritchey's chief operating officer and IS director, decided to rework the site so that the company could hear from its customers directly. He was looking for a software package that allows businesses to sell products and services over the Internet and collect information from consumers. Ellinwood found a product called Web Trader (from SBT Corp.), but it was too expensive for Ritchey Corp. to buy the software. Therefore, Ellinwood struck a deal with SBT: a lower price on the software in exchange for his willingness to test the package and put SBT's logo on Ritchey's Web site. It took one year and only $7,500 to turn the static Web site into an interactive marketing tool.

First, Ellinwood set up customer surveys on the Web site. To induce customers to participate, the company offers a chance to win free products. Visitors are asked to enter their names and addresses and then to answer questions about the company's products. Web Trader automatically organizes and saves the answers in a database. Then the information is used for marketing decision making and advertisement. Ellinwood can easily change the questions to learn customers' opinions about any of the 15 new products Ritchey develops each year. In the past, the company knew little about how consumers might react to a new product until it was in the stores. "The process could save us as much as $100,000 a year on product development," Ellinwood says.

To educate retailers and consumers about the technological advantages of Ritchey's high-end components over competitors' parts, Ellinwood created an electronic catalog. Visitors can browse through this product catalog, which includes detailed descriptions and graphics of Ritchey's products.

As of this writing Ritchey does not yet sell directly to individuals online, because the company wants to maintain its existing distribution system. However, dealers can place orders on the site, and they can learn about new products quickly, so they no longer push only those products about which they know the most.

3.2 The Consumer Behavior Model

The opening vignette illustrates to us the benefits a company can derive from changing its Web site from passive to interactive. Now the company can hear from its customers directly. Furthermore, the company can learn a lot about the customers and at the same time educate them. Why is a relatively small company making all these efforts?

As you may recall from chapter 1, companies today operate under increasing business environment pressures. The major pressures are labeled *the 3Cs:* competition, customers, and change. The customers are treated like royalty, as companies try to lure them to buy their goods and services. Finding and retaining customers is becoming the major critical success factor of most businesses.

The presence of the 3Cs is not new. Companies have been "fighting" for customers for decades. What is new is the intensity of the competition, the strength of the customers, and the magnitude of the changes. All of this boils down to a strategy: You need to control the 3Cs to succeed, or even to survive.

EC can be viewed as a new distribution channel that competes against the conventional ones. Furthermore, as soon as a company succeeds in its EC in a certain area, many competitors will try to follow suit, as in the case of Amazon.com. Thus, the task of attracting customers to an online company can be difficult, because it is necessary first to convince them to shop online and then to choose your company over the online competitors. Where customers shop and for what becomes the key to the success of any business, including those in cyberspace.

In this chapter we describe the new relationships that companies such as Ritchey Design are attempting to build with their customers. The key to building such relationships is understanding consumer behavior.

CONSUMER BEHAVIOR

Market researchers have been trying for decades to understand **consumer behavior** (East 1997). Their findings are summarized in a model of consumer behavior. We adjusted this model for the EC environment.

The Model of EC Consumer Behavior

According to the model of EC consumer behavior shown in Figure 3.1, the purchasing decision process is basically a customer's reaction to stimuli (on the left). The process is influenced by the buyer's characteristics, the environment, the technology, the EC logistic, and so on. The figure lists some of the variables in each category and also shows the chapter in this book (in parentheses) in which the topic is further discussed.

For example, the issue of marketing stimuli in EC is discussed in chapter 4 (advertisement and promotions). In chapters 9 and 12 the pricing decision is elaborated upon. Sellers are not able to control some of the other stimuli. In this chapter we deal mainly with consumer-related issues—namely, personal characteristics, the decision process, relationship building, and customer service.

Before we explore the details of the model we need to discuss who EC consumers are, their purchasing types, and customer relations in direct sales and in intermediary-based markets.

FIGURE 3.1 Electronic Commerce Consumer Behavior Model.

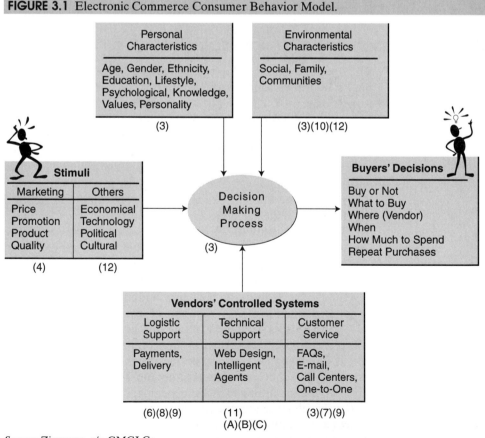

Source: Zinezone, c/o GMGI Co.

Consumer Types

Electronic Commerce consumers can be divided into two types: individual consumers, who get much of the media attention, and organizational buyers, who do most of the shopping in cyberspace. Organizational buyers include governments, private corporations, resellers, and public organizations. Organizational buyers' purchases are not intended for personal consumption. Rather, products or services they buy are generally used to create other products (services) by adding value to the products. Also, products may be purchased for resale without any further modifications.

Consumer behavior, which has a profound impact on the way online systems are developed, can be viewed in terms of two questions: Why is the consumer shopping, and what is in it for the consumer? As these questions imply, an online shopping experience can be valuable (accomplishing something), or valueless (simply browsing). Marketing researchers have categorized shopping experiences into two dimensions: *utilitarian*, carrying out a shopping activity "to achieve a goal" or "complete a task"; and *hedonic*, carrying out a shopping activity because "it is fun and I love it." An understanding of hedonic and utilitarian shopping can provide insight into many EC consumption behaviors that are normally not taken into account in the design and layout of electronic websites and marketplaces.

Purchasing Types and Experiences

Consumers can be categorized into three types: Impulsive buyers, who purchase products quickly; patient buyers, who purchase products after making some comparisons; and analytical buyers, who do substantial research before making the decision to purchase products or services. Also, there are window shoppers, who just browse.

DIRECT SALES, INTERMEDIARIES, AND CUSTOMER RELATIONS

Most companies do not sell directly to consumers but to intermediaries—wholesalers, dealers, distributors, retailers, or resellers. Whether your company sells consumer products through retail outlets or factory machinery direct to the purchasing agents at large industrial firms, defining the nature of *all* your "customers" is a first step. Even if a company does not sell directly to the end user of its product, it still has an interest in creating a better relationship with that end user. It is the end user—the ultimate consumer—who supports everyone in a network of value-creating relationships.

Ford Motor Company sells almost all of its cars to dealers, not to consumers, but it does recognize, nevertheless, that the ultimate drivers of Ford vehicles think of themselves as having a relationship with Ford. Hewlett Packard sells testing equipment to the purchasing agents at large microchip-manufacturing companies, but the ultimate users of these products are the bench engineers who develop new products and test current ones. In developing EC marketing and advertisement strategy, it is critical to define first who your target customers are: the end users, the intermediaries, or both.

Now, let us return to the model of Figure 3.1 and look at the environmental and personal variables.

3.3 Personal Characteristics and the Demographics of Internet Surfers

The variables that influence the decision-making process include environmental variables, which are described briefly in this section; characteristic variables, which are also described in this section; and vendors' controlled variables, which are discussed in subsequent sections of this chapter and in other chapters. Knowing about these variables can help vendors to design marketing and advertisement plans.

ENVIRONMENTAL VARIABLES

The environmental variables can be grouped into the following categories:

- *Social variables.* Social variables play an important role in EC purchasing. People are basically influenced by family members, friends, coworkers, and "what's in fashion this year." Of special importance in EC are *Internet communities* (chapter 12) and discussion groups that communicate via chat rooms, electronic bulletin boards, and news groups. These topics are discussed in various places in the text.
- *Cultural variables.* It makes a big difference if you live near Silicon Valley in California or in the mountains in Nepal. The interested reader is referred to Hasan and Ditsa (1999), who provide some insights regarding the impact of culture on IT adoption.
- *Psychological variables.* These variables are briefly mentioned in several places throughout the book. The reader who is interested in details is referred to East (1997).
- *Other environmental variables.* Other environmental variables include the available information, government regulations, legal constraints, and situational factors. Also, notice that environmental variables are included in the "other stimuli" of Figure 3.1.

PERSONAL CHARACTERISTICS AND INDIVIDUAL DIFFERENCES

Several variables are unique to individual customers; they include consumer resources, age, knowledge, gender, educational level, attitudes, motivation, marital status, personality, values, lifestyle, and more. Also important for EC are Internet usage and users' profiles. Only some of these data as they relate to EC are available. More data are available, however, on Internet consumer demographics.

Several consumer demographics provide an indicator of buying habits. The major demographics presented here include gender, age, marital status, educational level, ethnicity, occupation, and household income. Sufficient data for EC consumer demographics were not available at the time this book was written. Therefore, most of the data presented here are related to Internet surfers (potential buyers) and are not about actual buyers. However, it is logical to assume a close association between Net surfers and EC buyers.

The major source of Internet surfing data is the Graphic, Visualization, and Usability (GVU) Center at Georgia Tech University. This center conducts periodic surveys on Internet surfers' demographics. Many other organizations provide Internet data—for example, see www.statmarket.com, www.forrester.com, www.ey.com (their annaul surveys), and www.jup.com.

The following is a presentation of the major demographic variables as found by GVU in October 1998 (10th survey).

Gender

In 1998, in the United States, men were still the dominant users of the Internet at 61.3 percent, leaving the proportion of female users at 38.7 percent. Europe is considerably less gender balanced, with female use accounting for only 16.3 percent. For other parts of the world, women account for 30.5 percent. Younger respondents are most likely to be female: 43.8 percent of people 11 to 20 years of age, compared with 33.9 percent of people 50 years of age and over. However, this situation is changing rapidly, as can be seen in the statistics of those who have surfed the Internet for less

TABLE 3.1   Products/Services Women Would Like to Purchase on the Internet

Women's Purchases by Category

Purchases Category	Percentage of Total Category Purchases (299)	Percentage of Total Respondents Buying (116)
Computer Software	15%	39%
Books	14%	35%
Music	11%	28%
Magazines	11%	28%
Flowers	11%	28%
Women's Clothing	7%	19%
Computer Hardware	5%	12%
Games	5%	11%
Videos	4%	10%
Crafts & Craft Supplies	4%	10%
Toys	3%	9%
Home Furnishings	2%	6%
Children's Clothing	2%	4%
Men's Clothing	2%	4%
Art	2%	4%
Jewelry	1%	3%
Furniture	1%	2%
Total	100%	

Source: Fram and Grady (1997), p. 194.

than a year. In this category, there are more females than males (51.7 percent versus 48.3 percent).

Women are doing the majority of shopping offline and although they shop less than men on the Web today, the trend shows that they are quickly increasing their Web purchasing. A 1997 study of women online show that their cyber shopping patterns are similar to those of men (Table 3.1). It also indicates that women do about 75 percent of all online supermarket shopping. The study shows, however, that techno-savvy women do not seem to have much agreement on the types of merchandise they would like to see on the Web. They are somewhat apathetic about buying on the Net and find buying fashion merchandise online to be difficult. Most important, women find only little difference between the quality of goods found in local stores or catalogs and those sold on the Web. Finally, women view Web prices to be about the same or higher than those of local retailers.

Age

The average age of surfers in the United States is 35.1 years. For Europeans it is dramatically different with many more in the 21 to 30-year-old age range. This distribution is very similar to the United States prior to the emergence of the major Internet Service Providers (ISPs) such as AOL, CompuServe, and Prodigy. The users with the most online experience tend to be in the 21 to 30-year-old age range in general. An example of how this can affect purchasing is provided in Application Case 3.1.

APPLICATION CASE 3.1

Purchasing and Baby Boomers

Honda Motorcycle was selling a million bikes a year in the mid-1980s. But by the early 1990s, the numbers dropped by half. Honda was puzzled and anxious for an explanation.

The firm discovered the immense Baby Boomer generation of 76 million consumers had now been replaced in the youth market by the "Baby Bust" generation of consumers—which is only half its size. "Simply put, we're missing some 38 million consuming Americans in the Baby Bust generation," Bill Gronbach, a manager in a marketing research firm, said. It was not that teenagers stopped liking bikes, but there simply were not as many of them to keep the market strong.

The same problem happened to Levi Strauss. In November 1998, the manufacturer announced that it would lay off 7,000 workers—a third of its North American manufacturing workforce—because of a drop in demand for its blue jeans. "They thought that the five-pocket jeans would sell in perpetuity," Gronbach said. The numbers indicate that jeans are still popular, particularly with 20 year-old people—but there are fewer of them around. There were 3.3 million babies born in 1977—1 million fewer babies than were born 20 years earlier at the height of the Baby Boom. These people are now 22 years old, completing college, and starting to shop around.

Marital Status

The largest group of users are married (41.1 percent), and the next largest is the single group at 38.7 percent. The remaining group covers separated, divorced, or unknowns. European users are more likely to be single, probably because they are younger. Marital status may be an influencing factor in EC, because family purchases differ from that of singles.

Educational Level

Although the average education level of Web users has been declining in the United States, most users are still highly educated: 80.9 percent have at least some college education, and 50.1 percent have obtained at least a bachelor's degree. Users who have been on the Internet for four years or more are much more likely to have advanced degrees, such as masters and doctorates, than newer users.

Ethnicity

Internet users continue to be predominantly white, at 87.4 percent in the United States. There was a slight increase in the 1998 survey in the percentage of Asian users compared with previous surveys. Younger users are more racially diverse than are older respondents.

Occupation

The largest category of users work in education-related fields, at 26.2 percent, followed by computers at 22.3 percent and other professionals at 21.7 percent. European males are more likely to be in computer-related jobs than users in the USA; and European females are more likely to be in education than European males, who are most likely to be in computer positions. However, overall, only 7.6 percent of those who were online in the past year hold computer jobs, compared with 35.9 percent of those who have been online four years or longer. This clearly indicates a trend for diversification of users' occupations.

Household Income

In 1998, the average household income of surfers in the United States was $52,500, which is slightly higher than the 1997 figure. Overall, 46.2 percent of users reported income of at least $50,000. More experienced users tend to earn more than new users. Among those with over $50,000 in earnings, 47.1 percent are considered Internet experts, compared with 30.7 percent of novice users.

Internet Usage Profile

It is interesting to know how individuals access and use the Internet. Here we will look at Internet access options, length and frequency of Web use, and access cost, all of which can be typical indicators of EC shopping capabilities:

- *Internet access options.*   The majority of U.S. users, 62.6 percent, access the Web primarily from their homes. However, the largest category of Europeans, 58.0 percent, access the Web primarily from work or school. The number of home users in Europe has been increasing at a slow but steady rate. Overall, growth in home use has been mainly fueled by people who first use the Web at work and then are transferring the use into their homes, making it available to a new set of users, namely, their families. Lately, a new category of users has emerged—those that specifically seek out home Web access, such as retirees and children. In developing countries, many people access the Internet from kiosks. Shopping kiosks are being installed at 7-11 stores as well as in regular malls and public areas.
- *Length and frequency of use.*   Web users not only spend many hours on the Web, they also do it in multiple sessions, with the majority (87.9 percent) of users accessing the Web daily. Frequency of access also increases with years spent on the Internet, but even for the newest users, the largest category accesses the Web one to four times a day. Users with the most online experience tend to spend more hours on the Web. The most active users, spending 10 to 20 hours a week, make up 32.7 percent of all users. Those who use the Web for more hours amount to 26.4 percent, whereas 40.9 percent use it for fewer hours. As noted in chapter 4, most users give up television time in favor of Internet surfing.
- *Access cost.*   Cost of accessing the Internet includes the cost of the computer/terminal, communication cost (including a modem and telephone connection), and access to material on a Web site (such as paying to view certain material and paying for downloading). Here, *access cost* refers mostly to communication and connection costs using common carriers and an ISP. More than two-thirds of users (67.2 percent) pay for their own Internet access; 30.8 percent have their connection paid for by their employers. European users are more likely to have their access paid for by their place of work than U.S. users. Also, older users are much more likely to pay for their own connection, 86.3 percent, whereas younger users have their connections paid for by their parents or schools. Regardless of their Internet experience, users are equally likely to pay for their own access. More experienced users, usually those in the computer field, are more likely than new users to have an additional Internet connection paid for by their employers. Internet access cost in some countries is fixed per month, whereas in others it is by the hour or a combination of the two. Per-hour cost may slow the spread of EC.

CONSUMER BUYING PATTERNS

The final topic in this section involves direct EC data. More than three-quarters of respondents (76.2 percent) in the GVU survey in 1998 reported that they had ordered a product or service by filling out a form on the Web. U.S. males and experienced Internet users were more likely to have done this than other categories of users.

Internet surfers were more likely to have made an online purchase in the last six months of 1998 than a paper catalog purchase in the same period. Compared with retail purchases, computer products are less likely to be purchased online than in stores. However, travel arrangements (36 percent) is showing a slight edge over retail (35.4 percent). The highest rates of online purchases were reported in books, magazines, and software costing less than $50.

The largest percentage (32.5 percent) of those who made purchases over the Web in the last six months of 1998 spent between $100 and $500 followed by 29.5 percent of users who spent more than $500. Interestingly, when considering the years of experience on the Internet, the lowest category of spending—less than $50—decreases steadily as experience is gained, and the highest category of spending—above $500—is a mirror image of the lowest. There are slight differences in the spending patterns of women and men. Men are almost equally likely to spend at the $100 to $500 level, but women are more likely to purchase in the under $50 category and less likely to purchase above the $500 level.

It is interesting to note that the more experience people have with the Internet, the more they are spending there, as shown in the self-explanatory Figure 3.2.

The two most cited reasons for *not* making purchases on the Web are security and the difficulty of judging the product quality. Some users, about 9.3 percent, do not make purchases because they've heard that buying on the Web is not reliable, trustworthy or secure; but only 1.9 percent have actually had an unfavorable experience. In fact, having such a negative experience was the least-cited reason for not making more purchases on the Web; finally, 4.5 percent of users consider the process complicated.

FIGURE 3.2 Amount Spent on the Web.

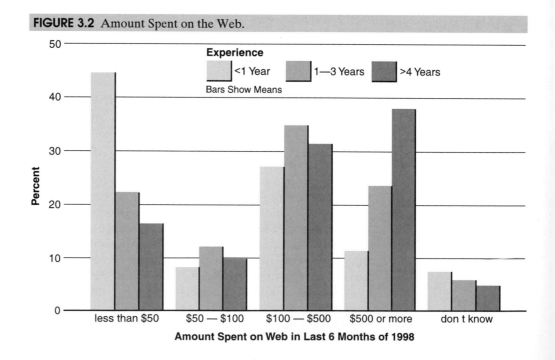

3.4 Consumer Purchasing Decision Making

We return again to Figure 3.1. As can be seen in the figure, the central part that determines **consumers' decision making** is the purchasing decision process. Before we discuss this topic, it is necessary to clarify the role people play in the decision-making process. The major roles are as follows (Kotler and Armstrong 1999):

- *Initiator:* the person who first suggests or thinks of the idea of buying a particular product or service
- *Influencer:* a person whose advice or views carry some weight in making a final buying decision
- *Decider:* the person who ultimately makes a buying decision or any part of it—whether to buy, what to buy, how to buy, or where to buy
- *Buyer:* the person who makes an actual purchase
- *User:* the person who consumes or uses a product or service

Advertisement and marketing strategies become very difficult when more than one individual plays these roles. How marketers are dealing with such an issue is beyond the scope of this book.

Several models have been developed in an effort to describe the purchasing decision-making process. These models provide a framework for learning about the process in an attempt to predict, improve, or influence consumer decisions. The models are also used as guidelines for research purposes. We will introduce only two models here.

THE PURCHASING DECISION-MAKING MODEL

A general purchasing decision-making model for consumers is shown in Figure 3.3. It consist of five major phases. In each phase we can distinguish several activities and, in some of them, one or more decisions. The five stages are (1) need identification, (2) information search, (3) alternatives evaluation, (4) purchase and delivery, and (5) after-purchase evaluation. Although these stages offer a general guide to the consumer decision-making process, do not assume that consumers' decision making will always proceed in such order. In fact, the consumer may revert back to a previous stage or end the process at any time.

FIGURE 3.3 Purchasing Decision-Making Process.

The first stage, need identification, occurs when a consumer is faced with an imbalance between actual and desired states of a need. A marketer's goal is to get the consumer to recognize such imbalance and convince the consumer that the product or service the seller offers will certainly fill in the gap between the two states. After identifying the need, the consumer searches for information about the various alternatives available to satisfy the need. Here we differentiate between a decision of what product to buy (product brokering) and from whom to buy it (merchant brokering). These two decisions can be separate or interrelated. This stage is basically an information search. An information search can occur internally, externally, or both. The internal information search is the process of recalling information stored in the memory. In contrast, an external information search seeks information in the outside environment, typically in Internet databases. In the external search, catalogs, advertising, promotions, and reference groups will influence consumer decision making. Product search engines, such as www.compare.com, can be very beneficial at this stage. The consumer's information search will eventually generate a smaller set of preferred alternatives. From this set, the buyer will further evaluate the alternatives (stage 3) and, if possible, will negotiate terms (this can be a complex task). In this stage, a consumer will use the information stored in memory and obtained from outside sources to develop a set of criteria. These criteria will help the consumer evaluate and compare alternatives. In the next stage the consumer will make the purchasing decision, arrange payment and delivery, buy warranties, and so on.

Finally, there is a postpurchase stage of customer service (e.g., maintenance) and evaluation of the usefulness of the product. This process can also be seen as a life cycle in which, at the end, the product is disposed of.

TABLE 3.2   Consumer Decision Support System

Decision Process	CDSS Facilities	Generic Internet and Web Facilities
Need recognition	Agents and event notification	Banner advertising on order Web sites URL on physical material Discussions in news groups
Information search	Virtual catalogs Internal search on Web site Structural interaction and question/answer sessions Links to (and guidance on) external sources	Web directories and classifiers External search engines Focused directories and information brokers
Evaluation	FAQs and other summaries Samples and trial Provisions of evaluative models Pointers to (and information on) existing customers	Discussions in news groups Cross site (i.e., firm) comparisons Generic models
Purchase	Product or service ordering Payment methods Arrangement of delivery	Electronic cash and virtual banking Logistics providers and package tracking
After-purchase evaluation	Customer support via e-mail and news groups E-mail communication and response	Discussions in news groups

THE CUSTOMER DECISION MODEL IN WEB PURCHASING

The model presented in Figure 3.3 is generic. How is such a process viewed in cyber-space? One attempt to answer this question was made by O'Keefe and McEachern (1998), who proposed a framework called Consumer Decision Support System (CDSS). According to their framework, which is shown in Table 3.2, each of the phases of the purchasing model can be supported by both CDSS facilities and generic Internet and Web facilities. The CDSS facilities support the specific decisions in the process, whereas the generic technologies provide information and enhance communi-cation. This framework can help companies in using Internet technologies to improve, influence, and control the process. Specific implementation of this framework is demonstrated throughout the text.

A MODEL OF INTERNET CONSUMER SATISFACTION

Consumer behavior on the Internet may be more complex due to the involvement of Web technology. A comprehensive framework for such a situation was developed by Lee (1999). His model, shown in Figure 3.4, is based on the assumption that a repeat Web purchase is mainly determined by customer satisfaction. Understanding these and similar models is essential for the appropriate development of consumer relation-ships and for increasing customers' satisfaction, as is discussed in the forthcoming sections.

FIGURE 3.4 A Comprehensive Model of Internet Consumer Satisfaction.

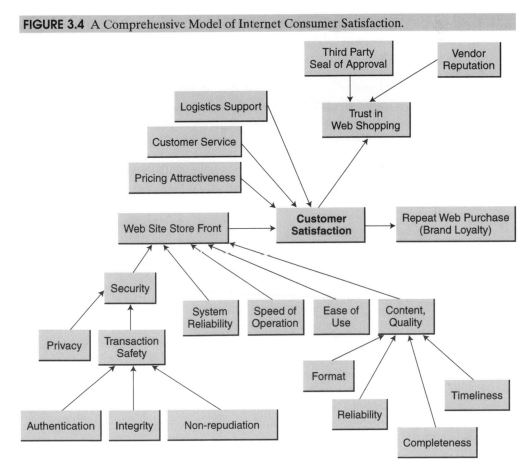

Source: Lee (1999).

3.5   One-to-One and Relationship Marketing

The availability of EC provides companies with unprecedented opportunity to conduct **one-to-one marketing.**

ONE-TO-ONE MARKETING: AN OVERVIEW

The Basic Idea

One-to-one marketing is a type of relationship marketing. **Relationship marketing,** according to Mowen and Hinor (1998), is the "overt attempt of exchange partners to build a long term association, characterized by purposeful cooperation and mutual dependence on the development of social, as well as structural, bonds" (p. 540). It includes the concepts of loyalty and trust, which we discuss later in this section. But not everything that could be called relationship marketing is in fact one-to-one marketing. To be a genuine one-to-one marketer, a company must be able and willing to change its behavior toward an individual customer, based on what they know about that customer. So, one-to-one marketing is basically a simple idea: "Treat different customers differently." It is based on the fact that no two customers are the same.

One-to-one marketing involves much more than just sales and marketing, because a firm must be able to change how its products are configured or its service is delivered, based on the needs of individual customers. Smart companies have always encouraged the active participation of customers in the development of products, services, and solutions. For the most part, however, being customer oriented has always meant being oriented to the needs of the typical customer in the market—the average customer. In order to build enduring one-to-one relationships, a company must continuously interact with customers, individually.

The actual, detailed mechanics of building a one-to-one relationship depend on understanding the various ways customers are different, and how these differences should affect the firm's behavior toward particular, individual customers. One reason so many firms are beginning to focus on one-to-one marketing is that this kind of marketing can create high customer loyalty and, as a part of the process, help the firm's profitability.

A company can make its own customers more loyal—one customer at a time—by establishing a learning relationship with each customer, starting with your most valuable ones. Think of a learning relationship as a relationship that gets smarter with every new interaction. The customer tells you of some need, and you customize your product or service to meet this need. With each interaction and recustomization, you get better at fitting your product to this particular customer. Thus, you are making your product more valuable to *this* customer. Then the customer will stay loyal to you.

How One-To-One Relationships Are Practiced

One of the benefits of doing business over the Web is that it enables companies to better understand their customers' needs and buying habits, which in turn enables them to improve and frequently customize their future marketing efforts. For example, Prodigy offers to its subscribers a personal librarian service in the form of a search engine capable of prioritizing information by subject of interest and Amazon can e-mail you an announcement of new books published in your area of interest.

Although many companies have similar programs, it is much more beneficial to institute a corporate-wide policy of building one-to-one relationships around the Web. There are several ways to do it (e.g., Peppers et al. 1999). The GartnerGroup, an IT consulting company, proposed what they call The New Marketing Cycle of Relationship Building. Their proposal, which is shown in Figure 3.5, views relationships as a two-way street in which customer information is collected and placed in a database.

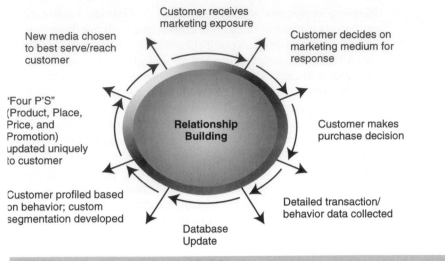

Customer receives
marketing exposure

New media chosen
to best serve/reach
customer

Customer decides on
marketing medium for
response

'Four P'S"
(Product, Place,
Price, and
Promotion)
updated uniquely
to customer

**Relationship
Building**

Customer makes
purchase decision

Customer profiled based
on behavior; custom
segmentation developed

Detailed transaction/
behavior data collected

Database
Update

FIGURE 3.5 The New Marketing Model.

Source: GartnerGroup.

Then a customer's profile is developed and the so-called four marketing P's (product, place, price, and promotion) are updated on a one-to-one basis. Based on this, appropriate advertisement is prepared, possibly leading to a purchase by the customer. The detailed transaction is then added to the database and the cycle repeats.

ISSUES IN EC-BASED ONE-TO-ONE MARKETING

Of the many issues related to implementing EC-based one-to-one marketing we will address only a few here. They include loyalty, trust, and referrals. For details and other topics see Allen and Yaekel (1998) and Peppers et al (1999).

Customer Loyalty

Customer loyalty is the degree to which a customer will stay with a specific vendor or brand. It is an important element in consumer purchasing behavior (e.g., see Reichheld 1996). Customer loyalty is one of the most significant contributors to profitability. By keeping customers loyal, a company can increase its profits because customers will buy more and sales will grow. Also, it costs about five to eight times more to acquire a new customer than to keep an existing one. A company's market position is strengthened because the customers are kept away from the competition. The company becomes less sensitive to price competition when it assumes that the customers will not be too sensitive to minor differences in price. Furthermore, increased loyalty can bring cost savings to a company in many ways: lower marketing costs, lower transaction costs (such as contract negotiation and order processing), customer turnover expenses, and lower failure costs such as warranty claims and so on. Loyal customers have a specific opinion about what to buy and from whom. Loyal customers buy regularly over a cross-section of specific products or services and often are immune to competitors' efforts. Also, loyal customers refer other customers to the site. During the past decade, customer loyalty in general has been decreasing. The introduction of EC accelerated this trend because customers' ability to shop, compare, and switch has become extremely easy, fast, and inexpensive, given the aid of search engines, mall directories, and intelligent agents (section 3.8). Customer loyalty can be increased by increasing customers' satisfaction. This can be done in several ways, including the provision of one-to-one marketing and meeting the customer's cognitive needs.

Meeting customers' cognitive needs. Gaining information about customers and potential customers' needs and converting such needs into demand is more feasible in EC than any other marketing channel. For those products that require more sophisticated service or information before and after purchase, addressing the cognitive need of the customers is an advantage. On the other hand, addressing the customer's cognition and perceptual process may be a hurdle in EC because EC experiences cannot be compared with a direct sales experience in a grocery or department store. Because shopping is an interpersonal activity, customer service in EC should not ignore the cognitive aspect of a vendor and customer interaction. To take into account such perceptual process among different buyers, Zellweger (1997) points out different knowledge segments of customers. The main difference lies in buyers' understanding of a specific product or service: novice, intermediate, and expert product skill levels. Internet-based customer service should be organized in a way that helps a novice buyer select the most general topics and progress toward more specific details until a product matches their need, whereas customers with more advanced knowledge should have the option of using shorter, more direct routes.

Trust in Electronic Commerce

Trust is the psychological status of involved parties who are willing to pursue further interactions to achieve a planned goal. A trading party makes itself vulnerable to the other party's behavior. In other words, the parties assume risk. In the marketspace, sellers and buyers do not meet face to face. The buyer can see a picture of the product but not the product itself. Promises of quality and delivery can be easily made—but will they be kept? To deal with these issues it is necessary to have a high degree of trust between buyers and sellers. Maintaining the high level of trust for vendors in EC is critical unless they are already established entities in the non-cyber-business environment. Trust is particularly important in global EC due to the difficulties of taking legal actions in case of a fraud and the different cultures and business environments involved.

In addition to trust between the buyer and seller, it is necessary to have trust in the EC infrastructure and in the EC environment. Here we discuss mainly the consumers' trust in the vendor.

Shapiro et al's (1992) trust model typifies three forms of trust:

1. **Deterrence-based trust** is related to the threat of punishment. The threat of punishment is likely to be a more significant motivator than the promise of reward.
2. **Knowledge-based trust** is grounded in the knowledge of the other trading partner (trustee), which allows the trustor to understand and predict the behavior of the trustee. The key factor in this trust is the information derived out of a relationship over time that permits a trustor to predict the behavior of a trustee or vice versa; also, brand recognition is very important in EC. For example, when you buy from Disney online or Walmart online, you probably will have a great trust. Obviously, you need to be assured that Disney is the seller and not an imposter.
3. **Identification-based trust** is based on empathy and common values with the other trading partner's desire and intentions, to the point that one trading partner is able to act as an agent for the other.

How does one establish the necessary level of trust for EC? Desired level of trust is determined by the following factors (Shapiro et al 1992): the degree of initial success that each party experienced with EC and with each other; well-defined roles and procedures for all parties involved; and realistic expectations as to outcomes from EC. On the other hand, trust can be decreased by any user uncertainty regarding the technology, by lack of initial face-to-face interactions, and by lack of enthusiasm among the parties. In fact, it is extremely difficult to measure the level of trust because it involves multiple parties, far apart both in time and location, as well as difficulties in measuring the nature of the mental process involved. Some theoretical and practical extensions of Shapiro's were made by Lewicki and Bunker (1996).

EC security mechanisms and technology can help solidify trust. Security issues are discussed in detail in chapters 8 and 11. In addition to relying on security techniques, it is necessary for EC vendors to disclose and update the latest business status and practices to potential customers and build transaction integrity into the system, as well as to guarantee information protection through various communication channels. Moreover, as is discussed in chapter 10, there is considerable amount of fraud on the Internet. This fraud is leading to mistrust, especially when unknown parties are involved. In chapter 10 we describe this issue and the measures that are being taken to reduce fraud and increase trust. This can be done by trusted third parties such as TRUST-e, iescrow, etrust, and so on. For comprehensive treatment of EC trust see Ratnasingham (1998) and Hoffman et al, (1999).

The Value of EC Referrals

As part of a beta test to launch a new online shipping service, FedEx sent an e-mail message to selected customers inviting them to try the new service. To their surprise, FedEx found that a large, unexpected number of people, who were not on the e-mail list, began using the service. This demonstrates how powerful the Internet referral network can be. Many FedEx customers who have started using the online shipping service report that they learned about it after receiving a package sent by the new Web service. Thus, for companies like 1-800-Flowers and FedEx, the word-of-mouth potential is multiplied because every transaction initiated by one person or company is completed through delivery to another.

Businesses that run exclusively on the Internet, such as DeJa News, Amazon, and E*TRADE, rely heavily on referrals to deliver people to their sites. DeJa News, a newsgroup with thousands of links to other sites, advertises online and has attracted a lot of followers from the positive, unsolicited reviews they regularly receive in the media. Such word-of-mouth advertising in 1998 made DeJa News the 30th busiest site on the Internet. It has also placed the company on many personal home pages as one of the favorite places to visit. World Hire, a Web site for employers and job seekers, also relies heavily on referrals. People learn about the service from either a news group such as DeJa News or other Internet links and search engines.

3.6 Delivering Customer Service in Cyberspace

When going through the purchasing process described in Figure 3.3, the customer may need some help. For example, in the need-recognition phase customers sometimes require assistance in finding out what they need. Then, they try to find out what to buy in order to satisfy the need. Customers have questions about product characteristics before they buy a product and about proper maintenance after they buy it. Sellers must be able to help the customers in any and all of the phases. Such help is a major task in customer service.

Customer service is a series of activities designed to enhance the level of customer satisfaction—that is, the feeling that a product or service has met the customer's expectations. Customer service helps shoppers to resolve problems they encountered in any phase of the purchasing decision-making process (Figure 3.3), or the product life cycle, to be described soon. Whereas traditional service puts the burden on the customer to direct a problem or inquiry to the right place and receive information bit by bit, EC delivers improved customer service, frequently by automating it.

In the early years of EC, adopters did not demand high levels of customer service, so the first generation of customer service was fairly simple. The next-generation customer service, however, requires the best, most powerful programs and software to be effective and satisfy the increased expectations of customers. If customer service options and solutions do not maintain the same level of excitement and interaction as the advertising and sales presentations, the level of intensity declines and the vendor runs the risk of losing customers. Therefore, EC marketers must quickly respond to the different and increasing requirements of consumers.

As part of the demand for higher levels of service, customers may want to receive "entertainment" values on the Internet. Customers invest money in hardware, software, and Internet access. They take time to learn systems and are ready to commit to a purchase when they feel happy by being entertained and being able to get a quick response and good service. The challenge for EC businesses is to continue "the sale" after the purchase transaction. This helps in increasing customers' loyalty.

EC plays a dual role in customer service. First, it provides customer service to a process that is done completely offline. For example, if you buy a product offline and you need expert advice on how to use it for a usual application, you may get the instructions online. Such delivery of information, according to the EC definition in chapter 1, is by itself EC, although not a pure one. Second, it provides help to online transactions. Regardless of its form, customer service needs to be delivered throughout the product life cycle.

PRODUCT LIFE CYCLE AND CUSTOMER SERVICE

Customer service in EC becomes more critical, since customers and merchants do not meet face to face (Sterne 1997). According to McKeown and Watson (1998), customer service should be provided during the entire product life cycle, which is composed of the following four phases:

1. *Requirements:* Assisting the customer to determine needs (e.g., photographs of a product, video presentations, textual descriptions, articles or reviews, sound bites on a CD, and downloadable demonstration files). All of these can be provided electronically.
2. *Acquisition:* Helping the customer to acquire a product or service (e.g., online order entry, negotiations, closing of sale, downloadable software, and delivery).
3. *Ownership:* Supporting the customer on an ongoing basis (e.g., interactive online user groups, online technical support, frequently asked questions and answers, resource libraries, newsletters, and online renewal of subscriptions).
4. *Retirement:* Helping the client to dispose of a service or product (e.g., online resale, classified ads).

Many activities conducted in each of these phases are shown throughout the book.

TYPES OF CUSTOMER SERVICE FUNCTIONS AND TOOLS

As seen in chapter 2, customer service on the Web can take many forms. Types of customer service include answering customer inquiries, providing search and comparison capabilities, providing technical information to customers, allowing customers to track order status, and of course allowing customers to place an online order, and so on. The following describes different kinds of customer service in more detail.

Answering Customer Inquiries

Consumers place great importance on the ability to get free information on demand. Detailed information, as well as general browsing, readily available at the click of a mouse on a point of interest providing such a service during the prepurchase phase, becomes as important as the purchase itself. Innovative use of links and keywords need to be the norm for building Web sites that keep the consumer coming back for more. The Internet provides the ability to embed numerous links to other information sites to get further useful information or transactions. For example, in 1-800-Flowers, customers get useful information from experts or get involved in online contests to win prizes. This added value motivates them to choose 1-800-Flowers as their floral delivery service. To make this process more efficient, one can use intelligent agents (section 3.8).

Providing Search and Comparison Capabilities

One of the major problems in EC is to find what you want. With the thousands of stores online and thousands of new ones added constantly, it is difficult for a customer to find what they want even inside a single mall. Once product (service) information is found, the customer usually wants to compare prices. Several sites provide efficient search engines for such purposes.

Providing Technical and Other Information

Interactive experiences need to be tailored to induce the consumer to commit to a purchase. The follow-up experience of service takes a partnering role in developing market research that will enable the business to capitalize on the preferences and needs of the Web customer. For example, General Electric's Web site provides detailed technical and maintenance information and sells replacement parts for discontinued models for those who need to fix outdated home appliances. Such information and parts are quite difficult to find offline. Another example is Goodyear.com, which provides information about tires and their use (see their tire school on the web).

As is shown in chapter 5, travel is big online. Airlines and hotels are offering consumers the advantage of direct booking. Customer service includes providing maps, price comparisons, push technology that sends you e-mail information about cheap tickets to your favorite destinations, weather, travelers' experiences, news, and so on.

Letting Customers Track Accounts or Order Status

Customers can view their account balance at a financial institution and check their merchandise shipping status anywhere, at any time. The traditional banker's hours have left the scene, and individual and business customers can check balances, transfer funds between accounts, and make and monitor investments at their own convenience (for details see chapter 5). Similarly, you can easily find the status of your stock portfolio, loan application, and so on. FedEx and other shippers allow customers to track their packages. If you ordered books from Amazon or others, you can find the anticipated arrival date. Amazon even goes one step further; it notifies you by e-mail the acceptance of your order, the anticipated delivery date, and later, the actual delivery date. Many companies follow the Amazon model and provide similar services.

Allowing Customers to Customize and Order Online

The ability to place an order at any time over the Internet has expanded business hours to be round-the-clock for both vendors and consumers. Dell Computer and Gateway 2000 have revolutionized purchasing of computers. Consumers are shown prepackaged "specials" and are given the option to "custom-build" systems. Add-ons, troubleshooting, and frequently encountered problems are handled with ease on these sites. The ability to download manuals and problem solutions at any time is another innovation of electronic customer service.

Music Blvd takes the same approach with music. Web sites such as www.music-maker.com or www.customdisk.com allow consumers to handpick individual titles from a library and customize a CD, a feature that is not offered in traditional music stores. Instant delivery of any digitized entertainment is a major advantage of EC. In gm.com, General Motors details the technical information and business procedures necessary for buying a new car as well as parts.

Web sites, such as www.gap.com, allow you to "mix and match" your entire wardrobe. Personal sizes, color and style preferences, dates for gift shipment, and so on, can be manipulated to increase sales and the probability of repeat business. Finally, JCPenny and Levi's allow customers to be physically measured at stores. Orders for the customized clothes are then transferred electronically to the production lines.

SOME TOOLS OF CUSTOMER SERVICE

There are many innovative Web-related tools to enhance customer service. Here are some of them.

Personalized Web Pages

Many companies are creating Web sites that allow customers to create their own individual Web pages. These pages can be used to record purchases and preferences. Also, customized information can be efficiently delivered to the customer, such as product information, add-on purchases, and warranty information. The information is easily disseminated when the customer logs on to the EC Website. Not only can the customer pull information as needed or desired, but also information is pushed to him or her. The customer database records purchases, problems, and requests. This information can then be utilized by the business to enhance both product lines and facilitate service to the customer. Information that formerly may have been collected one to three months after a transaction was consummated is now collected in real or almost real time, and it can be traced and analyzed for an immediate response. Transaction information can also be stored, accessed, and manipulated to support marketing of more products and to match valuable information about product performance and consumer behavior. Such information can be sorted and grouped for use by product, customer, or any other criteria. An example of such a Web site is that of American Airlines (see Application Case 3.2).

FAQs

Frequently asked questions (FAQs) is the simplest and least expensive tool to deal with repetitive customer questions. Customers use this tool by themselves (on the Web) which makes the delivery cost minimal. However, anything nonstandard requires an e-mail. Also, FAQs are not customized yet. (They may be one day; the system will know your profile and present to you a customized FAQ sheet.) Therefore, there is no personalized feeling or contribution to one-to-one relationship marketing.

A Chat Room

Another tool that provides customer service, attracts new customers and increases customers' loyalty is a *chat room*. For example, at Virtual Vineyard's chat room, www.wine.com you can discuss issues with both company experts and wine lovers. (For futher discussion of chat rooms, see chapters 4 and 11.)

American Airlines Builds the Largest Personalized Site on the Internet

American Airlines unveiled in late 1998 a new feature on its Web site, www.AA.com, considered by some as the most advanced site for personalized one-to-one interactions and transactions on the Net. The most innovative feature of the new site is its ability to generate personalized Web pages for each of the 650,000 (in 1998) American Airlines registered travel-planning customers.

How can AA handle such a large amount of information and provide real-time customized Web pages for each customer? The answer is: intelligent agents.

The site was developed by Broadvision (www.broadvision.com), a major developer of Internet applications for one-to-one marketing, using a system called One-to-One Application.

One-to-One is a complex software application for the development and real-time operation of Internet business applications. There are many components that contribute to achieving the goal of personalizing each Web page. One of the core components is the intelligent agents, which dynamically match customer profiles (built on information supplied by the customer, observed by the system, or derived from existing customer databases) to the database of contents. The output of the matching process triggers the creation of a real-time customized Web page, which in the case of AA can contain information on home airport and preferred destinations.

By using intelligent-agent technology, American Airlines is building a considerable edge over its competitors. Personalizing Web pages is becoming more important because of its potential in increasing customer loyalty and cementing excellent relationships with customers.

E-mail and Automated Response

The most popular tool of customer service is e-mail. Inexpensive and fast, e-mail is used to disseminate information (e.g., confirmations), to send product information (see chapter 4), and to conduct correspondence regarding any topic, but mostly inquiries from customers.

The ease with which e-mails are sent results in a flood of e-mail. Some companies receive tens of thousands of e-mails a week, or even a day. To answer these e-mails manually is too expensive and time-consuming. Customers want quick answers, usually within 24 hours (a policy of many organizations). Priced at about $50,000 (in 1998), you can buy an automated e-mail reply system that provides answers, from several vendors (e.g., www.egain.com). Such a system scans (if necessary) incoming regular mail and interprets and automatically responds to customer inquiries using intelligent agents.

The e-gain system, for example, looks for certain phrases or words such as "complaint" or "information on a product" and can tap into a knowledge base to generate a response. In cases in which human attention is needed, the query is assigned an ID number and passed along to a customer agent, who can tap into a knowledge base for faster response.

A key feature of a customer service system is audit and tracking capabilities, which allow managers to set goals for customer service and monitor progress as well as to find the information needed for intelligent agents.

Help Desks and Call Centers

One of the most important tools of customer service in general is the help desk. Customers can drop in or communicate by telephone, fax, or e-mail. Because initially the communication was done by telephone, the remote help desk is called the call center.

Today's **call center** is a comprehensive customer service entity in which EC vendors take care of customer service issues communicated through various contact channels. New products are extending the functionality of the conventional call center to e-mail and to Web interaction, integrating them into one product. For example, eFrontOffice (www.efrontoffice.com) combines Web channels, such as automated e-mail reply, Web knowledge bases, and portal-like self-service, with call center agents or field service personnel. Such centers are sometimes called **telewebs.** An example of how a web-based call center (or teleweb) works is provided in Application Case 3.3.

For both consumers and businesses, the Internet is a medium of instant gratification. Delays could easily send customers or potential customers elsewhere. More and more Internet users demand not only prompt replies but proactive alerts. For example, travel Web site Travelocity sends out a page with updated gate and time information if a customer's flight is delayed. An online mortgage lender, loanshop.com, focuses on the teleweb center for the future of sales and support in a natural language-based application. To use the system, customers submit structured e-mail messages in which they answer a number of questions. If the system cannot answer a query automatically, the e-mail is routed to an integrated queue of phone calls, e-mail, and faxes in the teleweb center. A comprehensive description of Web-based call centers, including information on leading vendors, is available at Orzech (1998).

Some of the hurdles a call center needs to address includes deploying technologies such as e-mail management software; creating knowledge bases for FAQs; integrating phone and e-mail into a single center; training customer service representatives who can manage such a function in an effective way; and dealing with foreign languages whenever necessary.

Providing well-trained customer service representatives who have access to data such as customer history, purchases, and previous contact with the call center agents is another way to improve service. In this way a company can maintain personal touch with the online customer. An example is Bell Advanced Communication in Canada, whose subscribers can submit requests to resolve technical questions over the Web. Consumers fill out an e-mail form with drop-down menus that help to pinpoint the problem. The e-mail is picked up by the call center, which either answers the question immediately or tries to respond within one hour. "From a customer service perspective, it provides good context. It keeps the personal aspect alive," says Maggi Williams, director of business development. This form of online "managed comprehensive contact" also gives Bell insight into what kind of information customers are interested in, which may, in turn, generate selling or marketing opportunities.

EXAMPLES OF SUPERB CUSTOMER SERVICE

How do companies make customers more satisfied? And what role does the Internet play in the process? Some examples are provided in Application Case 3.4 on page 94.

APPLICATION CASE 3.3

Canadian Tire Provides Superb Customer Service via an Integrated Call Center

Canadian Tire Acceptance Ltd. (CTAL), the financial services division of the $4 billion Canadian Tire Corp., Ltd., serves 4 million of Canadian Tire's credit card holders. In 1998 it became the primary call center of the company, expecting to increase sales and enhance customer retention by eliminating annoying and time-consuming call transfers and ensuring that customers were treated on an individual basis.

"The call center is a strategic asset," says Mary Turner, vice president of customer services at CTAL. "This is our main point of contact with the customer. We have to maximize it."

Canadian Tire operates 10 call centers, each dealing with a different business area (general information and retail, wholesale, service, and so on) or a geographical zone. The demands are heavy. CTAL's 10 call centers operate 24 hours a day, 7 days a week, and respond to more than 16 million calls a year. Call center representatives are expected to provide personalized service while handling a diverse set of customer needs—responding to more than 200 types of customer requests. CTAL's new system ensures that any representative can resolve any customer need without handoffs to other departments.

CTAL has several key business objectives:

- greater customer loyalty to Canadian Tire as a result of enhanced service;
- personalized customer attention and reduced transfers;
- rapid introduction of new products or changes to existing business services;

- reduced training requirements for customer service representatives; and
- integration of all customer touch points via a single system capable of handling Web, e-mail, and call center interactions.

The primary goal is to create a customer service environment that enables a complete set of customer-focused services in which the company understands customer behavior and needs and offers timely introduction of new services valued by the customers.

"When we began the project, we took a look at our operations and saw too many independent call centers," Turner continues. "It seemed that every time we introduced a new product or service, we set up a new call center. We decided to streamline operations to make it possible for customers to reach the right representative whenever they call." CTAL's new call center technology integrates data from multiple sources and media.

The call center integrates the telephone, fax, e-mail, and the Web. One of its major capabilities is to build customer profiles and act on them when needed, providing one-to-one relationships. The call center can be viewed as an interaction center that immediately recognizes the individual customer and integrates data that reflects on the relationship. Although the Web-based call center is still new, it is expected to pay for itself quickly. (For further details, see Peppers et al. 1999.)

3.7   Market Research for EC

Market research is aimed at finding information that describes the relationship between consumers, products, marketing methods, and marketers in order to discover marketing opportunities and issues, to establish marketing plans, to better understand the purchasing process, and to evaluate marketing performance. Market research includes gathering information about topics such as the economy, industry, firms, products, pricing, distribution, promotion, and consumer purchasing behavior.

Representative Examples of Superb Customer Service

1-800-Flowers offers on its Web site three ways to buy: telephone, retail shops, and online. This way the site provides flexibility as well as attracting new, first-time customers who were previously unaware of the services. Special online marketing programs leverage brand marketing by calling attention to the online capability in its offline promotions, including direct mail, television, and printed media. The company extended the use of e-mail for order confirmation and customer communication. This turned out to be quite effective because customers appreciate the fact that someone actually received their order and quickly responded to them. Providing games and giving incentives such as discounts for early holiday buying also promote repeat orders. Several value-added programs featuring frequent flier or other tie-in reward offers provide additional motivation to keep customers happy.

For Amazon.com, convenience, selection, value, and special services contribute to very high customer loyalty. Amazon.com, as described in chapter 2, sells through its Web site to more customers than any other book retailer on the Internet. More than one-third of Amazon's customers have bought two or more times. What changed customer buying patterns in this case is the convenience of buying on the Internet. Furthermore, customers find a large assortment of books at a discounted price that they cannot get anywhere else. In addition, Amazon uses e-mail as a low-cost vehicle for order confirmation and to personalize its service. For example, the company records each customer's topic and author prefer-

ences in a database and regularly sends out e-mail communications whenever a new book arrives that may appeal to that customer. Online editorials also keep customers coming back to the site to get reviews about books they are considering. This interactive function has been effective in building faithful followers for Amazon.com. Finally, there is high level of trust in the brand. The name Amazon is well known worldwide despite the fact that the company was established only in 1995.

Federal Express (FedEx) views the Internet as a front door to its service offerings. The company initially created a Web site to enable customers to track their packages, and then it found that more than 30,000 customers used the service in its first week of operation. Giving the customers an alternate method of tracking packages took the pressure off its customer service representatives and gave customers an incentive to choose its service over competitors. Based on the popularity of its tracking program, FedEx later added shipping-administration capability that allows customers to visit the FedEx Web site, calculate delivery cost, fill in a shipping form, arrange for courier pickup, or find a local drop-off point. When customers enter the Web site, they are delighted to find something in the real world occurring as a result of what they did in the cyberworld. This has led to a high percentage of repeated visits to their site, including customers who use the service daily. The use of e-mail is also improving FedEx's customer communication by giving customers direct access to customer service professionals and not just telephone operators.

The generic marketing research process is shown in Figure 3.6. It includes four major phases: First, define the problem to be investigated (e.g., why grocery online is expanding slower than books online) and the research objective (e.g., find the major reasons, rank them by importance). The second phase involves a research methodology (e.g., a sample survey) and data collection plan. In phase three, data are collected. In the last phase, data are analyzed and integrated.

Various marketing research tools have been used by businesses, educational institutions, and governments to acquire numerous data on people, specifically consumers. For example, you can find business representatives in physical shopping malls with

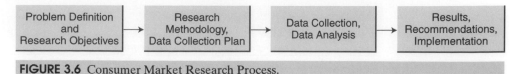

FIGURE 3.6 Consumer Market Research Process.

questionnaires collecting information on clothing, consumer products, or Internet usage; or you can taste food to determine how good it is. In addition, you will find surveyors in supermarkets, at the front door of your house, or at churches, airport terminals, or theaters. These places have high traffic, and replicating the surveys in various cities can give fairly generalized results. Another conventional way of conducting market research is by telephone surveys, in which an interviewer calls a prospective client, current customers, or a randomly selected sample of customers regarding a specific product or service. There are also questionnaires that are mailed to a specific person in a company or to households.

Furthermore, focus groups and other types of primary research methods can be useful for identifying differences in attributes, benefits, and values of various potential markets. Analyzing these differences in consumers is important when companies seek new target markets.

In the next section, we focus on online marketing research and consumer purchasing behavior in EC. Because EC also has to identify an appropriate customer group for specific products and services, it is important first to understand the grouping of consumers in different ways, whether it is for traditional offline marketing research or online. This grouping is called segmentation.

MARKET SEGMENTATION

Market segmentation is the process of dividing a consumer market into logical groups for conducting marketing research decision making, advertisement, and sales. A consumer market can be segmented in several ways—for example, according to geography, demographics, psychographics, and benefits sought. It is done in order to formulate effective marketing strategies that appeal to specific consumer groups.

In the past, most marketing approaches have targeted such segmentations; only in a few cases were companies able to identify individual consumers. However, improved methods of market research based on information technologies allow marketers today to collect, store, and analyze detailed and personal information in a cost-efficient way. Wal-Mart, for example, is reported to have current purchasing data on several million customers in their data warehouse.

The process of segmenting the consumer market involves several different classifications, as shown in Table 3.3.

An important task involved in market segmentation is analyzing consumer-product relationships. Marketers need to investigate the product concept and consider what types of consumers are likely to purchase and use this product and how they differ from those less likely to purchase and use the product. In EC, however, geographic segmentation is somewhat less meaningful.

When conducting segmentation, relationships must be checked carefully. For example, consumer lifestyles shape psychographic segmentation. That is, consumers are first asked a variety of questions about their lifestyles and then are grouped on the basis of the similarity of their responses. Lifestyles are typically measured by having

TABLE 3.3 Consumer Market Segmentation Tasks in the United States (a partial list)		
Segmentation Bases/Descriptors		
Geographic	Region	
	Size of city, county, or Standard Metropolitan Statistical Area (SMSA)	
	Population density	
	Climate	
Demographic	Age	Occupation
	Sex	Education
	Family size	Religion
	Family life cycle	Race
	Income	Nationality
Psychosocial	Social class	
	Lifestyles	
	Personality	
Cognitive, Affective, Behavioral	Attitudes	Involvement
	Benefits sought	Loyalty status
	Readiness stage	Usage rate
	Perceived risk	User status
	Innovativeness	Usage situation

consumers answer questions about activities such as work and family, interests including hobbies and community work, preferences and opinions.

Psychographic segmentation surveys usually generate rich information about consumers (appendix 3A). Although psychographic segmentation assumes that the more you know and understand about consumers, the more effectively you can address your marketing needs, psychographic studies often reach different conclusions about the number and nature of lifestyle categories. For this reason, the validity of psychographic segmentation is sometimes questioned. This information is related to the use of intelligent agents, such as www.firefly.net, which is described in section 3.9.

Marketing research, including EC market research, can be conducted by conventional methods (e.g., Burns and Bush 1998 and Churchill 1999), or it can be done with the assistance of the Internet, as discussed next.

ONLINE MARKET RESEARCH

The Internet is a powerful and cost-effective tool for conducting market research regarding consumer behavior, identifying new markets, and testing consumer interest in new products. Although telephone or shopping mall surveys will continue, interest in interactive Internet research methods is on the rise. **Online market research** utilizing the Internet is frequently more efficient, faster, and cheaper, and you have the ability to get a more geographically diverse audience than those found in offline surveys. Furthermore, the size of a market research sample is the key determinant of research design. The larger the sample size, the larger the accuracy and the predictive capabilities of the results. On the Web, one can conduct a very large research study much cheaper than with other methods (20 percent to 80 percent less). For example, telephone surveys can cost as much as $50 dollars per respondent. This may be too expensive for a small company that needs several hundred respondents. An online survey will cost a fraction of this. An overview of Internet market research is provided in Application Case 3.5.

Internet-based market research is often done in an interactive manner by allowing personal contacts with customers, and it provides marketing organizations with greater ability to understand the customer, market, and the competition. For example, it can identify early shifts in products and customer trends, enabling marketers to identify products and marketing opportunities and to develop those products that customers really want to buy. It also tells management when a product or a service is no longer popular. The next discussion describes some methods of conducting online market research.

ONLINE MARKET RESEARCH METHODS

The Internet provides an efficient channel for fast, cheap, and reliable collection and processing of marketing information, even in a multimedia format. Methods used on the Net range from one-to-one communication with specific customers, usually by e-mail, to moderated focus groups conducted in chat rooms, and to surveys placed on Web sites. A typical Internet-based marketing research process is shown in Table 3.4 on page 99.

Interaction with customers can be done over the Web site using games, prizes, (see opening vignette), quizzes, or sweepstakes. Using questionnaires, information is collected from customers before they are allowed to play games, win prizes, or download free software. However, according to the eighth GVU Survey (1998) more than 40 percent of the information people place on questionnaires is inaccurate or incorrect. Therefore, appropriate design of Web questionnaires and incentives for true completion are critical for the validity of the results. Professional pollsters and marketing research companies frequently conduct online voting polls.

Online market researchers have to address numerous issues. For example, customers may refuse to answer certain questions. Also, the administration of questionnaires can be lengthy and costly. Furthermore, you risk losing people who do not complete online questionnaires because they have had some technical problems. Some users may not have the latest, fastest computers or a fast way to connect to the Internet. For example, long download times and slow processing of Web-based questionnaires lead only to frustration on the part of the customers; it can convince them not to return to your site, leading to lost respondents and future sales.

Web surveys can incorporate radio buttons, data-entry fields, and check boxes, which keep respondents from selecting more than one choice or adding comments where none was intended; skipping questions is done automatically, based on respondents' previous answers rather than in the form of written instructions to the respondent. Responses can be validated as they are entered; and other elements can be added, such as graphics, logos, and links to other Web pages. Also, data reentry errors are eliminated and statistical analysis can be done in minutes. Data from prospective participants can also be collected across international borders. In addition, the participants have the flexibility of responding any time, at their own convenience. Real-time information and reporting can also be accomplished.

Tracking Customer Movements on the Internet

To avoid many of the problems cited earlier, especially the providing of false information, it is possible to learn about customers by observing their behavior rather than interacting with them and asking them questions. Many marketers keep track of consumers' Web movements using **cookie** files attached to a user's browser to help

---

APPLICATION CASE 3.5

Marketing Research on the Internet

Like the Internet itself, performing marketing research on the Net is still in its infancy. But as the use of the World Wide Web and online services becomes more habit than hype for a small but desirable fraction of U.S. consumers, online research is becoming a quick, easy, and inexpensive way to tap into their opinions.

Online researchers don't pretend that Web surfers are representative of the U.S. population. Online users tend to be better educated, more affluent, and younger than the average consumer, and a higher proportion are male. However, these are highly important consumers to companies offering products and services online. They are also some of the hardest to reach when conducting a research study. Online surveys and chat sessions (or online focus groups) often prove effective in getting elusive teen, single, affluent, and well-educated audiences to participate.

Online research isn't right for every company or product. For example, mass marketers who need to survey a representative cross-section of the population will find online research methodologies less useful. "If the target for the product or service you're testing is inconsistent with the Internet user profile, then it's not the medium to use," Paul Jacobson of Greenfield Online, an online research company, points out. "Is it the right medium to test Campbell's Chunky Soup? Probably not, but if you want to test how people feel about Campbell's Web site, yes."

When appropriate, online research offers marketers two distinct advantages over traditional surveys and focus groups: speed and cost-effectiveness. Online researchers routinely field quantitative studies and fill response quotas in only a matter of days. Online focus groups require some advance scheduling, but results are practically instantaneous.

Research on the Internet is also relatively inexpensive. Participants can dial in for a focus group from anywhere in the world, eliminating travel, lodging, and facility costs, making online chats cheaper than traditional focus groups. For surveys, the Internet eliminates most of the postage, phone, labor, and printing costs associated with other survey approaches.

However, using the Internet to conduct marketing research does have some drawbacks. One major problem is knowing who's in the sample. Tom Greenbaum, president of Groups Plus, recalls a cartoon in *The New Yorker* in which two dogs are seated at a computer: "On the Internet, nobody knows you are a dog," one says to the other. "If you can't see a person with whom you are communicating, how do you know who they really are?" Greenbaum says. Moreover, trying to draw conclusions from a "self-selected" sample of online users, those who clicked through to a questionnaire or accidentally landed in a chat room, can be troublesome. "Using a convenient sample is a way to do research quickly, but when you're done, you kind of scratch your head and ask what it means."

To overcome such sample and response problems, NPD Group and many other firms that offer online services construct panels of qualified Web regulars to respond to surveys and participate in online focus groups. NPD's panel consists of 15,000 consumers recruited online and verified by telephone; Greenfield Online picks users from its own database, then calls them periodically to verify that they are who they say they are. Another online research firm, Research Connections, recruits in advance by telephone, taking time to help new users connect to the Internet, if necessary.

Even when using qualified respondents, focus group responses can lose something in the translation. "You're missing all of the key things that make a focus group a viable method," says Greenbaum. "You may get people online to talk to each other and play off each other, but it's very different to watch people get excited about a concept." Eye contact and body language are two direct, personal interactions of traditional focus group research that are lost in the online world. Although researchers can offer seasoned moderators, the Internet format—running, typed commentary and online "emoticons" (punctuation marks that express emotion, such as :-) to signify happiness) —greatly restricts respondent expressiveness. Similarly, technology limits researchers' capability to show visual cues to research subjects. But just as it hinders the two-way assessment of visual cues, Web research can actually permit some participants the anonymity necessary to elicit an unguarded response. "There are reduced social effects online," Jacobson says. "People are much more honest in this medium."

Some researchers are wildly optimistic about the prospects for marketing research on the Internet; others are more cautious. One expert predicts that in the next few years, 50 percent of all research will be done on the Internet. "Ten years from now, national telephone surveys will be the subject of research methodology folklore," he proclaims. "That's a little too soon," cautions another expert. "But in 20 years, yes."

Source: Kotler and Armstrong (1999), p. 115. Portions adapted from Ian P. Murphy, "Interactive Research," *Marketing News*, January 20, 1997, pp. 1, 17. Selected quotes from "NFO Executive Sees Most Research Going to Internet," *Advertising Age*, May 19, 1997, p. 50. Also see Brad Edmondson, "The Wired Bunch," *American Demographics*, June 1997, pp. 10–15; and Charlie Hamlin, "Market Research and the Wired Consumer," *Marketing News*, June 9, 1997, p. 6.

track a Web surfer's movements online, whether consumers are aware of it or not. For example, Internet Profile Corporation collects data from client/server logs and provides periodic reports that include demographic data such as where customers come from or how many customers have gone straight from the home page to ordering. The company translates Internet domain names into real company names and includes

TABLE 3.4 Conducting Online Market Research

Process of Conducting the Research	1. Define the research issue and the target market.
	2. Identify news groups and Internet communities to study.
	3. Identify specific topics for discussion.
	4. Subscribe to the pertinent groups, register in communities.
	5. Search discussion group topic and content lists to find the target market.
	6. Search e-mail discussion group lists.
	7. Subscribe to filtering services that monitor groups.
	8. Read FAQs and other instructions.
	9. Enter chat rooms, whenever possible.
Content of the Research Instrument	1. Post strategic queries to groups.
	2. Post surveys on your Web site. Offer rewards for participation.
	3. Post strategic queries on your Web site.
	4. Post relevant content to groups with a pointer to your Web site survey.
	5. Post a detailed survey in special e-mail questionnaires.
	6. Create a chat room and try to build a community of consumers.
Target Audience of the Study	1. Compare your audience with the target population.
	2. Determine your editorial focus.
	3. Determine your content.
	4. Determine what Web services to create for each type of audience.

Source: Based on Vassos (1996), pp. 66–68.

general and financial corporate information in their reports. Tracking customers' activities without their knowledge or permission may be unethical or even illegal. For a discussion about cookies and tracking see chapter 10.

Limitations of Online Research

Concerns have been expressed over the potential lack of representativeness of samples composed of online users. As indicated earlier, online surfers tend to be mostly "baby busters" and "baby boomers"—wealthy, employed, and well educated. Although this is good for some marketers, the research results are not extendable for other marketers. Another important issue concerns the lack of clear understanding of the online communication process and how online respondents think and interact in cyberspace.

Online research is not suitable for every client or product. Although the Web user demographic is rapidly diversifying, it is still skewed toward certain population groups, such as those with Internet access. In addition, if you are a manufacturer of a consumer product such as laundry detergent, Internet research may not be an ideal research tool for you, because it may not reach enough of your target market. Depending on the demographic or target audiences a company wants, it is important to verify who the target people are so you can go after the right kind of sample. Web-based surveys typically have a lower response rate than e-mail surveys; and there is no respondent control for public surveys. If your target respondents are allowed to be anonymous, it may encourage these respondents to be more truthful in their opinions. The same attribute, however, may prevent researchers from knowing whether the respondent is projecting a false online image. It is not clearly known yet what kind of effect the electronic medium has on respondents' thinking and attentiveness—whether it is a stimulation or an impediment. Finally, there are still concerns about secure transmission of information, which may have an impact on the truthfulness of the respondents.

DATA MINING

Customer data accumulates daily in an ever increasing quantity. Large companies such as retailers, telecommunication companies, PC makers and car manufacturers build large data warehouses to store such information (e.g., see Gray and Watson 1998). To sift through the large amount of data (e.g., in order to analyze buying habits), marketers use **data mining** tools.

Data mining derives its name from the similarities between searching for valuable business information in a large database—and mining a mountain for a vein of valuable ore. Both processes require either sifting through an immense amount of material or intelligently probing it to find exactly where the value resides. Given databases of sufficient size and quality, data mining technology can generate new business opportunities by providing these capabilities:

- *Automated prediction of trends and behaviors.* Data mining automates the process of finding predictive information in large databases. Questions that traditionally required extensive hands-on analysis can now be answered directly and quickly from the data. A typical example of a predictive problem is targeted marketing. Data mining can use data on past promotional mailings to identify the targets most likely to favorably respond to future mailings. For example see Application Case 3.6
- *Automated discovery of previously unknown patterns.* Data mining tools identify previously hidden patterns. An example of pattern discovery is the

analysis of retail sales data to identify seemingly unrelated products that are often purchased together, such as baby diapers and beer. Other pattern discovery problems include detecting fraudulent credit card transactions and identifying anomalous data that may represent data entry keying errors.

The following are the major characteristics and objectives of data mining:

1. Relevant data are often difficult to locate in very large databases.
2. In some cases the data are consolidated in a data warehouse and data marts; in others they are kept in databases or in Internet and intranet servers. Data mining tools help remove the information "ore" buried in corporate files or archived in public records.
3. The "miner" is often an end user, empowered by "data drills" and other power query tools to ask ad hoc questions and get answers quickly, with little or no programming skill.
4. "Striking it rich" often involves finding unexpected, valuable results.
5. Data mining tools are easily combined with spreadsheets and other end-user software development tools; therefore, the mined data can be analyzed and processed quickly and easily.
6. Data mining yields five types of information: (a) association, (b) sequences, (c) classifications, (d) clusters, and (e) forecasting.

Data miners can use several tools and techniques. The most well-known tools of data mining are:

Neural Computing.   Neural computing is a machine learning approach by which historical data can be examined for patterns. Users equipped with neural computing tools can go through huge databases and, for example, identify potential customers for a new product, or search for companies whose profiles suggest that they are heading for bankruptcy.

APPLICATION CASE 3.6

British Telecom Uses Data Mining

British Telecom is a large telecommunication company in the UK. Its 1.5 million business users make about 90 million calls a day. The company provides 4,500 products and services. The company was looking for the best way to reach out and touch individual customers. The solution was a customer data warehouse. The company was using neural computing technology known as MPP (massively parallel processing). The data warehouse contained initially 3 GB of RAM. The system is used by the company to analyze buying habits of its customers to better understand customer needs and target market opportunities. Using the system, the company identified pur-chasing profiles for individual products, packages of products, and customers. One area is to identify customers that could be at risk of capture by the competition. The data mining is especially good for identifying trends in products that have a high sales value, such as intranets. This improves the relationship between marketing and sales. Now the sales force is guided on where to put their resources. Prior to data mining, marketing involved analyzing data that were six month's to a year old. Now sales people can trust marketing information because they now have almost real-time marketing information.

TABLE 3.5 Data Mining Applications	
Industry	*Application*
Retailing and sales	Predicting sales; determining inventory levels and schedules distribution.
Banking	Forecasting levels of bad loans, fraudulent credit card use, and credit card spending by new customers; predicting customer response to offers.
Airlines	Capturing data on where customers are flying and the ultimate destination of passengers who change carriers in midflight; thus, airlines can identify popular locations that they do not service and check the feasibility of adding routes to capture lost business.
Broadcasting	Predicting what is best to air during prime time and how to maximize returns by interjecting advertisements.
Marketing	Classifying customer demographics that can be used to predict which customers will respond to a mailing or buy a particular product.

Intelligent Agents.   One of the most promising approaches to retrieving information from the Internet or from intranet-based databases is the use of intelligent agents.

Association Analysis.   This is an approach that uses a specialized set of algorithms that sorts through large data sets and expresses statistical rules among items.

A Sample of Data Mining Applications.   According to a GartnerGroup prediction (www.gartnergroup.com), by 2000 at least half of all the Fortune 1000 companies worldwide will be using data mining technology. Data mining can be very helpful as shown by the examples of Table 3.5.

3.8   Intelligent Agents for Consumers

Intelligent and software agents play an increasingly important role in EC. In chapter 2 we demonstrate how intelligent agents help in finding and comparing products. **Intelligent agents,** and their subset software agents (appendix C), are computer programs that help the users to conduct routine tasks, search and retrieve information, support decision making, and act as domain experts. Agents sense the environment and act autonomously without human intervention. This results in a significant saving of time (up to 99 percent) to users. There are various types of agents, ranging from those with no intelligence **(software agents)** to **learning agents,** which exhibit some intelligent behavior.

Agents are used to support many tasks in EC. For example, Wang (1999) describes eight types of agents that assist B2B electronic commerce. Maes et al. (1999) provides an overview of EC agents, some of which are described in this section. Also, there is an increased number of commercial applications such as Inktomi Shopping Engine, My Yahoo, My Simon and Junglee. One of the primary reasons for using such agents is to overcome the tremendous amount of information overload. In going through the purchasing decision process described earlier, for example, a customer must examine large numbers of alternatives, each of which is surrounded by considerable amounts of information.

In this section we will concentrate on intelligent agents for assisting customers. However, before we do it, it will be beneficial to distinguish between search engines, which can be classified as software agents, and the more intelligent types of agents.

A *search engine* is a computer program that can automatically contact other network resources on the Internet, search for specific information or keywords, and report the results. For example, FAQs can be organized into an intelligent database for easy retrieval. Combined with e-mail, FAQs can be developed on a site by searching for and collecting similar questions. People tend to ask for things in the same general manner. For instance, requests for product information or pricing are asked by many. This type of request is considered repetitive, and it is costly to handle when done by a human. Automation provided by the search engines delivers answers economically and efficiently by matching questions with FAQ templates, which include standard questions and "canned" answers to them.

Unlike search engines, an intelligent agent can do more than just "search and match." For example, it can monitor movement on a Web site to check whether a customer seems lost or ventures into areas that may not fit his or her profile, and the agent can notify the customer and frequently provide assistance. Depending on their level of intelligence, agents can do many other things, some of which are demonstrated here. Of the many agents that can help consumers, we cover only a few representative ones. For other applications see Mutch and Johnson (1999).

INTELLIGENT AGENT FOR INFORMATION SEARCH AND FILTERING

Intelligent agents can help to determine what to buy to satisfy a specific need and where to buy it. This is achieved by looking for specific product information and critically evaluating it. One of the first intelligent agents available on the market for this task was PersonaLogic, an agent that helps consumers decide what product best fits their requirements by narrowing down the selection through a **filtering process.** Consumers specify requirements and constraints and the system returns a list of products that best meets their desire.

Another product that helps people to find what they want is Firefly. Firefly's Passport generates a **customer profile.** It is like a smart card, which stores information about who you are, what you like, and what you do not like. By using your Passport at different sites that use Firefly software (such as Barnes and Noble, My Yahoo, and Filmfinder), you can have access to personalized content, community, and services— while maintaining your privacy.

Firefly (www.firefly.net) uses a collaborative filtering process that can best be described as word of mouth to build the profile. The consumer is asked to rate a number of products, and the system then matches his or her ratings with the ratings of other consumers and, relying on the ratings of other consumers with similar tastes, recommends products that he or she has not yet rated. In other words, Firefly uses the opinion of like-minded people to make recommendations (Internet Exercise 10). Another agent of this type is ZineZone, described in Application Case 3.7.

INTELLIGENT AGENTS FOR PRODUCTS AND VENDOR FINDING

Intelligent agents help consumers decide where to buy by comparing merchants' offers. A pioneering intelligent agent for online price comparison was Bargainfinder. This agent was only used in online CD shopping. The agent queries the price of a specific CD from a number of online vendors and returns a list of prices. However, this system has encountered many problems because vendors who do not want to compete on price only have managed to block out the agent's requests.

The blocking problem has been solved by Jango (from NetBot/Excite). This agent originates the requests from the user's site instead of from Jango's. This way vendors have no way to determine whether the request is from a real customer or from the

APPLICATION CASE 3.7

ZineZone Helps in Information Search

ZineZone.com aggregates Web contents, organizes it into sections, and allows users to search for information related to their interests. The site's channels include culture, extreme sports, and "mind-body." In the mind-body section, users can, for example, participate in a chat forum titled "Is marijuana medicinal?" Those with a penchant for Tai Chi will find their search yields articles from sources such as the University of Capetown Tai Chi Clubs and links to Larry Stone's Martial Arts Center. Users can also enter their interests to create a page of continually updated articles.

ZineZone collects information about users and creates profiles that are used to push personalized advertisement. With the click of a mouse, admirers of Ms. Giove can outfit their bikes with the gear she recommends or buy a CD from her favorite band, the eardrum-blasting Rage Against the Machine. As usual, there is no free lunch; for example, those interested in Internet policy issues will get free articles from relevant sites such as CNet but will also get an electronic application form for a Visa card.

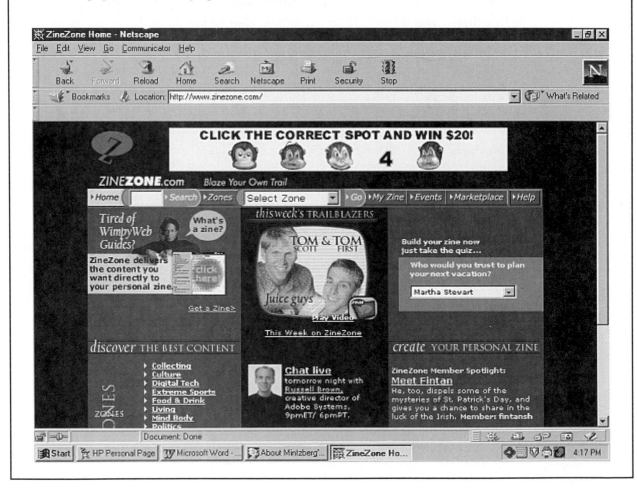

agent. Jango is also more complete than Bargainfinder as it includes more categories of products like computers, software, appliances, groceries, flowers, and even Beanie Babies. Furthermore, Jango provides product reviews in addition to price comparisons. Several other agents compete with Jango. They include Inktomi Shopping Agent, My Simon, and Junglee (of Amazon.com). (For further discussion see chapter 2.)

Another agent-based mediator worth mentioning is the Kasbah. In Kasbah, users wanting to sell (or to buy) a product assign the task to an agent, who is then sent out to proactively seek buyers (or sellers). In creating the agent, users must specify constraints including desired price, highest (or lowest) acceptable price, and a date by which to complete the transaction. The agent's goal is to complete an acceptable transaction based on these parameters. This agent can also negotiate on the part of the buyers, as will be discussed next.

NEGOTIATION AGENTS

As indicated earlier, the prepurchasing phase may involve negotiation in which price and other terms of transactions are determined. Intelligent agents can be particularly useful in this stage because they can take away some of the real-world problems associated with negotiation, such as the frustration some customers experience in the process and the technical limitations of being physically in different locations. There are several negotiation agents under development. Some will negotiate with humans while others will negotiate with other agents. For example, a buyer agent may negotiate with agents of several sellers. One area where such agents are being developed is in supporting auctions.

Auctions are one of the most popular activities on the Web because they easily overcome the problem of being physically dispersed. However, almost all auctions require users to personally execute the bidding. This is not the case of AuctionBot, in which users can create intelligent agents that will take care of the bidding process. In AuctionBot, users create auction agents by specifying a number of parameters that vary depending on the type of the auction selected. After that, it is up to the agent to manage the auction until a final price is met or the deadline of the offer is reached.

Kasbah is another environment in which intelligent agents are involved in the negotiation process. Kasbah agents (http://ai.mit.edu) are capable of negotiating with each other following specific strategies assigned by their creators. Three strategies are possible: anxious, coolheaded, and frugal. Each of them correspond to a different equation to increase (in case of buying) or decrease (if selling) the price over time. This method is simple, and therefore easy to understand by users. However, this agent's usefulness is limited by the fact that price is the only parameter considered. A better agent called Tete-@-tete has been developed by the creators of Kasbah and is described next.

Tete-@-tete is unique compared to other online negotiation systems because the agents here negotiate a number of different parameters with each other: price, warranty, delivery time, service contracts, return policy, loan options, and other value-added services. Another innovative feature of this system is that, unlike the Kasbah where negotiation is conducted along the lines of simple increase or decrease functions, negotiation of Tete-@-tete agents is argumentative. That is, agents use information acquired during the first two stages of the purchasing decision model (Figure 3.3) to evaluate each single offer. This, de facto, integrates the three stages of the decision purchasing model. This integrating approach makes Tete-@-tete the most advanced agent-based environment currently (1999) available. As of 1999 the system was not used commercially. A lot needs to be done, especially in terms of setting communica-

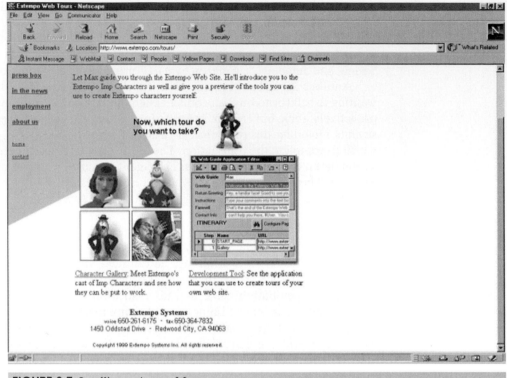

FIGURE 3.7 Intelligent Agent: Max.

tion standards and allowing agents to move freely in a networked environment before we can see commercial applications.

INTELLIGENT AGENTS FOR CUSTOMER SERVICE

Several intelligent agents enhance customer service by helping search as was shown earlier and by providing help to shoppers. For example, call center applications could be an effective way of portraying a comprehensive view of customer information. Extempo Improvisational built a prototype intelligent agent that provides a personal touch with a natural language interface, Max, as seen in Figure 3.7.

LEARNING AGENTS

A **learning agent** (also called remembrance) is capable of learning individuals' preferences and making suggestions. An example is Memory Agent, developed by IBM. Memory Agent uses a neural network technique called associative memory, which learns by creating a knowledge base of attributes of cases. This makes the system very small, fast, and scalable. Also, unlike other neural network-based agents, which use backward propagation, and require large number of historic cases to build and test the network, Memory Agent needs a small number of cases to start making suggestions.

A similar agent is Learn Sesame (from Open Sesame). This agent uses learning theory by monitoring customers' interactions. It learns customers' interests, preferences, and behavior and delivers customized services to them accordingly. Groaphens, from Netperceptions, personalizes content and creates customer loyalty programs with learning agent technology. Finally, Plangent is an agent that "moves around and thinks" (from Toshiba). It is classified as a "knowledge" agent because it performs tasks relying on a knowledge base of "actions."

Plangent has movement and planning capabilities as it moves around a network, determines the best course of action in various situations, and acts by itself. Its intelligent capabilities are guaranteed by the ability of the agent to decide its own behavior to achieve a predetermined goal. The technique used is called "planning," and it involves selecting appropriate "action" from a knowledge base of actions stored in each node of the network and in the agent itself. Plangent also has adaptability attributes, since it can go through as many different iterations of the planning process as necessary to achieve its goal. Like Memory Agent, Plangent, too, has been developed using the Java technology. The main reason behind this is the attempt to achieve 100 percent mobility among the network modes (PCs, laptops, mainframes, and so on.).

3.9 Organizational Buyer Behavior

The same product can well be B2C in a typical retail EC transaction or B2B. For example, both types of consumers may buy the same book, camera, or computer with differing purposes. Although the number of organizational buyers is much smaller than the number of individual buyers, their transaction volumes are far larger, and the terms of negotiations and purchasing are more complex. In addition, the purchasing, as seen in chapter 6, may be more important than advertising for organizational buyers. Factors that affect individual consumer behavior and organizational buying behavior are quite different, as seen in Table 3.6.

A BEHAVIORAL MODEL OF AN ORGANIZATION BUYER

The behavior of an organizational buyer can be described by a model similar to that of an individual buyer (Figure 3.1). However, some influencing variables differ (e.g., the family and Internet communities may have no influence). What is added in this model is an organizational module that includes the organization purchasing guidelines and constraints (e.g., contracts) and the system used. Also, interpersonal influences such as authority are added. Finally, the possibility of group decision making must be consid-

TABLE 3.6 Major Characteristics of Retail Buyers versus Organizational Buyers		
Characteristic	*Retail Buyers*	*Organizational Buyers*
Demand	Individual	Organizational
Purchase volume	Smaller	Larger
Number of customers	Many	Fewer
Location of buyers	Dispersed	Geographically concentrated
Distribution structure	More indirect	More direct
Nature of buying	More personal	More professional
Nature of buying influence	Single	Multiple
Type of negotiations	Simpler	More complex
Use of reciprocity	No	Yes
Use of leasing	Lesser	Greater
Primary promotional method	Advertising	Personal selling

Source: Lamb, et al. (1998), p. 194.

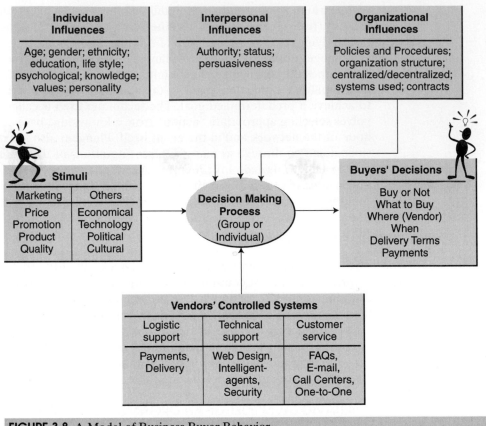

FIGURE 3.8 A Model of Business Buyer Behavior.

ered (see Figure 3.8). In chapters 6 and 7 we present an online procurement model, and we describe the role of the extranet in facilitating organizational purchasings. For a detailed discussion of organizational buyers see chapter 6 in Kotler and Armstrong (1999).

MANAGEMENT ISSUES

The following issues are germane to management:

1. **Understanding consumers.** Understanding the customers, specifically what the customer needs are and responding to those needs, is the most critical part of consumer-centered marketing. To meet customer demands, make consumers satisfied, and retain them to be loyal, management needs to monitor the whole process of marketing, sales, maintenance, and follow-up service.
2. **Consumers and technology.** Complex lives and lifestyles, a more diverse and fragmented population, and the power of technology all contribute to changing consumer needs and expectations of the EC age. Moreover, consumers today want more control over their time. Technology enables consumers to get things done more quickly and when they want to. Vendors should understand these relationships and utilize them in their marketing efforts.
3. **Response time.** Acceptable standards for response in customer service must be set. For example, customers want acknowledgment within 24 to 48 hours. Most companies want to provide this response time and do it at a minimum

cost of time and personnel. Offering service online allows companies ease and convenience at a reasonable cost. The initial investment in technology and software may be offset by a reduction in the number of customer service representatives needed and, more important, in savings resulting from customer retention.

4. **Justifying customer services.** The traditional models of the cost of services relative to the cost of product may not be appropriate for the cyberspace. Investment in software, hardware, and continuous improvement must be made and justified. The new model needs to take into account the benefits from the reduction in response time and the reduction in personnel needed.

5. **Timely information.** In many cases, using the Internet will dramatically change the customer base and growth patterns. It may be difficult to measure and compare anticipated results solely based on historical data. New parameters for success must be developed along with a new mind-set for customer service. Not only will customer service relate to the specific product or service offered, but information systems will now be part of the product/service offered and maintained. Therefore, management should strive to get right and rich up-to-the-minute information about customers in a timely manner through effective market research since market research provides information about who your customers (or potential customers) are and what, when, and why they buy.

6. **Intelligent agents.** Any company engaged in EC must examine the possibility of using intelligent agents at minimum to enhance customer service, and possibly to support market research. Commercial agents are available on the market at a reasonable cost. For heavy usage, consider building one yourself (see www.botspot.com).

7. **Developing relationship marketing.** Online market research and direct interaction with consumers will change retailers' relationships in many different ways. First, it presents an opportunity to develop deeper and more intimate relationships with consumers. This is possible as a result of tracking purchase and preference data and synthesizing that information to predict what other products and services the customers may need. Second, it enhances the ability to minimize "switching"—consumers moving among marketing channels and vendors. Third, it has the potential to capture an increased share of consumers' dollars by expanding the scope of products and services.

Summary

The compilation of this chapter helps you in attaining the following learning objectives:

1. **Essentials of consumer behavior.** Consumer behavior in EC is similar to that of any consumer behavior. It describes a stimuli-decision process-purchasing decision model. However, it also includes a significant vendor-controlled component that deals with logistics, technology, and customer service.

2. **Characteristics of customers.** Customers are the most critical factor for the success of business to consumer EC. Knowing what they are, what they need, and how to address those needs is important. Although most of the available data relates to Internet surfing in general rather than to EC in particular, we can make inferences from general Internet usage.

3. **Consumer decision-making process.** Understanding the process of consumer decision making and formulating an appropriate strategy to influence their behavior is the essence of marketing effort. For each step in the process, sell-

ers can develop appropriate strategies. Also, it is possible to use intelligent agents to automate some activities in these steps. Various models are available to describe or explain this process.

4. **Building one-to-one relationships with customers.** In EC there is an opportunity to build one-to-one relationships that do not exist in other marketing systems. Of special interest are the approaches to boost loyalty and increase trust. Product customization, personalized service, and getting the customer involved (e.g., in feedback, order tracking, and so on) are all practical in cyberspace.

5. **Implementing customer service.** Retaining customers by satisfying their needs and even creating new needs is the core of customer service. Customer service on the Web is provided by e-mail, on the corporate Web site, in customized Web pages, in integrated call centers, and by intelligent agents. Online customer service is media rich, effective, and less expensive than the services offered offline.

6. **EC market research.** Understanding market segmentation and grouping consumers into different categories is a necessity of effective EC market research. Several methods of Internet market research are available. They provide for fast, economical, and accurate research due to large samples involved. The two major approaches for data collection are to get information voluntarily or to use cookies to track customers' movements on the Internet. Finally, Internet-based market research has several limitations, such as data accuracy.

7. **Intelligent agents.** Gathering and interpreting data about consumer purchasing behavior can be done with software agents. Intelligent agents can also generate automatic e-mail replays, analyze customers' movement on the Internet, and support customer service and market research. Advanced agents can even learn about customer behavior and needs.

8. **Organizational buyer behavior model.** Organizational buyers must consider organizational factors in their purchasing decisions. For large-ticket items the decision may be made by a group. Also, interpersonal variables, such as authority and status, affect the decision.

Keywords

- Call centers
- Consumer behavior
- Consumer decision making
- Cookies
- Customer loyalty
- Customer profile
- Customer service
- Data mining
- Filtering process
- Intelligent agents
- Learning agent
- Market research
- Market segmentation
- One-to-one marketing
- Online market research
- Relationship marketing
- Software agents
- Telewebs
- Trust (in EC)

Questions for Review

1. Describe the typical profile of Internet users.
2. List the typical characteristics of individual retail buyers.
3. Describe the purchasing decision-making process.
4. Explain the concept of customer loyalty.
5. Describe what trust is in EC and how to increase it.
6. Explain how a call center is enhanced with Internet technology.
7. List typical examples of intelligent agents for consumers and their benefits.
8. Define market segmentation and provide examples.

9. Explain the goals of market research.
10. List the major methods of Internet-based market research.
11. Provide an example of an online market research tool.
12. Define data mining and describe its use in market research.

Questions for Discussion

1. What are major differences among U.S. and European Web surfers?
2. What would you do to maintain customer loyalty for the highly competitive retail clothing industry on the Web?
3. When would a consumer deviate from the standard decision-making process? Provide specific examples and explain what you would do as a marketer in each case.
4. What would a novice retail buyer need to do when surfing an automobile company Web site? Can an intelligent agent help? How?
5. Explain how to control, if possible, ever-increasing customer expectations. Provide some examples.
6. What are potential limitations of online market research? Can they be overcome? How?
7. What would you tell an executive officer of a bank about several critical success factors for retaining customer loyalty by using the Internet?
8. What can a vendor do to increase the trust level of customers online?
9. Why is data mining becoming an important element in EC? How is it used in learning about consumer behavior? How can it be used to facilitate customer service?

Internet Exercises

1. Compare the following two online grocery stores to see how they stack up against their bricks-and-mortar competitors in terms of cost of service and overall quality: http://www.netgrocer.com and http://www.pinkdot.com.
2. Enter www.priceline.com. Review the strategies used to attract and retain customers. What additional effort could priceline.com exercise to retain its customers?
3. Find recent Web-based call center and help desk products. Start with www.clarify.com.
4. Survey two department store Web sites, such as JCPenney (www.jcpenney.com) and Sears (www.sears.com). Write a report that highlights the different ways they provide their customer service program through online capability.
5. Surf the Home Depot (www.homedepot.com) Web site and identify whether (and how) the company provides service to the different levels of customers (e.g., a novice versus an expert).
6. Investigate whether a brand name plays a major role in maintaining online customer loyalty compared with traditional shopping in the coffee and tea markets. Check www.spinelli-coffee.com as an example.
7. Enter amazon.com and identify all customer services provided for free.
8. Go over a market research Web site such as www.acnielsen.com and discuss what might motivate a consumer to provide answers for the questions being asked.
9. Surf www.e-land.com and list the types of consumer information you can collect from the site.
10. Enter www.firefly.net and share your experiences about how the information you provide might be used by the company for marketing in a specific domain (e.g., the clothing market).
11. Get a guest pass from www.e-valuations.com and cruise the site. Discuss the types of data they are gathering. Are there any implications for privacy?
12. When would some of the market research data not be quite valid? Consider a global EC case by looking at World Market Watch, www.wmw.com.
13. Enter www.netdialog.com and review the services they provided. Sign up for their gold paper: online customer management. Prepare a summary of the paper.

Team Exercises

1. Team members are assigned one each to an overnight delivery service company (FedEx, DHL, UPS, and so on). Check all customer service features for each one. Write a report on common and unique services in the industry.
2. Let each team member apply demographic and psychosocial grouping to three different geographical areas of populations. Where would you find such data? If no data are available, how would you apply Internet technology to collect data?
3. Find 3 to 5 companies whose business is to enhance trust (in addition to www.ordertrust.com, www.ieserow.com, and www.etrust.com). Assign each member to one or two companies. Find the services they offer and prepare a report that will describe how trust is built by using a third party.

REAL WORLD CASE

Kansas City Power and Light Company

Due to recent deregulation and competition, power companies are losing market share rapidly. A critical issue for their survival is to provide better and more competitive customer service. Kansas City Power & Light (KCPL) is not an exception. The company has built a Web site (www.kcpl.com) that lets more than 400,000 customers check their own power usage, pay their bills, learn how to keep electric costs down, and much more. Douglas Morgan, vice president of information technologies, says, "We have competitors with offices in our city, and they are preparing to take our customers. We believe the Net is going to be a very positive force in expanding our products and services. It's still far too soon to tell if KCPL's Web initiative will help the century-old utility hang on to customers. . . ."

At the beginning, no one at KCPL understood the difference between publishing in hard copy and publishing online. So they just took printed brochures and put them on the Web site. Then they added a place for press releases. Soon the company started to learn a great deal about what works online and what does not. For example, they placed the links on the lower left-hand side (they should be on the right). Quickly they found that the static Web site was ineffective. They realized they must talk to customers and try to learn what kind of value-added services might be made available through the Web. What began as a relatively modest effort to get something up online—and perhaps sell some additional products and services— expanded as the company learned what customers wanted.

"The customers started to drive the Web site development toward being able to pay their bills online. Another thing that came out of those discussions was that the customers were aware of what deregulation meant. The customers were looking to KCPL to provide them with information to help them decide what to do." Morgan realized that when it came to giving customers immediate feedback on their use of electric power, KCPL can have an advantage over virtually all other power companies. In 1994 the company had invested heavily in the installation of a wireless automatic meter-reading system that gave utility employees sitting in front of computers at corporate headquarters real time access to meter readings for more than 400,000 businesses and homes. Unlike most automatic meter-reading systems, which check power usage only once a month, KCPL's system could check any meter anytime. By hooking that data into the Web site, the utility company could give customers with Internet access the ability to monitor their power usage in real time. The site provides formulas to figure out the average cost per hour needed to operate appliances and suggestions for saving energy. Customers can figure if their bill is higher than it should be. This application, called AccountLink, was phased in to residential and commercial customers in 1998.

When there is a problem or a disruption in service, KCPL also turns to the Web. The automated meter-reading system can tell KCPL repair units if a problem is in the customer's house or in the wires leading to the house. Each meter is equipped with a "last gasp" alarm, which alerts customer representatives when the flow of power stops. The wireless system saves the company about 105,000 field service trips a year.

The site also posts some marketing and sales information that had previously been available only in hard copy. There is a section for information of special interest to senior citizens and special needs customers, and there are explanations about the cold-weather program, which helps protect customers from electric power termination during the winter months. By mid-1998, the KCPL site had signed up more than 1,800 residential users and 800 commercial users for AccountLink. ■

Source: Condensed from *CIO Magazine* (July 1, 1998).

CASE QUESTIONS

1. Carefully review the actions KCPL has taken to address customer service issues and relate them to the set of guidelines presented in the customer service section of the chapter. Are there any additional actions KCPL can implement to enhance the level of customer service?
2. Go over the Web site of KCPL (www.kepl.com) and discuss how effective

and customer friendly it is. Any improvements you can suggest?
3. Compare this case with the opening vignette and comment.
4. How are one-to-one relationships being developed?
5. Should the Web site be integrated with the company-telephone-based call center? Will the cost be justified?

References

C. D. Allen and B. Yaeckel, *Internet World Guide to One-to-One Marketing (Internet World Series)* (New York: John Wiley & Sons, 1998).

P. Benassi, "TRUSTe: An Online Privacy Seal Program," *Communications of the ACM* 42 (2:1999).

J. A. Berry and G. Linoff. *Data Mining Techniques for Marketing, Sales and Customer Support* (New York: Wiley, 1997).

A. B. Blankenship et al., *State of the Art of Marketing Research* (Lincolnwood, IL: NTC Business Books, 1998).

J. Bradshaw, *Software Agents* (Menlo Park, CA: MIT Press, 1997).

A. C. Burns and R. F. Bush, *Marketing Research*, 2d ed. (Upper Saddle River, NJ: Prentice Hall, 1998).

G. Churchill, *Marketing Research*, 7th ed. (Fort Worth, TX: The Dryden Press, 1999).

R. East, *Consumer Behavior* (London: Prentice Hall, 1997).

E. Fram and E. Grady, "Internet Shoppers: Is There a Surfer Gender Gap?" *Direct Marketing* (January 1997):46–50.

Graphics, Visualization, & Usability (GVU) Center in Georgia Institute of Technology, *10th Survey,* 1998 (www.cc.gatech.edu/gvu).

P. Gray and H. J. Watson: *Decision Support in the Data Warehouse* (Upper Saddle River, NJ: Prentice Hall, 1998).

R. H. Guttman et al., "Agent-Mediated Electronic Commerce: A Survey," *Knowledge Engineering Review* (June 1998).

H. Hasan and G. Ditsa, "The Impact of Culture on the Adoption of IT: An Interpretive Study," *Journal of Global Information Management* (January/February 1999).

C. F. Ho and W. H. Wu, "Antecedents of Customer Satisfaction on the Internet: An Empirical Study of Online Shopping," *Proceedings of the 32nd HICSS* (January 1999).

D.L. Hoffman et al, "Building Consumer Trust Online," *Communication of the ACM,* (April 1999).

R. Kalakota and A. Whinston, *Electronic Commerce—A Manager's Guide* (Reading, MA: Addison Wesley, 1997).

R. Kalakota and A. B. Whinston, eds., *Readings in Electronic Commerce* (Reading, MA: Addison Wesley, 1997).

M. Komenar, *Electronic Marketing* (New York: John Wiley & Sons, 1997).

P. Kotler and G. Armstrong, *Principles of Marketing*, 8th ed. (Upper Saddle River, NJ: Prentice Hall, 1999).

C. Lamb et al. *Marketing*, 4th ed. (Cincinnati, OH: South Western College Publishing, 1998), p. 194.

C. Lamb, J. Hair Jr., and C. McDaniel, *Marketing*, 4th ed. (Cincinnati, OH: South Western Publishing, 1998).

E. Lawrence, et al., *Internet Commerce: Digital Models for Business* (New York: John Wiley & Sons, 1998).

M. K. O. Lee, A "Comprehensive Model of Internet Consumer Satisfaction," unpublished working paper, City University of Hong Kong, 1999.

D. Leebaert, *The Future of the Electronic Marketplace* (Boston: MIT Press, 1998).

R. J. Lewicki and B. Bunker, "Developing and Maintaining Trust in Work Relationships," in R. M. Kramer, and T. R. Tyler, eds. *Trust in Organizations* (Thousand Oaks, CA: Sage, 1996).

G. L. Lohse and P. Spiller, "Electronic Shopping," *Communications of the ACM* 41 (7: July 1998).

P. Maes et al., "Agents that Buy and Sell," *Communication of the ACM* (March 1999).

P. G. McKeown and R. T. Watson, *Metamorphosis—A Guide to the www and Electronic Commerce* (New York: John Wiley & Sons, 1998).

B. K. Moon, J. K. Lee, and K. J. Lee, "A Next Generation Multimedia Call Center on the Internet: IMC," *Proceedings of the International Conference on Electronic Commerce*, Seoul, Korea, 1998.

P. Morley, *Handbook of Customer Service* (Brookfield, VT: Gower Pub., 1997).

J. C. Mowen and M. Minors, *Consumer Behavior,* 5th ed. (Upper Saddle River, NJ: Prentice Hall, 1998).

R. M. O'Keefe and T. McEachern, "Web-Based Customer Decision Support System," *Communications of the ACM* (March 1998).

D. Orzech, "Call Centers Take to the Web," *Datamation* (June 1998).

D. Peppers, et al., *The One-to-One Fieldbook* (New York: Currency and Doubleday, 1999).

J. Peter and J. Olson, *Consumer Behavior and Marketing Strategy*, 4th ed. (Burr Ridge, IL: Richard Irwin Publishing, 1996), pp. 488–90.

M. E. Porter, *Competitive Advantage: Creating and Sustaining Superior Performance* (New York: Free Press 1985).

P. Ratnasingham, "The Importance of Trust in Electronic Commerce," *Internet Research* 8(4:1998).

F. F. Reichheld, *The Loyalty Effect* (Boston: Harvard Business Press, 1996).

D. Shapiro et al. "Business on a Handshake," *The Negotiation Journal*, Oct. 1992.

J. Sterne," *World Wide Web Marketing*, New York: Wiley & Sons, 1999.

E. Turban et al, *Information Technology for Management*, 2nd ed. (New York: John Wiley & Sons, 1999).

J. Vassos, *Strategic Internet Marketing* (Indianapolis, IN: QUE Publishing Co., 1996).

S. Wang, "Analyzing Agents for Electronic Commerce," *Information Systems Management* (Winter 1999).

J. Ware, *The Search for Digital Excellence* (New York: McGraw-Hill, 1998).

F. Wiersema, *Customer Service: Cases of Excellence* (New York: Harper Business, 1998).

Zellweger, "Web-Based Sales: Defining the Cognitive Buyer," *Journal of Electronic Markets,* 1997 (www.electronicmarkets.org).

APPENDIX 3A

Example of an Online Market Research Tool for Segmentation

A well-known psychographic segmentation was developed by SRI International in California. The original segmentation divided consumers in the United States into nine groups and was called VALS™, which stands for values and lifestyles and helps identify who to target-market, uncover what your target group buys, locate where concentrations of your target group live, identify how best to communicate with your target group, and gain insight into why the target group acts the way it does. Values and lifestyles has been applied in a variety of areas: new product/service design, marketing and communications, targeting, product positioning, focus-group screening, promotion planning, advertising, and media planning.

In VALS, the consumers are asked whether they agree or disagree with statements such as, "My idea of fun at a national park would be to stay at an expensive lodge and dress up for dinner" or "I could stand to skin a dead animal." Consumers are then clustered into different groups based on their answers.

VALS™ (values and lifestyles) is an advanced version of the "original" VALS (see Figure 3.9). VALS consumer groups are organized along two dimensions: The vertical dimension represents resources, which include income, education, self-confidence, health, eagerness to buy, and energy level. The horizontal dimension represents self-orientation and includes three different types: principle-oriented consumers, who take an intellectual approach to life and are guided by their views of how the world is or should be; status-oriented consumers, who are guided by the opinions of others in respected peer groups; and action-oriented consumers, who are guided by a desire for social or physical activity, variety, and risk taking. Each of the VALS groups represents from 9 percent to 17 percent of the United States adult population. Marketers can buy VALS product services and media data from custom VALS surveys and from linkages VALS has with other consumer database companies such as Simmons Market Research and Scarborough Research.

FIGURE 3.9 VALS2 Questionnaire.

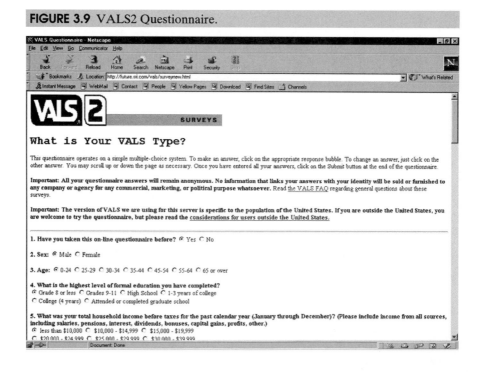

Advertisement in Electronic Commerce

Learning Objectives

Upon completion of this chapter, the reader will be able to:

- Describe the objectives of Web advertisement, its types, and characteristics.

- Describe the major advertisement methods used on the Web, ranging from banners to chat rooms.

- Describe various Web advertisement strategies.

- Describe various types of promotions on the Web.

- Discuss the benefits of push technology and intelligent agents.

- Understand the major economic issues related to Web advertisement.

- Describe the issues involved in measuring the success of Web advertisement as it relates to different ad pricing methods.

- Compare paper and electronic catalogs and describe customized catalogs.

- Describe Web advertisement implementation issues ranging from ad agencies to the use of intelligent agents.

4.1 CD-Max Uses E-Mail Lists to Advertise

CD-Max Enterprises (Carson, California) is a two-person business specializing in CD-ROM development. The company operates a resource site for information about CD-ROMs and a CD-ROM Shopper's Guide (www.cdrom-guide.com). The site generates about 40,000 hits a day.

The business started in 1996 and grew slowly. The idea of putting together an e-mail list of site visitors did not occur to Charles Simmons, the president, until about a year after the site had gone "live" on the Web. So, he and his partner generated a list and serviced it themselves. Furthermore, he found that the list is valuable to other advertisers, so he tried to sell it to them. Actually, it was necessary to create 50 lists to fit different advertisers. Soon he found that the job of creating and maintaining the lists,

117

as well as trying to sell them to potential advertisers, was a lot more work than the two partners could handle.

Simmons decided to outsource the job to others. He discovered there are companies that do most of the administrative tasks associated with online lists, such as keeping addressees current or finding buyers for the lists created by CD-MAX. He finally hired NetCreation (www.netcreation.com), a list management company (Brooklyn, New York), to manage the e-mail lists.

Promotional e-mail is becoming a big business, which is why companies are buying e-mail lists. The lists, a valuable source of new customer leads, are used as a direct marketing tool. In Section 4.3 we will show how they are being used.

Charles Simmons found very quickly that his decision to use NetCreation was wise. The outsourcer developed 275 lists from the names collected at CD-Max, which generated considerable income when sold. In 1998, the site was generating about 700 new names per day for the lists. The company's largest list, for CD-ROMs, has over 20,000 names. Average list size is about 1,500. "We're currently [1998] renting about 20,000 names per month," Simmons says.

In late 1998, Simmons began trying to gather matching zip codes of addresses to the e-mail lists, "since a number of advertisers have expressed interest" in that data. By collecting zip codes, marketers can determine city and state location "and make some inferences" about the demographics of the lists.

While Simmons will not disclose figures, he said that the list sales "surpassed" his expectations and selling e-mail lists became a lucrative business for his company.[1]

4.2 Web Advertisement

AN OVERVIEW

The CD-Max opening vignette illustrates the use of e-mail as an advertisement medium. By using e-mail lists, advertisers can focus on special interest groups and even on individuals, which is useful in direct marketing. Sending promotional material to people is done either with the consent of the recipients, i.e., they are asked to receive the promotions, or mailing is done without the receiver's consent. The latter case is called **spamming,** and it will be discussed later in this chapter as well as in chapter 10.

Advertising is an attempt to disseminate information in order to effect a buyer-seller transaction. In a traditional sense, advertising was impersonal, one-way mass communication or mass marketing, which was paid for by sponsors. Telemarketing and direct mail were attempts to personalize advertising in order to make it more effective. These **direct marketing** approaches worked fairly well but were expensive. The Internet redefined the meaning of advertising. The Internet has enabled consumers to *interact* directly with advertisers and advertisements. In interactive marketing, a consumer can click with his or her mouse on an ad for more information or send an e-mail to ask a question. The Internet has provided the sponsors with two-way communication and e-mail capabilities, as well as allowing the sponsors to target specific groups on which they want to spend their advertising dollars, which is more accurate than traditional telemarketing. Finally, the Internet enables a truly one-to-one advertisement.

A comparison of the above concepts is shown in Table 4.1.

In the previous chapters we discussed the importance of **interactive marketing** and the reasons why consumers prefer it. In this chapter we will show how it is implemented online. Let's start by providing some essential advertising terminology.

[1]*Source*: Based on L. Freeman "What's in a Name?," *CI0* (February 1998).

TABLE 4.1 From Mass Advertisement to Interactive Advertisement

	Mass Marketing	*Direct Marketing*	*Interactive Marketing*
Best outcome	Volume sales	Customer data	Customer relationships
Consumer behavior	Passive	Passive	Active
Leading products	Food, personal care products, beer, autos	Credit cards, travel, autos	Upscale apparel, travel, financial services, autos
Market	High volume	Targeted goods	Targeted individuals
Nerve center	Madison Ave.	Postal distribution centers	Cyberspace
Preferred media vehicle	Television, magazines	Mailing lists	Online services
Preferred technology	Storyboards	Databases	Servers, on-screen navigators, the Web
Worst outcome	Channel surfing	Recycling bins	Log off

Source: Based on *InformationWeek* (Oct. 3, 1994), p. 26.

INTERNET ADVERTISING TERMINOLOGY

There is considerable confusion regarding the terminology used for Web advertising. Hence, the following glossary can help:

1. **Ad views (also page views or impressions):** the number of times users call up a page with a banner during a specific time (e.g., "ad views per day"). The actual number of times the ad was seen by users may differ because of "caching" (which increases the real number of ad views) and browsers that view documents as text only (which decreases the number of ad views).
2. **Banner:** a graphic display on a Web page used for advertisement. The size of the banner is 5.0″ to 6.25″ × 0.5″ to 1.0″ and is measured in pixels (width × height). An ad is linked to an advertiser's Web page; when one "clicks" on the banner, one will be transferred to the advertiser's site.
3. **Clicks (or ad clicks):** every time a visitor clicks on an advertising banner to access the advertiser's Web site.
4. **Click ratio:** ratio indicating the success of an advertising banner in attracting visitors to click on the ad. For example, if a banner received 1,000 impressions and there are 100 "clicks," the click ratio is 10 percent.
5. **Cookie:** a program, stored on the user's hard drive, without disclosure or the user's consent. Sent by a Web server over the Internet, the information stored will surface when the user's browser again crosses the specific server combination (chapter 10).
6. **CPM:** cost-per-thousand impressions. The cost of delivering an impression to 1,000 people (or homes).
7. **Effective frequency:** the number of times an individual is exposed to a particular advertising message in a given period of time.
8. **Hit:** Webspeak for any request for data from a Web page or file, often used to compare popularity/traffic of a site in the context of getting so many "hits" during a given period. A common mistake is to equate hits with visits or page views. A single visit or page view may be recorded as several hits, and depending on the browser, the page size, and other factors, the number of hits per page can vary widely.
9. **Impressions:** *ad or page views*. This is the exposure to an ad.
10. **Interactive advertisement:** any advertisement that requires or allows the viewer/consumer to take some action. In the broadest sense, even clicking

on a banner is an interaction. However, usually we define action as sending a query or looking for detailed information.

11. **Meta tag:** tag giving a spider (search engine) specific information, such as keywords or site summaries; part of the HTML code. These tags stay behind the scenes—the end user never sees them. A Web author may surround sentences, even whole paragraphs, with these tags. Certain spiders then read the information in the tags as a way to help them index the site. Unfortunately, meta tag information is not always reliable. It may or may not accurately reflect the content of the site.

12. **Page:** an HTML document that may contain text, images, and other online elements, such as Java applets and multimedia files. It may be statically or dynamically generated.

13. **Reach:** the number of people or households exposed to an ad at least once over a specified period of time.

14. **Visit:** a sequence of requests made by one user in one visit to the site. Once a visitor stops making requests from a site for a given period of time, called a time-out, the next hit by this visitor is considered a new visit.

WHY INTERNET ADVERTISEMENT?

There are several reasons why companies advertise on the Internet. To begin with, television viewers are migrating to the Internet. The media follows, acknowledging that the goal of any advertiser is to reach its target audience effectively and efficiently. Advertisers recognize that they have to adapt their marketing plans to account for the ever-growing number of people spending increasing amounts of time online, frequently at the expense of other media.

Research conducted in fall 1996, found that three-quarters of PC users were willing to give up television to spend more time on their computers. The migration of so many from television seems very impressive. Add to this the fact that the Internet users are well educated with high incomes, it is only logical to conclude that Internet surfers are a desired target for advertisers.

Other reasons why Web advertising is growing rapidly are:

- Ads can be updated any time with a minimal cost; therefore, they are always timely.
- Ads can reach very large numbers of potential buyers globally.
- Online ads are sometimes cheaper in comparison to television, newspaper, or radio. The latter are expensive since they are determined by space occupied, how many days (times) they are shown, and on how many national and local television stations and newspapers they are posted.
- Web ads can efficiently use the convergence of text, audio, graphics, and animation.
- The use of the Internet itself is growing very rapidly.
- Web ads can be interactive and targeted to specific interest groups and/or individuals.

The last two points will be expanded upon later.

As of 1998 these characteristics began to convince large consumer products companies to shift an increasing amount of advertising dollars away from traditional media to Web advertisement. Toyota is a prime example of the power of the Internet. Saatchi and Saatchi, a major ad agency, developed the Web site for Toyota (www.toyota.com) and placed traffic-luring banner ads on other popular Web sites, such as www.espn.com. Within a year, the site overtook Toyota's 800 number as its best source of sale leads.

THE INTERNET VERSUS TRADITIONAL METHODS

The major traditional advertisement media are TV (about 36 percent), newspapers (about 35 percent), magazines (about 14 percent), and radio (about 10 percent). Each of these has its advantages and disadvantages. The Internet can be viewed as just another media with its advantages and limitations. Table 4.2 compares the Internet as an advertisement media against the traditional media.

TABLE 4.2   Advantages and Limitation of Internet Advertisement As Compared to Traditional Media

Medium	Pros for Generating Advertising Revenue	Cons for Generating Advertising Revenue
TV	• Intrusive impact—high awareness getter. • Ability to demonstrate product and feature "slice of life" situations. • Very "merchandisable" with media buyers.	• Ratings fragmenting, rising costs, "clutter." • Heavy "downscale" audience skew. • Time is sold in multiprogram packages. Networks often require major upfront commitments. Both limit the advertiser's flexibility.
Radio	• Highly selective by station format. • Allows advertisers to employ time-of-day or time-of-week to exploit timing factors. • Copy can rely on the listener's mood or imagination.	• Audience surveys are limited in scope, do not provide socioeconomic demographics. • Difficult to buy with so many stations to consider. • Copy testing is difficult, few statistical guidelines.
Magazines	• Offer unique opportunities to segment markets, demographically and psychographically. • Ads can be studied, reviewed at leisure. High impact can be attained with good graphics and literate, informative copy.	• Reader controls ad exposure, can ignore campaign, especially for new products. • Difficult to exploit "timing" aspects.
Newspapers	• High single-day reach opportunity to exploit immediacy, especially on key shopping days. • Reader often shops for specific information when ready to buy. • Portable format	• Lack of demographic selectivity, despite increased zoning—many markets have only one paper. • High cost for large-size units. • Presumes lack of creative opportunities for "emotional" selling campaigns. • Low-quality reproduction, lack of color.
Internet	• Internet advertisements are accessed on demand 24 hours a day, 365 days a year, and costs are the same regardless of audience location. • Accessed primarily because of interest in the content, so market segmentation opportunity is large. • Opportunity to create one-to-one direct marketing relationship with consumer. • Multimedia will increasingly create more attractive and compelling ads. • Distribution costs are low (just technology costs), so the millions of consumers reached cost the same as one. • Advertising and content can be updated, supplemented, or changed at any time, and are therefore always up-to-date. Response (click-through rate) and results (page views) of advertising are immediately measurable. • Ease of logical navigation—you click when and where you want, and spend as much time as desired there.	• No clear standard or language of measurement. • Immature measurement tools and metrics. • Although the variety of ad content format and style that the Internet allows can be considered a positive in some respects, it also makes apples-to-apples comparisons difficult for media buyers. • Difficult to measure size of market, therefore difficult to estimate rating, share, or reach and frequency. • Audience is still small.

Source: Based on Meeker (1997), pp. 1–10.

INTERNET IS THE FASTEST GROWING MEDIUM IN HISTORY

In 1997, a study titled "The Internet Advertising Report" (Meeker 1997) examined the adaptation rate of the Internet, compared to three traditional media: radio, network television, and cable television. Meeker examined the length of time it took for each to reach 50 million U.S. users. The results are shown in Figure 4.1.

As the figure shows, the length of time it took for the Internet to reach 50 million users was about 5 years, which is remarkable considering that it took radio 38 years, television 13 years, and cable television 10 years. According to these statistics, the Internet is the fastest growing media of communication, and its growth potential as a means of communication is very high.

OBJECTIVES AND GROWTH OF INTERNET ADVERTISEMENT

The objectives of advertising on the Internet are the same as those of any other advertising, namely, to persuade customers to buy a certain product or service. Thus, it is seen as an alternative (or a complementary) medium to traditional advertising media. Customers' awareness of this alternative is growing rapidly. Although Internet advertisement is only 1 percent to 2 percent of the total $100 billion a year advertisement bill in the United States, it is growing rapidly. *Business Week* (September 23, 1996) estimated the 1995 expenditures to be about $43 million. This amount grew to over $350 million in the first quarter of 1998 alone (www.iab.net). The estimate for 1999 is around $2 billion.

The largest U.S. advertiser, Proctor & Gamble, announced in 1998 that the company is shifting a substantial amount of its advertisement budget to the Internet (Application Case 4.1). According to the Internet Advertising Bureau (IAB) (www.iab.com), the top categories for Web ad spending in 1998 were computers (27

FIGURE 4.1 Adoption Curves for Various Media—The Web Is Ramping Fast.

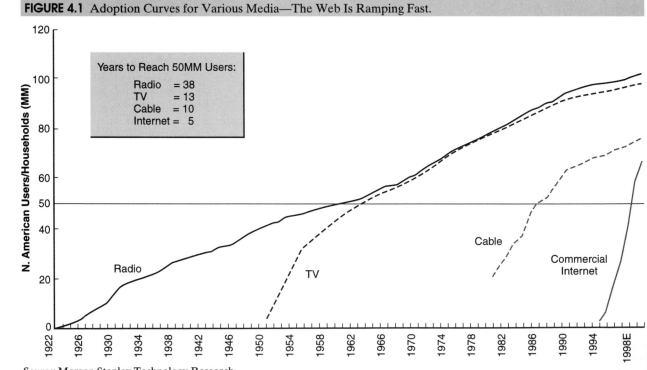

Source: Morgan Stanley Technology Research.

Procter & Gamble Co.'s (P&G) Interactive Marketing

The world's largest advertiser is actively experimenting with Web advertisement. Here are some of the company's 1998 and 1999 initiatives:

- P&G provided seed money and was an early advertiser at the ParentTime at Work channel on PointCast, in an effort to reach working women.
- It financed phys.com, a women's health and fitness site, with *Conde Nast Magazine.*
- P&G moved to give two of its existing brand Web sites greater visibility by integrating them into other facets of marketing.
- In May 1998, it launched a spot for the detergent Tide by Saatchi & Saatchi Worldwide, New York,

featuring an ad checking out Tide's Web site for stain removal help.
- It also used in-store messages issued by Catalina Marketing Corp.'s checkout coupon system to steer buyers of baby products to its Pampers site.

It is interesting to note that P&G buys advertisement space based on how many times an ad is clicked on. This is in contrast with the customary fee, which is based on impressions—every time a page with an ad banner is seen. For further discussion see section 4.6.

percent), consumer products (25 percent), telecom (14 percent), financial services (13 percent), and news media (10 percent).

TARGETED (ONE-TO-ONE) ADVERTISEMENT

As stated earlier, one of the major advantages of Internet advertising is the ability to customize ads to fit individual viewers. One company that pioneered such advertising is Double Click (Application Case 4.2).

One-to-one targeted advertisement and marketing can be expensive. However, it can be rewarding. For example, according to Taylor (1997), successful targeted ads were proven very effective for Lexus cars ($169/car sold). Targeting ads to groups rather than to individuals can also be very cost-effective.

TYPES OF INTERNET ADVERTISEMENT

According to the IAB, banner ads accounted for 55 percent of all Internet ad spending in 1998. Content sponsorship accounted for 40 percent of the spending. All other types (section 4.3) account for the remaining 5 percent. It should be noted that some advertisement is provided as a public service.

4.3 Advertisement Methods

Several of the major methods used for advertisements are:

BANNERS

Banner advertising is the most commonly used form of advertising on the Internet. As you surf your way through the information superhighway, banners are everywhere. The file size of the image should be about 7kb to 10kb. The smaller the file size, the quicker it loads. Designers of banners pay a lot of attention to the size of the image because long downloading times may cause a viewer to become impatient and move on before the banner is fully displayed. Typically, a banner contains a short text or graphical message to promote a product. Advertisers go to great lengths to design a banner

Targeted Advertisement: The Double Click Approach

One-to-one targeted advertisement can take many forms. Assume that 3M Corp. wants to advertise its $10,000 multimedia projectors. It knows that potential buyers are people who work in advertising agencies or in IS departments of large corporations or companies that use Unix as their operating system. 3M approaches Double-Click Inc. and asks the firm to identify such potential customers. How does DoubleClick find them? Clever and simple.

As of 1997, DoubleClick (www.doubleclick. net) monitors people browsing the Web sites of several hundred cooperating companies such as Quicken, Travelocity, Virtual Comics, and Books That Work. By inspecting Internet addresses of the visitors to these companies' Web sites and matching them against a database with about 100,000 Internet domain names that include a line-of-business code, DoubleClick can find those people working for advertising agencies. By checking the browsers, it can also find out which visitor is using a Unix system. While DoubleClick cannot find out your name, it can build a dossier on you, attached to an ID number that was assigned to you during your first visit to any of the cooperating sites. As you continue to visit the sites, an intelligent software agent builds a relatively complete dossier on you, your spending, and your computing habits. This process is done with a device known as cookie, a file created at the request of a Web server and stored on the user's hard drive, so the Web site can "remember" your past behavior on the Internet.

DoubleClick then prepares an ad about 3M projectors. The ad is targeted for people whose profile matches the criteria listed earlier. If you are a Unix user or an advertising agency, on your next browsing trip in any of the participating Web sites, you will be surprised to find exactly what you wanted: information about the multimedia project. How is all this financed? DoubleClick charges 3M for the ad. The fee is then split with the Web sites that carry the 3M ads, based on how many times the ad is matched with visitors.

In 1998, DoubleClick expanded the service, called Dynamic Advertising Reporting and Targeting (DART), to the leading online publishers in the advertising industry. Furthermore, the company expanded the service from pinpoint target and ad design to advertisement control, ad frequency determination, and providing verifiable measures of success.

that catches consumers' attention. With the progress of Internet programming we are starting to find banners with video clips and sound. Banners contain links that, when clicked on, transfer the customer to the advertiser's home page. There are two types of banners: *keyword banner* and *random banner*. **Keyword banners** appear when a predetermined word is queried from the search engine. It is effective for companies who want to narrow their target audience. **Random banners** appear randomly. Companies that want to introduce their new products (e.g., a new movie or CD) use random banners.

A 1998 study by AOL showed that 9 out of 10 people responded favorably to banner advertisement and about 50 percent of the viewers recall ads immediately after seeing them (www.adage.com, March 15, 1998).

Benefits

A major advantage of using banners is the ability to customize them to the target audience. One can decide which market segments to focus on. Banners can even be customized to one-to-one targeted advertisement. Also, "forced advertising" marketing strategy is utilized, which means customers are forced to see it. The disadvantages are high overall cost. If a company demands a successful marketing campaign, it will need to allocate a large percentage of the advertising budget to acquire a high volume of CPM. In addition, one of the major drawbacks of using banners is that limited information is allowed. Hence, advertisers need to think of a creative but short message to attract viewers.

An important factor an advertiser needs to scrutinize is the size of the banner. One needs to make sure that the image size the exchange uses is appropriate for the intended location and that the file size and animation limits are correct. An image with a large file size or unlimited animation looping may require several minutes of downloading time. This could prevent the remainder of the Web page from being displayed until the image is finished, resulting in impatient visitors who leave the site before the Web page is shown.

There are several different forms of placing banner advertising on the Internet on others' web sites. The most common forms are: Banner Swapping, Banner Exchanges, and Paid Advertising.

Banner Swapping

Banner swapping means that company A agrees to display a banner of company B in exchange for company B displaying company A's ad. It is a direct link between Web sites. Every time B's Web page is accessed, A's banner will be displayed, giving the viewer the opportunity to click on it and be transferred to A's Web site.

This is probably the least expensive form of banner advertising to establish and maintain, but it is also difficult to arrange. One must locate a site that one believes could generate a sufficient amount of quality traffic; a match between the swapping parties is a must. Then, one must contact the owner/Webmaster of the site and inquire if they would be interested in a reciprocal banner swap.

Banner Exchanges

Frequently banner swapping does not work because a match is not possible. If there are several companies involved, however, a multicompany match may be easier to find. For example, out of three companies, A can display B's banner, but B cannot display A's banner optimally. However, B can display C's banner, and C can display A's banner. Such bartering may involve many companies. **Banner exchange** organizations arrange for the trading of three or more partners. It works similarly to that of a regular bartering exchange. A firm submits a banner to the exchange service and displays a link on one of its Web pages, which will display a different banner each time the page is accessed. Each time the participant displays a banner for one of the exchange's members it receives a credit. After a participant has "earned" enough credits, its banner is displayed on an appropriate member's site. Most exchanges offer members the opportunity to purchase additional display credits. Many of the exchanges also permit the participants to specify what type of site the banner can be displayed on, thus allowing the advertiser to target what type of audience will see the banner ad.

Most exchanges offer a credit ratio of approximately 2:1. This means for every two banners displayed on your site, your banner will be displayed once. You may wonder why the ratio is not 1:1. The banner exchange company must generate revenue to cover its operating expenses and to offer additional services, so they sell about 50 percent of all banners. For example, Link Exchange (www.linkexchange.com) offers help in banner design, provides membership in newsgroups, delivers HTML tutorials, and even runs contests. The exchanges either sell the extra ad space or use it themselves to promote their services. Link Exchange acts as a banner ad clearinghouse for more than 200,000 small Web sites (in 1998) that form a network of partners. The sites are organized into 1,600 categories. Link Exchange monitors the content of the ads of all its members.

Some exchanges will not allow certain types of banners; hence, the decision on whether or not to participate is important. Overall, banner exchanging can be very valuable and should be considered by advertisers.

Paid Advertisement

Purchasing banner ad space on the Internet is quite similar to buying ad space in other media. However, in many cases, this option may be more expensive than the traditional ones. Also, on the Internet you are limited to the size of the ad and the amount of content (text and graphics) the ad may contain. This is to ensure that viewers do not become impatient waiting for the ad to appear and leave before it is fully displayed.

SPLASH SCREEN

A **splash screen** is an initial Web site page used to capture the user's attention for a short time as a promotion or lead-in to the site home page or to tell the user what kind of browser and other software they need to view the site.

The major advantage of a splash page over any other advertising method is that one can create innovative multimedia effects or provide sufficient information for a delivery in one visit.

SPOT LEASING

Search engines often provide space (spot) in their home page for any individual business to lease. The duration of the lease depends upon the contract agreement between the Web site host and the lessee. Unlike banners, which show up at various times, the ad place on the spot will always be there; hence, competition is reduced. The disadvantage of spot leasing is that the size of the ad is often small and limited, causing some viewers to miss the ad. Also, the cost can be very high.

URL (UNIVERSAL RESOURCE LOCATORS)

The major advantage of using URL as an advertising tool is that it is free. Anyone can submit its URL to a search engine and be listed. Also, by using URL the targeted audience can be locked and the unwanted viewers can be filtered because of the keyword function. On the other hand, the URL method has several drawbacks. First, due to intense competition, a company's listing at the top of the list of a search engine can easily be replaced by others. Moreover, different search engines index their listings differently. Some search engines honor meta tags and some do not. One may have the correct keywords, but if the search engine indexed its listing using the "title" or "content description" in the meta tag, then the effort could be fruitless.

E-MAIL

Another way to advertise on the Internet is to purchase e-mail addresses and send the company information to those on the list as was shown in the CD-Max case. The advantages of this approach are its low cost and the ability to reach a wide variety of targeted audiences. Most companies develop a customer database to whom they send e-mails. Of the many e-mail distribution service companies, one should note www.sparnet.com, which uses enhanced e-mail. As indicated earlier, using e-mail to send ads may involve spamming (see chapter 10).

E-mail is emerging as a marketing channel that affords cost-effective implementation and better, quicker response rates than other advertising channels. Marketers should be racing to embrace the medium. What happens, though, when every marketer starts inundating prospects and customers with mail? How much e-mail will this result in? How will consumers deal with it? What areas must marketers focus on to ensure e-mail marketing success?

Undoubtedly, the quantity of e-mail that consumers receive is exploding. According to a study by Jupiter Communications, messages per consumer will increase from 1,166 per user per year in 1998 to 1,606 per user per year by 2002. In light of this, marketers employing e-mail must take a long-term view and work toward the goal of motivating consumers to continue to open and read messages they receive. This is especially important as even now nearly one-third of consumers read e-mail only from senders with whom they have a relationship. As the volume of e-mail increases, consumers' tendency to screen messages will rise as well.

When considering who they should be talking to, marketers must supplement existing database information with data relevant to e-mail campaigns. When deciding what the mail concerns, marketers must integrate inbound customer service e-mail solutions with their outbound marketing efforts. Finally, in regard to the "how," or the execution, of the message, marketers must develop e-mail-specific copywriting skills and the ability to deliver multimedia-rich e-mail.

A list of e-mail addresses can be a very powerful tool because you are targeting a group of people you know something about. To create your own mailing list, consult www.onelist.com (the service is free) or www.revnet.com.

CHAT ROOMS

Electronic chat refers to an arrangement where participants exchange messages in real time. The software industry estimates that several hundred thousand Web sites have millions of chat rooms.

A *chat room* is a virtual meeting ground where groups of regulars come to gab (see chapter 11 for technological explanation). The chat rooms can be used to build a community to promote a political or environmental cause, to support people with medical problems, or to let hobbyists share their interest. And since many customer-supplier relationships have to be sustained without face-to-face meetings, online communities are increasingly being used to serve business interests, including advertising (chapter 12 and www.roguemarket.com).

A vendor frequently sponsors chat rooms (look for the logo). Chat capabilities can be added to a business site for free by letting software chat vendors host your session on their site. You simply put a chat link on your site and the chat vendor does the rest, including the advertising that pays for the session.

The main difference between an advertisement that appears on a static Web page and one that comes through a chat room is that the latter allows advertisers to cycle through messages and target the chatters again and again. Also, advertising can become more thematic. You can start with one message and build upon it to a climax, just as you would do with a good story. Chatters are used to seeing multiple ads on their screens, so they are bound to take notice.

In a 1998 report, Montgomery Security estimated that by 2000 Internet chats are expected to generate 7.9 billion hours of online use, leading to $1 billion in advertising revenue. The advertisement in a chat room merges with the activity in the room and the user is conscious of what is being presented. The message of advertisers is reaching the audience.

Chat rooms are also used as one-to-one connections between a company and their customers. For example, Mattel sells about one-third of its Barbies to collectors. These collectors use the chat room frequently and are likely to pay attention to Mattel's or others' advertisements there.

OTHER FORMS

Online advertisement can be done in several other ways ranging from advertisements in newsgroups to the use of kiosks (O'Keefe 1997). Advertisement on Internet radio is just beginning, and soon advertising on Internet television will commence. Of special interest is the advertisement to *Internet communities'* members (chapter 12). The community sites such as www.geocities.com offer direct advertisement (you can actually buy the advertised products). There are also ads that link you to other sites that might be of interest to the type of community member. Targeted ads also go to the members' Web pages.

4.4 Advertisement Strategies

Several advertisement strategies can be used over the Internet. Before we describe them, it will be useful to present some important considerations in Internet-based ad design.

CONSIDERATIONS IN THE INTERNET-BASED AD DESIGN

Some commonly accepted commandments of advertising on the Internet are advocated by Choi et al. (1998) and by others. Representative examples are:

- *Advertisements should be visually appealing.* In mass media, advertisements should be colorful to catch the reader's attention. On the Internet, this principle can be realized by adopting interactive and moving Web content that can grab the visitor's attention and draw repeated visits.
- *Advertisements must be targeted to specific groups or to individual consumers.* Ads should be customized and speak on a personal level.
- *The content should be valuable to consumers.* Web pages should provide valuable information, avoiding useless and large files that slow downloading time.
- *Advertisements must emphasize brands and a firm's image.* Ads should emphasize how your firm and its products and services differ from other competition.
- *Advertisements must be part of an overall marketing strategy.* Firms should actively participate in all types of Internet activities, such as newsgroups, mailing lists, and bulletin boards. All activities constitute a strategy. Also, online advertisements should be coordinated with offline advertisements.
- *Advertisements should be seamlessly linked with the ordering process.* When the customer has become interested after having seen the ads, the advertised items should be able to be ordered and paid for conveniently, preferably online.
- *Designing Internet ads.* Successful Web site design is an art as well as a science. It is actually a difficult task. For example, a study of Web ads done by the University of Michigan business school students for a Web company, Athenia Associates, showed that ads placed in the lower right-hand corner of the screen, next to the scroll bar, generate 228 percent higher **click-throughs** than ads at the top of the page. The study also found that ads placed one-third of the way down the page increased click-through 77 percent over ads at the top of the page, where ads are usually positioned. Andrew Kind, Webmaster with Athenia, attributed the higher click-throughs to the ads' positioning in the "click zone," where a user's mouse is naturally drawn. Information about the study is available at http://www.webreference.com/dev/banners. In many cases it is best to solicit the help of an expert or consultant to design Internet ads. Gehrke and Turban (1999) identified 50 variables that may increase (or decrease) shoppers' satisfaction with the Web page and consequently their willingness to read ads.

The 50 variables were divided into five categories. The authors conducted experiments to find their relative importance. Several of the most important variables in each category are listed below together with recommendations.

- *Page-Loading Speed*
  - Graphics and tables should be simple and meaningful. They need to match standard monitors.
  - Thumbnail (icon graphs) are useful
- *Business Content*
  - Clear and concise text is needed. A compelling page title and header text is useful.
  - The amount of requested information for registration should be minimal.
- *Navigation Efficiency*
  - Well-labeled, accurate, meaningful links are a must.
  - Sites must be compatible with browsers, software, etc.
- *Security and Privacy*
  - Security and privacy must be assured.
  - Rejecting cookies option is a must.
- *Marketing Customer Focus*
  - Clear terms and conditions of the purchases, including delivery information, return policy, etc., must be provided.
  - Confirmation page after a purchase is needed.

When the designed ads are in line with the above commandments, we can implement Internet-based advertisement in one, or as a combination, of the following strategy(ies).

PASSIVE PULL STRATEGY

Usually, customers will look for a site and visit it only if it provides helpful and attractive contents and display. This strategy when Web pages are waiting for a customer's passive access, is referred to as *passive pull strategy*. The passive pull strategy is effective and economical when advertising to open, unidentified potential customers worldwide. However, since there are so many Web pages open to all customers, there is a need for a directory that can guide customers to targeted sites. For instance, refer to the site Advertising World (http://advertising.utexas.edu/world). This is a noncommercial site that can guide customers. In this sense, portal search engine sites like Yahoo can be regarded as an effective aid for advertisement. These sites are all equipped with directories for the registered sites.

A site may be either a pure advertisement site (which means it does not offer order entry and payment capabilities) or a complete retailing storefront (like Amazon) as described in chapter 2. The ads in the latter case can be directly linked to sales. In this case, the ad can be regarded as the first step of sales activity on the Internet. When the site is an e-mall, we can see its own directory and search engines, which help find the desired products and services. In this sense, the directory in the e-mall can be regarded as the second step in the passive pull strategy.

ACTIVE PUSH STRATEGY

If customers do not visit the merchants' sites voluntarily, merchants need to actively advertise to the targeted customers. One option of this strategy is sending e-mails to the relevant people. The first issue to be considered by merchants adopting this strategy is how to obtain the mailing list of the target customers. Companies like DoubleClick (www.doubleclick.com) have started to generate mailing lists to meet this need. For a comprehensive list of such companies, refer to the direct marketing menu in Advertising

World (http://advertising.utexs.edu/world). For a case study of utilizing the mailing list service from Double Click, refer to Application Box 4.2. Mailing list generation is done in different ways, as was shown in the opening vignette. Companies are also using agent technology and cookies, as we will discuss in sections 4.5 and 4.8.

ASSOCIATED AD DISPLAY STRATEGY

With a banner, a display may be organized independently of who reads it and what is read. If the merchant can identify the person and the characteristics of accessed pages, displaying an associated ad can be a very effective advertisement. Let us call this the *associated ad display strategy*. For example, in using MapQuest (www.mapquest.com), which supports hotel reservations, the user may select an indexed category such as "lodging" within a city. Then, a Radisson ad may be displayed. These kinds of targeted ads cost about $40 per thousand impressions, compared with $25 per thousand impressions for other ads. Another example of associated ad display can be found at Amazon. When the customers read about a book, a list of books under the title "Customers who bought this book also bought . . ." is displayed (Figure 4.2). To support this kind of service, Amazon's system must have the capability of data mining from past records and storage in the database. The ad display can be directly ordered seamlessly. In this sense, this strategy can be regarded as just-in-time strategy.

ADS AS A COMMODITY

According to this strategy, an ad is sold as a product, using the approach of CyberGold (www.cybergold.com) and others. Interested consumers read the ads in exchange for direct payment made by the advertisers. Consumers fill out data on personal interests, then CyberGold distributes targeted banners based on the personal profiles. Each banner is denoted with the amount of payment for reading it. If interested, the reader clicks the banner to read it and, passing some tests on its contents, is paid for the effort. Readers can sort and choose what they read, and the advertisers can vary the

FIGURE 4.2 An Example of Associated Ad Display at Amazon.

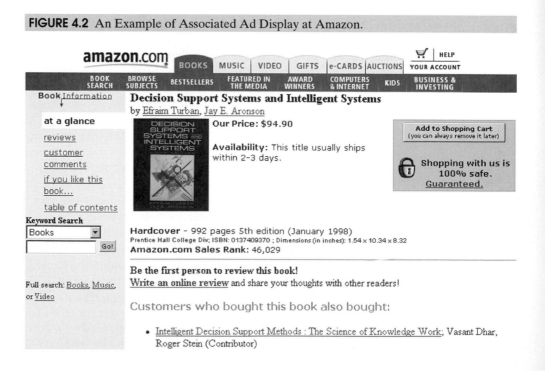

payment level reflecting the frequency and desirability of readers. Payments can be cash ($1 per banner) or discounts on the products sold. Also see www.gotoworld.com.

An illustrative screen of CyberGold is shown in Figure 4.3. This screen explains:

1. Who is paying the customers and why
2. How customers get paid

FIGURE 4.3 An Illustrative Screen of CyberGold.

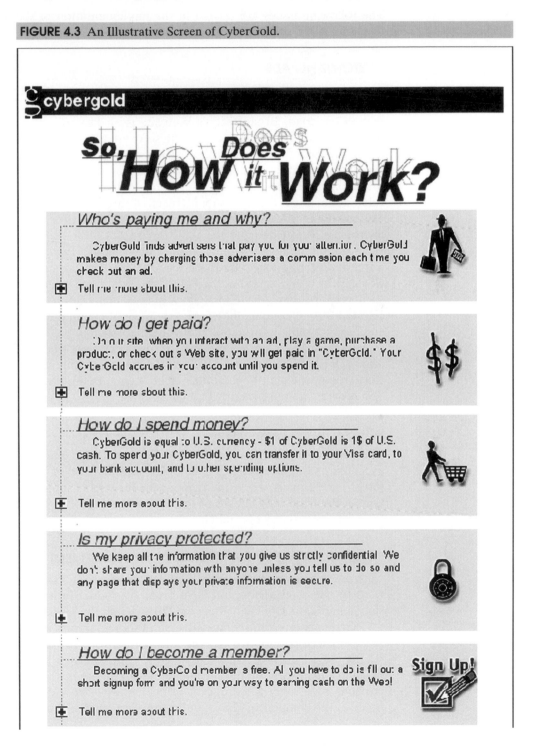

3. How customers can spend the paid money
4. How the privacy of the customer is protected

For details regarding CyberGold's strategy see Ware et al. (1998).

IMPLEMENTING THE STRATEGIES

The following issues are related to the implementation of the above advertisement strategies.

CUSTOMIZING ADS

There is too much information on the Internet for customers to view. So filtering the irrelevant information by providing *customized ads* can be a way to reduce the information overload. BroadVision's Web site is an example of a customized ad service platform (www.broadvision.com). The software One-to-One allows the rapid creation and alteration of secure and robust visitor-centric Web sites. The heart of One-to-One is a customer database, with registration data and information gleaned from site visits. Marketing staff can use One-to-One on their own desktops to set up and modify rules about how the site should react. Using this feature, a marketing manager can customize display ads based on users' profiles. For an example of how www. micromass.com customizes ads, see Exercise 2.

Another model of customized ad can be found in PointCast (www.pointcast.com), a free Internet news service that broadcasts personalized news and information (section 4.5). A user establishes the PointCast system and selects the desired information, such as sports, news, headlines, stock quotes, etc. The information described must be selected from the menu; therefore, you may not get all the information you want, and you may get some information that you do not need.

A salesman expert system provides a special example of advertisement. The system CYBER-SES (Lee et al. 1998) seeks the compatible items and parts when a purchase requires a set of compatible components. Being displayed as a compatible option provides an opportunity for advertisement.

INTERACTIVE AD STRATEGIES

The ads on the Internet can be passive (view only) or interactive. Interaction may be executed online using chatting and call center service or asynchronously using Web screens and e-mails. These interactions can be used to supplement passive Web pages. One of the major advantages of the Web is the ability to provide various types of interactive options at a reasonable cost.

COMPARISON ADS AS A MEDIUM OF ADVERTISEMENT

Customers need to compare many alternative products and services. Suppose you want to buy a television and have found a product in a Web catalog or e-mail, as shown in Figure 4.4. Then you would like to find the least expensive place to buy the TV. Comparisons with competitive vendors are shown in Figure 4.5, on page 134. An issue here is who provides the information for the ads. One possible policy is to let the e-mail managers provide such information as a free service for the brands listed in a mall without any specific request. The other policy is to generate the comparisons as a reply to a request of "Compare" for a designated product. In this process, the competitors have an incentive to pay for the comparing ad. The Meta-

FIGURE 4.4 An Illustrative Product with the "COMPARE" Button.

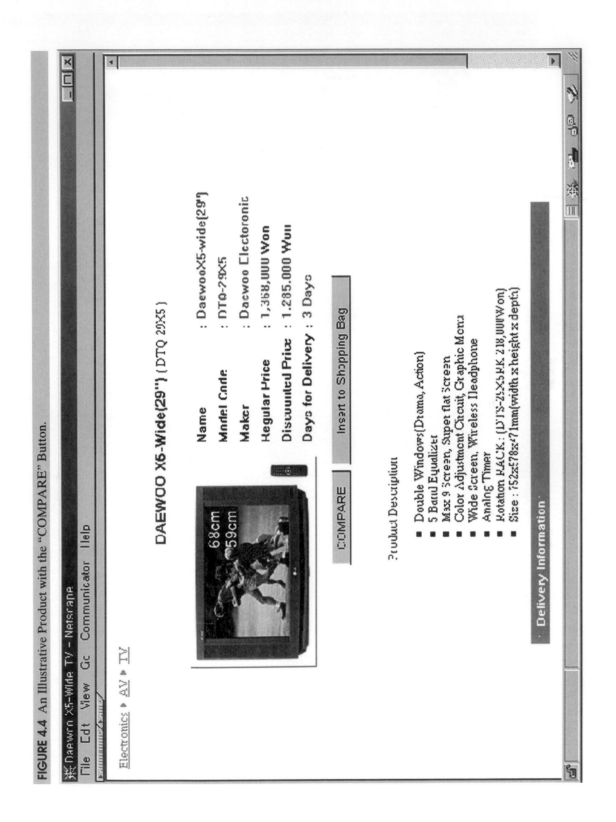

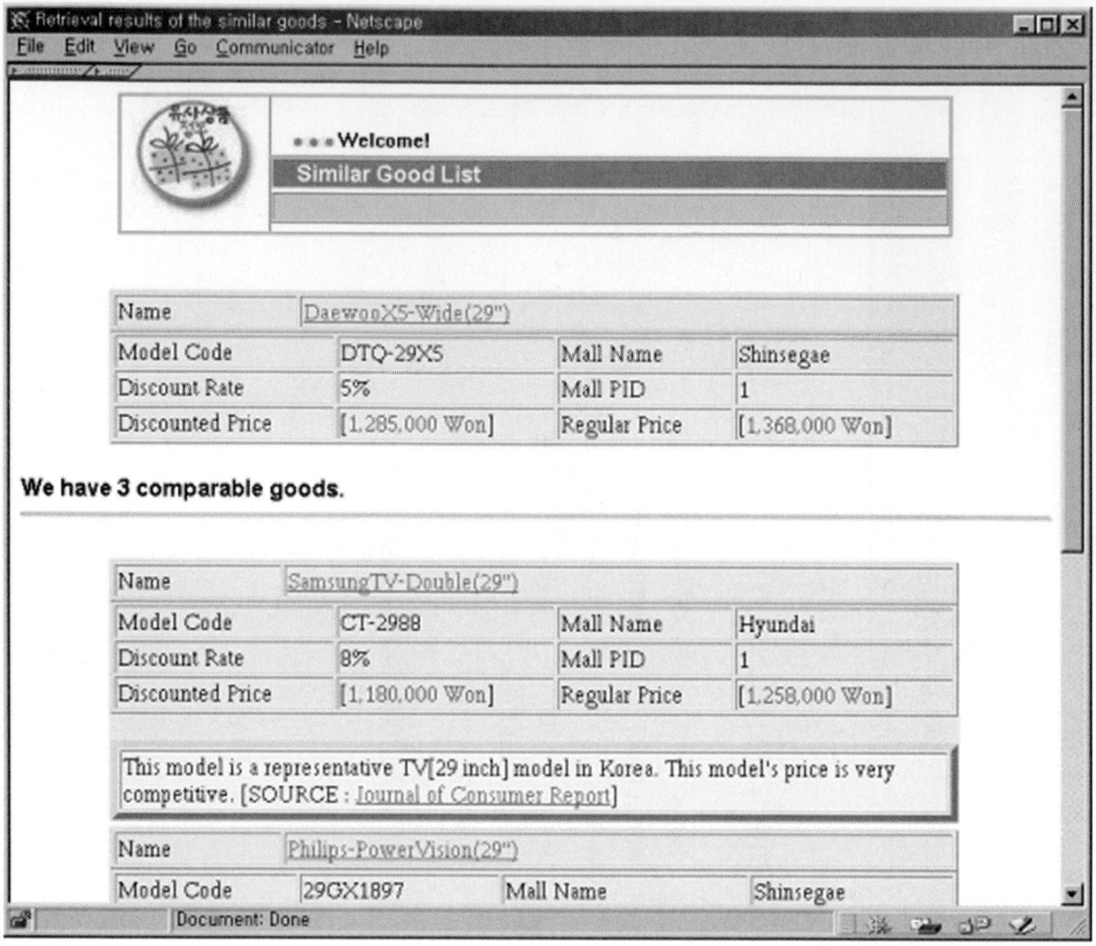

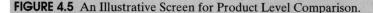

FIGURE 4.5 An Illustrative Screen for Product Level Comparison.

Malls Architecture (Lee and Lee 1998) has pursued the provision of such comparison service not only in one mall but over multiple independent e-malls, using the architecture shown in Figure 4.6.

ATTRACTING VISITORS TO A SITE

There are many ways to attract visitors to a Web site. Here we will discuss some of them.

Making the Top List of a Search Engine

In any search engine, there is a page for submitting URLs. By submitting a URL the search engine spider can crawl through the submitted site, following and indexing all related content and links. Because the spider indexes the full text of the pages, there is no need to submit a list of keywords. Nor does one need to give the search engine summaries or descriptions; they are generated automatically.

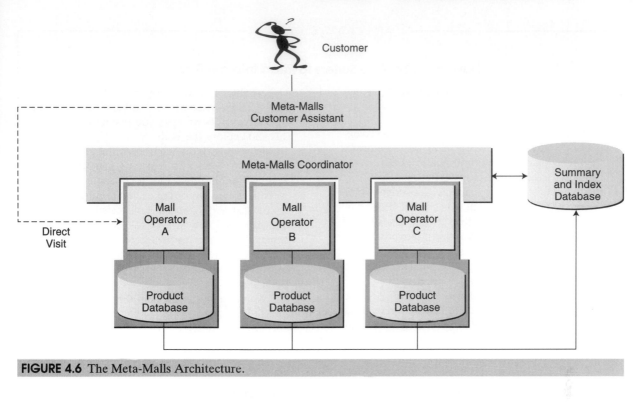

FIGURE 4.6 The Meta-Malls Architecture.

Improving a Company's Ranking on the Search Engines' Lists

By simply adding, removing, or changing a few sentences, the Web designer may alter the way a search engine's spider ranks its findings. For this reason, when designing or redesigning a Web site, the designer needs to think about the search queries the company wants people to use when they try to find the site. Then the designer creates a site that will be responsive to those queries.

For example, a user is searching for "Hawaiian Bed and Breakfast." The user will receive a list of 20 top locations. Now the user needs to find a particular site among the 20 sites retrieved by the search engine. The problem is how to be included in the top 20 and then how to attract the user to the site. To do so, the advertiser must not emphasize the way the ocean looks from a bedroom window but emphasize key terms, such as bed, breakfast, Hawaii, and weeklong getaways. In addition to being included in the top URL list, companies attract visitors by running special events and promotions.

ONLINE EVENTS, PROMOTIONS, AND ATTRACTIONS

It was the winter of 1994, the term EC was not yet known, and people were just starting to discover the Internet. Yet, one company demonstrated that there is a new way of doing business—on the Internet. DealerNet, which was selling new and used cars in physical lots, had a virtual showroom. It let people "visit" dozens of dealerships and compare prices and features. At that time it was a revolutionary way of selling cars. Furthermore, to get people's attention, DealerNet gave away a car, and it gave it away over the Internet.

APPLICATION CASE 4.3

How to Entice Web Surfers to Read Internet Ads

There are dozens of innovative ideas; here are some examples:

1. Yoyodyne Inc. conducts giveaway games, discount contests, and sweepstakes, whose entrants agree to read product information of advertisers ranging from Major League Baseball to Sprint Communication. For example, Yoyodyne organized a contest in 1997 in which H&R Block paid $20,000 toward the winner's federal taxes (H&R Block helps in tax preparation). Yoyodyne also offers multisponsor games.
2. Netzero and others offer free Internet access in exchange for viewing ads.
3. At www.egghead, real people help you. At www.lucent.com live people talk to you over the phone "pushing" material and ads to your computer.

4. Cybergold (www.cybergold.com), Goldmine (www.goldmine.com), and others connect you with advertisers who pay you real money to read ads and explore the Web.
5. Riddler (www.riddler.com) provides an opportunity to play games in real time and win prizes. People also play games for no prizes at all.
6. Netstakes runs sweepstakes that require no skills in contrast with contests. You register only once and can randomly win prizes (http://webstakes.com). Prizes are given away in different categories. The site is divided into channels; each has several sponsors. They pay Netstakes to send them traffic. Netstakes runs online ads, both on the Web and in many e-mail lists that people requested to be on.

This promotion was unique at that time and it was a total success, receiving a lot of media attention. Today, such promotions are regular events on thousands of Web sites. Contents, quizzes, coupons, and givaways, designed to attract visitors, are integral to Internet commerce as much, or even more than, offline commerce. Application Case 4.3 lists some innovative examples.

Running promotions on the Internet is similar to running offline promotions. Some of the major considerations, according to Chase (1998) and O'Keefe (1997), are:

1. The target audience needs to be clearly understood.
2. The target audience needs to be online surfers.
3. The traffic to the site should be estimated, and a powerful enough server must be prepared to handle it.
4. Assuming the promotion is successful, what will the result be? This assessment is needed for your budget and promotion strategy.
5. Consider co-branding. Many promotions succeed because they bring together two or more powerful partners.

BARGAINS, SPECIAL SALES, AND FINANCIAL INCENTIVES

Bargain hunters can find lots of bargains on the Internet. Special sales, auctions, and coupons, some of which are described in chapter 5, are frequently combined with ads. Of special interest are sites such as www.coolsavings.com, www.hotcoupons.com, www.supercoups.com, www.clickrewards.com, www.cybergold.com, and www.windough.com. A popular lottery site is www.worldlotto2000.com. If you like to help the Red Cross try www.pluslotto.com.

Finding Your Way Around

Several sites compile current contents by theme, prize, entry deadlines, and so on. They also provide search engines for finding sweepstakes.

4.5   Push Technology and Intelligent Agents

PUSH TECHNOLOGY

The explosion of the Internet phenomenon has led to a growing acceptance of electronic messaging and news transmission. In response to this trend, several new vehicles for information transmission are appearing on the Internet. Prominent among them is the concept of **push technology,** which allows for the direct delivery of information to an individual's computer desktop. The typical Internet format involves a *pull format;* users must seek out information through a search engine or other delivery system and then pull the information out to them. In contrast, push technology allows for the direct delivery of content to an end user. This delivery can occur through a scrolling ticker-tape bar, a screen saver, or as an imbedded window on the desktop. The term "push" comes from "server push," a term used to describe the streaming of Web page contents from a Web server to a Web browser.

The benefits to the subscriber of push technology is that instead of spending hours searching the Web, they can have the information they are interested in delivered automatically to their desktop via Web technology and the Internet. A computer *point-casts* (as opposed to broadcast) information of interest directly to the user. The push concept is becoming an important concept in the marketplace today. Whereas in the past manufacturers mass-produced products, today they are mass-customized to suit customers' needs. The same is true of broadcasting. Broadcasting is analogous to mass-production and **pointcasting** is analogous to mass customization. Only the information that is most relevant to the user is transmitted directly to him or her.

To have information pointcasted to a user's personal computer, the user gets involved in three steps: creation of a prespecified profile, selection of appropriate content, and downloading the selection. The prespecification of a user profile occurs when users register for a push delivery service. They then download client software on their computer that can be customized to deliver only certain channels or categories such as international news, sports, financial data, and so on. In this step the transmission of information is tailored to the user's preferences. The users can even specify how often they want this information transmitted to their PC. After a profile is submitted to the push delivery service and stored in a database, special software programs monitor Web sites and other information sources for the pertinent and relevant information that is requested by the user.

Upon finding information of interest to the user, the push programs download the information to the push client, notifying him or her by e-mail, playing a sound, displaying an icon on the desktop, sending full articles or Web pages, or by displaying headlines on a screen saver.

This process is designed for convenience and efficiency. Often the service is free to the PC user. It is the advertisers that "flip the bill" for organizations that offer push technology. One example of a pioneering push delivery system is PointCast Network. PointCast uses a screensaver format to deliver news selected by the user. News and information is compiled from over 700 quality sources worldwide and packaged in over 45 channels. When a user initially establishes his or her system, he or she selects the types of desired information (for example, sports, news, headlines, stock quotes). As the pioneer of push technology, PointCast received a great deal of publicity. However, since Yahoo and other companies offer competing services, the company shifted its attention to other Internet ventures (see *Interactive Week,* December 14, 1998).

There are four types of push technology. The first one, *self-service delivery*, gives Web surfers the tools to download pages for later viewing. Another type, *aggregated delivery,* acts like television networks or commercial online services in that it provides users with a wide variety of content and advertising choices packaged in a single offering. A third popular push technology, *mediated delivery,* lets Internet users control what information they receive from participating marketers and publishers by selecting from a menu of choices on the mediator's Web site. The last model is *direct delivery,* in which the PC desktop interface pulls information off the net itself.

PUSH ON THE INTRANET

One natural extension of the initial push technology is that many organizations are realizing that there is a need in today's competitive environment to distribute customized news to workers who need the information on a timely basis. Thus, companies are using push technology to set up their own channels to pointcast important internal information to either their own employees (on intranets) and/or to their supply chain partners (on extranets). Push offers corporations a cheap and easy way to deliver everything from training materials to a cafeteria menu. Direct marketers are also using push technology to deliver promotions to the desktops of targeted customers.

The material delivered may include information packaged by outside vendors and then disseminated internally. Alternatively, it can be the result of monitoring specific information in the corporate databases.

Microstrategy (www.microstrategy.com) developed a decision support software that sweeps corporate databases daily for automatic sending of relevant information to employees and managers, for example, tracking inventory and shipments. Delivery is done through e-mail or voice-synthesized voice mail.

THE FUTURE OF PUSH TECHNOLOGY

A major drawback of push technology is the bandwidth requirements. Since information is being constantly downloaded, it puts a tremendous stress on system resources. Several experts predict that the technology will never really fly. Others see a trend for specialized applications. Here are some examples:

- TIBCO software helps to create push technology by collecting corporate information from ERP and other data sources and distributing it throughout the enterprise.
- TIBCO also pushes event-driven multicasting using TIBCO.net, as well as the idea that on an intranet, the information for the particular group or individual may be of interest to others. TIBCO points out that push changes the emphasis from database-centric to information-centric computing, with automated information delivery.
- FirstFloor Software's Smart Delivery integrates documents and Web pages into business applications. Many of its customers have large field sales organizations. To support those customers' salespersons, Smart Delivery can automatically update files and notify users of new or changed documents.
- Lanacom's Headliner integrates headline information from more than 400 sites with information coming from internal databases and other internal sources. The emphasis is on creating highly personalized solutions.
- DeskTop Data combines push and pull technologies. Push technology alerts users to real-time news and important business events; users can then pull the underlying documents if needed. (This is a paid subscriber service, and no advertising is shown.)

- Both BackWeb and PointCast can be viewed as consumer push companies that also have business strategies. For example, BackWeb has an alliance with Lotus Domino, and PointCast is integrated with Microsoft's Active Desktop.
- The cost of push technology, like that of other advertisement-related methods, needs to be justified. Unfortunately, measuring the benefits of advertisement is a complex issue, as we will show in section 4.6.

INTELLIGENT AGENTS

In previous chapters we have described how companies, such as Firefly, collect information about consumers. The purpose of such collections is to create a customer's profile. If the company knows the profile, it can tailor an ad to the customer or ask the customer if he or she would like to receive product information. This type of agent is called *product brokering*. It alerts the users to new releases or recommends products based on past selections or constraints specified by the buyer. Examples would be the agents of Amazon.com, Fastparts, and Classified2000. In addition to Firefly Network, other vendors such as Net Perceptions, Personal Logic, Broadvision, and others build such agent systems. An example is provided in Application Case 4.4.

Another agent application exists in the area of interactive smart catalogs, for example, where experimental work was developed by Stanford University, Hewlett-Packard, and CommerceNet. The goal was to demonstrate the efficiencies and added capabilities afforded by making catalogs accessible on the Web in a form that allows potential customers to locate products according to descriptions of their specifications and for data in the catalogs to include descriptions of function as well as structure. The setup lets users focus quickly on their area of need and obtain a "personalized" view of it. By linking information about a product and its attributes throughout the entire distribution chain, buyers can view "virtual" catalogs in real time as new products become available. Consumers need truly interactive personalized smart catalogs to enhance the shopping experience. Future advances in personalized interactive catalogs will make it easier to locate products and their attributes throughout the value chain.

APPLICATION CASE 4.4

Fujitsu Uses Agents for Targeted Advertising in Japan

At the end of 1996, Fujitsu was using a new agent-based technology called Interactive Marketing Interface (iMi) that allows advertisers to interact directly with targeted customers and provide valuable services and information. The system enhances the customers' Internet experiences.

Interactive Marketing Interface allows advertisers to interact directly with specific segments of the consumer market through the use of software agents, while ensuring that consumers remain anonymous to advertisers. Consumers submit a personal profile to iMi, indicating such characteristics as product categories of interests, hobbies, travel habits, and the maximum number of e-mail messages per week they are willing to receive. In turn, by e-mail customers receive product announcements, advertisements, and marketing surveys from advertisers based on their personal profile information. By answering the marketing surveys or acknowledging receipt of advertisements, consumers earn iMi points, redeemable for gift certificates and phone cards.

4.6 Economics and Effectiveness of Advertisement

Justifying advertisement on the Internet is more difficult than for conventional advertisement. One of the major reasons for this is the difficulties in measuring the results of advertising. Several methods are available for measuring advertisement, conducting cost-benefit analysis, and for pricing ads. They are discussed below.

EXPOSURE MODELS THAT ARE BASED ON CPMs

Traditional pricing has been based on CPMs. So far, this model has been the standard advertising rate-pricing tool for Web sites as well. While CPM charges on the Web vary widely, on average they have been at higher levels than they are in most other media because of the small supply of highly trafficked Web sites.

Since advertisers pay an agreed-upon multiple of the number of "guaranteed" impressions (page views), it is very important that impressions are measured accurately in the context of the advertising business model. This limits the site's responsibility for ad delivery, and the ad revenue generated is simply the product of the traffic volume times a multiple, which is generally priced in terms of CPM, which can range from $10 to $100 (in 1999). The price charged is different for different search engines and other popular sites. For example, in 1999 Excite charged $68 per CPM and Lycos charged $50 to $60 per CPM. Generally, CPMs seem to average on the order of $45, resulting in a fairly low cost of $0.045 per impression viewed.

The wide price spread suggests that the Web can function both as a mass medium and a direct-marketing vehicle and that context, audience, technology, and anticipated results all play a part in determining what price an advertiser will pay. A few well-branded sites in a very broad range of categories (such as news, entertainment, and sports) will dominate, and these sites will be able to charge a premium for ad space.

Some companies, such as USA Today, charge their clients according to the number of hits (about 3 cents per hit in 1999). As explained earlier, there could be several hits in one impression.

CLICK-THROUGH

Ad pricing based upon click-through is an attempt to develop a more accountable way of charging for Web advertising (see http://www.pawluk.com/pages.htm). The payment for a banner ad is based on the number of times a visitor actually clicks on it. However, a relatively small proportion of those exposed to a banner ad actually click on the banner. DoubleClick Inc. reports that only 4 percent of visitors who are exposed to a banner ad the first time click on the ad. Thus, payment based upon click-through guarantees not only that the visitor was exposed to the banner ad but actively decided to click on the banner and become exposed to the target ad (Hoffman and Novak 1996). Space providers object to this method, claiming that viewing an ad itself may lead to a purchase later or to an offline purchase.

INTERACTIVITY

This is a new measure proposed by Novak and Hoffman (1997). While a payment based upon click-through guarantees exposure to target ads, it does not guarantee that the visitor liked the ad or even spent any substantial time viewing it. This proposal suggests basing the pricing upon the amount the visitor *interacts* with the target ad. Such an interactivity measure could be based upon the duration of time spent viewing the ad, the number of pages of the target ad accessed, or the number of repeat visits to the target ad.

Back in 1996, Modern Media, an interactive advertising agency, had developed a pricing model in which its clients paid not for exposures or click-through but only for activity at the client's Web site. This has raised a controversy surrounding the Web media. Web publishers were arguing that the problem with activity-based measures like click-through or interactivity is that the Web publishers cannot be held responsible for activity related to an advertisement. They also argued that traditional media, such as newspapers or television, charge for ads whether or not they lead to sales. So why should the interactive condition be applied on the Net?

Advertisers and their agencies, on the other hand, argued that since the Web medium allows for accountability, models can and should be developed that measure actual consumer activities. A standard solution will eventually be reached in the future or different approaches will be used by different companies.

ACTUAL PURCHASE

Marketers are interested in outcomes, and the ultimate outcome is a purchase. It is obvious that 1,000 people visiting a site is worth something, but a site that only 5 people visit can be worth much more if they are actually shopping there. It is also important to know the amount of money customers actually spend.

In an outcome-based approach to pricing, Web advertising begins by specifying exactly what the marketer would like the target ad to do. Examples of typical outcomes include influencing attitudes, motivating the consumers to provide information about themselves, or leading the consumer to an actual purchase. For example, if a customer purchased a book at amazon.com after he or she saw Amazon's ad at America Online's Web site, then America Online receives a referral fee of say 8 percent of the purchase price of the book.

OTHER METHODS

Several other methods exist, such as:

- The use of the gross number of visits (occasions on which a user looks up a site) as a possible measure of effectiveness is also inadequate. (Visiting an entertaining site may not result in a purchase.)
- The number of "unique users" at a site during a specific time can be calculated by recording some form of user registration or identification (to overcome the problem of one user paying several visits to one site). An ad placed in such a site has a greater potential of attracting a viewer, but there is no guarantee that a purchase will be made.
- Many advertisers charge a fixed monthly fee, regardless of the traffic. Others use a hybrid approach; some combination of the above.
- An interesting approach is to let the market determine prices. This is done via auctions. Both www.onsale.com and www.adauction.com schedule auctions for ads. Publishers post information about available space and buyers bid on it.

4.7 Online Catalogs

An important factor in EC is the manner in which products or services are presented to the users. This is frequently done via online catalogs.

EVOLUTION OF ONLINE CATALOGS

Printed paper has been the medium of advertisement catalogs for a long time. However, recently electronic catalogs on CD-ROM and on the Web have gained popularity. For merchants, the objective of **online catalogs** is to advertise and promote products and services, whereas the purpose of catalogs to the customer is to provide a source of information on products and services. **Electronic catalogs** can be searched quickly with the help of software agents. Also, comparisons involving catalogs' products can be made very effectively. For a comprehensive discussion of online catalogs see chapter 9 in Kosiur (1997).

Electronic catalogs consist of product database, directory and search capability, and a presentation function. On the Web-based e-malls, Web browser, along with Java and sometimes virtual reality, play the role of presenting static and dynamic information.

The majority of early online catalogs were online replication of text and pictures of the printed catalogs. However, online catalogs have evolved to be more dynamic, customized, and integrated with selling and buying procedures. As the online catalog is integrated with order taking and payment, the tools for building online catalogs are being integrated with merchant sites (tools for building storefronts and e-malls are described in chapters 2 and 11).

Electronic catalogs can be classified according to three dimensions:

1. The dynamics of the information presentation. Two categories are distinguished.
   - Static catalogs: The catalog is presented in textual description and static pictures.
   - Dynamic catalogs: The catalog is presented in motion pictures or animation, possibly with sound to supplement static content.
2. The degree of customization. Two extremes are distinguished.
   - Ready-made catalogs: Merchants offer the *same* catalog to any customer.
   - Customized catalogs: Deliver customized content and display depending upon the characteristics of customers.
3. The degree of integration of catalogs with the following business processes:
   - Order taking and fulfillment.
   - Electronic payment systems.
   - Intranet work flow software and systems.
   - Inventory and accounting systems.
   - Suppliers' or customers' extranet.
   - Paper catalogs.

COMPARISON OF ONLINE CATALOGS WITH PAPER CATALOGS

The advantages and disadvantages of online catalogs are contrasted with those of paper catalogs in Table 4.3. Although there are significant advantages of online catalogs, such as ease of updating, ability to integrate with the purchasing process, and coverage of a wide spectrum of products with a strong search capability, there are still disadvantages and limitations. Most of all, customers need computers and the Internet

TABLE 4.3   Comparison of Online Catalogs with Paper Catalogs

Type	Advantages	Disadvantages
Paper Catalogs	• Easy to create a catalog without high technology • Reader is able to look at the catalog without computer system • More portable than electronic catalog	• Difficult to update changed product information promptly • Only a limited number of products is displayed • Limited information through photographs and textual description is available • No possibility for advanced multimedia such as animation and voice
Online Catalog	• Easy to update product information • Able to integrate with the purchasing process • Good search and comparison capabilities • Able to provide timely, up-to-date product information • Provision for globally broad range of product information • Possibility of adding on voice and motion pictures • Cost savings • Easy to customize • More comparative shopping • Ease of connecting order processing, inventory processing, and payment processing to the system	• Difficult to develop catalogs, large fixed cost • There is a need for customer skill to deal with computers and browsers

to access online catalogs. However, since computers and Internet access are spreading rapidly, we can expect a large portion of paper catalogs to be replaced by or at least supplemented by electronic catalogs. On the other hand, considering the fact that printed newspapers and magazines have not diminished due to the online ones, we can guess that the paper catalogs will not disappear in spite of the popularity of online catalogs. There seems to be room for both media. However, in B2B, paper catalogs may disappear more quickly, as shown in Application Case 4.5.

ADVERTISING IN ONLINE CATALOGS VERSUS ELECTRONIC MALLS

Some catalogs on Web sites provide text and pictures without linking them to order taking. Refer to Calvin Klein ads in www.pobox.upenn.edu/~davidtoc. The site has an electronic directory with a large number of electronic catalogs. However, there is no reason why the catalogs cannot be linked with order taking or at least e-mail contacts. So, the dedicated advertising site seems to be a transient form of e-mall. However, some ads about company image can only be linked with e-mall, because the ads do not correspond to a specific product. For instance, Coca-Cola's Web site (www.cocacola.com) is not appropriate for taking Coke's orders online. It just reminds people about the taste of Coca-Cola. However, you can buy Coke's collector items and more.

Tools for building online catalogs are: iCat's Commerce Online (iCat), Boise's Marketing Service (Boise), IBM's Net.commerce (IBM), and Oracle's ICS (Oracle). See chapter 11 for details.

AMP's Online Catalogs Cut the Cost to One-Sixth

With annual revenues of more than $5.2 billion, AMP, an electronics components manufacturer, spent more than $7 million each year to mail and update 400 specialty catalogs to its distributors around the world and another $800,000 in fax-back phone costs. These catalogs cover about 134,000 electrical and mechanical components.

In the past, AMP had only enough resources to update about one-half of their 400 catalogs each year, so many catalogs had a life-cycle of two years, even though products changed more often than that. The estimate of the cost of setting the online catalogs up and running is $1.2 million, roughly one-fifth of the previous printing costs. Of the $1.2 million, software and hardware costs were $300,000 to $400,000, with the remainder spent for language translation and catalog development.

Source: Compiled from Kosier (1997), pp. 173–83.

CUSTOMIZED CATALOGS

A *customized catalog* is a catalog assembled specifically for a company, usually a customer of the catalog owner. It can be tailored to individual shoppers in some cases as well. There are two approaches to customized catalogs.

The first approach is to let the customers identify the interesting parts out of the total catalog as is done by companies such as One-to-One (www.broadvision.com) and PointCast (www.pointcast.com). Then, customers do not have to deal with irrelevant topics. A tool that aids customization is LiveCommerce from Open Market (www.openmarket.com/livecom). See the demos of their customers.

LiveCommerce allows the creation of catalogs with branded, value-added capabilities that make it easy for customers to find the products they want to purchase, locate the information they need, and quickly compose their order. Product offerings can be specialized for each customer's organization or for individuals with specific needs. Every customer company can view a custom catalog with individualized prices, products, and display formats. An e-mall manager who uses LiveCommerce can control a complete range of information that the customer sees and link the online catalog with related computing resources. LiveCommerce features a specialized catalog language that offers complete control over the look and feel of catalogs. This combination of power and flexibility allows a catalog to be quickly and easily modified to meet the evolving needs of customers.

The second approach is to let the system automatically identify the characteristics of customers based on their transaction records. For collecting data, *Cookie* technology is used to trace the transactions. However, to generalize the relationship between the customer and items of interest, data mining technology and support by intelligent systems, such as a neural network, is necessary. This second approach can be effectively combined with the first one.

As an example of the second approach, let us review a scenario of using a tool by Oracle called ICS in a customized catalog:

Joe logs on to the Acme Shopping site, where he has the option to register as an account customer and record his preferences in terms of address details, preferred method of payment, and interest areas. Acme Shopping offers a wide range of products, including electronics, clothing, books, and sporting goods. Joe is only interested in clothing and electronics. He is not a sportsman or a great book lover. Joe also has some very distinct hobby areas—one is photography.

After Joe has recorded his preferences, the first page of the electronic store will show him only the clothing and electronics departments. Furthermore, when Joe goes into the electronics department, he only sees products related to photography—cameras and accessories. But some of the products are way out of Joe's price range, so Joe further refines his preferences to reflect that he is only interested in electronics that relate to photography and cost $300 or less.[2]

Such personalization gives the consumer a value-added experience and adds to the compelling reasons for revisiting the site, building brand loyalty to that Internet store. Against the backdrop of intense competition for Web airtime, personalization provides a valuable way to get the consumer matched to the products and information they are most interested in as quickly and painlessly as possible. An example of how corporations customize their catalogs for corporate clients is provided in Application Case 4.6.

4.8 Special Advertisement Topics

Of the many issues related to Web advertisement, we touch only upon a few.

HOW MUCH TO ADVERTISE?

Like any other advertisement, Internet advertisement needs to justify itself; otherwise you may spend more than you need. It is important that companies know what their advertisement objectives are. The rationale is straightforward. A lack of objective evaluation about the Web may lead to problems of image and information overkill. Also, if what is expected from Web advertising cannot be articulated in broad terms and systematically evaluated in terms of deliverability by the medium, there may be no point in using the Web. Once it has been determined that using the Web as an advertising vehicle could indeed benefit a company in achieving its objectives, management's attention should turn to learning about the Web. They need to understand what the Web is and how it works, and they must realize the need for long-term commitment to the medium and short-term dynamics in information display. Only then can they decide how much to spend on Internet advertisement.

Transplanting television ad objectives into Web objectives does not seem to suffice. Web ads are dictated by different dynamics. Television, radio, newspapers, and magazines rely on in-your-face advertising and intrusions into a person's consciousness. Web advertisement may impact people differently because of the interactivity. Firms need to assess whether they have the commitment—manpower, time, and financial resources—needed to stay on course once they have decided to adopt the Web. Lack of commitment is likely to result in typical Web sites that disappointingly lead nowhere or constantly inform the visitor that they are under construction. Web sites are never truly finished; they require constant and dynamic changes to attract visitors.

For individuals and businesses, it may be wise to utilize the services of an established ad agency knowledgeable in the specialized medium of Internet advertising. Such an agency may have much more of an idea of what type of ads will actually influence the viewers, thereby generating the desired traffic to your Web site.

---

[2]*Source*: Oracle's white paper (1998), p. 6.

Electronic Catalogs at Boise Cascade: B2B

Boise Cascade Office Products is a $3 billion office products wholesaler whose customer base includes over 100,000 large corporate customers and 1 million small ones. All together the company sells over 200,000 different items. The company's paper catalog of 900 pages is mailed to customers once each year. Throughout the year, minicatalogs are sent to customers tailored to their individual needs based on past buying habits and purchase patterns.

In 1996, the company placed its catalog online. Customers view the catalog at www.bcop.com and can order straight from the site or they can e-mail in orders. The orders are shipped the next day. Customers are then billed. In 1997, the company generated 20 percent of its sales through the Web site. In late 1999, the figure was above 30 percent. The company acknowledges that its Internet business is the fastest growing segment of its business and that it expects to reach 70 percent of its total sales in just a few years.

The company prepares thousands of customers' customized catalogs. It used to take about six weeks to produce a single customer catalog, primarily because of the time involved in pulling together all the data. Now the process of producing a Web catalog takes one week. One major advantage of customized catalogs is pricing. In paper catalogs that everyone shares, you cannot show the specific price for each buyer, which is based on the type of the contract signed and the volume of goods being purchased.

The company estimates that electronic orders cost approximately 55 percent less to process than paper-based orders. The attached figure shows the process of working with the electronic catalogs.

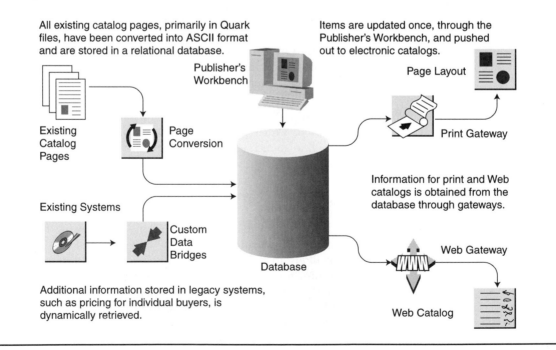

All existing catalog pages, primarily in Quark files, have been converted into ASCII format and are stored in a relational database.

Publisher's Workbench

Existing Catalog Pages

Page Conversion

Existing Systems

Custom Data Bridges

Database

Additional information stored in legacy systems, such as pricing for individual buyers, is dynamically retrieved.

Items are updated once, through the Publisher's Workbench, and pushed out to electronic catalogs.

Page Layout

Print Gateway

Information for print and Web catalogs is obtained from the database through gateways.

Web Gateway

Web Catalog

AUDITING AND ANALYZING WEB TRAFFIC

Before your company decides to advertise on someone's Web site, it is important that you know that the number of hits, click-throughs, or other data you are working with are legitimate because the potential for manipulation of data is large. An audit is critical; it validates the number of ad views and hits claimed by the site, assuring advertisers that they are getting their money's worth. An impartial, external analysis and review is crucial to advertisers to verify the accuracy of the page impression counted by the site.

A longtime friend of advertisers is the Audit Bureau of Circulation (ABC), established in 1914 as a not-for-profit association by advertisers, advertising agencies, and publishers who came together to establish advertisement standards and rules. They created ABC to verify circulation reports by auditing circulation figures and, as a result, to provide credible and objective information to the buyers and sellers of print advertising.

ABC provides services such as:

- A forum for buyers and publishers to come together to determine information critical to the buying and selling process.
- Circulation audits. An ABC audit is an in-depth examination of a publisher's Web records to assure buyers that circulation claims are accurate.
- Dissemination of circulation data, both in print and in electronic format, for ABC members' use.
- Continual improvement of its products and services so they remain relevant to buyer and publisher members.

The ABC is now adapting to Web advertisement. Several other independent third-party Internet auditing companies are in operation, such as PCMeter, BPA, and Audit.

An example of auditing is provided in Application Case 4.7. As you can see, in addition to circulation, other relevant information is provided.

Related to such auditing is rating of sites. This is done by companies such as Accure, Accipiter, Ipro, Netcount, Interse, Hotstats and Cnet (these are discussed further in the exercise section.)

Self-Monitoring of Traffic

Several vendors sell software that allow Webmasters to monitor and implement advertisement on their own Web sites. Examples are NetGravity, NetIntellect and Webtrends (these are discussed further in the Internet exercise section #6).

INTERNET STANDARDS

With so many creative ways to advertise on the Web, it would seem that the last thing anyone would want to do is make it more standardized and regulated. But, paradoxically, that's the way much of the Web ad industry is heading.

One proposed standard that will affect advertising deals with cookies. A *cookie,* as described earlier, is a mechanism that allows a Web site to record your comings and goings, usually without your knowledge or consent. This information can be used, for example, to automatically attach an ID number for a subscription-only site or to collect information about an online shopper's preferences so that electronic marketers can target their offerings to that individual. A committee of Internet users and technologists developed a cookies standard, which at the time of this writing (Fall 1999)

APPLICATION CASE 4.7

Sample of an Audit Report

The following is a summary of an audit quarterly report issued by BPA Audit (www.bpai.com) for Internet.com (Mecklermedia Corp.) for the period ended September 30, 1998.

PURPOSE

This BPA International Interactive Audit Report provides an independently verified summary of a census of activity recorded at Internet.com. This audit report includes verification of all traffic and demographics of nonregistered users. All verified counts are based on and have been audited for counts only as reported separately herein.

SITE CONTENT

Internet.com provides Internet-related daily news and information resources. Key features include: InternetNews.com, providing eight unique news categories that are updated daily; CWS-Apps, a buyer's guide of Windows application software; and The List, a directory of Internet service providers on the Web. Other features include BrowserWatch, WebDeveloper.com, and Java Boutique.

INDEPENDENT AUDITORS' OPINION

BPA International required and has examined the complete and entire access log files of this Web site for the period covered by this report. Sample or extracts of log files are not accepted.

BPA's examination of site usage, and accurate tracking by log files was made in accordance with generally accepted auditing standards and accordingly included tests and confirmations of actual access by site's users. BPA International used multiple software analysis tools for this Web site audit.

Based on such examination, it is BPA International's opinion that the statements set forth in this report present fairly and accurately the access of this Web site in conformance with generally accepted auditing principles.

REPORT'S HIGHLIGHTS

Total Quarterly Page Requests = 45,636,851
Average Daily Page Requests = 495,156
July, 12.9 million; Aug, 15.6 million; Sept, 17 million
Weekly Demand by Day: Range from 247,000 (Saturday) to 601,000 (Tuesday)
Hourly Usage: Low Usage 12 midnight–7 A.M. about 130,000/hr to about 280,000/hr during 9 A.M.–5 P.M.

---

was under review by the Internet Engineering Task Force. The proposal encourages, for example, browser vendors to make the utilization of cookies and its prevention more apparent to users. Some 72 percent of online users have never even heard of cookies, according to a survey of 300 people conducted by market research firm CyberDialogue in 1998. The proposal seeks to take control of the cookie away from online publishers and marketers.

Ad management companies are now drafting a counterproposal. Therefore, the cookie debate will not be settled soon, and there are sure to be more standards proposed that will affect Web advertising in the future.

LOCALIZATION

Localization is the process of converting media products developed in one country to a form culturally and linguistically acceptable in countries outside the original target market. It is usually done by a set of guidelines called *internationalization*. Web page translation (chapter 12) is only one aspect. There are several more. For example, a jewelry manufacturer that displays its products on a white background was astonished to find that this may offend customers in other countries that want a blue background. If you aim at the global market (there are millions of potential customers out there), you must make an effort to localize your Web pages. This may not be a simple task because of the following factors:

- Some languages use accented characters. If your product includes an accented character, it will disappear when you convert it to English, for example.
- Hard-coded text and fonts cannot be changed, so they remain in their original format in translated material.
- Graphics and icons are different when you cross borders. For example, a U.S. mailbox looks like a trash can in Europe.
- To be translated into Asian languages, significant cultural issues must be addressed.
- Dates that are written mm/dd/yy in the United States are written dd/mm/yy in many other countries.
- Consistent translation over several documents is difficult.
- To help with localization, you may want to hire a consultant (for example, see www.transware.ie).

THE MAJOR WEB AD PLAYERS

Meeker (1997) has identified several unique Internet market subsegments, comprising five major categories (besides the companies that create and operate Internet sites that are funded, in whole or in part, by advertising dollars):

1. *Advertising agencies and Web site developers*—companies involved in the generation of Internet advertising campaigns, from campaign planning to media buying, as well as developers of sites that allow companies to promote their brands and develop an online consumer presence. Since advertising is essentially the promotion of the company and its products and services, on the Web this is achieved either through buying advertising space at other sites or simply designing a site that serves the same purpose.
2. *Finding market research providers*—in such a new field, advertisers, publishers, investors, and other interested parties are all looking for real data about what is happening, how big it is, and where it is going. These are companies that are tracking the evolution of Internet technology with a focus on its impact on business and certain industries, including the Web advertising arena.
3. *Traffic measurement and analysis companies*—to validate advertising media buys on the Internet, advertisers need to be able to justify and verify the investment they make. Traffic analysis companies fill that need by offering software and services to aid publishers in tracking and executing advertising delivery on their Web sites.
4. *Networks/rep firms*—these companies provide value-added services for Web advertisers and publishers alike by brokering the distribution of advertisements and overseeing their delivery.
5. *Order processing and support*—companies that provide outsourcing services to Internet publishers and service providers.

4.9   Managerial Issues

1. *Make versus Buy.*   Web advertisement is a complex undertaking. Therefore, outsourcing should be seriously considered. Start with O'Keefe's book (1997) and the list of sources there. Examine the Interactive Publishing Alert that contains an index of Web sites, their advertising rates, and reported traffic count before you select a site on which to advertise. Also consult third-party audits.

2. *Finding the Most Visited Sites.*   One way to determine where to advertise is to check the site's traffic. Several places report the traffic on popular Web sites such as Yahoo or Netscape. Good sources for such lists are: www.100hot.com, www.web21.com, and www.pcmag.com/special/Web100/top100f. Advertisers can also access www.arbitron.com to find survey results, by metropolitan areas, about Internet advertisements.

3. *Company Research.*   Companies should research the Web thoroughly before meeting with an Internet marketing/advertising service. With so many services available, they should be researched, too. In addition, currently most ad networks provide little or no control to the advertiser regarding the execution of an ad campaign. An ad network should provide a convenient way for Web publishers to manage a portfolio of Web pages or sites.

4. *Commitment to Web Advertising and Coordination with Traditional Advertisement.*   Once a company is totally committed to advertising on the Web, it must remember that a successful program is multifaceted. It requires input and vision from marketing, cooperation from the legal department, and strong technical leadership from the corporate information systems (IS) department. A successful Web program also requires top management support. Finally, coordination with the traditional advertisement is a must (e.g., advertise your Web address on television).

5. *Ethical Issues.*   Several ethical issues relate to advertisement online. One issue that received lots of attention is spamming, which is subject to new legislation (chapter 10). Another issue is the selling of mailing lists and customer information. Some people believe that not only do you need the consent of the customers but that you should share with them the profits derived.

6. *Integrating Advertisement with Ordering and Other Business Processes.*   This is an important requirement. If you go to Amazon's site, you are directed to the shopping cart, then to the catalog, then to ordering and paying. Such integration should be seamless.

Summary

The completion of this chapter helps you in attaining the following learning objectives:

1. **Describe the objectives and characteristics of Web advertisement.**   Web advertisement attempts to attract surfers to advertiser's site where they can receive lots of information, interact with the sellers, and in many cases place an order. Distinctive features are customized ads to fit groups of similar interest and even individuals. Also, dynamic presentation by rich multimedia.

2. **Describe the major advertisement method.**   While banners is the most popular, other methods are frequently used. Notable are registration of the URL with search engines, e-mail, splash screens, newsgroups, and spot leasing.

3. **Describe the various advertisement strategies.**   The major strategies are: (passive pull)—let customers find ads by themselves; use push technology or e-mail list to send ads to customers; ads associated with the information searched by customers are automatically displayed; customers are paid to view ads (as in a commodity); ads are customized on a one-to-one basis.

4. **Describe various types of promotions on the Web.**   Web promotions are similar to offline promotions. They include giveaways, contests, quizzes, entertainment, coupons, and so on. Customization and interactivity distinguishes the Net from conventional promotions.

5. **Describe benefits of push technology and intelligent agents.**   Push technology allows the collection and delivery of desired information and sending it to customers, including advertisement on demand. The customization of information saves time and energy for users. When material is sent for free, it usually includes banner ads. The intelligent agents are used to identify customer profiles and to tailor ads to these customers.

6. **Describe the major economic issues related to Web advertisement.**   The major issue is justification, and it is related to the fees paid and pricing mechanism. Also, the allocation of money among the various Web alternatives (e.g., banners versus e-mail) is important.

7. **Measuring the success of advertisement and pricing ads.**   The traditional concept of paying for exposure (by CPM) is used on the Internet, but it is being challenged. The difficulty is pricing the ads. Some of the methods are paying by the number of hits or impressions (page views), which is basically an exposure to the ads, or paying for actions, such as click-through (to reach the advertiser's site). Ideally, an attempt is made to trace interaction on the advertiser's site, including actual purchasing.

8. **Compare paper and electronic catalogs and describe customized catalogs.**   The major advantages of electronic catalogs over paper ones are the lower cost, high speed, possibility to include animation and videos, and to attach audio. Online catalogs are also easy to update and can be integrated with ordering, inventory, and payment processing. Finally, creating customized catalogs becomes economically feasible. Customized catalogs are used mainly in B2B since large customers get different price schemas and may get customized products as well.

9. **Describe implementation issues.**   The major issues described here are finding appropriate advertisement level, auditing Web traffic, using ad agencies, using advertisement standards, localization of content, and dealing with spamming.

Keywords

- Advertisement
- Ad views
- Banner
- Banner exchange
- Click (ad click)
- Click ratio
- Click through
- CPM (cost per thousand impression)

- Cookie
- Direct marketing
- Electronic catalog
- Hit
- Impressions
- Interactive advertisement
- Interactive marketing
- Keyword banners
- Localization

- Meta tags
- Online catalogs
- Pointcasting
- Push technology
- Random banners
- Reach
- Spamming
- Splash screen
- Visit

Questions for Review

1. Describe Internet advertisement.
2. List the advantages of Internet advertisement.
3. Describe a banner.
4. List the major methods of Internet advertisement.
5. Describe the role of intelligent agents in advertisement.
6. List the advantages of electronic catalogs over paper catalogs.
7. Describe push technology and its benefits.
8. List the major measures of advertisement success (and basis for payments).
9. Describe Meta-Mall Architecture.
10. How can one advertise in a chat room?
11. Why is the pull technology a passive strategy?
12. From whom can a company obtain the e-mail list to send ads?
13. How can we escape from the flood of junk e-mails?
14. What is the associated ad display strategy?
15. How can an ad be sold as a commodity?
16. What is the typical model of customized ad strategy?
17. How can the product comparison process be used as an opportunity of advertisement?

Questions for Discussion

1. Compare banner swapping to a banner exchange.
2. Compare and contrast "pulling" information to "pushing" it.
3. In what ways does push technology resemble mass customization?
4. Explain the need to audit Internet traffic.
5. Discuss why banners are so popular in Internet advertisement.
6. Compare and contrast Internet and television advertisements.
7. Describe how a banner exchange works and how it can be customized.
8. How is the chat room used for advertisement?
9. What is the purpose of entertainment in EC?
10. Describe the steps of push technology and relate pointcasting to advertisement.
11. Why might the use of CPM to charge advertisers be inappropriate for the Internet?
12. Compare the use of "click-through" with more interactive approaches as a basis for charging ads.
13. Why would one want to standardize a cookie?
14. Should all online catalogs be tightly linked with order taking and payments?
15. Is the online catalog a part of an e-mall? When is this not realistic?
16. Do catalog personalizations based on past transaction records truly reflect the customer's preference?
17. How can push and pull advertisements work together?
18. How can an e-mall operator select an associated ad display if there is more than one advertisement applicant for a certain situation?

Internet Exercises

1. Visit the chat room of Lotus, called Domino Chat, and describe its capabilities. Analyze the advertisement on this site. Also, check the chat room of 1-800-FLOWERS. Compare the two. Finally, find general information about chat rooms (for example, http://cws.internet.com and www.icat.com). Prepare a report.
2. Find information about banners in the following sites:
   - www.linkexchange.com
   - www.coder.com

- www.sharat.co.il/services/services.html
- www.doubleclick.net/advertisers

Identify all the benefits and issues related to Internet banner advertisement.

3. Enter the Web site of www.ipro.com and find what Internet traffic management, Web results, and auditing services are provided. What are the benefits of each? Find at least one competitor in each category (such as www.netratings.com). Compare services offered and prices.

4. Examine the status of the growth of Web advertisement. Surf the sites of www.iab.net, www.jup.com, www.forrester.com, and www.adage.com. Prepare a report and project the growth for the next 5 years.

5. Investigate the services provided in chat rooms. Start with www.talkcity.com and list its services. Why do some vendors provide free chat rooms? Examine www.yack.com. Why are their chat listings so popular?

6. Investigate the tools for monitoring your Web site. What are the major capabilities provided? Start with www.Webarrange.com, www.Webtrends.com, and www.netgravity.com.

7. Investigate the status of push technology by visiting companies such as www.backweb.com, datachannel, marimba, netdelivery, pointcast, verity, myyahoo, myway, newscast, and tibco.

8. Consult an electronic catalog site such as Calvin Klein ads in www.pobox.upenn.edu/~davidtoc, and consider the possibility of extending the catalog with order taking and payment. Is such an extension reasonable?

9. Consult the iCat site and list the steps of building an electronic catalog.

10. For a chance to win $25,000, or at least have fun, register with www.windough.com. Prepare a report on the success of the site to attract the attention of surfers.

11. Enter www.hotwired.com and try to identify all the methods used for advertisement. Can you find those planned for targeted advertisement?

Team Assignments

1. It is said that Web ads are mushrooming due to the following trends:
   - E-mail gains respect
   - Women's sites launched
   - Ad serving broadens
   - Measurement of ads' success improves
   - EC is growing rapidly
   - Web expands its reach

   Find evidence that supports these trends, such as new companies, statistics, and experts' testimonials. Prepare a report.

2. Measuring Web traffic and verifying how many ad impressions are delivered is critical to the success of Web ads. Visit the following companies, find their products and services, and comment on them: NetRatings (plan), relevant knowledge (media metrix), ABC interactive, BPA interactive, and ipro. Also evaluate Matchlogic (True Count Service).

3. Generate a banner for your company. Several vendors provide you with free banner generation software. Your mission is to create a banner using a vendor of your choice, such as www.coder.com (click on instant banner). A good overview is provided at coder's "documentation" pages. Make use of the many options provided. Report on your experiences.

4. The use of classifieds is on the increase. The problem is how to find what you need or where to place the ads. Companies such as www.classifind.com may assist you. Investigate the issue of classified ads with its many aspects, including the role of Yahoo and AOL. Examine the issue of national use local advertisement.

Exercises

1. Enter www.micromass.com/demoworld/cardemo. Fill in the questionnaire and examine the customized ad generated by the "IntelliWeb." How well was the fit for you as a consumer? Also check the ad coder and healthcare demos.
2. Some say that companies such as Link Exchange constitute a threat to ad agencies. Others disagree. Examine the services of Link Exchange and compare it to the services of an Internet agency. Write a concluding report.
3. Sign up with www.hvaa.com/guessthe.htm. Try to win a $50 U.S. savings bond by estimating the damage to a pictured car on the site. Use the hints provided.
4. Plan a contest and other promotions for your company, or for a company you are familiar with. Start with www.Webmagnet.com (be sure to read "Ideas For You").

REAL WORLD CASE

Chevron's World
of Car Characters

To have its brand more easily recognized, especially among children, Chevron Corp., a major oil and gas company, ran an animated toy car promotional campaign that was centered around a Web site: www.chevroncars.com. It built one of the freshest, most innovative corporate Web sites. Within three months, traffic at the site increased from about 1,500 hits per day to over 150,000 hits per day (over 10,000 percent). The site won the 1997 Best of the Internet (BOTI) Award and generated about 100 suggestions per day from viewers, mostly children, ranging from ideas for new claymation characters to having the consumer actually design "the goods they want to consume."

Among the highlights of Chevroncars are a service for delivering seasonal and other e-mail cards to friends; a squirrel that points out commercial messages and tasks for which children may need adult permission; a grocery store where users can grab a cart and buy a plastic version of Chevron's animated vehicles or other Chevron items; a playground with games like crossword puzzles, connect the dots, and concentration-style matching games; and an area to print out stickers.

The game allowing users to check how they did against players nationwide seems to be the hands-down favorite. If you get the wrong answer, the site provides an empathetic "bummer" response.

The site has a definite commercial and branding message: to show that Chevron is a responsible, necessary, and even fun type of business; to demonstrate that Chevron is ecologically aware and doing things like protecting baby owls nesting in pumps; and to let users find out how a company like Chevron operates.

More is still to come on Chevroncars. The Road Adventure game will be expanded, and the company is thinking of ways to use the site to promote Chevron's math and science awards and to help teachers locate videos and other educational materials.

So what's the most popular part of the site? Shopping for the toy cars, of course. The largest buying group tends to be the parents of children between 3 and 9; then come 18- to 21-year-olds, followed by "kids" 35 years and older.

For a national gasoline company in just 26 markets, however, the real success of Chevron's site comes in the brand recognition it affords for both existing and future customers. And the fun message also reflects the changing nature of the gasoline business—pumps give way to complexes including commercial markets, car washes, fast-food chains, and even hotels. The company feels that the site's success has more to do with listening to what people want than any master plan. ■

CASE QUESTIONS

1. Why does the company believe that the site's success was not the result of any master plan?
2. Explain the logic of using claymation cars to advertise the sale of gasoline.
3. The company used the claymation cars in their television ads. Visit www.chevroncars: and examine the advantages over the television ad (if you have not seen it, try to find information about it).
4. Why is Chevron targeting 5- to 12-year-olds? They certainly do not buy gasoline, and by the time they drive cars, we will see many changes in gasoline sales.
5. From what you have learned in this chapter, what do you think are the factors that contribute to the site's success?
6. Investigate the role of animated characters in advertisement. Try: www.agentmart.com. Also go to www.argolink. com/genie/demos and other Microsofts agent. Finally, visit the agent characters gallery.

References

"A Strategic Approach to Internet Commerce," *Open Market*, 1998, www.openmarket.com/livecom/datasht1.cfm.

About Boise URL: *www.bcop.com.*

M. Abrams, ed., *World Wide Web: Beyond the Basics* (Upper Saddle River, NJ: Prentice Hall, 1998).

"Advertising World," 1998, www.advertising.utexas.edu.

Catalog Interoperability Study: Issues, Practices, and Recommendations, *CommerceNet* (February 27, 1998).

L. Chase, *Essential Business Tactics on the Net* (New York: J. Wiley, 1998).

S. Choi, et al., *The Economics of Electronic Commerce* (Indianapolis, IN: Macmillan Technical Publishing, 1997).

J. Eighmey, "Profiling User Responses to Commercial Web Sites," *Journal of Advertising Research*, 37 (3: 1997).

D. Gehrke and E. Turban, "Success Determinants of E-commerce Web Site Design," *Proceedings of 32 HICSS,* Hawaii, January 1999.

D. L. Hoffman and T. P. Novak, "Marketing in Hypermedia Computer Mediated Environments: Conceptual Foundations," *Journal of Marketing* (July 1996).

iCAT White Paper, 1998, URL:http://www.imagesoftco.com/iCatWP.htm.

R. Kalakota and A. B. Whinston, *Readings in Electronic Commerce* (Reading, MA: Addison-Wesley, 1997).

W. Kassay, "Global Advertising and the World Wide Web," *Business Horizons* (May/June 1997).

A. M. Keller, "Smart Catalogs and Virtual Catalogs" in *Readings in Electronic Commerce*, by R. Kalakota and Andrew Whinston (Reading MA: Addison-Wesley, 1997).

D. Kosiur, *Understanding Electronic Commerce* (Seattle: Microsoft Press, 1997).

J. K. Lee, et al., "A Comparison Shopping Architecture Over Multiple Malls: The Meta-Malls Architecture," *Proceedings of the International Conference on Electronic Commerce '98*, Seoul, Korea, 149–54.

S. K. Lee, et al., "Customized Purchase Supporting Expert System: UNIK-SIS," *Expert Systems with Applications,* 11 (4:1996).

N. Meeker, *The Internet Advertising Report* (New York: Morgan Stanley Corporation, 1997).

Morgan Stanley's Web site (www.ms.com) in early January 1997.

T. P. Novak and D. L. Hoffman, "New Matrices for New Media: Toward the Development of Web Measurement standatds" *World Wide Web Journal,* (Winter 1997).

S. O'Keefe, *Publicity on the Internet* (New York: John Wiley & Sons, 1997).

Oracle, *ICS White Paper*, 1998, oracle.com/products/ics/html/ics_wp.htm.

D. Peppers, et al., *The One-to-One Fieldbook* (New York: Currency/Doubleday, 1999).

J. Sterne, *World Wide Web Marketing* (2nd ed.) New York: Wiley & Sons, 1999.

C. P. Taylor, "Is One-to-One the Way to Market?" *Interactive Week* (May 12, 1997).

E. Turban, et al., *Information Technology for Management*, 2ed. (New York: John Wiley & Sons, 1999).

J. Ubois, "The Art of the Audit," *Internet World* (December 1995).

C. Vinzant, "Electronic Books Are Coming at Last!" *Fortune* (July 6, 1998).

J. Ware, et al., *The Search for Digital Excellence* (New York: McGraw-Hill, 1998).

H. Williamson, "The Pull of Push," *Webmaster* (July 1997).

"World Watch: International Business/The Pacific," *Los Angeles Times* (May 30, 1996), p. 4D.

www.commerce.net: Digital Marketplace, 1998.

www.homebusinesssmart.com/promotion/promo07.htm.

www.internetnews.com: Internet Advertising report, 1998.

www.towson.edu/~crest/internet.htm.

www.2000.ogsm.vanderbilt.edu.

Y. Yuan, et al., "The Relationship between Advertising and Content Provisions on the Internet," *European Journal of Marketing* (July/August 1998).

CHAPTER 5

Electronic Commerce in Service Industries

Learning Objectives

Upon completion of this chapter, the reader will be able to:

- Understand how broker-based services are performed online.

- Describe online travel tourism services and their benefits.

- Discuss the impact of EC on the travel industry.

- Describe the online job market, its drivers, and benefits.

- Describe the electronic real estate market.

- Understand how stock trading is done online and its benefits.

- Discuss cyberbanking, its drivers, and capabilities.

- Discuss implementation issues of online financial services and their future.

- Describe electronic auctions, their benefits, implementation, and impacts.

- Describe some innovative applications in the service industries.

- Discuss the future of intermediaries and their role in cyberspace.

5.1 Ordering Journals Electronically

Universities and many other organizations order periodicals for their libraries constantly. New periodicals appear every day, people change their preferences, and the librarians are busy. Typically, a university will contact an agent to place the orders. The agent, who is in contact with hundreds of publishers, consolidates orders from several universities and then places orders with the publishers. This process is both slow and expensive for the library, which pays a 3 percent commission and loses a 5 percent discount that the publisher passes on to the agent.

In 1996, the University of California at Berkeley pioneered an electronic ordering system, which enabled the university to save about $365,000 per year. Furthermore, the ordering cycle time was cut by as much as 80 percent, providing subscribers with the magazines one to three months earlier.

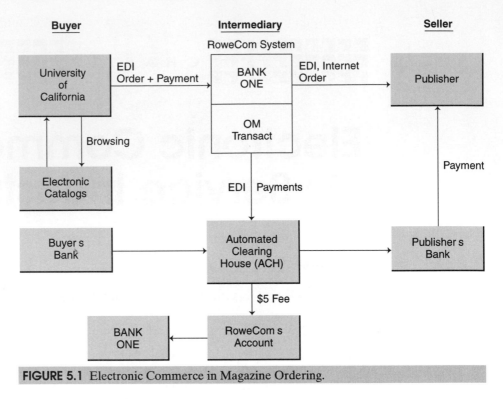

FIGURE 5.1 Electronic Commerce in Magazine Ordering.

RoweCom Inc. (www.rowe.com) manages the electronic ordering. Its software system, called Subscribe, enables a university to submit electronically its encrypted orders and a secure payment authorization to a central computer by EDI. The program verifies the order and the authorization, transfers the order by EDI to the publishers, and the payment authorization to the automated clearinghouse for EFT from the buyers' bank to the sellers' bank. The process is shown in Figure 5.1.

The cost to the university is $5 per order. For an average periodical with an annual subscription fee of $400, this ordering cost is more than 80 percent lower than if a human agent is used (5$ versus $32). The system includes BANK ONE managing software and EC back-office software called OM Transact from Open Market Inc. (chapter 11).

In 1999, the company offered over 43,000 magazines from more than 13,000 publishers, and more than 5 million books can be ordered by what is called Kstore. The company serves mostly organizations. Some of the benefits are lower cost, time savings, electronic renewals of notices, better subscription management, and easier interfaces.

5.2 Broker-Based Services

The opening vignette illustrates the use of EC in a **broker- (or agent) based service** and some of the potential benefits of EC as well as the changes that EC may introduce in existing business processes. Brokers usually work for a commission, acting as intermediaries between buyers and sellers of services. The buyers can be individuals or organizations. Some of the most notable services are travel agencies, job placement agencies, real estate agencies, insurance agencies, and stock market brokerages.

Agents basically make the markets. Some of the markets, such as stocks and travel, may be at nonnegotiated prices, but a variety of prices exist. Employment agencies basically match jobs with candidates, and real estate agents are involved in matching, negotiating, and contracting. The opening vignette showed a market for magazines that are offered at a fixed price.

Brokers provide many services. For example, travel agents are information brokers that pass information from product suppliers to customers. They also take and process orders, collect money, provide travel assistance (such as obtaining visas), and assist with insurance, possibly providing health and safety suggestions.

SERVICE INDUSTRIES VERSUS MANUFACTURING AND PRODUCT RETAILING

In chapter 1 we present a model that classified EC along three dimensions (Figure 1.1). As you may recall, we defined pure EC as a case where the product, the agent, and the process are all digital. When products are traded we can have pure EC only if we can digitize the product, such as in selling software or music. When we deal with a pure PC, the potential advantages are the greatest, since automating the entire process (including delivery) can result in a substantial cost reduction. When products are traded, the delivery must be physical in most cases, making pure EC impossible. However, when the service industry is concerned, pure EC can be used in most cases so that the savings are much larger than in selling most physical products.

Companies in the service industries, such as banks and stock brokerage houses, started to sell online even before the Internet. The major reason was the possible digitization of the entire process. At the beginning the vendors, such as banks, provided a disk with client software. The software, which the users installed on their PCs, provided the user with access to the vendor's database, over private lines, and later over the Internet. Later on the companies allowed their customers to download the software, instead of sending them a disk. Today, there is no need for the software, since the browser is used to fulfill all the functions necessary for the trade.

Similarly, at the beginning, travel and real estate agents provided data using their information systems, which were installed in their offices. They delivered information to the customers, but the customers had to come to the agent's office to view an online video clip or to see photos of a hotel or a house for sale. Today, such information is available anywhere and anytime over the Internet.

Electronic commerce provides customers with an opportunity to have a direct access to the providers of services or to superagencies. Thus, most of the value-added tasks of the agents or brokers can be automated. As more and more people use EC, different types of agencies will probably be the most endangered organizations, as their jobs are increasingly seen as being replaceable by technology. In this chapter we cover some of the major electronic agent-based services including travel, employment, and real estate. The chapter continues with a presentation of some related topics. Specifically, we look at electronic auctions (auctioneers can be viewed as agents) and at-home banking. We also provide examples of other online services. Finally, we discuss the future of intermediaries.

5.3 Travel and Tourism Services

The travel industry is expanding rapidly around the globe. Forrester Research Inc. predicts that by 2000, close to 25 percent of all B2C Internet commerce will be related to tourism. Any experienced traveler knows that good planning and shopping around can save a considerable amount of money. The same air ticket may have cost $400 or as much as $1,200. It is not uncommon to find people in a luxury hotel who have paid twice what others have for a similar room. The Internet is an ideal place to plan, explore, and arrange almost any trip. Potential savings are available through special sales and the elimination of travel agents by buying directly form the providers.

Some major Web sites are: www.expedia.com (affiliated with Microsoft) www.travelocity.com; and American Airlines, (using their Sabre reservation system); www.previewtravel.com; www.reservations.com; www.itn.net; www.thetrip.com; www.travelweb.com; www.priceline.com; and www.lonelyplanet.com. Services are also provided online by all major airlines' vacation services, large conventional travel agencies, car rental agencies, hotels (e.g., see www.bestwestern.com), and tour companies. Publishers of travel guides, such as www.fodors.com, provide considerable amounts of information on their Web sites.

SERVICES PROVIDED

If you open the Web page of AOL you will find "travel" on the main menu. By clicking on travel you will get some idea of the various services provided. The home page of a virtual travel agency, such as Expedia, tells you about some of the services available. You will note that some of the services are customized per the consumer's request.

Virtual travel agencies will offer you almost all the services you will find in a conventional travel agency, ranging from information to reservation and purchasing of tickets for your trips, accommodations, and entertainment. In addition to regular services, you will find services most conventional travel agencies do not offer, such as tips provided by people who have experienced certain situations (like a visa problem), electronic travel magazines, fare comparisons, currency conversion, **fare tracking** (free e-mail alerts on low fares to your favorite destinations), worldwide business and places locator, shopping for travel accessories and books, experts' opinions, major international and travel news, driving directions in the United States and several other countries (see www.status.com), chat rooms and bulletin boards, and frequent flier deals and personal milage. In addition, there are several other innovative services, which we discuss below.

Auctions, Bids, and Special Sales

American Airlines, Cathay Pacific, and Aer Lingus have been conducting online auctions in which passengers bid for tickets. American (www.americanair.com) auctions tickets to certain destinations at low-volume seasons. Cathay (www.cathay-usa.com) auctions tickets on competitive routes, showing current bids on its Web site. A limited amount of tickets sell for as much as half price. Aer Lingus (www.aerlingus.ie) auctions tickets that expire in a week or so. Special discount sales are available at all times. Several airlines offer last-minute discounts.

Priceline (www.priceline.com) asks you to specify a price you are willing to pay for airfare and/or accommodations. You must guarantee that you will buy what they find you at or below your price. Other airline companies allow you to bid only on certain types of tickets.

Virtual Community of Travel Fanatics

The *Conde Traveler* magazine created a Web site to leverage their brand name. They also use it for an Internet community of travelers (Champy et al. 1996).

BENEFITS AND LIMITATIONS

The benefits of online services to travelers are enormous. The amount of free information is tremendous and it is accessible anytime from any place. Substantial discounts can be found, especially if you have time and patience. You can take fantasy trips and get the feeling of being there. Soon, the addition of virtual reality will help you to enjoy virtual trips. You do not have to go to the travel agency and you can have lots of fun.

Online travel has its limitations. First, many people do not use the Internet. Second, Web sites want to sell, not to provide information. Therefore, the amount of time and the difficulty of using virtual travel agencies are not inconsequential. Finally, complex trips require specialized knowledge and arrangements, which must be done by a travel agent. Therefore, the need for travel agents as intermediaries is assured, at least in the immediate future. However, as we will show later, intelligent agents may lessen some of these limitations, reducing the reliance on travel agents.

CORPORATE TRAVEL

Corporations can use all the above services. However, many large corporations have additional special discounts arranged with travel agencies. To further reduce costs, companies can make arrangements that enable employees to plan and book their own trips. An example of such an arrangement is shown in Application Case 5.1.

APPLICATION CASE 5.1

Carlson Travel and American Express Automate Corporate Travel

Carlson Travel Network of Minneapolis is the largest travel agency in the United States. It provides an agentless service to corporate clients, the first of which was the General Electric Company. A computerized system allows GE employees to book trips by filling out a form on their PCs on GE's intranet. The system is available 24 hours a day. The intranet connects with the computer reservation system of major airlines, car rental companies, and hotel chains. The automated system enables GE to negotiate special rates for their employees. It also generates detailed spending reports. Complex travel itineraries are still handled manually, but they account for less than 5 percent of the total trips. The system saves GE several million dollars each year.

Carlson (www.carlson.com) is using IT to gain a competitive advantage over pure online agencies. It gives their human agents even more travel inventory than online shoppers can find anywhere else. They also use high-speed connections to integrate all the data and deliver it faster using superb communication networks, intranets, and extranets. Customers who are at a Carlson agent's site can get a callback within minutes. The company also offers unique "specials," such

as discounted unsold rooms from top hotels. Carlson believes that they have the most efficient way to distribute aggregated travel information. The company provides their corporate customers with travel management training in an attempt to make the customers dependent upon their services.

The corporate travel market is growing very rapidly. One new service is e-Travel, which provides software to automate and manage online booking. American Express teams with Microsoft and MCI to provide an interactive corporate travel reservation system called AXI, which displays airline seat charts, maps to hotels, information about nearby health clubs, and destination weather information. While trying to reduce cost to the corporate client, AXI creates a profile for each traveler and his or her preferences and, thus, tries to satisfy both travelers and the corporate travel managers. Both American Express and Carlson compete with the airlines and their travel companies. For example, Sabre Group Holding provides considerable discounts to corporations. Finally, the airlines themselves offer incentives to those who buy electronic tickets directly at the source.

THE IMPACT OF EC ON THE TRAVEL INDUSTRY

Electronic commerce, as shown in chapter 1, may have major effects on individual companies. These impacts can be combined for each company and then extended to an industry. Bloch and Segev (1997) analyzed the impact of EC on the travel industry using Porter's framework of competitive advantage (1985). According to Porter's model there are five forces that impact competition in any industry: new entrants, substitute product (or services), the bargaining power of buyers, the bargaining power of suppliers, and the rivalry of the competing companies in the industry. Bloch and Segev constructed an analysis framework that pertains to the travel industry. They first focus on the environment, then on competitive responses, and finally on one firm's strategy.

Such analysis could fit other industries but is especially suitable to the travel industry. (For a competitive analysis of the airline industry see Callon 1996.) As a matter of fact, the introduction of electronic tickets resulted in a significant commission cuts in 1998 and 1999. And, since 1995, there is a clear trend for fewer travel agencies. The business pressures described in chapter 1 are impacting the travel industry, which is one of the largest industries affected. The industry is clearly transformed by IT. The computerized airline reservation system is the largest nonmilitary information system, and this system is now accessible by customers directly via the Internet, taking away some functions traditionally performed by travel agents.

Bloch and Segev's analysis views the travel industry from a *supply* chain point of view (Figure 5.2). Four major actors are involved. Each of them can be classified into subcategories depending on the purpose of the travel (such as leisure or business) or the nature of the arrangement (like tours, individuals, or groups).

Reviewing some of the applications described earlier (like buying a ticket online or receiving information on low-cost tickets by push technology), Bloch and Segev identified impacts on the industry such as:

- Offering of lower-cost trips
- Providing a more personalized service
- Helping customers understand the products by using multimedia
- Saving money in a paperless environment
- Increasing the convenience of getting information at home
- Supporting a customer-focused strategy (such as targeted advertisement and integration of products)

These impacts may create opportunities for new products and/or vendors. An example is travel agencies online, such as Expedia (www.expedia.com). Other impacts related to intermediaries in general are discussed later in this chapter.

FIGURE 5.2 The Travel Industry Chain.

Source: Bloch and Segev (1997). Reproduced with permission of IEEE, ©1997.

APPLICATION CASE 5.2

Zeus Tours and Yacht Cruises Inc. Uses EC

Zeus is a relatively small, private travel company ($30 million annual sales) specializing in tours and cruises. The company uses the Net both as a marketing tool and as an interoffice bulletin board.

Zeus has been using IT for years. For example, it implemented multimedia CD-ROM to distribute cruise information to customers. Now it is using both the CD-ROM and the Net to supplement the traditional communication methods. Here is what the company is doing on the Web (www.zeustours.com):

- Sends Web-generated sales leads to 18,000 travel agents
- Continuously offers specials to individuals (honeymoon specials, seniors, two for the price of one, and so on)
- Places press releases on the Web site
- Makes bookings available online
- Provides communication via e-mail
- Makes extensive information available by country
- Makes customer comments about the company available
- Provides push-based service will be available

Source: Condensed from Rogers (1997) and from www.zeustours.com (1999).

Finally Bloch and Segev (1997) classify the EC impacts on the individual company in the travel industry into 10 categories ranging from product promotion to new products and new business models. They predict that travel agencies, as we know them today, will disappear. Only their value-added activities will not be automated, and these will be performed by a new breed of organizations. For example, they will serve certain targeted markets and customers (see Van der Heijdence 1995 and also the Carlson's application described earlier in this chapter, for details). Travel superstores, which will provide many products, services, and entertainment, could enter the industry, as well as innovative individuals who will operate from their homes. See Application Case 5.2 for an example of how a small tour company utilizes EC.

THE FUTURE

There is no doubt that EC will play an even greater role in the travel industry. One area that is very promising is that of intelligent agents.

An example of potential collaborating agents is provided by Bose (1996), who proposed a framework for automating the execution of collaborative organizational processes performed by multiple organizational members. The agents emulate the work and behavior of human agents. Each of them is capable of acting autonomously, cooperatively, and collectively to achieve the collective goal. The system increases organizational productivity by carrying out several tedious watchdog activities, thereby freeing humans to work on more challenging and creative tasks. Bose (1996) provides an example of a travel authorization process that can be divided into subtasks delegated to several intelligent agents.

Intelligent agents could be involved in buyer-seller negotiations as shown in the following scenario:

You want to take a vacation in Hawaii. You called a regular travel agent who was too busy; finally, he gave a plan and a price that you do not like. A friend told you to use an intelligent agent. Here is how it works:

- *Step 1.* You turn on your PC and enter your desired destination, dates, available budget, special requirements, and desired entertainment.

- *Step 2.* Your computer dispatches an intelligent agent that "shops around," entering the Internet and communicating electronically with the databases of airlines, hotels, and other vendors.
- *Step 3.* Your agent attempts to match your requirements against what is available, negotiating with the vendors' agents. These agents may activate other agents to make special arrangements, cooperate with each other, activate multimedia presentations, or make special inquiries.
- *Step 4.* Your agent returns to you within minutes, with suitable alternatives. You have a few questions; you want modifications. No problem. Within a few minutes, it's a done deal. No waiting for busy telephone operators and no human errors. Once you approve the deal, the intelligent agent will make the reservations, arrange for payments, and even report to you about any unforeseen delays in your departure.

How do you communicate with your agent? By voice, of course. This scenario is not as far off as it may seem. You will probably be able to do just that by 2001.

5.4 Employment Placement and the Job Market

The job market is one of the largest markets in the world where employers are looking for employees with specific skills and individuals are looking for a job. In a simplistic way we can view employees as selling their skills to organizations, frequently at a negotiated price. The job market is very volatile where the supply and demand are frequently unbalanced. Job matching is done in several ways, ranging from ads in classified sections of newspapers to the use of corporate recruiters and commercial employment agencies and headhunting companies.

Since the inception of the Internet, the job market has been moved to the Internet, where thousands of employment agencies operate, hundreds of thousands of employers advertise on their home pages, and an estimated 5 million job seekers (in 1999) place their résumés on the Internet.

DRIVING FORCES OF THE ELECTRONIC JOB MARKET

The following are some of the deficiencies of the *traditional* job market, in which most activity is conducted through newspaper ads.

1. Cost—classified ads are expensive.
2. Life cycle—unless renewed, at an additional cost, the life of the ads is days or weeks only.
3. Place—most ads are local. Nationwide ads are very expensive. International ads are even more expensive.
4. Minimum information—because of the high cost, the information provided is minimal and may not appeal to some job seekers.
5. Search—it is very time consuming to find all relevant available jobs or applicants. It is especially difficult to find information on jobs out of town.
6. Finding applicants—most job seekers, in the pre-Internet era, did not place ads about their availability. Some sent unsolicited letters with résumés. This situation made it difficult for companies to find employees with special skills. They had to use employment agencies and pay them high commissions.
7. Matching—it was difficult to match candidates to open jobs as well as to match supply and demand. Usually, it was done within a city or a country.

8. Lost and dated material—some applications or letters of response tended to get lost or arrive late. A letter in a big city may take two weeks to travel a few blocks.
9. Speed—communication by mail is slow and so is the processing of a large number of applications. Frequently, employers lost good employees, since by the time the application was processed, the applicant had taken another job. Similarly, applicants accept less desirable jobs because they are afraid to wait too long.

As a result, the traditional job market was inefficient.

THE INTERNET JOB MARKET

The Internet offers a perfect environment for job seekers and companies searching for hard-to-find employees. The job market is especially effective for technology-oriented jobs; however, there are thousands of other companies that advertise available positions, accept résumés, and take applications over the Internet. The job market is used by the following:

- *Job seekers.* Job seekers can reply to employment ads. Alternatively, they can take the initiative and place résumés on their own home pages or on others' Web sites, send messages to members of newsgroups asking for referrals, and use recruiting firms such as Career Mosaic (www.careermosiac.com/cm), Hot jobs (www.hotjobs.com), and Monster Boaral (www.monster.com). For entry-level jobs and internships for newly minted graduates, job seekers can use www.jobdirect.com. VaultReports.com offers information about 1,000 employers and 40 industries in New York City. It offers a free matching service.
- *Job offers.* Many organizations advertise openings on their Web site. Others use advertising. Possibilities range from others' popular sites to online services, bulletin boards, and recruiting firms. Employers can conduct interviews and administer tests on the Web.
- *Recruiting firms.* Thousands of job placement brokers are active on the Web. They use their own Web pages to post available job descriptions and advertise their services in e-malls and on others' Web sites. Recruiters use newsgroups, online forums, bulletin boards, Internet commercial résumé services, and providers such as CompuServe and AOL (see their E-Span service at www.espan.com).
- *Government agencies and institutions.* Government agencies advertise openings in the government as well as help job seekers to find jobs elsewhere, as is done in the Philippines (Application Case 5.3, pg. 166).

THE ADVANTAGE OF THE ELECTRONIC JOB MARKET

The Internet facilitates a solution to the nine market inefficiencies described earlier (See review question #20) The major advantages for job seekers are:

- Ability to find information on a large number of jobs worldwide
- Ability to communicate quickly with potential employers
- Ability to write and post résumés for large-volume distribution
- Ability to search for jobs quickly from any place at any time
- Ability to obtain several support services at no cost
- Ability to learn how to use your voice in an interview (www.greatvoice.com)

Web Site Matches Workers with Jobs in the Philippines

The Philippines is a country with many skilled employees but with few open jobs. In January 1999, the government created a special Web site that matches people with jobs. The site is part of the Department of Labor computerized project, and it is provided free. For those people who do not have computers or Internet access, the government created hundreds of kiosks located throughout the country. The system is also connected with Philippine embassies, especially in countries where there are many overseas Filipino workers, so they can find a job and return home.

Government employees help the applicants who do not know how to use the system. This gives them a chance to find a job that would best suit their qualifications. At the heart of the system is a matchmaking capability.

For the matchmaking process, a database stores all the job vacancies based on data fed in by different employers or companies. Another database stores the applications fed into the system. The system matches qualified applicants with companies. The system also automatically does a ranking based on the matches.

The job-matching feature differentiates this site from other online job sites. Everything is done electronically, so the results can be seen in seconds.

Source: Based on *Computerworld Hong Kong* (January 14, 1999).

For employer's the advantages are as follows:

- Ability to advertise to a large number of job seekers
- Ability to save on advertisement costs
- Ability to lower the cost of processing (using electronic application forms)
- Ability to provide greater equal opportunity for job seekers
- Ability to find highly skilled employees

See www.headhunter.net for extensive recruitment services.

THE LIMITATIONS OF THE ELECTRONIC JOB MARKETS

Probably the biggest limitation is the fact that many people do not use the Internet. This limitation is even more serious with non-technology-oriented jobs. To overcome the problem, companies may use both traditional approaches and the Internet. However, the trend is clear—over time, more and more of the job market is moving to the Internet.

Security and privacy may be another limitation. As we have discussed earlier, this limitation is diminishing with security improvements. The electronic job market may also accelerate people's movements to better jobs, resulting in high and expensive turnover. (To see what employers can do about that, refer to discussion question 14.)

EXAMPLES OF SERVICES ON THE NET

The following are the major services available on the net:

- *Finding a job.* Most sites offer lists of available jobs by location, by job classification, or by other criteria. A search engine is also provided by many sites. Once a job is found, an electronic application form can be filled out and a résumé can be attached and e-mailed.

- *Writing and posting résumés.* Several sites help you to write your résumé properly and then post it on the Web (for examples, see www.resume-link.com and www.jobweb.com). Using a personality test, www.discoverme.com matches candidates with jobs.
- *Career planning.* Career advice is also available on the Internet. Although personalized guidance by counselors (for a fee) is just starting to emerge, there are several Web sites that provide substantial information at no cost. For example, the Smart Business Supersite (www.smartbiz.com) provides links to many sources for further research, for accessing job listings, and for finding for-fee counselors. Comprehensive job sites include: www.career-path. com, which covers classified jobs from dozens of newspapers, and www.occ.com/.
- *Newsgroups.* Large numbers of newsgroups are dedicated to finding jobs (and keeping them). Here are some examples:

ba.jobs.contract	Issues involving contract employment
misc.job.misc	Discussion about employment, workplaces, careers
misc.jobs.offered	Announcements of available positions
misc.jobs.offered.entry	Job listings only for entry-level positions
misc.jobs.resumes	Postings of résumés and "situation wanted" articles
ba.jobs.misc	Discussions about the job market in the Bay Area
biz.jobs.offered	Position announcements
bionet.jobs.wanted	Requests for employment in the biological sciences
ba.jobs.resumes	Résumé postings for California Bay Area jobs
la.jobs	Los Angeles area job postings
www.aboutwork	A chat room and discussion group

EXAMPLE OF CAREER SERVICES ON THE NET

Internet Professional Association (now part of www.veriotexas.net) provides many services online including:

- *Recruiters Online Network.* A virtual association of recruiters, employment agencies, search firms, and employment professionals worldwide.
- *StaffNET.* A virtual association of firms and individuals engaged in contract (or interim) work, a fast-growing field.
- *Global employment network.* An association of search professionals engaged in international job search and placement.
- *Employment opportunities.* A listing for both individuals and organizations. Free to individuals posting résumés and to members of IPA.
- *The Intranet job market.* Many companies conduct an internal electronic job market. Openings are posted for employees to look at, and search engines enable managers to identify talents even if the people were not looking actively for a job change.

USING INTELLIGENT AGENTS

The large number of available jobs and résumés makes it difficult both for employers and employees to search the Net. Intelligent agents are used to solve this problem for both groups:

- *For employees.* A free service that searches the Internet's top job sites and databases for job postings based on users' profiles is offered at www.jobsleuth.com. Users can create as many as five different profiles based on more than 100 different job categories, geographic region, and key words. The users receive a daily e-mail containing job opportunities from over a dozen top job sites around the Internet (e.g., Career Mosaic), that match their career interests. This saves the users a tremendous amount of time.

- *For employers.* A special search engine helps employers to find resumes that match job descriptions written by employers. The search is done by intelligent agents as in the case of www.resumix.com. Here is how the company describes its product on its Web site:

"From the time a position becomes available or a resume is received, Resumix gives you the control while dispersing the work. Hiring managers can open jobs; operators can scan resumes; and you can search for a candidate or identify employees for training programs, redeployment opportunities, or new initiatives.

The core of this powerful system is Resumix's *Knowledge Base*. As an expert system, it goes beyond simply matching words. The Knowledge Base works for you to interpret a candidate's resume, determining their skills based on context, and matching those skills to the position criteria. For example, you might be looking for a Product Manager. Being a member of the American Marketing Association (AMA) might be one of the desirable skills for the job. However, with a basic keyword search, you might get candidates who have listed AMA but are really members of the American Medical Association or American Meatpackers Association. Not very relevant to your search. Resumix Knowledge Base would select only the condidates with relevant skills."

5.5 Real Estate: From Virtual Realtors to Virtual Reality

Real estate transactions are an ideal area for EC for the following reasons. First, you can view many properties on the screen, saving time for you and for the broker. Second, you can sort and organize properties according to your criteria and preview the exterior and interior design of the properties, shortening the search process. Finally, you can find detailed information about the properties and frequently get even more detailed real estate listings than brokers will provide. In some locations brokers allow the use of databases available only on private networks from their offices, but in many cities such information is available on the Internet from your home. For example, www.realtor.com allows you to search a database of over 1 million homes all over the United States. The database is composed of local multiple listings of all available properties and properties just sold in hundreds of locations. Cushman and Wakefield of New York also use the Internet for selling commercial property (Real World Case, end of this chapter).

Builders now use virtual reality technology on their Web sites to demonstrate three-dimensional floor plans to home buyers; "virtual models" enable buyers to "walk through" three-dimensional mock-ups of homes.

There are many innovative applications in the real estate market. One is presented in Application Case 5.4.

APPLICATION CASE 5.4

Finding Super Deals

In 1998, the rising real estate prices in southern California made it harder to find a really good deal. However, the foreclosure and trustee sale market presents an incredible opportunity, even for the inexperienced first-time buyer. There are 1,500 to 2,000 foreclosed properties every week in several price ranges and in many neighborhoods—the problem is how to find such information. Purchasing lists from government agencies, banks, and so on can be very expensive and hard to find. The solution is to go to the Web.

Visit the site of AM Holding (www.amholding.com) and you will find the daily notices of default and trustee sales listings. Users as well as brokers, real estate lawyers, banks, and financial institutions, can search for location, price range, and property type. The lists are very detailed and further information is available through links. The site provides a beginner's guide for those who have never tried it before. The monthly subscription cost is less than 25 percent of paper listings while the offerings and the services are much greater.

REAL ESTATE APPLICATIONS

The real estate industry is just starting to discover EC. Here are some services with representative Web addresses:

1. International Real Estate Directory and News is the most comprehensive web site at www.ired.com.
2. A national listing of real estate properties can be found at www.cyberhomes.com.
3. Go to www.comspace.com for a commercial real estate directory.
4. To assist you in buying or selling a home, try www.assist2sell.com.
5. For mortgage comparisons and calculations and other financing information or for mortgage applications, go to www.eloan.com; or www.iown.com.
6. If you are searching residential real estate in multiple databases see www.homescout.com or http://realestate.yahoo.com.
7. Real estate related maps are available on: www.mapquest.com and http://realestate.yahoo.com.
8. To automate the closing of real estate transactions, which is overwhelmed by paperwork, try www.datatrac.net.
9. The National Association of Realtors, www.realtor.com, has links to house listings in all major cities.
10. To find out how much of a house you can afford, consult www.replace.com.
11. Mortgage brokers can pass loan applications on the Net and receive bids from lenders that want to issue the mortgages.
12. To find mortgage interest rates online, use www. bankrate.com, www.eloan.com, or www.quickenmortgage.com.
13. To rent an apartment or a house, try www.rent.net. Several services are available including a virtual walk-through of some listings.
14. Loans are approved over the Web by several lenders, e.g., www.arcsystems.com.

Electronic Commerce can be useful not only to large companies but also to small ones as shown in Application Case 5.5.

How One Deal More than Paid for the Web Site of Colliers Arnold

Colliers Arnold is a commercial realtor in Florida (www.arnoldcompanies.com). To improve relationships with existing clients, the company established a Web site in 1995, posting demographic studies, press releases, and photos of available properties. The company was surprised to find out that it was immediately receiving 2,000 hits per day, but, like direct mail, only 5 inquiries were worth pursuing. This may result in substantial profit due to the large commission that can be generated even from one sale as in the case of Rockwell Corporation. Interested in leasing a property listed on the Web site, Rockwell sent an e-mail inquiry. Soon, a 5-year lease was signed, bringing Colliers a commission of $16,000, more than enough to pay back the $10,000 investment in the Web site.

Although the real estate industry was slow to use the Web, the situation is changing rapidly. Colliers is expanding its Web site, which includes information about specific areas' business climate, labor pool, consumer market, and transportation infrastructure. Most of the information is available free from local economic development agencies on Florida's southwest coast, where Colliers operates. Colliers closed several deals in addition to Rockwell, yet the company believes that the major benefit it derives is from providing customer service (discussion question 18).

Source: Condensed from B. Klein, "Florida Commercial Realtor Siphons 5 Web Leads a Day," *NETmarketing* (March 1997) http://netb2b.com.

In general, online real estate is supporting rather than replacing existing agents. Thousands of agents opened personal sites showing their listings. Due to the complexity of the process, real estate agents are still charging high commissions. However, several Web sites started to offer lower commission services. For example, see www.assistsell.com.

5.6 Trading Stocks Online

ONLINE STOCK TRADING

It is predicted that by 2002, more than 20 million people in the United States will trade stocks, bonds, mutual funds, and commodities online. Why is this so? It makes a lot of dollars and sense, that is why (Schonfeld 1998).

An online trade typically costs between $7 and $20 compared to an average fee of $100 from a full-service broker and $35 from a discount broker. There is no waiting on busy telephone lines, and the chance of making mistakes is small since there is no oral communication in a frequently very noisy environment. Orders can be placed from anywhere, any time, day or night, and there is no biased broker to push you. Furthermore, you can find a considerable amount of free information regarding investing in a specific company or in a mutual fund.

Several discount brokerage houses initiated extensive online stock trading, notably Charles Schwab, in 1995. Full-service brokerage companies such as Merrill Lynch, followed in 1998/1999. By 1999, there were more than 100 brokerage firms offering online trading. The volume of trading has increased significantly in the last three years, but the brokerage firms now need fewer employees.

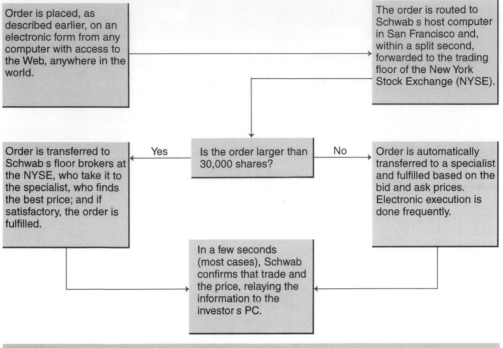

FIGURE 5.3 Trading Stocks Electronically.

How does online trading work? Let's say you have an account with Schwab. You access Schwab's Web site (www.schwab.com), enter your account number and password, and click on stock trading. Using a menu, you enter the details of your order (buy, sell, margin or cash, price limit, or market order). The computer tells you the current "ask" and "bid" prices, much as your broker would do over the telephone, and you can approve or reject the transaction.

The process your order goes through is illustrated in Figure 5.3. You may conduct the trade through a gateway such as AOL or Microsoft. Some well-known companies that offer online trading are E∗TRADE, Ameritrade, Waterhouse, Datek Online, Suretrade, Discover, and Lombard. E∗TRADE offers many services and also challenges you to participate in a simulated investment game (Internet exercise 8 in this chapter). For further details on brokers and services provided online, see chapter 8 in Farrell (1996).

Of the many brokers online, of special interest are Datek.com, which provides extremely fast executions, and webstreet.com, which charges no commissions on trades of 1,000 shares or more on NASDAQ. However, the most innovative service is that of E∗TRADE, whose home page is shown in Figure 5.4. Note that in early 1999, E∗⁼ TRADE started its own mutual funds online. E∗TRADE is expanding rapidly in several countries, enabling global stock trading.

INVESTMENT INFORMATION

There is almost an unlimited amount of information, mostly available for free, in many Web sites. Here are some examples:

- For municipal bond pricing, see www.bondmarkets.org.
- For overall market information and many links, see www.cyberinvest.com.

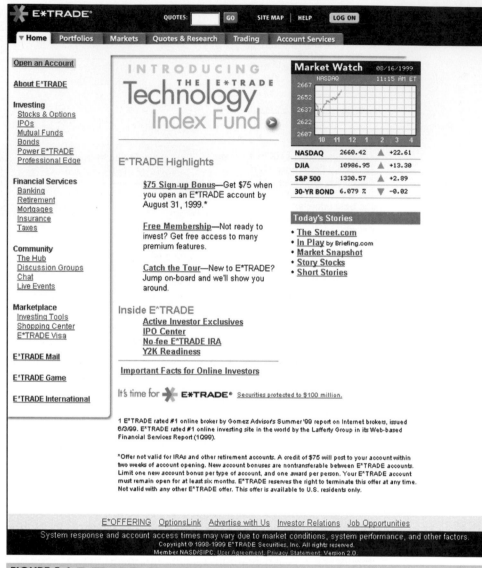

FIGURE 5.4 E∗TRADE's Home Page and Capabilities.

- For free Gurus' advice, see www.upside.com.
- For stock screening and evaluation, try www.marketguide.com.
- Articles from the *Journal of the American Association of Individual Investors* can be read on www.aaii.com.
- For reports on the latest findings and pricing of IPOs, go to www.ipocentral.com and www.ipodata.com.
- For chart lovers, try www.bigcharts.com.
- For mutual funds evaluation and other interesting investment information, see www.morningstar.net.
- Almost anything that you need will be provided to you by www.yahoo.com.
- Earning estimates and much more are found on www.firstcall.com.
- For current news and much more, try www.cnnfn.com.

Most of these services are provided free, together with financial news, global investment, portfolio tracking, investor education, and much more.

INITIAL PUBLIC OFFERINGS (IPOs) AND THE INTERNET

The first successful Internet IPO was that of a beer-making company called Spring Street Brewing. The owner created a special company, Wit Capital Corporation, to offer initial and secondary securities trading over the Internet. Several other successful offerings followed. For example, Internet Venture Inc. raised $5 million in the spring of 1998 (www.perki.net and www.ivn.net). Also, Direct IPO (www.directipo.com) is active in this area. Virtual Wall Street brings together investors and companies interested in raising capital via direct public offering (DPO) rather than using an underwriting syndicate. Auctions on IPOs are being conducted by www.openipo.com.

INDIVIDUAL INVESTORS AND DAY TRADING

As described in chapter 1, EC may have a major impact on both individual investors and day traders. Electronic commerce provides tools that enable some individuals to perform as good or even better than financial institutions. For possible impacts see Lim (1997).

RELATED MARKETS

In addition to stocks, online trading is expanding to include financial derivatives, commodities, mutual funds, and more. Futures exchanges around the world are positioning themselves for what many market participants now agree will be dominated by electronic trading.

Online trading is frequently combined with online banking, the topic of our next section.

5.7 Cyberbanking and Personal Finance

Electronic banking, also known as **cyberbanking,** virtual banking, home banking, and **online banking,** includes various banking activities conducted from home, business, or on the road, instead of at a physical bank location. Electronic banking has capabilities ranging from paying bills to securing a loan electronically. It started with the use of proprietary software and private networks but was not particularly popular until the emergence of the Web.

Electronic banking saves time and money for users. For banks, it offers an inexpensive alternative to branch banking and a chance to enlist remote customers. Many banks are beginning to use home banking, and some use EC as a major competitive

---

Cyberbanking at Wells Fargo

Wells Fargo is a large California-based bank (over 1,700 branches). The bank has been known for generations for its financial services, dating back to the days of the wild, wild West. Wells Fargo's declared competitive strategy is cyberbanking. They plan to move millions of customers to the Internet and close hundreds of branches. A visit to the Wells Fargo Web site (www.wellsfargo.com) indicates the richness of services available.

The services are divided into five major categories: online (personal) banking, personal finance services, small business, commercial banking, and international trade. In addition, there are employment opportunities and even shopping. The bank offers many services in all categories. Most interesting are the services that cover all the needs of small businesses, which are extremely user friendly and can run even on an old 386 computer. The bank also saves money for the customer by offering lower rates.

The bank facilitates shopping by offering a virtual mall in which you can buy from the Wells Fargo Museum Store.

---

strategy. One such bank is Wells Fargo, whose use of EC is described in Application Case 5.6. Overall, 7 million online bank accounts were open in 1999 (20 million are projected by 2002).

Some of the advantages of home banking are:

- *Get current account balances at any time.* You can easily check the status of your checking, savings, and money market accounts.
- *Obtain charge and credit card statements.* You can even set up your account to pay off cards automatically every month.
- *Pay bills.* Electronic payments from your accounts are normally credited the same day or the next. The cost of paying bills electronically may well be less than the postage involved in sending out a large number of payments each month.
- *Download account transactions.* It is easy to import them directly into a money management program such as "Quicken."
- *Transfer money between accounts.* No more waiting lines, deposit slips, and running to the ATM.
- *Balance your accounts.* If you are the kind of person who forgets to record ATM withdrawals, online banking may help you get organized. Just download the transactions and import them into your register.
- *Send e-mail to your bank.* Got a problem with your account? You can send a quick note to your online bank representative.
- *A new meaning for "banker's hours."* You can manage your money and bills on your own schedule.
- *Handle your finances when traveling.* You can access accounts when you are on the road and even arrange for bill payments to be made while you are gone.
- *Additional services.* Customers of some banks, receive free phone banking with their online banking service, all for a $6.95 monthly fee. Union Bank of California throws in free checking, ATM withdrawals, and bill paying (for one year). Several banks, including Bank of America, waive your regular checking charges if you sign up for online banking.

Electronic banking offers several of the benefits listed in chapter 1, both to the bank and to its customers, such as expanding the customer base and saving the cost of paper transactions (Mahan 1996). In addition to regular banks that are adding online services, we see the emergence of virtual banks solely dedicated to Internet transactions. The Security First Network Bank (SFNB) was the first such bank offering secure banking transactions on the Web (www.sfnb.com). The home page looks like the lobby of a bank. The bank offers savings and checking accounts, certificates of deposit, money market accounts, joint accounts, check imaging, and other services. To attract customers, SFNB offers relatively high interest yields for CDs and money market accounts and allows access to information from various locations. If you have an account with your parents, for example, and you are away from home, both you and your parents can view the account and add or withdraw funds. You can transfer money between accounts, review past statements and credit card transactions, pay bills, check balances in all your accounts and credit cards, and calculate the interest to be paid on loans and credit cards. In March 1998 SFNB sold its online banking operations to Royal Bank of Canada. The Canadian bank needs the online services to serve its customers while they are vacationing in the United States. SFNB created a software company, which is marketing the online banking software to many banks.

Other virtual banks are www.netbank.com and www.compubank.com. It is interesting to note that banks are involved in stock trading (for examples, see www.bank.com) while stockbrokers are doing banking (for example, see E*TRADE.com). (Before sending money to any cyberbank, especially those that promise high interest rates for your deposits, make sure that the bank is a legitimate one. Several cases of fraud have already occurred.)

International and Multiple-Currency Banking

International banking and the ability to handle trading in multiple currencies is critical for international trades. Although some international retail purchasing can be done by giving your credit card number, other transactions may require international banking support. Two examples of such cross-border support follow.

1. **Hong Kong Bank** has developed a special system called HEXAGON to provide electronic banking in Asia. Using this system, the bank has leveraged its reputation and infrastructure in the developing economies of Asia to become a major international bank rapidly, without developing an extensive new branch network. For details see Peffers and Tannanainen (1998).
2. **Mark Twain Bank** in the United States is using electronic cash to support trading in 20 foreign currencies. Teamed with DigiCash, the bank attracts international traders. For details, see www.marktwain.com.

Bank of America and most other major banks offer international capital raising, cash management, trades and services, foreign exchange, risk management investments, merchant services, and special services for international traders. Of special interest is Next Card (www.nextcard.com). You can apply online for a credit card, in one minute find out if you qualify, and get a card number in 30 seconds. Furthermore, NextCard can show you the balances on your other credit cards—automatically, once you have been approved, without even asking you for the cards' numbers.

IMPLEMENTATION ISSUES IN BANKING AND ONLINE TRADING

The implementation of banking and online trading are interrelated, and in many instances we can see that one financial institution offers both services. Here are some implementation issues.

Securing Financial Transactions

Financial transactions such as home banking and online trading must be highly secured. In chapter 8, we discuss the details of securing EC payment systems. In Application Case 5.7, we provide an example of how Bank of America provides security and privacy to their customers.

Using the Extranet

Many banks allow their large business customers more personalized service by allowing them access to the bank's intranet. One example, NationsBank Corporation, allows its customers access to accounts, historical transactions, and any other related data, including Intranet-based decision support applications, which may be of interest to the customers. NationsBank also allows its small-business customers to apply for loans through its Web site (www.nationsbank.com/smallbiz).

APPLICATION CASE 5.7

Security at Bank of America Online

Bank of America (B of A) provides extensive security to its customers. Here are some of the safeguards provided by the bank:

1. Customers accessing the system from the outside must go through encryption provided by SSL and digital certification verification (chapter 8). The certification assures you that each time you sign on you indeed are connected to the Bank of America. Then the message goes through an external firewall. Once the logon screen is reached, a user ID and a password are required. This information flows through a direct Web server, then goes through an internal firewall to the application server.

2. The bank keeps the information accurate; corrections are made quickly.

3. Information is shared only for legitimate business purposes among the company's family of partners. Sharing information with outside companies is done with extreme care.

4. The bank does not capture information provided by customers, conducting "what-if" scenarios using the bank's planning tools.

5. The company uses "cookies" to learn about the customers. However, customers can control both the collection and use of the information.

6. The bank provides suggestions on how to increase security (e.g. "use a browser with 128-bit encryption").

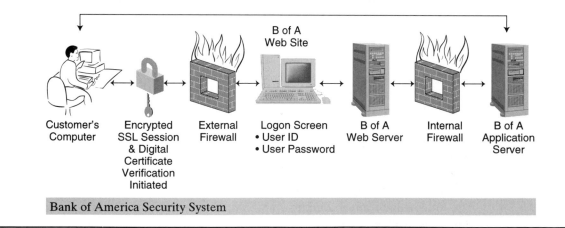

Bank of America Security System

Imaging Systems

Several financial institutions (NationsBank, for example) allow customers to view images of all incoming checks, invoices, and other related online correspondence. Image access can be simplified with the help of a search engine.

Pricing Online versus Offline Services

Computer-based banking services are offered free by some banks, while others charge $5 to $10/month. Also, there is a problem of how to price individual transactions (such as fee per check, per transfer, and so on). Some banks offer the same fees while others offer either higher or lower fees. For a discussion of this topic see Kingson (1997).

The Future of Banking

A 1998 study by the Boston Consulting Group (BCG), titled "The Information Superhighway and Retail Banking," painted a challenging picture for today's banking institutions. Rapid obsolescence will be the norm in the immediate future, since the online transaction cost can be as low as 1 percent of an offline one. Therefore, it is necessary to have a successful online banking strategy that will depend on factors such as:

- building alliances quickly with banks, software vendors, and information providers.
- effective outsourcing without neglecting to build in-house skills, particularly with respect to customer information systems;
- focusing on the profitable customer to provide broad channels for services and products;
- keeping a central role in the payment environment.

The study suggests that banks have three core strategies to pursue. They can become one of three types: customers' agents, product manufacturers, or integrated players.

Customers' agents. There will be a number of banks that will see themselves as unable to achieve economies of scale due to disadvantages in product manufacturing and processing. In many cases they may choose to leave that part of the business. Consistent with this option would be a strategy to offer customers the widest possible choice, including products from multiple sources, and to provide the customer with information-integrated services.

Product manufacturers. Conversely, some banks will see themselves as able to achieve economies of scale in product development, manufacturing, and processing and may choose to position themselves as either a branded or unbranded wholesaler of product and processing services. According to Bobby Mehta, vice president, the Boston Consulting Group, "The onset of online banking will strengthen a trend that can already be seen in a number of product segments (residential mortgages and credit card issuance) and in core processing services for small and medium-sized institutions."

Integrated players. Remaining as integrated players will be an option only for banks with a strong brand as well as a strong position from manufacturing to delivery. The study states "the banks may determine that if they sold third party products to increase choices for their customers, sales would not increase sufficiently to off-set lost margins. An example of such a player from outside banking is Fidelity Investments, although even such a strong player is bowing to customer demand for choice through its Funds Network offering." In the medium term, say the authors, many banks will adopt a hybrid strategy, but every player needs to make crucial decisions about which areas are strategically too risky to outsource and which capabilities need to be built up in-house.

Personal Finance Online

Banking can be beneficial to both businesses and individuals. Individuals often combine home banking with portfolio management and personal finance. Also, brokerage firms such as Schwab offer such personal finance services as retirement planning. However, specialized personal finance vendors offer more diversified services (Tyson 1997). For example, both Quicken (from Intuit) and Money (from Microsoft) offer many calculators and the following capabilities:

- Bill paying and electronic check writing
- Tracking bank accounts, expenditures, and credit cards
- Portfolio management, including reports and capital gains (losses) computations
- Investment tracking and monitoring of securities
- Quotes and tradeline historical and current prices
- Budget organization
- Record keeping of cash flow and profit and loss computations
- Tax computations and preparations (e.g., try www.jacksonhewitt.com and www.taxlogic.com)
- Retirement goals, planning, and budgeting

Although Quicken is the most popular personal finance software, there are more sophisticated packages, such as Wealth Builder (from Reuters) and CAPTOOL (from TechServe). All of these products are available as independent software programs for the Internet or are coupled with other services such as those offered by AOL.

BILLING ONLINE

In August 1998, 90 percent of people surveyed in the Bay Area in California indicated a desire to pay bills on the Internet. Mostly people prefer to pay online monthly bills, such as telephone, utilities, credit cards, cable television, and so on. The recipients of such payments are even more eager than the payers to receive money online since they can reduce processing costs significantly.

The following are the major existing payments systems:

- *Automatic payment of mortgage payments.* This method has existed for several years. The payee authorizes its bank to pay the mortgage, including tax and escrow payments.
- *Automatic transfer of funds to pay monthly utility bills.* Since fall 1988, the city of Long Beach has allowed its customers to pay their gas and water bills automatically from their bank accounts. Many other utilities worldwide provide such an option.
- *Paying bills from online banking accounts.* Such payments can be made into any bank account. Many people pay their monthly rent and other bills directly into the payee's bank accounts. Many utilities provide for online payment or plan to do so soon.
- *A merchant-to-customer direct billing.* Under this model, a merchant like American Express, posts bills on its Web site, where customers can view and pay them. This means that the customers have to go to many Web sites to

pay all the bills. Several utilities in Los Angeles allow customers to pay bills on the utilities' Web site, charging customers 20 cents per transaction, which is less than the price of a stamp.

• *Using an intermediary.*   According to this model, a third party like MSFDS (Microsoft and First Data Corporation) consolidates all bills related to each customer in one site and in a standard format. Collecting a certain commission, the intermediary makes it convenient both to the payee and payer to complete transactions. This latest model is of interest to many vendors, including E∗TRADE and Intuit.

5.8   Auctions: From Theory to Practice[1]

Auctions, an established method of commerce for generations, deal with products and services for which the conventional marketing channels are ineffective or inefficient. They can expedite the disposal of items that need liquidation or quick sale, they offer trading opportunities for both buyers and sellers that are not available in the conventional channels, and they assure prudent execution of contracts.

The Internet provides an infrastructure for executing auctions much cheaper, with many more involved sellers and buyers. Individual consumers and corporations alike can participate in this rapidly growing and very convenient form of electronic commerce. The Internet auction industry is projected to reach $52 billion in sales by 2002.

TYPES OF AUCTIONS

There are several types of auctions, each with its motives and procedures. Klein (1997) classified them into four major categories as shown in Table 5.1.

Traditional auctions, regardless of their type, have several limitations. For example, they generally last only a few minutes or even seconds for each item sold. This rapid process may give potential buyers little time to make a decision, so they decide not to bid; therefore, sellers may not get the highest possible price, and bidders may not get what they really want, or they pay too much. Also, in many cases, the bidders do not have much time to examine the goods. Since bidders must usually come to the auction site, many potential bidders are excluded. Similarly, it may be complicated for sellers to move goods to the auction site. Commissions are fairly high, since a place needs to be rented, the auction needs to be advertised, and the auctioneer and other employees need to be paid. Electronic auctioning removes these deficiencies.

ELECTRONIC AUCTIONS

Electronic auctions have been in existence for several years. Notable are the auctioning of pigs in Taiwan and Singapore (Neo 1992), cars in Japan and the auctioning of flowers in Holland, which was computerized in 1995 (Kambil and vonHeck 1998), but these were done on local area networks. Auctions on the Internet started in 1995. They are similar to offline auctions, except that they are done on a computer. Host sites on the Internet act like a broker, offering services for sellers to post their goods for sale and allowing buyers to bid on those items. Most auctions open with a starting bid, which is the lowest price the seller is willing to accept. Detailed information on every item for sale is available online. For high-value items, additional information may be obtained by e-mail. Bidders look at the descriptions and then start the bidding

---

[1] This section is based on Turban (1997).

TABLE 5.1 Motives of the Participants in Different Auction Types

Auction Type	Coordination mechanism	Price discovery	Allocation mechanism	Distribution mechanism
Buyer role	Short-term acquisition of resources, e.g., for demand peaks, auction as a mechanism to achieve an equilibrium	Often experts/professional collectors trying to acquire rare items at a reasonable price	Bargain hunting, gambling motive	Bargain hunting, gambling motive; possible side motive: charity
Supplier role	Short-term allocation of resources, load balance	Exposing items for sale to a charity sufficient breadth of demand, hope for a high price	Clearance of inventory	Attention, direct sales channel, public relations; possible side motive: charity
Auctioneer/ Intermediary role	Often electronic auction without auctioneer	Achieve high breadth and depth of the auctions, high trading volume results in high returns, competitive advantage over other auctions	Achieve high breadth and depth of the auctions, high trading volume results in high returns, competitive advantage over other auctions	Limited role because of supplier-buyer relation; possible function as service provider for the supplier side

Source: Klein (1997), p. 4. Used by permission.

by sending an e-mail or filling out an electronic form. The biddings, which may last for a few days, are shown on a page at the host's Web site and updated continually to show the current highest bids. Names of bidders are kept coded to maintain privacy. Most auctions are live; you compete in real time against others.

Many sites have certain etiquette rules that must be adhered to in order to conduct fair business. Haggle Online (www.haggle.com), which allows private individuals to put up their merchandise for sale (free of charge, summer 1998), has a page dedicated to rules for users.

There are several auctioning methods (see list at www.onsale.com). For example, some auctions use a "straight sales" method. The price for the good is listed and the first approved bidder gets the item at the listed price. In many cases the "Yankee method" is used in which sellers usually offer several identical items simultaneously. Bidding increases incrementally and the items are sold to the highest bidders. In the Dutch (or reversed) auction, prices decline until a buyer makes a bid (go to KlieKloc.com for gold and jewelry sales). Bid.Com International of Ontario Canada patented the Dutch (declining-price) auction technology.

Most auctions are open to the public. Items auctioned frequently are computers and other electronic parts, artwork, antiques, rare coins, vacation packages, airline tickets, and many other products. The www.usaweb.com site provides a search engine, Bidfind, where you type in the item you are looking for and the engine lets you know in what sites the item is auctioned. Some auctions are open only to dealers. These include used cars and foreclosed real estate sold by the U.S. government. There were about 500 companies doing auctions in 1999 on the Internet (a representative list is available at www.usaweb.com/auction.html). In 1999, Amazon.com and Dell Computers entered the auction business as well. Also, 3rd party companies, such as auction universe and itrack, monitor auction sites for customers (for free).

BENEFITS AND LIMITATIONS

Auctions allow individual sellers or companies to sell their goods efficiently and with little action or effort required. The sellers only need to enter the information about their merchandise into a form and send it to the host. After that, the auctioneer does all of the work. This creates a greater range of potential buyers. Extra cash can be earned and excess inventories can be sold quickly through this process. The main benefit to buyers is that they can get a huge variety of goods, especially collectibles and antiques that are not available locally. Also, buyers can find quality goods for largely discounted prices. This creates an opportunity for companies to have an additional channel of marketing.

The major limitations of online auctions are the inability to physically see the items and the possibility of fraud. Also, in many online auctions, a less competitive atmosphere may prevail on the Net since the elapse time is much longer. Finally, according to the FBI, there is more fraud in online auctions than in any other activity on the Internet.

IMPACTS

Some of the impacts of electronic auctions are presented in Figure 5.5. The figure shows the components of the auctions, the participants, and the process. The impacts are summarized in Table 5.2.

Some interesting auction sites are: www.onsale.com, www.auction.net, www.auction-web.com, www.bidfind.com (search engine), www.auctionhunter.com, www.ebay.com, www.winebid.com, www.ubid.com, www.firstauction.com, www.cityauction.com. The online software vendor www.egghead.com operates auctions as well.

Since many of the auction sellers are unknown, it is necessary to check the reliability of the auction sites. Also, one may want to use escrow services, such as www.tradesafe.com and www.iescrow.com, to assure quality and deliveries.

BUSINESS-TO-BUSINESS AUCTIONS

While most people are aware of B2C auctions, there are large numbers of auctions that are B2B in nature. Some companies use auctions to liquidate surpluses or obsolete material others use it as an additional marketing channel.

FIGURE 5.5 The Components of Auctions.

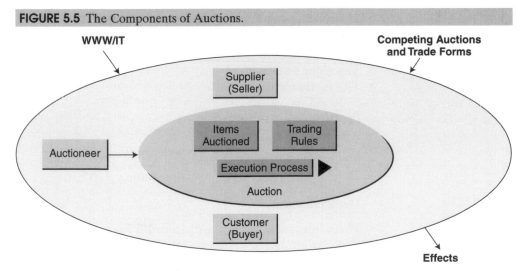

Source: Modified from Klein (1997), p. 4.

TABLE 5.2 Summary of Impact Areas

Parameter	Impact of the Web
Auctioneer	Lower entry barriers; opportunity for direct sales.
Access rules	Customizable; theoretically millions of potential customers can be reached.
Items auctioned	Focused product segments can be auctioned off; the technology extends the complexity of the product description.
Trading rules	The trading rules reflect the lack of a guaranteed service.
Execution process	For digital products the entire trading cycle can be handled on the Web; for physical products the trading process and the physical logistics of the trade objects can be separated, leading to a reduction of costs.

Source: Modified from Klein (1997), p. 5.

Two B2B auction models are emerging: third-party auction sites, which take a business's surplus goods on consignment and sell them to the highest bidder, and auctions that are added on to a business's EC site. Initially, auctions on both types of sites focused on selling computer equipment. For more on B2B auctions see chapter 6.

Independent sites, such as one run by FairMarket, Inc. (www.fairmarket.com), provide value by promoting their sites, drawing a larger crowd of bidders, and boosting sale prices. On the other hand, auctions at computer reseller Ingram Micro Inc. (www.ingram.com) are open only to existing customers. They are designed to cement relationships between the company and its traditional buyers.

Both sites tout the same cost-saving advantages; however, instead of getting roughly 8 cents on the dollar selling pallets full of out-of-date but still functional software and hardware to brokers, vendors can get closer to 50 percent of the wholesale price auctioning each item to individual users.

There are advantages and disadvantages to both auction models.

Third-Party Auction Sites
Advantages:

- Auction is open to more buyers, which can lead to higher prices.
- The seller does not have to develop a new sales channel.

Disadvantages:

- The seller loses control.
- The auction site takes a fee.

Proprietary Auction Sites
Advantages:

- Customers realize deep discounts.
- The company can make substantial money.

Disadvantages:

- There is a cost associated with the establishment and maintenance of a site.
- Skills to attract an audience and to keep auctions running need to be acquired.

5.9 Online Publishing, Knowledge Dissemination, and Other Services

Many other services are available on the Internet. In this section we will briefly discuss online publishing, knowledge dissemination, and other services.

ONLINE PUBLISHING

Online publishing is the electronic delivery of newspapers, magazines, news, and other information through the Internet. It is often related to advertisement since it is provided free in most cases, to attract people to certain sites where advertisement is conducted.

Developed in the late 1960s, online publishing was designed to provide online bibliographies and selling knowledge that was stored in online databases. Publicly funded online publishing originated for the purpose of medical, educational, and aerospace research programs Today, online publishing has different purposes. It is related to worldwide dissemination of information and to advertisement as well. The potential of new interactive technologies and other Internet applications aided the growth of online publishing.

Since 1995, some organizations have learned to use online publishing for gaining competitive advantage and market share. However, this was not always the case. Other organizations did not understand customer behavior regarding the uses of online publishing as a business tool. High technology without proper and impressive content was not enough to attract and retain customers' attention. Business organizations eventually realized that paying attention to the customers' needs and wants was an important factor in making online publishing a business tool.

Online Publishing Today and Tomorrow

One of the oldest examples of disseminating information by online publishing is the publishing of scholarly works for peer review. Today, online publishing is mainly used for disseminating information and for conducting sales transactions interactively. Magazine and newspaper publishers such as *Ad Week, PC Magazine, The Wall Street Journal*, and *The Los Angeles Times* are examples of the uses of online publishing for the dissemination of information. In the future, online publishing will include more customized material that the reader will receive free or will pay for.

Publishing Modes and Methods

Online publishing includes newspapers, magazines, news, textbooks, music, artwork, video clips, and movies. Several online publishing methods are in use. They include the online archive approach, new medium approach, publishing intermediation approach, and dynamic or just-in-time approach.

The *online archive approach* is a digital archive such as library catalogs and bibliographic databases. It basically makes paper publications available online. The *new medium approach* is used by those publishers that view the Web as a medium for creating new material. This form of publishing adds extra comprehensiveness to any issue or topic that traditional magazine publishing cannot offer. One way that the new medium does this is through its ability to integrate hypertext links that offer related stories, topics, and graphics. It also can be easily customized. The new medium approach also offers up-to-date material including breaking news. An example is HotWired (www.hotwired.com), which complements a paper version of *Wired Magazine*.

The *publishing intermediation approach* can be thought of as an online directory for news services. Publishing intermediation is an attempt to help people locate goods, services, and products online. Netscape provides services that are an example of this approach. The *dynamic* or *just-in-time approach* is another method of online publishing. With this approach content can be created in real time and transmitted on the fly in the format best suited to the user's location, tastes, and preferences. What makes dynamic publishing so "dynamic" is its ability to customize the content transmission of its Web pages to satisfy the users' preferences. The just-in-time portion of this approach refers to the ability to allow Java's applets and planned content to stream into the user's computer as they are needed and then destroy themselves once their function is no longer necessary.

Edutainment

Online publishing has also grown into other areas of usage with concepts such as edutainment and push technology. **Edutainment** is a combination of education, entertainment, and games. One of the main goals of edutainment is to make the student become an active learner instead of a passive one. With active learning a student is more involved in the experience of learning and, therefore, it makes the learning experience richer and the knowledge gained more memorable. The idea behind edutainment is that it is a type of embedded learning. It helps students to learn without them knowing it. Edutainment covers various subjects for the active learner, such as mathematics, reading, writing, history, and geography. Edutainment games are targeted to varying age groups ranging from three-year-olds to adults and is also used in corporate training over intranets. Examples of edutainment vendors are Broaderbound Software Inc. and Software Toolworks.

There are managerial issues to consider with edutainment in online publishing. Educational games are delivered mostly as CD-ROMs. However, since 1998 there is an increasing number of companies that offer edutainment online in a distance-learning format.

KNOWLEDGE DISSEMINATION

Online publishing is closely related to the concept of knowledge dissemination, which can be done in several ways. In this section we briefly look at two applications: virtual teaching and online consulting.

Virtual Teaching and Universities

The concept of **distance learning,** or learning at home, is not new. Educational institutions have been offering correspondence degrees for decades. Lately, IT in general and the Web in particular expanded the opportunities for distance learning. The concept of open universities or **virtual universities** is expanding rapidly, and hundreds of thousands of students in dozens of countries from Great Britain to Israel to Thailand are studying in such institutions (see McIlvaine 1997). Some universities, such as California State University at Domingaz Hills, offer hundreds of courses and degrees to students in a dozen countries. Other universities are offering limited courses and degrees but use innovative teaching methods and multimedia support (Application Case 5.8).

The virtual university concept allows universities to offer classes worldwide. Moreover, we may soon have integrated degrees, where students, customizing a degree that will best fit their needs, will be able to take courses at different universities.

The concept of online learning is shown in Figure 5.6. Notice the diversified forces that create the need for online learning.

APPLICATION CASE 5.8

Interactive MBA at City University of Hong Kong

As of May 1999 students in Hong Kong can study for their MBA any time, anywhere, and at any pace. This unique program integrates two technologies—the Web and interactive television. The objective of the program is to provide participants with a hi-tech-based, innovative and interactive learning experience to improve their managerial and professional competence. The program is composed of 17 standard courses: 8 core courses, 6 advanced, and 3 integrated. Each course includes 45 lecture hours delivered on an interactive television (iTV), (TV on demand). The students choose what lecture to watch and when they want to watch it. In addition to the lectures, all support material, exercises, and so on are provided on the Web. The students can interact electronically with the instructors and with each other, using e-mail and chat rooms. The program is supported by Hongkong Telecom, which provides broadband access service at 1.5 Mbps download speed (about 30 times the speed of a fast regular modem). For details about the program and the technology, check   www.itvhk.com/broadband/special   and www.imba.cityu.edu.hk.

This innovative program includes high-quality television videos. Web-based interactive discussions on course topics facilitated online by instructors and tutors and hyperlinked multimedia course materials (including video footage of course lectures) allow for immediate feedback.

FIGURE 5.6 Education as Electronic Commerce: Forces Driving the Transition.

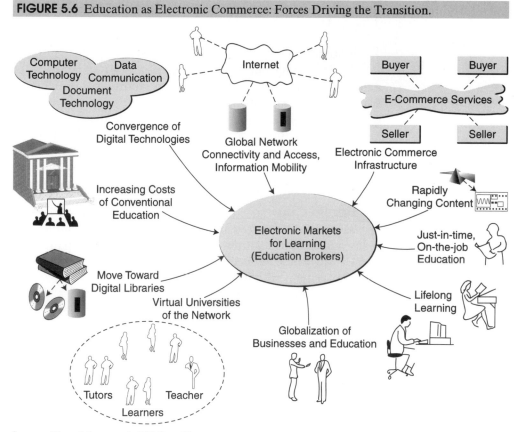

Source: Hamalainen et al. (1996), p. 30.

Online Consulting

This is a rapidly growing field in which tens of thousands of experts of all kinds sell their expertise, for a relatively low price, on the Internet. Here are some examples:

- *Medical advice.* Companies such as www.mediconsult.com, provide consultation with top medical experts. You can ask specific questions and get an answer from a specialist in a few days.
- *Management consulting.* Many consultants are selling their accumulated expertise from knowledge bases. A pioneer in this area is Anderson Consulting (www.knowledgespace.com; Internet Exercise 7). Such services are used mainly by corporations due to the high service fees.

Delivery of *legal advice* by consultation services to businesses has considerable prospects. For example, Atlanta-based law firm Alston & Bird coordinates counsel with 12 law firms for a large health-care company and many other clients. The company created a knowledge base that contains the best practices information. This information is available to law firms. Many lawyers offer inexpensive consulting services online. However, be careful; some of them may not give you the right advice.

Many companies offer extensive *financial advice.* For example, Merrill Lynch Online (http://askmerrill.com) provides free access to the firms research reports and analysis.

OTHER SERVICES ONLINE

There are thousands of unique services online. The following illustrative examples are discussed below.

Insurance

An increasing number of companies offer standard insurance policies such as auto, home, life, or health at a substantial discount. Furthermore, services offer free comparisons of what is available. Several large insurance and risk management companies offer insurance contracts online. While many people do not trust the faceless insurance agent, others are eager to take advantage of the reduced premiums. For example, a visit to www.insurerate.com will show a variety of services offered online. A 1998 study by www.forrester.com estimated total online insurance sales will reach over $1.1 billion in 2002. This figure seems to be very conservative.

Health Care

Many health services are provided online, for example, www.officemed.com provides information regarding eligibility, inquiry, and patient referral transaction services. Using these services, providers are able to perform secure, interactive health-care transactions with insurance payers.

Healtheon Corp, (www.healtheon.com) created a virtual health-care network linking health-care information systems and supporting enrollment, eligibility, referrals, and authorized laboratory and diagnosis test ordering, clinical retrieval, and claim processing. Medtel (www.medtel.com) offers a variety of services in the telemedicine field.

Future Exchanges

Future exchanges around the world are moving to electronic trading. For example, the Chicago Board of Trade, the world's largest futures exchange, is offering full-time electronic trading.

Matchmaking

Many of the previous services can be classified as agentbased, where agents play the role of matchmaker. Some more examples follow.

Several Web sites provide venture capital or information about it. The site www.garage.com matches potential investors with entrepreneurs.

College Edge Match Maker matches potential students with colleges and universities based on size, location, sport offered, degree sought, and more. It provides all the information including application forms (http://excite.collegeedge.com/matchmaker/match.asp). (Search: college matchmaker).

Match.com (www.match.com) is an online matchmaking service serving the singles community with chat rooms, bulletin boards, and more.

Digital Delivery of Documents

Delivering documents online in a secure environment is a new business offered by the U.S. Postal Service, United Parcel Service (UPS), and small companies such as e-Parcel (www.eparcel.com). For example, UPS offers door-to-door secure document delivery using 128-bit encryption and software for digital signature, authentication, and notarization and nonrepudiation (chapter 8). The secured service requires a UPS client computer at each end of the transaction. Another product (called Courier) is less secured and can move documents between any two computers. In effect, the delivery company is used as a third-party trusted service. E-Parcel offers certified electronic delivery service as of 1999. It is interesting to note that FedEx decided not to offer such a service (of course, they may change their mind later).

Electronic Stamps

There is no need to go to the post office to buy stamps any more as www.estamp.com will allow you to securely download postage straight from the Web. Users store the postage on their PC, and print out the equivalent of stamps in any denomination on envelopes or packages. Other companies that sell stamps are www.stampmaster.com and Pitney Bowes Inc., who controls the traditional postage meter market. The U.S. Postal Service favors the electronic stamps since they include better antifraud safeguards. Compaq Computer Corp. delivers the required technology on some of their PCs; most of the customers are expected to be businesses.

5.10 The Impact on Intermediaries and Their Changing Roles

Intermediaries traditionally provided trading infrastructure (such as a sales network), and they managed the complexity of matching buyers' and sellers' needs. The introduction of EC resulted in the automation of many of the tasks provided by the intermediaries. Does this mean that travel agents, real estate brokers, job agency employees, insurance agents, and other such jobs will disappear? We referred to the process of cutting out the intermediaries in retailing as **disintermediation** (chapter 2). Is disintermediation coming to brokers as well? Possibly. If we read the opening case of this chapter, we can see that the traditional purchasing agent may have no role in the new system. On the other hand, only large customers will be able to afford such a magazine purchasing system; smaller buyers may need the traditional agent. In the case of auctions, we can see that the intermediaries have a completely different role.

Bloch et al. (1996) believed that the agents' role will be changed, emphasizing value-added services such as:

- assistance in comparison shopping from multiple sources;
- providing total solutions by combining services from several vendors; and

- providing certifications and trusted third-party control and evaluation systems.

Such value-added services require an integration approach. Integration is the ability to sell a package of products to customers based on a very fine understanding of their needs, similar to the purchasing of a basket of stocks. For example, a travel agent that will take care of the complete trip, including booking the golf course and buying tickets for the show is using the integration approach. Another example is Carlson Travel, which provides services and products not available on the Internet. A bank will offer a basket of financial services, and a job placement will be supplemented by résumé writing, advice on tax implications, and the necessary transfer rights of pension and insurance. This may result in new entrants to an industry, those who are integrators and/or information brokers. Some issues that could impact the future of intermediaries are:

- The success of intelligent agents. In addition to the travel intelligent agents, there are agents to support job matching and to interpret résumés, and so on. The more intelligent the software agents are, the less you will need human agents.
- Consumer attitudes and behavior are important. If you have gratifying experiences with online insurance, stock purchasing, or with Expedia, would you ever return to using a human agent?

There will be lots of changes in the role of agencies. Take SABRE as an example. SABRE provided an infrastructure to hundreds of thousands of travel agents. Now there will be fewer agents, so the infrastructure is less important, but the content of information that SABRE sells is becoming their business cornerstone. Intermediaries will move from providing transactions to providing knowledge. Knowledge dissemination is one of the major applications of EC.

Some companies try to cut off disintermediation. For example, Merrill Lynch is trying to augment relationships between advisors and clients, which regular online trading companies cannot provide. For this reason many of the company's clients continue their trusted relationship and do not move to the less expensive online brokers. This approach is called **reintermediation** by some.

The issue of intermediaries in an agent-based transaction is part of a broader issue of the role Internet intermediaries will play. According to an answer to a FAQ at the Center for Research in Electronic Commerce at the University of Texas at Austin, there are two roles of electronic marketing intermediaries: The first role is to extend what we are familiar with in physical markets into the virtual world. For example, search services and e-malls are virtual counterparts of directory services, yellow pages, and buying guides. Certification authorities play similar roles of notaries identification-issuing agencies, insurers, and so on. Electronic cash banks and digital credit card services extend payment clearing functions into the Internet.

The other type of intermediation is evolving from the unique capabilities or needs of the networked market. This may involve breaking down the value-creating chain of the physical market into separate entities or combining them into a different type of service. For example, retailers have functions other than distribution. A posh department store transmits a message about the products it carries and their quality. Does a fancy Web site tell as much? A Web intermediary may sell quality information and nothing else. A toy retailer not only distributes but also presents lines of products toy buyers are interested in examining and comparing. Thus, an intermediary is needed if we are to avoid visiting each and every manufacturer of a toy item.

A retailer sells products as well as reputation about quality. Sometimes, that reputation might be a more important function of that business. For example, we presume superb quality of news if it appears on CNN or the *New York Times*. But will we accept news from those on the Internet we've never heard of? CNN and NYT are in reality just intermediaries who collect, repackage, and distribute news and information. In the information age, they cannot (or should not) wish to dominate the market. Online versions of CNN and NYT may emerge as the trusted source of digital information, but their value-creation processes are influenced by the needs of the physical market: cost of gathering information, being selective due to the constraints of time and space, the idiosyncrasies of broadcast and print media, predominant ad-supported business models, and so on. However the news business changes, the greatest asset of CNN and NYT is their reputation for quality, by which they can become the ultimate information intermediary in the digital economy.

5.11 Managerial Issues

Several managerial issues are related to the implementation of online service industries. Some examples are:

1. **Out-of-town recruitment.** This can be an important source of skilled people. Using video teleconferencing you can interview from a distance. For many jobs you can use telecommuters. This strategy could be a major one as we enter the twenty-first century.

2. **Privacy.** As applicants' information travels over the Internet, security and privacy become even more important. It is management's job to secure applicants' information.

3. **International legal issues.** Recruiting people online from other countries (and sometimes even from different states) may not be simple. The validity of contracts signed in different countries needs to be checked with legal experts. The same applies for travel arrangements involving foreign countries and to real estate transactions made from a distance.

4. **Ethics.** Ethical issues are extremely important in an agentless system. In traditional systems agents play an important role in assuring ethical behavior of buyers and sellers. Will the rule of etiquette be sufficient? Only time will tell. (See: www.ano.edu.au/people/rogerclarke/ec/annbibl.html).

5. **The intermediaries and their role.** It will take a few years before the new roles of the Internet intermediaries will be stabilized as well as their fees. Also, the emergence of support services, such as escrow services in auctions, will have an impact on the intermediaries and their role.

Summary

The compilation of this chapter helps you in attaining the following learning objectives:

1. **How broker-based services are performed online.** The customers communicate their wish online. In some cases there is an automatic match of the customer needs and the services offered. The broker role is being changed to that of market maker and a provider of added values not available on the Web. Commissions are reduced drastically since the market becomes more perfect. Customers have direct access to a provider and can even negotiate deals.

2. **How online travel/tourism services operate.** Most services available in a physical travel agency are also available online. In addition, customers get much more information, usually quicker. Customers log on to a virtual agency, prepare their desired trip plan, and receive bids from providers. They can even set a maximum price they are willing to pay for transportation, accommodations, events, and more. They can compare the prices, participate in auctions and chat rooms, and view videos and maps.

3. **The impact of electronic commerce on the travel industry.** Electronic commerce creates much stronger competition among travel agencies and providers of services, resulting in lower prices and lower commissions. The industry is being transformed to direct marketing operations. The role of travel agents is changing, and many will disappear. The survivors will be those whose service is changing to value-added. More automation is anticipated due to intelligent agents, including active bids, auctions, and negotiations.

4. **The online job market, its drivers, and benefits.** The online job market is growing rapidly with millions of jobs matched annually with job seekers. The major drivers of online job markets is the ability to reach a large number of job seekers at low cost, to provide detailed information online, to take applications, and even to conduct tests. Also, using intelligent agents, résumés are checked and matches are made quickly. Benefits occur to employers, job seekers, government agencies, and successful employment agencies.

5. **The electronic real estate market.** The online real estate market is basically supporting rather than replacing existing agents. However, time and effort of both buyers and sellers can be saved. You can buy distant properties much easier, and lately you can get less expensive services. Eventually, commissions on regular transactions will decline.

6. **Online stocks, bonds, and commodities trading.** One of the fastest growing online businesses is online trading. It is inexpensive, convenient, and supported by a tremendous amount of financial and advisory information. Trading is very fast and efficient, almost fully automated, and it is moving toward 24 hours of global trading. Day trading is rising rapidly and the traditional brokers are disappearing slowly. Also, IPOs are moving to the Net.

7. **Cyberbanking and its benefits.** Branch banking is on the decline due to the less expensive, more convenient online banking. The world is moving toward online banking; today most routine services are done from home. Banks are pressuring customers to move online and can reach customers in remote places; customers can bank with faraway institutions. This makes the financial markets more efficient.

8. **Implementing online financial services.** Financial services are moving online, frequently in an integrated fashion: stocks, banking, personal finance, and insurance, all in one stop. Strong growth is seen in all financial services, especially in automatic billing and security trading.

9. **Electronic auctions: implementation, benefits, and impacts.** Auctions online are exploding. Sellers may reach millions of bidders and pay small commissions; buyers can find what they want from their homes. Auctioneers change their role to market makers, and shares of eBay, Onsale, and uBid are skyrocketing. Liquidations, collectors' items, and a chance to sell almost anything drive this market. Auction types are diverse, and mechanisms to increase trust and reduce fraud are being developed. Even intelligent agents are employed in monitoring auctions and in placing bids strategically.

10. **Innovative service industries applications.** Hundreds of other services are coming online. Notable are online publishing, knowledge dissemination, distance learning and training, insurance, document management, electronic stamps, matchmaking, astrology online, and much, much more.
11. **The changing roles of intermediaries.** In most cases the conventional intermediation will disappear or change. Direct marketing will eliminate many types of intermediaries. The survivors will basically be providers of value-added services, and market makers and organizers.

Keywords

- Agent-based services
- Cyberbanking
- Distance learning
- Disintermediation
- Edutainment

- Electronic auctions
- Electronic banking
- Fare tracking
- Intermediaries (intermediation)
- Online banking

- Reintermediation
- Virtual realtors
- Virtual universities

Questions for Review

1. Define agent-based services.
2. Define fare tracker.
3. List the major services of an electronic travel service.
4. List the limitations of online travel services.
5. List the driving forces of the electronic job market.
6. What are the major advantages of electronic job seeking to the candidate? To the employers?
7. List the major benefits of trading online.
8. List the various options of paying bills electronically.
9. List the benefits of electronic auctions to the buyers, to the sellers.
10. List the types of online publishing.

Questions for Discussion

1. Why is travel such a popular Internet application?
2. What are the major motivations for an airline to sell electronic tickets?
3. Why are so many Web sites providing free travel information?
4. Discuss the potential impact of a virtual travel agency on a traditional one.
5. What are the implications of a virtual travelers' community?
6. Distinguish between corporate and individual travel as conducted on the Internet.
7. Compare online stock trading to offline trading.
8. Examine the section about the "future of banking." Select a large bank in your area. Which of the three strategies is this bank most likely to follow. Why?
9. Analyze Bloch and Segev's impact model. Give examples that will show its validity.
10. What role could intelligent agents play in online travel and why?
11. What other services are similar to job placement? Can they be provided online? Why or why not?
12. Why do Internet services provide free advice on how to write a résumé?
13. Intelligent agents are reading résumés and bringing their content to the attention of potential employers. Why is this done?
14. The online employment services make it easy to change jobs; therefore, turnover rate may increase. This could result in a high cost of recruiting and training new employees, and paying higher salaries and wages. What can companies do to ease the problem?

15. What strategic advantage is provided to airlines that offer online discounted tickets? Why some airlines use auctions instead of a discount?
16. How can companies offer very low commissions for buying stocks online (as low as $5 per trade—some even offer no commission for certain trades)? Why? Speculate on the long run. Will commissions increase or continue to decrease?
17. It is said that some banks are going online because they are forced to do so. Others banks are very happy to lead the way. Why do banks use different online strategies?
18. Why does Colliers Arnold (Application Case 5.6), believe that the major value of their Web site is customer service and not the direct additional sales?
19. Compare electronic to physical auctions.
20. Review the nine deficiencies of a traditional job market as listed in section 5.4. For each deficiency, explain how it is going to disappear or at least be minimized if the Internet is used.
21. Compare real estate agents to stock market agents in EC.
22. Why is knowledge dissemination on the Internet growing so rapidly.

Internet Exercises

1. Access www.sourcer.com. Find information about software support for recruitment. Try the following demos:
   - Sorcy.Zip (about 900K). You can change the WAV file to record your own announcement.
   - So Tour.Zip (about 970K). Unzip and run the program through your program manager.
2. Enter www.oakland.edu and find the Internet career guide. You will find more than 100 references to career-oriented sites, organized alphabetically. Use the reference list to find:
   - A summer internship
   - Job openings in Bethlehem, Pennsylvania
   - A computer analyst's job in Hong Kong
   - Related software (Oak repository)
   - Information about job fairs in your city or state (www.careermag.com)
3. Make your résumé accessible to millions of people. Try www.webplaza.com. Find some help to rewrite your résumé. Consult www.jobweb.org in planning your career. Get prepared for a job interview (www.hotjob.com).
4. Determine your career vision by completing the self-assessment questionnaire at www.careerpath.com. Do you feel that the scoring and recommendations are of value to you?
5. Use the Internet to perform the following tasks:
   - Sign up with Expedia and tell them you want to travel from your city to Hawaii. Wait a few days to receive low-price flight suggestions on your e-mail.
   - Track a flight in real time (www.thetrip.com), by flight number, by airline, and by city.
   - Find the lowest possible fare for a trip from Los Angeles to Paris, France, leaving on a weekday, staying 10 days, and returning on a weekday.
   - Use Expedia's Hotel Wizard to find a hotel in London. Use the currency converter to figure your nightly cost.
   - Find a map of Jerusalem, Israel, a list of attractions, and an entertainment guide.
6. Enter www.homeowners.com/index2.html or a similar site and compute the mortgage payment on a 30-year loan at 7.5 percent fixed. Also check current rates. Estimate your closing costs on a $200,000 loan. Compare the monthly payments of the fixed rate with that of an adjustable rate for the first year. Finally, compute

your total payments if you take the loan for 15 years at the going rate. Compare it to a 30-year going rate. Comment on the difference.

7. Enter 30 free subscriptions to www.knowledgespace.com. Use the service to write a report on the topics of mass customization and global EC.

8. Access www.etrade.com and register for their Internet stock game. You will be bankrolled with $100,000 in a trading account every month. Also, identify all the services offered by E*TRADE and comment on them. You can also play a simulation investment game with www.cnnfn.com which offers an "investment challenge" game.

9. Enter www.wellsfargo.com and examine their global and B2B services. For each service that is being offered, comment on the advantages of online versus offline options.

10. Examine the progress of consolidated billing. Start with www.ebill.com, money central.msn.com and www.intuit.com. Identify other contenders in the field. What are the standard capabilities that they all offer? What are some unique capabilities?

11. Enter www.etrade.com and find how you can trade stocks in countries other than the one you live in. Prepare a report. (You can send an e-mail to them).

12. How about building a Web site for your mortgage company? Try http://webworks.glyphix.com or www.pacpartners.com. Look at demo sites and sample sites.

Team Exercises

1. Each team member will represent a broker-based area (e.g., real estate, insurance, stocks, job finding). Each member will find the new development in the assigned area in the last three months. Look at the vendor's announcement and search with Yahoo or another search engine. Examine news at cnnfn.
   The group will prepare a report on common developments in broker-based areas and on unique areas of development.

2. Business-to-business auctions are growing rapidly. Each team member is assigned to a different type of auction: third-party auction site, proprietary auction site, conducting bids on the Internet, others. Visit sites such as www.fairmarkert.com and usaweb.com. Conduct a comparative analysis.

3. Refer to the opening vignette. Have one team member investigate the status of Subscribe, another one check on OM Transact (at www.openmarket.com), and one connect by e-mail with rowe.com. Prepare a report on the status of the project, the role of the software, and the advantages over the conventional ordering system.

REAL WORLD CASES

Cushman and Wakefield Uses an Intranet to Communicate Effectively

Cushman and Wakefield Inc. of New York is a real estate broker and property management company specializing in commercial properties. The company employs 2,000 employees in 40 locations in the United State and overseas. The company was facing two problems: first, how to make the ever-changing corporate policies and human resources information easily accessible to its employees, and second, how to provide detailed data on thousands of commercial properties around the world to all its brokers. In contrast to residential real estate, where the buyers and the sellers are usually in the same city, in commercial real estate a specific property can be purchased by a buyer in another location.

A solution to the first problem was attempted with CD-ROMs. But because of the frequent changes in policies and procedures, the system collapsed. The solution to the second problem was to use paper catalogs and faxes. This solution proved to be clumsy, expensive, and difficult to maintain and update. The company decided to use an intranet solution.

The company has a WAN infrastructure that connects its headquarters with five large cities using high-speed T1 lines. In addition, it uses high-speed modems to connect its 40 branch offices to a central communication server. With an expense of less than $10,000 (for an Internet server, browsers, and so on), the company has initiated its intranet. The reason for such a low cost was the existence of networks, programs, and hardware.

Using the existing TPC/IP-based network, the intranet was created in three months and has been growing incrementally. In the beginning, the intranet provided only passive access to human resource documents. Later, the company added a property-tracking site-solution database, which includes pictures and text regarding all properties for sale or lease. By adding an online chat forum, the company improved the communication among its employees. Finally, the existing e-mail system was incorporated into the intranet. Users access the system through a customized Graphical User Interface (GUI) client interface, and they can query the database with a Web browser.

The system provides the company with a strategic business application advantage. It is being expanded to allow other brokers to communicate with the corporate brokers and view available properties. This is where the intranet meets the Internet. As a matter of fact, the company has a small Web site (www.cushwake.com) that provides information to the general public about the company and its business. ∎

Source: Condensed from *Information Week,* March 26, 1996.

CASE QUESTIONS

1. Why was the intranet the best solution for the company's problems?
2. How was it possible to install an intranet so inexpensively?
3. How can a chat room improve communication?
4. How can the company brokers communicate with outside brokers using an intranet/Internet mix?

Web Takes Banking to Sea

The Navy Federal Credit Union serves 1.7 million customers. Many of these customers are on active duty, serving on hundreds of ships, sometimes at sea for months at a time. Others are dispersed in military bases all over the world.

Using satellites and other technologies, the U.S. Navy created a sophisticated communications system that allows its customers online banking from any place at any time. The network is connected to 150,000 ATMs worldwide, including ATMs on all Navy vessels.

Users can view their accounts, transfer money, pay bills, and apply for loans on the Internet. The system is integrated with an intranet so that the 3,700 employees of the credit union can communicate with the headquarters, regardless of their location. Also, the intranet is used for training and facilitating the loan application process.

These secured services are provided through a wireless Internet link connected to the Department of Defense satellite system. This gives the credit union members the ability to access bank accounts and take care of household finances from the various ships.

The system provides superb customer service, and at the same time, the cost of the new client/server-based system is significantly lower than that of the old mainframe-based system. However, the new system still uses the old legacy system. The contacts are made through a Web interface, making the legacy system accessible through browsers. The intranet consolidates the administrative and member services in an easy-to-read GUI, regardless of the back-end application systems to which it may be tied (like payroll and accounts payable). ∎

CASE QUESTIONS

1. How is the cost benefit of such a system measured?
2. The system is linked to global systems such as the U.S. Armed Forces Financial Network as well as to Plus Systems Inc. (a public network). Why?
3. What is the role of the intranet in this case?
4. What type of EC is this?

References and Bibliography

S. Alexander, "The Search Is Online," *Careers* (Fall 1997).

J. P. Bailey, "The emergence of electronic market intermediaries," *Proceedings, HICSS*, Hawaii, 1998.

K. M. Bayne, "Recruiting Via Internet on the Rise," *Advertising Age* (October 1997).

M. Bloch, and A. Segev, "The Impact of Electronic Commerce on the Travel Industry," *Proceedings, HICSS 31*, Hawaii, 1997.

M. Bloch et al., "Leveraging Electronic Commerce for Competitive Advantage: a Business Value Framework," in *Proceedings of the Ninth International Conference on EDI-IOS*, June 1996; Bled, Slovenia.

K. Bose, "Intelligent Agents Framework for Developing Knowledge-based DSS for Collaborative Organizational Processes," *Expert Systems with Applications* 11 (3:1996).

J. Bradshaw, *Software Agents* (Menlo Park, CA: AAAI Press/MIT Press, 1997).

J Champy et al., "Creating the Electronic Community," *Information Week* (June 10, 1996).

J. D. Callon, *Competitive Advantage Through Information Technology* (New York: McGraw-Hill, 1996).

C. Dahle, "Going Places," *Webmaster Magazine* (August 1997).

J. Davis, "E*TRADE's Portal Play," *Business 2.0*, premiere issue (Fall 1998).

P. B. Farrell, *Investor's Guide to the Net* (New York: Wiley, 1996).

M. Fitch, "Cruise the Web to Land the Job of Your Dreams," *Money* (May 1997).

M. Hamalainen et al., "Electronic Marketing for Learning: Education Brokerages on the Internet," *Communications of the ACM* (June 1996).

R. Helton, "Using the Internet and the Web in Your Job Search: A Complete Guide," *Database* (August/September 1997).

P. Jacobs, "American Express Travel and Wal-Mart: Breaking Digital Ground," *InfoWorld* (July 28, 1997).

F. E. Jandt and M. B. Nemnich, eds., *Using the Internet and the Web in Your Job Search*, 2^d ed. (Indianapolis: Jistwork, 1999).

S. Klein, "Introduction to Electronic Auctions," *Electronic Markets* 7 (4:1997).

A. Kambil and E. van Heck, "Reengineering the Dutch Flowery Auctions: A Framework for Analyzing Exchange Organizations," *Information Systems Research* (March 1998).

J. King, "Web Site Offers Job Lists, Search Services for Free," *ComputerWorld* (January 13, 1997).

B. J Kingston, "Pricing Home Banking Services: A Puzzle for Vacillating Bankers," *American Banker* (December 1997).

R. Koonce, "Using the Internet as a Career Planning Tool," *Training and Development* (September 1997).

S. Lim, "The Impact of the Web on Individual Investors and Electronic Stock Market Trading" at www.employees.org (go to slim).

J. S. Mahan, "Electronic Commerce and the Future of Banking," *The Bankers Magazine* (March/April 1996).

M. J. Mandel and T. Gutner, "Your Next Job," *Business Week* (October 13, 1997).

A. McIlvaine, "Cyber Scholars," *Human Resource Executive* (October 6, 1997).

B. S. Neo, "The Implementation of an Electronic Market for Pig Trading in Singapore," *Journal of Strategic Information Systems* (December 1992).

K. Peffers and V. K. Tunnainen, "Expectation and Impacts of a Global Information Systems: the case of a Global Bank from Hong Kong" *Tour of Global IT ManagementVol 1 #4, 1998.*

M. E. Porter, *Competitive Strategy, Techniques for Analyzing Industries and Competitors* (New York: The Free Press, 1980).

A. Rogers, "Travel Gods Smile on Zeus," *Information Week* (September 1, 1997).

M. Sarkar et al., "Intermediaries and Cybermediaries: A Continuing Role for Mediating Players in the Electronic Marketplace," *Journal of Computer-Mediated Communication* 1(3:1995).

E. Schonfeld, "Schwab-Put It All Online," *Fortune* (December 7, 1998).

S. Timewel, "Shopping for Money," *Banker* (August 1996).

J. G. M. Van der Heijden, "The Changing Value of Travel Agents in Tourism Networks: Towards a Network Design Perspective," in Stefan Klein et al., *Information and Communication Technologies in Tourism* (New York: Springer-Verlag, 1996): 151–59.

E. Turban, "Auctions on the Internet," *Electronic Markets* 7 (4:1997).

K. H. Wadsworth, "Cyber Malling: A Retail Death Sentence?" *Journal of Property Management* (March/April 1997).

CHAPTER 6

Business-to-Business
Electronic Commerce

Learning Objectives

Upon completion of this chapter, the reader will be able to:

■ Describe the applications of B2B EC.

■ Identify key technologies for B2B EC.

■ Classify the architectural models of B2B EC.

■ Describe the characteristics of the supplier-oriented marketplace.

■ Describe the characteristics of the buyer-oriented marketplace.

■ Describe the characteristics of the intermediary-oriented marketplace.

■ Discover the benefits of B2B EC in procurement reengineering from the GE case.

■ Describe the importance of JIT delivery in B2B EC.

■ Distinguish the characteristics of Internet-based EDI from traditional EDI.

■ Design a method of integrating EC with back-end information systems.

■ Analyze the role of agents for B2B EC.

■ Describe marketing issues in B2B.

■ Specify the characteristics of the solutions for B2B EC.

6.1   Procurement Revolution at General Electric

General Electric's material costs increased 16 percent between 1982 and 1992, while GE's products' prices remained flat for a few years and then started to decline. In response to these cost increases, GE began an all-out effort to improve its purchasing system. The company analyzed its procurement process and discovered that its purchasing was inefficient, involved too many transactions, and did not leverage GE's large volumes to get the best price. In addition, more than one-quarter of its 1.25 million invoices per year had to be reworked because the purchase order, receipt, and invoice did not match.

General Electric has taken a number of steps to improve its purchasing, and the most recent one involves the Internet. Factories at GE Lighting used to send hundreds of requisitions for quotations (RFQs) to the corporate sourcing department each day for low-value machine parts. For each requisition, the accompanying blueprints had to be requested from storage, retrieved from the vault, transported to the processing site, photocopied, folded, attached to paper requisition forms with quote sheets, stuffed into envelopes, and mailed out. This process took at least seven days and was so complex and time-consuming that the sourcing department normally sent out bid packages only to two or three suppliers at a time.

TPN AT GE LIGHTING DIVISION

In 1996, GE Lighting piloted the company's first online procurement system, the Trading Process Network (TPN 1999b) Post (tpn.geis.com). Now, the sourcing department receives the requisitions electronically from its internal customers and can send off a bid package to suppliers around the world over the Internet. The system automatically pulls the correct drawings and attaches them to the electronic requisition forms. Within two hours from the time the sourcing department starts the process, suppliers are notified of incoming RFQs by e-mail, fax, or EDI (section 6.9) and are given seven days to prepare a bid and send it back over the extranet to GE Lighting. The bid is transferred over the intranet to the appropriate evaluator and a contract can be awarded the same day.

BENEFITS OF TPN

As a result of implementing TPN, GE has realized a number of benefits:

- Labor involved in the procurement process declined by 30 percent. At the same time, materials costs declined 5 percent to 20 percent due to the ability to reach a wider base of suppliers online.
- Of the staff involved in the procurement process, 60 percent have been redeployed. The sourcing department has at least six to eight free days a month to concentrate on strategic activities rather than on the paperwork, photocopying, and envelope stuffing it had to do when the process was manual.
- It used to take 18 to 23 days to identify suppliers, prepare a request for bid, negotiate a price, and award the contract to a supplier. It now takes 9 to 11 days.
- With the transaction handled electronically from beginning to end, invoices are automatically reconciled with purchase orders, reflecting any modifications that happen along the way.
- General Electric procurement departments across the world now share information about their best suppliers. In February 1997 alone, GE Lighting found seven new suppliers through the Internet, including one that charged 20 percent less than the second lowest bid.

SIDE BENEFITS TO SUPPLIERS

General Electric reports that TPN benefits extend beyond its own walls. A computer reseller, Hartford Computer Group, reports that since joining TPN, it has increased exposure across the different GE business units so that its business with the company has grown by over 250 percent. At the same time, TPN has introduced Hartford Computer Group to other potential customers.

As of October 1997, eight divisions of General Electric use TPN for some of their procurement needs. The company bought over $1 billion worth of goods and supplies over the Internet during 1997; by 2000, the company expects to have 12 of its business units purchasing their nonproduction and maintenance, repair, and operations materials (MRO) over the Internet, for an annual total of $5 billion. General Electric estimates that streamlining these purchases alone can save the company $500 to $700 million annually.

OPEN AS A PUBLIC BIDDING SITE

Now GE has opened the site tpn.geis.com as a public bidding site and has 2,500 registered suppliers as of December 1998 (see Blankenhorn 1997b for more details).

6.2 Characteristics of B2B EC

The GE story demonstrates a case of B2B EC as defined in chapter 1. It demonstrates how EC can revolutionize the procurement process. It also shows the diversified benefits of EC and two of GE's strategies: start EC in one division and slowly go to all divisions, and use the site as a public bidding market generating income for GE.

Business-to-business electronic commerce implies that both the sellers and buyers are business corporations, while *business-to-consumer electronic commerce* implies that the buyers are individual consumers. Business-to-business EC is expected to grow to $1,330.9 billion by 2003 and continue to be the major share of the EC market (Freeman 1998, Retter and Calyniuk 1998). The percentage of Internet-based B2B EC compared to total B2B commerce will expand from .2 percent in 1997 to 2.1 percent in 2000 and 9.4 percent in 2003. Computing electronics, utilities, shipping and warehousing, motor vehicles, petrochemicals, paper and office products, food, and agriculture are the leading items in B2B EC. See Table 6.1.

Business-to-business EC covers a broad spectrum of applications that enable an enterprise or business to form electronic relationships with their distributors, resellers, suppliers, and other partners. As Handfield and Nichols (1999) suggest, B2B applications will offer enterprises access to the following sorts of information:

- *Product*—specifications, prices, sales history
- *Customer*—sales history and forecasts
- *Supplier*—product line and lead times, sales terms and conditions
- *Product process*—capacities, commitments, product plans
- *Transportation*—carriers, lead times, costs
- *Inventory*—inventory levels, carrying costs, locations
- *Supply chain alliance*—key contacts, partners' roles and responsibilities, schedules
- *Competitor*—benchmarking, competitive product offerings, market share
- *Sales and marketing*—point of sale (POS), promotions
- *Supply chain process and performance*—process descriptions, performance measures, quality, delivery time, customer satisfaction

By using B2B EC, businesses can reengineer their supply chain and partnership.

SUPPLY CHAIN

Even though there are many B2B applications, the relationships between businesses can be best understood in the supply chain context. Consider something as mundane as the manufacture and distribution of cereal. The overall process is shown in Figure 6.1 (Handfield and Nichols 1999). The process actually consists of a number of interrelated processes and roles: all the way from the acquisition of grain from farmers (or some other grain suppliers), to the processing of the grain into cereal, the packaging of

TABLE 6.1 Forecasted Revenue of the Internet-based B2B EC (dollars in billions)

Industry Sector		1997	2000	2003
Computing, electronics	Total revenue	$477.8	$693.1	$1,005.4
	Internet revenue	$8.7	$121.4	$395.3
	Internet pct. of total	1.8%	17.5%	39.3%
Motor vehicles	Total revenue	$915.9	$1,150.5	$1,445.3
	Internet revenue	$1.5	$22.7	$212.9
	Internet pct. of total	0.2%	2.0%	14.7%
Petrochemicals	Total revenue	$987.3	$1,142.9	$1,323.0
	Internet revenue	$2.1	$22.6	$178.3
	Internet pct. of total	0.2%	2.0%	13.5%
Utilities	Total revenue	$490.2	$567.5	$656.9
	Internet revenue	$3.2	$32.2	$169.5
	Internet pct. of total	0.7%	5.7%	25.8%
Paper/office products	Total revenue	$826.7	$981.8	$1,166.0
	Internet revenue	$0.6	$6.4	$65.2
	Internet pct. of total	0.1%	0.7%	5.6%
Shipping/warehousing	Total revenue	$312.6	$334.7	$358.3
	Internet revenue	$0.5	$6.8	$61.6
	Internet pct. of total	0.2%	2.0%	17.2%
Food/agriculture	Total revenue	$1,489.6	$1,627.7	$1,778.6
	Internet revenue	$0.1	$6.3	$53.6
	Internet pct. of total	0.0%	0.4%	3.0%
Other	Total revenue	$4,411.9	$5,314.4	$6,412.0
	Internet revenue	$2.0	$32.7	$194.4
	Internet pct. of total	0.0%	0.6%	3.0%
TOTAL	Total revenue	$9,911.9	$11,812.6	$14,146.5
	Internet revenue	$18.6	$251.1	$1,330.9
	Internet pct. of total	0.2%	2.1%	9.4%

Source: Forrester Research Inc. and Anders (1998).

FIGURE 6.1 Supply Chain of Cereal.

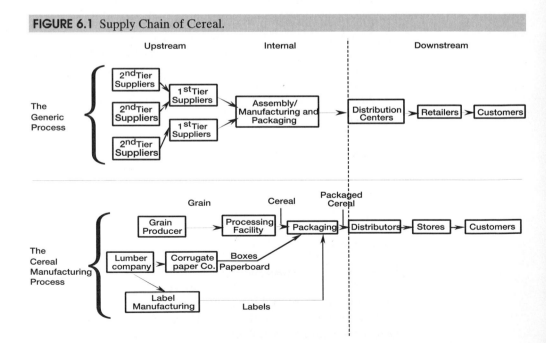

Source: Compiled from Handfield and Nichols (1999).

the cereal into boxes, the transportation of the packaged cereal to distributors and grocers, and eventually the purchase by end consumers.

Taken together these processes and roles are called a *supply chain.* The supply chain encompasses all the activities associated with the flow and transformation of goods from the raw materials stage all the way to the end user. As shown in Figure 6.1, the supply chain can be broken into three parts—*upstream activities* involving material and service inputs from suppliers, *internal activities* involving the manufacturing and packaging of goods, and *downstream activities* involving the distribution and sale of products to distributors and customers. In the 1990s business managers have come to recognize that management and control of the upstream and downstream activities— which involve relationships with partners who are technically outside the enterprise— are as important as the internal activities involved in the actual production of products.

Historically, many of the processes in the supply chain, especially the upstream and downstream activities, have been managed with paper transactions (e.g., purchase requisitions and orders, invoices, and so forth). This is where B2B EC applications come into play. They can serve as supply chain enablers that can offer a distinct competitive advantage.

ENTITIES OF B2B EC

The Internet can provide the most economical B2B EC platform for linking companies without additional network implementation. This chapter will describe the various applications and architectures of B2B EC on the Internet. Since **supply chain management** encompasses "the coordination of order generation, order taking, and order fulfillment/distribution of products, services, or information" (Kalakota and Whinston 1997), the involved companies can be studied both from the customers' and from the purchasers' point of view. Thus, B2B EC can contribute to lower purchase costs, reduced inventory, enhanced efficiency of logistics, as well as to increased sales and lowered sales and marketing costs.

The key entities in B2B EC and their concerns are the following:

* *Selling company*—with marketing management perspective
* *Buying company*—with procurement management perspective
* *Electronic intermediary*—a third-party intermediating service provider (the scope of service may be extended to include the order fulfillment)
* *Deliverer*—who should fulfill the JIT delivery
* *Network platform*—such as the Internet, intranet, and extranet
* *Protocols and communication*—such as EDI and comparison shopping, possibly using software agents
* *Back-end information system*—possibly implemented using the intranet and Enterprise Resource Planning (ERP) systems.

The content of these entities will be covered one by one in the following sections of this chapter. However, the related intranet and extranet will be covered in chapter 7. Now let us discuss the relationship between B2B EC and the following perspectives: electronic marketing, procurement management, electronic intermediary, JIT delivery, EDI, intranet, extranet, integration with back-end information systems, and online services to business.

Electronic Marketing

The B2B EC platform can be used to sell the company's products and services to business customers on the Internet. This business model can be named supplier-oriented marketing (or seller-oriented marketing) because customers visit the Web site that the supplier has prepared. The concept of this model is described in the Cisco case later in this chapter. From the supplier's point of view, a Web site equipped with an electronic catalog is basically the same as that for B2C EC. Thus, the concepts and technologies described in chapter 2 for retailing can be equally applied here. The only differences are that: (a) the customers are companies to whom the integration of order information with the procurement management systems is crucial; (b) each corporate buyer may have its own catalog and price schedule; and (c) the corporate buyer behavior differs from that of an individual one. In chapter 2, the critical success factors of direct marketing with the supplier-oriented marketplace are described in the Dell and Ford cases. In these cases, the customers can be both individual consumers and businesses owing to the nature of the items sold—computers and cars. However, certain groups of items, such as industrial equipment, are purchased only by businesses. Network router is an example, because it is used only in business.

Procurement Management

From the purchasing company's point of view, B2B EC is a medium of facilitating **procurement management** such as reduced purchase price and reduced cycle time. To implement B2B EC from the procurement management's point of view, the buyer-oriented marketplace (or customer-oriented marketplace) can be used in this model—where the buyers announce the RFQs to potential suppliers for competitive purchasing. The concept of this model is described in a case study with GE Trade Process Network later in this chapter. To the suppliers, participating to the customer-oriented marketplace and winning the bid is the major concern.

Electronic Intermediaries

The electronic intermediaries for consumers mentioned in chapter 2 can also be referenced for B2B EC, replacing the consumers with business customers. Both individual consumers and businesses purchase a group of items such as books, stationery, and personal computers. In this case, consumers and business buyers can share the intermediary. However, certain items, such as industrial equipment and parts, are purchased only by businesses. For instance, the parts for jumbo jets are purchased only by business. An example in which Boeing plays the role of intermediary between airline customers and 300 part suppliers is described later in this chapter. This business model is an example of an intermediary-oriented marketplace. Since the purchasing party is a business who has to deal with many suppliers and intermediaries, an integrated and tailored buyer's directory linked with relevant suppliers and intermediaries is needed.

Just-in-Time Delivery

The **just-in-time (JIT) delivery** of parts to manufacturing buyers is crucial to realize JIT manufacturing. Since online direct marketing requires an internal JIT manufacturing system, the JIT delivery and advanced confirmation of suppliers' inventory are essential elements for B2B EC. Just-in-time delivery was not a critical issue in B2C EC, so it was not handled as a central theme of EC yet. However, as the importance of B2B grows, the study on JIT delivery should be emphasized. This issue is covered later in this chapter with a discussion of a FedEx case.

Electronic Data Interchange

Electronic data interchange (EDI) is the electronic exchange of specially formatted standard business documents such as orders, bills, approval of credit, shipping notices, and confirmation sent between business partners. EDI is used primarily to transfer electronically repetitive business transactions. The EDI translator is necessary to convert the proprietary data into standard format. In the past, EDI ran on expensive **value added networks (VANs).** The VAN is, however, confined to large trading partners. As a result, large companies doing business with thousands of small companies were unable to use EDI. However, the situation is changing rapidly with the emergence of Internet-based EDI as we describe later in this chapter. So Internet-based EDI is an important technology for B2B EC.

Intranet

The intranet is a dedicated Internet to a company whose access is protected by a server called a *firewall* (chapters 7 and 11). Since the intranet is an effective platform of implementing Web-based workflow and groupware, this platform is becoming a standard for the corporate information systems. Therefore, integration of a B2B EC platform with an intranet-based corporate information system is a very important issue. The concept of the intranet, and success stories and considerations for implementing intranets, are described in detail in chapter 7.

Extranet

The B2B EC platform may be either a dedicated network between the associated parties or a public network similar to the Internet. The Internet is the most economical and seamlessly accessible platform for B2B EC. However, security is a concern. The extranet, which can implement the virtually private network (VPN) technology between involved companies on the Internet, answer the concern. For more about the extranet and its applications, refer to chapter 7.

Integration with Back-end Information Systems

Back-end information systems may be implemented using intranet-based workflow, database management systems (DBMS), application packages, and ERP. In the supplier-oriented marketplace setting, the **integration of EC** with suppliers' **back-end information systems** is relatively easy because the suppliers keep the platform for both EC and their back-end systems in their servers. However, it is not easy for the buyers to trace their transactions that are scattered in various suppliers' servers. By the same token, in the customer-oriented marketplace setting, business buyers, but not suppliers, can integrate EC with their back-end information systems easily. In the intermediary-oriented marketplace setting, neither buyers nor sellers can organize their transactions easily. This difficulty is a challenge to the participating buyers and sellers in B2B EC but is a good opportunity for the intermediary. The status of integration with the leading ERP system providers and research direction toward this end are discussed later in this chapter.

Online Services to Business

The online services for travel and tourism, employment placement and job market, real estate, trading stocks, cyberbanking, insurance, and auctions are explained in chapter 5. These online services can be used both by consumers and by businesses. For a comprehensive study about the **online services for businesses,** read chapter 5. In addition, there are services that support B2B, such as matching buyers and sellers.

6.3 Models of B2B EC

In this section, the business models of B2B are described. The first three models are classified depending upon who controls the marketplace: the supplier, customer, or intermediary. Other important business models are virtual corporation, networking between headquarter and subsidiaries, and online services to business.

SUPPLIER-ORIENTED MARKETPLACE

The most common B2B model is the **supplier-oriented marketplace.** Most of the manufacturer-driven electronic stores belong to this category. In this model, both individual consumers and business buyers use the same supplier-provided marketplace as depicted in Figure 6.2. The architecture for this B2B model is basically the same as that for B2C EC, and the purchasing process is similar.

Successful Cases and Challenge

Successful examples of this business model are Dell (chapter 2), Intel (chapter 1), and Cisco and IBM (discussed later in this chapter). It is reported that Dell sold 90 percent of their computers to business buyers, and Cisco sold $1 billion worth of routers, switches, and other network interconnection devices in 1998 mainly to business customers through the Internet. The sites with this model may be sustained as long as the vendor has a superb reputation in the market and a group of loyal customers. Thousands of other companies are using this model. One of the major issues for smaller companies is how to find buyers. This issue is described in the electronic marketing in B2B section.

However, this model may not be convenient to large and repetitive business buyers, because the buyers' order information is stored in the suppliers' servers and is not easily integrated with the buyer's corporate information system. So it is necessary to provide a buyer-owned shopping cart, which can store the ordered information and can be integrated with the buyer's information system. This is particularly important, because buyers have to visit several sites for comparison shopping. This characteristic requires that the B2B EC platform will differ from the B2C EC platform. This issue is described in detail later in this chapter.

Electronic Auctions

Another application of the supplier-oriented marketplace is the proprietary auction sites like the computer reseller Ingram Micro (www.ingram.com). These sites are open only to approved customers. They are designed to cement relationships be-

FIGURE 6.2 Supplier-Oriented B2B Marketplace Architecture.

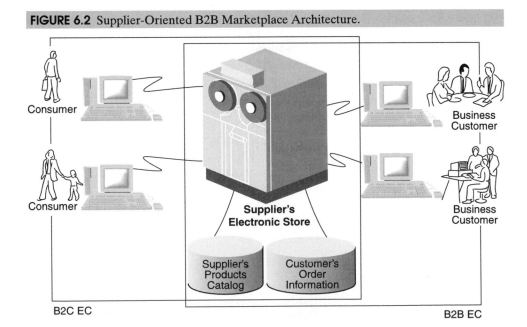

tween the company and its regular buyers. Sellers can get rid of surplus goods, and business customers can realize deep discounts. Also, as described in chapter 5, liquidators can get 600 percent more than if they use offline auctions. In chapter 5 we introduce online auctions.

BUYER-ORIENTED MARKETPLACE

Under the platform of supplier-oriented marketplace, the buyer's acquisition department has to manually enter the order information into its own corporate information system. Searching e-stores and e-malls to find and compare suppliers and products can be very costly to companies like GE, who purchase thousands of items on the Internet. Therefore, such big buyers would prefer to open their own marketplace, which we call the **buyer-oriented marketplace,** as depicted in Figure 6.3. Under this model, a buyer opens an electronic market on its own server and invites potential suppliers to bid on the announced RFQs, as the GE case illustrates. This model offers a greater opportunity to committed suppliers.

Successful Case and Challenge

An example of a successful case of this category is GE as illustrated earlier. Boeing Inc. is another example. Finally, www.shoppoint.co.kr invites suppliers to bid on many parts, all over the Web. As the number of such sites increases, suppliers will not be able to trace all such tender sites. The situation will be improved with the introduction of online directories that list the open RFQs. Another way to solve this problem is the usc of software agents, which can reduce the human burden in the bidding process as we describe later in this chapter.

FIGURE 6.3 Buyer-Oriented B2B Marketplace Architecture.

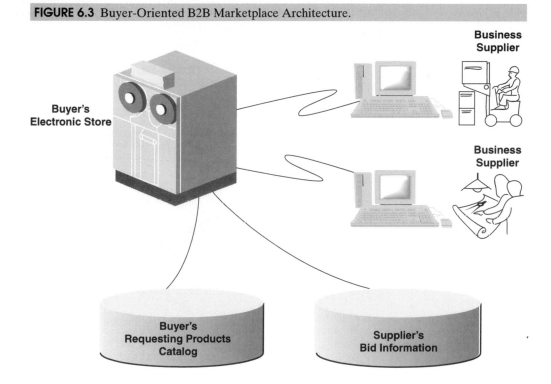

INTERMEDIARY-ORIENTED MARKETPLACE

The third business model is establishing an electronic intermediary company, which runs a marketplace where business buyers and sellers can meet as depicted in Figure 6.4. This concept is similar to intermediary-based e-malls or e-stores developed for B2C EC (chapter 2). Let us call these sites the **intermediary-oriented marketplace.**

Successful Cases and Challenge

Typical cases of intermediary malls are Boeing's PART, ProcureNet, Manufacturing.net, and Industry.net. Boeing's PART links airlines with 300 key suppliers of Boeing's maintenance parts.

ProcureNet was launched by Fisher Technology Group in Pittsburgh, a major industrial distributor, and it targets MRO (maintenance, repair, and operations) purchases. ProcureNet, which went online in March 1996, has 30 seller sites with 100,000 products listed in electronic catalog. The service gets about 1 million hits a month. ProcureNet does not require registration; however, only buyers whose company information has been validated in advance can place orders with selling companies. The service also offers contract pricing (Blankenhorn and Strazewski 1997).

Industry.net had about 275,000 members from 36,000 organizations in 1998. The service receives about 10,000 visitors a day directed to 53 seller company sites. Industry.net charges participating sellers from $2,000 to $250,000 for the Web home site searchable online catalogs and ordering links with corporate buyers. Buyers with contractual relationships can place orders using e-mail forms (Blankenhorn 1997b).

When the participating buyers and sellers are businesses, coupling the intermediary-oriented B2B EC platform with their corporate information systems is a must, particularly for large and repetitive buyers and sellers. Most B2B electronic intermediaries are not equipped with this capability yet, but it should be developed in the next-generation B2B EC platform. Intermediary marketplace are frequently delivered on an extranet such as in the case of ANX (Chapter 7) and Chemlex (chapter 12).

FIGURE 6.4 Intermediary-Oriented B2B Marketplace Model.

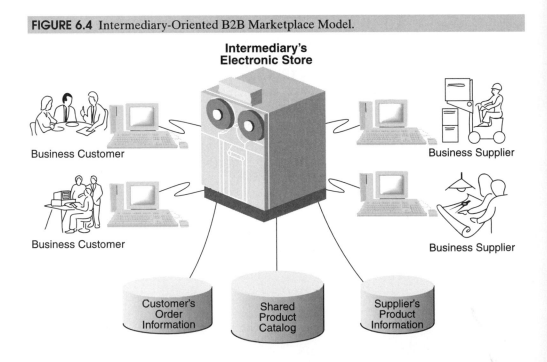

Third-Party Electronic Bidding, Auctions, and Bartering

The third-party intermediary can run the electronic bidding and auction sites. General Electric's TPN Post opened its own bidding site to other buyers so that they can post their requests for quotations. The TPN site can also, therefore, be regarded as an intermediary-oriented marketplace. Auction sites like A-Z Used Computers (www.azuc.com) and FairMarket belong to this category.

VIRTUAL CORPORATION: NETWORKING BETWEEN BUSINESS PARTNERS

One of the most interesting reengineered organization structures is the virtual corporation (VC). A **virtual corporation** is an organization composed of several business partners sharing costs and resources for the purpose of producing a product or service. According to Goldman et al. (1995), permanent virtual corporations are designed to create or assemble productive resources rapidly, frequently, concurrently, or to create or assemble a broad range of productive resources. The creation, operation, and management of a VC are heavily dependent on the B2B EC platform.

However, VCs are not necessarily organized along the supply chain. For example, a business partnership may include several partners, each creating a portion of products or service in an area in which they have special advantage, such as expertise or low cost. So the modern VC can be viewed as a network of creative people, resources, and ideas connected by online services and/or the Internet.

The major goals that VCs pursue are:

- Excellence: Each partner brings its core competence, so an all-star winning team is created.
- Utilization: Resources of the business partners are frequently underutilized. A VC can utilize them more profitably.
- Opportunism: A VC can find and meet market opportunity better than an individual company.

The B2B EC platform, like the Internet and extranet, makes the VC more successful, because the communication and collaboration among the dispersed business partners are key to making it happen. On this platform, the business partners can use e-mail, desktop video conferencing, knowledge sharing, groupware, EDI, and EFT.

For instance, IBM Ambra formed a VC to take advantage of an opportunity to produce and market a PC clone. Each of five business partners played the following roles: engineering design and subsystem development, assembly on a build-to-order basis, telemarketing, order fulfillment and delivery, and field service and customer support. As the B2B EC platform propagates, more companies will be able to make VCs. More examples (Steelcase Inc. and The Agile Web, Inc.) can be found in Turban et al. (1999) and the AeroTech case in Upton and McAfee (1996).

NETWORKING BETWEEN HEADQUARTERS AND SUBSIDIARIES

The B2B EC platform can help the communication and collaboration between headquarters and subsidiaries or franchiser and franchisee by providing e-mail, message boards and chat rooms, and online corporate data access around the globe no matter what the time zone is. The platform helps the franchiser create the global brand marketing and management for franchisees. The on-demand training program can also be shared by franchisees. Advanced extranets can link headquarters to franchisees and approved suppliers, making it easier for them to do business and reduce overhead and duplication.

Marriott International's Extranet Links Global Franchisees

Marriott International has 1,500 hotels in 50 countries, and 600 of them are franchises. Marriott achieved revenue of about $10 billion in 1998. The company first went on the Internet in 1995 with an online brochure. Their marketing strategy is "whatever customers want to buy, we make that available." This became possible by using the EC platform.

Internet, Intranet, and Extranet
Marriott started a passive Web site, www.marriott.com. Through this site, orders of $3 mil-

lion a month were received. Marriott adopted the corporate intranet for the company's 20,000 management employees worldwide. Finally, the intranet was extended to an extranet to help the worldwide franchisees and company properties. Owing to the extranet, the franchises can access Marriott's corporate intranet for better communication and operations (Intel 1999a, 1999b).

Leading businesses are moving quickly to realize the benefits. For example:

- Tricon Restaurant International, which operates 10,000 KFC, Pizza Hut, and Taco Bell restaurants in 83 countries, uses both B2C and B2B EC platforms in global brand marketing and management.
- The real estate franchiser RE/MAX uses the B2B EC platform to improve communications and collaboration among its nationwide network of independently owned real estate franchisees, sales associates, and suppliers.
- Marriott International, the world's largest hospitality company, started with an online brochure and then developed an advanced EC initiative aimed at linking corporations, franchisees, partners, and suppliers, as well as customers, around the world, as illustrated in Application Case 6.1.

ONLINE SERVICES TO BUSINESS
There are many online services available for businesses, although individual customers can share some of the services. The online service industry is described in chapter 5. Among the various online services, the ones mostly used by business are:

- *Travel and tourism services:*   Many large corporations have special discounts arranged with travel agents. To further reduce costs, companies can make special arrangements that enable employees to plan and book their own trip online. For instance, Carlson Travel Network of Minneapolis provides an agentless service to corporate clients like General Electric (chapter 5). The GE employees can fill out the application at their intranet. The system allows a special rate for employees reserving airline tickets, rental cars, and hotels.
- *Real estate:*   Since business real estate investment can be very critical, the Web site cannot replace the existing agents. Instead, the Web site helps in finding the right agents. However, some auctions on foreclosed real estate sold by the government may be opened online only to business. Similarly, used cars are auctioned to dealers only.
- *Electronic payments:*   Firm banking on the Internet is an economical way of making business payments. The EFT using financial EDI on the Internet is

the most popular method business uses. The payment transaction cost on the Internet is cheaper than that of any other alternatives (chapter 8).

- *Online stock trading:*   Corporations are important stock investors. Since the fees for online trading are very low (as low as $5.00) and fixed, regardless of the trading amount, the online trading brokerage service is a very attractive option to business investors.

- *Electronic auction to business bidders:*   Some electronic auctions are open only to dealers, for instance, used cars and foreclosed real estate sold by the government. For the auction of flowers to dealers, see chapter 12. The comprehensive list of auction sites is available at www.usaweb.com/auction.html.

- *Online publishing and education:*   Online publishing is not the monopolistic asset of business. However, businesses subscribe to certain professional magazines. The on-demand electronic education program can provide a useful training opportunity for busy employees.

- *Online loan and capital makers:*   Business loans can be syndicated online from the lending companies. IntraLink Corp. provides a solution for syndicates, and BancAmerica offers IntraLoan's matching service to business loan applicants and potential lending corporations (chapter 7). Moreover, some sites, like www.garage.com, provide information about venture capital.

- *Other online services:*   Business is the major user of online consulting, legal advice, health care, delivery requests, electronic stamping, escrowing, and so forth.

6.4   Procurement Management Using the Buyer's Internal Marketplace

As described in the previous sections, a unique feature of the B2B EC platform (that does not exist in the B2C EC platform) is the buyer-oriented marketplace and its use for procurement reengineering. Let us investigate procurement management in depth and examine the business models for it. To do this, we need to distinguish the buyer's internal marketplace from the open bidding sites. General Electric's TPN is an example of a buyer-oriented marketplace with a bidding site.

BUYER'S INTERNAL MARKETPLACE

In the buyer's internal marketplace, the procurement department needs to define the scope of products or projects to buy and invite vendors to bid. The bid prices are pre-offered and stored in the buyer's internal electronic catalogue. There are no purchase determined at this stage. Instead, specifications of the products and their prices will be installed in the intranet-based Web and are accessible by the employees of the buying company. The final buyer (not the procurement department) can very effectively compare the available alternatives in the electronic catalogs, and an organizational purchasing decision can be tightly coupled with the internal workflow management system. There is no delay waiting for bids, and, thus, the bidding cycle time converges to an instant. The internal electronic catalog can be updated manually or in the future by using software agents.

MasterCard and KIST (Korea Institute of Science and Technology) are examples of earlier models of the customer's internal marketplace. The customer's internal marketplace model can be very effectively applied for low-valued items with highly repetitive purchases from committed suppliers, avoiding the storage of inventory.

ISSUES IN PROCUREMENT MANAGEMENT

Purchasing and Supply Management (P&SM) professionals now advocate innovative purchasing as a strategic approach to increase profit margins. Many organizations are discovering that every dollar saved in P&SM contributes directly to the bottom line. Some of the tactics used in this transformation, which are facilitated by the Web are: volume purchase, buying from approved suppliers, selecting the right supplier, group purchasing, awarding business based on performance, improving quality of existing suppliers, doing contract negotiation, forming partnerships with suppliers, and reducing paperwork and administrative cost.

INEFFICIENCY IN PROCUREMENT MANAGEMENT

Approximately 80 percent of an organization's purchases constitute 20 percent of the total purchase value. It is also common to hear purchasing people complain that they expend 80 percent of their time on 20 percent of the total purchase value. A high percentage of this time is spent on non-value-added activities such as performing data entry, correcting errors in paperwork, expediting delivery, or solving quality problems. As such, they do not have sufficient time to pay full attention to upstream activities. Organizations then try to redress this imbalance by implementing new purchasing policies and ISO 9000 procedures. However, all of them face the uphill task of enforcement because these structured procedures require more work and time to execute. For the 20 percent of high value items, purchasing personnel need to spend a lot of time and effort on upstream procurement activities such as qualifying suppliers, building rapport with strategic suppliers, and carrying out supplier evaluation and certification. This is not a single task and therefore procurement reengineering is often needed.

GOALS OF PROCUREMENT REENGINEERING

What many organizations fail to understand is that a fundamental change in their internal processes must be implemented to maximize the full benefits of procurement reengineering. The two critical success factors that most organizations overlook are to cut down the number of routine tasks and to reduce the overall procurement cycle through the use of appropriate technologies such as workflow, groupware, ERP packages, as well as the B2B EC models. By automating and streamlining the laborious routine of the purchasing function, purchasing professionals can focus on more strategic purchases, achieving the following goals:

- Reducing purchasing cycle time and cost
- Enhancing budgetary control
- Eliminating administrative errors
- Increasing buyers' productivity
- Lowering prices through product standardization and consolidation of buys
- Improving information management; e.g., supplier's information and pricing information
- Improving the payment process

THE MAJOR SOLUTION: B2B EC

The immediate benefit that electronic procurement can bring about is in the purchase of MRO items. All the existing manual processes of purchase requisition creation, requests for quotation, invitation to tender, purchase order issuance, goods receiving,

MasterCard's Procurement Card Case

Pleased with the progress of a six-month pilot program, MasterCard International expanded the use of its online buying program throughout the company. Requisitioners placed thousands of transactions over nine months in 1998 with the company's preferred suppliers using Elekom Corp.'s procurement system (www.elekom.com). The system allows requisitioners to select goods and services from MasterCard's own electronic catalog containing more than 10,000 items, to electronically place orders with suppliers, and to pay for products using the MasterCard corporate procurement card. The software, initially used by more than 250 requisitioners, was rolled out to 2,300 users in 1998.

"Given the positive results from using the system over the past few months, it is a logical progression to deploy it companywide. Our objectives for this project were to consolidate buying activities from multiple sites, improve process costs, and reduce our supplier base," said Jim Cullinan, vice president for global purchasing of MasterCard. In conjunction with the expanded deployment, MasterCard plans to add suppliers and catalog content to the system.

---

and payment can be streamlined and automated. However, to implement such automated support, the people involved in the procurement need not only to use internal workflow, groupware, and the internal marketplace but also the suppliers' Web sites. In this sense, the seamless support of procurement management using intranet (for internal marketplace) and extranet (for bid site) is recommended.

CUSTOMER'S INTERNAL MARKETPLACE CASES

Korea Institute of Science and Technology implemented a customer's internal marketplace model to enhance the purchasing process of items like personal computers, office supplies, and chemicals used in laboratories. The procurement department's role is completely eliminated, and the cycle time is reduced from 20 days to 1. The following short case from MasterCard illustrates the model (see Application Case 6.2).

6.5 Supplier-Oriented Marketplace: Cisco Connection Online Case

As mentioned earlier, the supplier-oriented marketplace for B2B EC can be successful if the supplier has a sufficient number of loyal business customers and the frequency of orders is not formidable from the buyer's point of view. Cisco's marketplace belongs to this category. Let us investigate Cisco Connection Online (CCO), which operates the market (Maddox 1998).

CISCO CONNECTION ONLINE

Cisco sold more than $1.0 billion online out of a total $6.4 billion worth of routers, switches, and other network interconnect devices during its 1997 fiscal year. Cisco's Web site has evolved over several years, beginning with technical support for customers and developing into one of the world's largest Internet commerce sites. Today, Cisco offers nearly a dozen Internet-based applications to both end-use customers and reseller partners.

Customer Service

Cisco began providing electronic support in 1991 using the Internet. Software downloads, defect tracking, and technical advice were the first applications. In the spring of 1994, Cisco put its system on the Web and named its site Cisco Connection Online. By 1998, Cisco's customers and reseller partners were logging onto Cisco's Web site about 1 million times a month to receive technical assistance, check orders, or download software. The online service has been so well received that nearly 70 percent of all customer service inquiries are delivered online, as are 90% of software updates.

Online Ordering

Cisco builds virtually all its products to order, so there are very few off-the-shelf products. Before the Cisco Web site, ordering a product has been lengthy and complicated. Cisco began deploying Web-based commerce tools in July 1995, and as of July 1996, the Internet Product Center allowed users to purchase any Cisco product over the Web. In 1999, the same customer's engineer could sit down at a PC, configure a product online, know immediately if there are any errors, and route the order to its procurement department.

Cisco's large customers can take advantage of the features of immediate and automatic access to Cisco's online ordering, configuration, and technical support tools. However, because of their large purchasing volumes, they do not want to access Cisco's Web site each time they place an order or have a question. A program that was launched in November 1997 interactively links the customer's and Cisco's computer systems over the Internet and private networks, so that the configuration and price can be validated at the customer's own PC even before the order is placed. This approach can be possible if the customer commits to Cisco.

With online pricing and configuration tools, about 98 percent of the orders go through Cisco's system, saving time for both Cisco and their customers. Lead times were reduced from 4 to 10 days to 2 to 3 days, and customers' order submission productivity has increased an average of 20 percent. In the first five months of its operation in 1996, Cisco booked over $100 million of sales on the Internet alone. For the first 10 months of 1997, the figure grew tenfold, topping $1 billion. In December 1997, online sales reached over $260 million. Cisco closed 1998 with $4 billion in annualized online sales.

Finding Order Status

Each month in 1998 Cisco's Web site received about 150,000 order status inquiries such as: "When will the order be ready? How should it be classified for customs? Is it eligible for NAFTA? What export control issues apply?" Cisco gives customers the tools on its Web site to find the answers by themselves. In addition, Cisco records a shipping date, the method of shipment, and the current location of each product. The company's primary domestic and international freight forwarders regularly update Cisco's database electronically with the status of each shipment, typically by EDI. The new information in the database automatically updates Cisco's Web site, keeping the customer current on the movement of each order. As soon as an order ships, Cisco sends the customer a notification message by e-mail or fax.

Benefits

- *Reduced operating cost:* Cisco estimates that putting its applications online in 1998 saved the company $363 million per year, or approximately 17.5 percent of the total operating costs.

- *Enhanced technical support and customer service:* With 70 percent of its technical support and customer service calls handled online, Cisco's technical support productivity has increased by 200 percent to 300 percent per year.
- *Reduced technical support staff cost:* The online technical support reduced technical support staff costs by roughly $125 million.
- *Reduced software distribution cost:* Customers download new software releases directly from Cisco's site, saving the company $180 million in distribution, packaging, and duplicating costs. Having product and pricing information on the Web and Web-based CD-ROMs saves Cisco an additional $50 million in printing and distributing catalogs and marketing materials to customers (savings are per year).

The Future and Lessons

Cisco expected online sales to grow to 60 percent of total volume during 1999. If analysts' projections that Cisco's overall sales would grow to $10.5 billion by July of 1999 were correct, then its online sales would reach $5 billion to $6 billion by then as well. By using the Internet, Cisco would be able to increase the sales to business while reducing costs associated with order processing, customer service, technical support, and confirming order status.

6.6   Buyer-Oriented Marketplace: GE's TPN Case Revisited

The most popular type of buyer-oriented marketplace is the buyer's bidding site. As an example, note the functionality of GE's TPN (tpn.geis.com)—the electronic bidding site built to enhance GE's procurement process. Read in the opening section of the chapter about how the TPN Post helped GE's procurement process. Note that GE's TPN is open to other buyers who want to post their RFQs there.

ELECTRONIC BIDDING PROCESS

Under the buyer-oriented marketplace model, sellers can no longer sit and wait for visits from business buyers, as in seller-oriented e-malls. Instead, the bid site provides a chance for the sellers to participate in the bidding process of GE according to the following procedure:

1. Buyers prepare bidding project information
2. Buyers post the bidding projects on the Internet (RFQs)
3. Buyers identify potential suppliers
4. Buyers invite suppliers to bid on projects
5. Suppliers download the project information from the Internet
6. Suppliers submit bids for projects
7. Buyers evaluate the suppliers' bids and may negotiate electronically to achieve the "best deal"
8. Buyers accept the bids that best meet their requirements

BENEFITS TO BUYERS

The GE TPN Post system can improve the productivity of the buyer's sourcing process and allow buyers to access quality goods and services from around the world. This larger pool of suppliers fosters competition and enables the buyers to spend more time negotiating the best deals and less time on administrative procedures. The benefits of joining GE TPN Post as buyers are:

- Identifying and building partnerships with new suppliers worldwide
- Strengthening relationships and streamlining sourcing processes with current business partners
- Rapidly distributing information and specifications to business partners
- Transmitting electronic drawings to multiple suppliers simultaneously
- Cutting sourcing cycle times and reduce costs for sourced goods
- Quickly receiving and comparing bids from large number of suppliers to negotiate better prices

Since GE has opened TPN to other buyers, this benefit can be shared with other companies; but GE can earn fees from them.

BENEFITS TO SELLERS

Sellers in the GE TPN Post system can gain instant access to global buyers with over $1 billion in purchasing power. Sellers may dramatically improve the productivity of bidding and sales activities. The benefits of joining GE TPN Post as sellers are:

- Boosted sales
- Expanded market reach
- Lowered costs for sales and marketing activities
- Shortened selling cycle
- Improved sales productivity
- Streamlined bidding process

LESSONS

The process of electronic bidding and its benefits to buyers and sellers are examined. Since other large companies can easily duplicate this benefit, this kind of buyer-oriented marketplace will grow more popular. This will attract more vendors to cyberspace for B2B electronic marketing.

6.7   Intermediary-Oriented Marketplace: Boeing's PART Case

Boeing's PART case demonstrates the intermediary-oriented B2B marketplace. Boeing plays the role of intermediary in supplying maintenance parts to airlines. Unlike other pure intermediaries like ProcureNet and Industry.net, revenue as an intermediary may be a minor concern to Boeing. Supporting the customers' maintenance through this electronic intermediary service seems the major goal. That is why this model is very important to many assembling companies who provide parts for maintenance.

GOAL OF BOEING'S PART PAGE

The purpose of this electronic intermediary, Boeing's PART, is to link airlines who need maintenance parts with suppliers who are producing the parts for Boeing's aircraft (Teasdale 1997). Boeing's online strategy is to provide a single point of online access through which airlines (the buyers of Boeing's aircraft) and maintenance providers can access the data about parts needed to maintain and operate aircraft, regardless of whether the data is from the airframe builder, component supplier, engine manufacturer, or the airline itself. Thus, Boeing is acting as an intermediary between the airlines and part suppliers. With data from 300 key suppliers of Boeing's airplane parts, Boeing's goal is to provide its customers with one-stop shopping with online maintenance information and ordering capability.

SPARE PARTS BUSINESS USING TRADITIONAL EDI

Ordering spare parts has been a multistep process for many of Boeing's customers. An airline's mechanic informs the purchasing department when a part is needed. Purchasing approves the purchase order and sends it to Boeing by phone or fax. At this point the mechanic does not need to know who produced the part, because the aircraft was purchased from Boeing as one body. However, Boeing has to find out who produced the part and then ask the producer to deliver the part (unless Boeing happens to keep an inventory of the part). The largest airlines began to streamline the ordering process nearly 20 years ago. Because of the volume and regularity of their orders, the largest airlines established EDI connections with Boeing over VANs. Not all airlines were quick to follow suit, however. It took until 1992 to enlist 10 percent of the largest customers, representing 60 percent of the volume, to order through EDI. The numbers have not changed much since then due to the cost and complexity of VAN-based EDI.

DEBUT PART PAGE ON THE INTERNET

Boeing views the Internet as an opportunity to encourage more of its customers to order parts electronically. With the initial investment limited to a standard PC and basic Internet access, even its smallest customers can now participate. Because of its interactive capabilities, many customer service functions that were handled by the telephone are now handled over the Internet.

In November 1996, Boeing debuted its PART page on the Internet, giving its customers around the world the ability to check parts availability and pricing, order parts, and track order status, all online. Less than a year later, about 50 percent of Boeing's customers used it for parts orders and customer service inquiries. In its first year of operation, the Boeing PART page handled over half a million inquiries and transactions, from customers around the world.

BENEFITS OF PART PAGE

Boeing's primary objective for the PART page was to improve service to its customers. Boeing also expects to realize significant operating savings as more of its customers use the Internet. In addition, the PART page could lead to new sales opportunities. Boeing's spare parts business processed about 20 percent more shipments per month in 1997 than it did in 1996 with the same number of data entry people. In addition, as many as 600 phone calls a day to telephone service staff have been eliminated because customers access information about pricing, availability, and order status online. Over time, Boeing anticipates that the PART page will result in fewer parts being returned due to administrative errors. Furthermore, airlines may buy Boeing aircraft the next time they make an aircraft purchase.

PORTABLE ACCESS TO TECHNICAL DRAWINGS/SUPPORT

Airline maintenance is spread out over a wide geographical area. It takes place everywhere in the world the airline flies. At an airport, maintenance activities may take place at the gate, in the line-maintenance department, or at the maintenance operations center. Mechanics are traditionally forced to make repeated, time-consuming trips to the office to consult paper or microfilm reference materials. A single manual may contain as many as 30,000 pages.

For this purpose, in April 1996 Boeing On Line Data (BOLD) went into operation, incorporating not only engineering drawings but manuals, catalogs, and other technical information. As of October 1997, BOLD had 7,500 users in 40 airline customers and another 60 customers in the pipeline. In addition, Portable Maintenance Aid (PMA), which solves the issue of portable access, was developed. Owing to BOLD and PMA, mechanics or technicians are able to access all the information they need to make decisions about necessary repairs at the time and place they need the information.

BENEFITS TO BOEING'S CUSTOMERS

Because they are such recent initiatives, little data is available on the full impact of BOLD and PMA. However, early users report benefits such as:

- *Increased productivity:* Spending less time searching for information freed up engineers and maintenance technicians to focus on more productive activities. One U.S. airline saved $1 million a year when it gave 400 users access to Boeing's BOLD program. Seeing the results of the initial implementation, the airline expanded the service to 2,000 users. A European airline estimated that it will save $1.5 million from BOLD in the first year, due to a nearly 4 percent boost in production and engineering staff productivity.
- *Reduced costs:* With information available online at the gate through PMA, rather than in the crew office, delays at the gate resulting from missing information can be reduced. The European airline mentioned earlier estimates that PMA will reduce flight delays by 5 percent to 10 percent.
- *Increased revenues:* Every 3,000 hours, an airline does a schedule C maintenance check that can keep an airline grounded for up to a week. Idle aircraft cost tens of thousands of dollars a day. Not having information readily available can lengthen the process. The longer the maintenance check, the less revenue opportunity. Through BOLD and PMA, the European airline estimates it will save 1 to 2 days per year for each aircraft, resulting in $43 million in revenue increase.

6.8 Just-in-Time Delivery: FedEx InterNetShop Case

WHY JIT DELIVERY FOR B2B EC

This section investigates the JIT delivery issue in B2B EC. Business customers who run their factories according to the JIT manufacturing principle critically need JIT delivery. In such a case, delivering materials and parts on time is a must. Using EC, it is highly possible to assure JIT deliveries. Just-in-time delivery can be realized by the coordinated effort of delivery-service company and supplier's inventory policy. For example, National Semiconductor was able to deliver to customers JIT by outsourcing the delivery service to FedEx (Application Case 6.3, pg. 218).

Since most companies have to outsource the delivery service, let us review the FedEx case in this section to see how they implement quick delivery service for their customers. Quick delivery does not necessarily mean JIT delivery, but the system for quick delivery is the backbone of JIT delivery. For the B2B EC environment, the advanced confirmation of the delivery date at the contract stage is very important, which has not yet been emphasized in the B2C EC environment.

FEDEX: A DELIVERY COMPANY

A number of delivery and logistics companies, including FedEx, UPS, the U.S. Postal Service, and others are using the Internet in key business processes. FedEx delivers 2.5 million packages daily to 211 countries around the world with an on-time delivery rate of 99 percent. The example of FedEx illustrates the role played by the Internet and private networks in improving efficiency and customer satisfaction.

FEDEX ON THE INTERNET FOR CUSTOMER'S TRACKING REQUEST

In July 1996, FedEx launched FedEx InterNetShip, extending online tracking capabilities to the Internet. Within 18 months, 75,000 customers were using the service. Today, a fedex.com customer can request a parcel pickup or find the nearest drop-off point, compute shipping cost, print packing labels, request invoice adjustments, and track the status of their deliveries without leaving the Web site. Recipients of deliveries can request that FedEx send them e-mail when the package has shipped.

PROPRIETARY NETWORK FOR PROGRESS ENTRY: COSMOS

The company's Web site is just the tip of the iceberg of FedEx's extensive use of networks. Its own proprietary network, FedEx COSMOS, handles 54 million transactions a day. Through the information available on the network, the company can keep track of every package every step of the way from the point at which a customer requests a parcel pickup to the point at which it reaches its final destination. When a customer enters a pickup request, a courier is notified electronically of the time and location. Once at the customer's office, the courier uses a handheld system to scan the bar code on the package, recording that the package has been picked up. FedEx employees record and track the package progress electronically from the van to a FedEx plane to a sorting center where it gets sorted and loaded onto another FedEx plane, to the truck that it gets unloaded onto, to the customer's home or office.

VALUE-ADDED SERVICE TO ENSURE THE CUSTOMER'S DELIVERY COMMITMENT

FedEx also plays a role in other companies' core logistics processes as described in chapter 1. In some instances, FedEx operates the merchant server on which a retailer's Web site runs. In others, FedEx operates warehouses that pick, pack, test, and assemble products, as well as handle the delivery, which sometimes involves consolidating products with other shipments and clearing customs. For customers with valuable or perishable products, the orders have to be filled almost immediately. The information network that enables FedEx's core business to meet its delivery commitments is the foundation for its growing logistics business, as well.

SUPPORTING CUSTOMER'S TAILORED TRACK SYSTEM

Hundreds of thousands of tracking requests per month come from over 5,000 Web sites to fedex.com. These FedEx customers can add a product-tracking feature to the other services they offer to their online customers. If a customer buys a router from Cisco Systems and wants to know when it is supposed to arrive, instead of making a phone call to get the details, he or she can go to Cisco's Web site, enter the order number, and find out that the router is on a FedEx truck and will arrive the next morning. This information appears directly in the Cisco site in a matter of seconds. This service is called *embedded extranet* (chapter 7).

BENEFITS TO FEDEX

FedEx's proprietary network forms the foundation of the company's EC today. As more companies sell tangible goods over the Internet with the promise of quick delivery, FedEx can gain more benefits from the increased business opportunities. For competitive reasons, FedEx has not publicly shared the full extent of benefits it has realized from information technology and electronic networks, except to say that it has enabled FedEx to continuously lower its delivery cost. However, FedEx provided some examples:

Outsourcing On-Time Delivery: National Semiconductor Experience

Up until 1993, National Semiconductor (Nat-Semi) dealt with a variety of different companies to get products from Asian factories to customers across the world, including freight forwarders, customs agents, handling companies, delivery companies, and airlines. In 1993, they decided to outsource this entire process to FedEx. Today, virtually all of NatSemi's products, manufactured in Asia by three company factories and three subcontractors, are shipped directly to a FedEx distribution warehouse in Singapore. Each day, NatSemi sends its orders electronically to FedEx, which makes sure the orders get matched to products and the products are delivered directly to the customers when promised. By going with FedEx as a one-stop shop for their logistics needs, NatSemi has seen a reduction of the average customer delivery cycle from four weeks to one week, and their distribution costs dropped from 2.9 percent of sales to 1.2 percent.

- *Avoided costs:* If not for FedEx PowerShip, FedEx would have had to hire an additional 20,000 employees to pick up packages, answer phone calls at the call centers, and key in air bills. With PowerShip, a good deal of the routine tasks are automated or transferred from FedEx to the customer. Couriers spend less time recording information at the customer site, and phone service representatives spend less time answering calls from customers who now place orders and track their own shipments online.
- *Lower operating costs:* Customers use FedEx InterNetShip to track over 1 million packages per month (and the volume increases at double-digit percentage levels month to month). Without the system, approximately half of these calls would have gone to FedEx's toll-free number, resulting in high expenses.
- *Better customer service:* Customers still have a choice in how they interact with the company, whether by phone, fax or other means. Nearly 950,000 customers (in 1998) find it easier and more convenient to communicate with FedEx electronically.

6.9 Other B2B Models, Auctions, and Services

Many innovative B2B models were developed over the years. In this section we will deal only with some of them and describe some B2B services.

Before we present these topics it is important to note that companies, especially if they are large ones, can use several models. IBM uses a supplier model for its products, a buyer model for procurement, and other models for various other activities.

BUSINESS-TO-BUSINESS AUCTIONS

Earlier in this chapter we briefly referred to both buyer-oriented and supplier-oriented auctions. Here we will look further into this topic. Business-to-business auctions are growing very rapidly due to the following benefits they provide:

Generating Revenue

- New sales channel that supports existing online sales. For example, Weirton Steel Corp. doubled its customer base when it started auctions, see Fickel (1999).
- New venue for disposing of excess, obsolete, and returned products quickly and easily.

Increasing Page Views

- Auctions give sites "stickiness." Auction users spend more time on a site and generate more page views than other users.

Acquiring and Retaining Members

- All bidding transactions result in additional registered members.

There are three major types of B2B auctions according to Forrester Research:

1. *Independent auctions*. In this case companies use a third-party auctioneer to create the site and sell the goods. (e.g., www.fairmarket.com, www.imx exchange.com, and www.auctiongate.com).
2. *Commodity auctions*. In this case many buyers and sellers come together to a third-party Web site. For example, access energy, utilities, and telecommunications are sold at www.band-x.com. The Dutch flower market (chapter 12) is another example. Typical intermediaries are www.metalsite.net and www.fastparts.com.
3. *Private auctions by invitation only*. Several companies bypass the intermediaries and auction their products by themselves. Ingram Micro has its own site, www.auctionblock.com, for selling obsolete computer equipment to its regular business customers.

For further information on B2B auctions, see Fickel (1999).

MANAGED INTERACTIVE BIDDING

The bidding process conducted by companies such as GE and Boeing lasts a day or more and is managed by the companies themselves. In some cases the bidders bid only once. In other cases the bidders can see the lowest bid and change theirs. In such a case the bid is viewed as an auction. Bidding can be managed by an intermediary as shown in Application Case 6.4 (page 220).

Bartering

Related to auctions and bids is *electronic bartering,* the exchange of goods and/or services without the use of money. There are several intermediaries that arrange for bartering (e.g., www.barterbrokers.com). The intermediaries try to match partners, sometimes three or more. Corporate bartering exceeds $100 billion annually in the United States, and much of it can be done electronically. Companies barter office space, idle facilities and labor, products, and banner ads.

FACILITATING AUCTIONS AND BARTERING

Businesses can conduct auctions on an intermediary site. Here is an example of services the intermediary can provide, according to www.fairmarket.com.

APPLICATION CASE 6.4

How FreeMarket Operates: A New B2B Model

Imagine this scenario: United Technologies Corp. needs suppliers to make $24 million worth of circuit boards. Twenty-five hundred suppliers were identified as possible contractors. These were found in electronic registries and directories. The list was submitted to FreeMarkets On-Line Inc. (www.freemarket.com). FreeMarkets experts reduced the list to 1,000, based on considerations ranging from plant location to the size of the supplier. After further analysis of plant capacity and customers' feedback, the list was reduced to 100. A detailed evaluation of the potential suppliers resulted in 50 qualified suppliers who were invited to bid.

Three hours of online competitive bidding was conducted. FreeMarkets divided the job into 12 lots, each of which was put up to bid. At 8:00 A.M., the first lot valued at $2.25 million was placed on the Net. The first bid was $2.25 million, which was seen by all. Minutes later, another bidder placed a $2.0 million bid. Using the reverse (Dutch) method, the bidders further reduced the bids. Minutes before the bid closed, at 8:45 A.M., the 42nd bidder placed a $1.1 million bid. When it all ended, the bids for all 12 lots totaled $18 million (about 35% savings to United Technologies).

To finalize the process, FreeMarkets conducted a very comprehensive analysis on several low bidders of each lot, attempting to look at other criteria in addition to cost. FreeMarkets then recommended the winners and collected its fees.

Source: A. Jahnke, "How Bazaar," *CIO Magazine,* August 1, 1998.

No Resources Required

- No additional hardware, bandwidth, engineering resources, or IT personnel.
- No opportunity costs associated with the redeployment of the necessary resources or hiring costs associated with the acquisition of additional resources.

Own and Control Auction Information

- No intermediary branding, looks like the merchant site.
- Control the valuable Web traffic, page views, and member registration data.
- Set all auction parameters: transaction fee structure, user interface, and reports.
- Easy integration within the merchant site for cohesive auction functionality.

Fast Time to Market

- Have a robust, customized auction up and running immediately, and maintains sale in the future.

Other services provided both buyer and seller functionalities:

Searching and Reporting

A complete set of tools is available to the merchant that allows it to search and report on virtually every relevant auction activity. A summary "At a Glance" report, a comprehensive set of standard reports, and additional ways to analyze more complex information is provided through the Administrative Module. Reports can be exported to Excel or other programs.

Billing and Collection

Merchant-specific shipping weights and charges can be input for automatic calculation of shipping charges. End user credit card data can be required to place a bid. All credit card data is encrypted for secure transmission and storage. All billing information can be easily downloaded for easy integration with existing systems.

BUSINESS-TO-BUSINESS SERVICES

Many companies provide services that are intended to facilitate B2B. Some of these services are provided by intermediaries, others by specialists. Here are some examples.

CommerceNet

CommerceNet (www.commerce.net) is a global nonprofit membership organization that aims to meet the needs of companies doing EC. It targets promoting and supporting emerging communities of EC.

CommerceNet established a forum for companies doing EC to meet and exchange their experiences, while introducing the latest technology to them to facilitate their business. It does contain information about members, which can be buyer or supplier companies. However, no specific product information is stored in its database. In fact, CommerceNet mainly acts as a services provider, not dealing with any of the individual transactions.

CommerceNet also certifies Internet-enabled EDI products.

Open Buying on the Internet

The Open Buying on the Internet (OBI) Consortium (www.openbuy.org) is a nonprofit organization dedicated to developing open standards for B2B Internet commerce. Membership in the consortium, an independent collaborative managed by CommerceNet, is open to buying and selling organizations, technology providers, financial institutions, and other interested parties on an annual fee basis.

ConnectUS

ConnectUS is an online service designed for use by companies paying with corporate purchasing cards. It is basically a for-fee database, operated by Thomas Publishing Co. and General Electric Information Systems, allowing companies to search for suppliers anywhere in the world. The service may cut up to 90 percent of the transaction cost for the average ($150) purchase. ConnectUS also aids companies in overcoming the shortfalls of purchasing card programs, which are difficult to audit, sometimes resulting in vendor overpayment.

ConnectUs provides all the necessary information that supports card purchasing and facilitates trades done with EDI. (See Corporate Cashflow, April 1997). The service is now offered as part of www.geis.com and www.thomasregister.com systems.

The Global Business Alliance Incorporated

The Global Business Alliance Incorporated has established a network that helps firms line up suppliers, negotiate contracts, solicit joint venture partners, arrange for delivery of goods, and make payments. The network, called IBEX (International Business Exchange), is supported by large banks and corporations such as AT&T, Viacom, and Microsoft.

IBEX yellow pages contain data on over 12 million corporations worldwide. Users provide a desired profile of the potential partners, and intelligent software agents search the database for a match. IBEX's system includes full message encryption and password control for transmitting e-mail, faxes, and payment authorization over the Internet.

By design, each IBEX partner functions as an EDI hub. It is especially useful for small companies that do not have the resources necessary for efficient EC. About 1.5 million subscribers are likely to join IBEX by 2000. The major advantage to small businesses is the ability to tap new markets around the world at a low cost ($250 access fee and $25 per transaction, versus 20 percent finder's fee elsewhere). General Electric is one of the major partners in IBEX and allows IBEX users to access GE's TPN.

World Insurance Network

World Insurance Network (WIN) is a globally managed network created by the insurance industry in England in an effort to facilitate EC between insurance brokers and underwriters. It advocates systems solutions that replace paper, fax, copier, courier, and mail with IT, by telling its members how to implement EC.

The Financial Services Technology Consortium and the Smart Card Forum (SCF)

The Financial Services Technology Consortium (FSTC) and the Smart Card Forum (SCF) are organizations of banks, financial institutions, computer and telecommunications firms, and government and private research laboratories that jointly pursue EC research related to electronic banking and payment systems. Some projects are interbank check imaging, electronic checks, fraud prevention and control, and the creation of standards and protocols.

Joint Transmission Services Information Network

Several hundred utilities have developed very secure systems (or a virtual private Internet) for secure transmission of sensitive data among the members.

Others

Hundreds of other services are available, ranging from finding business partners in Asia (www.asiansources.com) to organizing specialty markets over the extranet (www.chemdex.com).

6.10 From Traditional to Internet-Based EDI

The majority of B2B transactions are conducted by EDI and/or extranets. An example is shown in Figure 6.5. In this section, EDI and its transition to the Internet platform will be described. The extranet is covered in chapter 7.

TRADITIONAL EDI
EDI and Standards

Electronic data interchange has been around for almost 30 years in the non-Internet environment. It is a system that standardizes the process of trading and tracking routine business documents, such as purchase orders, invoices, payments, shipping manifests, and delivery schedules. Electronic data interchange translates these documents into a globally understood business language and transmits them between trading partners using secure telecommunications links (Figure 6.6). The most popular standard is United Nations EDI for Administration, Commerce, and Trade (EDIFACT). In the United States, the most popular standard is ANSI X.12. Traditional EDI users (most Fortune 1,000 or global 2,000 companies) use leased or dedicated telephone lines or a VAN, such as those run by IBM and AT&T, to carry these data exchanges. To distinguish it from Internet-based EDI, we call EDI on the non-Internet platform traditional EDI.

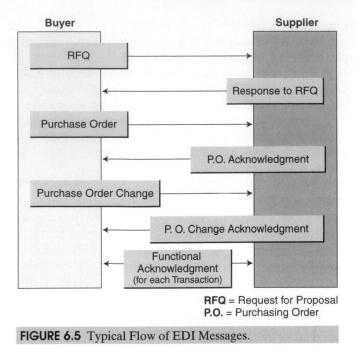

FIGURE 6.5 Typical Flow of EDI Messages.

FIGURE 6.6 Traditional and Web-Based EDI.

Traditional Electronic Data Interchange (EDI)

Web-based EDI

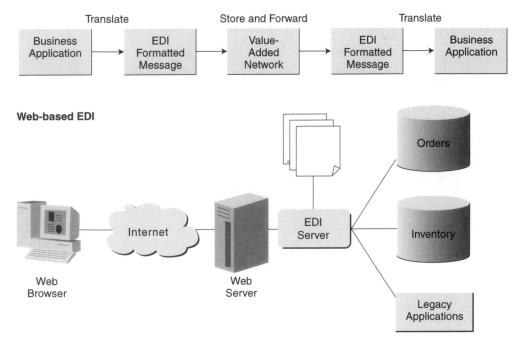

Applications of EDI

Traditional EDI has changed the landscape of business, triggering new definitions of entire industries. Well-known retailers, such as The Home Depot, Toys R Us, and Wal-Mart, would operate very differently today without EDI, since it is an integral and essential element of their business strategy. Thousands of global manufacturers, including Proctor and Gamble, Levi Strauss, Toyota, and Unilever, have used EDI to redefine relationships with their customers through such practices as quick response retailing and JIT manufacturing. These highly visible, high-impact applications of EDI by large companies have been extremely successful.

Limitations of Traditional EDI

However, despite the tremendous impact of traditional EDI among industry leaders, the current set of adopters represents only a small fraction of potential EDI users. In the United States, where several million businesses participate in commerce every day, fewer than 100,000 companies have adopted EDI (in 1998). Furthermore, most of the companies have had only a small number of their business partners on the EDI, mainly due to its high cost. Therefore, in reality, most businesses have not benefited from EDI, the major factors being:

- Significant initial investment is needed
- Restructuring business processes is necessary to fit EDI requirements
- Long start-up time is needed
- Use of expensive private VAN is necessary
- High EDI operating cost is needed
- There are multiple EDI standards
- The system is complex to use
- There is a need to use a converter to translate business transactions to EDI standards

These factors suggest that traditional EDI—relying on formal transaction sets, translation software, and VANs—is not suitable as a long-term solution for most corporations, because it does not meet the following requirements:

- Enables more firms to use EDI
- Encourages full integration of EDI into trading partners' business processes
- Simplifies EDI implementation
- Expands the capabilities of online information exchange

Therefore, a better infrastructure is needed; such infrastructure is **Internet-based EDI.**

INTERNET-BASED EDI

Why Internet-based EDI

When considered as a channel for EDI, the Internet appears to be the most feasible alternative for putting online B2B trading within the reach of virtually any organization, large or small. There are several reasons for firms to create EDI ability over the Internet:

- The Internet is a publicly accessible network with few geographical constraints. Its largest attribute, large-scale connectivity (without demand to have any special company networking architecture) is a seedbed for growth of a vast range of business applications.

- The Internet global internetwork connections offer the potential to reach the widest possible number of trading partners of any viable alternative currently available.
- Using the Internet can cut communication costs by over 50 percent.
- Using the Internet to exchange EDI transactions is consistent with the growing interest of business in delivering an ever-increasing variety of products and services electronically, particularly through the Web.
- Internet-based EDI can complement or replace current EDI applications.
- Internet tools such as browsers and search engines are very user-friendly, and most users today know how to use them.

Types of Internet-based EDI

The Internet can support EDI in a variety of ways.

- Internet e-mail can be used as the EDI message transport in place of VAN. For this end, the Internet Engineering Task Force (IETF) is considering standards for encapsulating the messages within Secure Internet Mail Extension (S/MIME).
- A company can create an extranet that enables trading partners to enter information in Web form whose fields correspond to the fields in an EDI message or document.
- Companies can utilize the services of a Web-based EDI hosting service in much the same way that companies rely on third parties to host their commerce sites. Netscape Enterprise is illustrative of the type of Web-based EDI software that enables a company to provide their own EDI services over the Internet, while Harbinger Express is illustrative of those companies that provide third-party hosting services.

Prospect of Internet-based EDI

Companies who currently possess traditional EDI have had a positive response to Internet-based EDI. A 1998 Forester Research, Inc. survey of 50 Fortune 1,000 companies showed that nearly half of them planned to use EDI over the Internet by the end of the decade. By late 1997, 8 percent were already moving to Internet-based EDI, another 12 percent were piloting systems, and 32 percent were considering them. The companies polled said that an average of 16 percent of their traffic will move from VAN and leased lines to the Internet by 2000. Some EDI participants are turning to Internet-based systems to eliminate costly VANs. In traditional EDI, they also have to pay for network transport, translation, and routing of EDI messages into their legacy processing systems. Frequently, companies combine traditional EDI with the Internet by having their Internet-based orders transmitted to a VAN or service provider that translates the data into an EDI format and sends it to their host computers. The Internet simply serves as an alternative transport mechanism to a more expensive lease line. The combination of the Web, XML (appendix B-4), and Java makes EDI worthwhile even for small, infrequent transactions. Whereas EDI is not interactive, the Web and Java were designed specifically for interactivity as well as ease of use.

6.11 Integration with Back-End Information Systems

Since most commercial sites are seller-oriented marketplaces, integration with the buyer's back-end information systems is a challenging issue to be resolved for effective procurement management. The typical back-end information systems tend to be developed on the intranet (with e-mail, workflow, and groupware capabilities), DBMS, legacy systems, and ERP. Integration of EC with the intranet is relatively simple as far as the firewall can control the unauthorized access to the internal network (chapter 7). The DBMS providers tend to support the Web-based DBMS. The Web page can be dynamically generated from the database just like reports are generated from the database. So our keen concern is in the way to integrate the EC platform with ERP software.

ENTERPRISE RESOURCE PLANNING SYSTEM

Enterprise Resource Planning (ERP) is an enterprise-wide application software that can provide a centralized repository of information for the massive amount of transactional detail generated daily. It integrates core business processes from planning to production, distribution, and sales. A popular ERP solution is SAP's R/3. However, the early versions of ERP solution focused on the intranet-based groupware, so effective integration with EC was not established. The approaches taken for the integration between EC and ERP are the inside-out approach, outside-in approach, and open electronic cart approach.

Inside-Out Approach: Extend ERP Outward

The leading ERP vendors, such as SAP, PeopleSoft, Oracle, Baan, and J.D. Edwards, offer the way to extend their applications to users through a Web interface as depicted in Figure 6.7. For instance, SAP offers a B2B Internet-commerce system to

FIGURE 6.7 Architectures of Integrating EC with ERP.

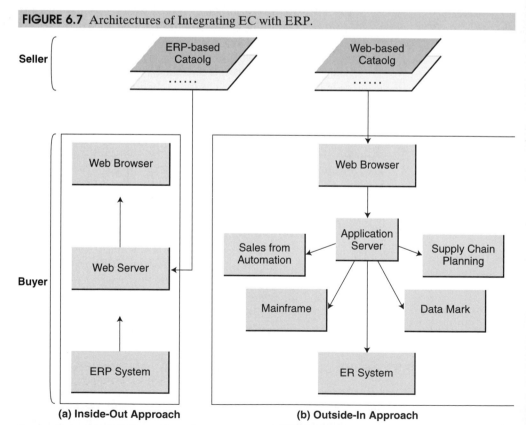

(a) Inside-Out Approach   **(b) Outside-In Approach**

Source: Compiled C. Sellman, Extending E-Business to ERP (Advisor Media, Inc., San Diego, CA, January 1999).

be used within the R/3 system, and the strategic partner, Commerce One, provides additional commerce functionality to operate with SAP. The SAP B2B Procurement solution (BBP) is provided as part of the SAP supply chain optimization planning and execution initiative. Each desktop within an organization is able to use a single entry screen to purchase goods and check pricing from multiple suppliers, availability, and delivery times. This cuts out middlemen and reduces costs. Commerce One announced the MultiSupplier Catalog (MSC). The catalog system provides buy-side information to connect multiple suppliers and integrates with the R/3 Material Management Module. It is also accessible from SAP BBP, when available. This approach assumes that both parties involved in a B2B EC are equipped with the ERP software (Nelson 1998).

When the e-business solution requires a simple mapping of ERP functionality to a Web interface, this inside-out architecture can be highly effective. It lets companies distribute ERP transaction capabilities to a wide audience of Web users without requiring that they load any specific client software on their PCs. However, companies should consider whether inside-out architecture enables them to integrate best-breed technologies. Also, most companies use multiple back-end systems in addition to their ERP system, such as legacy systems or data warehouse. However, the inside-out approach is difficult to integrate with multiple systems, and when the e-business processes do not map directly with the ERP system, the inside-out approach breaks down.

Outside-In Approach

In this approach, rather than extending the reach of ERP-based business processes through a Web server, the outside-in approach uses a robust software named application server, which has the ability to integrate multiple systems into an e-business solution as depicted in Figure 6.7. The outside-in architecture is better suited for complex e-business with multiple back-end and front-end applications. Following the outside-in approach, the e-business application resides within the application server rather than within the individual back-end systems. Typical application servers are Application Server (Netscape), Enterprise Server (Microsoft), Domino (Lotus), Websphere (IBM), and Enterprise Server (Sun). However, the outside-in approaches are limited by the capabilities of the application server platforms upon which they are built (Sullivan 1999a).

Open Electronic Cart Approach

In this approach, the buyer keeps a shopping basket, which resides at the buyer's PC. Items from multiple sources can be tentatively selected and stored in the buyer's electronic cart (e-cart). The order can be made and stored in the e-cart as well. However, the e-cart has an open file format, so the ERP or any legacy systems can be interfaced easily. This architecture is simple and economical and suits the B2B EC environment well (Lee and Lee 1998).

6.12 The Role of Software Agents for B2B EC

AGENT'S ROLE IN THE SELLER-ORIENTED MARKETPLACE

In chapter 2, software agents are used to aid the comparison-shopping process. The major role of software agents there is collecting data from multiple commercial sites. These software agents mainly collect information from the seller-oriented marketplace, so they can be used both for consumers and business buyers.

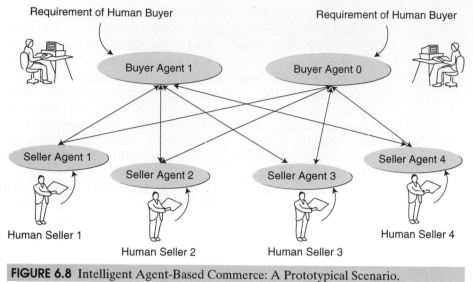

FIGURE 6.8 Intelligent Agent-Based Commerce: A Prototypical Scenario.

Source: J. K. Lee, and W. Lee (1997).

AGENT'S ROLE IN THE BUYER-ORIENTED MARKETPLACE

When a large number of customers want to collect a request for quote (RFQ) from multiple potential suppliers in the buyer-oriented marketplace, answering such numerous inquiries manually will become physically impossible and uneconomical. Therefore, software agents need to assist both buyers and sellers. To make agent-based commerce possible, intelligent buyer agents and seller agents need to be developed, as depicted in Figure 6.8.

Agents need to have the capability of meta-problem solving (the ability to understand how to react to the received message and what to say for the context) and communication controller (interpret the other agent's message and synthesize messages understandable to the other agents). UNIK-AGENT in Figure 6.9 adopted this architecture (Lee and Lee 1997). A special issue on agents was published by *Communications of the ACM* (March 1999), which includes the review on the agents that buy and sell (Maes et al. 1999).

Agents need to use commonly agreed-upon agent communication languages, (ACL) like KQML (knowledge query manipulation language; Finin et al. 1993). Agent Communication Languages consists of performatives and parameters. For instance, *tell* is a performative, and *sender* and *receiver* are parameters. To develop a dedicated ACL for EC, we need to augment the parameters to incorporate the generic terms necessary for EC and product specification. Agents also need to understand the protocol of contract types that the involved agents will follow for each bid. The contract type definition needs to be standardized worldwide to support the compatible communication among agents. For more information about agents, refer to appendix C.

6.13   Electronic Marketing in B2B

In the previous sections we described the various models of B2B and discussed several issues related to B2B implementation. However, we did not discuss the issue of B2B marketing, namely, how a company can find customers for its products. In fact, companies compete strongly in the B2B market. The discussion about advertisement (chap-

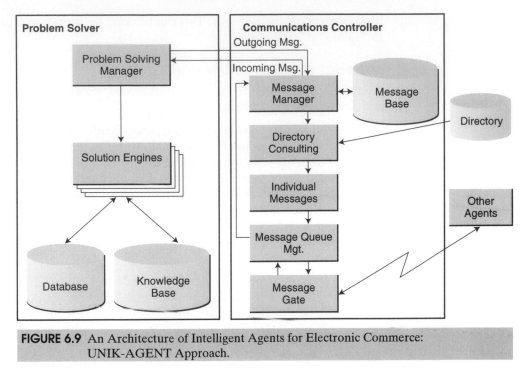

FIGURE 6.9 An Architecture of Intelligent Agents for Electronic Commerce: UNIK-AGENT Approach.

Source: J. K. Lee, and W. Lee (1997).

ter 4) and market research and buyers' behavioral issues described in chapter 3 need to be adapted to the corporate environment. Here are some related issues, most of which are adapted from Silverstein (1999).

DIRECT MARKETING TO REACH FUNCTIONAL BUYERS

In the typical business organization, buying decisions, especially for products over a few thousand dollars, are made by groups of individuals. As a result, direct marketers need to extend the reach of their programs to different functional areas and perhaps even different levels within a functional area.

There are multiple buyers and influencers in any organization who play a role in the buying decision. You may know with reasonable certainty who your primary target is, but secondary targets can be just as important to reach. You may have to reach business buyers and influencers in three basic management areas (functional management, financial management, and general management) and do it at middle to upper managerial, as well as technical, levels. To do it companies need accurate e-mail lists, which they can develop by viewing companies' Web sites and reviewing annual reports and other public documents.

RELATIONSHIP MARKETING

Business buyers are not always ready to buy products or services when you are ready to sell them. Factors you cannot control, such as the company's budgeting process, the need for additional approvals, or purchasing procedures, may have a direct impact on plans to purchase. There may be a casual interest in the product but not an immediate need.

The smart B2B direct marketer compensates for this uncertainty by making sure a program of regular, ongoing communications (often called a continuity program) is in front of prospects periodically. This can be done by direct e-mail and by placing the information on the Web site.

AUDIENCE STRATEGY AND MAILING LISTS

Audience strategy drives the process of evaluating and selecting mailing lists. There are three basic kinds of lists:

1. *Your house list*. The house list is typically made up of customer and prospect names (with appropriate segmentation) collected by a variety of methods: input from the sales force, trade shows, leads from various media, and so on.
2. *Response list*. These are lists with names of individuals who responded to you by e-mail, filling out Web questionnaires, and so forth. Typical response lists include subscribers, buyers, and member lists.
3. *Compiled list*. These lists are compiled from a variety of sources, including telephone directories.

ELECTRONIC/INTERACTIVE MEDIA

Electronic or interactive media presents the B2B direct marketer with the most exciting creative potential. There are three basic media, each with its own creative considerations: CD-ROMs, e-mail, and the Web. Electronic mail and the Web are Internet-based media. The CD-ROM medium offers opportunities to execute full-fledged multimedia promotions with scripted copy, music, and full-motion video. From a direct marketing perspective, CD-ROMs should incorporate plenty of interactivity and, if appropriate, facilitate response. They are also increasingly being used to "connect" to the Internet; for example, an electronic catalog can be housed on a CD and, through a link to a Web address, can be automatically updated. This technique draws a prospect or customer to the marketer's Web site for additional information.

Currently, e-mail is a text-only medium, although graphic e-mail is on the horizon. The Web is the interactive area receiving the most attention from direct marketers. Creatively, the Web combines the qualities of several direct marketing media with some of its own unique ones. It is similar to direct mail in that it can accommodate integrated copy and graphics. Like broadcast and CD-ROM, the Web also facilitates the use of sound and multimedia, but the Web is unique in its construction and its instant interactivity.

HOW TO BUILD YOUR E-MAIL LISTS AND MARKETING DATABASE

Perhaps the area with the most payback potential is your house list—or what should be your marketing database. The list can be enhanced with marketing intelligence about each of the individuals on it. In building e-mail lists make sure to avoid:

- entries that have wrong contacts,
- lists that are composed of many different unorganized lists,
- a list that is embarrassingly out-of-date,
- a list that cannot be segmented,
- a list that is not being used often enough.

INTERNET MARKETING STRATEGIES

Several potential marketing strategies can be used in B2B. Silverstein (1999) classifies them into the following five categories:

1. Generating and qualifying leads with the Internet.
2. Using Internet events to promote products and services.
3. Executing instant fulfillment on the Internet.
4. Generating orders through the Internet.
5. Enhancing customer relationships with the Internet.

Some of these topics were discussed in chapters 3 and 4. For further discussion see Silverstein (1999).

6.14 Solutions of B2B EC

In this chapter, we have seen several business models and architectures useful for B2B EC. Now, let us compare the key **required features of B2B EC** to those of B2C EC. Currently, most B2B EC platforms are mainly developed with the idea of supplier-oriented marketplaces, so this platform for B2B EC is not significantly different from the platform for B2C EC (Davis 1997). In the future, however, B2B EC needs to be equipped with the following eight features to distinguish it from B2C EC. These eight features also provide a fertile opportunity for B2B EC research (Lee 1998a). These features are discussed below.

1. *Management of buyer information at buyer sites to integrate with corporate information systems:* The platforms for the supplier-oriented marketplace store the customers' information in the suppliers' servers. Business buyers cannot effectively manage the procurement information at their servers, resulting in poor integration with the buyer's information system. Thus, the B2B EC platform needs to store the buyer's ordered information in the buyer's server.

B2C EC Platform	B2B EC Platform
• Buyer's information stored in the seller's server.	• Buyer's information needs to be stored in the buyer's server to integrate with the buyer's information system, such as intranet, workflow, and ERP.
• Limited bookkeeping is supported.	• Complete bookkeeping is necessary.
• Web technology using a thin client is usually in use.	• Web technology with thick client is needed. Java and External Helper Programs at client PC are necessary.

2. *Comparison shopping with buyer's own e-cart*: The supplier-oriented marketplace stores the shopping cart in the supplier's server. However, to compare the items from multiple e-stores, it is convenient to pick the items for the buyer's e-cart tentatively so that the buyer's organizational decision making can be supported by the information in the cart.

B2C EC Platform	B2B EC Platform
• Customers need to visit many e-malls.	• Meta-malls architecture is needed for customers to reduce the effort of visiting many sites (Lee and Lee 1998b).
• Every e-mall asks customers to use the proprietary shopping bag and digital wallet.	• Standard shopping bag and digital wallet that can work independently of e-malls are necessary.

(continued)

B2C EC Platform	B2B EC Platform
• A software agent merely helps the search process.	• Comparison shopping needs to be treated as multiple criteria decision support.
• Customer membership registration is requested for each mall.	• Shared customer membership is necessary to allow the comparison of multiple malls with a single registration.

3. ***Just-in-time delivery***: The business who operates the assembly line in JIT manner needs JIT delivery.

B2C EC Platform	B2B EC Platform
• Inventory availability is not displayed.	• Dynamic inventory availability should be displayed to customers.
• Precise delivery date is less critical.	• Precise delivery date should be dynamically confirmed at ordering time.
• Ordering system is separated from inventory system.	• Integration of orders with inventory, production scheduling, and delivery scheduling systems is essential.

4. ***Buyer-oriented directory***: The supplier-oriented directory is not easy to use from the business buyer's point of view. The buyer needs to construct a buyer-oriented directory that will be maintained by software agents.

B2C EC Platform	B2B EC Platform
• Seller-oriented directory is popular.	• To big buyers, buyer-oriented directory should be offered.
• Major motivation of EC is sales promotion.	• Additional motivation is reengineering the acquisition process.
• Either buyer- or seller-oriented directory is developed.	• Intermediary directory is necessary to coordinate seller- and buyer-oriented directories.

5. ***Formal contract with bidding process***: Business contract needs more formal documentation and protocol. The buyer may need to attach an electronic invoice for their organizational decision and audit.

B2C EC Platform	B2B EC Platform
• Ordering without formal contract is sufficient for order fulfillment.	• Formal contract with electronic documents that include specific terms and conditions is necessary.
• Free contract protocol.	• Legitimate contract protocol needs to be conformed.
• Electronic versions of traditional bidding and auction are implemented.	• More creative contract protocol can be innovated.

6. ***Organizational purchasing decision***: To assist the organizational purchasing decision-making process, the workflow should be integrated with the B2B EC platform.

B2C EC Platform	B2B EC Platform
• Purchasing is an individual buyer's decision.	• Purchasing is an organizational buyer's decision.

B2C EC Platform	B2B EC Platform
• Buying decision process does not need coordination.	• Buying decision is made as a combination of synchronous group decision (using Web conference and Internet phone) and asynchronous group decision (using workflow tools).

7. *Agent-based commerce*: Agents need to be more intelligent to understand and respond appropriately. The language for agent-based commerce needs to be standardized for global B2B EC.

B2C EC Platform	B2B EC Platform
• Human interactively involved in the buying decision.	• Buyer's and seller's software agents assist communication to minimize human involvement.
• Software agent in one site may not understand the norm of the counterpart agents.	• Mutually agreed contract type conformation is necessary to establish understandable communication among agents.
• Buyers have to search around the seller's products catalog, configuring manually.	• Seller agents assist the configuration process based on the buyer's requirement specification.
• Seller's data mining is popular.	• Buyer's data mining is additionally necessary.

8. *Secure large payment*: Business purchase needs large payment, and the credit card is too expensive for electronic payments. Electronic fund transfer with a smart-card-based certification seems an appropriate payment method for B2B EC.

B2C EC Platform	B2B EC Platform
• Credit card is popular, which charges the relatively high fee to sellers.	• Electronic check and EFT will become popular. Fees are traditionally paid by payer. Security, certification, and nonrepudiation will become more critical. Therefore, registered delivery, which keeps the important transaction record at the third party, will become popular (see chapter 8).

6.15 Managerial Issues

1. *Focus of EC management:* Select from the three business models of B2B EC (supplier-oriented, buyer-oriented, and intermediary-oriented marketplaces). Each individual company should select an appropriate model depending upon the major emphasis of management.
2. *Sales promotion:* To promote sales, adopt the supplier-oriented marketing approach, and consider joining the other popular, intermediary-oriented marketplaces, as well.
3. *Purchase process reengineering:* To reengineer the purchasing process, establish a customer-oriented marketplace if the sales volume is big enough to attract the attention of major vendors. Otherwise, join the third-party intermediary-oriented marketplace.

4. *JIT delivery:* Outsource to a reliable delivery service provider. Make sure the advanced assurance of JIT delivery can be committed.

5. *New electronic intermediary business:* Open an electronic brokerage or retailing of industrial supplies.

6. *Provision of solutions:* Since the technology for B2B EC is at the embryonic stage, the solution providers have a huge opportunity for selling new products.

7. *Business ethics:* Since B2B EC counts on the sharing of mutual information, business ethics are a must. Accessing unauthorized parts should not be attempted, and privacy of partners should be protected both technically and legally.

Summary

The compilation of this chapter helps you in attaining the following learning objectives:

1. **Applications of B2B EC.** Users of B2B EC, both sellers and buyers, are businesses. The B2B EC platform is an effective media for managing the supply chain, telemarketing, procurement, intermediary, JIT delivery, networking with business partners, networking between headquarter and subsidiaries, and online services.

2. **Key technologies for B2B EC.** The B2B EC platforms employ EDI, intranet, extranet, and integration with back-end information systems, as well as the Internet.

3. **Architectural Models of B2B EC.** Three typical architectural models are supplier-oriented marketplace, buyer-oriented marketplace, and intermediary-oriented marketplace.

4. **Characteristics of supplier-oriented marketplace.** A supplier offers an e-store to promote sales. The customers are both consumers and business buyers. This is a popular type of initial electronic marketplace. Auctions are becoming popular to clear the surplus. Suppliers manage the ordered information, so business buyers cannot effectively organize their ordered information in this architecture.

5. **Characteristics of buyer-oriented marketplace.** A buying company opens a bidding site to enhance its purchasing procedure. This model is a unique entity of B2B EC that does not exist in B2C EC. The electronic bidding can reduce the purchasing cost and cycle time. The customer-oriented marketplace is an effective medium for buyers, but sellers have to search for the sites with relevant tenders. (Use smart search engines).

6. **Characteristics of intermediary-oriented marketplace.** A third party for buyers and sellers opens an intermediary e-store. The electronic intermediary may be used for both consumers and business buyers, depending upon the type of products. The third-party electronic auction and bidding sites are gaining popularity. An assembly company may also play the role of intermediary between its customers and part suppliers. This can enhance the customers' maintenance.

7. **Benefits of B2B EC to procurement reengineering.** The benefits of B2B EC to procurement reengineering are reduced procurement labor, reduced materials costs, redeployment of the staff involved in the procurement process, secured time for strategic activities by reducing manual works, reduced cycle time, automatic reconciliation of invoices with purchase orders, and discovery of new suppliers.

8. **Importance of JIT delivery in B2B EC.** The manufacturing systems have to accommodate make-to-order and mass customization because the customers

can order directly from manufacturers. To run the company in this setting, JIT manufacturing is essential and the parts should be delivered in a JIT manner. Offering a tracking system to customers is a way to report the status of delivery.

9. **Characteristics of Internet-based EDI.** Traditional EDI systems were implemented in VAN, limiting the accessibility of small companies. Internet-based EDI can offer wide accessibility to most companies in the world. Three types of Internet-based EDI can be used. First, the Internet is used in place of VAN. Second, Web form fields replace the EDI message format. Third, a Web-based EDI hosting service is used.

10. **Method of integrating EC with back-end information systems.** EC can be easily integrated with the initiating side but not with the responding side. For instance, in the supplier-oriented marketplace, it is not easy for the buying companies to organize the ordered information, because the information is scattered to various sellers' servers. Therefore, a buyer-owned shopping cart, which can interface with the back-end information systems, is necessary.

11. **Role of agents for B2B EC.** The agents (buyer agents) for retailing are used to search for the items in the supplier- and intermediary-oriented electronic marketplaces. This can be used for the B2B EC environment as well. However, the agents (seller agent) that help the sellers are necessary in the buyer-oriented electronic marketplace. Therefore, the collaboration between buyer agents and seller agents has become necessary.

12. **Issues of B2B marketing.** As in B2C, companies need to continuously search for new customers and make sure that the existing ones will stay loyal. Some of the ways of doing so are similar to what sellers do for B2C; others are unique for business customers. Sellers must find who the real buyers are so they can direct appropriate advertisement. Audience and interactive media are useful and creation of a detailed database is a must. Segmentation is used in many cases. Five Internet marketing strategies were found to be successful.

13. **Characteristics of the solutions for B2B EC.** The solutions for B2B EC need to support the following capabilities: integrating the buyer's order information with back-end information systems, buyer's own shopping cart to aid comparison shopping over multiple sources, JIT delivery, buyer-oriented directory, formal electronic contract, organizational purchasing process, and securing large payment.

Keywords

- Agents for B2B EC
- Business-to-business electronic commerce (B2B EC)
- Buyer-oriented marketplace
- Electronic data interchange (EDI)
- Enterprise resource planning (ERP)
- Integration of EC with back-end information systems
- Intermediary-oriented marketplace
- Internet-based EDI
- Just-in-time (JIT) delivery
- Online services in business
- Procurement management
- Required features for B2B EC
- Solutions for B2B EC
- Supply chain management
- Supplier-oriented marketplace
- Value added networks (VANS)
- Virtual Corporation

Questions for Review

1. Describe the relationships between B2B EC with supply chain management, procurement management, electronic marketing, intranet, and extranet.
2. List the business models of B2B EC.
3. Explain how using B2B EC can enhance the procurement process.

4. Describe how Cisco succeeded in selling their products and providing services to their customers.
5. Explain how GE reengineered its procurement process.
6. Describe how Boeing plays the role of intermediary between their customers and parts suppliers.
7. Explain how FedEx meets the quick delivery requirement by using the Internet.
8. Define EDI.
9. Describe the advantage of Internet-based EDI over traditional EDI.
10. Explain the role of agents in searching and comparing items of buyers' interest.
11. Explain the required features for the B2B EC platform.
12. Describe the various perspectives of B2B EC solutions.

Questions for Discussion

1. Can both consumers and businesses use the supplier-oriented marketplace?
2. Can both consumers and businesses use the buyer-oriented marketplace?
3. Can businesses continue to use the supplier-oriented e-malls platform for B2B EC? To what extent is this proposition correct, and what is the limitation?
4. How can buying companies from the supplier-oriented workplace integrate the order information with the corporation's procurement systems?
5. GE has opened its TPN for procurement process reengineering.
   - Can other big corporations follow the same strategy? Why or why not?
   - Can small businesses follow the same strategy as well? If not, what should their strategy be?
   - What could be the response of vendors to the proliferating buyer-oriented marketplaces?
6. What should be the architecture that will assure JIT delivery at the time of ordering?
7. How do companies eliminate the potential limitations and risks associated with Internet-based EDI?
8. How can the software agents work for multiple sellers and buyers? What kind of communication language can the agents use?
9. What are the required features of a desirable B2B EC platform?
10. To what extent, do current B2B solutions meet the required features?

Questions for Cases

1. *Read the GEs TPN Post case in the opening section (section 6.1)*

   1. Describe the original motivation of developing TPN Post.
   2. Identify the benefits of TPN in terms of procurement processing time, labor cost, and purchasing price.
   3. Identify the benefits to the joining suppliers.
   4. Visit tpn.geis.com and find the plan of extending the applications.
   5. Discuss whether TPN's success story can be replicated in other companies. Why and why not?

2. *Read the Cisco Connection Online (CCO) case in section 6.5.*

   1. What is the business model of CCO?
   2. What are the percentages of volume handled by CCO?
   3. What kinds of inquiry are supported when customers check their order status?
   4. What are the benefits of CCO to Cisco and customers?
   5. What are Cisco's prospective online sales?

3. *Read GE's TPN Post Case (section 6.6)*

1. What is the business model of GE's TPN Post?
2. What is the bidding process in TPN?
3. What motivates buyers to join the TPN?
4. What are the pros and cons of opening the TPN to other buyers?
5. What are the benefits of joining TPN as sellers?

4. *Read Boeing's PART Case (section 6.7)*

1. What is the role of Boeing in the PART page case?
2. What are the benefits to the airlines?
3. How can the mechanics (customers who order) at the various repair sites access the electronic manual information?
4. How can BOLD and PMA work together with PART to serve the moving mechanics?
5. What are the benefits to Boeing of deploying the PART page?
6. Can ProcureNet and Industry.net compete with Boeing's PART in selling the parts of Boeing's aircraft?

Team Exercises

1. For each case above, explore why these companies were able to succeed with the Internet-based business model. Select a key competitor in each case, and study why the competitor could not respond effectively to the opportunities of Internet technology, if that is so.
2. Select a company you can access. Design a desirable architecture for a B2B EC platform for the company, considering the required features described in section 6.12.

Internet Exercises

1. Enter www.cisco.com and www.dell.com, and examine the sites from the business buyer's perspective. Find out how to order on the supplier-oriented marketplaces. Design a way to integrate the electronic marketplace with the ERP system of the buying company.
2. Enter tpn.geis.com and review the bidding process of TPN. Describe the preparations your company should make in order to bid on GE jobs.
3. Enter www.commerceone.com and review the capability of BuySite and MarketSite. Find out how Commerce One supports the integration of the multiple sellers' electronic catalogs for a specific buyer.
4. Enter www.allsystem.com to review All-System Aerospace International Inc., who handles the aircraft parts of several vendors. Evaluate whether this site can compete with Boeing's PART system from the aircraft repairman's point of view.
5. Find the URL of FedEx's InterNetShip site using a search engine. List the scope of support that the customers can enjoy, such as checking the status of deliveries.
6. Try the sites www.fastparts.com, www.ariba.com, www.tandem.com, www.trilogy.com, www.freemarkets.com, www.electricnet.com, www.harbinger.com, and www.ecweb.com. Describe a business model of B2B EC with each site.

R E A L   W O R L D   C A S E

Fruit of the Loom's Distributors

Fruit of the Loom (www.fruit.com) is known for its underwear clothing but also sells T-shirts, sweatshirts, and boxer shorts. Unlike the underwear business, in which the company sells products directly to large retailers such as Wal-Mart, the Activewear division, which manufactures blank T-shirts, uses several dozen distributors. These distributors sell the shirts to about 30,000 screen printers and embroiderers, who decorate the shirts and sell them to the public and/or retailers, who then market them to customers.

This market is very competitive and complex. The distributors sell other products as well, including T-shirts made by Fruit of the Loom's competitors. Therefore, the relationships between Activewear and its distributors are critical. To boost these relationships, Fruit of the Loom decided to develop and maintain an individual Web commerce site for each of their 40 key distributors on an extranet. Each site includes a color electronic catalog,

inventory level information, buyers' credit availability, and ordering forms. Both the shirt printers and the retailers enter the distributors' sites to facilitate their own back-office operation of inventory and billing. The distributors are allowed to advertise and sell other vendors' products on the Web site. This way Fruit of the Loom commits itself to supporting a system that benefits all channel members in a link that starts with its own site.

Fruit of the Loom hopes to gain favor with the distributors, many of whom do not have the time or money to build their Web sites. The system also includes a model that automatically suggests Fruit of the Loom's substitute products for products not in stock. Even though building and maintaining 40 sites incurs a cost, Fruit of the Loom believes that the investment pays for itself. Fruit of the Loom also uses its experience to generate profit by setting up Web sites for other companies. ■

CASE QUESTIONS

1. Why is Fruit of the Loom using distributors for T-shirts and not for underwear?
2. Why does Fruit of the Loom allow their distributors to use the Web sites for selling competitors' products?
3. Is the EC system bringing Fruit of the Loom closer to its customers? Why or why not?
4. Fruit of the Loom did all the Web development work in-house. Is this a reasonable strategy? Why?
5. Why is this application considered an extranet?

References

G. Anders, "Click and Buy," *The Wall Street Journal* (December 7, 1998): R4.

D. Blankenhorn, "GE's e-Commerce Network Opens Up to Other Marketers," May 1997a, *NetMarketing* (www.netb2b.com).

D. Blankenhorn, "New Industry.net Owners to Return to Information Roots," December 1997b, *NetMarketing* (www.netb2b.com).

D. Blankenhorn, and L. Strazewski, "Web Malls Add Online Purchasing," May 1997, *NetMarketing* (www. netb2b.com).

Commerce One, 1999 (www.commerceone.com).

C. Davis, "Most B-to-B Sites Don't Meet Customer Needs: Gartner," September 1997, *NetMarketing*, (www.netb2b.com).

Elekom Procurement, 1999 (www.elekom.com).

P. Fabris, "EC Riders (GE's TPN), *CIO Magazine* (July 15, 1997).

L. Fickel, "Online Auctions: Bid Business" *CIO Web Business Magazine* (June 1, 1999).

T. Finin et al. "Specification of the KQML Agent Communication Language," DARPA Knowledge Sharing Initiative, External Interface Working Group, 1993.

L. Freeman, "Net Drives B-to-B to New Highs World-wide," *NetMarketing*, January 1998 (www.netb2b.com).

J. E. Frook, "Web Links with Back-End Systems Pay Off," *Internet Week*, July 13, 1998 (www.internetwk.com).

S. Goldman et al., *Competitors and Virtual Organizations* (New York: Van Nostrand Reinhold, 1995).

R. Handfield and E. Nicols, *Supply Chain Management* (Upper Saddle River, NJ: Prentice Hall, 1999).

Intel Corp., "Franchising Meets the Internet," March 4, 1999a (www.intel.com/businesscomputing/Ebusiness/bizbiz/franchise.htm).

Intel Corp., "Marriott International Checks In," March 4, 1999b (www.intel.com/businesscomputing/Ebusiness/bizbiz/marriott. htm).

R. Kalakota, and A. B. Whinston, *Electronic Commerce: A Manager's Guide* (Reading MA: Addison-Wesley, 1997).

T. Lappin, "The Airline of the Internet," *Wired* (December 1996): 234–40.

E. Lawrence et al., *Internet Commerce. Digital Models for Business* (New York: John Wiley & Sons, 1998).

J. K. Lee, "Next Generation Electronic Marketing Environment: ICEC Perspective," *Proceedings of International Conference on Electronic Commerce '98*, 1998a (www. icec.net): 6.

J. K. Lee, and W. Lee, "An Intelligent Agent Based Contract Process in Electronic Commerce: UNIK-AGENT Approach," *Proceedings of 13th Hawaii International Conference on System Sciences* (1997): 230–41.

J. K. Lee, Y. U. Song, and J. W. Lee, "A Comparison Shopping Architecture over Multiple Malls: The Meta-Malls Architecture," *Proceedings of International Conference on Electronic Commerce '98* (1998b): 149–154.

K. Maddox, "Cisco Wins Big with Net Ordering," *NetMarketing*, 1998 (www.netb2b.com/cgi-bin/cgi_article/monthly/ 97/05/01/article.html).

P. Maes, R. H. Guttman, and A. G. Moukas, "Agents That Buy and Sell," *Communications of ACM,* 42 (3:March 1999): 81–91.

M. Nelson, "SAP Adds Module for I-Commerce," *Info-World,* 21 (27: July 6, 1998).

T. Retter and M. Calyniuk, *Technology Forecast: 1998* (Price Waterhouse, March 1998).

B. Silverstein, *Business-to-Business Internet Marketing* (Gulf Breeze, FL: Maximum Press, 1999).

C. Silwa, "Software Improved Net Purchasing Process," *ComputerWorld*, December 1998 (www.computerworld.com).

D. Sullivan, "Extending E-Business to ERP," *e-business Advisor* (January 1999a): 18–23.

D. Sullivan, "Take ERP on the Road," *e-business Advisor* (January 1999b): 24–27.

S. Teasdale, "Boeing Extranet Speeds Ordering Process for Spare-Parts Buyers," *NetMarketing*, June 1997 (www.netb2b. com).

Trading Process Network, 1999a (tpn.geis.com).

Trading Process Network, "Extending the Enterprise: TPN Post Case Study—GE Lighting," 1999b (tpn.geis.com/tpn/resouce_center/casestud.html).

E. Turban, E. McLean, and J. Wetherbe, *Information Technology for Management*, 2d ed., (New York: John Wiley & Sons, 1999).

D. M. Upton and A. McAfee, "The Real Virtual Factory," *Harvard Business Review* (July/August 1996): 123–33.

N. Weil, "MCI Offers Web-based Purchasing Service," 1998 (www.computerworld.com/home/news.nsf/all/9809303world).

W. Weston, "Commerce One Debuts SAP-oriented Tools," 1998 (News.com, June 12, www.news.com/News/Item/ 0,4,23566,00.html).

CHAPTER 7

Intranet and Extranet

Learning Objectives

Upon completion of this chapter, the reader will be able to:

- Describe the relationship among the Internet, intranet, and extranet.
- Describe the role of firewalls for intranets and extranets.
- Discuss the functions of intranets.
- Discuss the applications of intranets.
- Describe the industries that use intranets.
- Discover typical cases of intranet applications.
- Identify the key elements of extranets.
- Identify the key technologies for tunneling.
- Discuss the applications of extranets.
- Describe typical industries that use extranets.
- Discuss the business models for extranet applications.
- Describe the architecture of embedded extranets.

7.1 Automotive Network Exchange—The Largest Extranet

In September 1997, the big three U.S. carmakers and two dozen other auto industry companies began piloting what could become the world's largest extranet, the Automotive Network Exchange (ANX). The ANX promises to cut costs by billions of dollars and change the way the auto supply chain does business (Davis, Dalton, and Wilder 1997). Backed by General Motors, Ford, and Chrysler, ANX allowed companies in the automotive market to swap supply and manufacturing data. As many as 30 companies and dealers participated in the trial, but the commercial network ultimately would involve more than 10,000 companies globally.

BENEFITS OF ANX

Applications will include procurement, CAD/CAM file transfers, EDI, e-mail, and groupware. The ANX organizers believe that the network's EDI element alone will slice $71 from the cost of designing and building a car. That translates into an industry-wide savings of $1 billion a year. Each of the "big three" expects to save millions by consolidating communications links onto the ANX. Not only will the companies pay for fewer T1 lines and satellite connections, but standardizing the protocol will also reduce support costs.

The extranet will help auto suppliers reduce the time it takes to turn around an order. The faster the parts and subassemblies come in, the faster the cars leave the assembly line. Ford Co., for example, hopes to compress some work-order communications from three weeks to five minutes. "We may well convert our entire WAN to ANX," says Rick Collins, a senior IS consultant at Paccar Inc., a maker of custom semitrailer trucks.

VIRTUALLY PRIVATE NETWORK FOR ANX

The ANX is the most visible B2B implementation of virtual private networks (VPNs) that run over the Internet across the country and eventually the globe. As for security, all participants must have tools compliant with the **Internet Protocol (IP) security** standards (chapter 11), which cover encryption, authentication, and encryption key management. Each packet that travels over the ANX is encrypted and authenticated. After one year, Ameritech, Bell Canada, EDS, and MCI disclosed at Autotech '98 that they had met the specific performance requirements needed to be certified network providers for the ANX (Dalton and Davis 1998). The ANX was on live on November 1, 1998, and is now operational, meeting participants' expectations overall. General Motors moved 300 suppliers from private links to ANX in December 1998, and the suppliers are also enthusiastic about the ANX.

7.2 Architecture of the Internet, Intranet, and Extranet

The ANX vignette illustrates how the major players and competitors in an industry may team up to create a unified industry-wide extranet that benefits everyone. The Internet, intranet, and extranet are the most popular platforms for EC. In this chapter, we investigate these technologies, their benefits, costs, deployment strategies, and case studies. The Internet is the most common platform for B2C EC (chapter 2); the intranet is the most common platform for corporate internal management; and the extranet is the most common platform for B2B EC (chapter 6). It will be beneficial to provide definitions of the Internet, intranet, and extranet and contrast them. The common protocol that provides interoperability between the Internet, intranets, and extranets is TCP/IP. Table 7.1 compares and contrasts the three technologies.

THE INTERNET

The **Internet** is a public and global communication network that provides direct connectivity to anyone over a local area network (LAN) or **Internet Service Provider (ISP).** The Internet is a public network that is connected and routed over gateways.

TABLE 7.1 Characteristics of the Internet, Intranet, and Extranet

Network Type	Typical Users	Access	Type of Information
The Internet	Any individual with dial-up access or LAN	Unlimited public; no restrictions	General, public, and advertorial
Intranet	Authorized employees only	Private and restricted	Specific, corporate, and proprietary
Extranet	Authorized groups from collaborating companies	Private and authorized outside partners	Shared in authorized collaborating groups

Source: Compiled from Szuprowicz (1998), p. 24. Used by permission.

End users are connected to local access providers (LANs or ISPs), who are connected to Internet access providers, to network access providers, and eventually to the Internet backbone. Since access to the Internet is open to all, there is a lack of control that may result in an unruly proliferation of information. Owing to the vast scope of public and advertising information, users need effective and efficient search engines to navigate the sea of information (see chapter 11).

THE INTRANET: AN INTRABUSINESS DELIVERY SYSTEM

An **intranet** is a corporate LAN or wide area network (WAN) that uses Internet technology and is secured behind companys' firewalls (a kind of access control server—see chapter 11), as depicted in Figure 7.1. The intranet links various servers, clients, databases, and application programs like Enterprise Resource Planning (ERP). Although intranets are developed on the same TCP/IP protocol as the Internet, they operate as a private network with limited access. Only authorized employees are able to use it. Intranets are limited to information pertinent to the company and contain exclusive and often proprietary and sensitive information. The firewalls protect the intranets from unauthorized outside access; the intranet can be used to enhance the communication and collaboration among authorized employees, customers, suppliers, and other business partners. Since the intranet allows access through the Internet, it does not require any additional implementation of leased networks. This open and flexible connectivity is a major capability and advantage of intranets. Intranets provide the infrastructure for many **intrabusiness commerce** applications as will be shown later in this chapter.

THE EXTRANET

An **extranet,** or "extended intranet," uses the TCP/IP protocol networks of the Internet, to link intranets in different locations as shown in Figure 7.2. Extranet transmissions are usually conducted over the Internet, which offers little privacy or transmission security. Therefore, when using an extranet, it is necessary to improve the

FIGURE 7.1 Architecture of Intranet.

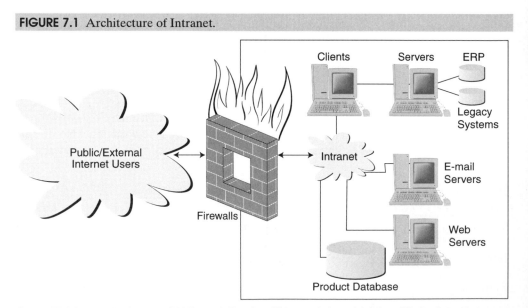

Source: Kalakota and Whinston (1997), p. 41. Reprinted by permission of Addison Wesley Longman; © 1997 by Addison-Wesley Publishing Company.

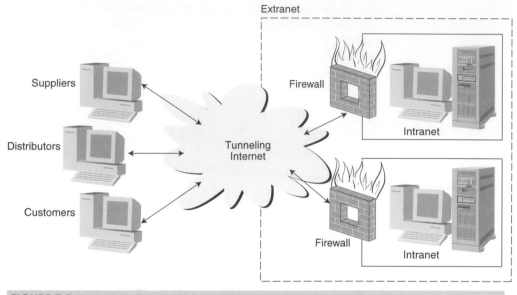

FIGURE 7.2 Diagrammatic Contrast of the Internet, Intranet, and Extranet.

security of the connecting portions of the Internet. This is done by creating tunnels (chapter 11) of secured data flows, using cryptography and authorization algorithms. The Internet with tunneling technology is known as a **virtually private network (VPN).**

Extranets provide secured connectivity between a corporation's intranets and the intranets of its business partners, materials suppliers, financial services, government, and customers. Access to intranets is usually limited by agreements of the collaborating parties, is strictly controlled, and it is only available to authorized personnel. The protected environment of the extranet allows groups to collaborate, sharing information exclusively and exchanging it securely. Since an extranet allows connectivity between businesses through the Internet, it is an open and flexible platform suitable for supply chain management. To increase security, many companies replicate the databases they are willing to share with their business partners and separate them physically from their regular intranets. However, even separated data need to be protected. This protection is provided by special architecture.

ROADS AHEAD

The following sections cover the key technologies and applications of intranets and extranets. For a review of technology per se, refer to chapter 11. Sections 7.3–7.6 cover intranet applications, and 7.7–7.11 cover extranet software and applications.

7.3   Intranet Software

According to Forrester Research, in April 1997, 64 percent of Fortune 1,000 companies already had an intranet. Another 32 percent were building them (Maddox 1997). According to the tracking of Zona Research Inc., sale of intranet software in 1996 was $476 million and by 1998 had topped $8 billion. With such rapid growth, many software developers were trying to capture part of this business.

To build an intranet, we need Web servers, browsers, Web publishing tools, back-end databases, TCP/IP networks (LAN or WAN), and firewalls, as shown in Figure

7.1. A **firewall** is software and/or hardware that allows only those external users with specific characteristics to access a protected network (chapter 11). Additional software may be necessary to support the Web-based workflow, groupware, and **Enterprise Resource Planning (ERP),** depending upon the individual company's need. The security schemes for the intranet, which are basically the same as the ones for the Internet, are described in chapters 8 and 11.

7.4 Applications of Intranets

In this section, we will review the applications of intranets from three perspectives: generic functions, application areas, and industry specific intranct solutions.

GENERIC FUNCTIONS OF INTRANET

The major generic functions that intranets can provide (SurfCONTROL 1997) are

- *Corporate/department/individual Web pages*
- *Database access:* Web-based database
- *Search engines and directories:* assist keyword-based search
- *Interactive communication:* chatting, audio, and videoconferences
- *Document distribution and workflow:* Web-based download and routing of documents
- *Groupware:* fancy e-mail and bulletin board
- *Telephony:* intranets are the perfect conduit for computer-based telephony
- *Integration with EC:* interface with Internet-based electronic sales and purchasing
- *Extranet:* linking geographically dispersed branches, customers, and suppliers to authorized sections of intranets creates happier customers, more efficient suppliers, and reduced staff costs

These functions provide for a large number of applications.

INTRANET APPLICATION AREAS

According to a survey conducted by *InformationWeek* with 988 responding managers (Chabrow 1998), information that is most frequently included in intranets are corporate policies and procedures, document sharing, corporate phone directories, human resource forms, training programs, customer databases, product catalogs and manuals, data warehouse and decision support access, image archives, purchase orders, enterprise suits, and travel reservation services. Refer to the diagram in Figure 7.3, which displays the percentages of such applications. Among the above applications, customer databases, product catalogs and manuals, purchase orders, and travel reservation services are directly related to electronic marketing and purchasing.

Using the above information, intranets can be applied to (Robinson 1996):

- *Electronic commerce:* Sales and purchasing can be done online.
- *Customer service:* UPS, FedEx, and other pioneering companies have proved that information about product shipments and availability make customers happier.
- *Reduced time to market:* Easy online access for product development speeds teamwork.
- *Enhanced knowledge sharing:* Web pages can enhance knowledge sharing.
- *Enhanced group decision and business process:* Web-based groupware and workflow is becoming the standard intranet platform.

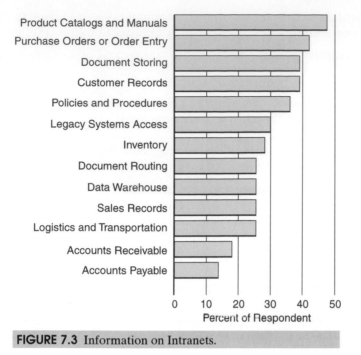

FIGURE 7.3 Information on Intranets.

Source: Compiled from Chabrow (1998). Used by permission.

- *Empowerment:* Everything should be available to everyone with the right to know.
- *Virtual organizations:* Web technology at both ends removes the barrier of incompatible technology between businesses.
- *Software distribution:* Use the intranet server as the application warehouse and avoid many maintenance and support problems.
- *Document management:* Employers can access pictures, photos, charts, maps, and other documents regardless of where they are stored.
- *Project management:* Share the reports and check the projects' progress.
- *Training:* The Web page is a valuable source of providing knowledge to novices.
- *Facilitate transaction processing:* The data are entered efficiently through the intranet Web only once, and internal control can be applied consistently throughout the system.
- *Eliminate paper-based information delivery:* Eliminating the paper in a firm can result in lower cost, easier accessibility, and greater efficiency.
- *Administrative process support:* The internal management of production, inventory, procurement, shipping, and distribution can be effectively supported by linking these functions in a single threaded environment—intranet—and these functions can also be seamlessly integrated with the interorganizational extranets.

INDUSTRY-SPECIFIC INTRANET SOLUTIONS

Intranet solutions are frequently classified by industry instead of technology, because the technology is no longer a bottleneck for implementation. The development of business models has become a critical concern for the managerial success of intranets.

According to the classification of InformationWeek Online, the top 100 intranet and extranet solutions can be classified by industry as follows (Solution Series 1998).

- *Financial services:* banking, brokerages and other financial services, insurance
- *Information technology*
- *Manufacturing:* chemicals and oil, consumer goods, food and beverage, general manufacturing, and pharmaceuticals
- *Retail*
- *Services:* construction/engineering, education, environmental, health care, media, entertainment, telecommunications, transportation, and utilities

Internet applications are very diversified. The 46 industry-specific intranets are listed in appendix 7.1. We can see there is no limit to industries using the intranet. It is interesting to note that the extranet has become the best user of intranets in 1999. This implies that the internal use of the intranet has matured, changing the focus to the extranet as of 1999.

7.5 Intranet Application Case Studies

Now, let us investigate some typical application cases in depth, including their return on investment (ROI).

INTRANET CASE STUDIES WITH ROI ANALYSIS

International Data Corporation (www.idc.com) compiled a collection of successful intranet cases of world-class companies such as Amdahl Corporation; Booz, Allen & Hamilton; Cadence Design Systems Inc.; Deere & Company; Lockheed Martin Corporation; Silicon Graphics, Inc.; and Southern California Gas Company.

Each case includes background of the company, business challenges, before-intranet technology, intranet cost, intranet strategy, after-intranet technology, subjective benefits (optional), lessons learned, and analysis of ROI. The detailed cases are available at the site home.netscape.com/comprod/announce/roi96_idc.html. The Cadence Design Systems Inc. case is summarized at the end of this chapter (Real World Case).

SHORT INTRANETS APPLICATION CASES

In this section, we present several examples[*] of intranet applications.

FedEx—Package Tracking

FedEx has a system linking more than 60 internal Web sites that were created by and for employees. The integrated intranets allow communication between divisions and corporate headquarters on issues important to employees and customers. The company is continuing to expand the intranet by adding servers in all of its locations so that the 30,000 office employees will be networked.

A unique part of the FedEx intranet is the package tracking system that allows customers to access FedEx's intranet to find the status of a package that they have shipped or one that they are expecting. By allowing customers themselves to find this information, customer service agents are able to concentrate on problem solving rather than answering routine inquiries. The customer cannot access any other part of the intranet, so confidential information is secure. This implementation has been estimated to save FedEx over $2 million annually. For the FedEx case from a JIT perspective, see Application Case 1.4 in chapter 1 and also chapter 6.

*From Szuprowicz (1998). Used by permission.

FedEx went one step further with its intranet. It cooperated with retailers that ship products directly to customers, by setting up computer systems that place and ship orders. The retailer fills the order and FedEx handles the shipping. Everything is done within the computer system, including inventory control, and FedEx implements and even maintains these systems. Complete efficiencies are gained by this integration, and all parties involved move the entire EC process forward.

Moen—Connected ERP

Moen Corp. (North Olmstead, Ohio) launched an intranet called CinfoNet in 1997. Moen needed to share information quickly and easily, especially with a huge SAP R/3 system that was implemented at that time. The development team was made up of three employees and several consultants. A favorite user application was the product database. Initially, 70 percent of Moen's 2,500 employees had access to the intranet. When R/3 was implemented, 100 percent were on the intranet. To make CinfoNet a complete success, existing electronic documents were converted to the new system.

Compaq Computer Corp.—Investment Assistant

Compaq's employees use the intranet to access the company and to communicate, but it has another unique feature. The staff can also access the human resources database for such information as their retirement account. Employees can then choose to reallocate the investments that they have in the account; they have a great deal of latitude and control over their retirement plans and how they perform. This enables them to choose where their money goes, and they are individually responsible for the performance and the growth of their funds. In addition, they can choose benefits, learn about training programs, and much more.

Silicon Graphics, Inc.—Share Huge Internal Web Sites

Silicon Graphics makes high-end graphics workstations. Their intranet system, called Silicon Junction, is accessed by over 7,000 employees. It includes 800 specialized internal Web sites containing more than 144,000 pages of technical information. There is also access to all corporate databases. Previously this access was not possible. Information that used to take days to access can now be obtained in a few minutes, simply by using links, pointing, and clicking.

SHARE KNOWLEDGE AMONG CORPORATE EMPLOYEES:
COOPERS AND LYBRAND

Coopers and Lybrand, one of the six largest CPA, taxation, and consulting firms, developed a special Knowledge Curve Intranet. It originated as a service for company consultants and corporate tax professionals who handle taxes for Fortune 1,000 corporations. It is a development of an online service that was introduced in 1993 and was shifted to the Web in 1997.

The Knowledge Curve is now integrated with the Tax News Network (TNN), an extranet for tax consultants for whom Coopers & Lybrand created a one-stop interactive information source on the constantly changing tax laws and regulations. The network contains tax information from numerous sources, integrating internal and external and even competing resources. In addition, it includes full text of various tax analyses, legislative tax codes, and major business newspapers. It is available to 75,000 employees and consultants of Coopers & Lybrand worldwide who use Lotus Notes Domino as a standard communications and collaboration system.

The company combined a series of automated Notes and third-party applications, to replicate internal documents that are published on TNN across company Notes

TABLE 7.2   Evaluation Criteria of Intranet Platform

Criteria	Description
Scalability	The efficient transaction read/write capability should be ensured as the number of users and access increases.
Interoperability	Enterprise Web, data warehouse, message and mail manager, online transaction processing, and other nodes should have a high interoperability on the network.
Configurability	Vendors must provide a broadly configurable array of enterprise servers that do not require major box swaps as enterprise requirements change.
Compatibility	The server family must not only meet expandable configuration requirements but also standard industry specifications to protect application investment.
Manageability	As the trend increases, systems must address the major operational management problems concerning configuration, problem diagnosis, and installation.
Availability	The enterprise servers must be able to sustain tens to hundreds of thousands of accesses and transactions with minimal downtime.
Reliability	The hardware reliability, data integrity, systems integration, and operational error immunity are essential.
Distributability	Whether in two- or three-tier client/server architecture, the enterprise servers must embrace clients appropriately.
Serviceability	Increase uptime by mandating online serviceability through the use of hot-swappable components, remote diagnostics directly connected to vendor service centers, and predictive diagnostics.
Stability	The generation changes in technology and architecture must minimize upgrade disruption and preserve investment protection.

servers. Company researchers can post their tax findings within Notes bulletin boards and set up database replication systems in Notes, which can be transformed into separate Notes databases on the extranet. The TNN extranet requires potential members to register and receive a password. The extranet runs on three servers located at the Information Access Company data center in Medford, Massachusetts, where backbone communications facilities are particularly suitable for efficient worldwide transmission. This is an example of a corporate knowledge base deliverable on an intranet and extranet.

7.6   Considerations in Intranet Deployment

Intranets (and extranets) are implemented in a distributed environment. Therefore, it is recommended that the intranet server platforms meet the 10 evaluation criteria listed in Table 7.2: scalability, interoperability, configurability, compatibility, manageability, availability, reliability, distributability, serviceability, and stability (Light 1996).

7.7   The Extranets

Now let us shift our attention to the extranet, the extended intranet that connects multiple intranets through a secured tunneling Internet. Let's start by viewing an example in Application Case 7.1.

BASIC CONCEPT OF EXTRANETS

Extranets combine the privacy and security of intranets with the global reach of the Internet, granting access to outside business partners, suppliers, and customers to a controlled portion of the enterprise network. Extranets are becoming the major plat-

Toshiba's Extranet Keeps Dealers on Time

The Problem

Toshiba America works with 300 dealers. Dealers that needed parts quickly had to place a telephone or fax order by 2:00 P.M. for next-day delivery. To handle the shipments, Toshiba's Electronic Imaging Division (EID) (fax machines and copiers) spent 1.3 million on communications and charged $25 per shipment to the dealers. In addition, dealers had to pay the overnight shipping fee. A cumbersome MS-DOS order-entry system was created in 1993, but no significant improvement was achieved.

The Solution

In August 1997, Toshiba created a Web-based order-entry system using an extranet. Dealers now can place orders for parts until 5:00 P.M. for next-day delivery. The company placed the warehouse in Memphis, Tennessee, near

FedEx headquarters. Dealers can also check accounts receivable balances and pricing arrangements, read service bulletins, press releases, and so on. Once orders are submitted, a computer checks for the parts availability. If a part is available, the order is sent to Toshiba's warehouse in Memphis over a dedicated leased line. Once at the warehouse site, the order pops up on a hand-held RF (radio frequency) monitor. Within a few hours the part is packed, verified, and packaged for FedEx. See Figure 7.4.

The Results

Using the extranet, the cost per order has declined to about $10. The networking cost of EDI has been reduced by more than 50 percent (to $600,000/year). The low shipping cost results in 98 percent overnight delivery, which increases customer satisfaction.

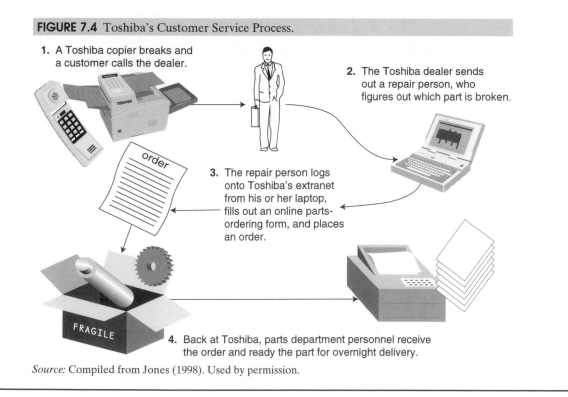

FIGURE 7.4 Toshiba's Customer Service Process.

1. A Toshiba copier breaks and a customer calls the dealer.

2. The Toshiba dealer sends out a repair person, who figures out which part is broken.

3. The repair person logs onto Toshiba's extranet from his or her laptop, fills out an online parts-ordering form, and places an order.

4. Back at Toshiba, parts department personnel receive the order and ready the part for overnight delivery.

Source: Compiled from Jones (1998). Used by permission.

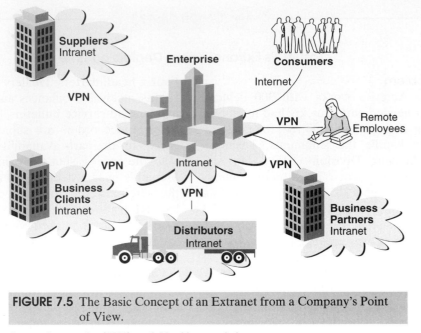

FIGURE 7.5 The Basic Concept of an Extranet from a Company's Point of View.

Source: Szuprowicz (1998), p. 6. Used by permission.

forms for B2B EC replacing or supplementing EDI. They provide the flexibility of serving internal and external users as depicted in Figure 7.5.

POTENTIAL OF THE EXTRANET MARKET

Since intranets are included in extranets, the forecasted potential of extranets is frequently combined with that of the intranets. According to a study by the Gartner Group (www.gartner.com), extranets are expected to be the platform of choice of more than 80 percent of B2B EC by 2001. This increasing acceptance is expected to surpass B2C EC, which is also expected to be conducted across intranets, by about 40 percent. Most of the B2C EC traffic will be done on the regular Internet. However, many companies, such as FedEx, will allow consumers to enter their intranets.

The telecommunication carriers, such as AT&T, MCI, and Sprint, and the leading Internet access providers, such as Bolt, Beranek, & Newman (BBN) and UUNet, already offer special corporate extranet services. These services provide secure data transmission within VPNs and extensive performance-monitoring systems. According to the Internet research firm of Killen & Associates (Palo Alto, California), sales of intranet and extranet software, hardware, and services reached $7.76 billion in 1997 and it is expected to reach $20 billion by 2000 (Szuprowicz 1998).

PLANNING EXTRANETS: COORDINATION AND SECURITY

While extranets are easy to use, implementing an efficient extranet requires extensive coordination between the company and its business partners. Legacy systems, databases, and other corporate resources must be interconnected for outside access and protected from unauthorized intruders. Companies must approach extranet design and development with a needs analysis to identify the best business opportunities.

The success of the extranet depends on the security measures implemented for the system. The extranet is useless without the ability to securely transmit sensitive data between the intranet and authorized partners. Although 100 percent security is impossible, discerning actual threats from perceived threats and then selecting appropriate measures will help secure the communication environment. Is selecting the strongest possible security for the entire extranet and associated intranets the best strategy? Not necessarily, because the stronger the security measures, the more hardware and software resources are required to maintain an acceptable performance level. A balance between security levels and return on investment analysis is an important component of an initial investigation to conduct extranet development.

Once a thorough needs analysis is completed, the feasibility of outsourcing must be checked. For most companies, the best strategy is to acquire a complete extranet package from a vendor such as Bay Networks, Lotus Development, Microsoft, or Netscape Communications. Select an ISP that provides high performance, low-latency connectivity, dial-in availability, and written service-level guarantees.

7.8 The Structure of Extranets

This section elaborates on the structure of extranets, including a review of tunneling technology and VPN.

ELEMENTS OF EXTRANET

Extranets are comprised of a wide variety of components and participants, and there are several possible configurations. These include intranets, Web servers, firewalls, ISPs, tunneling technology, interface software, and business applications. The tunneling principle is the basic concept that makes the extranet possible. **Tunneling** means that data transmissions across the Internet can be made secure by authenticating and encrypting all IP packets. Several tunneling protocols are available, but IP Security proposed by IETF (Internet Engineering Task Force) is one of the more popular protocols (Szuprowicz 1998). See chapter 11 for the protocols.

Extranets are configured by two basic methods:

1. They can be implemented using a direct leased line with full control over it, linking all intranets.
2. A secure link (tunnel) can be created across the Internet, which can be used by the corporation as a VPN, usually at a much lower cost.

Besides the security issue, the effectiveness of an extranet depends on the degree to which it is integrated with legacy systems and databases. In many instances, integrating with legacy systems involves integrating a System Network Architecture (SNA)—the backbone of legacy systems in many corporations—with TCP/IP, the Web backbone. The technical differences between the two systems are often sources of conflict.

7.9 Extranet Products and Services

CATEGORIES OF EXTRANET PRODUCTS AND SERVICES

Extranet products and services are available in four categories:

1. **Extranet development tools** provide the means and facilities to design extranet servers, a client-base, security, EC applications, and electronic catalogs.
2. **Extranet hosting and network connectivity** provide secure ISP connections to Internet backbones and host extranet services for corporations.

3. **Extranet services** provide extranet design expertise with proprietary tools or turnkey services for building and operating extranet-based services for corporate clients.
4. **Virtual private networks** provide components specifically designed for connecting remote operators and creating IP WANs for corporations.

These products and services are designed to develop, host, and enable extranets, and their numbers are increasing rapidly. Categories overlap significantly as vendors enter associated market segments—particularly among extranet hosting companies that provide extranet development tools and management services. In some cases, the differences between extranet products and services are decreasing.

EXTRANET TOOLS AND SERVICES PROVIDERS

The extranet development tools include a range of products from relatively simple EC software to sophisticated catalog servers that combine software and hardware products. The representative tool providers are listed in the book's Web site.

There are four types of extranet service providers (Szuprowicz 1998). Representative extranet services are listed in the book's Web site (www.prenhall.com/turban).

1. **Consultants** who develop extranet networks for clients
2. **Developers** who are using generally available development tools or proprietary products
3. **System integration** firms that provide turnkey solutions, including design, development, ISP connectivity, and extranet hosting operations as a single source
4. **Internet service providers** who already operate the Internet backbones

Representative VPN products and providers are listed in the book's Web site. Many telecom carriers now offer VPN services for Internet-based, B2B communications. These carriers use their own private network backbones to which they have added security features, intranet connectivity, and new dial-up capabilities for remote services. According to Forrester Research (www.forrester.com), VPN carrier service revenues were less than $40 million in 1997 but are expected to increase rapidly to $1.5 billion by 2000. At that time, 40 percent of all business Internet sales are expected to involve VPN services linking intranets. Major services and providers are listed in the book's Web site (www.prenhall.com/turban) (Szuprowicz 1998).

7.10 Applications of Extranets

The generic functions of extranets are basically the same as those of the intranet, although an extranet can cover more than one intranet. The key extended function of an extranet is, as the name implies, that the geographical dispersed dedicated networks (whether LAN or WAN) can be connected through the Internet. The current WAN on the proprietary network may be replaced by an extranet mainly because of its low cost and the use of Internet tools.

BENEFITS OF EXTRANETS

According to Szuprowicz (1998, p. 126, used by permission), there are five categories of extranet benefits. They are:

1. Enhanced communications
   - Improved internal communications
   - Improved business partnership channels

- Effective marketing, sales, and customer support
- Collaborative activities support

2. Productivity enhancements

- Just-in-time information delivery
- Reduction of information overload
- Productive collaboration between work groups
- Training on demand

3. Business enhancements

- Faster time to market
- Simultaneous engineering potential
- Lower design and production costs
- Improved client relationships
- New business opportunities

4. Cost reduction

- Reduced error
- Improved comparison shopping
- Reduced travel and meetings
- Reduced administrative and operational costs
- Elimination of paper publishing costs

5. Information delivery

- Low-cost publishing
- Leveraging of legacy systems
- Standard delivery systems
- Ease of maintenance and implementation
- Elimination of paper publishing and mailing costs

INDUSTRY SPECIFIC EXTRANET SOLUTIONS

The application of extranets are classified by industry. The popularly applied industries are information services, computers, financial services, travel, industry/manufacturing, business and professional, real estate, and consumers. The percentage that operates extranets is listed in Figure 7.6 (Davey 1997). Business models with 54 industry-specific extranet solutions are summarized in appendix 7.2 (Solution Series 1998).

7.11 Business Models of Extranet Applications

Let us investigate the business models that applied the extranets effectively. We have selected 11 typical representative models with cases (Szuprowicz 1998, pp. 212–234; used by permission). Other extranet examples are provided in the opening vignette (ANX case), Application Case 7.1 (Toshiba case), chapter 6 (GE and Boeing cases), and chapter 12 (Chemdex case) in the B2B EC context.

CONNECT BUSINESS CUSTOMERS TO SELL PARTS: AMP

AMP of Harrisburg, Pennsylvania, is a large electric-connectors distribution company with annual sales of over $5 billion, conducting business in 50 countries. The company sells nearly 80,000 different products, including fiber-optic connectors, printed wiring boards, splices, and switches. In 1996, AMP launched an extranet called AMP Connect, which is based on electronic catalogs with product descriptions, three-

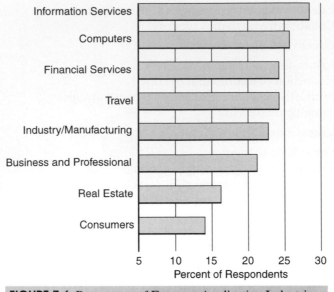

FIGURE 7.6 Percentage of Extranet Application Industries.

Source: Compiled from Davey (1997).

dimensional models, and comparative charts and tables of all its products. The company operates one of the most advanced Web sites. The information is available in eight languages and the site receives 100,000 hits daily from approximately 15,000 business customers worldwide.

This application is a good example of connecting a company with its customers through the extranet. AMP Connect is used to place orders and has given the company a forum for communicating with wholesalers, distributors, resellers, and customers that will eventually become a transactional extranet system.

CONNECT DEALERS' KIOSK: GENERAL MOTORS

This giant automaker wants to change the way automobiles are marketed by using an extranet accessed in kiosks and personal digital assistants (PDAs). The interactive kiosks are installed in dealerships and shopping malls. The extranet uses the GM-Access network, which connects 8,600 North American dealers with GM factories. GM-Access is implemented worldwide using the Pulsar satellite system, which is operated by Hughes Network Systems.

The goal is to link interactive kiosks to GM's legacy infrastructure. Ideally, these will be instantly updated whenever GM changes the configuration or price of a car. The cost of the kiosk system is estimated to be $1.3 million, and the overall project is expected to cost more than $1 billion.

CONNECT WITH SUPPLIERS FOR PURCHASE: VHA, INC.

The Irving, Texas, alliance of 18 hospitals and 1,400 health-care organizations is developing an extranet to collaborate and access an electronic catalog of products for approximately 22,000 dial-up users. VHA members of this alliance purchase more than $8 billion in products annually under contracts from 350 suppliers.

Initial use of VHAsecure.net is for access to VHA health-care organizations and the Internet. In the future, VHA members will buy and sell merchandise and offer a wide range of medical, legal, and pharmaceutical research capabilities. The extranet will eventually allow all VHA members to purchase directly from suppliers.

VHAsecure.net allows all VHA members to exchange information through a ubiquitous, secure environment. VHA chose IBM as its ISP because of its experience with data networking. Security was a particularly important issue because of the sensitive nature of clinical information. Hospitals, clinics, home health companies, and managed care facilities in numerous locations are involved, and patient information must remain private.

The VHA extranet is expected to cost $100 million when completed and is being built by IBM Global Services, which will also operate the system for VHA during the next five years. IBM constructed the Internet backbone for VHA and will manage the company's firewalls and routers. This is a good example of an industry-wide partnership similar to that described in the ANX opening vignette.

TRACKING SHIPPING STATUS: CSX TECHNOLOGY

In 1996 a railroad company, CSX Technology, developed a highly publicized intranet for tracking cross-country train shipments from point to point. The company is now expanding this intranet as an extranet, TWSNet Premium, which will eventually link more than 200 freight shippers and forwarders. The extranet allows CSX customers to trace shipments, initiate work orders, and view pricing data over the Internet. CSX plans to include the large suppliers of transportation services such as railroads, trucks, container ships, and barges to TWSNet Premium.

The TWSNet Premium is also open to non-CSX customers who require Web-based solutions for managing inbound shipping or outbound delivery information as part of their supply-chain management. The extranet allows tracking of shipments to the line-item level, simplifying identification of bottlenecks or problems. A global reporting system analyzes carrier performance and trends. It also allows users to perform precise demand forecasting, while a special programming interface enables integration with legacy systems.

REDUCE DESIGN CYCLE TIME BY CONNECTING SUPPLIERS: ADAPTEC, INC.

Adaptec, Inc. is a $1 billion microchip manufacturer supplying critical components to electronic equipment makers. The company outsources the manufacturing tasks concentrating on product research and development. Outsourcing production, however, puts the company at a disadvantage with competitors that have their own manufacturing facilities and can optimize their delivery schedules. Before it implemented the extranet, Adaptec required up to 15 weeks to deliver products to customers; competitors were able to deliver similar chips in only 8 weeks.

The longer delivery time was mainly caused by the need to coordinate design activities between Adaptec headquarters in California and its three principal fabrication factories in Hong Kong, Japan, and Taiwan. The company reduced its chip production cycle times by shortening order-to-product-delivery time from 15 weeks to between 10 and 12 weeks. The enabling solution is an extranet and enterprise-level supply chain integration software that incorporates automated workflow and EC tools.

One initial benefit included the reduced time required to generate, transmit, and confirm purchase orders. This was done by using e-mail to communicate with manufacturers across several time zones thereby automatically beginning the flow of raw materials, which in turn reduced invoicing and shipping time. In addition to business transaction documents, Adaptec can send chip design diagrams over the extranet, enabling the manufacturers to prepare for product changes and new designs. This faster communication method required Adaptec to adjust its decision-making processes that were based on the old assumption that at least two weeks were needed to put an order into production.

REDUCE PRODUCT DEVELOPMENT TIME BY CONNECTING SUPPLIERS: CATERPILLAR, INC.

Caterpillar Inc., a multinational heavy machinery manufacturer, was an early extranet adopter. The company operated an intranet that was accessible by customers who wanted to make changes to customized vehicles. In the traditional mode of operation, such changes increased cycle time because the process involved paper document transfers among managers, salespeople, and technical staff.

Using an extranet, the company demonstrated in 1998 how a request from a farm company for a customized tractor component received through a dealer was handled by designers and suppliers all in a very short time. Suppliers produced and delivered the final product directly to the customers. Caterpillar is developing extranet applications as competitive tools to shorten product development cycles. During 1998, the company connected its engineering and manufacturing divisions with its active suppliers, distributors, overseas factories, and customers, all in a global extranet.

Caterpillar customers, for example, can use the extranet to retrieve and modify detailed order information while the vehicle remains on the assembly line. This ability to collaborate remotely between customer and product developers decreases cycle time delays resulting from additional rework time. The system is also used for expediting maintenance and repairs.

LINK THE WORLDWIDE CHAINS' EMPLOYEES: KINKO'S, INC

Kinko's Inc. is a global photocopying retail chain headquartered in Ventura, California, which in 1999 operated more than 900 stores with close to 253,000 employees. It developed an extranet to offer Internet access in its stores and PC rental time to its customers. Using IP tunneling, Kinko's offers secure and virtually private IP channels that link Kinko's stores with each other and with the corporate headquarters. The company compared the cost of an alternative leased-line-based network and determined that a fully meshed network costs more than extranet deployment cost.

Each Kinko's store connects to the Internet with a 64-Kbps channel of an Integrated Services Digital Networks (ISDN) link. When intranet traffic is transmitted, a router in the store establishes a secure tunneled connection to the main office for access to confidential data, such as credit information, sales reports, and company policies and procedures. The main office can also connect to another store by dialing the remote router and sending instructions to establish a secure link.

LINK BUSINESS PARTNERS: COUNTRYWIDE HOME LOAN

Countrywide Home Loans of Pasadena, California, is the nation's largest independent mortgage lender, with nearly 330 branch offices nationwide. It is using extensive Internet, intranet, and extranet solutions that serve its employees, business partners, and consumers.

Every day, Countrywide processes thousands of transactions that are influenced by continuous fluctuations in lending rates and product offerings. To improve processing, the company has embarked on a long-term project to eliminate paper from its operating environment. The system provides a completely open, networked environment that seamlessly ties into the mountains of legacy data that must be accessed by people using various computer platforms, both inside and outside the corporate firewall.

Countrywide's IS department has developed a corporate-wide intranet system serving more than 5,000 employees at the company's headquarters and branch locations. This far-reaching network provides employees with online access to product guidelines, forms, and corporate information. Countrywide programmers develop intranet applications for such corporate functions as mortgage origination, mortgage servicing, and back-office operations.

The company has also developed a powerful extranet accessible only to Countrywide's lending partners, brokers, and real estate agents. These parties require secure access to valuable information, such as account and transaction status, loan status, company contacts, and company announcements. A total of 500 Countrywide lenders use Netscape Navigator client software to access the extranet, which uses a sophisticated routing program. This program automatically identifies each lender and provides them with their own customized information on premium rates, discounts, and special arrangements.

The same server deployed for the extranet is also being used to develop a host of customer-oriented applications for use on a publicly accessible Internet site. These applications come online as part of a Web service offered free by Countrywide. For example, consumers can calculate home mortgage rates based on any number of market variables and product offerings. Countrywide integrated its consumer Web services with massive legacy databases that contain pertinent information on loan offerings, loan rates, and mortgage products.

EMBEDDED EXTRANET: FEDEX'S EXTRANET EMBEDDED TO CISCO

Cisco depends on FedEx for the delivery of ordered products to customers. Cisco cannot provide information about the status of a delivery because FedEx manages the delivery process. Cisco or the customer has to access FedEx's computer system to trace the progress. This causes inconvenience to the customers of any company that outsources the delivery service. To overcome this problem, FedEx developed an embedded extranet architecture as depicted in Figure 7.7.

FedEx provides dynamic links between their sites and business partners to transparently deliver information to users from multiple sites. For instance, Cisco's customer issues an order status query to Cisco's Web page. Then Cisco's Web site queries FedEx's database and transmits to FedEx's server over the embedded extranet. Cisco's Web site thus transparently returns a status report to the customer, and Cisco's customers do not need to access FedEx's Web site. The embedded extranet is a very promising architecture to support supply chain management.

FIGURE 7.7 Architecture of Embedded Extranet.

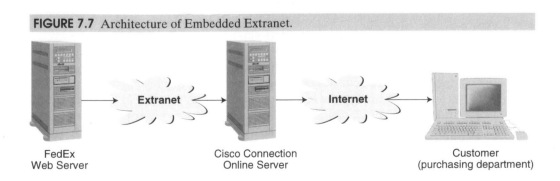

FedEx
Web Server

Cisco Connection
Online Server

Customer
(purchasing department)

CONNECT WITH SERVICE INSTITUTIONS: INTRALOAN

The extranets can connect outside services like financial institutions. Compaq Computer secured a $4 billion syndicated loan mostly over the Web in 1997. National Semiconductor also borrowed $200 million on the Web (Jones 1997). The loans were handled by two groups of banks led by BancAmerica Security, Inc., which is the brokerage arm of BankAmerica Corp. (www.bankamerica.com).

BancAmerica used IntraLoan, an extranet application from IntraLinks Inc. (www.intralink.com), to coordinate the activity of 35 lending institutions investing in the Compaq loan. The extranet handles the paperless distribution of information about the loan and serves as a secure e-mail connection for the parties involved. About 40 percent of institutions investing in the Compaq loan used the extranet.

The extranet eliminated time zone problems and printing and shipping costs. The extranet let investors cut and paste relevant portions of the loan documents into the reports they used to get internal loan approval. IntraLink also offers links to research sites such as the Securities and Exchange Commission's EDGAR Web site and other online resources.

IntraLoan can eliminate phone, fax, and the time it takes to communicate with investors, and its password-protected service is more secure than paper distribution. IntraLink has priced its extranet service below $10,000—the typical paper distribution costs of syndicated loans. Since July 1997, IntraLink has handled on the extranet tens of billions of dollars of loans' requests.

7.12 Managerial Issues

Management no longer worries about whether or not to adopt the intranet/extranet but is concerned about how to utilize them successfully for business. Intranets/extranets are already a fact of life in many large corporations. Thus, management needs to review its own company's position in dealing with a variety of issues in installing the intranet/extranet. The following are guidelines for managerial review.

1. **Find business opportunities by utilizing the intranet and extranet.** For example, consider connecting the customers, suppliers, and internal branches that are geographically dispersed.
2. **Analyze whether the connectivity requirement suits the intranet or extranet.** It is mainly dependent upon whether the network is composed of one LAN or multiple LANs. The former is suitable for intranet and the latter for extranet. Individuals' remote access should also be considered.
3. **Plan the most secure and economical choice for implementation.** Consult the technical persons inside and outside of the company for implementation. Review the current proprietary or leased network and determine if it can be replaced by intranet and extranet. It may reduce costs and widen connectivity for the customers and suppliers.
4. **Select the best outsourcers for implementation.** Compare the outsourcers who can implement the intranet/extranet. The extranet solution providers can cultivate new opportunities in this big market.
5. **Selling the intranet.** Corporate intranets can serve as a wonderful resource pool, where employees can do many things ranging from taking classes to updating benefit plans. Too often, employees are not using the intranet to its fullest capacity. Businesses are exploring innovative ways to market their intranet to their employees. For example, some companies are making pre-

sentations to employees, others give prizes, yet others created an "Intranet Day." (For more information see *InternetWeek*, May 3, 1999, p. 27).

Summary

The compilation of this chapter helps you in attaining the following learning objectives:

1. **Relationship among the Internet, intranet, and extranet.** The Internet is a public and global network open to anybody. An intranet is a corporate network whose access is protected by firewalls. An extranet is an extended intranet, which links the remote intranets, or individuals, over the VPNs built on the Internet.
2. **Role of firewalls for intranets and extranets.** The firewall controls the access, filters packets, and provides proxy service to protect the internal network. It is installed at the gateway of the internal network.
3. **Functions of intranets.** Intranets provide corporate Web pages, database access, search engines and directories, interactive communication, document distribution and workflow, groupware, telephony, integration with EC, and extranets.
4. **Applications of intranet.** Intranets can be applied to EC, customer service, reduced time to market, knowledge sharing, enhancement of group decision and business processes, empowerment, virtual organization, software distribution, project management, and training.
5. **Industries that use intranets.** Any industry and any company can use an intranet. But typical industries include financial services, information technology, manufacturing, retail, and services.
6. **Typical cases of intranet applications.** The cases covered in this chapter include Cadence Design (real world case), FedEx, Moen, Compaq, Silicon Graphics, and 46 cases in appendix 7.1.
7. **Key element of extranet.** Besides the firewalls that intranets need, the extranet needs tunneling technology, which makes the Internet secure enough to use as a VPN among the distant intranets.
8. **Key technologies for tunneling.** Authentication and encryption of IP packets route on the Internet.
9. **Applications of extranets.** Enhanced communication, productivity enhancement, business enhancements, cost reduction, and information delivery.
10. **Industries that use extranets.** Information services, computers, financial services, travel, industry/manufacturing, business and professional, and real estate.
11. **Business models for extranet applications.** Connect with business customers, connect with dealers, connect with suppliers for purchasing, track shipping status, reduce design cycle time by connecting suppliers, reduce product development time by connecting suppliers, link the worldwide chains, link business partners, and connect with service institutions.
12. **Embedded extranet.** One site connected to the Internet has an embedded extranet of another company so that the company in the back can provide information to the customers seamlessly.

Keywords

- Enterprise Resource Planning (ERP)
- Extranet
- Firewalls
- Internet
- Internet Protocol (IP)
- Internet Protocol Security
- Internet Service Provider (ISP)
- Intrabusiness commerce
- Intranet
- Tunneling
- Virtually Private Network (VPN)

Questions for Review

1. Define the Internet, intranet, and extranet.
2. How do the architectures of the Internet, intranet, and extranet differ from one another?
3. What are the roles and types of firewalls for intranets and extranets?
4. List the kinds of intranet software that are available in the market.
5. Describe the generic functions of intranets.
6. List the major purposes of intranets application.
7. What are the existing industry-specific application models of intranets?
8. Define the forecast of the extranet market.
9. List the key planning factors of extranets.
10. Describe the major components of an extranet.
11. Describe the concept and methods of tunneling.
12. Define the VPN.
13. List the application categories of extranets.
14. What kinds of information are dealt with on the extranets?
15. List the major industry-specific extranet solutions.
16. List the major business models of extranets.

Questions for Discussion

1. How can the external users like customers and suppliers access the intranets?
2. How can the VPN operates as a secure extranet?
3. How can the multiple extranet service providers participating in the ANX project maintain consistency?
4. Can the extranet eventually replace the role of leased-line-based WAN?
5. Describe the process of planning the intranet and extranet systems.
6. Find a benchmarking case of extranet that connects business customers.
7. Find a benchmarking case of extranet that connects dealers.
8. Find a benchmarking case of extranet that connects suppliers for efficient purchasing.
9. Find a benchmarking case of embedding extranet that allows the tracking of shipping status.
10. Find a benchmarking case of extranet that reduces the product development time by connecting business partners, including committed suppliers.
11. Find a benchmarking case of linking business partners and service institutions.
12. What is the business opportunity of an ISP in the extranet market?

Internet Exercises

1. Enter one of the interesting intranet sites listed in appendix 7.1. Identify the business model and the adopted technology for implementation.
2. Enter one of the interesting extranet sites listed in appendix 7.2. Identify the business model and the adopted technology for implementation.
3. Select a real-world large retailer. Identify whether the retailer is appropriate for adopting the Internet, intranet, or extranet. Find a similar case from the list in the industry-specific intranet/extranet solutions in the appendix to this chapter.
4. Suppose you are a supplier to automakers. How will you react to the ANX project? How can you take a competitively advantageous position in this situation?
5. Propose an intranet/extranet system that has a secure communication network on the Internet among branch offices dispersed throughout the world (hint: Kinko's case).
6. Suppose a manufacturer counts on an outside shipping company. How can the manufacturer convey to customers the shipping status on its own Web site? Propose a network architecture for this purpose.

7. To reduce the cycle time of product development, how should we establish the cooperation system with suppliers (hint: Caterpillar case)?
8. How can a company support its dealers' need to meet customers' needs seamlessly (hint: General Motors case)?
9. Show a business model of syndicating a business loan on the Internet (hint: IntraLoan case)?

Team Exercises

1. Make two teams (A and B) of five members or more each. Person 1 plays the role of an assembly company (A-View for team A and B-View for team B) of television monitors. Persons 2 and 3 play the role of domestic parts suppliers to the assembling company, and Persons 4 and 5 play foreign parts suppliers. Now, both A-View and B-View want to sell the televisions directly to consumers. Let each team design the network environment for this situation and present their study to the audience, who evaluates each team's result.
2. Select a particular company that the team can access. Prepare a proposal to reengineer the supply chain using the intranet and extranet.

R E A L   W O R L D   C A S E

Cadence Design Systems—
ROI of Intranet 1,766 Percent

Cadence Design Systems Inc. is a leading supplier of Electronic Design Automation (EDA) software tools and professional services for managing and accelerating the design of semiconductors, computer systems, networking and telecommunications equipment, consumer electronics, and other electronic-based products. The San Jose-based company employs more than 3,000 people in offices worldwide to support the development requirements of the world's leading electronic manufacturers.

Business Challenge

Early in 1995 Cadence recognized that the business model for EDA products was beginning to evolve from tools orientation to one where the value placed on software and consulting services holds the potential for the largest revenue growth. Rather than sell a single product, Cadence wanted to support the customer's entire product development cycle.

To understand and address this changing model, Cadence identified two areas of customer interaction: sales and delivery. The new sales strategy required the sales force to have an in-depth understanding of Cadence's product line of almost 1,000 products and services. With two separate organizations interacting with a customer, coordination and communication were needed to ensure an effective and consistent relationship built on a real understanding of the customer's issues.

Adopt Intranet Technology

Throughout 1995, Cadence worked with a consulting firm specializing in intranet solutions to create a Web-based single point of information for supporting the sales organization. This system, called OnTrack, uses a home page with links to other pages, information sources, and custom applications to map each phase of the sales process with supporting materials and reference information. By adopting

OnTrack, Cadence achieved the high return on investment of 1,766 percent.

With OnTrack, the sales rep now has a single unified tool that provides all of the information and data needed to go through the sales process from prospecting to closing a deal and account management. In addition, global account teams have their own home page where they can collaborate and share information. However, OnTrack is more than a static road map. A sales rep can initiate workflow automatically, eliminating the hurdle of needing to know who to call. Information on a customer or competitor is now available instantly through access to an outside provider of custom news. The sales rep can simply search, using a company name, to get everything from financial information to recent news articles and press releases.

All creators of information in the company, from sales reps to marketing and management, are responsible for maintaining the information contained in OnTrack. With a wide range of people entering data, a simple-to-use information submission process was needed. To avoid the need to understand HTML, forms were created to allow submission or modification of any part of the information in the OnTrack system. Anyone with appropriate access can now add a new message to the daily alerts, modify a step in the sales process, or update a customer presentation by using these custom tools. Feedback is also a key part of OnTrack. Reports are generated highlighting frequently accessed pages and documents. Even frequent searches are reviewed with an eye toward including new information and making critical information easier to access.

Lessons Learned

Many lessons can be learned through adopting the OnTrack system.

- Balancing the cost of training against the return is a difficult task. Although the use of a browser and the navigation of a Web page required minimal training, the application of the OnTrack system to the daily activities of a sales rep was not easy. OnTrack supported a reengineering of the sales process, and Cadence believed that demonstrating the use of OnTrack in supporting the sales rep might have accelerated the use of the system.

- For Cadence, the key to success was the holistic approach taken to unifying the technology with the process. Rather than mandate a new process, or install a new software system, the combination of an easy-to-use technology, a refined process, and the appropriate personnel and support systems created a single coherent system that could support the new sales paradigm.

- Cadence worked to design a process and infrastructure that could satisfy 80 percent rather than 100 percent of the sales situations. This strategy helped the company in two ways. First, it is often more effective to refine a system after gaining experience than to attempt to design the perfect system from the beginning. Second,

creating a process that can address all possible exceptions is often an exercise in futility. One reason Cadence has achieved such a high return on investment is its focus on supporting the bulk of work process rather than the entire process.

- Relatively low cost was needed to implement OnTrack. Cadence leveraged its existing infrastructure and wisely hired outside experts to create the application rather than devoting internal resources. This choice allowed the company to focus its efforts on defining the process and tools needed to support the sales force rather than designing software.

- The greatest impact is the result of the shortened training time for new sales reps. A new salesman stated that he had learned in two days from OnTrack what it took months to learn at a previous company. With 40 new reps hired in the first year, and 40 planned for each of the next two years, reducing the ramp-up time for new sales personnel had a substantial impact on additional profits to Cadence. ∎

Source: Compiled from Campbell (1996)

CASE QUESTIONS

1. What was the purpose of adopting an intranet for Cadence?
2. What is the function of the OnTrack system?
3. What are the benefits realized by adopting OnTrack?
4. Describe the holistic approach taken by Cadence.
5. Describe the outsourcing strategy of Cadence.
6. Describe the training requirement for the intranet system OnTrack.

References

D. Bayles, *Extranets: Building the Business-to-Business Web* (Upper Saddle River, NJ: Prentice Hall, 1998).

R. Bernard, *The Corporate Intranet* (New York: John Wiley & Sons, 1997).

J. Bort and B. Felix, *Building an Extranet: Connect Your Intranet with Vendors and Customers* (New York: John Wiley & Sons, 1997).

D. Cameron, *Intranet Security* (Charleston, SC: Computer Technology Research Corp., www.ctrcorp.com, 1997).

I. Campbell, "The Intranet: Slashing the Cost of Business," 1996 (home.netscape.com/comprod/announce/roi96_idc.html#cadence).

J. Cashin, *Intranet Strategies and Technologies for Building Effective Enterprisewide Intranet Systems* (Charleston, SC: Computer Technology Research Corp., 1998).

E. Chabrow, "Instruments of Growth," *InformationWeek* (October 5, 1998).

G. Dalton and B. Davis, "ANX Gets Certified Network Providers," *InformationWeek* (August 31, 1998).

T. Davey, "Extranets Unlock Your Business," *InformationWeek* (June 9, 1997).

B. Davis, G. Dalton, and C. Wilder, "Automotive Extranet Set for Test Drive," *InformationWeek* (September 1, 1997).

J. S. Gonzalez, *The 21st Century Intranet* (Upper Saddle River, NJ: Prentice Hall, 1998).

S. Grisworld, *Corporate Intranet Development* (Rocklin, CA: Prima Publishing, 1997).

S. L. Guengerich, D. Graham, and M. Miller, *Building the Corporate Intranet* (New York: John Wiley & Sons, 1996).

C. Harrison, A. Caglayan, and C. G. Harrison, *Agent Source Book: A Complete Guide to Desktop, Internet, Intranet Agents* (New York: John Wiley & Sons, 1997).

M. Hills, *Intranet Business Strategies* (New York: John Wiley & Sons, 1996).

B. Hopkins, *How to Design and Post Information on a Corporate Intranet* (Hampshire, UK: Gower Pub. Co., 1997).

K. Jones, "Copier Strategy As yet Unduplicated," *Interactive Week* (February 9, 1998), a Ziff-Davis publication.

K. Jones, "Extranet Eliminates Loan Paperwork," *Interactive Week* (September 29, 1997).

R. Kalakota and A. Whinston, *Electronic Commerce: A Manager's Guide* (Reading, MA: Addison Wesley, 1997).

A. Laalo, "Intranets and Competitive Intelligence: Creating Access to Knowledge," *Competitive Intelligence Review* 9(4), 1998.

D. Levinson, *Extranets—A New Way to Reach Customers, Partners & Suppliers* (Sybase, Inc., 1997).

M. Light, "The Internet and Enterprise Intranets: The Impact on Distributed Computing," *Inside Gartner Group This Week* (July 10, 1996).

T. Lister, "Ten Commandments for Converting Your Intranet into a Secure Extranet," *UNIX Review's Performance Computing* (July 1998).

P. Loshin, *Extranet Design and Implementation* (Berkeley, CA: Sybex, 1997).

K. Maddox, "Intranet Opens New Opportunity," *Net-Marketing* (www.netb2b.com) (April 1, 1997).

M. Miller, A. Roehr, and B. Bernard, *Managing the Corporate Intranet* (New York: John Wiley & Sons, 1998).

D. Minoli, *Internet and Intranet Engineering* (New York: Computing McGraw-Hill, 1997).

J. Mullich, "Intranet Runs Cold to Hot," *PCWeek* (February 9, 1998).

B. Pfaffenberger, *Building a Strategic Extranet* (New York: IDG Books Worldwide, 1998).

F. Reggins and H. Rhee, "Developing the Learning Network Using Extranets," 1997 (riggins-mgt.iac.gatech.edu/papers/learning.html).

A. Richardson, *The Intranet: Opportunities within the Corporate Environment* (Elsevier Science Online, 1997).

J. Robinson, "Intranet 100: The Revolution Is Here," *InformationWeek* (November 18, 1996), pp. 106–108.

Solution Series, "Intranet/Extranet 100," *InformationWeek* (www.informationweek.com/703/03sslist.html) (October 5, 1998).

SurfCONTROL, "The Intranet—A Corporate Revolution," 1997 (www.intranet.co.uk/papers/intranet/intranet.html).

B. Szuprowicz, *Extranet and Intranet: E-commerce Business Strategies for the Future* (Charleston, SC: Computer Technology Research Corp., 1998).

E. Turban, E. McLean, and J. Wetherbe, *Information Technology for Management*, 2d ed. (New York: John Wiley & Sons, 1999).

R. L. Wagner and E. Englemann, *Building and Managing the Corporate Intranet* (New York: McGraw-Hill, 1997).

Industry-Specific Intranet Solutions

Industry	Company	Intranet Solutions
Banking	Bankers Trust (www.bankerstrust.com)	The BT Connect 98 intranet lets 20,000 employees in 50 countries assess performance and set career goals, enroll in training classes, and keep abreast of job openings.
	Canadian Imperial Bank of Commerce (www.cibc.com)	An intranet procurement system lets 40,000 employees in 1,400 offices buy supplies and other items.
	Citibank (www.citibank.com)	Citibank's intranet gives employees access to catalogs in order to streamline purchasing.
	NationsBank (www.nationsbank.com)	An intranet links sales associates to a decision support system to identify new products to sell to major clients.
Brokerages	Charles Schwab (www.schwab.com)	The Schwab intranet lets financial analysts at the discount brokerage access information about clients so they can respond faster to their needs, which, in turn, boosts business.
Chemicals and Oil	Amoco Chemicals (www.amocochem.com)	An intranet lets staffers share their knowledge of how to do their jobs with employees who are new to their own positions.
	British Petroleum (www.bp.com)	The multinational oil company uses an intranet to disseminate benefit and career-training information to 53,000 employees worldwide.
	Olin Chlor Alkali Products (www.olin.com)	The chlorine and caustic soda maker uses an intranet to develop, deliver, and track mandatory OSHA training. Employees can also use the intranet to share innovative ideas.
	Texaco (www.texaco.com)	Employees worldwide use video-conferencing over an intranet.
Construction and Engineering	Hovnanian Enterprises (www.khov.com)	The home builder uses an intranet to provide employees at temporary construction sites with project information.
Consumer Goods	Eastman Kodak (www.kodak.com)	The photographic equipment maker offers course registration and online training on its intranet.
	Rollerblade (www.rollerblade.com)	The maker of popular inline skates uses an intranet to develop products and control inventory.

(continued)

Industry	Company	Intranet Solutions
	Sony Music (www.sonymusic.com)	An intranet distributes music to sales representatives and talent scouts.
	Warner Music Group (www.wbr.com)	Employees use an intranet to share the latest information about artists and the sales, manufacturing, and distribution of recordings.
Education	St. John's University (www.stjohns.edu)	An intranet that spans three campuses lets professors collaborate on course development and gives students, faculty, and staffers access to university records and library catalogs. Eventually, students will be able to use it to purchase tickets to athletic events, and to pay tuition, room and board, and other fees.
	State University of New York at Buffalo (www.buffalo.edu)	An intranet provides a virtual service center where students can request phone repairs, check course status, and check on tuition aid.
Environmental	General Services Administration (www.gsa.gov)	An intranet lets employees buy supplies through a Web procurement system.
	Jacksonville Sheriff's Office (www.coj.net)	An intranet gives law enforcement officers access to a satellite mapping system, crime data, and mug shots of suspects and criminals.
Food and Beverage	Case Swayne (www.case-swayne.com)	The specialty-foods maker uses an intranet to post job listings, policies, benefits handbooks, and company news.
	Quaker Oats (www.nestle.com)	The food company uses an intranet to create schedules for factory workers and production lines.
	Turner Foods (www.turnerfoods.com)	The company's intranet gives citrus grove managers real-time weather information to help them plan field operations.
Food and Travel	Auto Club of Southern California (www.aaa-calif.com)	This affiliate of the American Automobile Association uses an intranet to train 7,000 employees in 100 offices in 4 states.
	Domino's Pizza (www.dominos.com)	An intranet keeps all stores current on news, research, and buying habits. Stores can also use the intranet to order supplies.
	Harrah's Entertainment (www.harrahs.com)	An intranet connects the databases of 19 casinos to help operators identify and compensate members of its Total Gold customer-reward program.

Industry	Company	Intranet Solutions
General Manufacturing	Becton Dickinson (www.bd.com)	This medical-equipment maker employs a worldwide intranet for knowledge management.
	Cintas (www.cintas-corp.com)	This uniform maker uses an intranet to develop products and control inventory.
	Cooper Industries (www.cooperindustries.com)	Employees at the company's hardware and tools unit can access sales, manufacturing, purchasing, and distribution control systems on its intranet.
	Marshall Industries (www.marshall.com)	This electronics-parts manufacturer's intranet lets employees store data and get up-to-date information on customers and suppliers. The company's extranet gives customers and suppliers a secure way to access individualized services and information and order products.
	Philips Electronics (www.philips.com)	An intranet facilitates communication between the customer service, technical service, and product design departments at headquarters at production facilities in Matamoros, Mexico, and at a warehouse in Brownsville, Texas.
	Universal Sewing Supply (www.universalsewing.com)	The intranet allows employees in the main headquarters to communicate with a branch office in the Dominican Republic.
Health Care	Austin Regional Clinic (www.austinregionalclinic.com)	Health-care professionals use wireless technology to input patient data into medical records that are shared over an intranet.
	Florida Hospital (www.flhosp.org)	An intranet lets health-care professionals tap into files and medical records; it also provides communication with three other local hospitals.
	Sarasota Memorial Hospital (www.smh.com)	From the bedside to the emergency room, health-care workers use an intranet to input admissions and patient-assessment information.
Information Technology	FastLane Technologies (www.fastlanetech.com)	The intranet at the administration software maker lets employees track their job performance privately and allows them to voice their thoughts, concerns, and questions about the company.
	Novell (www.novell.com)	Nearly 5,000 employees in more than 40 countries use the InnerWeb intranet to communicate and collaborate on projects.

(continued)

Industry	Company	Intranet Solutions
Insurance	The Hemisphere Group (www.hemispheregroup.com)	Independent insurance agents nationwide use the company's intranet to share strategies with colleagues.
Media/Entertainment	Dow Jones Interactive Publishing (www.dowjones.com)	An intranet lets sales representatives demonstrate at customer sites how company information products can be combined with customers' intranets.
	Lexis-Nexis (www.lexis-nexis.com)	The information publisher's intranet improves workflow and communications among employees with daily news briefings, self-serve employee data modifications, and event registration.
Pharmaceuticals	Eli Lilly (www.lilly.com)	Scientists use an intranet, which offers data mining, visualization, and knowledge-management applications, to collaborate, share information, and take courses online.
	Fisher Scientific International (www.fisher1.com)	The company launched a ProcureNet intranet to price contracts in real time, process payments, and manage EDI transactions.
	Pfizer Pharmaceuticals Group (www.pfizer.com)	Through the PPG Online intranet, 5,000 marketing, medical, and sales-training employees share information and ideas.
Retail	Barnes & Noble (www.barnesandnoble.com)	Business customers can link their intranets to the bookseller's internal network, so their employees can access books and manuals previously approved for purchase.
	Hannaford Brothers (www.hannaford.com)	An intranet links 140 stores in this Northeast supermarket chain and helps track sales, figure inventory, and swap inventory analysis.
	Home Depot (www.homedepot.com)	Using handheld devices, employees at the hardware retailer can order items over the corporate intranet to restock shelves.
	Kmart (www.kmart.com)	An intranet links in-store kiosks to the discount retailer's back-end system to let shoppers buy large appliances.
Telecommunications	MCI (www.mci.com)	An intranet lets more than 3,000 employees take virtual classes at networkMCI University, the training arm of the telecommunications giant.

Source: Compiled from Solution Series (1998). Used by permission.

Industry-Specific Extranet Solutions

Industry	Company	Extranet Solutions
Brokerages	First Data (www.firstdatacorp.com)	An extranet lets this transaction processing services company serve customers such as banks and brokerages.
	Merrill Lynch (www.ml.com)	Analysts and other employees at this investment firm use an extranet to manage deals and bill customers; eventually, the extranet will accommodate 26,000 workers.
	Northern Trust (www.ntrs.com)	This billing-services company uses an extranet to invoice retailers for food vendors such as Frito Lay.
	PricewaterhouseCoopers (www.pwcglobal.com)	The accounting and professional services company uses an extranet to offer a full range of business advisory services for global, national, and local companies and institutions.
Chemicals and Oil	Chevron Global (www.chevron.com)	Two hundred jobbers and independent distributors use an extranet to access pricing information, receive invoices, and make payments.
Consumer Goods	Epic Records (www.epiccenter.com)	An extranet lets Epic artists access a back-end system that lets them communicate with their fans over the Internet.
	Warner/Chappell (www.warnerchappell.com)	An extranet allows customers to license company music.
Education	Education News & Entertainment Network (www.enen.com)	Employees at Fortune 1,000 companies get training over an extranet that lets teachers and students interact in real time.
Environmental	Enviryx Environmental LLC (www.enviryx.com)	An extranet lets companies access environmental, health, and safety information and outsource their government-reporting, chemical-tracking, and inventory-reporting requirements.
	Government & Legal Corporate Service Co. (www.cscinfo.com)	Large law firms and corporations in all 50 states access CSC's extranet to retrieve legal and government documents.
	Department of Labor's Pension Benefit Guarantee (www.dol.gov)	This government group uses an extranet to track the trustee and pension plans of bankrupt companies and issue statements for them.
Food and Beverage	Nabisco (www.nabisco.com)	The cookie maker uses an extranet to manage its supply chain, which links

(continued)

Industry	Company	Extranet Solutions
		plants, suppliers, sales offices, trucking companies, and distributors.
	Nestlé (www.nestle.com)	An extranet lets employees of the food company order supplies through catalogs and lets managers approve purchases. Centralized reports help the company track purchases, negotiate better prices, and reduce paperwork.
General Manufacturing	Alcoa (www.alcoa.com)	Global distributors use a secured extranet to place manufacturing orders.
	Boeing (www.boeing.com)	Customers, suppliers, and employees use an extranet to do everything from perusing company maps to ordering airplane parts.
	Goodway Graphics (www.goodwaygraphics.com)	Customers can submit orders for customized documents through the printer's extranet and receive delivery in 24 hours.
	Harley-Davidson (www.harley-davidson.com)	An extranet lets dealers cut processing of warranty claims from three weeks to three days. Dealers can also get technical documents on demand.
	Lockheed Martin's Tactical Aircraft Division (www.lmco.com)	An extranet with multimedia conferencing features lets the airplane maker confer with partners British Aerospace and Northrop Grumman as they build a next-generation jet fighters.
	Raytheon Systems (www.raytheon.com)	The defense contractor's extranet allows authorized employees to procure supplies from designated vendors.
	Saab Cars USA (www.saabusa.com)	Dealers use the car manufacturer's extranet to better manage parts and inventory.
	Toyota USA (www.toyota.com)	Toyota's Technical Education Network extranet lets the automaker provide community colleges with the latest educational materials on manufacturing and servicing automobiles.
	TRW (www.trw.com)	An extranet lets the maker of automotive and defense systems technology buy supplies from 25 business partners for use in plants in North America and Europe.
	U.S. Surgical (www.ussurg.com)	An extranet lets health-care customers order products from catalogs; the company uses the extranet to work with suppliers to build parts for its products.

Industry	Company	Extranet Solutions
	Visio (www.visio.com)	Employees at this manufacturer of drawing products use an extranet to purchase nonproduction goods and services.
	Visteon Automotive System (www.visteonet.com)	The maker of Ford auto parts uses an extranet, which connects 82,000 employees, to manage its supply chain.
Health Care	Cobe BCT (www.cobebct.com)	Medical technicians worldwide use an extranet to get the information and training they need to run sophisticated medical devices.
Information Technology	Automated Concepts (www.autocon.com)	This systems integrator's extranet provides training for mobile employees, such as consultants working at customers' sites, and lets managers supervise projects remotely.
	Bay Networks (www.baynetworks.com)	The networking hardware manufacturer's extranet, eNet Connections, tailors product, pricing, sales information, and industry and technical news to individual customers.
	CompuCom Systems (www.compucom.com)	An extranet lets customers order and track PC products.
	Dell Computer (www.dell.com)	Sales representatives use an extranet to give customized multimedia presentations about company products to their small-business customers.
	Entex Information Systems (www.entex.com)	An extranet lets suppliers in 29 countries keep the PC systems integrator's staff updated on the status of shipments.
	Hewlett-Packard (www.hp.com)	The HP Open Pix extranet lets customers, resellers, and fulfillment houses manage the sale, licensing, and servicing of software.
	J.D. Edwards World Solutions (www.jdedwards.com)	EnterpriseNet extranet lets business partners, customers, and employees collaborate on the development of enterprise software.
	Safeguard Business Systems (www.safeguard.org)	An extranet for management software lets customers track the status of orders and balances, saving the company $100,000 a year in labor costs.
	Seagate Technology (www.seagate.com)	Customers of the disk and tape-drive maker use an extranet to view the status of orders, shipments, credit updates, product warranties, and pricing.

(continued)

Industry	Company	Extranet Solutions
	USWeb (www.usweb.com)	An extranet lets the Internet integrator collaborate with many parties during its acquisition of other companies.
	Worldmachine Technologies (www.worldmachine.com)	Clients of the Internet integrator can use an extranet to check progress reports and invoices and share project-design documents.
	Xerox Business Systems (www.xerox.com)	An extranet lets customers submit documents for multiple distribution through Xerox Documents Direct, a service that distributes documents electronically.
Insurance	Insurance Holdings of America (www.insuranceholdings.com)	An extranet supports insurance policy sales, delivery, and underwriting to individual and corporate clients.
Media/Entertainment	Discovery Communications (www.discovery.com)	Discovery Communications' extranet delivers up-to-the-minute programming and promotional information to cable television partners.
	United Artists Theater Circuit (www.uatc.com)	An extranet gives managers of 400 theaters access to applications that analyze and track ticket sales and reservations.
Pharmaceuticals	PharMark (www.pharmark.com)	Employees use an extranet to identify patients whose drug-use patterns place them at risk for adverse health outcomes.
	VWR Scientific Products (www.vwrsp.com)	The company's extranet supports a purchasing system that provides pricing for 250,000 customers.
Retail	NuSkin International (www.nuskin.net)	Individual and business distributors can use an extranet to order supplies from this cosmetics maker online and track their own sales.
	Rite Aid (www.riteaid.com)	Pharmaceutical companies and other suppliers can use an extranet to track inventory levels of their products at 4,000 company drugstores.
Telecommunications	GTE (www.gte.com)	Developing a one-on-one relationship with a single customer, the extranet lets the University of Southern California enter orders for telephone equipment and services.
Transportation	Alaska Airlines (www.alaska-air.com)	Agents and passengers use an extranet to obtain information on flight arrivals and departures, fares, and frequent-flier accounts.

Industry	Company	Extranet Solutions
	American Airlines (www.aa.com)	Frequent fliers can use the company's extranet to track their miles and customize their travel profiles.
	CSX Transportation (www.csx.com)	The Transportation WorkstationNet extranet lets customers and 3,000 employees order, plan, and track rail shipments.
	Federal Express (www.fedex.com)	The Project Grid (Global Resource for Information Distribution) extranet lets employees and customers track packages.
	UniGroup (www.unigroupinc.com)	Customers can use an extranet to track shipments on Mayflower Transit and United Van Lines. The company also plans to use the extranet for knowledge and sales-certification training for agents.
Utilities	Maritime Electric (www.maritimeelectric.com)	Customers can use the Canadian company's extranet to apply for and receive a personal identification number; then they can check their latest power bill and receive an account summary of any credit or debit.
	Southern Co. (www.southernco.com)	The company's extranet lets customers check their power usage and obtain billing information.
	Tennessee Valley Authority (www.tva.gov)	Employees and customers use an extranet to share contract information and shipment and payment status. The extranet is also used for distribution of surplus materials and for power brokering.

Source: Compiled from Solution Series (1998). Used by permission.

CHAPTER 8

Electronic Payment Systems

Learning Objectives

Upon completion of this chapter, the reader will be able to:

- Describe the typical electronic payment systems for EC.
- Identify the security requirements for safe electronic payments.
- Describe the typical security schemes used to meet security requirements.
- Identify the players and procedures of the electronic credit card system on the Internet.
- Discuss the relationship between SSL and SET protocols.
- Discuss the relationship between EFT and debit cards.
- Describe the characteristics of a stored-value card.
- Classify and describe the types of IC cards used for payments.
- Discuss the characteristics of electronic check systems.
- Discuss how many IC cards will be adequate.

8.1 Is SET a Failure?

The most common Internet payment method for the B2C EC is credit cards. However, a concern for customers is security while sending over the Internet, credit card information, including name, card number, and expiration date. Buyers also are concerned with privacy. They do not want others to know who they are, or what they buy. They also want to be sure that no one will change their order and that they are connected to the real vendor and not to an imposter.

At present most companies use **SSL (Secure Socket Layer)** protocol to provide security and privacy. This protocol allows customers to encrypt their order at their PC. However, this protocol does not provide customers all the protection they could have.

Visa and MasterCard have jointly developed a more secure protocol, called **SET (Secure Electronic Transaction).** Theoretically, it is a perfect protocol. For example, a typical difference between SET and the widely used SSL is that SSL does not include a customer certificate requiring special software (called **digital wallet**) at the client site.

SSL is built into the browser, so no special software is needed. The Visa and Master-Card plan was to accept messages only if they conformed to SET protocol.

However, SET did not propagate as fast as most people expected because of its complexity, slow response time, and the need to install the digital wallet in the customer's computer. Most cyber banks and e-stores stayed with SSL protocol, even though some e-stores, like Wal-Mart Online, support both SSL and SET protocols. Moreover, according to a survey by Forrest Research, only 1 percent of electronic businesses plans to migrate to SET by 1999.

MasterCard said that the digital wallet would be distributed as embedded software in the next version of Windows. However, Visa decided not to wait. Thus, Visa agreed to offer a credit card processing gateway embedded in the barebones SSL encryption protocol. Wells Fargo, one of the largest Web banking companies uses a SET-free payment processing service that adds certificates to SSL data encryption. The certificates are stored in smart cards that can be slipped into a special keyboard with a built-in slot.

Is SET a failure? Or should we just wait a little longer until the digital wallet in the smart card is more widely used and SET becomes easier for us?

8.2 Electronic Payments and Protocols

The opening case illustrates to us one of the major issues in EC: payments and their security. Secured payment systems are critical to the success of EC and they are the subject of this chapter.

When buying a hamburger in a fast-food restaurant, we pay with several dollars of paper bills and may receive some coins back. To have a nice dinner at a French restaurant, we may pay with a credit card. To pay the electric utility bill, we send a paper check. These are typical offline payment methods. It is estimated that approximately 55 percent of consumer transactions in the United States are paid by cash and 29 percent by check. Credit, debit, and other electronic transactions account for 15 percent of all consumer transactions. The resources the United States spends on processing these payments amount to $60 billion annually, which corresponds to 1 percent of the gross national product.

The emergence of electronic shopping on the Internet has necessitated new payment methods. Cash cannot be a medium of payment between remote buyers and sellers in cyberspace. Therefore, the credit card has become the most popular payment method for consumer-initiated cybershopping. Figure 8.1 illustrates an online credit card payment screen. The computer asks you to input the card number, holder's name, and expiration date. In most e-malls, the answer to these questions are encrypted. However, not all consumers are confident with the safety of online message delivery. Therefore, sellers are obliged to offer multiple options for transmission of credit card information, so that buyers can select their preferred method (Application Case 8.1). The customer may send the card information online or by making a toll-free telephone call.

SECURE ELECTRONIC TRANSACTION PROTOCOL FOR CREDIT CARD PAYMENT

A major question is "Is the encryption secure enough to protect confidentiality and authentication?" You may recall that the merchant in every offline credit card transaction has the customer's credit card information. This implies that the credit card information may be abused. The same is true in Internet commerce. Here the risk is even greater, since hackers may read the card's information while it travels on the Internet. The risk of faked use of another person's credit card is inherent unless a protocol can

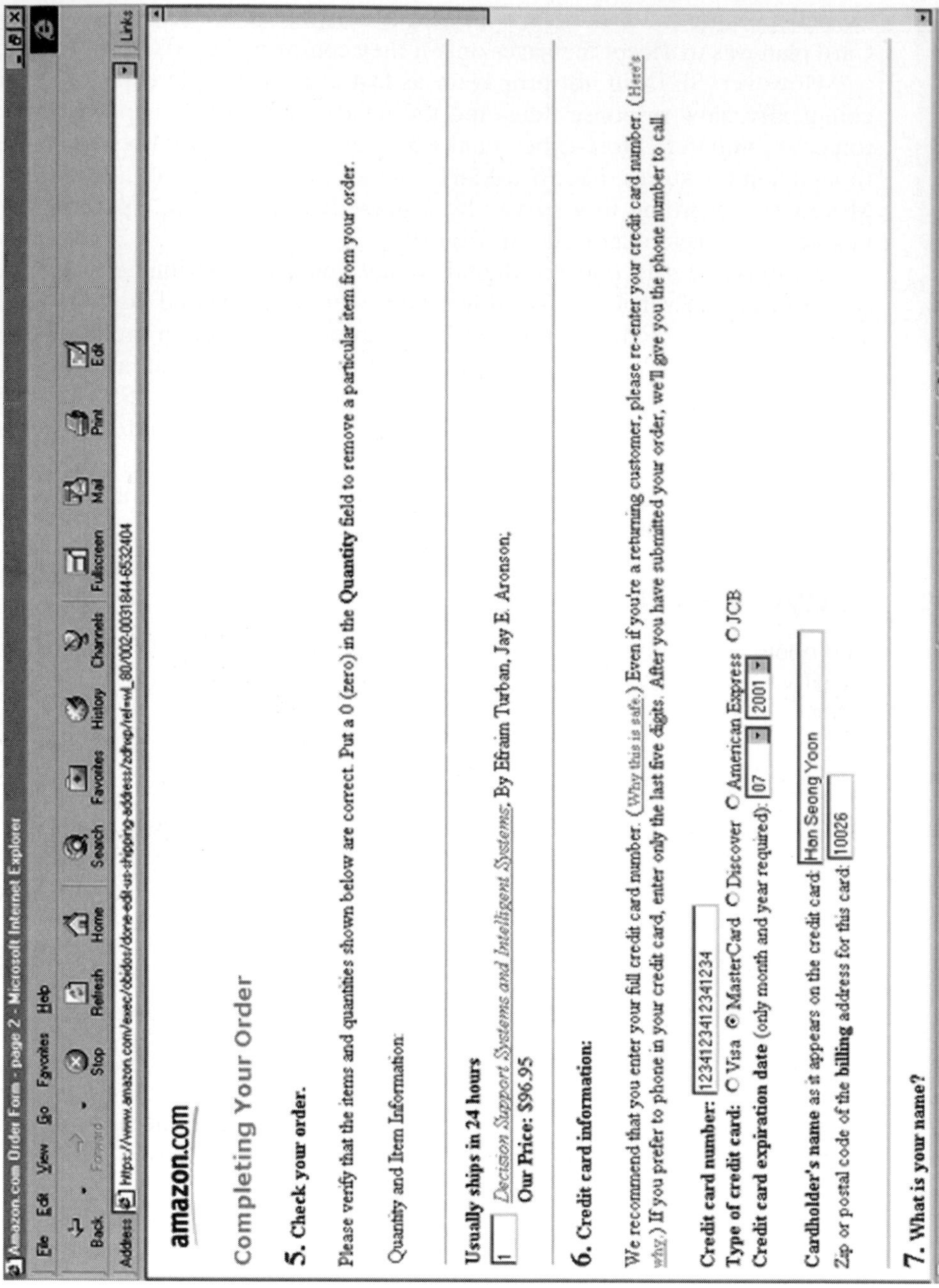

FIGURE 8.1 An Illustrative Online Credit Card Payment at Amazon, the Popular Cyber Bookstore.

APPLICATION CASE 8.1

Merchants Offer Multiple Payment Options

Even though electronic payments are rapidly becoming popular, many customers are still afraid of providing their credit card information online. While customers are getting acquainted with the new systems, merchants should offer multiple payment options during this transition period. Sophisticated payment schemes should not become a deterrent to customers' access. Customers should be allowed to type in the card information online as well as to call a toll-free telephone number, for instance. Some sites even accept a fax, e-mail, or printed mail in a sealed envelope.

The call center, with its labor costs, and the cost of processing fax, e-mail, and printed mail mean SET-protocol-based payment will eventually become the most economical for merchants. Nevertheless, few commercial sites are dedicated only to SET protocol, which requires downloading a "digital wallet." Most customers are not patient enough and some cannot perform the technical installation process. So merchants have had to open alternative user-familiar payment methods. Merchants need to follow the customers learning curve in selecting payment methods.

---

confirm the truthfulness of the cardholder on the other side of cyberspace. Can sending card information by fax, telephone, e-mail, or sealed envelope avoid this risk? Of course not. In fact, appropriate encryption techniques are the most secure protection against wiretapping during transmission.

Not only does security during transmission need to be resolved but also authentication of the cardholder. Even a password cannot completely eliminate risk if an ill-intentioned person has registered with a fake name. Consumers need to show an authenticating certificate that may be stored in a smart card so that counterfeiters cannot abuse the card information even though the information might have been exposed. This is what SET protocol is trying to achieve. SET is presented in section 8.4.

ELECTRONIC FUND TRANSFER AND DEBIT CARDS ON THE INTERNET

Electronic fund transfer (EFT), a popular electronic payment method, transfers a money value from one bank account to another in the same or a different bank. EFT has been in use since the 1970s through automated clearinghouses (ACHs). Today, we can also use an Internet-based EFT, which implies that the connection between cyberbanks and security protection during the transmission is a must. The architecture of Internet-based EFT and its relationship with debit cards is also described in section 8.5. The necessity of certificates for EFT cardholders and the need to merge multiple certificates to one smart card are also described in section 8.5.

STORED-VALUE CARDS AND E-CASH

Suppose a consumer has purchased a digital picture or listened to music on the Internet for a $0.25 fee. How is he or she going to pay for it? The minimum cost to process a credit card payment is about $1.00, which should be charged to the seller (according to First Virtual (1999), an Internet-based payment intermediary). This means that there is no way to sell such small items unless a more economical payment method is developed. This is why the so-called micropayment method is necessary. Electronic cash can be an answer to this problem. It is used similarly to the way **stored-value**

cards are used to pay for buses, subways, and public phones. The question is how to adapt and integrate the non-Internet-based e-cash available on smart cards with the Internet-based cyberbanking system. This topic is presented in section 8.6.

ELECTRONIC CHECK SYSTEMS

Paper checks are the most popular payment method for remote payees in several countries, including the United States. The high processing costs of paper checks is a problem, however. An average paper check transaction costs $0.79, which is twice the cost of an ACH service. It seems necessary to develop a more economical **electronic check (e-check)** processing system. However, since the cost of current check issuance is born by banks, there is no strong incentive for the payers to use e-checks, which will reduce the float due to the high speed of electronic circulation. Nevertheless, the e-check system is expected to become a major payment medium, especially for the B2B EC environment, in which payment amounts are large.

Since an e-check system without float is fairly similar to EFT, it is necessary to compare the characteristics of the two types of electronic payments. Also, there are several issues related to the implementation of e-checks. For example, the default risk inherent in the checking system is an issue. We need to investigate the possibility of reducing the default rate by utilizing the capabilities of intelligent agents in e-checking systems. These issues are described in section 8.7. Let us now investigate each payment method one at a time.

8.3   Security Schemes in Electronic Payment Systems

Before we explore each electronic payment method, it is helpful to review the security schemes that are commonly used in electronic payment methods. Security issues are also covered in chapter 11. Four essential security requirements for safe electronic payments are:

1. **Authentication:** a method to verify the buyer's identity before payment is authorized.
2. **Encryption:** a process of making messages indecipherable except by those who have an authorized decryption key.
3. **Integrity:** ensuring that information will not be accidentally or maliciously altered or destroyed during transmission.
4. **Nonrepudiation:** protection against customers' denial of orders placed and against merchants' denial of payments made.

SECURITY SCHEMES

The key security schemes adopted for electronic payment systems are encryption, digital signature, message digest, and use of certificates and certifying authorities. There are two types of encryption: secret key and public key encryption.

Secret Key Cryptography

For many years, people used a security system based on a single secret key. In this **secret key** encryption scheme, also known as **symmetric encryption,** or **private key encryption,** the same key is used by a sender (for encryption) and a receiver (for **decryption**). The most widely accepted algorithm for secret key encryption is the Data Encryption Standard (DES) (Schneier 1996). Some cryptographers believe that the DES

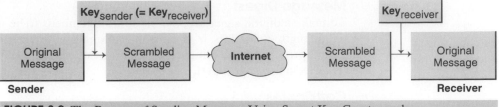

FIGURE 8.2 The Process of Sending Messages Using Secret Key Cryptography.

algorithm is penetrable. However, DES is believed to be secure enough because penetration would take several years at a cost of millions of dollars. The SET protocol has adopted the DES algorithm with its 64-bit key. The process of using a single key is shown in Figure 8.2. Note that the problem with a single key is that it needs to be transmitted to a counterpart. The public key encryption scheme described next overcomes the problem of exchanging a private key.

Public Key Cryptography

Public key encryption, also known as *asymmetric encryption,* uses two different keys: a public key and a private key. The public key is known to all authorized users, but the private key is known only to one person—its owner. The private key is generated at the owner's computer and is not sent to anyone. To send a message safely using public key cryptography, the sender encrypts the message with the receiver's public key. This requires that the receiver's public key be delivered in advance. The message encrypted in this manner can only be decrypted with the receiver's private key. The most popular algorithm with public key cryptography is the RSA (Rivest, Shamir, and Adelman) algorithm (see Schneier 1996) with various key sizes, like 1,024 bits. This algorithm has never been broken by hackers, so it is seen as the safest encryption method known to date. The process of using a public key is shown in Figure 8.3. Public key cryptography, RSA, is usually used to transmit the secret key of DES algorithm because the DES algorithm is more efficient and faster in handling encryption and decryption.

Digital Signature

Digital signature is used for the authentication of senders by applying public key cryptography in reverse. To make a digital signature, a sender (let's say Sally) encrypts a message with her private key. In this case, any receivers with her public key can read it, but the receiver can be sure that the sender is really the author of the message. A digital signature is usually attached to the sent message, just like the handwritten signature.

FIGURE 8.3 The Process of Sending Messages Using Public Key Cryptography.

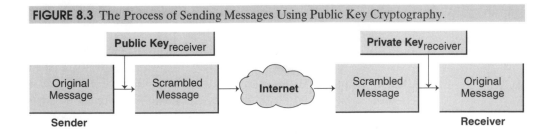

Message Digest

To make a digital signature, the base message needs to be normalized to a predetermined length of 160 bits, regardless of the length of the original message. This normalization process can be achieved by hashing the original message. This hashed message is called a **message digest.**

Certificates

A **certificate** usually implies an identifying certificate that is issued by a trusted third-party certificate authority (CA). A certificate includes records such as a serial number, name of owner, owner's public keys (one for secret key exchange as receiver and one for digital signature as sender) an algorithm that uses these keys, certificate type (cardholder, merchant, or payment gateway), name of CA, and CA's digital signature (Figure 8.4).

Certificate Authority

A **certificate authority** is a body, either public or private, that seeks to fill the need for trusted third-party services in EC. A CA accomplishes this by issuing digital certificates that attest to certain facts about the subject of the certificate. VeriSign is one the pioneering CAs (VeriSign 1999). The U.S. Postal Service is expected to play a major role as a CA. A CA may be certified by another trusted CA, making a hierarchy of CAs, as shown in Figure 8.5.

In the context of credit cards, the cardholder certificate authority (CCA) issues the certificate to cardholders, the merchant certificate authority (MCA) to merchants who operate e-stores, and the payment gateway certificate authority (PCA) to payment gateway service providers. The above CAs need their own certificates from a na-

FIGURE 8.4 An Illustrative Certificate.

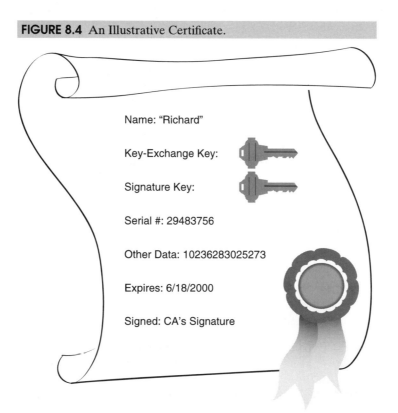

Name: "Richard"

Key-Exchange Key:

Signature Key:

Serial #: 29483756

Other Data: 10236283025273

Expires: 6/18/2000

Signed: CA's Signature

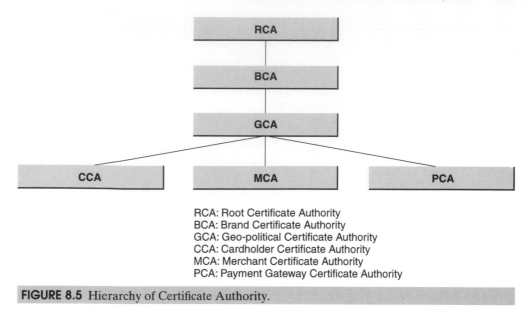

RCA: Root Certificate Authority
BCA: Brand Certificate Authority
GCA: Geo-political Certificate Authority
CCA: Cardholder Certificate Authority
MCA: Merchant Certificate Authority
PCA: Payment Gateway Certificate Authority

FIGURE 8.5 Hierarchy of Certificate Authority.

tionally designated CA, which is called a geopolitical certificate authority (GCA). For the international exchange of certificates, a brand certificate authority (BCA) like VeriSign needs to certify the GCA. Eventually, a single root certificate authority (RCA) needs to certify the BCAs. So far, it is not decided who will become the RCA. Application Case 8.2 lists 10 tips for selecting a CA. Cross-certification among CAs is becoming popular for international EC.

Digital Envelope

Digital enveloping is the process of encrypting a secret key (like the one for DES) with the receiver's public key. The DES key encrypted in this manner is called a **digital envelope,** because the DES key should be opened first to decrypt the message contents with the key.

Transaction Certificate and Time Stamp

A **transaction certificate** attests to some fact about the conduct of a transaction that can be used to prevent repudiation. Similarly, a **time stamp** is a cryptographically unforgeable digital attestation that a document was in existence at a particular time. A CA may keep these evidences at the CA's computer upon the request of customers.

The above security schemes include five security requirements:

1. A digital signature assures the sender's authentication and nonrepudiation.
2. At the receiver's site, the received message is hashed to generate a message digest and the digital signature is hashed to generate another message digest. By comparing these two message digests, integrity can be assured.
3. The DES algorithm along with the digital envelope using the RSA algorithm can assure secure encryption.
4. The receiver's certificate, which includes the secret-key exchange key, can assure the receiver's authentication and nonrepudiation.
5. The transaction certificate and time stamp stored in the third-party CA is the third-party evidence of authentication and nonrepudiation for both sender and receiver.

---

10 Tips for Selecting a CA

1. **Who owns the CA?** Look for well-known companies with a reputation for integrity.

2. **How are users authenticated?** Go with a CA that demands face-to-face verification and photo identification.

3. **How are certificates and keys generated?** This must be done in a secure environment using tamper-resistant hardware.

4. **How are certificates distributed?** Sending keys and PINs (personal identification numbers) separately keeps them from falling into the wrong hands.

5. **Are policies and procedures published on the Web site?** This gives potential customers a clue as to how the CA operates.

6. **How are certificates revoked?** Speedy revocation of compromised or stolen certificates prevents misuse and fraud.

7. **What's the certificate renewal process?** Regular revalidation makes for more security.

8. **Is there a disaster recovery plan?** A CA is mission critical, so around-the-clock availability is a must.

9. **Is the CA independently audited?** External checks help maintain the integrity of the service.

10. **Does the CA have cross-certification with other CAs?** This allows subscribers to reach business partners certified by other CAs. This is a major consideration for cross-border EC.

Source: Compiled from Eng (1999). Used by permission.

SECURE SOCKET LAYER PROTOCOL

Security schemes are adopted in protocols like SSL and SET. This section explains the general-purpose protocol SSL. SET, tailored to credit card payment on the Internet, will be explained in the next section. Since SET is established on top of SSL, understanding SSL is the foundation for understanding SET. The protocol Secure-HTTP (S-HTTP) applies SSL between Web servers and browsers, which communicate by HTTP protocol.

The SSL protocol performs message exchanges as shown in Figure 8.6. Assume that the sender is Sally, and the receiver is Richard. The steps of the process correspond to the numbers in Figure 8.6.

1. At Sally's site, the message to be sent is hashed to a previously fixed length for message digest.
2. The message digest is encrypted with Sally's private signature key using an RSA algorithm, and the output is a digital signature.
3. The digital signature and Sally's certificate are attached to the original message. In the meantime, a secret key using the DES algorithm at Sally's computer, encrypts the bundle with the key.
4. The symmetric key is encrypted with Richard's public key, which resides in Richard's certificate, received in advance. The result is a digital envelope.
5. The encrypted message and digital envelope are transmitted to Richard's computer over the Internet.
6. The digital envelope is decrypted with Richard's private exchange key.
7. Using the restored secret key, the delivered message is decrypted to the message, digital signature, and Sally's certificate.
8. To confirm the integrity, the digital signature is decrypted by Sally's public key (that resides in Sally's certificate), obtaining the message digest.

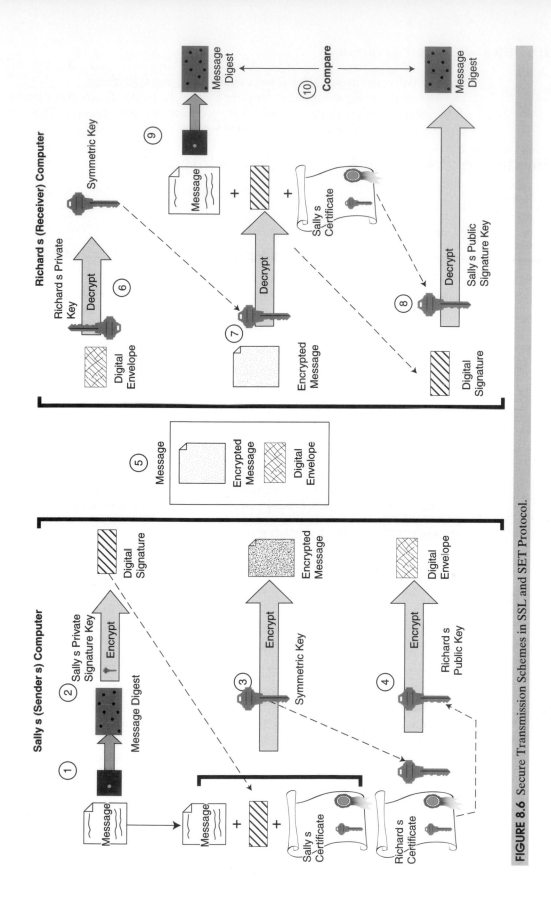

FIGURE 8.6 Secure Transmission Schemes in SSL and SET Protocol.

283

9. The delivered message is hashed to generate a message digest.
10. The message digests obtained by steps 8 and 9, respectively, are compared to confirm whether there was any change during the transmission. This step confirms the integrity.

8.4 Electronic Credit Card System on the Internet

Credit cards are the most popular payment method for cyberspace consumer shopping today.

THE PLAYERS

Before exploring the process of using credit cards online, let's identify the players in the credit card system. They are:

1. **The cardholder:** a consumer or a corporate purchaser who uses credit cards to pay merchants.
2. **The merchant:** the entity that accepts credit cards and offers goods or services in exchange for payments.
3. **The card issuer:** a financial institution (usually a bank) that establishes accounts for cardholders and issues credit cards.
4. **The acquirer:** a financial institution (usually a bank) that establishes an account for merchants and acquires the vouchers of authorized sales slips.
5. **The card brand:** bank card associations of issuers and acquirers (like Visa and MasterCard), which are created to protect and advertise the card brand, establish and enforce rules for use and acceptance of their bank cards, and provide networks to connect the involved financial institutions. The brand authorizes the credit-based transaction and guarantees the payment to merchants. Sometimes, the issuing bank performs the business of the brand.

THE PROCESS OF USING CREDIT CARDS

A typical process of using credit cards is shown in Figure 8.7. The procedure varies depending upon the agreement among the brand, issuer, and acquirer. The major steps in the process are:

1. Issue a credit card to a potential cardholder
   - A potential cardholder requests an issuing bank, from in which the cardholder may have an account, the issuance of a card brand (like Visa or MasterCard).
   - The issuing bank approves (or denies) the application.
   - If approved, a plastic card is physically delivered to the customer's address by mail.
   - The card is activated as soon as the cardholder calls the bank for initiation and signs the back of the card.
2. The cardholder shows the card to a merchant whenever he or she needs to pay for a product or service.
3. The merchant then asks for approval from the brand company, and the transaction is paid by credit. The merchant keeps a sales slip.
4. The merchant sells the slip to the acquiring bank and pays a fee for the service. This is called a *capturing process.*
5. The acquiring bank requests the brand to clear for the credit amount and gets paid. Then the brand asks for clearance to the issuer bank.
6. The amount is transferred from issuer to brand. The same amount is deducted from the cardholder's account in the issuing bank.

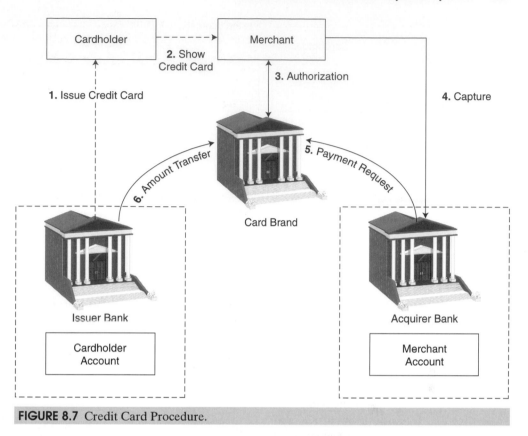

FIGURE 8.7 Credit Card Procedure.

In the conventional credit card system, the process just described is only partially automated, in the sense that the disqualified card information is transmitted to the merchants on printed paper and requests for authorization are sometimes made by telephone (in many countries). Moreover, merchants have to mail the paper sales slips to the acquirer bank for capturing. However, the entire process must be fully automated on the Internet in a secure manner. That is why SET protocol was devised.

SECURE ELECTRONIC TRANSACTION PROTOCOL

SET protocol was initially designed by Visa and MasterCard in 1997 and has evolved since then (MasterCard/Visa 1997). SET protocol meets the four security requirements for EC as SSL does: authentication, encryption, integrity, and nonrepudiation. In addition, SET defines the message format, certificate format, and procedure of message exchange as depicted in Figure 8.8.

In SET protocol, there are four entities: cardholder, merchant, CA, and payment gateway, as depicted in Figure 8.9, pg. 287. The roles of issuer, acquirer, and brand are beyond SET protocol specifications. The role of payment gateway is to connect the Internet and proprietary networks of banks. Each participating entity needs its own certificate. To keep the consumer's certificate in his or her personal computer or IC card, software called the **electronic wallet,** or *digital wallet,* is necessary. To connect the digital wallet with various merchants, interoperability is a very important characteristic to meet.

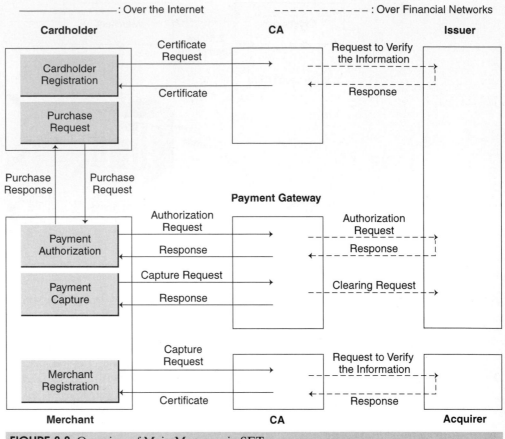

FIGURE 8.8 Overview of Main Messages in SET.

ELECTRONIC WALLET

Now the question is where to store the electronic wallet. To achieve perfect security, the electronic wallet has to be downloaded into the buyer's personal computer. Since the interoperability of the cardholder's digital wallet with any merchant's software is essential, a consortium of companies (Visa, MasterCard, JCB, and American Express) has established a company called SETCo (Secure Electronic Transaction LLC 1999). This company performs the interoperability test and issues a SET Mark as a confirmation of interoperability. IBM, Netscape, Microsoft, VeriSign, Tandem, and MetaLand provide such interoperable digital wallets.

STORAGE OF CERTIFICATES

If the private key and corresponding public key in a certificate are physically stored in the customer's personal computer, the customer can use the certificate only at the computer. However, if the certificate is stored in an IC card, the wallet can work if the IC card is inserted into a card reader attached to a computer. Therefore, storing the certificate in IC card seems to be the safest method. The initial SET 1.0 announced in May 1997 did not include standards about integrating with IC cards. SET 2.0 may include standards for integration with IC cards. C-SET (Chip-SET) protocol attempts to integrate SET protocol with the EMV (Europay, MasterCard, and Visa 1999) standard developed for e-cash on the IC card (Europay International 1999).

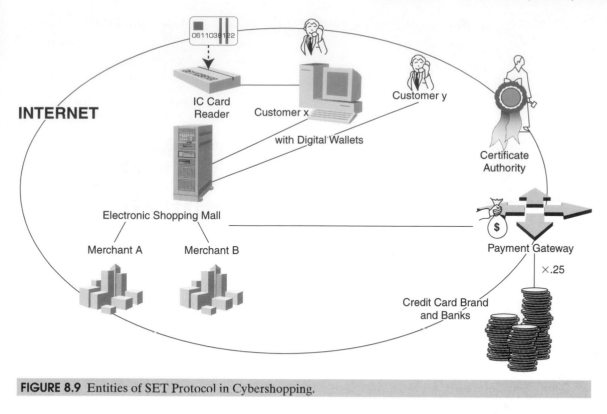

FIGURE 8.9 Entities of SET Protocol in Cybershopping.

The International Center for Electronic Commerce (ICEC 1999) has developed a system named *Smart-SET,* which integrates SET protocol with an IC card that can store multiple certificates.

SECURE SOCKET LAYER PROTOCOL FOR ELECTRONIC PAYMENT

Even though SET is a perfect solution for secure electronic payments, a relatively simple version of SSL is currently widely adopted. This is because SET protocol is complex and certificates are not widely distributed in a stable manner. Theoretically, the SSL protocol (Netscape 1996) may use a certificate but it does not include the concept of a payment gateway. Merchants need to receive both ordering information and credit card information because the capturing process initiated by the merchant. The SET protocol, on the other hand, hides the customer's credit card information from merchants and also hides the order information from banks to protect privacy. This scheme is called *dual signature.* Until SET becomes popular, a simple version of SSL is a very viable alternative.

8.5   Electronic Fund Transfer and Debit Cards on the Internet

As the second most popular electronic payment method on the Internet, EFT and the debit card are used.

ELECTRONIC FUND TRANSFER

Electronic fund transfer, designed to transfer a certain amount of money from one account to another, existed a long time before the initiation of Internet commerce. This money may be transferred to another bank as depicted in Figure 8.10. The customer's

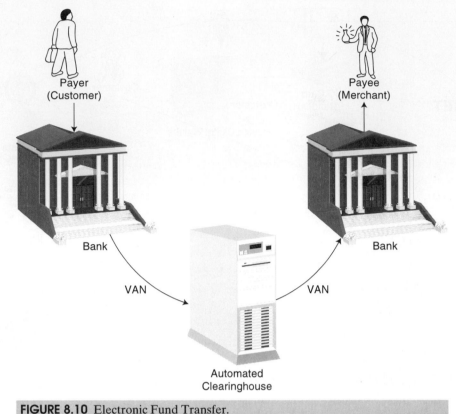

FIGURE 8.10 Electronic Fund Transfer.

terminal can be an automatic teller machine (ATM), PC, or telephone terminal. Traditionally, a dedicated financial VAN was used to link the banks through ACHs. Customers were expected to link up to the bank's server by a dial-up connection. The security on the VAN, as indicated earlier, is higher than that of the Internet.

As the Internet propagates and becomes a charge-free medium of public data communication, it is becoming the most economical medium of EFT. Many cyberbanks like Bank of America (Application Case 8.3) and Citibank also support Internet-based transfers. However, to transfer funds on the Internet safely, the encryption of messages is essential. Currently, most cyberbanks do not utilize certificates. To adopt the concept of a certificate for EFT, a SET-like protocol for pure cyberbanks and for legacy bank systems that are linked with the Internet through payment gateways, needs to be developed. A likely architecture of Internet-based fund transfer is depicted in Figure 8.11 (pg. 290). The certificate for EFT may also be stored in an IC card along with the certificates for credit cards. This feature will influence the architecture of the next generation of cyberbanks.

DEBIT CARD

A **debit card,** also known as a *check card,* is a card that authorizes the EFT. While a credit card is a way to pay later, a debit card is a way to pay now. When you use a debit card, the amount is immediately deducted from your checking or savings account. The debit card allows you to spend only what is in your bank account. Debit cards are accepted at many locations including grocery stores, retail stores, gasoline stations, and

---

APPLICATION CASE 8.3

Bank Online and Security Tips

Cyberbank is becoming a major medium of EFT over the Internet. Bank Online (from Bank of America) was ranked in 1998 as the nation's number-one online banking service (See Gomez Advisors' Internet Banker Scorecard, www.gomez.com). Bank Online offers Internet-based fund transfers and bill payments in addition to other banking services like checking your account balances. The services offered by Bank Online are:

Home Banking: allows customer to check account balances and transfer funds between linked accounts.

Convenient Time: open 24 hours a day and 7 days a week.

Inexpensive Bill Payment: available for monthly fee of $5.95. Free of charge if you have a certain account in the Bank of America.

BankAmericard Online Access: view up to 6 months of your account history, in real time.

PC Banking for Business: provides businesses with another way to access accounts conveniently and get timely information to control finances and manage cash flow.

Security on the Internet: In addition to the encryption scheme at the browser, Bank of America suggests the customer follow 5 rules to protect the customer's privacy and security. These can be recommended to any cyber-service with high security requirements.

Five Security Tips:
1. First and foremost, don't reveal your online pass code to anyone else. If you think your online pass code has been compromised, change it immediately online.
2. Don't walk away from your computer if you are in the middle of a session.
3. Once you have finished conducting your banking on the Internet, always sign off before visiting other Internet sites.
4. If anyone else is likely to use your computer, clear your cache or turn off and reinitiate your browser in order to eliminate copies of Web pages that have been stored in your hard drive.
5. Bank of America strongly recommends you use a browser with 128-bit encryption to conduct secure financial transactions over the Internet.

---

restaurants. You can use your card anywhere merchants display the debit card's brand name or logo. A debit card is an alternative to carrying a checkbook or cash.

Many ATM cards have the features of a debit card. Advantages of using debit cards are listed below (Manuel 1999):

- Obtaining a debit card is much easier than obtaining a credit card.
- Using a debit card instead of writing checks saves you from showing personal identification.
- Using a debit card frees you from carrying cash, traveler's checks, or a checkbook.
- Merchants accept debit cards more readily than checks, especially in other countries.

However, from the customer's point of view, it is not clear what the advantage of debit cards over credit cards is. Debit card purchases can have less protection than credit card purchases for items that are never delivered or are defective. Returning goods or canceling services purchased with a debit card is treated as if the purchase were made with cash or check. When a customer uses a debit card, however, no fee is charged to the merchant. So there is a strong incentive for merchants to offer discounts to encourage paying by debit card instead of credit card.

For the payments of B2B EC, the credit card is too expensive an option for sellers, so the debit card can be a popular alternative over checks. Later on in this chapter, we

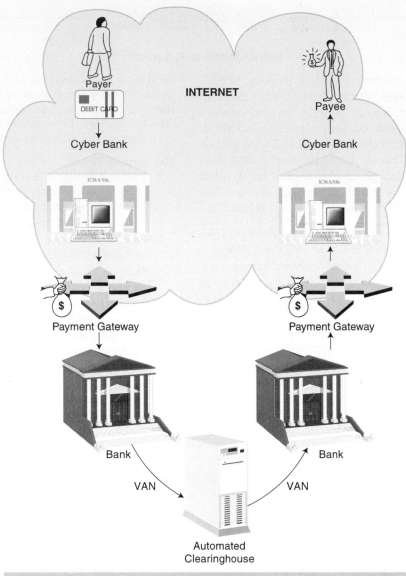

FIGURE 8.11 An Architecture of Electronic Fund Transfer on the Internet.

see the nature of e-check systems and their resemblance to debit cards, because the e-check is delivered at lightning speed.

A debit card can be used at the e-store just like a credit card. The certificate for a credit card may be shared for a debit card on the Internet. Again, the safest place to store the certificate for a debit card is an IC card. The IC card issue will be discussed in the next section.

FINANCIAL EDI

Financial EDI is nothing but an EDI used for financial transactions. For the EDI per se, refer to chapter 6. The EDI is a standardized way of exchanging messages between businesses, so the EFT can be implemented using a financial EDI system. Recently, the leading banks like Bank of America and Chase Manhattan have used financial

EDI on the Internet. Safe financial EDI needs to adopt the security schemes used for the SSL protocol. Extranet is another way of implementing secure financial EDI between financial institutions and businesses (chapter 7). Extranet encrypts the packets exchanged between senders and receivers using public key cryptography.

8.6   Stored-Value Cards and E-Cash

A major benefit of using e-cash is that high fees for small payments **(micropayment)** are avoided. Other benefits include anonymity, convenience, and support for multiple currencies across borders. Electronic cash has been popular on the IC card, but it is now becoming available on the Internet.

SMART CARDS

The concept of e-cash has been in use in the non-Internet environment under the name of **smart card** since the 1970s. Plastic cards with magnetic stripes on them have been used to store information such as personal identification numbers. Cards were also used to store a value of money, which decreased with use. Applications include telephone, transportation, and library copies. The current generation of smart cards includes IC chips with programmable functions. The value of money can then be depleted and recharged. Today, customers must keep separate e-cash cards, one for each application, and can recharge the card only at designated locations, such as a bank office or a kiosk. In the future, recharges will be done through your PC whether it is on the Internet or your bank's network. At the moment, the most widely known general-purpose smart cards are Mondex (Application Case 8.4) and VisaCash.

APPLICATION CASE 8.4

Mondex Makes Shopping Easy

Shopping with Mondex. Payments are made by slipping the Mondex card into a card reader in the retail terminal. Then funds are transferred immediately from the card to the terminal with no need for signatures or authorization. Newspaper vendors and small shops can use battery-powered terminals.

  Adding money to the card. The card can be recharged by debiting the money value to the card at specially adapted cash dispensers or by telephone. Mondex-compatible mobile phones will be able to act as your own personal mobile cash dispenser. Specially adapted pay phones will also be able to transfer funds. As well as loading up the card, you can lock it with a four-digit code to prevent misuse if stolen. Money on a locked card can only be spent by first unlocking the card with the four-figure code.

  Paying for a new era of electronic entertain-ment. Children, young people, and adults will all be able to use Mondex to pay for the new generation of Video-on-Demand films and video games supplied through the Internet. With Mondex you can only spend what is on the card.

  Paying on the Internet. Using the Mondex wallet, e-cash can be moved from one card to another—as simply as one person can give another person physical cash. Parents will be able to use the wallet to give electronic pocket money to their children. The wallet also lets you see details of your last 10 transactions—so you can finally find out just where your cash is going!

  Balance reader. A small electronic key tag allows you to find out how much money is on your card.

  Other properties. Mondex can store up to five different currencies at a time. (1999)

REPRESENTATION OF E-CASH SYSTEMS

To design an **e-cash** system, we need to identify how to represent and move the e-cash. One can think about two types: (1) electronic money with a unique value and identification number and (2) stored-value cards.

Electronic Money

Electronic money is analogous to paper money or coins. The pioneer of electronic money on the Internet was DigiCash (DigiCash 1999). Banks affiliated with DigiCash issue electronic bills, each with a unique identification. To prevent the duplication of bills, DigiCash has to trace the usage record of issued bills. This implies that each payment transaction must be reported to the bank, which makes the process as expensive as EFT. In addition, recording transaction history makes the process even more expensive than EFT. For this reason electronic money systems have not been widely adopted in real-world situations.

Another potential problem with DigiCash is the conflict with the role of the central bank's bill issuance. Legally, DigiCash is not authorized to issue more than an electronic gift certificate even though it may be accepted by a wide number of member stores. A similar approach was attempted by Net Cash (Medvinsky and Neuman 1993). The electronic purse may be stored either in the PC or in the smart card. The early version of DigiCash stored the electronic purse in the PC. DigiCash did not have a chance to store electronic money in the IC card.

Stored-Value Cards

In a stored-value card approach, there is no issuance of money. The debit card is nothing but a delivery vehicle of cash in an electronic form. In this sense, the stored-value card is the same as a prepaid card. Mondex (Mondex International 1999), VisaCash (Visa International 1999b), and several e-cash systems listed in Table 8.1 have adopted this approach. The stored-value card may be either anonymous or onymous. An advantage of an anonymous card is that the card may be transferred from one person to another, while the onymous card must not. The notion of a stored-value card is also implemented on the Internet without employment of an IC card. CyberCash has commercialized a stored-value card named CyberCoin as a medium of micropayment on the Internet (CyberCash 1999). Henceforth, when we say *e-cash,* it implies the stored money value on the IC card unless qualified differently.

TABLE 8.1   IC Card-Based E-Cash Systems

Countries	Name of E-Cash (Promoting Institution)	Started Date	Initiative	Type
Belgium	Proton (Banksys)	Feb. 1995	Bank's Consortium	Closed
U.K.	Mondex (Mondex UK)	July 1995	Mondex International	Open
The Netherlands	ChipKnip (Interpay)	Oct. 1995	Bank's Consortium	Closed
Germany	GeldKarte (ZKA)	May 1996	Bank's Consortium	Closed
U.S.A.	VisaCash (Visa)	Jul. 1996	Visa International	Closed
Portugal	Porta Moedas (SIBS)	Feb. 1995	Bank's Consortium	Closed
Denmark	Danmont (Danmont)	Sep. 1995	Bank's Consortium	Closed
Finland	Avant (Toimirasha Oy)	Feb. 1994	Bank's Consortium	Closed

CLOSED VERSUS OPEN E-CASH SYSTEM

E-cash systems can be either closed or open. A closed system implies that the cash value in the IC card can only be recharged from a bank's account, and the used money, which was collected in the memory of the IC card readers (like ones installed in the subway meters), will be transferred to the receiver's bank account. The direct transfer between IC cards is prohibited. On the other hand, the open system allows direct transfer of money value between IC cards. Because governments are afraid of the risk of lost traceability and money laundering, most systems other than Mondex have adopted the closed system as demonstrated in Table 8.1. It is interesting to note that MasterCard has substantial ownership in Mondex, while Visa commits to VisaCash, which is a closed system. Thus, it seems that there may not be a single global standard protocol in e-cash systems.

CONTACT VERSUS CONTACTLESS IC CARDS

Many IC cards are activated by contacting the IC chip with a card reader. However, by using remote-sensing IC cards, the readers can be accessed without physical contact. The e-cash withdrawal can be executed while the card is moving. Two types of contactless cards are recognized: a proximity card and an amplified remote-sensing card. The proximity card can be read up to one foot from the reader. Proximity cards are mainly used to access buildings and for paying bus fares and other transportation systems. The amplified remote-sensing card (also known as a *short-range dedicated card*) is good for a range of up to 100 feet, and it is used for tolling moving vehicles.

The bus card in many cities in the world from Seoul to Helsinki and subway cards in Hong Kong and other cities are examples of *proximity cards.* The nonstop pay system at Highway 91 in California and many other expressways worldwide are examples of *amplified remote-sensing cards* (Application Case 8.5). By using the card, the cars on Highway 91 can pay their toll without stopping. However, these cards cannot yet be recharged through the Internet.

In Pusan City in Korea, a hybrid card (which has two separate chips on one card) is used—one contact-type and one proximity card-type chip. A similar card is used in other cities in the world for mass transportation. For example, in Tokyo, you can use the same card for buses, trains, and taxis. In some systems, the contact-type chip is used for taxi fees, while the remote-sensing type is used for the subway and buses. The two chips are not internally connected with each other, however, and recharging the contactless chip through the Internet is not economically feasible due to the high cost of contactless reader/writers. This problem will be solved in the next generation of transportation cards, which will be a combi-card. This card will have a shared memory with both contact and contactless uses. The recharge will be realized through inexpensive contact-type readers attachable to the PC. The real-world case at the end of this chapter illustrates some applications of transportation cards.

INTEGRATING INTERNET AND NON-INTERNET PAYMENT SYSTEMS

A critical deficiency of current cyberbanks has been that cash cannot be delivered to customers at home. However, by adopting smart-card-based e-cash, e-cash can be recharged at home through the Internet and can be used on the Internet as well as in a non-Internet environment. IC-card-based e-cash can be an important medium of integrating cyberspace with the traditional commercial world.

APPLICATION CASE 8.5

Smart Tollway: Highway 91

Most of California's population lives around Los Angeles, where many commute one to three hours each day. Several million cars travel daily between residential areas and the city, creating air pollution, noise, and commuter stress.

Highway 91 is a major, eight-lane, east-west highway east of Los Angeles. Traffic is especially heavy during rush hours. To beat the traffic, some commuters formerly had to leave home as early as 4:30 in the morning, and the situation got worse as traffic increased. The State of California was running out of funds to add more lanes in time and therefore decided to resort to an innovative solution: allow a private company to build and operate a smart tollway parallel to Highway 91.

California Private Transportation (CPT) Company built six express lanes along a 10-mile stretch in the median of existing Highway 91 at a cost of $126 million. In exchange, CPT company will collect tolls on the road for 35 years while maintaining the road, including highway patrol. The express lane system has only one entrance and one exit, and it is totally operated with EC technology. Here is how the system works:

1. Only subscribers can drive on the road. A subscriber signs a contract with the company, prepays a certain amount, and receives an automatic vehicle identification (AVI) device, called a *transponder*, that is placed on the rearview mirror of the car. The device, about the size of a thick credit card, includes a microchip, antenna, and a battery.

2. A large sign over the tollway tells drivers the current fee for cruising the express lanes. In 1998, it varied from $0.50 in slow traffic hours to $2.75 during rush hours.

3. Sensors in the pavement let the tollway computer know that a car has entered; the car does not need to slow or stop.

4. The AVI device makes radio contact with a transceiver installed above the lane.

5. The transceiver relays the car's identity through fiber-optic lines to the control center, where a computer deducts the toll from the driver's prepaid account.

6. Surveillance cameras record the license numbers of cars without AVI devices. These cars can be stopped by police at the exit or fined by mail.

7. Video cameras along the tollway enable managers to keep tabs on traffic, for example, sending a tow truck to help a stranded car. Also, through knowledge of the traffic volume, pricing decisions can be made. Raising the price ensures the tollway will not be jammed.

8. Subscribers can get a free ride if they carpool (three or more riders) on a "three or more only" lane. This lane is monitored manually to ensure that three or more people are indeed in the car.

Subscribers and police are the only humans on the tollway; there are no tollbooths and there is no stopping.

The system saves commuters between 40 and 90 minutes each day, so it is in high demand. An interesting extension of this system is the use of the same AVI devices for other purposes. For example, they can be used in paid parking lots. And one day you may be recognized when you enter the drive-through lane of McDonalds and a voice asks you, "Mr. Smart, do you want your usual meal today?"

Recall that it was also necessary to store the private key and certificates in the IC card. The concern now is whether to integrate the certificates and stored money value in one card. The issue is not a matter of technology but of a business model. The business needs to consider the brand company (like Mondex and VisaCash), the bank (who will actually sell the cards to users), the CA (who needs to be involved to download the certificates to the cards), and the cardholder's motivation to pay with the IC card. Multiple alternatives for using IC cards seems to be the most important motivation for potential cardholders.

CEILING OF STORED VALUES AND MULTIPLE CURRENCIES

To prevent the abuse of stored values and illegal transfer of money across international borders, the law controls in some countries the maximum stored value on a card. For instance, in Singapore, S$500 is the ceiling; in Hong Kong, HK$3,000 is the ceiling. Stored-value cards like Mondex allow the storage of multiple currencies. Cards can be used for **cross-border payments** by selecting the agreed-upon currency between trading parties. Future cards will allow currency conversion.

8.7   Electronic Check Systems

The **e-check** system is basically an electronic implementation of the paper check system, as depicted in Figure 8.12. The security features in e-check systems are encryption, digital signature, and certificates. Thus, the security schemes for e-checks are basically the same as those in SET. Only the usage procedures are different. However, since the circulation time of e-checks may take only a few minutes, the e-check system becomes virtually similar to EFT.

According to the FSTC (Financial Services Technology Consortium) project (FSTC 1999), four scenarios of e-check systems are proposed, as depicted in Figure 8.13. Besides the deposit and clearing scenario, which was adopted in Figure 8.12, we can see that three other scenarios are also variations of EFT. A difference in Figure 8.12 from the traditional EFT is the existence of two certificates and a remittance invoice returned to the payer. Therefore, we need to investigate the characteristics of electronic payment methods to analyze the similarities and differences among them.

Since e-checks are more important in B2B EC, a highly secured payment system is needed, especially for large payments. For this purpose, the electronic checkbook—the counterpart of the electronic wallet, which stores credit card certificates and e-cash—needs to be integrated with the accounting information system (back office)

FIGURE 8.12 Procedure of FSTC Prototype.

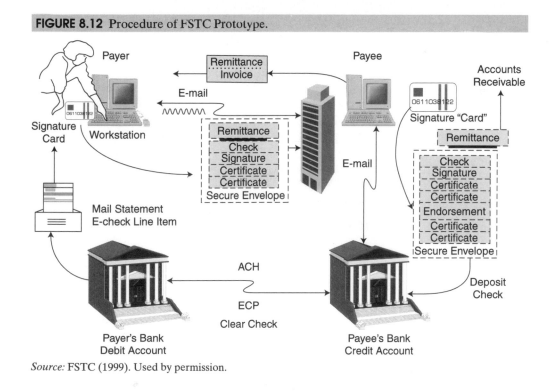

Source: FSTC (1999). Used by permission.

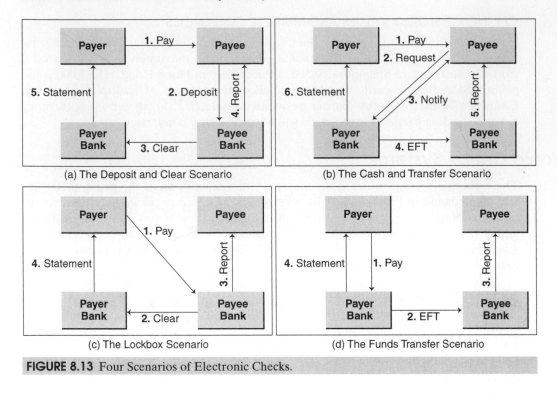

FIGURE 8.13 Four Scenarios of Electronic Checks.

of business buyers as well as the payment server of sellers. Also, the electronic invoice and receipt of payment need to be saved in the buyers' and sellers' computers for future retrieval. To keep track of the time and contents of important check issuances and receipts, the transaction certificate and time stamp need to be maintained by a trusted third party.

In 1998, a SafeCheck system was proposed, which uses an agent-based checkbook that resides on the checkholder's PC (Figure 8.14). Since the electronic checkbook can autonomously validate the authorization of check issuance, SafeCheck can prevent the ill-intentioned default-risky check issuance. This kind of control is not possible with paper checks. In the SafeCheck system, the number of blank check sheets and the ceiling amount of check issuance are determined by the level of the checkbook-holder's credit. Since SafeCheck does not need authorization for each check issuance, as the credit card system does, it can be used effectively in high-credit societies, reducing the cost of authorization (Lee and Yoon 1999). For more information about e-checks, refer to www.echeck.org.

8.8 Unified Payment Systems

INTEGRATING PAYMENT METHODS

As seen in the previous sections, some electronic payment systems share several characteristics and therefore can be consolidated. Two potential consolidations to be implemented are:

1. The online e-check is merging with EFT.
2. The e-check with a designated settlement date is merging with electronic credit cards.

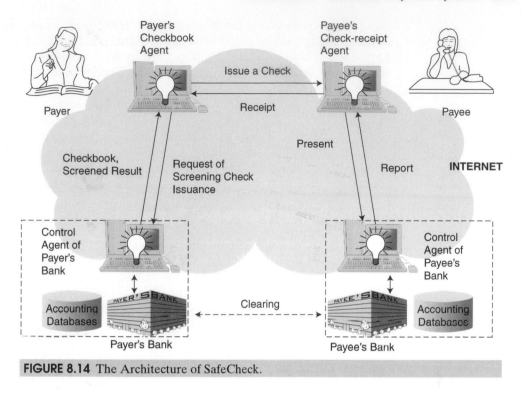

FIGURE 8.14 The Architecture of SafeCheck.

During the early stage of e-check service, the first cyberbank, Security First Network Bank (www.sfnb.com), provided a so-called Quick Payment Service. Upon request of paper check issuance on the Internet, paper checks were issued to the payees when the receivers were not equipped with the Internet. However, as the Internet became more popular, this service disappeared. Instead, Security First Network Bank challenged the cyberbanking services of traditional banks with lower service charges. The battle of more economical and secure payment service has begun in cyberspace as well. Compare what SFNB offers in contrast to the cyberbank offered by Bank of America (Application Case 8.3, pg. 289).

- Free tryout for six months: no monthly fees, no minimum balances
- 20 free electronic bill payments each month
- 10 free ATM withdrawals each month
- Free online images of cleared checks

The leading credit card brand, Visa, is experimenting with new services of VisaCash and ePay. VisaCash is a stored-value money card as mentioned earlier, and ePay is an EFT service (see Visa International 1999a). So the bank's traditional service area may be infringed on by credit card brand companies, which regard all payment services as their target business. Another issue to consider is bills payment; since bills can be paid over the Internet, conventional banks will have to join cyberbanking services to provide electronic payment service on the Internet (chapter 5).

HOW MANY CARDS ARE APPROPRIATE?

We have seen that an onymous card is necessary to keep the certificates for credit cards, EFT, and electronic checkbooks. Future cards will use fingerprints to identify the cardholder, so no one else can use it as e-cash (in implementation). On the other hand, the stored value in the IC card can be delivered in an anonymous mode. Should we keep the two in one card? Malaysia's Multimedia Super Corridor project pursues a One-Card system. The Relationship Card by Visa is also attempting a one-card system. The single card that includes both multiple certificates and e-cash is theoretically feasible. However, if the card is used frequently to pay for small amounts, the risk of losing the card may become higher. Therefore, it seems safer to have a separate anonymous e-cash card for daily micropayment. Because e-cash may be abused through money laundering, both anonymous and onymous IC cards need to have a ceiling. The inspection at international borders, where there is a limit on the amount of money transferred, could be difficult or even impossible if the money resides on a card. This problem can be minimized for e-cash that has a storage ceiling.

8.9 Prospect of Electronic Payment Systems

As the volume of EC becomes larger, the role of secure and economical online payments on the Internet will, accordingly, become more important. At the moment, the credit card payment for B2C trades with SSL protocol is the most widely adopted. However, SET protocol tailored to credit card payment may become one of the next-generation standards. For micropayment, smart-card-based e-cash will become more popular and will be recharged through the Internet from the cyberbanks, which will revitalize the benefit of cyberbanks.

As B2B occupies the major portion of EC, more economical payment methods like Internet-based funds transfer equipped with the benefit of check systems will become the major medium for large-amount payments. The credit card fee seems too high to transfer large amounts among credible corporations. This prospective trend should envision opportunities to payment businesses and corporate finance managers.

8.10 Managerial Issues

Managerial issues for electronic payment systems vary depending upon the business position.

1. **Security solution providers** can cultivate the opportunity of providing solutions for secure electronic payment systems. Typical ones include authentication, encryption, integrity, and nonrepudiation.
2. **Electronic payment systems solution providers** can offer various types of electronic payment systems to e-stores and banks. The SET solution of having the certificate on the smart card is an emerging issue to be resolved.
3. **Electronic stores** should select an appropriate set of electronic payment systems. Until electronic payment methods become popular among customers, it is necessary to offer traditional payment methods as well.
4. **Banks** need to develop cyberbanks compatible with the various electronic payment systems (credit card, debit card, stored-value card, and e-check) that will be used by customers at e-stores. Watch for the development of consistent standards in certificates and stored-value-card protocols.
5. **Credit card brand companies** need to develop standards like SET and watch the acceptance by customers. It is necessary to balance security with efficiency. Careful attention is needed to determine when the SSL-based solution will be replaced by the SET-based solution and whether to combine the credit card with the open or closed stored-value card.
6. **Smart card brands** should develop a business model in cooperation with application sectors (like transportation and pay phones) and banks. Having

standards is the key to expand interoperable applications. In designing business models, it is important to consider the adequate number of smart cards from the customer's point of view.

7. **Certificate authorities** need to identify the types of certificates to be provided. Banks and credit card companies need to consider whether they should become a CA.

Summary

The compilation of this chapter helps you in attaining the following learning objectives:

1. **Typical electronic payment systems for EC**—electronic credit card, EFT, debit card, stored-value card, and e-check.
2. **Security requirements for safe electronic payments**—authentication, encryption, integrity, and non**re**pudiation.
3. **Typical security schemes used to meet security requirements**—secret key cryptography, public key cryptography, digital signature, message digest, certificate, digital envelope, transaction certificate, and time stamp.
4. **Players of the electronic credit card system on the Internet**—cardholder, merchant, card issuer, acquirer, and brand.
5. **Relationship between SSL and SET**—SSL is a general-purpose security protocol that employs the security schemes listed in 3, above. SET is a specific protocol tailored to credit card payment procedures on top of the SSL. SET brings in a new entity, payment gateway, and defines the message formats and procedure.
6. **Relationship between EFT and debit cards**—*EFT* is a way of transferring money between accounts in the same or different banks. The *debit card* is a card that authorizes the EFT service online.
7. **Stored-value card**—an IC card that stores the value of money in numbers.
8. **Types of IC cards**—contact versus contactless and hybrid card versus combicard.
9. **Characteristics of E-check Systems**—the e-check system is similar to EFT in the EC environment.
10. **Adequate number of IC cards**—at minimum, one anonymous card to store e-cash and one anonymous card to store the certificates. The number depends upon the competition status of business models.

Keywords

- Acquirer
- Authentication
- Certificate
- Certificate authority (CA)
- Cross-border payments
- Debit card
- Decryption
- Digital envelope
- Digital signature
- Encryption
- Electronic cash (e-cash)
- Electronic check (e-check)
- Electronic credit card system
- Electronic fund transfer (EFT)
- Electronic (or digital) wallet
- Financial EDI
- Integrity
- Micropayments
- Nonrepudiation
- Private key
- Public key
- Symmetick key
- Secure electronic transaction (SET)
- Secure socket layer (SSL)
- Smart cards
- Stored-value card
- Time stamp

Questions for Review

1. List the four security requirements for safe electronic payments.
2. Describe the pros and cons of secret key encryption and public key encryption and their complementary use.
3. Define *digital signature* and *digital envelope*.

4. What is a CA?
5. Describe the security schemes adopted in SSL and SET.
6. Describe the players and procedures of the electronic credit card system.
7. Describe EFT and its relationship with debit cards.
8. Describe the difference between open and closed stored-value cards.
9. List the types of smart cards in terms of contact requirements and internal memory storage.
10. Define the concept of micropayment and provide examples of its use.
11. Define e-cash, and list the different types of e-cash.
12. Describe the e-check system and its resemblance to EFT and electronic credit cards.

Questions for Discussion

1. Compare SSL and SET.
2. Explain why traditional payment systems are inadequate for EC.
3. Why does a micropayment require a special payment system? How does such a system enable economical payments?
4. Compare and contrast e-cash and debit cards.
5. Why are micropayments so important for the future of EC? How can you pay 25 cents or a dollar electronically?
6. Which of the payment systems are best for B2C transactions? Which for B2B? Why?
7. Discuss some of the issues that are involved in cross-border transactions.
8. What are the advantages of the public key systems over the secret key?
9. Describe the role of certificates, digital signatures, and digital envelopes.
10. What are the differences between an e-check and a paper check?
11. Explain the role of a CA. Why is it necessary?
12. Explain the essentials of SET. Why is it becoming an international payment standard?
13. What is the difference between a regular debit card and a stored-value card?
14. How does Internet EFT differ from VAN-based EFT?
15. What are some of the issues of cross-border payments?
16. Compare and contrast the contact and contactless cards (proximity and amplified remote smart cards).
17. Discuss the pros and cons of the hybrid card and the combi-card, and evaluate the cost of recharging the stored-value card.
18. What are the characteristics of a public/private key system? Compare it to a single-key system.

Internet Exercises

1. Enter the home pages of Wal-Mart (www.wal-mart.com) and Amazon (www.amazon.com). Identify the acceptable payment methods in each site. What kinds of security measures has each site adopted?
2. Enter the cyberbanks like Bank of America (www.bankamerica.com), Wells Fargo Bank (www.wellsfargo.com), Citibank (www.citibank.com), and Security First Network Bank (www.sfnb.com). Compare the electronic payment systems supported in each cyberbank.
3. Enter the Web site of Mondex International (www.mondex.com). Examine the various capabilities of the Mondex card. Find information about Visa's e-cash wallet. (Go to Visa's site). Compare and contrast the two cards.
4. Describe how public and private keys are used in the following instances:
   a. Adam wants to send a message that only Barbara can read.
   b. Barbara wants to make sure that the message she received was written by Connie.

c. Adam wants to pay Barbara, who lives in another city, by e-cash. How can the transaction be secured?

d. How can a vendor who receives an e-check be sure that the check is real?

5. Enter the site of Cross-Border Council (www.nacha.org/xborder/cbc/tm). Prepare a report about the need for the council, how it works, and what their latest projects are.

Team Exercises

1. Form two teams to debate the protocols of stored-value cards. One team supports the closed system. The other team supports an open system. Let each team present its position with real-world cases like Mondex and VisaCash and argue with each other. Choose among the strategies of cultivating applications, card distribution, and recharge.

2. Form two teams to analyze the competition between card brand companies and banks in the electronic payment service industry. One team plays the role of a card brand company (like Visa); let them expand the business to EFT, debit card, and stored-value card service. The other team plays the role of a bank (like Bank of America); let them compete with the card brand company. Let each team debate the strengths and weaknesses of each side, and discover what they both have in common.

R E A L   W O R L D   C A S E

Transportation Cards in the Big Cities

Six Million Bus Cards in Seoul

Seoul Bus Association installed the contactless stored-value bus card in July 1996 for the first time in the world. The 8,013 buses of 442 routes owned by 86 companies joined this project. A total of 6 million cards were issued. About 39 percent of bus fares and 30 percent of deluxe bus fares were collected via the card. The cards are used 1.73 million times per day (900 million won) and are recharged 77,000 times per day (880 million won).

Because of its popularity, supplying the IC card caused a huge bottleneck. The card-issuing machine is able to produce 30,000 cards per day, which means it takes 200 days to provide 6 million cards. The offline 2,618 kiosks operated by humans are the outlets for card recharge. As of October 1998, the total investment in installing the card issuers, rechargers, clearing systems, and readers on buses was 16.8 billion won. Use of the card has been extended to cities around Seoul.

From Hybrid to Combi-Card in Pusan

The Hanaro Card (which means One Card in Korean) in Pusan City in Korea was designed for bus, subway, taxi, and tollgate fares in February 1998. The card is widely accepted for the bus, subway, and tollgates but not yet for taxis. More than 50 percent of fares are collected through the Hanaro Card, as summarized in the attached table. The card readers are installed in 3,003 urban buses, at 581 subway entrances in 34 subway stations, in 7,579 taxis, in 341 minibuses, and at 28 tollgates.

The card is basically a stored-value money card. There are two types of Hanaro Card: the hybrid (both contact and contactless chips are in the card) and contactless proximity (used for bus and subway).

The card can be purchased and recharged at subway stations, the issuing banks (Housing & Commercial Bank, Pusan Bank, and Community Credit Cooperative), and ATMs. It takes 2,000 won (less than two U.S. dollars) to buy a card. The minimum rechargeable amount is 5,000 won, with a ceiling of 70,000 won. This card is mainly used for micropayment.

Incentive to use the card is the convenience of not carrying coins and fare tickets. The card users get a 15 percent discount (25 percent for students) on subway fares, a 3 percent to 8 percent discount on major urban buses, and a 10-won discount for minibuses. The Hanaro Card has become a necessity for Pusan citizens. The bus companies also enjoy the traceability of revenue and the reduced cost of ticket handling.

However, collecting taxi fares is not widely accepted because the contact-type Hanaro Card requires online debiting. A taxi driver has to call over a wireless phone for every payment so that the amount can be transferred online to the taxi company's bank account. This system is very expensive to use and it seems the system adopted for bus and subway, which collects money during the day at a terminal and transmits the accumulated funds to the bank once a day, would be better. ■

Frequency of Using the Hanaro Card				
Classification	*Card Use per Day (thousand)*	*Total Passengers per Day (thousand)*	*Percentage Using Hanaro Card*	*Operational Status*
Urban Bus	1,050	2,100	50	Full
Subway	350	570	60	Full
Minibus	90	180	50	Full
Tollgate	30	200	15	Full
Taxi	30 persons	1,080	0.003	Partial

CASE QUESTIONS

1. What is the difference between a hybrid card and a combi-card?

2. Why is the combi-card essential to recharge e-cash through the Internet at home?

3. Why isn't the Mondex card get adopted for the bus and subway?

References

V. Ahuja, *Secure Commerce on the Internet* (London: Academic Press, 1996).

Bank of America, "Bank of America Home Page" (www.bankamerica.com), 1999.

D. Cameron, *E-commerce Security Strategies: Protecting the Enterprise* (Charleston, SC: Computer Technology Research Corporation, 1998).

L. J. Camp, M. Sirbu, and J. D. Tygar, "Token and Notational Money in Electronic Commerce," *Usenix Workshop on Electronic Commerce* (New York, 1995).

D. Chaum, "Achieving Electronic Privacy," *Scientific American*, 267 (2:1992): 76–81.

Citibank, "Citibank Home Page" (www.citibank.com), 1999.

CyberCash, Inc., "Introducing CyberCoin™" 1999 (www.cybercash.com/cybercash/shoppers/coingenpage.html).

DigiCash, "DigiCash—Publications," 1999 (www.digicash.com/ publish/publish.html).

J. A. Dorn, *The Future of Money in the Information Age* (Washington D.C.: Cato Inst., 1997).

R. C. Effors, *Payment Systems of the World* (NY: Oceana Publications, 1994).

C. Eng, "Certificate Authorities: The Keys to E-Commerce," *Data Communications* (February 1999): 48AA–48FF.

J. Essinger, *Electronic Payment Systems: Winning New Customers* (NY: Chapman & Hall, 1992).

Europay International, "Corporate Publication," 1999 (www. europay.com/Publication).

Financial Services Technology Consortium, "FSTC Home Page," 1999 (www.fstc.org).

First Virtual Holdings, "First Virtual Home Page," 1999 (www. fv.com).

A. Furche and G. Wrightson, *Computer Money: A Systematic Overview of Electronic Payment Systems* (Los Altos, CA: Morgan Kaufman Publishers, 1996).

A. K. Ghosh, *E-Commerce Security: Weak Links, Best Defenses* (NY: John Wiley & Sons, 1998).

D. B. Humphery, ed., "The U.S. Payment System: Efficiency, Risk, and the Role of the Federal Reserve," *Proceedings of a Symposium on the U.S. Payment System* (Dordrecht, Netherlands: Kluwer Academic Publishers, 1990).

International Center for Electronic Commerce, "ICEC Home Page," 1999 (icec.net).

J. K. Lee and Han S. Yoon, "Intelligent Agent-Based Virtually Defaultless Check System: SafeCheck System," forthcoming in *International Journal of Electronic Commerce* (1999).

P. Loshin and P. Murphy, *Electronic Commerce: Online Ordering and Digital Money* (Rockland, CA: Charles River Media, 1997).

D. C. Lynch and L. Lundquist, *Digital Money: The New Era of Internet Commerce* (NY: John Wiley & Sons, 1996).

C. A. Manuel, "Debit Cards: Beyond Cash and Checks," *National Consumers League,* February 1999 (www.natl-consumersleague.org/debitbro.htm).

MasterCard/Visa, *Secure Electronic Transaction (SET) Specification (Version 1.0)*, May 1997.

G. Medvinsky and B. C. Neuman, "Net-Cash: A Design for Practical Electronic Currency on the Internet," *Proceedings of First ACM Conference on Computer and Communications Security*, November 1993.

M. S. Merkow, K. Wheeler, and J. Breithaupt, *Building SET Applications for Secure Transactions* (NY: John Wiley & Sons, 1998).

Mondex International, "Mondex Technology," 1999 (www. mondex.com).

K. D. Nagel and G. L. Gray, *1999 Electronic Commerce Assurance Services* (San Diego, CA: Harcourt Brace Professional Pub., 1998).

Netscape, "SSL 3.0 Specification," 1996 (home.netscape.com/eng/ssl3/index.html).

D. O'Mahony, M. Peirce, and H. Tewari, *Electronic Payment Systems* (Norwood, MA: Artech House, 1997).

B. Schneier, *Applied Cryptography* (NY: John Wiley & Sons, 1996).

Secure Electronic Transaction LLC, "SET Secure Electronic Transaction LLC Home Page," 1999 (www. setco.org).

Security First Network Bank, "Security First Network Bank—The World's First Internet Bank," 1999 (www. sfnb.com).

B. J. Summers, *The Payment System: Design, Management, and Supervision* (International Monetary Fund, 1994).

E. Turban, E. McLean, and J. Wetherbe, *Information Technology for Management*, 2^d ed., (NY: John Wiley & Sons, 1998).

T. P. Vartanian, R. H. Ledig, and L. Bruneau, *"21st Century Money, Banking, & Commerce* (NY: Fried, Frank, Harris, Shriver & Jacobson, 1998).

VeriSign Inc., "VeriSign Digital ID Enrollment—Netscape Servers," 1999 (www.verisign.com/netscape).

Visa International, 1999a (www.visa.com/cgi-bin/vee/fm/epay.html?2+0).

Visa International, "Visa—VisaCash," 1999b (www.visa.com/cgi-bin/vee/nt/cash/main.html? 2+0).

Wal-Mart, "Wal-Mart Online Security Guarantee" (www.wal-mart.com/docs/security.shtml), 1999.

P. Wayner, *Digital Cash*, 2d ed. (London: Academic Press, 1997).

CHAPTER 9

EC Strategy and Implementation

Learning Objectives

Upon completion of this chapter, the reader will be able to:

- Describe the strategy planning process for EC.
- Understand the process of formulating EC strategies.
- Describe the role of CSF and justification of EC.
- Explain competitive intelligence on the Internet and in EC.
- Explain the steps and issues involved in EC implementation.
- Understand how to reassess EC projects.

9.1 IBM's E-Business's Strategy

IBM's declared strategy is to transform itself into an e-business in order to provide business value to the corporation and its shareholders. As stated earlier, IBM views e-business as being much broader than EC because it serves a broader constituency and a variety of Web-based processes and transactions. To assure successful implementation, IBM formed an independent division, called Enterprise Web Management, that has the following four goals:

- To lead IBM's strategy to transform itself into an e-business and to act as a catalyst to help facilitate that transformation.
- To help IBM's business units become more effective in their use of the Internet, both internally and with their customers.
- To establish a strategy for the corporate Internet site. This would include a definition of how it should look, feel, and be navigated—in short, create an online environment most conducive to customers doing business with IBM.
- To leverage the wealth of e-business transformational accumulated case studies to highlight the potential of e-business to customers.

Like many other companies, IBM started to use the Internet as a static digital brochure—or a publication model—basically posting information. Now, however, it is moving toward e-business, namely carrying out transactions of all kinds over the Internet, intranets, and extranets; transactions between IBM and its suppliers; among members of its Business Partner network; among its employees; and so on. IBM wants to become truly e-business oriented and to focus on how it can use this powerful networking technology to fulfill the diverse needs of its customers.

One of the major issues in moving to e-business was the reengineering of many of its core business processes on the Internet—including commerce, procurement, customer care, and knowledge management. The company is developing consistent companywide business strategies that leverage the size and scale of IBM's Web presence and investments. In addition, it is creating an Internet model that is both unified and user-centric. This involves the setting of site hosting and production standards related to design, functionality, and navigation.

The company targeted for reengineering those areas in which IBM can make the biggest return on investment and which are most practical to address. IBM focused its activities around seven key initiatives:

- Selling more goods over the Web—e-commerce.
- Providing all kinds of customer support online, from technical support to marketing backup—e-care for customers.
- Support for IBM's business partners over the Web—e-care for business partners.
- Dedicated services providing faster, better information for IT analysts and consultants, financial analysts, media, stakeholders—e-care for influencers.
- Improving the effectiveness of IBMers by making the right information and services available to them—e-care for employees.
- Working closely with customers and suppliers to improve the tendering process and to better administer the huge number of transactions involved—e-procurement.
- Using the Internet to better communicate IBM's marketing stance—e-marketing communications.

Some of these initiatives have already borne fruit. There is more to e-business than just how many dollars per day IBM sells on the Web, though. In the procurement area, for example, IBM is invoicing electronically to reduce the millions of paper invoices it sends out and to enable fast, competitive tendering from its suppliers. IBM has evaluated every step of the procurement process to determine where the use of the Web can add value. This has resulted in the identification of more than 20 initiatives—including collaboration with suppliers, online purchasing, and knowledge-management-based applications—in which the company can reduce cost and improve purchasing.

The major goal that IBM has set is to become the premier e-business. That means being the leader in each of the business process areas outlined above. Leadership in these areas will improve customer satisfaction and will allow it to grow more profitably. As the recognized leader in e-business, IBM also adds tremendous credibility to its e-business marketing campaign.[1]

9.2 Strategic Planning for EC

The opening vignette raises some interesting issues related to **strategic planning** for EC. First, IBM created an independent EC division; second, it introduced EC as a corporate culture; third, IBM leveraged its existing strengths; fourth, IBM tied EC with the reengineering of its processes; fifth, the company started seven different EC initia-

---

[1]*Source*: Compiled from *Inside IBM*, November 1998.

tives; sixth, IBM decided to be an EC leader; and seventh, it used return on investment as a criteria for selecting EC projects. The measuring of benefits and figuring ROI is difficult but essential for launching EC projects. (e.g., Folz 1999 and Whipple 1999).

It can also be seen in the opening vignette that the executives of successful EC companies seem to be strategic thinkers focusing on customers, markets, and competitive positioning, as well as on internal operations. Determination of a suitable EC strategy begins with identification of the opportunities and risks. The task of tracking the changing environments, understanding customer groups, and devising methods of meeting the needs of customer groups, requires formulating strategies and planning their implementation.

This chapter first describes how to analyze an industry environment and identify the relative position of the company as part of EC planning. Such planning proceeds with formulating strategic objectives to be achieved through the choice of various competitive strategies. This chapter also addresses the issue of project justification and measuring ROI, which are part of the planning process. Finally, implementation and assessment and reassessment issues are addressed.

Why does a company need strategic planning for EC and what are the available options? A company may decide (1) not to go for EC; (2) to do only passive advertising (as discussed in chapter 2); (3) to open online stores in addition to existing stores, typically called *e-tailing* (chapter 2); (4) to establish a separate online division within the company; or (5) to dissolve regular business and go for cyber-business only (as seen in the Egghead case in chapter 1). The choice depends not only on the nature of the business the company conducts but also on the environment the company is operating in and on the internal resources available. Its strategic plan includes a detailed analysis that supports a choice of one of the five alternatives just mentioned.

How do we conduct EC planning and implementation? One approach is to use a generic methodology. The one we elected to use here is composed of four main stages: industry and competitive analysis, strategy formulation, implementation, and assessment. These stages are interrelated in a cyclic movement, as shown in Figure 9.1. The following sections describe this cycle in detail. We begin with the first stage.

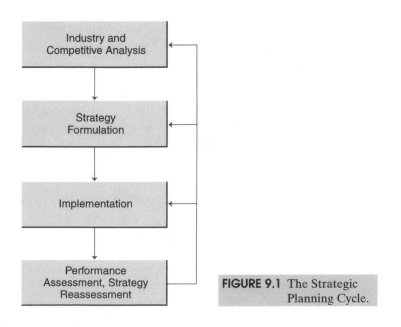

FIGURE 9.1 The Strategic Planning Cycle.

INDUSTRY AND COMPETITIVE ANALYSIS

Industry and competitive analysis for EC entails monitoring, evaluating, and disseminating information from the external and internal environments with respect to launching an EC project. Its goal is to identify the critical factors that will determine the success of the EC project. A popular way to conduct such an analysis is to start with environmental scanning using a SWOT analysis. **SWOT** is an acronym used to describe particular strengths, weaknesses, opportunities, and threats.

The external environment consists of opportunities and threats that are outside the organization and are not typically within the short-run control of top management. These can be related to the corporate strengths and weaknesses in a four-cell matrix, as shown in Figure 9.2. This matrix is referred to as the *SWOT matrix*.

The elements of SWOT are the following:

- In the **Opportunities (O)** block, the external current and future opportunities available for the company are examined.
- In the **Threats (T)** block, the external threats facing the company now and in the future are analyzed.
- In the **Strengths (S)** block, the specific areas of current and future strengths for the company are described.
- In the **Weaknesses (W)** block, the specific areas of current and future weakness for the company are stated.

For example, the study can find an opportunity to sell EC software developed for internal purposes to others or to add new products. The threat may come from competitors or from spreading some corporate resources too thin. A strength can be the company's programmers, whereas weakness may be the lack of experience in database integration. Once the preliminary analysis using SWOT or other methodologies is completed, we can proceed to strategy formulation.

FIGURE 9.2 SWOT Diagram.

Internal Factors / External Factors	Strengths (S)	Weaknesses (W)
Opportunities (O)	**SO Strategies** **Generate strategies here that use strengths to take advantage of opportunities**	**WO Strategies** **Generate strategies here that take advantage of opportunities by overcoming weaknesses**
Threats (T)	**ST Strategies** **Generate strategies here that use strengths to avoid threats**	**WT Strategies** **Generate strategies here that minimize weaknesses and avoid threats**

Source: Wheelen and Hunger (1998), p. 112. Used by permission.

STRATEGY FORMULATION

Based upon the results of the analysis of industry and competition, an EC strategy then needs to be developed. **Strategy formulation** is the development of long-range and strategic plans for the effective management of environmental opportunities and threats, in light of corporate strengths and weaknesses. It includes examining or redefining the corporate or project mission by specifying achievable objectives, developing strategies, and setting implementation guidelines for EC. It should be noted that "going EC" can be done in many ways, as demonstrated throughout this book. An EC initiative may include such EC projects as creating a storefront, extranet, or an electronic mall. Strategy formulation is relevant both for EC initiative in general and for individual EC projects.

An organization's mission states the purpose for the organization's existence. It tells what the company is providing through EC. Based on its EC mission, a company will formulate the objectives of each EC project. An *EC objective* is the measurable goal that the company wants to achieve with EC. First, a business should think about what it intends to accomplish by establishing a Web site. There are primarily three reasons why businesses establish Web sites: *marketing, customer support*, and *sales*. Determining the purpose of the site provides the framework for a company's EC strategy.

Most current sites on the Web can be considered merely a marketing presence or a passive advertisement, as was shown in the opening vignette of chapter 3. Other companies have found that the Internet is an effective way for offering customer service, providing product specifications, furnishing online answers to frequently asked questions, or building one-to-one marketing. Finally, a company may decide to be fully involved in EC for its entire line of business.

Regardless of its EC involvement level, a company has to develop strategies to meet its goals. For example, a strategy might be to make information easier to find for Web site visitors by using a specialized search engine, or a strategy could also be to utilize a Web-based call center to enhance customer service. Amazon's declared strategy is to stay online and not to open physical bookstores. Amazon also declared product diversification as part of its strategy.

In strategy formulation, we need to provide answers to questions such as: Does your business have a product that is a good candidate for EC (chapter 2)? There are certain products and services that lend themselves more readily to EC than others. The usual examples are commodities—a *commodity* is a product that the buyer knows, such as books, CDs, stock purchasing, and travel tickets. If your particular product can be shipped easily or transmitted electronically, it targets knowledgeable buyers, and its price falls within a certain range, then it is a good candidate for EC.

In addition to redefining the market for existing products and services, EC also provides the opportunity for entirely new products and services. Examples include network supply and support services, directory services, contract services, escrow and trust services, market makers, and many kinds of online information services. Although these various opportunities and benefits are all unique, they may also be interrelated to some extent. For example, improvements in competitiveness and quality of service may in part be derived from mass customization, whereas shortening of supply chains may contribute to cost saving and price reduction.

Unfortunately, many companies approach EC with no clear idea of where they are going. Often, they view the industry leaders' accomplishments superficially and try to imitate the front-runners. Such a shortsighted view may well be a waste of resources. What they fail to consider is the level of commitment to organizational redefinition that must occur behind the scenes. Attributing the success of an EC strategy to skillful marketing and wishful thinking is an illusion. Unless companies plan and reengineer their organizations appropriately, EC implementation may not be followed by sales. For example, let's look at some of the early Web sites for air ticket sales. They often served only as information providers for those who shop for the lowest discount airfares. Such shoppers leave the site, without any purchase, after collecting the information. If EC is to serve a company's mission, it must be considered part of a larger view of the enterprise—as an element in the organization's response to customer needs and how to capitalize on those needs.

Strategy formulation could include several other topics and as a result be too lengthy. To help in focusing on the essentials, one can use a methodology such as that of the critical success factors (CSF) described next.

CRITICAL SUCCESS FACTORS FOR EC

Critical success factors are the indispensable business, technology, and human factors that help to achieve the desired level of organizational goals. Since CSF are highly dependent on the company's situation, it is often helpful to start considering business environments and benefits of EC, then analyzing any risks involved in the EC project. Ghosh (1998) suggested a set of questions a company can ask, which consider how EC can benefit its customers. For example, the following are questions to consider when cost reduction and service enhancement are considered.

1. How can I use the information I have about individual customers to make it easier for them to do business with me?
2. How much does it cost me to provide services that customers could get by themselves over the Internet?
3. What help can I give customers by using the experience of other customers or the expertise of my employees?
4. Will I be at a significant disadvantage if my competitors provide these capabilities to customers before I do?

The answers to such questions can help plan for EC better and identify EC opportunities.

Many CSF may be relevant to EC projects. For example, in addition to organization, customer, and supplier aspects, technology and information system issues should not be underestimated as CSF. Integrating new Web applications with existing legacy systems for seamless database operation, queries, and transaction processing may be highly desirable but must be weighed against the cost and the challenge of implementation in many different hardware platforms and software applications. Several other CSF can be identified for specific circumstances. The major CSF for EC are summarized in Table 9.1.

A VALUE ANALYSIS APPROACH

The opportunities for a company that moves quickly to establish EC can be a threat to other companies that do not have EC. When customers start to use the Internet to conduct business, a new value for the selling company is created, and if the customers move from a competitor, this competitor may suffer a loss. One approach that can be used to assess the desirability of EC is to employ a formal value chain analysis (Porter 1985). A **value chain** is a series of activities a company performs to achieve its goal(s) at various stages of the production process, from resources' acquisition to product delivery. The added value of these activities contributes to profit and enhances the asset

TABLE 9.1 Critical Success Factors of EC Initiatives

—Specific products or services traded
—Top management support
—Project team reflecting various functional areas
—Technical infrastructure
—Customer acceptance
—User-friendly Web interface
—Integration with the corporate legacy systems
—Security and control of the EC system
—Competition and market situation
—Pilot project and corporate knowledge
—Promotion and internal communication
—Cost of the EC project
—Level of trust between buyers and sellers

value as well as the competitive position of the company in the market. To examine the implications of an EC project on the value chain of the products and services the company offers, one may answer value chain questions such as those in Application Case 9.1. Companies that seek to create additional value using their EC channels should consider the competitive market and rivalry in order to best leverage its EC assets. By answering the questions in Application Case 9.1 companies can assess the value added by EC, which is a part of its justification.

Another factor to consider is the relative position of the company in its industry's competitive market. One way for an EC vendor to achieve a more advantageous position is to *differentiate* itself by providing superior service at every point of contact with

APPLICATION CASE 9.1

Value Analysis Questions

a. Representative Questions for Clarifying Value Chain Statements

- Can I realize significant margins by consolidating parts of the value chain (such as inventory control) for my customers?
- Can I create significant value for customers by reducing the number of entities they have to deal with in the value chain?
- What additional skills do I need to develop in order to take over the functions of others in my value chain?
- Will I be at a competitive disadvantage if someone else moves first to consolidate the value chain?

b. Representative Questions for Creating New Values

- Can I offer additional information regarding transaction services to my existing customer base?
- Can I address the needs of new customer segments by repackaging my current information assets or by creating new business propositions using the Internet?
- Can I use my ability to attract customers to generate new sources of revenue, such as advertising or sales of complementary products?
- Will my current business be significantly harmed by other companies providing some of the value I currently offer on an à la carte basis?

Source: Ghosh (1998), compiled from pp. 130 and 132.

FIGURE 9.3 GartnerGroup and Relationship Marketing Model.

customers (see the GartnerGroup model in Figure 9.3). The idea is based on relationship marketing (chapter 3), and it divides customer interaction into four categories. Electronic commerce can effectively support all of them.

While the foregoing discussion emphasizes customer contact in the value chain, interaction with suppliers in the earlier stage of the chain can also significantly improve the efficiency of operation. Furthermore, such efficiency may be achieved by cost and time reduction, but it often requires changes in the company's organizational infrastructure as well as business procedures. Looking at value added activities provides only one aspect of EC justification. Looking at the costs and the risks is as critical, as will be shown next.

RETURN ON INVESTMENT AND RISK ANALYSIS

Some EC initiatives could be strong revenue generators but may not create new markets; others may create new markets but will not return a significant profit, at least in the short run. Moreover, some may streamline the distribution or supply channels creating competitive advantage, but may also run the risk of failure upon emergence of a strong new competitor's action. Therefore, resources required to create additional value through EC need to be examined with respect to cost-benefit analysis and the level of risks involved as we will see next.

The rate of **return on investment (ROI)** for an EC project is a ratio of the cost of resources required to the benefits generated by the EC project. It includes both quantifiable and nonquantifiable items. Although the cost of resources, such as hardware, software, and human resources, for an EC project is relatively easy to quantify, the returns (benefits) have been difficult to measure, as seen in many other information technology projects. Primary intangible benefits that the company can draw from EC include an effective marketing channel, increased sales, and customer service. Even profit, which is easier to measure, may be difficult to forecast in EC due to lack of experience and fast-changing conditions. As an example of the difficulties in computing the ROI, let us look at the case of an extranet, such as that of Lockheed Martin (Application Case 9.2).

The toughest part about calculating an extranet's ROI is assessing the extranet's impact on business processes internally and across organizational boundaries. How do you measure the gains in such a case? Is it possible to quantify the benefits? Although ROI projections play a critical role in investment decision making, many of the critical benefits may not be easily converted to numbers. Many companies get into EC not be-

APPLICATION CASE 9.2

Lockheed Martin Uses EC to Compete

To win a tactical fighter prototype contract from the Department of Defense (DOD) against Boeing, Lockheed Martin had to stay within the DOD's $28 million to $35 million per aircraft budget. To reduce the cost of collaboration with its subcontractors, Robert Stephens, Lockheed's IS manager, turned to an EC solution, an extranet. The secured Web site he deployed let managers at Lockheed's headquarters in Fort Worth, Texas, share project management updates with design teams at British Aerospace Ltd. in the United Kingdom and Northrop Grumman Corp. in Southern California.

In order to win additional contracts in 2001, Stephens has to document all productivity gains attributable to EC. As extranet projects grow in scope and expense, he faces increased pressure to show bottom-line returns on the investment in EC. While business partners/subcontractors are happy, it is not exactly clear how many new orders this happiness will generate. Also, it is not clear how many dollars an extranet will shave off the cost of doing business. If the investment in EC has been money well spent, Stephens wants his superiors and customers to know about it.

Measuring EC payoff is tricky; benefits are spread across functional units inside the company, and synergy with suppliers may generate benefits, too. The speed that the latter accrues depends on how quickly outsiders are willing to change the way they do business. Stephens found major savings in travel and training costs due to EC. "We're bringing in expertise when we need it, where we need it, without having to fly someone here to work side by side with us." For example, when a multicompany team writes a specification for a new part of a plane, the extranet serves as a common workplace, storing the input of everyone involved. When Lockheed engineers are on the road, they have instant access to relevant project data without the need to have a special hookup to Lockheed's private network. Even training courses, which used to be held offsite, are now available over the extranet."

Overall, Lockheed Martin management believe that the benefits of the extranet are enormous and the extranet strategy was right and inevitable for survival.

---

cause of the ROI but because they realize that an improved link to customers and suppliers is necessary. Such up-front need will often evolve into mission-critical systems that can revamp an organization's way of doing business. Most EC gets started in one function at a time: For example, the engineering department needs to collaborate better with suppliers, so they will start an extranet. Then the marketing department voices the problem of communicating with an international sales partner, for which they will start an EDI. Eventually, all this has to be integrated with the company's business procedures and information systems.

One attempt to address this issue in IT in general was made by Parker (1996), who classified generic IT values and risks into a) values: financial, strategic, and stakeholder; and b) risks: competitive strategy, organizational strategy, and uncertainty.

Most financial values are measurable to some degree. *Strategic values* include competitive advantage in the market and benefits generated by streamlining back-end or front-end business procedures. They are not easy to measure or quantify. *Stakeholder values* are reflections of organizational redesign, organizational learning, empowerment, and information technology architecture, which are unique to each company. On the risk side, *competitive strategy risks* are external due to joint venture alliances or demographic changes, among others. Finally, *organizational strategy risks* are uncertainty factors internal to the company, as opposed to external competitive

Marriott's Analysis Emphasizes Shareholders' Values

Courtyard by Marriott used to fax stacks of marketing reports to its various hotels, including 16 operating manuals, one of which is over 500 pages long. In 1998, the hotel started to operate the Source, an information system where employees from more than 380 Courtyard-owned and franchised hotels can find all the information from new and old manuals and reports on the Web. "We used to spend $50 to $100 to print each manual, so that's a big savings," says Craig Lambert, senior executive of the company. In addition, online employment forms have cut about

an hour off the time it takes hotel managers to bring a new hire on board. It sounds like a simple thing, but multiply that by several hundred hotels and 50 new employees per year and it becomes a lot of man-hours. According to Lambert, ROI projections played a major role in Courtyard's investment decision but were not the most important factor. "What was driving the EC project was the knowledge management part of it, not the ROI part of it. We wanted to have a source for our people to get answers that lets them do their jobs more productively."

risks. They cover short-term risks inherent in business reorganization and risks due to technical uncertainty and implementation risks. While all those values and risks need to be examined, considering any underlying assumptions for each factor and setting appropriate priorities among them would help formulate a desirable EC strategy.

An example of shareholder value that is more important than financial value, is provided in Application Case 9.3.

ELECTRONIC COMMERCE SCENARIOS

Once the strategic planning and the cost-benefit analysis are completed, an EC project can be implemented. However, before that it is necessary to consider both the external business environment and the availability of information technology resources. Hutchinson (1997) described four EC scenarios that can be used to accomplish the above task. The first is the open, global commerce scenario, where removal of intermediaries is a powerful force that flattens the value chain. The members-only subnet scenario applies mostly to B2B EC. The electronic middlemen scenario shows that suppliers in both business and consumer markets can make their products and services available through independent third-party distribution channels. Finally, in the new consumer marketing channels scenario, traditional broadcast, advertising, and consumer telephony collapse into a unified consumer-centric EC medium on the Internet. While EC proliferation would certainly allow any combination or variation of such scenarios, each company has to select the most appropriate model for its needs. The major IT and business events associated with each scenario are shown in Table 9.2.

The use of this model can help EC planners to determine the type of EC that best fits their organization.

STRATEGIC PLANNING FRAMEWORK: COMPETITIVE VERSUS COOPERATIVE STRATEGIES

To address customer needs and capitalize on those needs, strategies to approach the market should be considered first, regardless of the type of scenario. Business strategies in general, as well as in EC, can be competitive and/or cooperative. A **competitive startegy** assumes fighting against all competitors for the purpose of survival and to win, whereas a

TABLE 9.2   EC Scenario and Critical IT and Business Events

I. Open, Global Commerce Scenario

IT Events
- Internet standards expand to cover transaction security, content control, authentication, and new media; proprietary solutions marginalized.
- Internet standards become pervasive and embedded; intranets are hot.
- Highly distributed, fat-client architectures prevail.

Business Events
- Global third-party trade, logistics, and delivery support services are widely available on the Internet.
- Consumers and businesses pay most bills electronically.
- Digital cash widely accepted and widely used; smart cards are pervasive.
- Fewer transactions occur involving wholesalers and/or salespeople.

II. Members-Only Subnets Scenario

IT Events
- Intercompany connection standards vary widely between industries.
- Objective measures of Internet security and reliability prove elusive; "brownouts" common.
- EDI standards are extended and widely adopted.
- Web standards diverge; proprietary extensions and add-ons thrive.

Business Events
- Industry consortia build high-performance information networks.
- Cross-border commerce remains cumbersome.
- America Online and CompuServe thrive as independent network service providers.
- Access to and usage of the public Net plateaus at twice the 1996 numbers.

III. Electronic Middlemen Scenario

IT Events
- EC development focuses on transaction processing and interface.
- Distributors drive EC terms and interfaces for buyers.
- EC activity expands rapidly. Transactions made primarily with credit or debit cards.
- Transaction security is deeply embedded in access software.

Business Events
- Most EC dollar volume originates from a few sites; one-stop shopping popular.
- Electronic buying cooperatives and online professional services become popular with smaller enterprises.
- Consumers exchange personal information for coupons, discounts, and custom service.

IV. New Consumer Marketing Channels Scenario

IT Events
- Most EC activity is oriented to consumers; less B2B.
- Price of wireless and landline bandwidth converges and drops.
- Majority of households can access three or more networks.
- New compression techniques drive growth of networked multimedia.

Business Events
- Online transactions seen as less convenient; security not widely trusted.
- Basic international norms accepted for online advertising and other content.
- Multiple levels of interaction with advertisements are tracked and priced differently.
- Wireless links to databases and customers increase sales productivity.

Source: Hutchinson (1997), p. 57. Used by permission.

cooperative strategy plans for working together with specific competitors to gain advantage against other competitors. The following discussion covers both strategies.

Competitive Strategies

A competitive strategy can be planned either offensively or defensively. An **offensive strategy** usually takes place in an established competitor's market location. A **defensive strategy** one usually takes place in the firm's own current market position, as a defense against possible attacks by a rival(s). Two methods used commonly to attack a competitor's position with offensive strategies in EC are:

- *Frontal assault:* The attacking firm goes head-to-head with its competitor. It matches the competitor in most of the categories from price to promotion to distribution channel. To be successful, the attacker must not only have superior resources but also the willingness to persevere. This usually is a costly tactic. An example is Barnes & Noble, which has reacted to the swift entrance of Amazon.com into the online bookselling business, and Toys "Я" Us, which countered e-Toys.

- *Flanking maneuver:* Rather than going straight after the competitor's position with a frontal assault, a firm may attack a part of the market, where the competitor is weak. To be successful, the flanker must be patient and willing to carefully expand out of the relatively undefended market niche or else face retaliation by an established competitor. Stock traders like E∗TRADE, Ameritrade, and My Discount Broker, which are competing against the major conventional stock brokerage companies, are such examples. Another example in such a niche market is Virtual Vineyards, the online seller of premium and specialty wines and foods. Several online bookstores are attacking Amazon by specializing in technical books, old books, or children's books.

A second type of competitive strategy is *defensive.* According to Porter (1985), defensive strategies aim to lower the probability of successful attack, divert attacks to less threatening avenues, or lessen the intensity of an attack. Instead of increasing competitive advantage per se, they make a company's competitive advantage more sustainable by causing a challenger to conclude that an attack is unattractive. These tactics deliberately reduce short-term profitability to ensure long-term profitability. Two common defensive strategies are:

- *Raise structural barriers:* Entry barriers act to block a challenger's logical avenues of attack. They offer a full line of products in every profitable market segment to close off any entry points; raise buyer switching costs by offering low-cost training to users; raise the cost of gaining trial users by keeping prices low on items new users are most likely to purchase; or increase scale economies to reduce unit costs. Examples are Cisco Online in the networking and interconnection device market and FedEx, Dell Computers, and the auction site eBay in their comprehensive offerings. Toys "Я" Us uses the first strategy against e-Toys by offering an expensive Web site that e-Toys cannot afford.

- *Lower the inducement for attack:* Another type of defensive strategy is to reduce a challenger's expectations of future profits in the industry. An example is www.buycomp.com with their "lowest price on earth" strategy.

Cooperative Strategies

Cooperative strategies are used to gain a competitive advantage within an industry by working with other firms. A typical cooperative strategy involves a strategic alliance through joint venture or value chain partnership. This may be done through a company-controlled extranet, for example, as shown in chapter 7. A **strategic alliance** is a partnership of multiple corporations formed to achieve competitive advantages that are mutually beneficial. Companies may form a strategic alliance for a number of reasons, including: (1) to obtain technology and/or manufacturing capabilities, (2) to obtain access to specific markets, (3) to reduce financial risk, (4) to reduce political risk, (5) to achieve or ensure competitive advantage, (6) to utilize unused capacity, and (7) to combine areas of excellence. Chapter 7 presents several examples of industry-type extranets that provide strategic alliances. The major types of strategic alliance used in EC are:

- *Joint venture:*   A joint venture is a cooperative business activity, formed by two or more separate organizations for strategic purposes, that creates an independent business entity and allocates ownership, operational responsibilities, and financial risks and rewards to each member, while preserving their separate identity/autonomy. Joint ventures provide a way to combine temporarily the different strengths of partners to achieve an outcome of value to both. Disadvantages of joint ventures include loss of control, lower profits, probability of conflicts with partners, and the likely transfer of technological advantage to the partner. An example in the U.K. is retailer W. H. Smith, which together with British Telecom and Microsoft Network, developed and operates an Internet portal that provides a variety of entertainment and educational services. Softbank (Japan), which is teaming up with Microsoft and Yahoo in a joint venture to advertise and sell cars over the Net, is another example. This kind of alliance is also known as a **virtual corporation**.
- *Value-chain partnership:*   A value-chain partnership is a strong and close alliance in which a company forms a long-term arrangement with a key supplier or distributor for mutual advantage. Value-chain partnerships are becoming popular as more companies outsource activities that were previously done within the company. Examples of such partnership are Dell computers and 7-11 stores whose exclusive suppliers are located near their plants or stores. FedEx performs online-supported logistics activities, such as managing inventories and shipments, with many companies.
- *EC strategies in small businesses:*   Formulating strategies in small businesses is usually much less sophisticated than it is in large corporations. Senior managers tend to know the whole spectrum of business and possess the knowledge and authority for the destiny of the new EC venture. A fundamental reason for differences in strategy formulation between large and small companies lies in the relationship between owners and managers. The CEO of a large corporation has to consider and balance the diverse needs of the corporation's many stakeholders. The CEO of a small business, however, is very likely also to be the owner (or one of the owners). For further discussion on EC in small companies, see chapter 12.

9.3   Electronic Commerce Strategy in Action

In the previous section we presented some generic methodologies and showed their relevance to EC. In this section we will present the essence of EC strategy in action as proposed by Mougayar (1998).

WHAT QUESTIONS A STRATEGIC PLAN SHOULD ANSWER

At the end of the strategic planning, a company should be able to answer questions such as these:

- *How is EC going to change our business?*
  To answer this question, you have to accurately articulate at the strategic level the linkage between your current business objectives and your objectives in the marketspace.
- *How do we uncover new types of business opportunities?*
  There are two kinds of opportunities: those ones that allow you to extend your current model into the Internet, and those that are entirely birthed with the Internet in mind.
- *How can we take advantage of new electronic linkages with customers and trading partners?*
  The Internet allows you to expand the capabilities you currently have with current trading partners, and it allows you to link new partners faster than before by opening your intranets to them over extranets.
- *Do we become intermediaries ourselves?*
  By examining how each piece of your value chain may be affected, you can determine whether it is time to become an intermediary or defend a position weakened by the rise of a new intermediary.
- *How do we bring more buyers together electronically (and keep them there)?*
  Today it is a challenge to bring electronic buyers into your business and to keep them there, as seen in chapter 3. Keeping a customer is much cheaper than getting a new one. For your customer it becomes too tempting and easy to switch to a competitor when it is so easy to do it.
- *How do we change the nature of our products and services?*
  There is an evolution from physical goods to digital goods and to information-based products and interactive services. Can your company participate?
- *Why is the Internet affecting other companies more than ours?*
  It is hard to imagine a large corporation not being affected by the Internet. Is your company being negatively affected? Why?
- *How do we manage and measure the evolution of our strategy?*
  Once you have identified where to focus your priorities, you have to ensure that you are following up with a sustained management and measurement framework for monitoring and refining your success in the marketspace.

THE STEPS TO SUCCESSFUL EC PROGRAMS

In order to maximize the chances of EC success, Mougayar (1998) recommends assessing the following 10 steps and acting on perfecting the outcomes of each one.

Step 1: Conduct Necessary Education and Training

Communicating a new and perhaps complex way of doing business requires education. Executives and managers must be educated, as well as customers, prospects, and trading partners.

Step 2: Review Current Distribution and Supply Chain Models

It is necessary to examine the potential effect that EC will have on your distribution channels and supply chain management. For example:

- Can you increase the number of electronic connections, simplify interorganizational processes, and at the same time discover ways to shrink, speed up, or virtualize the value chain?
- What is likely to happen with your wholesalers, distributors, or retailers? Are they going to be disintermediated or are they likely to survive by trans-

forming their businesses into new types of intermediaries? Are you going to support their transition to electronic mediation, or do you plan on bypassing them (Fruit of the Loom case in chapter 6)?

Step 3: Understand What Your Customers and Partners Expect from the Web

It is necessary to know how many customers are able and willing to interface with you over electronic networks and to conduct transactions. If you know where and how your customers are buying in electronic marketplaces, you can then be in tune with their level. For example, Marshall Industries, Cisco, and Intel have had the luxury of starting with a captive audience, since their customers were used to the Internet well before it became known as the Web.

Step 4: Reevaluate the Nature of Your Products and Services

It is not enough just to sell physical products over the Internet. You must aggressively develop other types of products and services to increase your revenues in the electronic marketplace and solidify your position on several fronts. These include the addition of digital goods, interactive services, and information-based products and scrvices.

Step 5: Give a New Role to Your Human Resources Department

Internet commerce requires a cross-functional focus and must bc totally integrated with the overall business strategy. As a result, the role of each employee may be changed. What is the role of the human resources department in the new and evolving EC world? In addition to providing content for the company's intranet, three specific responsibilities have been identified.

1. Establishing corporate Internet/intranet policies.
2. Acting as a companywide certification authority. Innovative human resources departments are acting as the certification authorities for their own companies. They are responsible for issuing digital IDs to their employees.
3. Formalizing new job descriptions.

Step 6: Extend Your Current Systems to the Outside

Your Web site may have been the first beachhead you built to mark your entry into cyberspace. However, with the trend toward user-centric inquiries and intermediated marketplaces, it becomes important to link your products and services with other online catalogues, directories, and trading communities as well as integrate back-end business to your partners' and suppliers' intranets. The Web site got you there, but it won't keep you there; therefore, you must expand EC activities.

Step 7: Track New Competitors and Market Shares

In EC it is not clear who your competition is. Because of the volatility of old value chains, new services can be introduced by totally unexpected parties that become your new competition. Once you begin to get a clearer picture as to who your competitors really are in the new digital markets, you will need to begin to track them and their market share.

Step 8: Develop a Web-Centric Marketing Strategy

Even if your current marketing strategy has taken the Web into account, you must develop a marketing strategy that clearly targets the Web as a primary marketing channel. This is what American Greetings, Wells Fargo Bank, and Toys "Я" Us are doing. This includes using the Internet as a primary medium for all marketing communications activities, such as press releases, investor relations, and advertising. A new breed of advertising and marketing agencies are repositioning their offerings to include what they call "digital marketing," or "interactive marketing," as shown in chapters 3 and 4.

Step 9: Participate in the Creation and Development of Virtual Marketplaces

Beyond pushing your own distribution channels in the electronic markets that you are targeting, you have to think about creating your own virtual marketplaces. You can lead the creation of new marketplace communities that later become transaction and trading communities for your products and services.

Step 10: Instill EC Management Style

It is essential to move decision making from physical to electronic space. Think about EC as an entirely new territory, and give it new parameters of success and measurements. However, while doing that, do not forget about sound business management practices that generally still apply.

Most organizations now must compete in two marketplaces: a physical (traditional) one and the emerging electronic one, mediated by the Internet. Unless your business is entirely devoted to the Web, you will have to manage in both spaces.

Ware et al. Seven-Step Model

An alternative process was suggested by Ware et al. (1998) who proposed a seven-step strategy for developing EC. It focuses on the following basic questions:

- Where are you along the continuum of possible EC applications?
- Where do you want to go?
- How are you going to get there?

There are crucial questions to address if you want to take a strategic approach to the application of EC technologies. For example, how do companies increase their ability to exploit digital economy opportunities for a sustainable value? Having the proper framework is the key to building capabilities of identifying and capitalizing on the opportunities. Ware et al. have developed an assessment and planning methodology and an approach for clarifying goals and expectations. The methodology includes the following seven steps:

- Step 1: Create a map of scenarios for aligning business strategy and Internet initiatives in the future.
- Step 2: Communicate a vision from top management to drive Internet initiatives.
- Step 3: Identify and transform key value constellations, specifically, what business core practices and processes the Internet technologies could mostly affect. This step identifies possible opportunities, as shown in the IBM opening vignette.
- Step 4: Develop the portfolio of EC initiatives your company wants to pursue. (See the IBM opening case.)
- Step 5: Develop year-by-year objectives and plans for the chosen initiatives, including measures of effectiveness and their effect on the business.
- Step 6: Implement the change. The project participants must undergo the changes in attitudes and behavior required by such a system.
- Step 7: Monitor the overall plan, learn lessons, adjust, and improve.

9.4   Competitive Intelligence on the Internet

Competitive intelligence is an integral part of strategic planning and can be conducted by conventional methods and by using the Internet.

USING THE INTERNET TO CONDUCT COMPETITIVE INTELLIGENCE

The Internet can play a major role as a source of competitive information (competitive intelligence) and an increasingly important role in supporting competitive intelligence. Power and Sharda (1997) proposed a framework in which the Internet capabilities are shown to provide information for strategic decisions. According to the framework, the external information required and the methods of acquiring such information can be supported by the Internet and the strategic planning process.

Using Internet tools one can implement specific search strategies as illustrated in Application Case 9.4.

Note that overreliance on such information can be dangerous. The problem is that by searching the overwhelming amount of data, one assumes that everything that could be learned has been found. However, Internet searches are either full-text searches, keyword-searches, or directory searches. Full-text searches allow one to search for a phrase or character string of any length. Keyword searches allow Boolean combinations of keywords. Search engines, which are based on these technologies, find only 3 percent to 20 percent of all available important information. Directory search engines, such as Yahoo, use human editors to classify Web pages into hierarchical categories. An advantage of a directory search is that the category hierarchy en-

---

APPLICATION CASE 9.4

Competitive Intelligence on the Internet

The Internet can be used to help a company conduct competitive intelligence easily, quickly, and relatively inexpensively in the following ways:

1. **Review competitor's Web sites.** Such visits can reveal information about new products or projects, potential alliances, trends in budgeting, advertising strategies used, financial strength, and much more.

2. **Analyze related newsgroups.** Internet newsgroups help you find out what people think about a company and its products. For example, newsgroup participants state what they like or dislike about products provided by you and your competitors. You can also examine people's reactions to a new idea by posting a question.

3. **Examine publicly available financial documents.** This can be accomplished by entering a number of databases. While some databases charge nominal fees, others are free. The most notable is the Securities and Exchange Commission EDGAR database (www.sec.gov/edgarhp.htm).

4. **You can give prizes** to those visitors of your Web site who best describe the strengths and weaknesses of your competitor's products.

5. **Use an information delivery service (**such as Info Wizard, My Yahoo, or PointCast) to find out what is published on the Internet, including newsgroup correspondence about your competitors and their products. Known as *push technologies,* these services provide any desired information including news, some in real time, for free or a nominal fee.

6. **Corporate research companies** such as Dun & Bradstreet and Standard and Poor's, provide information ranging from risk analysis to stock market analysts' reports about your competitors, for a fee. These are available electronically.

7. **Solicit opinions in chat rooms** of both your company, your competitors, or of some communities.

ables an accurate search based on a specific topic, thus limiting the potential for errors in keywords or poorly indexed information.

USING PUSH TECHNOLOGY FOR COMPETITIVE INTELLIGENCE

Current information about companies can be found in their press releases and information they publish on their Web sites. Several vendors offer a free service to inform users of the latest news of many companies. For example, Yahoo provides a free service called "netcenter" that delivers up-to-date news on companies and topics selected by users. Also, online databases are a good source of information, especially for background research. However, they may not be the best source for fresh information. In response to the pressure of competition, commercial databases are beginning to incorporate **push technology** into their offerings. For example, Dialog Web (www.dialog-web.com) allows users to request updates of topics and have the latest records automatically delivered to users' e-mail addresses.

Push technology (chapter 4) can provide corporate snoopers with lots of information and saves search and monitoring time. There are several ways push technology can provide competitive intelligence information. The broadcast model (i.e., pure push) installs a push client on the user's PC, selects the channels of information, and then sets the service in motion. Selective (or automated) pull models have the user subscribe to certain types of information and then deliver the information specified on a periodic basis. Once set up, the service will change only when requested. Industry watchers such as the GartnerGroup offer to notify the user by e-mail when a new industry report is available. In the distributed push-pull model the service acts as a broker of information, notifying the end user when information on certain Web sites is updated or changed. In the interactive push model, the user can both receive or send information to members of a user list. The list is made up of users with common interests and to whom material is distributed in a timely manner. Push technology can also be used to disseminate data and intelligence over the company intranet.

However, for competitive intelligence professionals, push technology does not replace in-depth background research but rather keeps one up on current events within the search parameters. Despite the promise to reduce information overload, push has its downside. Users still tend to be overwhelmed by the delivered content, which can be 90 percent irrelevant. This may be controlled by carefully monitoring the information specifications and continual editing and refining of the search agents.

In addition to push technology, business intelligence companies offer packaged competitive analysis. For example, companysleuth.com is a business intelligence company that provides a wide variety of legal information about companies, and IDS.com provides a rich set of market data and insight for competitive intelligence. Companies like Fuld (www.fuld.com) or IDC, specializing in competitive intelligence, can be timely and effective sources of information for strategic decision making.

A major issue in online intelligence is the quality of information being received from the Internet push and other services. It is necessary to validate the reliability of those services. Once strategic planning, competitive intelligence, and cost-benefit activities are completed, it is time to implement the EC project.

9.5 Implementation: Plans and Execution

Before starting to implement what was prescribed by the strategy, it is necessary to build an **implementation plan** that will outline the steps to follow during implementation. Then one needs to get organized, usually starting with establishing a Web team;

Only then can one continue with the execution of the plan. In this section we deal with a few issues related to this process.

A PILOT PROJECT

Often, implementing EC requires significant investments in infrastructure. Therefore, a good way to start this is to undertake one or a few small EC pilot projects. Since pilot projects help discover problems early, the pilot project can be considered a part of the planning; modifications in the plan after the pilot is completed are likely. General Motors Corporation's pilot program (GM BuyPower) is an example. On its Web site, www.gmbuypower.com, shoppers can choose car options, check local dealer inventory, schedule test drives, and get best-price quotes by e-mail or telephone (Figure 9.4). This pilot project has been in existence since 1997 starting in four western U.S. states and expanding to all states in 1999. Meanwhile, Chrysler also went nationwide with its pilot Get-a-Quote program, while Ford's Build Your Own program is also operational.

If the pilot project is successful, the company may consider the issue of EC leadership, which is also part of planning.

ELECTRONIC COMMERCE LEADERSHIP

Should your company lead EC efforts in your industry or be a follower? It is interesting to note that even a small company can play a leadership role in EC. Of course, the offline leaders may decide to lead in EC efforts as well (Application Case 9.5, pg. 324).

FIGURE 9.4 GMBuyPower.com.

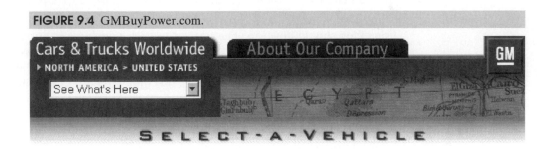

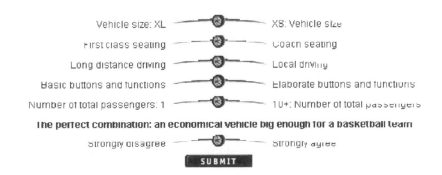

Examples of Market Leaders

Market leaders do not need to establish themselves in large markets to have a significant presence on the Internet, as we show in chapter 12. An example of a market leader in a niche market is Virtual Vineyards, the online seller of premium and specialty wines and foods (chapter 11). Another type of market leader is one that retains its offline establishments but intends to be a major player online utilizing its offline retail power on the Internet. Staples and Tower Records are good examples of such leadership. Though cdnow.com was first on the Net, Tower quickly established a sizable presence and captured a large portion of the market share. Staples, Tower, Wal-Mart, Toys "Я" Us, and others remain major players in the physical retail establishment arena but have broadened their business scope by retailing on the Internet. Rowe.com (chapter 5) is another market leader with intentions of keeping its offline facilities. The company markets a periodical and journal purchasing service to libraries, offering both on- and offline technologies to facilitate intermediary activities between libraries and magazine publishers. Rowe.com has a competitive advantage in that they have had no significant offline competition; now, any competitor establishing an online presence must sell both its name and the magazines at the same time, which is quite a formidable task. A similar case is SkyMall (see Real World Case 9.2). Finally Barnes & Noble created a powerful separate online business that in 1999 recaptured market share from Amazon.com.

UNCOVERING SPECIFIC EC OPPORTUNITIES AND APPLICATIONS

Many companies are eager to know what the right opportunities are and what applications they should develop. The answer to such questions is not simple. It requires an understanding of how digital markets operate, how Internet customers behave, how competition is created, what infrastructure is needed, what the dynamics of EC are, and much more. Once a company has this understanding, one can begin mapping opportunities that match current competencies and markets.

It is interesting to note that in addition to just selling existing products/services on the Internet, there are many opportunities to create new products and services, some of which are unrelated to an existing business. For example, Fruit of the Loom (chapter 6) developed Web sites for their wholesalers. Then they created a special organization that develops Web sites for any company that wants to develop one for its own wholesalers. In chapter 7 we learned how companies are organizing extranets in their industry (also refer to the Chemdex case, chapter 12). These are primarily B2B markets. One can organize the market and/or the sellers and/or the buyers. Other opportunities are listed below (Mougayar 1998, pp. 143, 144):

- *Matchmaking.* Matching buyers' needs with products and services from sellers, without former knowledge of either one.
- *Aggregation of services.* Combines several existing services to create a new service or category that didn't exist before.
- *Bid/ask engine.* Creates a demand/supply floating pricing system in which buyers and sellers bid and/or ask for prices (e.g., www.priceline.com).
- *Notification service.* Tells you when the service becomes available, when it becomes cheaper, or when it goes on sale in your neighborhood.
- *Smart needs adviser.* "If you want it at this price, you have to wait until September; or if you want this service, you may also want to consider this other one."

- *Negotiation.* Price, quantity, or features are negotiated according to a set of parameters.
- *Up-sell.* Suggests an additional product or service, so that if you buy both, you get a combined discount or an additional benefit.
- *Consultative adviser.* "Here's a tip on this new service you're about to purchase."

The process of finding EC applications is similar to the process of finding other IT applications (e.g., Turban et al. 1999). Some approaches to consider are:

- Brainstorming by a group of employees, using any method including electronic group support systems.
- Soliciting the help of experts, such as consultants.
- Reviewing what the competitors are doing.
- Asking the vendors to provide you with suggestions.
- Reading the literature to find out what's going on.
- Using analogies from similar industries or business processes.
- Using a conventional requirement analysis approach.

Once general planning and specific implementation plans are completed, we can proceed to actual implementation.

Which Business Model to Use?

The issue of uncovering opportunities is related to the issue of which model(s) to use. EC implementation can be done in several ways. A typical choice is that of Schubb Corp., which is shown in Application Case 9.6. (pg. 326)

CREATING A WEB TEAM AND ASSIGNING FUNCTIONAL SKILLS TO SUBPROJECTS

In creating a **Web team,** the roles and responsibilities of the team leader, user management, Webmaster, and technical staff should be defined. The project leader often has the strategic challenge of being a "visionary" regarding the tasks of aligning business and technology goals and implementing a sound enterprise EC plan. Such a plan is best arrived at by negotiation with those knowledgeable about particular data and information and how they should be structured and presented in an online, hypermedia environment. The details need to be developed by the joint efforts of different functional areas: IS, marketing, customer relations, purchasing, accounting, finance, human resources, security, and other operations. Such involvement will have a far-reaching impact on decisions regarding how the EC implementation plan is to be implemented. The project team can be managed in a matrix format by assigning functional expertise to subprojects, as shown in Table 9.3.

If a mechanism is put in place that brings together all relevant technical people, the rules concerning security, authentication, link management, markup language standards, and so on could be properly developed, updated on a regular basis, and satisfactorily applied toward drafting and interpreting an enterprisewide Internet policy. Such a mechanism is beneficial to the policy process in that it is more likely to produce a policy consistent with the enterprise's business goals and strategies.

Some companies go beyond organizing a Web team by establishing a completely independent online company, such as was done by Barnes & Noble in 1999. In other cases an IS group is in charge of building the Web for other functional areas or for the company's customers and/or suppliers. Finally, the use of an outside vendor as a site developer should be considered.

APPLICATION CASE 9.6

Strategic Directions at Schubb Corp.

Schubb Corp., a 115-year-old property and casualty insurance company, reviewed three EC strategies:

1. Create a new business model with EC as a major driver.
2. Spawn a secondary business model around EC; go directly to consumers.
3. Usc EC as a tool within the existing business model.

The first option was quickly discarded; the company had a successful business model with products matching distribution systems. The company sells differentiated products that require some degree of explanation and a deep understanding of customers' needs. Therefore, there is no logic in discontinuing a successful model.

The second model looked promising, but management did not want to disrupt the excellent relationship they have had with their agents and brokers. It also required building an infrastructure: a call center staffed around the clock, technologies for processing tasks that agents and brokers traditionally do, and more.

The company opted for the third alternative. This EC initiative helped Schubb to further differentiate its products and services, basically by providing superb customer service over the Internet. Schubb opened several Web sites, one for each special interest group (e.g., for wine collectors). Customers can view the status of their claims, and commercial clients can view their policies in full. Also, commercial customers are permitted into the data warehouse to view and use analytical tools to examine their policy-usage records.

The Web enables superb communication with agents and business partners and it allowed business expansion into 20 countries. Services include form creation, certification, validation, and more. A special value was the service to multinational corporations, which must be insured in several countries where different insurance regulations exist.

Source: Condensed from special supplement in www.itol.com, May 1, 1999.

EVALUATING OUTSOURCING

Implementing EC requires access to the Web, building the site, connecting it to the corporate existing information systems (front-end for order taking, back-end for order processing). Here comes the outsourcing decision, which may be very complex: Should you build your own EC infrastructure in-house, purchase a commercial EC software package or EC suite, or use a **Web hosting company** (a combination of the above is also possible)? Building your own software may be a complex and expensive solution compared with using a commercial software product or suite of products (see

TABLE 9.3 Assigning Functional Expertise to Subprojects

	Web Site Design	Building System Infsrastructure	Business Process Reengineering	Security and Control
Marketing	*		*	
Finance		*	*	*
Accounting	*		*	*
Information Technologies	*	*	*	*
Human Resource Management			*	*

chapter 11), which is usually quicker and less expensive. Many EC tools come with catalog page templates that can be used repeatedly and easily. Using a host company's rental space and frames may be less costly and quicker to build; however, loss of control over the design and operations of your EC store and the possibility of paying high monthly fees are the potential drawbacks. Another option is to hire a **Web design house** that specializes in EC design. A compromise between outsourcing and internal design might be to utilize a suite of software that integrates storefront functions into a single box. Examples of commercial software suites (chapter 11) are iCat Corp.'s Electronic Commerce Suite and Commerce Publisher; Open Market's Transact and LiveCommerce; Microsoft Corp.'s Site Server Commerce Edition; IBM Corp.'s Net.Commerce Pro; Saqqara Systems' StepSearch Professional; and AT&T's Web marketing solution (Application Case 9.7, page 328).

If you decide on a buy option, you also have to decide which specific package to use, from which vendor. This may be a complex, multicriteria decision since the suites differ in several areas: ease of configuration and setup, database and scripting support, payment mechanism, cataloging storefronts design, and work flow management. Some important features for future improvement are documented database support and integration ERP systems. In the area of database support, figuring out the data structures for your storefront and documenting data dictionaries and tables still (in 1999) difficult to do with existing software. More sophisticated packages are needed to monitor and process customer preferences and spending habits. Cross-matching a demographics database with logs detailing user habits and then coming up with an automated site response is another challenge. So is data mining. Tying a Web site to order fulfillment and customer service process, payment processing services, or legacy systems still requires significant custom development even with the better suites. Making a multimedia-rich Web catalog can be especially costly. Also, the presentation and maintenance of catalogs and their customization for customers (chapter 4) can be a difficult task. Finally, large systems need to be connected to the corporate data warehouse, ERP structure and data mining capabilities.

In addition, an e-store must be able to offer secure payment processing. Credit authorization and payment methods include credit cards, e-cash, or purchase orders. Specialized software that can authenticate the purchaser and verify the purchase should be considered. The software package chosen should also work with encryption technologies. There are many details involved in order processing such as shipping, taxes, and inventory management. An EC vendor should look for software that supports third-party shipping modules and tax calculation packages. See chapters 8 and 11 for details.

Another important area is the interface with business partners along the supply chain. All vendors need to set up a mechanism that allows them to collect money from many banks' cards. Amazon needs connection with publishers, and Ticketmaster with theaters, theme parks, and golf courses. This is an example of interfacing with suppliers.

How much does it cost to outsource? A reasonable electronic procurement system can begin at $25,000 for systems that do not link to other applications. Higher-end systems, which include top-tier features like application programming interfaces to existing legacy systems with the ability to handle different communication among multiple suppliers, can range from $250,000 to $2 million. With such high start-up costs expected and the current limitations of software packages, making a decision on buying versus building is critical. A viable alternative can be partial outsourcing, namely outsourcing some tasks and doing the rest in-house. Some companies outsource not only system development but system operations and maintenance as well. Leasing is also a viable option. Yahoo, Excite, Netscape and more offer a complete set of tools for about $100/month.

AT&T's Cyberspace Solution Helps Businesses Conduct Commerce on the Internet

Businesses large and small now can quickly and easily establish a full-featured electronic business on the Internet, thanks to a turnkey solution introduced by AT&T. AT&T's Web Marketing Solution integrates all the critical elements necessary for a successful Internet-based business: access, hosting, advertising, and one-stop customer care.

Outsourcing addresses the major challenges companies face in launching a Web-based business: building the site, attracting existing and potential customers, growing the market, and managing the operation. This is a powerful way for companies to unlock the potential of the Internet. They can expand their reach, get closer to their customers, and dramatically reduce their costs—with confidence that AT&T will provide a total solution for Web success. Dan Schulman, AT&T vice president for marketing for business services, said that Web Marketing Solution's customized Internet access software gives businesses "an unparalleled opportunity to attract existing customers to their Web site."

Building a site on the Internet. AT&T's World Wide Web (EW3) Service provides all the technical Web site infrastructure and management needed to host a reliable Web application. The service eliminates many of the complex and extensive steps required to establish, manage, and monitor a Web site, thereby allowing businesses to publish information on the Internet without having to own their servers.

Businesses can depend on AT&T to take care of connectivity issues, bandwidth requirements, server capacity, interface to the secure transaction platform, support for custom applications, state-of-the-art computers, network security, integrated site development tools, and Web site management services. In addition, AT&T's Creative Alliance Program links clients with skilled professional Web site creation and design services. For do-it-yourselfers, AT&T offers a two-day, in-depth class on Web site design and development.

Attracting customers with commerce-driven programs. With AT&T WorldNet Business-Reach Service, clients can provide their existing and potential customers or suppliers with customized software to bring them onto the Internet. The customized software also includes all the standard features of AT&T WorldNet Service, AT&T's value-added Internet access service.

Client Web sites may include AT&T's "Project iA" icon, which allows Internet surfers to click on the icon to initiate an immediate telephone conversation with a customer service agent. The agent can send images to a customer's screen to illustrate products or services being discussed. The phone conversation is provided over the AT&T network while images are simultaneously transmitted through the Internet.

Managing the operation. AT&T assigns a project manager to oversee the creation and installation of a client's Web business and to ensure it goes online as scheduled. A specialized customer care center serves as a single point of contact for the client's entire application. Additionally, as of November 1988, AT&T's Secure-Buy Service makes it possible to conduct secure online transactions, including order processing and credit card verification.

What is the cost to the client? It depends on the services used.

WEB CONTENT DESIGN

The Web team has to determine the specific content of the Web site. Table 9.4 lists features that can be considered in the Web site design (Minali and Minali 1998 and Treese and Stewart 1998).

Table 9.5 summarizes a set of considerations for a Web team to implement an EC project. Details can be found in Mougayar (1998), Minali and Minali (1998), and Pffafenberger (1998).

TABLE 9.4 Web Application Features	
—E-mall	—Video
—Unique Uniform Resource Locator	—File transfer capability
—EC/financial transactions	—Forms
—Shopping cart software	—Chat rooms
—Online catalogs	—Three-dimensional display
—Direct order procedures	—Statistics
—Dynamic databases	—Customer tracking
—Static databases	—E-mail response and forwarding
—Multimedia	—Animation
—Telephony	—Security
—Audio	

Source: Schulman and Smith (1997), p. 152.

SECURITY AND CONTROL IN EC

Maintaining the security and control of Web contents is an important factor that must be considered throughout the development process. It is necessary for a Web team to develop effective security and privacy guidelines. These should address the Internet features that must be monitored, policies on access and use, and disclosure of information through the Internet. (Details of the security issues are discussed in chapters 8 and 11.)

9.6   Project and Strategy Assessment

NEED FOR ASSESSMENT

Like any other project, Web projects need to be assessed during and after implementation. Several objectives exist for such **strategic reassessment.** The most important ones are listed below:

- Find out if the EC project delivers what it was supposed to deliver.
- Determine if the EC project is still viable in an ever-changing environment.
- Reassess the initial strategy in order to learn from mistakes and improve future planning.
- Identify failing projects as soon as possible and determine the reasons for failures to avoid the same problems on subsequent systems.

TABLE 9.5 Web Content Design Considerations	
—Services wanted	—Training for Web team
—Manpower and electronic content the company can provide	—Outside consulting
—Time to design your site	—System installation
—Time to create and program your site	—Server maintenance
—Extra fees for software development	—Application programming
—Fees for off-the-shelf application tools	—Place for Web hosting
—Size of the site	—Security for financial transactions
—Amount of traffic the site generates	—Bandwidth needs
—Management and control of content	—System capacity planning

Source: Schulman and Smith (1997), p. 153.

EC project and performance results are monitored and assessed so that corrective actions, problem resolutions, or an expansion plan can take place if needed. Assessing EC is not simple because in many situations, Web applications grow in unexpected ways, often expanding beyond their initial plan. For example, Genentec, a biotechnology giant, wanted merely to replace a homegrown bulletin board system. Genentec started with a small budget only to report that the internal Web had grown rapidly and become very popular in a short span of time, encompassing many applications. Another example is Lockheed Martin, which initially planned to put its corporate phone directory and information on training programs on the intranet; in a short time, many of its human resources documents were placed on the intranet as well. Soon after, the use of the Web for internal information expanded from administrative purposes to extranet applications.

Such extensions typically bring about many changes: Individuals and departments need to be responsible for publishing and maintaining the information that they create, especially with new business applications. From an enterprise's standpoint, such an assignment of responsibility creates numerous challenges. First, an enterprise must grant rights to various individuals and departments to create content. Second, it must establish policies and procedures that entrust a Web master to coordinate and oversee that the content is appropriate. Such content control is also important from a legal and ethical point of view. For example, Lockheed Martin allowed each department to design its own page, as long as it leveraged existing information and reflected corporate guidelines. All of these changes need to be reflected in the assessment.

While the expansion of Web projects on a large scale brings in many control and administrative issues, it is necessary to examine the entire Web project from a strategic perspective and review whether the project has achieved its intended goal and what should be done next. Such reassessment of the project can be examined both from the cost-benefit of the initial investment as well as from a future strategy formulation. This is not a simple task, especially when the Web project includes the Internet, intranet, and one or more extranets, as was shown in Figure 1.9 in chapter 1. Assessment and reassessment of projects must be based on some measurement of EC results.

MEASURING RESULTS

Each company measures success or failure by different sets of standards. Some companies may find that their goals were unrealistic, that their Web server was inadequate to handle demand, or that expected cost savings were not realized. On the other hand, some may have to respond to exploding application requests from various functional areas in the company. A review of the requirements and design documents should help answer many of the questions raised during the assessment. It is important that the Web team develops a thorough checklist to address both the evaluation of project performance and the assessment of a changing environment. Table 9.6 summarizes a set of pertinent questions in evaluating EC projects.

To assess the impact of an EC project on the company's mission and formulate a new set of strategies, it is useful to pose a set of questions such as those shown in Table 9.6 to both internal management and to customers. Other information may be relevant as well.

COLLECTING INFORMATION

One should collect all possible opinions from a diverse group of people. For example, monthly reports on bandwidth utilization and server hits from ISPs can be very helpful in determining future changes, expansion needs, and technological updates. It is also

TABLE 9.6 Questions to Evaluate an EC Project
—What were the goals? Were they met?
—What were the expectations? Were they realistic?
—What products and services did your company want to offer? Can the system deliver them?
—Did unanticipated problems occur? If so, how were those handled?
—What costs did you hope to reduce? Were you successful in doing so?
—Did other costs increase unexpectedly? If yes, why?
—What were the sales objectives? Were they realistic?
—Did you intend to reduce distribution costs?
—Did you intend to reduce travel expenses for corporate staff? Were you successful?
—Did Web and Internet communications reduce traditional communications costs, such as long distance and fax?
—Did you improve customer relations? If you did not, what went wrong?
—How can those errors be corrected?
—Was your project finished on time and on budget? If not, what went wrong?
—Are recurring costs within the budget? If not, can contracts be renegotiated?
—Was the budget realistic to begin with?
—Should the budget be revised for the next stage or budget cycle?
—Were additional people hired as expected?
—What do customers want that you are not providing? What will the additional services cost?
—What impact will the fulfilment of customers' needs have on the infrastructure, from bandwidth to software?
—What specific changes have taken place among your competitors that might affect what you are trying to accomplish?
—Have your suppliers provided adequate service?
—Has training of employees been adequate?
—What new internal needs have arisen that need to be addressed?
—Did you learn some things in the process that were valuable?

Source: Compiled from Schulman and Smith (1997), pp. 277–78.

critical to review the marketing program from different points of view. The answers could vary considerably to a question such as: How effective was the marketing plan for the EC project?

Your customers can provide invaluable information on whether the promised goods, services, and information were delivered on time. Feedback from customers can be solicited either electronically, by telephone, or in person. The first two options are more convenient. Contacts with customers will also provide a chance to compare your Web content to that of your competitors.

The *analysis* of the answers, some of which are quantitative and some qualitative, may be complex and lengthy. Furthermore, different approaches exist for such analysis, some of which are proprietary to consulting companies. Therefore we will not elaborate further on this topic.

FINALIZATION

With the gathered data, the actual ROI can be computed and compared to the projected one. Also, if any part of the sales expectations were not met, a review of your marketing efforts is in order. Were the right prospects targeted? Were they likely Internet or Web users? Was the Web site registered with the appropriate lists and search engines to ensure that prospects were likely to find your company? However, it is often difficult to distinguish the effect of online marketing and traditional offline effort in correctly identifying the Web impact.

Web assessment can be done in different ways. Most major consultants can help with their proprietary procedures. A theoretical model has been offered by Selz and Schubert (1997).

Based on the collected information, corrective steps might be required, from product offerings to pricing strategy or from Web promotion to a review of your software vendors. Once this is done a new strategy can be formulated.

9.7 Managerial Issues

1. **Considering the strategic value of EC.** Internet technology offers an unprecedented opportunity for EC. Management has to understand how EC can improve marketing and promotion, customer service, and sales. Furthermore, new business opportunities can be found through EC. To capitalize on the potential of EC, management needs to view EC from a strategic perspective, not merely as a technological advancement.

2. **Conducting strategic planning.** Strategic planning for EC starts with environmental scanning and competition analysis. Industry and market status will cause formulation of different strategies.

3. **Considering the risks.** Strategic moves have to be carefully weighed against potential risks. Identifying CSFs for EC and analyzing cost-benefit as well as ROI should not be neglected. Benefits are often hard to quantify, especially when they are more strategic than operational cost savings in nature. In such an analysis, risks should be addressed with contingency planning (deciding what to do if problems arise).

4. **Integration.** Electronic commerce may lead to the realignment of current business procedures and departmental units to maximize the long-term benefits for the company; integrating existing databases and legacy applications with Web-based new applications is not a trivial task (chapter 11). Because of such technical sophistication, as well the potential impact of the integration on the functional areas, senior management involvement is critical.

5. **Pilot projects.** When a company decides to go for a pilot project, creating a Web team representing all functional areas of the company is an important part of the implementation plan. After the pilot project is completed, it is necessary to reexamine the EC project strategies to assess the EC strategic planning efforts and its results.

Summary

The compilation of this chapter helps you in attaining the following learning objectives:

1. **Importance of strategic planning for EC.** Strategic planning clarifies what an EC project should do or focus on, with respect to the company's mission and the given business environment. Because of the comprehensiveness of EC, conducting formal strategic planning is a must.

2. **EC strategy formulation.** The strategy formulation process involves understanding the industry and competition as well as analyzing cost-benefit and ROI. It further gives guidance on whether to compete against others or to cooperate, such as forming an alliance in the market.

3. **CSF and EC justification.** Identifying the CSFs and relating them to the EC project is a critical step in strategic planning. Without such factors, an EC project is likely to fail.
4. **Competitive intelligence on the Internet.** Intelligent agents can help execute business intelligence in the market more efficiently. Intelligence on the Web can be done in many ways, such as environmental scanning, analyzing messages of news groups, carefully reviewing competitors' Web pages and analyzing publicly available online documents (such as EDGAR).
5. **Implementation steps and plans.** Creating a Web team representing various functional areas and planning for detailed technology tasks including Web hosting and security and control are important parts of an implementation plan. Other implementation issues are whether or not to outsource.
6. **Web assessment.** Feedback and corrective actions (if needed) for EC strategies are critical before launching a large project or expanding a pilot one.

Keywords

- Strategic planning
- Industry and competition analysis
- Strengths, weaknesses, opportunities, and threats (SWOT)
- Strategy formulation
- Critical success factors (CSF)
- Value chain
- Return on investment (ROI)
- Competitive strategy
- Cooperative strategy
- Offensive strategy
- Defensive strategy
- Competitive intelligence
- Push technology
- Implementation plan
- Web team
- Web hosting company
- Web content design
- Strategic alliance
- Strategy reassessment
- Virtual corporation

Questions for Review

1. Describe the objectives of strategic planning.
2. List the stages of strategic planning.
3. Describe what SWOT is.
4. Define the meaning and purpose of critical success factors in EC.
5. Describe what the value chain is in EC.
6. Explain what ROI is. Why is it important for EC?
7. Explain the concept of competitive strategies.
8. Explain the concept of cooperative strategies.
9. Define competitive intelligence.
10. Describe the procedures for implementing EC.
11. Explain the nature of EC project assessment.
12. Describe the reasons for EC infrastructure outsourcing.

Questions for Discussion

1. How would you start performing the industry analysis for a small business that wants to launch an EC project?
2. What are some typical difficulties you may encounter during an environmental scanning process?
3. Apply the SWOT approach to a small local bank for its electronic banking services.
4. What are the organizational level CSFs for a small local bank that is considering electronic banking?
5. What would be typical values EC can add to the product distribution channels of a major toy manufacturer?

6. What might be typical competitive strategies for a company trying to launch a bookselling business?
7. What might be typical cooperative strategies for a company trying to launch a bookselling business?
8. What would you tell an executive officer of a real estate company about the competitive intelligence capabilities in the real estate business as a justification for launching a new Web-based real estate business?
9. What are the factors companies should be looking for when selecting an EC software vendor?
10. How would you organize a Web team for a large retailer trying to launch a direct-selling business on the Internet?
11. Amazon.com decided not to open physical stores, while First Network Security Bank (FNSB) opened its first physical bank in 1999. Compare and discuss the two strategies.

Internet Exercises

1. Survey the different online travel agencies (e.g., cheaptickets.com, www.priceline.com, expedia.com, previewtravel.com, and so on) on the Web and compare their business strategies for customers. Especially focus on how they compete against physical travel agency offices.
2. Go over the history of Lycos Search Engine Company (lycos.com). What was wrong with its business strategy in its difficult times and what are the strategies that turned it around recently?
3. Go to Nissan Motor Corporation's Web site (nissan.com). Discuss how Nissan complements its promotion and sales program with its Web presence. What are the business values added by its Web site?
4. Enter www.companysleuth.com and discuss the types of competitive information the site offers. The service is offered free to anyone. Why? The same vendor offers the Electronic Library (www.elibrary.com) for a fee. How are these two services related? Why is the first one offered free?
5. Check the music CD companies on the Internet (e.g., cdnow.com) and find out if any of them focus on specialized niche markets as a primary strategy.
6. Go over the ISPs (e.g. http://thelist.internet.com) and compare the offerings of three companies for Web hosting.
7. Check the following search engines: Infoseek, Yahoo, and a third-party Web design service company. Discuss their major differences, if any.
8. American Greetings is the world's largest greeting card company. Until the early 1980s cards were sold mainly in specialty card stores (about 65 percent). However, by 1999 over 65 percent were sold at discount stores (e.g., Wal-Mart). Because of this fact and the strong competition, American Greetings profits declined sharply in 1999. You are assigned as a strategy consultant to assess the potential impact of EC on American Greetings' business. Use a SWOT approach and prepare a report. Use stock market and financial information available free on the Internet.

Team Exercises

1. Explain how a beauty shop/hair salon can take advantage of a Web presence for its business. Each team member visits a local beauty shop. What types of services can be on the Web? Discuss any possibilities in the area of marketing, customer service, and sales. Are there any EC activities in which the various vendors can collaborate? Prepare a report.
2. The relationship between manufacturers and their distributors regarding sales on the Web can be very strained. Direct manufacturer to consumer sales may cut into the distributors' business. Here are some examples of corporate strategies:

  a. Some companies, such as Levi's, do not allow department stores to sell their products online. (Policy was relaxed in late 1999).
  b. Some companies, such as most car manufacturers and Ritchey Design (chapter 3), do not sell on the Web in order not to upset their distributors.
  c. Other companies, such as www.wizards.com, sells both to retailers and individual consumers.
  d. Other companies, such as www.fruit.com, build Web sites for their distributors but do not interact directly with individual customers.

Each team member is assigned to a company in each of the four categories: study the strategies and compare and contrast.

3. Cisco Systems sells most or all its Internet hardware, routers, switches, and other gear on the Web. Its business model includes automating all the routine activities on the Internet. Sales support is automated by developing programs that answer queries online 24 hours a day. Thus, buyers serve themselves. This allows highly trained and scarce service engineers to deal with technical challenges rather than answering routine questions. Since 1995, sales have jumped fourfold. In addition, Cisco set up a program that lets customers choose and download software. Distributing software support over the Web, as opposed to transferring software to disks and mailing to customers, eliminated printing, handling, and postage costs. Overall, Cisco saves an estimated $325 million a year from automating its sales support and distribution support. Have each team member research one aspect of Cisco's EC activities. Then have the team prepare answers to the following:

  a. Assume you are conducting strategic planning for Cisco. Produce a table listing costs and benefits of such planning. List both quantifiable and nonquantifiable items.
  b. Check the Cisco Web site. Assume you were in charge of forming a Web team. Identify expertise/human resources you need from functional areas as well as the different types of tasks to be accomplished.
  c. If you were asked to develop strategic planning for a relatively weak competitor of Cisco, what types of strategies would you choose? Check the networking equipment industry status from a competitive intelligence perspective and discuss the alternatives for the competing company.
  d. Cisco started its EC efforts in mid-1996 and slowly expanded them. On the other hand, Intel Corp. (opening vignette, chapter 1) moved to EC only in late 1998 but did it very rapidly. Comment on the two strategies.

R E A L   W O R L D   C A S E S

Wizards of the Coast, Inc.[1]

The Wizards of the Coast, a developer of electronic games (www.wizards.com), decided to change its Web site in 1998 so orders could be taken there. It opened a store on the Internet for both retailers and individual consumers to have direct access to the Internet. The newly opened site provides the following opportunities to Wizards:

- Expand distribution to offer consumers and retailers direct access to products over the Internet.
- Overcome barriers associated with traditional methods for distribution; open up new worldwide markets without impacting existing channels.
- Offer new product presentations and promotions and enable growth for future capabilities, such as electronic software distribution, shopping privileges, and unique consumer promotions and services.

The company used the following implementation strategy:

- Offer a site with full security to detect and prevent fraudulent transactions.
- Ensure that front-end and back-end interfaces are user friendly and easy to navigate and maintain.
- Meet an aggressive design and development schedule to get to market quickly. Create a cost-effective solution that doesn't compromise standards for quality assurance, testing, and deployment.
- Subcontract the Web site development to a vendor.
- Offer a special storefront both for retailers and individual customers.
- Plan to offer a special storefront for employees.
- Take good care of customers by providing demos and freebies, a retail locator, and a call center.

The company used www.mindcorps.com as software vendor and builder. This resulted in a fast development time (less than eight weeks). Mindcorps also managed the deployment of basic end-system integration and the transaction pipeline. Electronic commerce lets Wizards offer new product presentations and promotions and plan for future efforts such as electronic software distribution, shopping privileges for association members, and unique consumer promotions and services.

While management extols the benefits of selling over the Internet, it is careful to add value through new features. Management wants to ensure that Wizards is sufficiently equipped to fully support any new offerings and to maintain a high level of customer service. From the inception of the online store, Wizards considered such factors as ensuring that promotions and brand awareness would not destroy any of the company's existing sales channels.

When a customer visits the Wizards' site, selects merchandise, and enters payment information, site server components in the plan pipeline are used. After the customer confirms the purchase, activity passes through the purchase pipeline, and ClearCommerce Merchant Engine components take over (an ordering/payment software). As the order passes through the purchase pipeline, fraud checking is invoked, real-time credit card processing begins, and information is logged to a database.

Wizards' site represents a high level of sophistication because Wizards successfully researched what to sell online and how to market it. The company also thought about what would happen when they grew and how to scale. They did the right planning.

The company offers several other services such as:

- Supporting several newsgroups.
- Using push technology to send information on a specific game or area of interest mailing lists.
- Providing a chat room and a messaging center.

---

[1] Adapted from Falla (1999).

- Providing a "reading room" with magazines and game reviews.
- Providing a global information desk with news

releases, job listings, information about conventions, tournaments, and more.
- Providing a search engine. ∎

CASE QUESTIONS

1. What barriers normally associated with traditional methods of distribution were overcome by EC?
2. Why is the company offering its Game Center and the other services (visit the site!)?
3. How come EC was not destroying existing distribution channels?
4. Why does the company need three different storefronts (consumers, retailers, employees)?
5. Identify all the CSFs of this site (list only). Compare with the CSFs presented in the chapter.

6. Visit www.mindscorps.com and review all their products and services.
7. Did Wizards succeed because they chose the right product to market and sell or because they used the right technologies/products? Would you have chosen a different set of tools?
8. Match the strategy and planning process here against what is described in the chapter.

SkyMall's EC Strategy

SkyMall, an Internet and airlines retailer (printed catalogs), unveiled a new EC strategy on April 12, 1999. "Our strategy is designed to capitalize on the exclusive relationships developed by our in-flight catalog business and last year's strong performance of our skymall.com site," said Robert Worsley, chairman and CEO. "We are convinced that consumers are not going to navigate and bookmark numerous sites to cover all their needs. Our ultimate goal is to build a comprehensive one-stop site that provides consumers with a broad selection of best-selling merchandise and travel-related services and content that is easy to navigate and provides unique and entertaining consumer experiences."

INFRASTRUCTURE STRATEGY

"A key component of our e-commerce strategy is to apply the knowledge we have developed from our existing business to further develop the infrastructure necessary to support our Web efforts. Specifically, we plan to upgrade the speed, performance and functionality of the Company's existing skymall.com site to ensure that by the fourth quarter the consumer experience at skymall.com meets or exceeds that of other major e-commerce sites."

CONTENT STRATEGY

"Merchandising plans call for SkyMall to increase the variety and selection of merchandise offered on the Web by two primary means. First, SkyMall plans to further leverage its relationships with its existing base of over 100 catalog vendors by adding more of their products to SkyMall's database, in addition to the best-selling items already available in the in-flight catalog. SkyMall has already made progress in this area in 1999, and has increased the number of products available through its Internet site to approximately three times the print catalog offering.

The company's second merchandising strategy is to secure product content in new categories that have not been traditionally covered by the catalog industry by securing relationships directly with the manufacturers and other major distributors of products.

To date, SkyMall has secured relationships with numerous manufacturers and other distributors in categories that include electronics, health-related products, and home furnishings. In connection with the second phase of the planned infrastructure upgrades, the Company anticipates that the products from many of these manufacturers will be available on its site."

TRAVEL

"Leveraging its relationships with its airline and other travel partners, SkyMall expects to launch a travel site in the third quarter of 1999. Through its airline and other relationships, the Company expects to be able to secure travel content and to provide various value-added services to travelers. Initial plans call for links between skymall.com's travel and shopping sites in order to increase awareness of both sites. Ultimately, the Company plans to incorporate shopping and travel into one comprehensive site."

MARKETING ALLIANCE STRATEGY

"SkyMall.com's e-commerce strategy is to implement marketing programs designed to improve brand awareness, drive traffic to its site and increase consumer spending. SkyMall believes the key to SkyMall's success in its in-flight catalog business has been to successfully secure and manage numerous partner relationships with major airlines and merchants.

SkyMall plans to use its partnership relationship experience to form additional strategic partnership alliances with third parties, such as financial service providers and media companies. By bringing SkyMall's product content to third parties to enable them to conduct e-commerce on a co-branded site, the Company believes it can also secure additional on- and offline channels for promotions to the customer bases of these third parties at little or no cost to SkyMall.

In turn, through these proposed alliances, SkyMall plans to give its partners access to some of the most demographically appealing consumers in the country through its existing in-flight catalog and hotel channels."

BROAD BAND TECHNOLOGIES

"Experts believe that the convergence of television and the Web will occur in the foreseeable future, creating the opportunity to provide a richer content experience to consumers via broad band technologies.

The Company believes that broad band technologies will allow it to expand its reach, customer base and enhance brand awareness, while offering much needed support to potential broad band partners."

WORKPLACE WEB INITIATIVE

"Given the increasing use of Internet in the workplace as well as the significant number of dual-income households, SkyMall believes that the corporate workplace is an ideal channel for further distribution of its products and services. The company plans to implement workplace marketing initiatives on Web-based intranet systems that deliver logo merchandise as well as other product content to consumers at work."

INVESTMENT SPENDING

"SkyMall plans to invest significantly in its e-commerce strategy and the investment is expected to cause SkyMall to experience a loss for 1999 ranging between $1.00 and $1.20 per share.

SkyMall plans to invest the $20 million of expense and $7 million of capital expenditures in four major areas: $5 million to staff the Internet development and support team and to operate the recently opened New York office, $10 million for sales and marketing of the new sites, $5 million for infrastructure and the management team to lead the Company's growth initiatives, and $7 million of capital expenditures for computer equipment and software development.

The Company expects to fund the e-commerce investment through catalog operations cash flow and its current cash position of approximately $4 million, as well as by re-negotiating its line of credit to increase its borrowing capacity. While these funds are expected to be sufficient to meet skymall.com's expansion objectives for 1999, the Company is continuing to explore other financing options."

SUMMARY

"Research shows that consumers are quickly accepting the Internet as a new shopping medium, with about half of the households in the U.S. that had Internet access making at least one purchase online in the last six months," stated Bob Worsley. "We believe the fourth quarter of 1999 will present us with important opportunities in this new era of Internet shopping and we plan to capitalize on these opportunities by executing the strategies we have discussed today." ∎

CASE QUESTIONS

1. A major objective of the strategy is to "drive traffic to the site."
   Explain why the company is expecting more visitors as a result of the strategy.
2. Can you make a few suggestions to the company about how to increase traffic even further?
3. The company is talking about "leveraging its relationship with its travel partners." What do they mean by that and how is it reflected in the strategy?

4. In one of the book's chapters there is a discussion about "redefining organizations" by developing new products and new business models. Relate the concept of redefining organizations to SkyMall's strategy.
5. What kind of infrastructure does SkyMall need? (Think about customers, business partners, products.)

References

J. Bower et al., *Business Policy: Managing Strategic Processes*, 8th ed. (Burr Ridge, IL: Irwin McGraw-Hill, 1995).

F. David, *Strategic Management: Concepts and Cases,* 7th ed. (Upper Saddle River, NJ: Prentice Hall, 1998).

J. Falla, "Launch a Successful E-Commerce Site," *e-business Advisor* (February 1999).

R. J. Folz, "Build an E-Commerce Site with True ROI," *e-Business Advisor* (February 1999).

A. K. Maitra, *Building a Corporate Internet Strategy* (New York: van Nostrand Reinhold, 1996).

J. E. Gaskin, *Corporate Policies and the Internet: Connection without Controversy* (Upper Saddle River, NJ; Prentice Hall, 1992).

S. Ghosh, "Making Business Sense of the Internet," *Harvard Business Review* (March/April 1998).

T. Guimaraes and C. Armstrong, "Exploring the Relations between Competitive Intelligence, IS Support, and Business Change," *Competitive Intelligence Review* 9 (3:1997).

A. Hutchinson, "E-Commerce: Building a Model," *Communications Week* (March 17, 1997).

S. Kalin, "Title Search," CIO Web Business Magazine (Feb. 1, 1999).

W. C. Lisse, "The Economics of Information and the Internet, *Competitive Intelligence Review* 9 (4:1998).

S. Liu, "Business Environment Scanner for Senior Managers: Towards Active Executive Support with Intelligent Agents," Proceedings 30th HICSS, Hawaii, January 1998.

E. Marlow, *Web Visions* (New York: Van Nostrand Reinhold, 1997).

D. Minali and E. Minali, *Web Commerce Technology Handbook* (New York: McGraw-Hill, 1998).

W. Mougayar, *Opening Digital Markets*, 2ᵈ ed. (New York: McGraw-Hill, 1998).

M. Parker, *Strategic Transformation and Information Technology* (Upper Saddle River, NJ: Prentice Hall, 1996).

B. Pffafenberger, *Building a Strategic Internet* (Foster City, CA: IDG Books, 1998).

M. Porter, *Competition in Global Industries* (Boston: Harvard Business School Press, 1986).

B. C. Power and R. Sharda, "Obtaining Business Intelligence on the Internet," *Long Range Planning* (April 1997).

M. E. Porter, *Competitive Advantage: Creating and Sustaining Superior Performance* (New York: Free Press, 1985).

P. Ruber, "Getting Smart with Business Intelligence," *Beyond Computing* (June 1998).

A. Raskin, "The ROIght Stuff," *CIO Web Business Magazine* (February 1, 1999).

M. Schulman and R. Smith, *The Internet Strategic Plan* (New York: John Wiley & Sons, 1997).

D. Selz and P. Schubert, "Web Assessment—A Model for the Evaluation and Assessment of Successful Electronic Commerce Applications," *Electronic Markets* 7 (3:1997).

G. W. Treese and L. Stewart, *Designing Systems for Internet Commerce* (Reading, MA: Addison-Wesley, 1998).

E. Turban ct al., *Information Technology for Management*, 2ᵈ ed (New York: John Wiley & Sons, 1999).

D. Young et al., "Strategic Implications of Electronic Linkages," *Information Systems Management* (Winter 1999).

J. Ware et al., *The Search for Digital Excellence* (New York: McGraw-Hill, 1998).

T. Wheelen and J. Hunger, *Strategic Management and Business Policy*, 6th ed. (Reading, MA: Addison-Wesley, 1998).

L. C. Whipple, "The Web's Return on Investment" *e-Business Advisor* (January 1999).

CHAPTER 10

Public Policy: From Legal Issues to Privacy

Learning Objectives

Upon completion of this chapter, the reader will be able to:

- List and describe the major legal issues related to EC.

- Understand the difficulties of protecting privacy and describe the measures taken by companies and individuals to protect it.

- Describe the intellectual property issues in EC and the measures provided for its protection.

- Describe some of the ethical issues in EC and the measures organizations take to improve ethics.

- Understand the conflict between Internet indecency and free speech and the attempts to resolve the conflict.

- Describe the issues involved in imposing sales tax on the Internet.

- Discuss the controls over exporting encryption software and the issues of government policies.

- Differentiate between contracts online and offline.

- Describe the measures available to protect buyers and sellers on the Internet.

10.1   EC-Related Legal Incidents

CONTRACTUAL ISSUES IN EC

ProCD sold a database program called SelectPhone containing information from 3,000 telephone directories. The company sold the same program to both commercial users and individual retail consumers, with a discount offered to the consumers. The discount was based, in part, on an agreement, or license, that restricted the use of the program to noncommercial purposes. Mr. Zeidenberg bought a retail version of the program and proceeded to resell it over the Internet, a blatant violation of the agreement. When sued by ProCD, Zeidenberg argued that the contract was not enforceable since he was unable to examine it until after he had purchased and opened the package (the agreement is shrink-wrapped with the software). The court responded by explaining that Zeidenberg bound himself to the terms by using the program when he had the opportunity to return it. The Supreme Court held that "Shrink-wrap licenses are enforceable unless their terms are objectionable on grounds applicable to contracts in general."

The Court reasoned that placing the terms on the outside of the box would require such fine print that the function of the information would be diminished. Conversely, if the postsale terms are additional to an already formed contract, then those terms are probably not enforceable as part of the agreement. The Court also recognized that an increasing number of software sales are performed by wire where the opportunity to review conditions may not occur until the "package" is in the possession of the consumer. As a result of these forward-looking facts and supposition of the direction of online software sales, the Court established a precedent that addressed a small portion of electronic contract law that paves the way for enhanced EC.

COPYRIGHT INFRINGEMENT ON THE WEB

David LaMacchia was a student at MIT who ran a computer bulletin board system that was accessible over the Internet. On this bulletin board he offered free copies of such copyrighted software as Word, Excel, and WordPerfect, among others. He was distributing the copyright-protected software without charge. When he was sued (*U.S. versus LaMacchia*), he was found not guilty since he did not benefit financially from the sales. The applicable law, the Copyright Infringement Act, stated that "the defendant must have willfully infringed the copyright and gained financially." Although he had definitely infringed the copyright, he could not be held liable for damages since there was no financial gain on his part. This was a loophole in the copyright act, and it was fixed after LaMacchia's trial.

10.2   Legal, Ethical, and Other Public Policy Issues

The opening vignettes illustrate two legal issues related to EC. The first one deals with the validity of contracts related to software purchase and distribution. This issue is especially important since software is a digitized product and its sales online are growing rapidly. In addition to contract validity, this vignette is related to the issue of intellectual property and software piracy. The second vignette deals with the issue of unethical (now illegal) distribution of software, which is related to intellectual property and software piracy.

Electronic commerce is so new that the legal, ethical, and other public policy issues that are necessary for EC's existence are still evolving. The second vignette illustrates a legal loophole that was fixed only after the incident occurred. Yet, such issues are extremely important to the success of EC as they encompass one of the major pillars that support EC applications (see Figure 1.2 in chapter 1). As a matter of fact, most of the surveys that attempt to find the inhibitors of EC consistently place legal and related public policy issues at the top of the list. For example, according to the Georgia Tech 1997 and 1998 surveys (www.gvu.gatech.edu/user_surveys), the most important issues facing the Internet were (in declining order of importance) censorship, privacy, navigation, taxation, and encryption. With the exception of navigation, all the other issues are discussed in this chapter.

LEGAL AND ETHICAL ISSUES: AN OVERVIEW

The implementation of EC involves many legal issues. These can be classified in several ways. We have segregated the EC-related legal issues in this chapter to include:

- *Privacy.* This issue is becoming the most important issue for consumers. And indeed, privacy statements can be found today in most large EC-related Web sites. Compliance with the Privacy Act of 1974 and its extensions are not simple, since the line between legal definitions and ethics is not always clear, as we show later.
- *Intellectual property.* Protecting intellectual property on the Web is very difficult since it is easy and inexpensive to copy and disseminate digitized information. Furthermore, it is very difficult to monitor who is using intellectual property and how. Copyright, trademarks, and other intellectual property issues are defined by federal legislation.
- *Free speech.* The Internet provides the largest opportunity for free speech that has ever existed. Yet, this freedom may offend some people and may collide with the Indecency Act. Again, the line is not always clear between what is illegal and what is unethical.
- *Taxation.* At the present time, it is illegal to impose new sales taxes on Internet business (at least until October 2001). A possible collision between federal and state legislation is possible, as well as between tax laws of different countries.
- *Consumer protection.* Many legal issues that deal with consumer protection, ranging from misrepresentation to different kinds of fraud, are related to electronic trade.
- *Other legal issues.* Several other EC legal issues exist, including topics such as validity of contracts, jurisdiction over trades, encryption policies, and Internet gambling.
- *Legal issues versus ethics.* In theory, one can distinguish between legal issues and ethical issues. If you do something that is not legal, you are breaking the law. If you do something unethical, you may not be breaking the law. Obviously, many illegal acts are unethical as well. The problem is that, in information technology (IT), it is not always clear what is illegal, and ethical issues may be debatable. The rest of this chapter deals with several topics that, under most circumstances, are both illegal and unethical. Before we explore these issues, let us examine the meaning of ethics.

ETHICAL ISSUES

Ethics is a branch of philosophy that deals with what is considered to be right and wrong. Over the years, philosophers have proposed many ethical guidelines, yet what is unethical is not necessarily illegal. Thus, in many instances, an individual faced with an ethical decision is not considering whether or not to break the law. In today's complex environment, the definitions of right and wrong are not always clear. Consider the following scenarios:

- A company developed profiles of potential customers from information collected with cookies and questionnaires and sold the list to advertisers. Some of the profiles were inaccurate; consequently, people received numerous pieces of inappropriate e-mail.
- Management allowed employees to use the Web for limited personal uses, then monitored usage without employees' knowledge.

- The president of a software development company marketed online a tax advice program, knowing it had bugs. As a result, some users filed incorrect tax returns and were penalized by the IRS.

Whether these actions are considered unethical depends on the organization, country, and the specific circumstances surrounding the scenarios.

The spread of EC has created many new ethical situations. For example, the issue of a company monitoring e-mail is very controversial (47 percent of the readers of *InformationWeek* believe companies have the right to do so, 53 percent disagree). Obviously, there are major differences among companies and individuals with respect to what is right and wrong.

There are also differences regarding ethics among different countries. What is unethical in one culture may be perfectly acceptable in another. Many Western countries, for example, have a much higher concern for individuals and their rights to privacy than some Asian countries. In Asia, more emphasis is, in general, placed on the benefits to society rather than on the rights of individuals. Some countries, like Sweden and Canada, have very strict privacy laws; others have none. For example, in 1997, Italy, Belgium, Spain, Portugal, and Greece had minimal legislation protecting an individual's right to control personal data in governmental or commercial databases. This obstructs the flow of information among countries in the European community. To overcome this problem, in 1998, the European Community Commission issued guidelines to all its member countries regarding the rights of individuals to access information about themselves and to correct errors.

Many companies and professional organizations develop their own **codes of ethics,** a collection of principles intended as a guide for its members (Oz 1994). For a discussion of the code of the Association for Computing Machinery (ACM), see Anderson et al. (1993).

The diversity of EC applications and the increased use of technology have created new ethical issues, as illustrated throughout this text. An attempt to organize IT ethical issues into a framework was undertaken by Mason (1986) and Mason et al. (1995), who categorized ethical issues into privacy, accuracy, property, and accessibility.

- *Privacy*—collection, storage, and dissemination of information about individuals.
- *Accuracy*—authenticity, fidelity, and accuracy of information collected and processed.
- *Property*—ownership and value of information and intellectual property.
- *Accessibility*—right to access information and payment of fees to access it.

Representative questions and issues in each category are listed in Table 10.1.

Mason et al. (1995) also developed a model for ethical reasoning that shows the process that leads to ethical judgment when an individual is faced with an ethical issue.

Legal and ethical issues are important for the success of EC. Two organizations that are active in this area are the Organization for Economic Cooperation and Development (www.oecd.org) and CommerceNet (www.commerce.net).

10.3 Protecting Privacy

Privacy means different things to different people. In general, **privacy** is the right to be left alone and the right to be free of unreasonable personal intrusions. A definition of **information privacy,** according to Agranoff (1993), is the "claim of individuals, groups,

TABLE 10.1 A Framework for Ethical Issues	
Privacy	*Accuracy*
• What information about oneself should an individual be required to reveal to others? • What kind of surveillance can an employer use on its employees? • What things can people keep to themselves and not be forced to reveal to others? • What information about individuals should be kept in databases, and how secure is the information there?	• Who is responsible for the authenticity, fidelity, and accuracy of information collected? • How can we ensure that information will be processed properly and presented accurately to users? • How can we ensure that errors in databases, data transmissions, and data processing are accidental and not intentional? • Who is to be held accountable for errors in information, and how is the injured party compensated?
Property	*Accessibility*
• Who owns the information? • What are the just and fair prices for its exchange? • Who owns the channels of information? • How should one handle software piracy (copying copyrighted software)? • Under what circumstances can one use proprietary databases? • Can corporate computers be used for private purposes? • How should experts who contribute their knowledge to create knowledge bases be compensated? • How should access to information channels be allocated?	• Who is allowed to access information? • How much should be charged for permitting accessibility to information? • How can accessibility to computers be provided for employees with disabilities? • Who will be provided with equipment needed for accessing information? • What information does a person or an organization have a right or a privilege to obtain—under what conditions and with what safeguards?

Source: Compiled from Mason (1986) and Mason et al. (1995).

or institutions to determine for themselves when, and to what extent, information about them is communicated to others."

Privacy has long been a legal and social issue in the United States and many other countries. The right to privacy is recognized today in virtually all U.S. states and by the federal government, either by statute or common law. The definition of privacy can be interpreted quite broadly; however, the following two rules have been followed fairly closely in past court decisions: (1) The right of privacy is not absolute. Privacy must be balanced against the needs of society. (2) The public's right to know is superior to the individual's right of privacy. These two rules show why it is difficult, in some cases, to determine and enforce privacy regulations. Federal privacy legislation related to EC is listed in Table 10.2.

The complexity of collecting, sorting, filing, and accessing information manually from several different agencies was, in many cases, a built-in protection against misuse of private information. It was simply too expensive, cumbersome, and complex to invade privacy. However, personal computers, powerful software, large databases, and the Internet have created an entirely new dimension of accessing and using data. The inherent power in systems that can access vast amounts of data can be used for the good of society. For example, by matching records with the aid of a computer, it is pos-

TABLE 10.2   Representative U.S. Federal Privacy Legislation

Legislation	Content
Privacy Act of 1974	Prohibits the government from collecting information secretly. Information collected must be used only for a specific purpose.
Privacy Protection Act of 1980	Provides protection of privacy in computerized and other documents.
Electronic Communications Privacy Act of 1986	Prohibits private citizens from intercepting data communication without authorization.
Computer Security Act of 1987	Requires security of information regarding individuals.
Computer Matching and Privacy Act of 1988	Regulates the matching of computer files by state and federal agencies.
Video Privacy Protection Act of 1988	Protects privacy in transmission of pictures.
Fair Health Information Practices Act of 1997	Provides a code of fair information.
Consumer Internet Privacy Protection Act of 1997	Requires prior written consent before a computer service can disclose subscribers' information.
Federal Internet Privacy Protection Act of 1997 (H.R. 1367)	Prohibits federal agencies from disclosing personal records over the Internet.
Communications Privacy and Consumer Empowerment Act of 1997 (H. R. 1964)	Protects privacy rights in online commerce.
Data Privacy Act of 1997 (H. R. 2368)	Limits the use of personally identifiable information and regulates spamming.

sible to eliminate or reduce fraud, government mismanagement, tax evasion, welfare cheats, family support filchers, employment of illegal aliens, and so on. The question is: What price must every individual pay in terms of loss of privacy so that the government can better apprehend criminals?

With the widespread use of the Internet and EC, the issue of privacy becomes more critical (Exercise 1). A special organization called the Electronic Privacy Information Center (www.epic.org) is trying to protect privacy. Also see Cavoukian and Tapscott (1997); Schneier and Banisar (1997); and Wang, Lee, and Wang (1998) for comprehensive coverage. Some issues of privacy are discussed next.

PRIVACY ISSUES

Online businesses constantly gather and use demographic information from users who are afraid that their personal data, including credit card numbers or their behavior on the Net, may be sold, used, or revealed in an inappropriate manner. Such fears keep many consumers from shopping online. Among the 77 percent of Internet users who have never purchased products online, 86 percent say that they have been holding back out of fear that others might use their credit card number, or other private information, without their consent. Obviously, this is a significant hindrance to the growth of EC.

There are several issues related to privacy, which we discuss here. One issue, spamming, we will discuss in Section 10.5.

HOW IS PRIVATE INFORMATION COLLECTED?

Here are examples of the ways someone can collect private information through the Internet:

- Reading your newsgroups postings.
- Finding you in the Internet directory.

- Making your browser record information about you.
- Recording what your browsers say about you.
- Reading your e-mail (Rainone et al. 1998).

Web site self-registration and the use of cookies are two of the major sources of information for companies seeking to collect personal data.

Web Site Self-Registration

Web sites can gather customer information through filled-out registration questionnaires. In a registration process, customers type in their private information, such as name, address, phone, e-mail address, or even interests and hobbies, in order to receive a password to participate in a lottery, to receive information, or to play a game. This information may be collected for planning the business, sold to a third party (sometimes an unknown party), and used in an inappropriate manner. Consequently, users have concerns over privacy information, although self-registration creates less concerns than cookies.

It is interesting to note that the Tenth User Survey by GVU (1988) found that 40 percent of all users have falsified information when registering online. Of all U.S. and European respondents, 66.49 percent reported that they don't register because they don't know how the information is going to be used. In addition, 62.78 percent don't feel that registration is worthwhile considering the content of the sites, and 57.57 percent stated that they don't trust the sites collecting this information from them. These reasons, along with others (lack of time, as well as unwillingness to report one's address, name, or e-mail), clearly illustrate why only 6.01 percent of all respondents always register when requested.

Cookies

A **cookie** is a piece of information that allows a Web site to record one's comings and goings. Cookies help Web sites maintain user states. This means that Web sites can "remember" information about users and respond to their preferences on a particular site, process transparent user passwords, and so on.

A cookie can be viewed as a temporary identity. Each time a person goes to a Web site, it is as though they are visiting it for the very first time. Cookies allow Web sites to maintain information on a particular user across HTTP connections.

More specifically, cookies allow Web sites (servers) to deliver simple data to a client (user); request that the client store the information; and, in certain circumstances, return the information to the Web site. Most leading browsers, including Netscape Navigator and Microsoft Internet Explorer, support cookies.

Web sites use cookies for various reasons. Sites such as Yahoo or Excite use cookies to personalize information. Some sites, such as Amazon.com or Microsoft, use cookies to improve online sales/services, while others, such as AltaVista or Double Click, attempt to simplify the way popular links or demographics are tracked. In addition, Web site designers can keep sites fresh and relevant to the user's interests by using cookies. For instance, an online newspaper may want to enable subscribers to log in without having to enter a password at every visit. An airline may want to keep track of a customer's seating preferences, so that it does not have to ask whether a window or aisle is desired each time a reservation is made. Cookies can be very handy for users, too. Some users do not mind having cookies used to make their Web browsing more convenient, they find it cumbersome to enter a password or fill out a form over and over again.

Cookies have brought about more concerns over privacy than self-registration be-

Public Policy: From Legal Issues to Privacy

cause cookies allow Web sites to collect private information such as users' preferences, interests, and surfing patterns on the Web sites users visit. Furthermore, personal profiles created by cookies are more accurate than self-registration because, as indicated earlier, almost half of users falsify information when registering. Therefore, cookie features have been very attractive for Internet marketers. The demand for cookies is unlikely to decline, and the concerns such as user privacy and legal enforcement have grown. The potential for abuse also exists. For example, if a user often visits Web sites associated with racial issues and his or her surfing pattern is revealed by an opposing party, his or her rights might be abused. In a legal example, some perpetrators engaging in pornography have been arrested by tracking their behavior online. Although these cases were considered a success, anxiety remains. What if the government or police track behavior on the Net without notice, consent, or just cause?

There are some solutions to cookies. First, users can delete cookie files stored in their computers. However, deleting cookie files entirely will cause users to start from scratch with every Web site they usually visit. It may, therefore, be preferable to open the cookies.txt file (in the case of Netscape) and remove only the entries users do not like, or go to the cookies folder (in the case of Microsoft Explorer) and delete the unwanted files from the servers.

The second solution is the use of anticookie software. Pretty Good Privacy's Cookie Cutter is free and uses filters to either block or allow cookies at a user's command. Luckman's Anonymous Cookie is also free for Windows 95 and 98 users and instantly disables all cookies in a user's cookie directory or cookie file allowing users to browse the World Wide Web anonymously. Cookie Crusher is free as well and automatically accepts or rejects cookies from user-selected sites. Cookie Monster is free for Macintosh users.

After the FTC hearing of June 1997 regarding privacy concerns online, among other topics, Netscape and Microsoft introduced new browsers: Netscape Communicator 4.0 and Microsoft Internet Explorer 4.0. Today's browsers contain an option allowing users to refuse all cookies without having to click through the warnings. In addition, Netscape Communicator has an option for a user who wants to accept only the cookie that is going to be returned to the domain on which the user is logged. This option is aimed at stopping third-party cookies used by advertisers.

The call for cookie regulation has come from the public, as proponents, and the vendor's sector, as opponents, and they have confronted each other. Consumers want to control what personal information is disclosed about them, to whom, and how that information will be used. On the other hand, the opposing side represents most industries, who want to keep collecting more accurate information and demographic data for future business use.

PRIVACY PROTECTION

How organizations collect and use personal information, together with their privacy protection practices, can be summarized in five principles, which provide guidelines for the collection and dissemination of personal information and which are shared by European countries, Canada, some other countries, and the United States. These five basic principles are:

1. **Notice/awareness.** Consumers must be given notice of an entity's information practices prior to collection of personal information. Consumers must be able to make informed decisions about the type and extent of their disclosures based on the intentions of the party collecting the information.

2. **Choice/consent.** Consumers must be made aware of their options as to how their personal information may be used as well as any potential secondary uses of the information. Consent may be granted through opt-out clauses requiring steps to prevent collection of information; in other words, no action equals consent. Consumers may grant consent through opt-in clauses, requiring steps to allow the collection of information.

3. **Access/participation.** Consumers must be able to access their personal information and challenge the validity of the data.

4. **Integrity/security.** Consumers must be assured that the data is secure and accurate. It is necessary for those collecting the data to take whatever precautions are required to ensure that data is protected from loss, unauthorized access, destruction, fraudulent use, and to take reasonable steps to gain information from reputable and reliable sources.

5. **Enforcement/redress.** There must always be a method of enforcement and remedy, otherwise there is no real deterrent or enforceability for privacy issues. The alternatives are government intervention, legislation for private remedies, or self-regulation.

The implementation of these principles may not be simple as is illustrated in Application Case 10.1.

PROTECTING YOUR PRIVACY

Here are nine suggestions about how you can protect your privacy:

1. Think before you give out personal information on a site.
2. Track the use of your name.
3. Keep your newsgroups posts out of archives.
4. Use the Anonymizer when browsing.
5. Live without cookies.
6. Use anonymous remailers.
7. Use encryption.
8. Reroute your mail away from your office.
9. Ask your ISP or employer about a privacy policy.

Anonymizers. One way to increase privacy is to surf the Web anonymously. A number of tools can be used to do so (Cranor 1999). This is done with the help of intelligent agents, which can work along with regulatory and self-regulatory frameworks to provide online privacy protection. (See Figure 10.1, page 350.)

Legislation. Legislation of private remedies has included the proposal of such acts as the Consumer Internet Privacy Act, which seeks to regulate the use of personal information by prohibiting third-party disclosure and expanding online subscriber rights. The Federal Internet Privacy Protection Act prohibits federal agencies from disclosing personal records or making identifying records about an individual's medical, financial, or employment history. The Communications Privacy and Consumer Empowerment Act is perhaps the most broad in scope and attempts to protect privacy rights in EC through a variety of measures. This act requires the FTC to report online privacy rights in EC including the collection and use of personal data. It also expands previous laws to include the facilitation and development of improved safety measures in online commerce and requires access providers to offer blocking software. Finally, it obligates the Federal Communications Commission to establish procedures to en-

---

APPLICATION CASE 10.1

Case of Microsoft and GeoCities Privacy Policies

Microsoft. Microsoft's Web site posts privacy policies explaining why Microsoft asks customers about themselves, what cookies are used for, and so forth. Among other things, it says that customers are in charge of deciding what Microsoft knows about them and that Microsoft uses customers' information to improve its site and refine its services. Moreover, it says although Microsoft may share customer information with its partner companies, it will not do so without the customer's consent. Also, customers can update and edit their information at the Personal Information Center, a service that should be obligatory rather than optional.

GeoCities. GeoCities has several million members, and industry reports have identified it as the third most frequently visited site on the Web. In August 1998, GeoCities agreed to settle Federal Trade Commission (FTC) charges that it misrepresented the purposes for which it was collecting personal identifying information. GeoCities misled its customers, both children and adults, by not telling the truth about how it was using their personal information. In order to become a member of GeoCities, individuals must complete an online application form that requests certain personal identifying information. Through this registration process, GeoCities created a database that held e-mail and postal addresses, member interest areas, and demographics, including income, education, gender, marital status, and occupation. The personal "mandatory" information was supposed to be used only in cases where members were provided with specific advertising offers and products or services they requested, and the "optional" information (education level, income, marital status, occupation, and interests) was not supposed to be released to anyone without the member's permission. In fact, this information was disclosed to third parties who used it to target members for solicitations beyond those agreed to by the member.

This is the first FTC case involving Internet privacy. Under the settlement, GeoCities agreed to post a clear and prominent privacy notice on its site telling consumers what information is being collected and for what purpose, to whom it will be disclosed, and how consumers can access and remove the information. GeoCities also must obtain parental consent before collecting information from children 12 and under. This provision conforms to current industry self-regulatory guidelines. This case is a wake-up call to all Internet marketers, because their information collection practices must be accurate and complete. The FTC will continue to monitor these Internet sites and bring enforcement actions when it is appropriate.

---

sure consideration of the needs of ISPs and their customers for efficient interconnection for packet-switched networks.[1]

The Data Privacy Act is another proposed legislation that seeks not only to limit the use of personal information but also to regulate the dissemination of spam. This act calls for an industry committee that would establish voluntary guidelines to limit the use and collection of personal information for commercial marketing purposes. Another committee would develop a registration system for spammers and devise a process for consumer complaints.

The role of government in the protection of privacy is ambiguous. Societal regulation and authority has proven to be a necessity, but not at the expense of individual freedoms and civil liberties. Ultimately, self-regulation and discretion may be the best

---

[1]By the time this book is printed some of this proposed legislation may have been enacted or rejected.

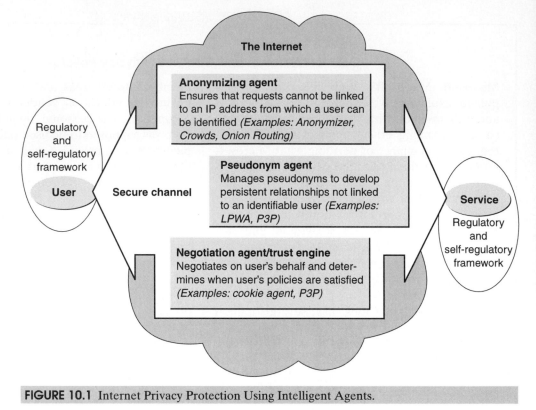

FIGURE 10.1 Internet Privacy Protection Using Intelligent Agents.

Source: Cranor (1999), pg. 30.

alternatives to reliance on outside oversight. Consumers must feel confident that policies, procedures, and avenues for redress of grievances are available before EC can reach its full potential.

FEDERAL TRADE COMMISSION (FTC) AUDIT

The FTC audited 1,400 U.S. commercial Web sites in March 1998 in order to measure the effectiveness of self-regulation; that is, whether Web sites are addressing consumers' privacy concerns through self-regulatory measures. Surveyed were the Web sites that were likely to be of interest to consumers, including health, retail, and financial sites and the most popular commercial sites. Specific practices examined were:

- *Notice* by the site of its information-gathering and dissemination policies.
- An opportunity for users to exercise *choice* over how their personal information is used.
- User *control* over personal information.
- *Verification* and *oversight* of claims made by the site.
- *Recourse* for resolving users' complaints.

As a result of the survey, the FTC found privacy protection on the Net to be *very poor*. In its June 1998 "Report to Congress on Privacy Online," the FTC concluded that the "industry's efforts to encourage voluntary adoption of the most basic fair information practices have fallen short of what is needed to protect consumers."

MOVEMENT OF ADVOCATE GROUPS AND INDUSTRY

As the FTC survey shows, the private sector is apathetic in the public movement toward information protection. Many businesses seem to prioritize business profits by collecting private information without disclosure rather than change their business strategy to reduce consumers' privacy concerns. The passive mood in the private sector has prompted some groups to advocate self-regulation in their attempts to facilitate EC.

ELECTRONIC PRIVACY INFORMATION CENTER (EPIC)

The Electronic Privacy Information Center, a public-interest research center in Washington, D.C., was established in 1994 to focus public attention on emerging civil liberties issues and to protect privacy, the First Amendment, and constitutional values. In February 1997, EPIC proposed a regulation that restricts the use of cookies. In the regulation, a user should be able to reject all cookies, know when cookies are being used, and manage cookies based on their origin or domain.

According to the American Civil Liberties Union (ACLU), monitoring computer users—**electronic surveillance**—is a widespread problem. The ACLU estimates that tens of millions of computer users are being monitored, many without their knowledge. While surveillance is one of the most extensively debated privacy issues, the practice is widely used.

Employees have very limited protection against employers' surveillance. Although several legal challenges are now under way, the law appears to support employers' rights to read e-mail and other electronic documents. Legislation now before the U.S. Congress attempts at least to require employers to inform employees that their on-the-job activities might be monitored electronically.

Information about individuals is being kept in many databases. When you apply for a new telephone, for example, you may be asked to fill in a two-page questionnaire. The questionnaire is reviewed and then stored in a database. Perhaps the most visible locations of such records are credit-reporting agencies. Other places personal information might be stored are banks and financial institutions; cable television, telephone, and utilities companies; employers; residential rental agencies and equipment rental companies; hospitals; schools and universities; supermarkets, retail establishments, and mail-order houses; government agencies (IRS, Census Bureau, your municipality); libraries; insurance companies; and online vendors. Records of purchasing, paying bills, transferring funds, buying stocks online, and more are available at vendors' databases.

There are several concerns about the information you provide to these record keepers. Under what circumstances will personal data be released? Do you know where the records are? Are these records accurate? Can you change inaccurate data? How long will it take to make a change? How are the data used? To whom are they given or sold? How secure are the data against unauthorized people?

Having information stored in many places increases the chance that the information is inaccurate, not up-to-date, or not secured properly.

One way to protect privacy is to develop **privacy policies,** or codes, which can help organizations avoid legal problems. In many organizations, senior management has begun to understand that with the ability to collect vast amounts of personal information on customers, clients, and employees comes an obligation to ensure that the information—and, therefore, the individual—is protected. A privacy code was issued on June 22, 1998, by most major Internet-related companies including IBM and Microsoft. Let us look at what a privacy policy looks like.

PRIVACY POLICY BASICS—A SAMPLE
Major areas of concern are:
Data Collection

- Data should be collected on individuals only to accomplish a legitimate business objective.
- Data should be adequate, relevant, and not excessive in relation to the business objective.
- Individuals must give their consent before data pertaining to them can be gathered. Such consent may be implied from the individual's actions (e.g., applications for credit, insurance, or employment).

Data Accuracy

- Sensitive data gathered on individuals should be verified before it is entered into the database.
- Data should be accurate and, where and when necessary, kept current.
- The file should be made available so the individual can ensure that the data are correct.
- If there is disagreement about the accuracy of the data, the individual's version should be noted and included with any disclosure of the file.

Data Confidentiality

- Computer security procedures should be implemented to provide reasonable assurance against unauthorized disclosure of data. They should include physical, technical, and administrative security measures.
- Third parties should not be given access to data without the individual's knowledge or permission, except as required by law.
- Disclosures of data, other than the most routine, should be noted and maintained for as long as the data are maintained.
- Data should not be disclosed for reasons incompatible with the business objective for which they are collected.

The Organization for Economic Cooperation and Development in Europe has probably provided the best-known set of guidelines intended to protect individuals' privacy in the electronic age (O'Leary 1995).

10.4 Protecting Intellectual Property

Intellectual property is the intangible property created by individuals or corporations, which is protected under copyright, trade secret, and patent laws. *Copyright* is a statutory grant that provides the creators of intellectual property with ownership of it for 28 years. They are entitled to collect fees from anyone who wants to copy or use the property. The U.S. Federal Computer Software Copyright Act (1980) provides protection for source and *object codes,* but one problem is that it is not clear what is eligible to be protected. For example, similar concepts, functions, and general features (such as pull-down menus, colors, or icons) are not protected by copyright law.

A *trade secret* is intellectual work, such as a business plan, which is a company secret and is not based on public information. An example is a corporate strategic plan. Laws about trade secrets are legislated at the state level in the United States.

A *patent* is a document that grants the holder exclusive rights on an invention for 17 years. Thousands of patents related to IT have been granted over the years. Examples of EC patents given to Open Market Corp. are Internet Server Access Control and Monitoring (5708780), Network Sales Systems (5715314), and Digital Active Advertising (5724424). Juno Online Services received an interactive ad patent (5809242).

COPYRIGHTS

Copyrighting is the major intellectual property issue related to EC.

Uniqueness of the Internet

Copyright laws need to be changed to reflect the uniqueness of the Internet. Initially, there were no laws governing computer software protection rights. To provide some protection, current copyright laws were used to safeguard software business. Problems arise because copyright laws were written for physical products and not for digitized software. Companies argue that cyberspace soon will be little more than a vast copying machine for pirated software, CDs, and movies, destroying thousands of jobs and $millions$ in revenue. Opponents fear that unbridled copyright power will threaten something equally important: the right to listen, read, and research without having to pay a toll any time a private citizen wants to gather information for his or her own use. A bill is required that both protects intellectual property and affords the kind of access to it that is protected under the Copyright Act.

Using Technology for Copyrights

It is possible today to codify copyrights in cyberspace. This technology could prevent circumvention of digital products. Software, movie, and record companies could, with a few lines of code, make it impossible to sample from larger works. For the user to do it would mean going around copy-protection schemes, which is illegal.

Legislation is currently considered that bans digital watermarks and validation codes. These are crucial in preventing online counterfeiting and could set back the growth of Internet business (Yeung 1998).

Copyright Protection Techniques

Besides providing laws to assist in both sides of the above debate, there are a few methods of prevention a business can take to protect its intellectual property. These methods are personalized products, frequent updating, making the window of possibility narrow, and offering freeware.

The most common intellectual property violation related to IT is software. However, there are several other potential violations of intellectual property, as shown in Application Case 10.2. (pg. 354)

One of the most difficult issues created by IT is who owns information? The information in large databases has been compiled by many people at different times. A comprehensive discussion of this issue is provided by Wells-Branscomb (1994).

Some Practical Methods

Several methods are available to protect digitized material, such as music, from being copied. One such method is by the use of **watermarks.** Digital watermarks are embedded invisible marks that can be represented by bits in digital content. The watermarks are hidden in the source data, becoming inseparable from such data. Solana Corporation's system is being integrated into tools, developed by Liquid Audio Corp., that converts audio files into a format that can be delivered over the Internet. While the watermarks cannot prevent the duplication of music, the product can help, for example, identify who is passing around pirated versions of songs downloaded from the Net. For details see Yeung (1998).

Copyright Protection versus Free Speech on the Internet

Gil Trevizo was a 25-year-old student who loves the television science-fiction series *Millennium*. He was able to get a bootlegged video of the first episode and other information and images regarding the show. He dedicated his Web site at the University of Texas to the show even before its big 1996 network premier. The show belongs to Twentieth Century-Fox, which has its own Web site dedicated to the show. The university switched off Trevizo's Internet account after Fox alerted them to the apparent piracy of its copyrighted material. Gil removed the material from his Web site.

Millennium's Internet fans were unhappy with the situation. The "First Unofficial *Millennium* WWW Site" went up before the second episode. Several dozen other fans activated protest sites before the third show aired on No-vember 8, 1996. A university did not control these fans, so their sites remained open. "They [Fox] are shutting us down," the protest sites proclaim, playing on a line instantly recognizable to fans of the *X-Files* series. "Free speech is out there."

Although Gil did not receive any economic benefits, Fox could have been hurt by his site. Fox spent over $100,000 on its *Millennium* Web site and wanted the fans to visit this site where promotional material is sold. If fans go to Gil's or similar sites, fewer visitors will come to the official site.

The problem is not unique to Fox. Thousands of Web sites are using unauthorized material, and it is unclear whether what is going on in cyberspace is governed by predigital copyright law.

Source: Based on A. Harmon, "Web Wars: Companies Get Tough on Rogues," *Los Angeles Times*, November 12, 1996, p. 1. Copyright 1996, Los Angeles Times. Reprinted by permission.

Legal Perspectives

Signed into law in December 1997, the most important legal development (till 1999) in the protection of intellectual property in cyberspace is the Electronic Theft (NET) Act. After the software industry lost $13.2 billion to pirates in 1997, this legislation imposed criminal liability for individuals who reproduce or distribute copies of copyrighted works. The language clarifies that reproduction or distribution can be accomplished by electronic means and that even if copyrighted products are distributed without charge, financial harm is experienced by the author of the software, as described in vignette 2 at the beginning of this chapter.

Because an individual does not personally benefit from the unauthorized distribution of software does not mean that it does not cost the developer, license or patent holder, and ultimately the honest consumer, more money. Software development companies have research and development costs to recover; the fewer units that are legally sold means that higher costs per unit must be passed on to honest consumers to make up for lost revenues. Consumers are penalized by **software piracy** and should support intellectual property rights in order to maintain a high level of product quality, integrity, and ongoing efforts in software development.

The Software Publishers Association is the principal industry trade organization working to prevent piracy. Other concerned groups are the Electronic Frontier Foundation and the World Intellectual Property Organization; both are striving to implement methods of securing copyrights while allowing an acceptable level of public access.

Another legal dichotomy in the electronic world is how to expand library and distance learning over the Internet without compromising copyrights. The Digital Copyright Clarification and Technology Education Act limits the scope of digital copyright infringement by allowing distance learning exemptions. This act addresses some of the shortfalls of the NET act, such as the inherent conflict with the fair use doctrine and the concept of contributory infringement. While the act provides civil liability for the "circumvention, removal, alteration, or falsification of copyright management information," it also provides that "individuals other than the author or owner of a digital work may make incidental copies if the copying does not conflict with the exploitation of the work, and does not prejudice the legitimate interests of the author."

This is essentially applying the doctrine of fair use to digital works available over the Internet and allows for the limited copying of material in specific situations. For example, a teacher may reproduce a single copy of a digital work for classroom use or multiple copies if certain requirements are met.

Internet access providers are anxious to know how far the liability issue extends for violations of digital copyright law; under the current law there is no liability for a pirate who links his or her site to a party from which to download software. One answer is the Online Copyright Liability Limitation Act, which seeks to protect Internet access providers from liability for direct and vicarious violation under specific circumstances in which they have no control or knowledge of infringement. This act also limits the remedy for contributory infringement to injunctive relief for such providers; however, it does provide civil liability for knowing misrepresentation of material. Internet access providers must act responsibly and make efforts to police piracy; not necessarily because of threats of litigation but because it is in their best long-term interest to do so.

The Digital Millennium Copyright Act codifies for the first time how copyright applies in cyberspace. The bill, passed by the House in 1998:

- Reasserts copyright in cyberspace.
- Makes illegal most attempts to defeat anticopying technology.
- Requires the National Telecommunications and Information Administration to review the effect the bill would have on the free flow of information and make recommendations for any changes two years after it is signed into law.
- Lets companies and common citizens circumvent anticopying technology when necessary to make software or hardware compatible with other products, to conduct encryption research, or to keep personal information from being spread by Internet cookies or other copy-protection tools.
- Forbids excessive copying of databases, even when those databases contain information already in the public domain.

International Aspects

Copyright laws in the digital age are being challenged, and international agreements are needed. In 1996, the World Intellectual Property Organization began to discuss the need for copyright protection of intellectual property delivered on the Internet. More than 60 member countries were trying to bridge cultural and political differences and come up with an international treaty. Part of an agreement readied in 1998 is called the "database treaty," and its aim is to protect the investment of firms that collect and arrange information. This organization is continuously working on the many still-unresolved issues.

DOMAIN NAMES

There are two controversies concerning **domain names.** One is whether top-level domain names (similar to com, org, and gov) should be added and the other is the use of trademark names by companies for domain names that belong to other companies.

Network Solutions Inc.

At the heart of all the controversy is Network Solutions Inc. (NSI), which has been contracted by the U.S. government to assign domain addresses. Until 1998 NSI assigned domain names for several top levels: .com, .net, .mil, .gov, .edu, and .org. The United States, as well as the rest of the world, are subject to NSI domain names. European critics are ready to relieve the United States of that responsibility. Europe is weary of the United States assuming the right to direct Internet governance and effectively subjecting the Internet to U.S. law. On June 1, 1998, the monopoly of NSI over domain names ended. Instead, the company created a registration system that it shares with several other competing companies. This may cause the registration price to drop.

The Council of Registrars (CORE), a European private sector group, and the Global Internet Project, a U.S. private sector group, want to increase the number of top-level names. One of the objectives is to create an adult-only top-level name that will prevent pornographic material from getting into the hands of children.

Both CORE and the Global Internet Project have the desire to repair the trade name disputes over domain names. Companies are using trade names of other companies as their domain address to help attract traffic to their Web site. For example, DC Comics is suing Brainiac Services Inc. for using one of their comic book names, Brainiac. Private sector groups will have to resolve this issue in the future before more lawsuits begin to surface. Major disputes involved the international scene, since the same corporate name may be used in different countries by different corporations.

10.5 Free Speech, Internet Indecency, and Censorship

The emergence of the Internet and EC generated one of the most heated debates of our times—free speech versus government censorship. This section will cover the highlights of this debate and the related issue of spamming.

THE FREE SPEECH VERSUS CENSORSHIP ISSUE

Many surveys indicate that the issue of censorship is one of the most important issues of concern to Internet surfers (usually number one or number two). **Censorship** refers to government's attempt to control, in one way or another, the material broadcast on the Internet. Here are some of the major elements of the debate regarding this issue.

Defining Freedom of Speech[2]

The First Amendment of the Bill of Rights in the Constitution of the United States reads as follows:

> Congress shall make no law respecting an establishment of religion, or prohibiting the free exercise thereof; or abridging the freedom of speech, or of the press; or the right of the people peaceably to assemble, and to petition the government for a redress of grievances.

The United Nations Universal Declaration of Human Rights in 1948 defined what constitutes human rights for the citizens of the world. Article 19 of that document addresses the right to freedom of expression:

> Everyone has the right to freedom of opinion and expression; this right includes freedom to hold opinions without interference and to seek, receive, and impart information and ideas through any media and regardless of frontiers.

---

[2] The discussion here is based on Abrams (1998).

Theoretically, free speech is guaranteed on the Internet to the world's people. If only it were so simple.

The Internet: The Ultimate Medium for Free Speech

"Free speech" has often been dictated by the voices of the few, the rich, and the powerful. The voices of the many, the not-quite-so-rich, and the not-nearly-as-powerful have heretofore not been given equal due. The Internet changes this tradition by allowing many voices, many cultures, and many opinions equal exposure. The Internet has opened doors to freedom of speech that have never been accessible before. The goal of free speech for all has only tacitly been achieved in the past.

The Internet ultimate freedom has been challenged by many parents and government officials. It resulted in the passage of the Communications Decency Act (CDA), a bill that proposes restrictions on telecommunications in the United States, including the Internet. However, this bill was found unconstitutional since it contradicts the First Amendment cited earlier.

The Debate about Free Speech on the Internet

At a symposium on free speech in the information age, Parker Donham (1996) defined his own edict entitled "Donham's First Law of Censorship." This semiserious precept states: "Most citizens are implacably opposed to censorship in any form—except censorship of whatever they personally happen to find offensive."

Nothing could more accurately describe the free speech debate than that quotation. Everyone is fundamentally for the right to free speech; the issue resides in the limits to free speech, what the boundaries are, and how we should enforce them.

On one side of the argument are governments protective of their role in society, parents concerned about exposing their children to inappropriate Web pages and chat rooms, and federal agencies attempting to deal with illegal actions like terrorism, gambling, and money laundering. On the other side are citizen action groups desiring to protect every ounce of their freedom to speak, individuals concerned about their right to information on the Internet, and organizations seeking to empower the citizens of the earth.

All groups want nothing except what is best from their position. The disagreements deal with the exact methods selected to achieve their goals. The debate can become very heated indeed when attempts are made to enact these methods into law. Generally there are provisions in law for two cases that limit free speech: obscene material and a compelling government interest (Abrams 1998).

All is relatively clear until the term "indecency" is thrown into the mix. The CDA, signed as part of a major telecommunications bill in the United States on February 1, 1996, defines indecency as: "any comment, request, suggestion, proposal, image, or other communication that, in context, depicts or describes, in terms patently offensive as measured by contemporary community standards, sexual or excretory activities or organs." This definition of indecency and its interpretation in the CDA have been found unconstitutional. Thus, with this rejection of censorship, the public argument on the true purpose and legal interpretation of indecency and the CDA commenced. The major arguments for and against the CDA are summarized in Table 10.3. (pg. 358)

PROTECTING CHILDREN

One of the major points in the free speech versus censorship debate is the potential damage to children. Citizens are very concerned about children viewing inappropriate material, such as pornographic, offensive, hate, and other potentially dangerous material. Also, merchants solicit information from children about their parents and family.

TABLE 10.3 Pro and Con Arguments on the CDA

Pro CDA	*Con CDA*
The CDA is solely intended to protect children from "harmful" material on the Internet.	"Harmful" material is already restricted from children by the obscenity laws. And furthermore, there are clear judicial rulings on what is "harmful" to children as opposed to what is indecent. ("Harmful to children" terminology was removed from a draft version of the CDA and replaced with "indecency.")
Courts should rule on what is included in the "indecency" clause and what is not. They argue the court rulings would limit the scope of the "indecency" clause to harmful material exposed to children.	The judges that ruled the CDA unconstitutional argued that the language of the CDA left open the possibility of restricting content that had artistic, educational, and political merit.
The Internet is wide open to children who may unintentionally (or intentionally) come across indecent content.	The Internet is unlike broadcast media such as radio and television in that active use of the Internet must be made to encounter such indecent material.
There will be legal restrictions applied to the Internet in some form if the CDA is ultimately proven unconstitutional by the Supreme Court, just as there have been restrictions applied to every other communication medium that has evolved in the past. Why resist restrictions that will only make the world safer and better for you and your children?	Unnecessary legislation imposed onto such a dynamic new medium could kill the very heart and soul of the medium itself. Protecting children from the indecent portions of the Internet can be achieved without hindering free speech with unnecessary laws. Why write new laws when proper ones already exist? What happened to the "least restrictive means possible?"

Source: Abrams (1998), Table 19-1, p. 349.

There are three approaches regarding the protection of children from inappropriate material on the Internet. The first view is that no information should be held back and parents should be responsible for monitoring their own children. The second is that the government only can truly protect children from this material, and the last approach is to hold the Internet providers responsible for all the material and information they provide. These approaches can be implemented for any surfer, not just children.

Parents Governing Their Own Children

Some believe the parents need to take responsibility to monitor, teach, and control the material to which their children have access. They can simply advise children about what they can see and instruct them about merchants' questionnaires. Advocates of this approach do not want a government agency to interfere. They argue that government mandated filters are too broad and wide; an array of nonharmful speech—everything from the Quaker home page to the American Association of University Women—has been blocked by filtering programs. Information that can be checked out of the library cannot be accessed through the Internet in the same library. They further argue that there are already federal laws in place that give the Department of Justice power to arrest and charge those who deal in obscenity and child pornography.

Government Protecting the Children

Those who want the government to control the material children view believe that the job can only be done through legislation. They want to see legislation that will force libraries and schools to use blocking filters. President Bill Clinton has made a strong effort to have no offensive material on the Net accessible to children. Legislation is also being proposed that will make some information illegal to put on the Internet, like bomb-building procedures. More difficult to control is the information solicited by merchants about parents, their income level, and lifestyles.

Responsibility for the Internet Providers

America Online, in its attempts to take responsibility, is trying to build a medium that is friendly to consumers, safe for families, and affordable for everyone. They rely very much on their own members to self-police the system and bring to their attention things that violate the terms of service. Some of the material AOL's policy prohibits is hate speech or truly offensive speech. They have applied their policy in situations like a KKK site or a serial-killer Web site. Some believe that the Internet providers, like AOL, should be held legally liable for all the material they allow to be accessed.

Forcing Internet providers to be accountable   In January 1998, a prosecutor in Munich, Germany, caused CompuServe, which provides its global subscribers with access to the Internet, to shut down 200 of the Net's sex-related newsgroups because they violated German law. Since the firm had no technical way to restrict Internet content only in Germany, it was obliged to impose the same restrictions on all of its 4 million subscribers worldwide. Some organizations are threatening to sue service providers for defamation or obscenity if they do not clean up their act. These watch groups believe that Internet providers can no longer be willfully blind; they are going to have to take responsibility for the services they provide.

Legal Perspectives in the United States

When the CDA was declared unconstitutional, both sides of the debate agreed that controls are needed; but who has censorship responsibility or, in fact, authority will be disputed for years. Several bills are designed so they will not clash with the First Amendment yet will provide protection. Here are some EC-related examples:

- The Child Online Protection Act was enacted as part of the Internet Tax Freedom Act in July 1998. This law requires, among other things, that companies verify an adult's age before showing online material that is deemed "harmful to minors." Verification can be accomplished through a credit card number or access number. Included in the bill is a requirement for parental consent prior to collecting personal information from a minor. The language of the bill, however, is so restricting that the "Starr Report" on President Clinton would probably be censored and access limited to only the most savvy senators.
- Another legislation is the Family Friendly Internet Access Act, which would require access providers to offer screening software at the time of sign-up that would enable customers to filter out material deemed inappropriate for children. Most providers offer this feature now for competitive reasons rather than altruism.
- The Internet Protection Act seeks to limit state and federal regulation of the Internet and at the same time prohibit ISPs from providing accounts to sexually violent predators.
- The Internet School Filtering Act also attempts to limit access to inappropriate material by controlling federal funds and grants to schools and libraries. Schools must provide blocking software that restricts indecent and harmful material from minors. Of course, the danger is that a lot of good information is blocked out along with the material considered unacceptable, and the con-

trol is given to the government rather than the educators. Some of the filtering techniques include blacklists, which do not allow disapproved material; whitelists, which allow only approved sites; word blocking; and blocking entire areas that are deemed inappropriate.

CONTROLLING SPAMMING

Spamming refers to the practice of indiscriminate distribution of messages (for example, junk mail) without permission of the receiver and without consideration for the messages' appropriateness. One major piece of legislation addressing marketing practices in EC is the Electronic Mailbox Protection Act. The primary thrust of this law is that commercial speech is subject to government regulation, and secondly, that spamming, which causes significant harm, expense, and annoyance, should be controlled.

Spam comprised 30 percent of all mail sent on America Online. This volume significantly impairs an already limited bandwidth slowing the Internet in general and, in some cases, shutting ISPs down completely. This act requires those sending spam to identify it as advertising, to indicate the name of the sender prominently, and to include valid routing information. Recipients may waive the right to receive such information. Also, ISPs would be required to offer spam-blocking software, and recipients of spam would have the right to request termination of future spam from the same sender and to bring civil action if necessary. (Now spam is less than 10 percent.)

A few other bills focused on similar objectives are the Unsolicited Commercial Electronic Mail Act, which requires all unsolicited e-mail to start with the word "advertisement" and include the name, address, and telephone number of the sender. The Netizens Protection Act seeks to expand the coverage of the Telephone Consumer Protection Act to include e-mail, unless there is a preexisting relationship between the sender and the receiver or the receiver requests the e-mail.

Spamming costs consumers time and money, yet to date there is no legal remedy available for such electronic harassment and bombardment of unsolicited advertisement. Screening software and the delete key may be an individual's best tools in self-defense on the electronic advertisement war front. Although consumers have rights that govern traditional means of advertising, such as the telephone, radio, and print, new technologies require new laws that inherently lag behind the applications, as it did with each of the aforementioned inventions.

How to Cut Spamming

Although companies are defenseless if spammers use their domain to falsify return addresses or transmit junk e-mail, there are a few things they (and "netizens") can do:

- Tell users not to validate their addresses by answering spam requests for replies if they want to be taken off mailing lists.
- Disable the relay feature on mail servers so mail cannot be bounced off the server.
- Delete spam and forget it—it is a fact of life and not worth wasting time over.

Several software packages can help you to fight spamming. For example, message filters have been invented to put "a ban on spam." Web sites such as www.getlost.com and www.junkbusters.com provides free software that block unwanted banner ads and protect you from cookies and other threats. America Online, for example, is using collaborative filtering technologies, also known as "agent technologies." The agent resides on your PC and watches what you view and where. This way the agent "learns" you and will filter material that is pushed to you by content providers, keeping only the items that match material you have seen before.

10.6 Taxation and Encryption Policies

In this section we touch upon two controversial issues in EC: taxation and encryption policy. These issues are extremely important since they are related to global EC as well as to fairness in competition, when EC competes with offline marketing channels and conventional mail orders where taxes are paid.

TAXATION POLICIES

Taxing EC is an important issue due to the large volume of trade forecasted for the next decade. Cities, states, and countries all want a piece of the pie.

The Taxation Exemption Debate

The Internet Tax Freedom Act passed the U.S. Senate on October 8, 1998, as bill S442. This act promotes EC through tax incentives by barring any new state or local sales taxes on Internet transactions during the next three years. Note: This law deals only with sales tax and not with federal or state income tax that Internet companies must pay. This act also carried an amendment known as the Children's Online Privacy Protection Act. This was added in an effort to prevent extension of tax benefits to pornographers.

The act also creates a special commission to study Internet taxation issues and recommend new policies to the president. This panel is required to submit an initial report by spring 2000. In the meantime, existing Internet taxes, taxes on mail-order goods, and other excise taxes already in place will remain unaffected.

Electronic commerce transactions are multiplying at an exponential rate, and the $500 billion to $3000 billion forecasted for 2003 means lots of potential sales tax. The taxation issues that involve 30,000 state and local jurisdictions in the United States, in addition to the innumerable international jurisdictions, will add numerous volumes to an already complex tax code. Applying existing law to new mediums of exchange is far more difficult than ever imagined. The global nature of business today suggests that cyberspace be considered a distinct tax zone unto itself with unique rules and considerations befitting the stature of the environment. This is in fact what has occurred. The three-year moratorium on taxation of Internet transactions is a fine temporary solution where no precedent exists; however, longer-range strategies must be developed quickly. Here are some complicating factors to consider: Several tax jurisdictions may be involved in a single transaction, not only on a domestic level but internationally. The implications of such involvement are tremendous; the identity of the parties involved and transaction verification is frequently a problem.

Non-EC industries feel that the Internet businesses must pay their fair share of the tax bill for the nation's social and physical infrastructure. They feel that the Internet industries are not pulling their own weight. These companies are screaming that the same situation exists in the mail-order business and that there are sufficient parallels to warrant similar legal considerations. In fact, in many states EC has already been treated the same as mail-order businesses. Others suggest using the established sales tax laws. "You've got a tax structure in place—it's called sales tax," said Bill McKiernan, chairman and CEO of software.net. "Just apply that to Internet transactions."

The probabilities for tax evasion are also potentially large. Tax havens and offshore banking facilities will become more accessible. Singapore has passed a law to establish itself as a legally and financially safe haven for the rest of the world for the EC industry, similar to Swiss banks' role in the financial industry.

There is debate about whether tax policies should promote businesses on the Information Superhighway or preserve those on Main Street. Many argue it is not the government's role to protect older industries that are threatened by emerging technologies. Laws were not enacted to protect blacksmiths when the automobile became popular.

Arguments exist concerning tax-free policies, especially if they last three years, that they are giving online businesses an unfair advantage. For instance, some argue that Internet phone services should be exempt from paying access charges to local telephone companies for use of their networks. In their effort to avoid sales taxes, Internet merchants like to point to the difficulty of tracking who should be paid what. The opposition argues that the same is true for telephone transactions, so existing laws should suffice. The same opposition asks, "Should EC business be allowed to operate without taxing consumers while regular telephone companies cannot?"

Proposed Taxation Solutions in the United States

The National Governors' Association, the National League of Cities, and the U.S. Conference of Mayors fought the Tax Free Bill for the Internet. The National Governors' Association estimates state governments now lose $3 billion to $4 billion a year on difficult-to-control, mail-order sales to out-of-state merchants. They figure that more will be lost through EC sales and are suggesting that the IRS might "come to the rescue" with a single and simplified national sales tax. That would reduce 30,000 different tax codes to "no more than 50." Net sales would be taxed at the same rate as mail-order or Main Street transactions. While states could set their one rate, each sale could be taxed only once. As stated, the details of Net taxation would be settled by a panel of industry and government officials that would send its recommendation to Congress by 2000.

The questions to be considered and answered relate to physical presence and taxing jurisdictions. International implications of expatriots and common carrier obligations versus communications in defining the taxability of the Internet are other gray areas requiring legal attention. Is the Internet a forum for the exchange of goods and services, a transfer agent of goods and services, or merely a telecommunications industry? How do these issues translate to the access providers? There are varying degrees of liability, responsibility, and taxable interests from each viewpoint, and thus far, the courts have only agreed to examine each issue on a case-by-case basis. Eventually, cyberlaw taxation policy will truly be greater than the sum of its parts; the legislative building blocks are slowly meshing with commercial interests and this will be critical to success.

ENCRYPTION POLICY

The 128-Bit Encryption Debate

Encryption technology makes EC secure and provides protection for copyrights. On September 23, 1998, the U.S. government allowed Compaq Corporation to export a 128-bit public key encryption for the banking industry in support of EC. This is a milestone for the encryption industry. Export 128-bit encryption is 3.09×10 to the 26th power times more difficult to decipher than the preceding legally exportable technology. For the past 20 years there was a limitation on exported encryption devices of 56-bit codes, but recent legislation allows 128-bit codes in specific circumstances, thus paving the way for the Compaq permit. The old government policies handicapped the field of encryption. A conflict is erupting between secure EC and the government's legal requirements.

Data Encryption Standard

Data encryption standard (DES) is a published federal encryption standard created to protect unclassified computer data and communications. The DES standard uses 56-bit keys and has been incorporated into industry and international standards. Many claim that the standard is too insecure for today's EC trade. The government believes that widespread access to 128-bit encryption technology will endanger national security and refuses to license any secure encryption product for export unless it utilizes "key recovery," law enforcement code for the ability of third parties (not originally intended to receive the message) to easily decrypt information. The technology is not available and the industry is unable to deliver this combination. Systems today use public and private keys; the FBI wants two private keys instead of one. Here are the positions of both sides:

Law Enforcement's Plea. Robert Litt, a Department of Justice attorney responsible for handling encryption issues, said, that "law enforcement's position has been consistently misrepresented and misunderstood." He believes that people think that the FBI wants to ban all encryption and that the CIA can crack any code. One conflict is the FBI's insistence on security throughout the process. Cryptographers would follow an audit trail to ensure that keys haven't been released improperly; however, law enforcement does not trust that process. Robert Litt continues, "If encryption is not controlled now, chances are that when the technology is truly widespread, law enforcement will press for other compromises to handle surveillance powers in other media."

First Amendment Right. In an attempt to legalize export encryption technology, some individuals argue software is speech and must be protected under the First Amendment. Their argument is that today's encryption technology makes it virtually impossible to break the code and is not a national security risk. Technology can encrypt so thoroughly that every computer on earth working in tandem would take trillions of years to decode it.

Business View. The Electronic Frontier Foundation (EFF) has a contest once a year to see who can crack a DES code the fastest and the cheapest. In 1998, the winner spent only $250,000 and did it in less than three days. The EFF efforts are attempting to reveal the insecurity of the current standard. They want growth in the industry, which they believe can only be delivered with more security. The EFF believes that software, networked communications, and cryptography industries are suffering. Because of the government's constraints, tests cannot be written and performed, preventing Internet businesses from growing faster.

Legal Perspectives

The legal issue of encryption techniques and applications must be viewed from two sides. National security demands a secure protocol for encryption codes, the limits of which are made public, and control over exports of encryption codes, devices, and techniques. Individual privacy and civil liberties dictate a large degree of freedom and discretion in communications and protection from unwarranted censorship or restriction from the government. Thus, legal policy toward security and encryption seeks to promote secure EC, since that is a key for public faith in online transactions, while concurrently regulating the sale, export, and extent of encrypting capability.

According to Ira Magaziner, the former White House chief advisor on Internet issues, "We can expect to see strong controls on encryption for some time." Measures such as the Secure Public Networks Act show that moderate regulation can accomplish seemingly conflicting goals of security through encryption and the public's right to free trade. This bill legalizes the use of encryption technology while prohibiting the government from accessing decrypted information without warrant or lawful authority. It criminalizes the use of encryption in some circumstances, such as during the commission of a crime. The bill also prohibits the federal government from mandating the use of encryption standards in the private sector, other than for interaction with the federal government.

One last proposal worth mentioning is the Security and Freedom through Encryption (SAFE) Act. This act seeks wider individual freedom by authorizing the domestic use and sale in interstate commerce of any encryption regardless of strength. It prohibits the federal or state creation of mandatory escrow systems for encryption keys as a precondition for licensing or certification except for law enforcement purposes. This act opens the door to uncontrolled exports of encryption technology, a step that may prove counterproductive at today's level of electronic trade and the existing trade gaps.

10.7 Other Legal Issues: Contracts, Gambling, and More

Privacy, intellectual property, and censorship receive a great deal of publicity because consumers easily understand them. However, there are several other legal issues related to EC. Here are some examples:

- What are the rules of electronic contracting, and whose jurisdiction prevails when buyers, brokers, and sellers are in different states and/or countries?
- How can gambling be controlled on the Internet? Gambling is legal in Nevada and other states. How can the winner's taxes be collected?
- When are electronic documents admissible evidence in courts of law? What do you do if they are not?
- Time and place can carry different dates for buyers and sellers when they are across the ocean. For example, an electronic document signed in Japan on January 5 may have the date January 4 in Los Angeles; which date is legal?
- Is a digital signature legal? (Refer to www.oecd.org.)
- The use of multiple networks and trading partners makes the documentation of responsibility difficult. How is such a problem overcome?
- Liability for errors, malfunction of software, or theft and fraudulent use of data may be difficult to prove. How is such liability determined?
- What is considered misrepresentation? Where should you take legal action against misrepresentation?
- Much of the law hinges on the physical location of files and data. With distributed databases and replication of databases, it is difficult to say exactly where the data are stored at a given time. How is electronic storage related to existing legalities?
- Online corporate reports are difficult to audit since they can be changed frequently and auditors may not have sufficient time to perform with due diligence. There are no established auditing standards. How should such auditing be conducted and what legal value does it have?
- How can money laundering be prevented when the value of the money is in the form of a smart card. (Japan limits the value of money on a smart card to about $5,000; other countries such as Singapore and Hong Kong set even lower limits.)
- Which government has jurisdiction over an EC transaction (Alberts et al. 1998)?
- Can a company link into a Web site without permission (see Application Case 10.3)?

APPLICATION CASE 10.3

Linking to Your Web Site

On April 28, 1998, Ticketmaster Corporation filed a suit against Microsoft charging that Microsoft's link to Ticketmaster's Web site infringes on its name and trademark by its mere presence on the Microsoft site. Meanwhile, Ticketmaster, claiming losses due to the linking, used a special computer code to block users from linking to its site from certain sites. Should Ticketmaster win, it may create a major problem for companies attempting to get permission to link (some Web sites have thousands of links) to other sites. Microsoft gave the service free to Ticketmaster. Microsoft refers their customers who visit their site, which provides entertainment information about different cities (http://entertainment.sidewalk. msn.com) to Ticketmaster.

Here is something to think about. If you place a famous name on your site, it will attract search engines and you can increase the visits to your site. If it is not illegal, is it ethical? (As the book was going to press, Microsoft agreed to sell its disputed "sidewalk" to Ticketmaster.)

Of the many issues, we will discuss only the first two here. For more information refer to Adam (1998).

ELECTRONIC CONTRACTS

A legally binding contract requires a few basic elements: offer, acceptance, and consideration. However, these requirements are difficult to establish when the human element in the processing of the transaction is removed and the contracting is performed electronically.

The Uniform Electronic Transactions Act seeks to extend existing provisions for contract law to cyberlaw by establishing uniform and consistent definitions to electronic records, digital signatures, and other electronic communications. This act is a procedural act that provides the means to effectuate transactions accomplished through an electronic medium. The language purposefully refrains from addressing questions of substantive law, leaving this to the scope of the Uniform Commercial Code (UCC).

The UCC is a comprehensive law regarding business conduct. The proposed amendment to the UCC is Article 2B, which is also designed to build upon existing law by providing a government code that supports existing and future electronic technologies in the exchange of goods or of services. This law was approved in 1999 and enactment by the states is expected in 2000. This law is one of the more significant EC legal developments.

The framework of common law provides clear language to address the issues of offer and acceptance required for formation of a contract. An online offer is manifested through electronic communication and describes the goods or services that will be delivered upon acceptance of terms. It was previously required that acceptance be made in an identical manner in which the offer was made; however, the UCC in section 2-206 now allows acceptance of an offer in any "reasonable manner." Therefore, an online offer may be accepted in a variety of ways. Agreements may be in effect and enforceable, even if the terms are not known until after the purchase, as illustrated in the following types of transactions.

Shrink-wrap agreements, or box top licenses, appear in or on the package containing the software. The user is bound to the license by opening the package even though he or she has not yet used the product or even read the agreement. This has been a point of contention for some time. The court felt that information such as warranties or handling instructions would provide more benefit to the consumer given the limited space available on the exterior of the package. The *ProcCD versus Zeidenberg* case supported the validity of shrink-wrap agreements when the court ruled in favor of the plaintiff, ProCD.

Click-wrap contracts are an extension of this ruling and are contracts derived entirely over the Internet. The software vendor offers to sell or license the use of the software according to the terms accompanying the software. The buyer agrees to be bound by the terms based on certain conduct; usually that conduct is retaining the product for a sufficient time to review the terms and return the software if unacceptable. In the case of *Hotmail Corporation versus Van's Money Pie Inc., et al.*, the U.S. District Court for the Northern District of California held that the defendants, Van's Money Pie, Inc., were bound to the terms of the agreement by clicking on the button "I agree." In this case the plaintiff, Hotmail, required customers to agree to their terms of service, which expressly prohibited the use of Hotmail e-mail accounts for the purpose of sending spam, or unsolicited e-mail. Users agree to these terms by a click-wrap agreement that is initiated after the consumer has an opportunity to review the terms of service. The agreement is performed and effected by simply clicking on a box that says "I agree."

The defendants, Van's Money Pie, sent e-mail advertising pornography to thousands of users after falsifying the return address, mark, and domain name to indicate that the spam was sent by Hotmail. Hotmail was inundated with complaints and responses from subscribers that effectively impaired their ability to conduct business by *(a)* using an inordinate amount of finite computer space, *(b)* delaying subscribers' ability to transmit legitimate e-mail, *(c)* tying up personnel resources to direct and respond to the complaints, and *(d)* damaged the reputation and goodwill of Hotmail.

Based on the above, Hotmail was successful in obtaining an injunction for breach of contract. However, the true enforceability of click-wrap agreements specifically was never really tested as the judge indicated that the evidence presented was sufficient to determine breach of the terms that were so obviously accepted by the defendants.

Intelligent Agents. Article 2B also makes clear that contracts can be performed even where no human involvement is present. It states: "*(a)* operations of one or more electronic agents which confirm the existence of a contract or indicate agreement, form a contract even if no individual was aware of or reviewed the actions or results. *(b)* In automated transactions, the following rules apply: (1) A contract may be formed by the interaction of electronic agents. A contract is formed if the interaction results in the electronic agents engaging in operations that confirm the existence of a contract or indicate agreement. The terms of the contract are determined under section 2B-209(b). (2) A contract may be formed by the interaction of an individual and an electronic agent." Article 2B also addresses language, timing, payments, forms, and other nuances particular to EC that are not currently covered in the existing UCC. Many solutions have not withstood the scrutiny of legal challenges in a court of law but as common law has developed from case law; cyberlaw must be tested and validated as technology is introduced and applications challenged.

GAMBLING

Gaming commissions have had a tough time regulating gambling laws in Nevada, on Indian reservations, on offshore casinos, in sport bars, and other places where gambling is legal. Technology makes this effort all the more difficult to monitor and enforce since the individuals abusing the rules have at least the same level of sophistication available as the law enforcement officials; in many cases they are even better equipped. The ease and risk of online wagering is evidenced by many recent cases of individuals losing their life savings without understanding the implications of what they are doing with their home PC.

The Internet Gambling Prohibition Act of 1998 was established to make online wagering illegal except for minimal amounts. This act provides criminal and civil remedies against individuals making, or in the business of, online betting or wagering. Additionally, it gives U.S. district courts original and exclusive jurisdiction to prevent and restrain violations and subjects computer service providers to the duties of common carriers. The impact of this act is to make ISPs "somewhat" liable for illegal currency movements and reportable transactions requiring documentation by the carriers.

Online casinos have all of the inherent dangers of physical gaming houses with the added risk of accessibility by minors or individuals of diminished capacity who may financially injure themselves without the constraints otherwise found in a physical environment. As is the case with most issues in cyberspace, self-regulation may be the best policy. Methods of wagering can be found all over the Internet. For example, at the World Sports Exchange (www.wsex.com), they advertise: "If you can use a mouse, you can place a wager." Ostensibly located in Antigua where gaming is legal, not only have they shown the ease of wagering but they have made it their slogan. Here an account can be established by wiring or electronically transferring funds, even sending a check will establish an electronic gaming account. This account is used to fund a variety of available wagers on all types of sporting events that can be viewed and effected online. The issue is that anyone that travels physically to Nevada or Antigua can play there legally. But what about electronic travel from places where gambling is illegal? Related to the control of gambling is the tax on winners' profits. Because it is now illegal to tax Internet transactions, should taxes be paid on electronic winnings?

10.8   Consumer and Seller Protection in EC

When buyers and sellers cannot see each other, and may even be in different countries, there is a chance that dishonest people might commit all types of fraud and other crimes over the Internet. During the first few years of EC we witnessed many of these, ranging from the creation of a virtual bank that disappeared together with the investors' deposits to manipulating stocks on the Internet. This section is divided into the following parts: fraud, consumer protection, seller's protection, and automatic authentication.

FRAUD ON THE INTERNET

Internet fraud and its sophistication have grown as much and even faster than the Internet itself, as we see in the following examples.

Online Auction Fraud. The majority (68%) of complaints registered at the National Consumers League (of Washington, DC) deals with auctions. Money is collected but the goods are not satisfactory, or even not delivered.

Internet Stocks Fraud. In fall 1998, the Securities and Exchange Commission (SEC) brought charges against 44 companies and individuals who illegally promoted stocks on computer bulletin boards, online newsletters, and investment Web sites (details on both settled and pending cases are at www.sec.gov). In most cases, stock pro-

How David Lee Was Cheated by an International "Investment" Group

David Lee, a 41-year-old Hong Kong resident, replied to an advertisement in a respected business magazine that offered him free investment advice. When he replied, he received impressive brochures and a telephone sales speech. Then, he was directed to the Web site of Equity Mutual Trust (Equity) where he was able to track the impressive daily performance of a fund that listed offices in London, Switzerland, and Belize. From that Web site he was linked to sister funds and business partners. He monitored what he believed were independent Web sites that provided high ratings on the funds. Finally, he was directed to read about Equity and its funds in the respected *International Herald Tribune*'s Internet edition items, which appeared as news items but were actually advertisements. Convinced that he would receive good short-term gains, he mailed US$16,000, instructing Equity to invest in the Grand Financial Fund. Soon he grew suspicious when letters from Equity came from different countries, telephone calls and e-mails were not answered on time, and the daily Internet listings dried up.

When David wanted to sell, he was advised to increase his investment and shift to a Canadian company, Mit-tec, allegedly a Y2K bug troubleshooter. The Web site he was directed to looked fantastic. But David was careful. He contacted the financial authorities in the Turks and Caicos Islands—where Equity was based at that time—and was referred to the British police.

Soon he learned that chances were slim that he would ever see his money again. Furthermore, he learned that several thousand victims paid billions of dollars to Equity. Most of the victims live in Hong Kong, Singapore, and other Asian countries. Several said that the most convincing information came from the Web sites, including the "independent" Web site that rated Equity and its funds.

Source: Based on a story in the *South China Morning Post* (Hong Kong), May 21, 1999.

moters falsely spread positive rumors about the prospects of the companies they touted. In other cases, the information provided might have been true, but the promoters did not disclose that they were paid to talk up the companies. Stock promoters specifically target small investors who are lured to the promise of fast profit.

Here is a typical example. In November 1996, a federal judge agreed to freeze the assets of the chairman of a little company, called SEXI (Systems of Excellence), and the proprietors of an Internet electronic newsletter, called SGA Goldstar. The latter illegally received SEXI stocks in exchange for promoting the stock to unwary investors. As a result, SEXI stock jumped from $0.25 to $4.75, at which time the proprietors dumped the shares (a "pump-and-dump" scheme). Cases like this, as well as ones involving nonregistered securities, are likely to increase because of the popularity of the Internet.

Other Financial Fraud. Stocks are only one of many areas where swindlers are active. Other areas include selling bogus investments, phantom business opportunities, and other schemes. Financial criminals have access to far more people, mainly due to the availability of e-mail. An example of a multibillion dollar international fraud is provided in Application Case 10.4.

Other Fraud in EC. Many nonfinancial types of fraud exist on the Internet. For example, customers may receive poor-quality products and services, may not get products in time, may be asked to pay for things they assume will be paid for by sellers, and much more.

The FTC Consumer Alerts

The FTC provides a list of 12 scams labelled the "dirty dozen" (the name of a famous movie) most likely to arrive by bulk e-mail (www.ftc.gov/bcp/conline/pubs/alerts/doznalrt.htm, July 1998, with examples in each category). They are:

1. **Business opportunities**—easy to start a business that will bring you a fortune. Also illegal pyramid schemes are being offered.
2. **Bulk mail solicitors**—selling you lists of e-mail addresses. If you use them you usually violate the terms of service of your ISP.
3. **Chain letters**—you are asked to send money to some people and your name is placed on a list. This is usually illegal to do.
4. **Work-at-home schemes**—it is usually worthless and costs you more money than you will make.
5. **Health and diet schemes**—you usually get worthless products that do not work.
6. **Effortless income**—do not believe these "easy to make money" opportunities. They will take your money.
7. **Free goods**—you pay to join a club and recruit others. It is usually an illegal pyramid scheme.
8. **Investment opportunities**—do not believe in investment with "no risk" and "high return." There are many scams to watch.
9. **Cable descrambler kits**—it usually does not work, and it is illegal.
10. **Guaranteed loans or credit on easy terms**—you usually pay application fees and then are turned down.
11. **Credit repair**—again, you pay a service fee but get no repair.
12. **Vacation prize promotions**—these electronic certificates are usually scams. You will be asked to upgrade and it will cost you a lot.

There are several ways buyers can be protected against EC fraud. The major methods are described next.

BUYER PROTECTION

Buyer protection is critical to the success of any commerce, especially electronic, where buyers do not see the sellers (*Internet World*, March 1997). Tips for safe electronic shopping include the following:

1. Look for reliable brand names at sites like Wal-Mart Online, Disney Online, and Amazon.com. and make sure that you enter the real Web site of these companies.
2. Search any unfamiliar site for address, telephone and fax numbers. Call up and quiz a person about the sellers.
3. Check the seller with the local chamber of commerce, Better Business Bureau (www.bbbonline.org), or TRUSTe, as described later.
4. Investigate how secure the seller's site is and how well it is organized.
5. Examine the money-back guarantees, warranties, and service agreements.
6. Compare prices to those in regular stores; too-low prices may be too good to be true.
7. Ask friends what they know. Find testimonials and endorsements (for examples go to www.virtualemporium.com).
8. Find out what you can do in case of a dispute.
9. Consult the National Fraud Information Center (http://nfic.inter.net/nfic).
10. Check www.consumerworld.org. There you will find many useful resources.
11. Do not forget that you have shopper's rights (see Application Case 10.5).

APPLICATION CASE 10.5

Internet Shopping Rights

Although the Web offers new ways to shop, you can still benefit from legal protections developed for shopping by telephone, mail, and other means. The two most important consumer protection laws for online shopping come from the U.S. government: the Mail/Telephone Order Rule and the Fair Credit Billing Act.

Mail/Telephone (e-mail) Order Rule. Sellers must deliver your goods within certain time periods or they can face penalties from the FTC. If the seller advertises or tells you a delivery date before you purchase, it must deliver by that date.

If the seller does not give you a delivery date, it must deliver within 30 days after receiving your order. If the seller cannot deliver by the required date, it must give you notice before that date, so you can choose either to cancel your order and receive a full and prompt refund or to permit the seller to deliver at a later date. If delivery problems continue, look up the resources below for additional rights and how to make a complaint.

Fair Credit Billing Act. Using your credit card on the Web is like using it at a store. The Fair Credit Billing Act gives you certain rights if there is an error or dispute relating to your bill. If there is an error on your statement, you can withhold payment for the disputed amount while you notify the creditor.

You can withhold payment when your bill contains a charge for the wrong amount, for items you returned or did not accept, or for items not delivered as agreed. Notify the creditor of the error promptly, no later than 60 days after the first bill on which the error appeared. Put it in writing. Describe the error clearly and include your name, address, and credit card number. After you send the notice, the creditor must give written acknowledgment within 30 days and must resolve the error within 90 days.

New Payment Methods: A Word of Caution. While consumer protections for traditional credit cards are well established, the protections for those who use new forms of "digital payment," "digital cash," and the like are unclear. Some resemble credit cards; others resemble ATM cards; still others are brand-new forms of payment. Look up the resources below for the latest information on new regulations that may be developed to protect consumers using these payment methods.

RESOURCES FOR FURTHER INFORMATION

- Federal Trade Commission: http://www.ftc.gov; click on "complaint form"; Tel: (202) 382-4357
- Abusive e-mail: Forward the mail to: uce@fte.gov
- National Fraud Information Center: consult with http://nfic.inter.net/nfic
- Consumer Information Center: examine http://www.pueblo.gsa.gov; Tel: (729) 948-4000
- Direct Market Association: call Tel: (202) 347-1222 for advice
- Internet Fraud Complaint Center: This is a new unit established at the FBI. It registers complaints online from consumers.

Disclaimer: This is general information on certain consumer rights. It is not legal advice on how any particular individual should proceed. If you want legal advice, consult an attorney.

Source: Based on L. Rose, "Internet Shopping Rights," *Internet Shopper* (Spring 1997), p. 104.

THIRD-PARTY SERVICES

Several public organizations as well as private companies attempt to protect consumers. Following are just a few examples:

TRUSTe's "Trustmark"

TRUSTe is a nonprofit group whose mission is to build user's trust and confidence in the Internet by promoting the policies of disclosure and informed consent. Through TRUSTe's program, members can add value and increase consumer confidence in online transactions by displaying the TRUSTe Advertising Affiliate Trustmark to identify sites that have agreed to comply with responsible information-gathering guidelines. Licensing fees of Trustmark range from $500 to $5,000 depending on the size of the online organization and the sensitivity of the information it is collecting. In addition, the TRUSTe Web site provides a "privacy policy wizard," which is aimed at helping companies readily create their own privacy policies.

The program is voluntary. By mid-1998, 130 prominent Web sites had signed on as TRUSTe participants, including AT&T, CyberCash, Excite, IBM, America Online, Buena Vista Internet Group, CNET, GeoCities, Infoseek, Lycos, Netscape, The New York Times, and Yahoo. The number of members in the program has increased dramatically. However, there still seems to be fear that signing with TRUSTe could expose firms to litigation from third parties if they fail to live up to the letter of the TRUSTe pact, and it is most likely to deter some companies from signing.

Better Business Bureau (BBB)

The BBB, a private nonprofit organization supported largely by membership, provides reports on business firms that is helpful to consumers before making a purchase. The BBB responds to millions of such inquiries each year. They have a similar program to TRUSTe's Trustmark for EC. Companies that meet the BBBOnLine Standards exhibit a BBBOnLine seal on their Web sites. The seal indicates that they "care" about their customers. Consumers are able to click on the BBBOnLine seal and instantly get a BBB report on the participating company.

Online Privacy Alliance

The Online Privacy Alliance is a diverse group of corporations and associations who lead and support self-regulatory initiatives that create an environment of trust and foster the protection of individuals' privacy online. They have guidelines for privacy policies, enforcement of self-regulation, and children's online activities. Major members are AT&T, Bell Atlantic, Compaq, Dell, IBM, Microsoft, NETCOM, Time Warner, and Yahoo. The Online Privacy Alliance supports the third-party enforcement programs, such as the TRUSTe and BBB programs. This is because these programs award an identifiable symbol to signify to consumers that the owner or operator of a Web site, online service, or other online area has adopted a privacy policy that includes the elements articulated by the Online Privacy Alliance.

AUTHENTICATION AND BIOMETRIC CONTROLS

In cyberspace, buyers and sellers do not see each other. Even when a videoconferencing is used, the authenticity of the person you are dealing with must be verified, unless you have dealt with the person before. If we can be assured of the identity of the person on the other end of the line, we can imagine improved and new EC applications:

- Students will be able to take exams online from any place, any time, without the need for proctors.
- Fraud recipients of government entitlements and other payments will be reduced to a bare minimum.
- Buyers will be assured who the sellers are and sellers will know who the buyers are with a very high degree of confidence.
- Arrangements can be made that only authorized people in companies can place (or receive) purchasing orders.
- Interviews for employment, possible marriages, and other matching applications will be accurate since it will be almost impossible for imposters to represent other people.
- Trust in your partners and in EC in general will increase significantly.

The solution for such authentication is provided by information technologies known as biometric controls for accessing an EC network.

Biometric controls provide access procedures that match every valid user with a unique user identifier (UID). They also provide an authentication method to verify that users requesting access to the computer system are really who they claim to be. A UID can be accomplished in one or more of the following ways:

- Provide something only the user *knows*, such as a password.
- Present something only the user *has*, for example, a smart card or a token.
- Identify something only the user *is*, such as a signature, voice, fingerprint, or retinal (eye) scan. It is implemented by biometric controls.

A *biometric control* is defined as an "automated method of verifying the identity of a person, based on physiological or behavioral characteristics" (Forte 1998). The most common biometrics are the following.

- *Face geometry (photo).* The computer takes a picture of your face and matches it with a prestored picture. In 1998, this method was successful in correctly identifying users except in cases of identical twins. (e.g., www.mr-payroll.com).
- *Fingerprints (fingerscan).* Each time a user wants access, matching a fingerprint against a template containing the authorized person's fingerprint identifies him or her.
- *Hand geometry.* Similar to fingerprints except the verifier uses a television-like camera to take a picture of the user's hand. Certain characteristics of the hand (e.g., finger length and thickness) are electronically compared against the information stored in the computer.
- *Blood vessel pattern in the retina of a person's eye.* A match is attempted between the pattern of the blood vessels in the retina that is being scanned and a prestored picture of the retina.
- *Voice (voiceprint).* A match is attempted between the user's voice and the voice pattern stored on templates.
- *Signature.* Signatures are matched against the prestored authentic signature. This method can supplement a photo-card ID system.
- *Keystroke dynamics.* A match of the person's keyboard pressure and speed against prestored information.
- *Others.* Several other methods exist such as facial thermography, using a PIN, and iris scan.

These methods have different levels of advantages and disadvantages measured on four characteristics (Figure 10.2). The closer you are to the center of the figure, the lower the value of the characteristics is. Compare your favorable method against the ideal one. Note that an *iris scan* is both very accurate and inexpensive.

SELLERS' PROTECTION

The Internet makes fraud by customers easier because of the ease of anonymity. Sellers must be protected against:

- Dealing with customers that deny that they placed an order.
- Customers downloading copyrighted software and/or knowledge and selling it to others.
- Being properly paid for products and services provided.
- Use of their names by others.

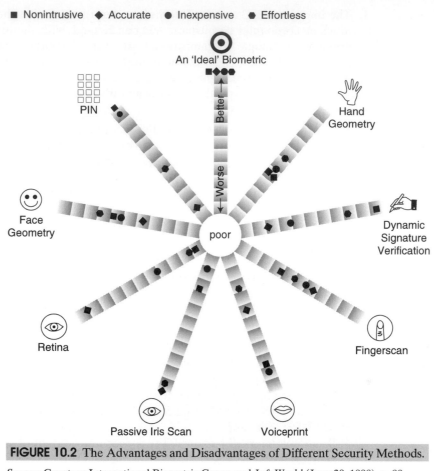

■ Nonintrusive ◆ Accurate ● Inexpensive ● Effortless

An 'Ideal' Biometric

PIN

Hand
Geometry

Better

Worse

Face
Geometry

poor

Dynamic
Signature
Verification

Retina

Fingerscan

Passive Iris Scan

Voiceprint

FIGURE 10.2 The Advantages and Disadvantages of Different Security Methods.

Source: Courtesy International Biometric Group and *InfoWorld* (June 29, 1998), p. 88.
PIN = Password and Personal Information Number

- Use of their unique words and phrases, names and slogans, and their Web address (trademark protection).

For a discussion of the issue see Swisher (1998). Also, third-party escrow and trust companies help to prevent fraud against both buyers and sellers.

10.9 Managerial Issues

Management attention must be directed to public policy issues such as privacy and legal and consumer protection surrounding EC. Here are some points to consider:

1. Multinational corporations face different cultures in the different countries in which they are doing business. What might be ethical in country A may be unethical in country B. Therefore, it is essential to develop a country-specific ethics code in addition to a corporate-wide one. Also, managers should realize that in some countries there is little legislation specifically concerned with computers and data.

2. Issues of privacy, ethics, and so on may seem to be tangential to running a business, but ignoring them may hinder the operation of many organizations. Privacy protection can cut into profits (Hildebrand 1996).

3. The impacts of EC and the Internet can be so strong that the entire manner in which companies do business will be changed, with significant impacts on procedures, people, organizational structure, management, and business processes. (Read "The Economic and Social Impact of Electronic Commerce" at www.oecd.org/subject/e_commerce.)

4. The following are typical points for an ethics policy or code concerning privacy and other issues:
   - Decide whether you want to allow employees to set up their own Web pages on the company intranet. If you do, formulate a general idea of the role you want Web sites to play. This should guide you in developing a policy and providing employees with a rationale for that policy.
   - Your policy should address offensive content and graphics, as well as proprietary information.
   - Your policy should encourage employees to think about who should and who should not have access to information before they post it on the Web site.
   - Make sure your Web content policy is consistent with other company policies.
   - Don't be surprised if the policies you develop look a lot like simple rules of etiquette. They should.

5. The following are some useful Web warnings:
   - Have attorneys review your Web content.
   - Issue written policy guidelines about employee use of the Internet.
   - Don't use copyrighted trademarked material without permission.
   - Post disclaimers concerning content, such as sample code, that your company does not support.
   - Post disclaimers of responsibility concerning content of online forums and chat sessions.
   - Make sure your Web content and activity comply with the laws in other countries, such as those governing contests.
   - Appoint someone to monitor Internet legal and liability issues.

Summary

The compilation of this chapter helps you in attaining the following learning objectives:

1. **The major legal issues related to EC.** The legal framework for EC is just beginning to solidify. Major issues include privacy, protecting intellectual property, controlling Internet indecency, preventing fraud, establishing a tax framework, controlling gambling, determining jurisdiction, and protecting both sellers and buyers.

2. **The issue of privacy on the Net.** The implementation of EC requires considerable customer information, some of which can be acquired by tracking the customer's activities on the Net. The issue is how to protect privacy and whose responsibility it is to do so. While legal measures are being developed, it is basically up to the companies that collect such information to provide the necessary measures.

3. **The issue of intellectual property on the Net.** It is extremely easy and inexpensive to illegally copy intellectual work (e.g., music, knowledge) and resell it or sell it on the Net without paying royalties to the owners. While the legal aspects are clear, monitoring and catching violators is difficult.

4. **Ethical issues in EC.** Lack of mature legal EC systems make ethical issues very important. Therefore, ethics codes of companies and guidelines of various organizations help to fill the gap between the needed legal system and the existing one. The problem is that ethics are subjective and their implementation depends on the circumstances.

5. **The conflict between Internet indecency and free speech.** It is easy to distribute indecent material on the Internet, but it is very difficult to control it. The government attempts to control what is delivered on the Internet through censorship were found unconstitutional, contradicting the First Amendment. Other legislation is insufficient or not in place yet. Who will protect the surfers, especially the children, from indecent or offending material and how is still debatable.

6. **To tax or not to tax?** While the federal government in the United States wants to have free trade without any tax or tariff on Internet transactions, almost every other local, state, or international government wants the opposite. The issue is the fairness to competitive traditional marketing systems, what kind of tax to impose, and how to allocate tax collected among several involved governments. In the meantime, there is a three-year moratorium in the United States and several other countries on new sale taxes on Internet transactions.

7. **The restriction on export of encryption software.** The issue is, does national U.S. security justify the imposition of export restriction of 128-bit software, which is necessary for some EC transactions. At the time of the writing of this book, the issue was still debatable.

8. **Contract online versus regular contract.** You definitely need a lawyer to examine the differences. If you do not know the details, you may be heading for trouble.

9. **Protecting buyers and sellers online.** Protection is needed because there is no face-to-face contact, because there is a great possibility for conducting fraud, because there are no sufficient legal constraints, and because new issues and scams appear constantly. Several organizations, private and public, attempt to provide protection that is needed to build the trust, which is essential for the success of wide spread EC.

Keywords

- Biometric controls
- Censorship
- Code of ethics
- Cookies
- Data encryption standard (DES)
- Domain names
- Electronic surveillance
- Encryption
- Ethics
- Information privacy
- Intellectual property
- Privacy
- Privacy policies
- Software piracy
- Spamming
- Watermarks

Questions for Review

1. Define ethics.
2. What are the four categories of ethics as they apply to IT and EC?
3. Define cookies.
4. Why do the government and corporations use surveillance?
5. Why is there so much information about individuals in databases?
6. Explain the potential ethical issues involved in using electronic bulletin boards.
7. Describe the content of a code of ethics (for privacy).
8. Define intellectual property.

9. List the major legal issues of EC.
10. Define privacy.
11. Define how one can protect oneself against cookies.
12. List the five basic principles of privacy protection.
13. Define a domain name. What are its various levels?
14. Define spamming.
15. Describe biometric controls.

Questions for Discussion

1. There are three ways to alert employees that information in their computers is under observation: (1) notify all employees upon recruitment that they may be observed while working on their computers; (2) notify employees once a year that they may be under surveillance; or (3) alert employees by a light or visible message on the computer screen (each time the computer is turned on) that they may be under observation. Which alternative would you prefer and why?
2. The IRS buys demographic market research data from private companies. These data contain income statistics that could be compared to tax returns. Many U.S. citizens feel that their rights within the realm of the privacy act are being violated; others say that this is an unethical behavior on the part of the government. Discuss.
3. Clerks at 7-Eleven stores enter data regarding customers (sex, approximate age, and so on) into the computer. These data are then processed for improved decision making. Customers are not informed about this nor are they being asked for permission. (Names are *not* keyed in.) Are the clerks' actions ethical? Compare with the case of cookies?
4. Many hospitals, health maintenance organizations, and federal agencies are converting, or plan to convert, all patients' medical records from paper to electronic storage (using imaging technology). Once completed, electronic storage will enable quick access to most records. However, the availability of these records in a database and on networks or smart cards may allow people, some of whom are unauthorized, to view one's private data. To protect privacy fully may cost too much money and/or considerably slow accessibility to the records. What policies could health-care administrators use in such situations? Discuss.
5. Explain why there are such diverse opinions regarding specific ethical issues even within the same company.
6. It is said that EC has raised many new privacy issues. Why is this so?
7. Discuss the various aspects of relationships between IT and e-mail surveillance.
8. Several examples in this chapter illustrate how information about individuals can help companies improve their businesses. Summarize all the examples provided in this chapter, and explain why they may result in invasion of privacy.
9. Why do many companies and professional organizations develop their own codes of ethics?
10. What are the two major rules of privacy? Why do these rules make privacy issues difficult to enforce?
11. The Kennedy Center Web site is being visited by millions of people who enjoy different forms of art. The Center had a plan to offer snippets of classical concerts, plays, and so forth so that the public could view some of its programs. Artists and their unions objected. They wanted royalties from the snippets, which the Center was unable to pay. The unions of the Center's employees are also complaining. They do not like the online ticketing introduced by the Center. Discuss the ethical (and possible legal) issues of the incident (*Webmaster*, May/June 1996).
12. Cyber Promotions Inc. attempted to use the First Amendment right in their flooding of AOL subscribers with junk e-mail. America Online tried to block the junk mail. The federal judge agreed with AOL that unsolicited mail that is annoying, a costly waste of Internet time, and often inappropriate should not be sent. Discuss

some of the issues involved, such as freedom of speech, how to distinguish between junk and nonjunk mail, and the analogy with regular mail.

13. Legal and ethical issues may differ. Why? When do they coincide?
14. Provide two privacy examples in EC where the situation is legal but not ethical.
15. What are some specific privacy issues related to EC?
16. Distinguish between self-registration and cookies in EC. Why are cookies a larger concern to individuals?
17. Compare and contrast mail orders (by paper catalogs) to Internet shopping. Why should one pay tax when one buys from a paper catalog but not when buying from an electronic one?
18. Relate the encryption restrictions to the First Amendment.
19. Why is the copyright issue on the Internet so unique?
20. Why are companies willing to pay millions of dollars for domain names (for example, Digital Equipment paid over $3 million for the AltaVista name).
21. Why was the Communication Decency Act considered unconstitutional?
22. Why is the Internet considered the ultimate medium for free speech.
23. Why does the government warn customers to be careful with their payments for EC products and services?
24. Some say that it is much easier to commit a fraud online than offline. Why?

Exercises and Debates

1. An information security manager had access to corporate e-mail. She routinely monitored the contents of electronic correspondence among employees. She discovered that many employees were using the system for personal purposes. Some messages were love letters, and others related to a football betting pool. The security manager prepared a list of the employees, with samples of their messages, and gave them to management. Some managers punished their employees. The employees objected to the monitoring, claiming that they should have the same right to privacy as they have using the company's interoffice mail system.

   a. Is monitoring of e-mail by managers ethical?
   b. Is the use of e-mail by employees for personal communication ethical?
   c. Is the submission of a list of abusers by the security manager to management ethical?
   d. Is punishing the abusers ethical?
   e. What should the company do in order to rectify the situation?
   Note: In January 1996, a district court in Pennsylvania reaffirmed that employers can read e-mail sent over their computer system, even if employees do not know about it. The court ruled that Pillsbury Company could fire a manager who used e-mail to lambaste some bosses as "backstabbing bastards." The district court ruled that Pillsbury had the right to read the e-mail, saying "the company's interest in preventing inappropriate and unprofessional comments" outweighed any privacy rights the employee had. The decision is similar to two earlier California cases that allowed company searches of e-mail.

2. There is a major debate regarding taxes on the Internet. Investigate the status of the Internet Tax Freedom Act. Summarize the reasons for its initiation and the arguments against it.

3. Prepare a list of EC activities that are impacted by the First Amendment versus censorship debate.

4. Investigate the issue of sellers' protection from dishonest buyers. Prepare a report.

5. Read the Real First Amendment at www.krusch.com/real/ladanyi and examine the issues raised by the author with respect to freedom of the press. Relate it to EC.

6. Concerning monitoring internet usage, many companies that provide their employees with Internet access are experiencing problems with employees spending

too much time on the Web. As a result, employers are monitoring Web usage. Debate the pros and cons of such an approach.

7. California is one of the few states that publishes data about doctors on the Internet (www.medbd.ca.gov). For example, the Web site can reveal disciplinary actions by hospitals (recommended by fellow doctors) as well as court and private judgments against physicians. Consumer groups are delighted. The doctors claim an invasion of their privacy. Who is right? You may want to find out more information about this topic on the Web.

8. A 27-year-old science teacher was peddling cyanide pills to suicidal Japanese. Nawaki Hashimoto used his credentials as a pharmacist to buy enough cyanide to kill 3,000 people. Then he opened a home page with a consultation room encouraging people to kill themselves. Hashimoto had a good business. He paid $25 and collected $2,600 from the first 8 people, one of who died before the police intervened. The Internet cyanide case alarmed people all over the world and reheated the debate over whether potentially harmful information, such as the proliferating sites on how to commit suicide, should be kept in check. The government in Japan is seriously considering closely monitoring the Internet. On the other side are those that say that the same crime can be committed by telephone or newspaper—but few people would dream of imposing stricter controls on them. What should the government do? Why? (Debate the issues.)

Internet Exercises

1. Your mission is to identify additional ethical issues related to EC. Surf the Internet, join newsgroups, and read articles from the Internet.

2. Two interesting terms in Internet terminology are *flaming* and *spamming*. Surf the Internet to find out more about these terms. How are they related?

3. Enter www.internetwk.com/links.

   a. Get a listing of industry organizations with privacy initiatives.
   b. Check out the W3Ci's Privacy Preferences Project.
   c. Find out more information about Firefly Network's privacy policies (www.firefly.net).

   Also, enter www.privacyrights.org to learn about privacy concerns.

4. Enter www.nolo.com.

   a. Click on Legal Encyclopedia. Try to find information about the legal issues of EC. Find information about international EC issues.
   b. Click on www.lawstreet.com. Try to find information about international legal aspects of EC.
   c. Support the above with a visit to www.legallink.org and with a search on Yahoo.

5. Find the status of the latest copyright legislation. Try http://fairuse.stanford.edu. Is there anything regarding international aspects of copyright legislation?

6. Enter www.ftc.gov and http://nfic.inter.net/nfic and identify some of the typical types of fraud and scams on the Internet.

7. Enter the Internet Service Providers' Web site (www.ispc.org) and find the various initiatives they take regarding topics discussed in this chapter.

8. Check the latest on domain names by visiting sites such as www.vo.org. Prepare a report.

9. Place an ad on the Internet and in some newsgroups that you want to buy something unique, such as the Brooklyn Bridge or the ship *Queen Mary*. Collect the responses and try to identify the type of fraud.

10. In order to confirm what you can and cannot place on your Web site without breaking the copyright law, consult www.cyberlaw.com and similar sites. Prepare a report.

11. Private companies such as www.thepubliceye.com and www.investigator.com act as third-party investigators of the honesty of your business. What do these companies do and why are the services of TRUSTe and BBBOnLine insufficient, making the services of these companies necessary?
12. Visit www.consumers.com. What protection can this group give that is not provided by BBBOnLine?
13. Visit www.consumerworld.org. What unique services are provided on this site?
14. Find the status of fingerprint identification systems. Try www.digitialpersona.com.
15. Download freeware from www.junkbuster.com and learn how to prohibit unsolicited e-mail. Describe how your privacy is protected.

Team Assignments

1. There is an increasing number of legal suits filed in the United States and in other countries that are related to EC. Have each group member search for specific cases (contracts, liability, and so forth.). Prepare a list of about 12 cases from the past year.
   a. How are these cases related to the topics in this chapter?
   b. What is the likelihood of the court decision in each case? Why?
2. Search the Internet and newspapers for stories regarding Internet fraud. Specifically, assign group members to find stories that match the 12 scams (the "dirty dozen") that the FTC warns about.

   Have the group prepare a report suggesting how to improve the warning statements against such scams.

References

M. Abrams, ed., *World Wide Web: Beyond the Basics* (Upper Saddle River, NJ: Prentice Hall, 1998).

N. R. Adam, ed., *Electronic Commerce: Technical, Business, and Legal Issues* (Upper Saddle River, NJ: Prentice Hall, 1998).

M. H. Agranoff, "Controlling the Threat to Personal Privacy," *Jour. of Information Systems Management* (Summer 1993).

R. J. Alberts et al., "The Threat of Long-Arm Jurisdiction to Electronic Commerce," *Communications of the ACM* (December 1998).

American Civil Liberties Union, "Fahrenheit 451.2: Is Cyberspace Burning?" 1997 (http://www.aclu.org/issues/cybcr/burning.html).

R. E. Anderson et al., "Using the New ACM Code of Ethics in Decision Making," *Communications of the ACM* (February 1993).

R. Bannan, "Net Tax Bill Sails by Committee to House Floor," *Interactive Week* (February 2, 1998).

T. D. Casey, "A New Threat to Privacy," *Interactive Week* (January 26, 1998).

A. Cavoukian and D. Tapscott, *Who Knows: Safeguarding Your Privacy in a Networked World* (New York: McGraw-Hill, 1997).

P. Cozzoling, "Everyone Wants to Tax the Net," *Business Week* (April 13, 1998).

L. F. Cranor, "Internet Privacy," Special Issue, *Communications of the ACM* (February 1999).

R. Dejoie et al., *Ethical Issues in Information Systems*, 2d ed. (Boston: Boyd and Fraser, 1995).

D. E. Denning, "To Tap or Not to Tap," *Communications of the ACM* (March 1993a).

———*Information Warfare and Security* (Reading, Mass: Addison Wesley, 1998).

W. Diffie and S. Landau, *Privacy on the Line: The Politics of Wiretapping and Encryption* (Boston: MIT Press, 1998).

D. Flint, "Internet Content Regulation," *The Computer Law and Security Report* (November/December 1998).

D. Forte, "Biometrics: Truths and Untruths," *Computer Fraud and Security* (November 1998).

GVU-*Graphics, Visualization,* and *Usability Center at Georgia Tech University*, 1998 (www.cc.gatech.edu/gv/user_surveys).

"Internet Censorship," Electronic Privacy Information Center, http://www.epic.org/free_speech/censorship/, (August 4, 1998): 1–4.

O. Hance and S. D. Bulz, *Business and Law on the Internet* (New York: McGraw-Hill, 1997).

L. E. Harris, *Digital Property* (New York: McGraw-Hill, 1998).

C. Hildebrand, "Privacy vs. Profit," *CIO* (February 15, 1996).

S. Hinde, "Privacy and Security—The Drivers for Growth of E-Commerce," *Computers and Security*, 17 (6:1998).

E. A. Kalman and J. P. Grillo, *Ethical Decision Making and Information Technology*, 2d ed. (New York: McGraw-Hill, 1996).

C. S. Kaplan, "The Year Saw Many Milestones in Cyberlaw," *Cyberlaw Journal* (January 1, 1998).

R. Karpinski, "Developers Head Privacy Concerns," *Electronic Commerce* (February 16, 1998).

A. Korzyk, "A Decision-Making Model for Security-Conducting Electronic Commerce," *NISSC* (1998).

R. O. Mason, "Four Ethical Issues of the Information Age," *MIS Quarterly* (March 1986).

R. O. Mason et al., *Ethics of Information Management* (Thousand Oaks, CA: Sage Publishers, 1995).

L. R. Mizell, *Invasion of Privacy* (Berkley, CA: Berkley Pub. Group, 1998).

D. E. O'Leary, "Some Privacy Issues in Knowledge Discovery: The OECD Personal Privacy Guidelines," *IEEE Expert* (April 1995).

E. Oz, *Ethics in the Information Age* (Dubuque, IA: Wm. C. Brown, 1994).

J. Osen, "The Thorny Side of Jurisdiction and the Internet," *Network Security* (November 1998).

T. Page, "Digital Watermarks as a Form of Copyright Protection," *The Computer Law and Security Report* (November/December 1998).

"Patents—STO's Internet Patent Search System," http://sunsite.unc.edu/patents/intropat.html (September 21, 1998).

S. H. Rainone et al., "Ethical Management of Employee E-mail Privacy," *Information Strategy: The Executive Journal* (Spring 1998).

W. Rodger, "Copyright Bill Moves to House Panel Vote," *Interactive Week* (June 22, 1998).

———, "Domain Name Plan: 'Too U.S.-Centric'," *Interactive Week* (March 16, 1998).

J. Rosenoer, *Cyberlaw: The Law of the Internet* (New York: Springer Verlag, 1996).

B. Schneier and D. Banisar, *The Electronic Privacy Paper* (New York: John Wiley & Sons, 1997).

T. J. Smedinghoff et al., eds., *Online Business: The SPA's Legal Guide to Doing Business on the Internet* (Reading, MA: Addison Wesley, 1996).

H. J. Smith et al., "Information Privacy: Measuring Individuals' Concerns about Organizational Practices," *MIS Quarterly* (June 1996).

G. V. Smith and R. L. Parr, *Intellectual Property* (New York: John Wiley & Sons, 1998).

R. Smith and R. H. Wientzen, "Privacy Sound Off: Regulation vs. Self-Regulation," *Internet Week* (September 21, 1998).

J. Stern, "The 10 Common Myths of Cookies," *Computer Fraud and Security* (July 1998).

K. Swisher, "Seller Beware," *Wall Street Journal* (December 7, 1998).

M. Tantum, "Legal Responsibility of Internet Service Providers," *The Computer Law and Security Report* (November/December 1998).

H. Wang, H. K. O. Lee, and C. Wang, "Consumer Privacy Concern about Internet Marketing," *Communications of the ACM* (March 1998).

A. Wells-Branscomb, *Who Owns Information? From Privacy to Public Access* (New York: Basic Books, 1994).

J. Whitemore, "Security and E-business: Is There a Prescription?" *NISSC* (1998).

M. M. Yeung, ed., "Digital Watermarking," Special Issue, *Communications of the ACM* (July 1998).

CHAPTER 11

Infrastructure for EC

Learning Objectives

Upon completion of this chapter, the reader will be able to:

- Describe the protocols underlying Internet client/server applications.

- Compare the functions and structures of Web browsers and servers.

- Discuss the security requirements of Internet and EC applications and how these requirements are fulfilled by various hardware and software systems.

- Describe the functional requirements for online selling and what the specialized services and servers are that perform these functions.

- Describe the business functions that Web chats can fulfill and list some of the commercially available systems that support chat.

- Understand the ways in which audio, video, and other multimedia content are being delivered over the Internet and to what business uses this content is being applied.

11.1 It Takes More than Technology

Regardless of their basic purpose—B2C or B2B—virtually all EC sites rest on the same network structure, communication protocols, Web standards, and security systems. This chapter focuses on the basic hardware and software infrastructure underlying the millions of sites used to sell to, service, and chat with both customers and business partners. While the commonality among EC sites certainly outweighs their differences, specialized servers and components are sometimes required, especially at sites with either substantial amounts of network traffic or unique selling or service needs. This chapter also considers some of these specialized components. In considering the underlying infrastructure, it is important to keep in mind that technology is not the real key. Since most sites utilize the same underlying technologies, this is not the distinguishing feature. Instead, the real key is the way in which the technology is employed and the attention given to the business aspects of the site.

VIRTUAL VINEYARDS: WHERE CONTENT IS THE KEY

One of the earliest B2C Web sites was Virtual Vineyards, established in January 1995 and still in operation today. As its name partially implies, the site specializes in selling wines from small producers with limited distribution and gourmet foods from around

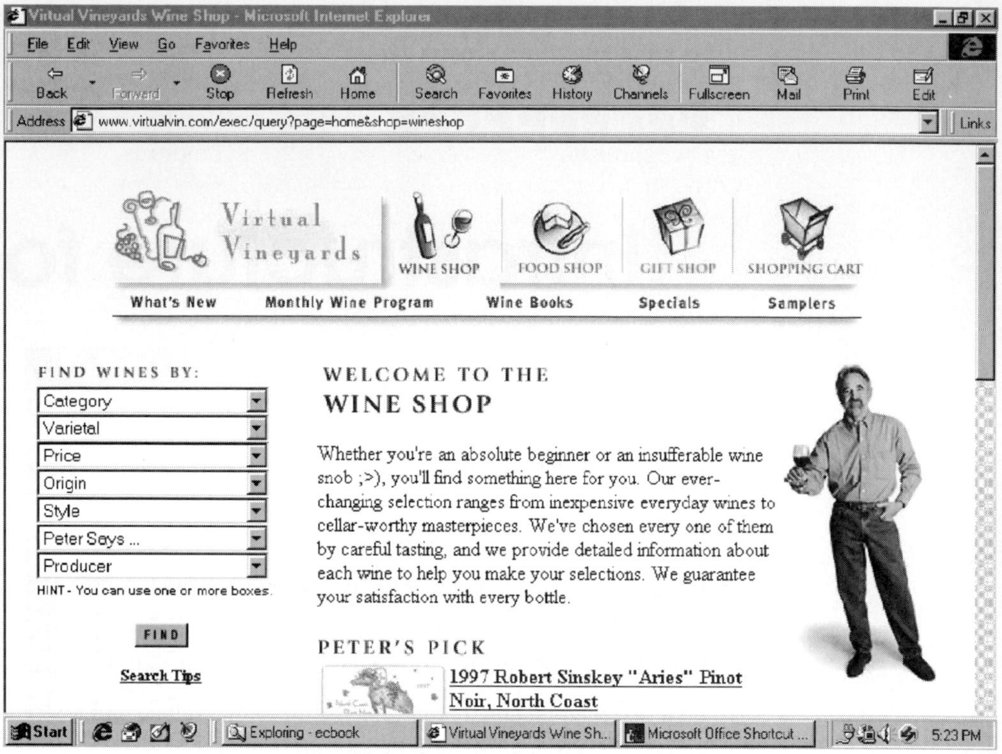

FIGURE 11.1 Virtual Vineyard's Wine Shop.

Source: www.virtualvin.com, 1999. Used by permission.

the world where many of the foods are made by hand in small batches. The combined number of wines and foods carried by the site varies but is currently less than 1,000 items. Each item is selected personally by the owners.

Figure 11.1 shows the starting Web page for Virtual Vineyard's wine shop. While the "look and feel" of the site has been modified frequently, the basic content has remained the same almost from inception. Like other successful online sales sites, this site provides:

- Simple, straightforward navigation from one page to the next.
- An electronic catalog of products for sale that can be searched by a variety of parameters.
- A virtual shopping cart where a customer can place items until he or she is ready for checkout.
- Secure payment either by credit card or CyberCash.

What distinguishes Virtual Vineyards from other sales sites is its focus on content and customer convenience. These characteristics are reflected in the following features:

- *Personal Profiles* that enable customers to view records of their purchases and to make notes about the purchases they make.
- *Monthly Programs* in which customers receive a selection of wines based on the color they select—white, red, or mixed—and the number of bottles they wish to receive—two, four, or six.
- *Virtual Sampler Sets* to help customers explore wines of varying prices that they might not otherwise try.

- *Tasting Charts* that provide a graphic representation of the flavor profile of each wine. These charts are created by one of the owners whose moniker is the "Cork Dork."

From a technical standpoint, it is important to note that all of the distinguishing features are built on straightforward Web standards. The pages at the Virtual Vineyard site are constructed from simple Web objects—text, forms, and graphics. On the server side of the equation, Virtual Vineyards employs a standard Web server configuration and straightforward database connections (appendix B details Web-based database access). What is important is not the technology but Virtual Vineyards' attention to customers.

In 1998 Virtual Vineyards became a member of the ShopperConnection along with CDNow, Cyberian Outpost, eToys, Reel.com, PreviewTravel, PC Flowers, Garden.com, and Datek Online (Davis 1999). The ShopperConnection is a network of retail sellers with Web linkages among the member sites. It is designed to increase brand awareness by associating the member sites with other powerful brands.

UNITED PARCEL SERVICE (UPS) SERVICES THE MASSES

United Parcel Service has been in the package distribution business since 1907. They are the worlds' largest package distribution company, transporting over 3 billion parcels and documents per year. For some time UPS has provided the means for customers to track their shipments—determining the status and whereabouts of a particular package. In the past, this was done primarily over the telephone. Servicing these calls was an expensive proposition (estimated at $2 per call). In 1995 UPS put up a Web site. Initially, it was a simple site running on a single Web server and consisting of a small collection of hard-coded, static Web pages. Then in 1996-97 they created a new Web site for servicing customers.

Besides general marketing information, this site provides customers with the means to do online tracking, to determine the cost and transit time for delivering a package, to schedule a package for pickup, and to locate the nearest drop-off facility. If a customer clicks on "Tracking," he or she is taken to the "form" displayed in Figure 11.2. Here, the customer simply enters the tracking number, hits the "Track" button, and receives status information about the designated package.

While the front end is simple enough, the back-end processing used to handle the request is a little complicated. When a request first reaches the UPS site, it is handed off to one of a handful of Web servers. The particular server that is selected depends on a variety of factors such as the current load on the various machines. Next, the selected server passes the request to the appropriate application server. In this case, the application is tracking. From there the application server passes the request to an IBM AS/400 computer, which is attached to the UPS tracking database. Actually, this database is the largest transaction database in the world and contains over 16 terabytes of data. The mainframe actually does the database search for the status information associated with the tracking number. Once the information is found, it is passed back up the line through the various servers to the customer's browser. Figure 11.3 provides a schematic of the whole operation.

The UPS Web site is designed to handle a substantial amount of network traffic. In 1998, the site experienced 82,000 sessions, 5.7 million hits, and 225,000 requests per day. By late 1998 the estimated net ROI was $10 million. Even though their technology is impressive, their ROI is primarily a function of the way in which UPS is servicing its customers, not the technology.

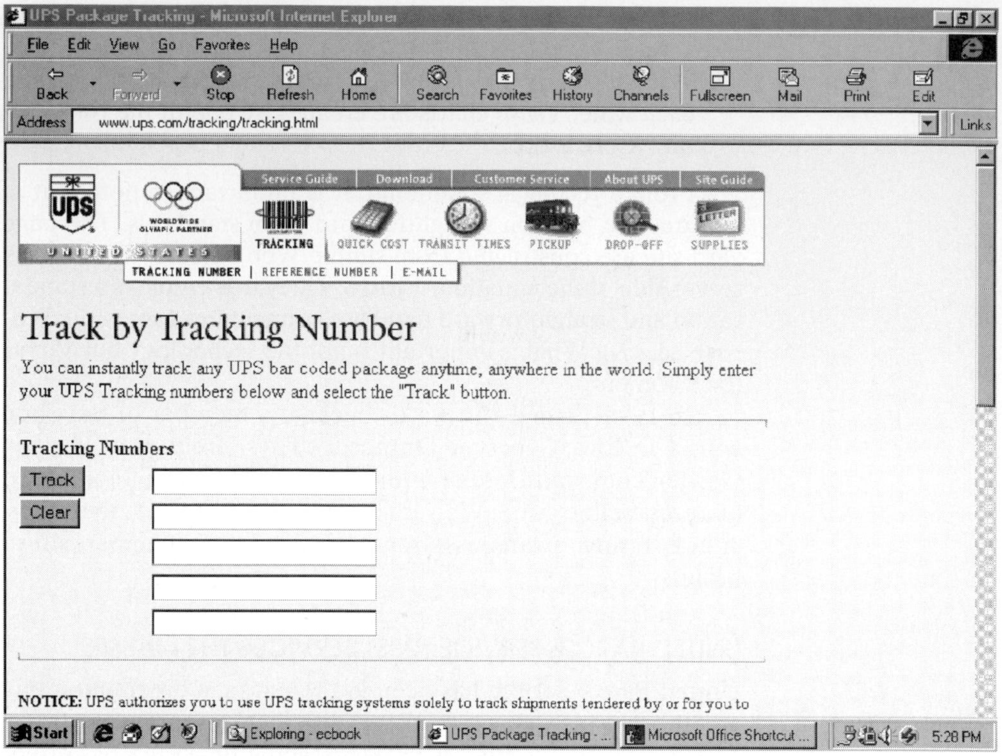

FIGURE 11.2 Package Tracking at UPS Web Site.

Source: www.ups.com, 1999. Used by permission.

FIGURE 11.3 Architecture of the UPS Web Site.

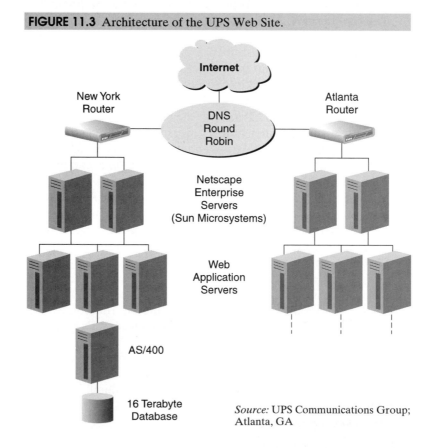

Source: UPS Communications Group; Atlanta, GA

11.2   A Network of Networks

Only a few years ago, businesses encountered major difficulties in delivering online information and applications even to their own employees, especially across geographically dispersed areas and to remote users. Today, businesses can easily deliver information to employees, customers, partners, and the public at large, regardless of location. Many observers point to the Web as the catalyst for this change. Yet, without the 30 or more years of development in the global network infrastructure we call the Internet, the Web would not have been possible.

While many of us use the Internet on a daily basis, few of us have a clear understanding of its basic operation. From a physical standpoint, the Internet is a network of thousands of interconnected networks. Included among the interconnected networks are: (1) the interconnected backbones that have international reach; (2) a multitude of access/delivery subnetworks; and (3) thousands of private and institutional networks connecting various organizational servers and containing much of the information of interest. The backbones are run by the **network service providers (NSPs),** including companies like MCI, Sprint, UUNET/MIS, PSINet, and BBN Planet. Each backbone can handle over 300 terabytes per month. The delivery subnetworks are provided by the local and regional **Internet Service Providers (ISPs).** The ISPs exchange data with the NSPs at the **network access points (NAPs).** Pacific Bell NAP (San Francisco) and Ameritech NAP (Chicago) are examples of these exchange points (Minoli and Minoli 1998). Figure 11.4 offers a high-level view of the interconnections among the ISPs, NAPs, and the backbones (Mudry 1995).

When a user issues a request on the Internet from his or her computer, the request will likely traverse an ISP network, move over one or more of the backbones, and

FIGURE 11.4 Internet Network Architecture.

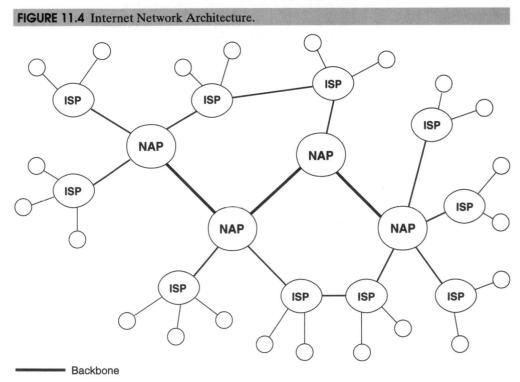

━━━━━ Backbone

Source: Mudry (1995). Used by permission.

across another ISP network to the computer containing the information of interest. The response to the request will follow a similar sort of path. For any given request and associated response, there is no preset route. In fact, the request and response are each broken into packets, and the packets can follow different paths. The paths traversed by the packets are determined by special computers called **routers.** The routers have updateable maps of the networks on the Internet that enable them to determine the paths for the packets. Cisco (www.cisco.com) is the premier provider of high-speed routers.

11.3 Internet Protocols

One thing that amazes people about the Internet is that no one is in charge. This is one of the reasons that enterprises were initially reluctant to utilize the Internet for business purposes. It is not like the international telephone system that is operated by a small set of very large companies and regulated by national governments. Instead, it is more like organized chaos that works because there is widespread de facto agreement among all the involved parties about the protocols underlying the operation of the interconnected networks, although the (voluntary) IETF has the responsibility of developing Internet specifications and standards. As Loshin (1997) notes,

> The problem of internetworking is how to build a set of protocols that can handle communications between any two (or more) computers, using any type of operating system, and connected using any kind of physical medium. To complicate matters, we can assume that no connected system has any knowledge about the other systems: there is no way of knowing where the remote system is, what kind of software it uses, or what kind of hardware platform it runs on.

A **protocol** is a set of rules that determines how two computers communicate with one another over a network. The protocols around which the Internet was designed embody a series of design principles (Treese and Stewart 1998):

- Interoperable—the system supports computers and software from different vendors. For EC, this means that the customers or businesses are not required to buy specific systems in order to conduct business.
- Layered—the collection of Internet protocols works in layers with each layer building on the layers at lower levels. This layered architecture is shown in Figure 11.5.
- Simple—each of the layers in the architecture provides only a few functions or operations. This means that application programmers are hidden from the complexities of the underlying hardware.
- End-to-end—the Internet is based on "end-to-end" protocols. This means that the interpretation of the data happens at the application layer (i.e., the sending and receiving side) and not at the network layers. It is much like the post office. The job of the post office is to deliver the mail, only the sender and receiver are concerned about its contents.

TCP/IP

The protocol that solves the global internetworking problem is the **Transmission Control Protocol/Internet Protocol (TCP/IP).** This means that any computer or system connected to the Internet runs TCP/IP. This is the only thing these computers and sys-

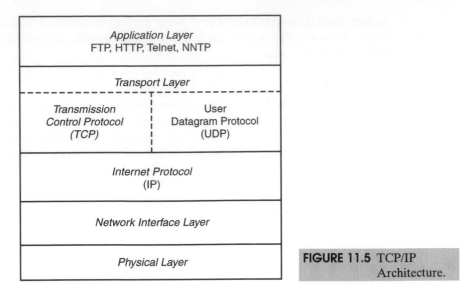

Application Layer FTP, HTTP, Telnet, NNTP
Transport Layer
Transmission Control Protocol (TCP)	User Datagram Protocol (UDP)
Internet Protocol (IP)
Network Interface Layer
Physical Layer

FIGURE 11.5 TCP/IP Architecture.

tems share in common. Actually, as shown in Figure 11.5, TCP/IP is two protocols—TCP and IP—not one.

The TCP ensures that two computers can communicate with one another in a reliable fashion. Each TCP communication must be acknowledged as received. If the communication is not acknowledged in a reasonable time, then the sending computer must retransmit the data. In order for one computer to send a request or a response to another computer on the Internet, the request or response must be divided into **packets** that are labeled with the addresses of the sending and receiving computers. This is where IP comes into play. The IP formats the packets and assigns addresses.

The current version of IP is version 4 (IPv4). Under this version, Internet addresses are 32 bits long and written as four sets of numbers separated by periods, e.g., 130.211.100.5. This format is also called dotted quad addressing. From the Web, you are probably familiar with addresses like www.yahoo.com. Behind every one of these English-like addresses is a 32-bit numerical address. The numerical addresses are assigned by the Internet Network Information Center (InterNIC).

With IPv4 the maximum number of available addresses is slightly over 4 billion (2 raised to the 32nd power). This may sound like a large number, especially since the number of computers on the Internet is still in the millions. One problem is that addresses are not assigned individually but in blocks. For instance, when Hewlett Packard (HP) applied for an address several years ago, they were given the block of addresses starting with "15." This meant that HP was free to assign more than 16 million addresses to the computers in the networks ranging from 15.0.0.0 to 15.255.255.255. Smaller organizations are assigned smaller blocks of addresses.

While block assignments reduce the work that needs to be done by routers (e.g., if an address starts with 15, then it knows that it goes to a computer on the HP network), it means that the number of available addresses will probably run out over the next few years. For this reason, various Internet Society boards began in the early 1990s to craft the **Next Generation Internet Protocol (IPng).** This protocol, which was renamed IP version 6 (IPv6), has just begun to be adopted and utilizes 128-bit addresses. This will allow 1 quadrillion computers (10 raised to the 15th power) to be connected to the Internet. Under this scheme, for instance, one can imagine individual homes having their own networks. These home networks could be used to interconnect and access not only PCs within the home but also a wide range of appliances each with their own unique address.

DOMAIN NAMES

Names like www.microsoft.com, which reference particular computers on the Internet, are called **domain names.** Domain names are divided into segments separated by periods. The part on the very left is the name of the specific computer, the part on the very right is the top-level domain to which the computer belongs, and the parts in between are the subdomains. In the case of www.microsoft.com, the specific computer is www, the top-level domain is com, and the subdomain is microsoft. Domain names are organized in a hierarchical fashion. At the top of the hierarchy is a root domain. Below the root are the top-level domains. Until 1997, there were seven top-level domains including com, edu, gov, mil, net, org, and int. Below each top-level domain is the next layer of subdomains, below which is another layer of subdomains, and so on. The leaf nodes of the hierarchy are the actual computers.

When users wishes to access a particular computer, they usually do so either explicitly or implicitly through the domain name, not the numerical address. Behind the scenes, the domain name is converted to the associated numerical address by a special server called the *domain name server.* Each organization provides at least two domain servers, a primary server and a secondary server, to handle overflow. If the primary or secondary server cannot resolve the name, the name is passed to the root server and then on to the appropriate top-level server (e.g., if the address is www.microsoft.com, then it goes to the com domain name server). The top-level server has a list of servers for the subdomains. It refers the name to the appropriate subdomain and so on down the hierarchy until the name is resolved. While several domain name servers might be involved in the process, the whole process usually takes microseconds.

The Internet Assigned Numbers Authority (IANA) controls the domain name system. Network Solutions, Inc. (NSI) issues and administers domain names for most of the top-level domains—com, edu, gov, net, and org. The overwhelming majority of the names issued in recent years have been in the com domain. Anyone can apply for a name. Obviously, the names that are assigned must be unique. The difficulty is that across the world several companies and organizations have the same name. Think how many companies in the United States have the name ABC. There is the television broadcasting company, but there are also stores like ABC Appliances. Yet, there can only be one www.abc.com. Names are issued on a first-come, first-serve basis. The applicant must affirm that they have the legal right to use the name. If disputes arise, then the company or organization with the earliest trademark wins. One of the ways that has been proposed to minimize the disputes over domain names is to allow additional top-level domains (e.g., tv, which would produce an address like www.abc.tv) and to permit additional companies to administer the new domains (Hakala and Richard 1996). This proposal has yet to be officially adopted.

INTERNET CLIENT/SERVER APPLICATIONS

To end users, the lower level protocols like TCP/IP on which the Internet rests are transparent. Instead, end users interact with the Internet through one of several client/server applications. As the name suggests, in a client/server application there are two major classes of software:

- Client software, usually residing on an end user's desktop and providing navigation and display.

- Server software, usually residing on a workstation or server-class machine and providing back-end data access services (where the data can be something simple like a file or complex like a relational database).

The most widely used client/server applications on the Internet are listed below. As noted in Table 11.1, each of these applications rests on one or more protocols that define how the clients and servers communicate with one another.

NEW WORLD NETWORK: INTERNET2 AND NEXT GENERATION INTERNET (NGI)

In the late 1970s there were about 100 million e-mail messages sent every year. By the late 1990s the figure is around 200 billion. Ten years ago data represented about 5 percent of all telecommunications traffic; now it is about 50 percent and will surpass voice traffic around 2005. The current data infrastructure and protocols—the infranet—are capable of handling today's Internet traffic but not for long. Two consortiums, as well as various telecoms and commercial companies like Cisco, are in the process of constructing the new world network. It will be capable of dealing with the next generation of Internet applications, which will be multimedia laden.

The first of the consortiums is the University Corporation for Advanced Internet Development (UCAID, www.ucaid.edu), which has 146 university members and various nonprofit affiliates. These members are in the process of building a leading-edge research network called Internet2. Internet2's architecture is based on a series of interconnected gigapops—the regional, high-capacity points of presence that serve as aggregation points for traffic from participating institutions. In turn, thesc gigapops are interconnected by the National Science Foundation's (NSF) very high performance Backbone Network (vBNS) infrastructure. Over time, Internet2 will migrate from IPv4 to IPv6 (see the above discussion on TCP/IP). The ultimate goal of Internet2 is to connect universities so that a 30-volume encyclopedia could be transmitted

TABLE 11.1 Internet Client/Server Applications		
Application	*Protocol*	*Purpose*
E-mail	Simple Mail Transport Protocol (SMTP) Post Office Protocol version 3 (POP3) Multipurpose Internet Mail Extensions (MIME)	Allows the transmission of text messages and binary attachments across the Internet.
File Transfer	File Transfer Protocol (FTP)	Enables files to be uploaded and downloaded across the Internet.
Chat	Internet Relay Chat Protocol (IRC)	Provides a way for users to talk to one another in real time over the Internet. The real-time chat groups are called channels.
UseNet Newsgroups	Network News Transfer Protocol (NNTP)	Discussion forums where users can asynchronously post messages and read messages posted by others.
World Wide Web (Web)	HyperText Transport Protocol (HTTP)	Offers access to hypertext documents, executable programs, and other Internet resources.

in less than a second and to support applications like distance learning, digital libraries, video teleconferencing, teleimmersion and collaborative tools, and virtual laboratories. By the end of 1998, nearly all the university members had Internet2 connections, ten gigapops were up and running, and some of the members were able to communicate over the vBNS.

The second effort to develop the new network world is the government-initiated and -sponsored NGI. Started by the Clinton administration, this initiative includes government research agencies such as the Defense Advanced Research Projects Agency (DARPA), the Department of Energy, the NSF, the National Aeronautics and Space Administration (NASA), and the National Institute of Standards and Technology. These agencies have earmarked research funds that will support the creation of a high-speed network, interconnecting various research facilities across the country. Recently, DARPA provided funding for the National Transparent Optical Network (NTON), which is a fiber-optic network test bed for 20 research entities on the West Coast including Nortel Networks, GST Telecommunications, Sprint, the San Diego Supercomputing Center, the California Institute of Technology, Lawrence Livermore Labs, Microsoft, and Boeing. The aim of the NGI is to support next-generation applications like health care, national security, energy research, biomedical research, and environmental monitoring.

Just as the original Internet came from efforts sponsored by NSF and DARPA, it is assumed that the research being done to create both Internet2 and the NGI will ultimately benefit the public Internet. While they will certainly impact the **bandwidth** among the ISPs, IAPs, and NAPs, it still does not eliminate the barriers across the last mile to businesses and homes.

11.4 Web-Based Client/Server

Over the past three or four years, the World Wide Web (WWW) has come to dominate the traffic on the Internet. The vast majority of EC applications are Web based. In such applications, the clients are called Web browsers and the servers are simply called Web servers. Like other client/server applications, Web browsers and servers need a way (1) to locate each other so they can send requests and responses back and forth and (2) to communicate with one another. To fulfill these needs, a new addressing scheme—the URL—and a new protocol—the HyperText Transport Protocol (HTTP)—were introduced.

Universal Resource Locators (URLs) are ubiquitous, appearing on the Web, in print, on billboards, on television, and anywhere else a company can advertise. We are all familiar with "www.anywhere.com." This is the default syntax for a URL. The complete syntax for an "absolute" URL is *access-method://server-name[:port]/directory/file*, where the access-method can be either http, ftp, gopher, or telnet. In the case of a URL like www.ge.com, for example, the access-method (http), port (80), directory, and file (e.g., home page.htm) take default values, as opposed to the following example where all the values are explicitly specified: *http://info.cern.ch:80/hypertext/DataSources/Geographical.html*. What this URL represents is the Web page "Geographical.html" on the server "info.cern.ch" stored in the directory "DataSources."

HYPERTEXT TRANSPORT PROTOCOL

Users navigate from one page to the another by clicking on hypertext links within a page. Behind most hypertext links is the location of a hypertext document. When the user does this, a series of actions takes place behind the scenes. First, a connection is made to the Web server specified in the URL associated with the link. Next, the browser issues a request to the server, say to "GET" the Web page located in the directory specified by the associated URL. The structure of the GET request is simply "GET url" (e.g., "GET www.ge.com"). The server retrieves the specified page and returns it to the browser. At this point, the browser displays the new page and the connection with the server is closed.

GET is one of the commands in the **HyperText Transfer Protocol (HTTP).** The HTTP is a lightweight, stateless protocol that browsers and servers use to converse with one another. There are only seven commands in the protocol. Two of these commands—GET and POST—make up the majority of the requests issued by browsers. The HTTP is stateless because every request that a browser makes opens a new connection that is immediately closed after the document is returned. This means that the server cannot maintain state information about successive requests in a straightforward fashion.

Although it is not apparent, **statelessness** represents a substantial problem for EC applications. The problem occurs because an individual user is likely to have a series of interactions with the application. Take, for example, the case of a buyer who is moving from page to page across a virtual shopping mall. As the buyer moves, he or she selects various items for purchase from the various pages, each time placing the selected item(s) in a virtual shopping cart. The question is: "If the server can't maintain information from one page to the next, how and where are the contents of the shopping cart kept?" The problem is exacerbated because the mall is likely to have several buyers whose interactions are interleaved with one another. Again, "How does the shopping application know which buyer is which and which shopping cart is which?" In this chapter we will not go into the details of how "state" is maintained in an application (this is addressed in appendix B). Instead, we simply note that it is up to the programmer who created the shopping application to write special client-side and server-side code to maintain state.

Every document that is returned by a Web server is assigned a **Multipurpose Internet Mail Extension (MIME)** header, which describes the contents of the document. In the case of an HTML page, the header is "Content-type: text/html." In this way, the browser knows to display the contents as a Web page. Servers can also return plain text, graphics, audio, spreadsheets, and the like. Each of these has a different MIME header, and in each case the browser can invoke other applications in order to display the contents. For instance, if a browser receives a spreadsheet, an external spreadsheet application will be invoked to display the contents.

WEB BROWSERS

The earliest versions of the Web browsers—Mosaic, Netscape 1.0, and Internet Explorer 1.0—were truly "thin" clients. Their primary function was to display Web documents containing text and simple graphics. Today, the two major browsers in the market—Netscape Communicator 4.0 and Microsoft's Internet Explorer 5.0 (IE 5.0)—are anything but thin, both offering a suite of functions and features. Table 11.2 outlines the major components available in both browsers.

The Netscape Communicator 4.0 suite consists of the browser plus the following components:

- *Messenger* for e-mail reading
- *Composer* for authoring HTML Web pages
- *Collabora* for news offerings
- *Calendar* for personal and group scheduling
- *Netcaster* for push delivery of Web pages

TABLE 11.2	Common Browser Components in Internet Explorer 5.0 and Netscape Communicator 4.0		
Text and Graphics	*Suite Components*	*Scripting*	*Objects*
HTML display and navigation	• POP-3 and IMAP4 e-mail clients • NNTP newsgroup reader • HTML Web authoring • Live collaboration • Push delivery systems • MIME support for a number of third-party components (e.g., reading Acrobat files)	JavaScript	Java Applets

The IE 5.0 suite of components consists of the browser along with the following tools:

- *Outlook Express* for e-mail reading
- *FrontPage Express* for authoring of HTML Web pages
- *NetMeeting* for collaboration

Unlike Communicator, IE 5.0 relies on the Channel Definition Format (CDF) standard to provide support for push delivery of Web pages. In addition to the Java Applet and JavaScript standards, IE also offers support for VB Scripting and ActiveX objects.

While offering similar functionality, Netscape and Microsoft have chosen to support different standards for many of these features. For example, both browsers support dynamic HTML (DHTML) but the two versions are incompatible (appendix A

APPLICATION CASE 11.1

Left Your Browser Behind?
Soon a Kiosk May Be Coming to the Rescue

A new class of applications is appearing that connects kiosks—a cabinet-bound PC with a touch screen, credit card reader, and a printer for receipts—with the Web. The applications for Web-based kiosks are varied. For example, at airports, kiosks provide a convenient way for business travelers who don't have their laptops or find it hard to connect to access e-mail or other Web-based information. Simiarly, at trade shows, kiosks (without cabinets) are being used by companies to offer visitors a way to access their Web sites.

One of the major providers of enclosed kiosk equipment is EMF Corporation of Redmond, Washington, who specializes in business applications for airports and stores. Plumbing and auto supply companies use their kiosks, for example, to put catalogs in stores, and Mailboxes Etc. uses them to sell Internet-based services such as business credit reports. The average price of an enclosed kiosk is about $5,500.

As EMF's vice president of sales commented, "Many people thought kiosks would die because of the Internet, but in fact it's the opposite. It's a delivery platform for Internet-based services." According to Frost and Sullivan Research, kiosk sales are predicted to reach $6.5 billion by 2000.

Source: Condensed from Blankenhorn (1997).

details DHTML). This means that companies who want to do business on the Web cannot be assured that their pages and applications will look, feel, or run the same in both browsers unless the pages employ the lowest common denominator of features and functions. Surprisingly, it is Microsoft who has chosen to work more closely with the Web standards bodies, and in all likelihood many of the advanced functions in IE will set the tone for the future. The problem is that IE only works with Windows and Macintosh, while Netscape is open to most of the major platforms.

WEB SERVERS

A Web server is not a hardware platform; it is a software program. In the Unix world this program is called an http daemon. In the Windows NT world the program is known as an http service. At last count there were over 75 different Web servers on the market. The primary function of all of these programs is to service HTTP requests. In addition, they also perform the following functions (Mudry 1995; Pffafenberger 1998):

- Provide access control, determining who can access particular directories or files on the Web server.
- Run scripts and external programs to either add functionality to Web documents or provide real-time access to databases and other dynamic data. This is done through various application programming interfaces like CGI.
- Enable management and administration of both the server functions and the contents of the Web site (e.g., list all the links for a particular page at the site).
- Log transactions that the users make. These transaction files provide data that can be statistically analyzed to determine the general character of the users (e.g., what browsers they are using) and the content in which they are interested.

While they share several functions in common, Web servers can be distinguished by:

- *Platforms*—some are designed solely for the Unix platform, others for Windows NT, and others for a variety of platforms.
- *Performance*—there are significant differences in the processing efficiency of various servers, as well as the number of simultaneous requests they can handle and the speed with which they process those requests.
- *Security*—in addition to simple access control, some servers provide additional security services like support for advanced authentication, access control by filtering the IP address of the person or program making a request, and support for encrypted data exchange between the client and server.
- *Commerce*—some servers provide advanced services that support online selling and buying (like shopping cart and catalog services). While these advanced services can be provided with a standard Web server, they must be built from scratch by an application programmer rather than being provided "out of the box" by the server. Commerce servers are discussed later in this chapter.

COMMERCIAL WEB SERVERS

While there are dozens of Web servers on the market, three servers predominate: Apache server, Microsoft's Internet Information Server (IIS), and Netscape's Enterprise Server. The following section provides a brief description of each.

- *Apache*—a free web server from www.apache.com. Although this server runs on Windows NT, it runs best on a variety of Unix hardware including low-end PCs running the Linux operating system, has a number of functions and features found with more expensive servers, and is supported by a large number of third-party tools. Despite the price, this server requires a substantial amount of Unix experience to install and administer. There is a comme cial version available from C2Net, called Stronghold (stronghold.c2.net/products), that provides SSL security and costs $995.
- *Microsoft Internet Information Server*—a free server that is included with Windows NT (which effectively means that it costs $995—the cost of NT). Like other Windows products, IIS is easy to install and administer. It also offers an application development environment, Active Server Pages (ASP), and an application programming interface (ISAPI) that make it possible to develop robust, efficient applications easily. Unlike most Unix-based servers, IIS can run on inexpensive equipment. From a benchmarking standpoint, IIS outperforms the other contenders.
- *Netscape Enterprise Server*—Netscape offers a number of Web servers. The Enterprise server costs $995 and is aimed at sites that service a large number of hits (some as high as 100 million per day). Enterprise runs on both Unix and Windows NT. The ease of installation and maintenance rivals IIS. It also offers a wide variety of features that make it simple for the authors of documents to publish and control access to those documents without the assistance of a Webmaster.

WEB SERVER USAGE SURVEY

Since late 1995, a company called Netcraft (www.netcraft.com) has been conducting monthly surveys to determine the market share of the various servers (by numbers connnected to the Internet). This is done by polling known Web sites with an HTTP request for the name of the server software. Table 11.3 shows the survey results for selected months beginning in January 1996 and ending in January 1999.

While the results are not based on a complete census of Web servers on the Internet, they do indicate a series of interesting things:

- The number of Web servers has increased substantially over the past couple of years with no signs of letting up in the near future. The implication is that the Web will continue to proliferate at breakneck speed for the foreseeable future.
- The Unix operating system still predominates on the Web in spite of the inroads made by Windows NT. Although the operating system is not noted, this point is supported by the fact that Apache, which runs primarily on Unix, has over 50 percent market share.

TABLE 11.3   Netcraft Survey of Web Server Market Share (Ns in Millions)

Server	January 1996 N = 74	January 1997 N = 646	January 1998 N = 1,835	January 1999 N = 4,062
Apache	19.7%	41.4%	45.4%	54.2%
Microsoft IIS	0.0%	7.7%	20.7%	23.4%
Netscape	12.4%	9.9%	5.5%	4.2%
O'Reilly WebSite	3.8%	2.3%	2.2%	1.7%
NCSA	35.7%	10.8%	3.8%	1.2%

- Apache has been and still is the market leader, even though Microsoft's IIS has shown the largest percentage growth over the past few years.
- Web servers that are specially designed for commercial or security purposes have only a very small share of the market.

11.5 Internet Security

CORNERSTONES OF SECURITY

Security is often cited as a major barrier to EC. Prospective buyers, for example, are leery of sending credit card information over the Web. Prospective sellers worry that hackers will compromise their systems. While the need for security intensifies as a business moves into "transaction-oriented" EC, even marketing sites are not immune to harm from security breaches. The National Computer Security Association (NCSA) has identified four cornerstones of secure EC. Included are:

- *Authenticity*—Is the sender (either client or server) of a message who they claim to be? In TCP/IP the basic means of verifying the identity of a user is a password, but passwords can be guessed and intercepted. Internet Protocol addresses can also be screened to prevent unauthorized access. Yet, IP has no way of verifying that a packet has actually come from a particular domain. By means of a technique called IP spoofing, a hacker can send a message that appears to come from a particular domain when in fact it does not or he or she can alter a URL on a Web page so that subsequent accesses appear as if they were being handled by a trusted site, when in fact they are not.
- *Privacy*—Are the contents of a message secret and only known to the sender and receiver? Breaches to privacy can occur both during and after transmission. Once a message is received, the sender must be assured that its contents remain private. Here, the term *contents* is used in its broadest sense. For example, even when a user accesses a page from a Web site, a log is made of the transaction. The log records information like the time and date, the address of the user's machine, and the URL of the previous page the user was viewing. If the user is accessing the Web by an ISP, the ISP's server can potentially maintain every site visited by the user. In the same vein, many commercial sites utilize cookies to maintain information about users. In most cases, there are legitimate uses for cookies. However, some advertisers have made unscrupulous use of cookies to track the viewing habits of users. The greatest threat to privacy is not the information that is obtained in underhanded ways. Instead, it is the information that users freely provide to Web sites that can be most compromising.
- *Integrity*—Have the contents of a message been modified (intentionally or accidentally) during transmission? The TCP/IP transmits data packets in plain text. Because the packets associated with a given message often traverse a number of routers and lines as they move from client to server and back again, they are susceptible to capture and modification while en route. For instance, a hacker might modify the address where the contents of a Web form will be submitted. The user might fill in a credit card number on a form, click "Submit," and unknowingly transmit the information to the hacker's server.
- *Nonrepudiation*—Can the sender of a message deny that they actually sent the message? If you order an item through a mail-order catalog and pay by check, then it is difficult to dispute the veracity of the order. If you order the

same item through the catalog's 1-800 number and pay by credit card, then there is always room for dispute, although caller id can be used to identify the phone from which the order was placed. Similarly, if you use the catalog's Web site and pay by credit card, then you can always claim that it was not you who placed the order although the access log file that the server creates and updates automatically records the sender's Internet address (log files are discussed in Section 11.9). The key to nonrepudiation is a "signature" that makes it difficult to dispute that you were involved in an exchange.

In short, securing an EC site requires that the cornerstones be secured. At a minimum, this means that the privacy of data and messages must be protected, identities must be verified and verifiable, and unauthorized access must be controlled. Ensuring the overall security of an EC site is an extremely complex task for which there are a number of guides. See, for example, Stein (1998) and Garfinkel and Spafford (1996). In the next sections we look at three solutions—encryption, digital signatures and certificates, and firewalls—that provide the foundation for client and server security in an EC application.

ENCRYPTION

One way to ensure the confidentiality and privacy of messages is to make sure that even if they fall into the wrong hands they cannot be read. This is where **cryptography** comes into play. While cryptography dates to the ancient Greeks, today's systems rely on sophisticated mathematical formulas and computer algorithms. Regardless of the level of sophistication, all cryptography has four basic parts:

1. *Plaintext*—the original message in human-readable form.
2. *Ciphertext*—the plaintext message after it has been encrypted into unreadable form.
3. *Encryption algorithm*—the mathematical formula used to encrypt the plaintext into ciphertext and vice versa.
4. *Key*—the secret key used to encrypt and decrypt a message. Different keys produce different ciphertext when used with the same algorithm.

Cryptography enables not only text but also binary information—video, sound, and executable software modules—to be encrypted for secure transmission across the Internet.

Different algorithms can be used to encrypt messages. Even if the algorithm is known, the message is still secure as long as the key is unknown. It is possible to guess a key simply by having a computer try all the possibilities until the message is decrypted. This is why the length of the key is the main factor in securing a message. If a key were only 4 bits long (e.g., 0101), then there would be 16 possibilities ($2^4 = 16$). For some time keys had a length of 56 bits (i.e., $2^{56} \approx 72$ quadrillion possibilities). During this period computers were incapable of cracking the key through brute force. Today, this is no longer the case. High-speed computers can try millions of guesses in a second. Brute force is also speeded by the use of parallel processors each working on a smaller segment of the possible keys. The actual length of key that is employed depends on a variety of factors. One of these factors is the useful life of the data. For example, information about an individual's credit history must remain confidential beyond the life of the individual. On the other hand, a credit card number only needs to remain confidential during the life of the card.

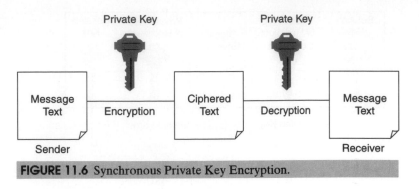

FIGURE 11.6 Synchronous Private Key Encryption.

For much of history, encryption algorithms were symmetrical, which means that the same key was used to both encrypt and decrypt a message (Figure 11.6). This means that the sender and receiver had to agree in advance on the key. Symmetrical key encryption is also called **private key encryption.** There are a wide variety of symmetrical encryption algorithms. The most widely used symmetrical encryption algorithm was the DES, which was sanctioned by the National Institute of Standards and Technology (NIST) for use with unclassified government documents. The DES employed 56-bit keys. While DES is still used, other algorithms have been invented because of its susceptibility to brute force attack. For example, RC2, RC4, and RC5 are a series of encryption algorithms invented by RSA Data Security. Their keys range in length up to 2,048 bits.

One difficulty with symmetrical or private key encryption is that many Internet messages are sent between people or people and machines that have never met. Another difficulty is that Web servers are accessed by many people. If a server's private key is distributed to thousands of users, there is no way that the key will remain secret for long. For these reasons, a new type of algorithm, called public key encryption, was invented in 1976 by Whitfield Diffie and Martin Hellman.

Public key encryption, also known as asymmetrical encryption, utilizes a pair of keys—one public and one private. The public key is made available to anyone who wants to send an encrypted message to the holder of the private key. The only way to decrypt the message is with the private key. In this way messages can be sent without agreeing on the keys in advance. The process of **public key encryption** is diagrammed in Figure 11.7.

FIGURE 11.7 Public Key Encryption.

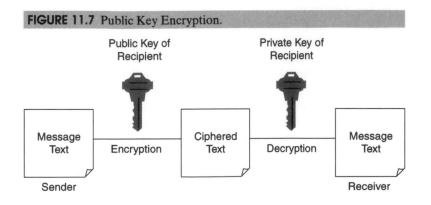

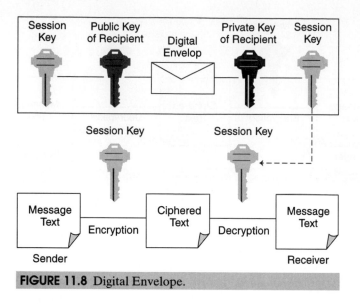

FIGURE 11.8 Digital Envelope.

Unlike symmetrical encryption, there are only a couple of algorithms for encrypting public key messages. One of these is RSA, named after its inventors Ronald Rivest, Adi Shamir, and Leonard Adelman. RSA Data Security holds the patent on RSA. Employing key lengths ranging from 512 to 1,024 bits, RSA is the most widely used algorithm for encrypting Web and e-mail messages. The main problem with all public key algorithms is their speed. Symmetrical algorithms are qualitatively faster than public key algorithms because they require shorter keys. This is why a combination of symmetrical and public key encryption is used with real-world applications. The combination of a symmetrical and public key encryption is known as a **digital envelope.** The basic idea is to use public key encryption to create and send a symmetrical key to the message recipient. The symmetrical key is then used to encrypt and decrypt the message. The overall process is outlined in Figure 11.8.

DIGITAL SIGNATURES: AUTHENTICITY AND NONDENIAL

How can you ensure that a message is actually coming from the person you think sent it? Similarly, how can you ensure that a person has no way of denying he or she sent a particular message? One part of the answer is a **digital signature**—the network equivalent of a personal signature that cannot be forged. Digital signatures are based on public key encryption.

The use of a digital signature is illustrated in Figure 11.9. The basic idea is that messages encrypted with a private key can only be decrypted with a public key. Essentially, the sender creates a phrase (like John J. Jones) and encrypts it with his or her private key. This phrase is then attached to the message and the combined message is encrypted with the recipient's public key. Upon receipt, the message is first decrypted with the recipient's private key. The signature phrase is decrypted with the sender's public key. If the phrase is successfully decrypted, then the recipient knows that the message could have only been sent by the holder of the sender's private key. Of course, at this point there is no guarantee that the sender is actually the sender. It could be someone who has stolen the private key. This is where digital certificates come into play.

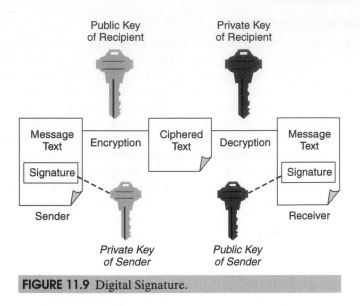

FIGURE 11.9 Digital Signature.

DIGITAL CERTIFICATES AND CERTIFICATE AUTHORITIES (CAs)

If you have to know someone's public key to send them a message, where does it come from and how can you be sure of their actual identity. **Digital certificates** verify that the holder of a public and private key is who they claim to be. The structure of a digital certificate is governed by the IETF's X.509 standard.

Digital certificates are issued by third parties called **certificate authorities (CAs).** Individuals or companies apply for digital certificates by sending the CA their public key and identifying information. The CA verifies the information and creates a certificate that contains the applicant's public key along with identifying information. The CA uses their private key to encrypt the certificate and sends the signed certificate to the applicant. Now when someone wants to send the applicant a message, they first request the recipient to send their signed certificate. The sender uses the CA's public key to decrypt the certificate. In this way the sender can be more confident of the true identity of the recipient. After decrypting the certificate, the sender uses the embedded public key to encrypt the message. In this way, the only public key that the sender really has to know ahead of time is the CA public key.

CAs and signed certificates form the basis of an emerging public key infrastructure. Certificates now exist to authenticate Web sites (site certificates), individuals (personal certificates), and software companies (software publisher certificates). There are also a growing number of third-party CAs. VeriSign (www.verisign.com) is the only CA open to the public and issues three classes of certificates. Class 1 verifies that an e-mail actually comes from the user's address; Class 2 checks the user's identity against a commercial credit database; and Class 3 requires notarized documents. In the future, the U.S. Post Office's Cylink will issue public certificates. Companies such as GTE (www.cybertrust.gte.com), BBN, and Netscape already offer systems and software that enable companies to issue their own private and in-house certificates. In this way companies can verify the identity of users of their own networks.

SECURE SOCKET LAYER

If the average user had to figure out how to use encryption, digital certificates, digital signatures, and the like, there would be few secure transactions and, in turn, few purchases made on the Web. Fortunately, all of these issues are handled in a transparent fashion by Web browsers and Web servers. This is done primarily through a special protocol called **secure socket layer (SSL)** that encrypts communications between browsers and servers. At one time there was an alternative protocol known as S-HTTP. For a number of reasons S-HTTP found little support. Today, SSL version 3.0 has been adopted by both Netscape and Microsoft.

Secure socket layer is a protocol that operates at the TCP/IP layer. This means that any application that relies on TCP/IP—such as the Web (HTTP), UseNet newsgroups (NNTP), and e-mail (SMTP) can be secured by SSL. Secure socket layer supports a variety of encryption algorithms and authentication methods. The combination of algorithms and methods is called a *cipher suite*. When a client contacts a server, the two negotiate a cipher suite, selecting the strongest suite the two have in common. For Web pages, the negotiation process is initiated when the user clicks on a link whose URL begins with https rather than http (e.g., https://www.ups.com, as opposed to http://www.ups.com). From then on, all their communications are encrypted.

SECURE ELECTRONIC TRANSACTIONS

The SSL makes it possible to encrypt credit card numbers that are sent from a consumer's browser to a merchant's Web site. There is more to making a purchase on the Web than simply passing a credit card number to a merchant, however. The number must be checked for validity, the consumer's bank must authorize the card, and the purchase must be processed. The SSL is not designed to handle any of the steps beyond the transmission of the card number. A cryptographic protocol that is designed to handle the complete transaction is **secure electronic transaction (SET),** which was jointly developed by Visa, Mastercard, Netscape, and Microsoft. The SET protocol provides authentication, confidentiality, message integrity, and linkage, and it relies on public and private keys for the consumer and the merchant and supports the following features (Stein 1998):

- cardholder registration
- merchant registration
- purchase requests
- payment authorizations
- payment capture
- charge backs
- credits
- credit reversal
- debit card transactions

The only commercial products that currently provide SET transactions are Verifone Corporation's vWallet application for consumers and the vPOS extension to Microsoft's Merchant Web server. In the future, Netscape and Microsoft browsers will provide support for SET.

FIREWALLS: ACCESS CONTROL

One of the major impediments to EC has been concern about security expressed by companies who are afraid to open their networks and servers to the outside world. A number of companies have sidestepped the issue by letting outside companies host their Web sites. In this way they eliminate the possibility of a hacker breaking into their internal systems, although hackers can still play havoc with the contents of the Web site. For those companies hosting their own sites, one of the immediate concerns is controlling access to network services both inside and outside the company. Companies need to ensure that intruders cannot gain access to critical applications by **tunneling** through the Web site to exploit weaknesses in the network operating system, security system, or application software and databases.

For most applications the primary means of access control is password protection. Passwords are notoriously susceptible to compromise. Users have a habit of sharing their passwords with others, writing them down where others can see them, and choosing passwords that are easily guessed. On top of these problems, when the Web requests the user to enter a password to access protected documents or applications, the browser transmits the password in a form that is easily intercepted and decoded. One way to combat this problem is to make sure that even if the passwords are compromised, the intruder only has restricted access to the rest of the network. This is one of the roles of a firewall.

A **firewall** is a network node consisting of both hardware and software that isolates a private network from a public network. There are two basic types of firewalls: dual-homed gateways and screen-host gateways. In a **dual-homed gateway** a special server called the **bastion gateway** connects a private internal network to the outside Internet. The gateway server has two network cards so that data packets reaching one card are not relayed to the other card (Figure 11.10). Instead, special software programs called **proxies** run on the gateway server and pass repackaged packets from one network to the other. There is a proxy for each Internet service that a company provides. For instance, there is an HTTP proxy, an FTP proxy, and so on. In addition to controlling inbound traffic, the firewall and proxies control outbound traffic. With a **screen-host gateway** a network router is used to control access to the bastion gateway. The router ensures that all inbound traffic must pass through the bastion gateway. A popular variant of the screened-host is the screened subnet gateway (Figure 11.11), in which the bastion gateway offers access to a small segment of the internal network. The open subnet is known as the demilitarized zone. The idea behind the screened subnet is that there is no way for outside traffic to gain access to any of the other hosts on the internal network.

In addition to the control offered by application-level proxies, those firewalls that utilize routers also provide control through packet filtering. **Packet filters** are rules

FIGURE 11.10 Bastion Host Gateway.

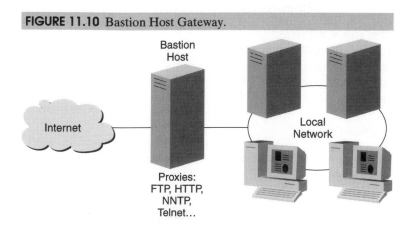

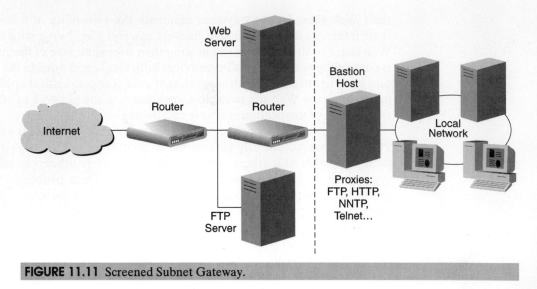

FIGURE 11.11 Screened Subnet Gateway.

that can accept or reject incoming packets based on source and destination IP addresses, source and destination port numbers, and packet type. Packet filtering can also be used to reject any packet from the outside that claims to come from an address inside the network. If a bastion host does not have a proxy for a particular application, then packet filters can serve as the default access control for these other applications.

Firewall systems can be created from scratch. However, most companies rely on commercial firewall systems. Among the better-known commercial firewall products are DEC's AltaVista, Secure Computing Corporation's Borderware, CyberGuard Corporation's Firewall, Raptor Systems' Eagle, Checkpoint Software Technologies' Firewall-1, Trusted Information System's Gauntlett, and On Technology's ON Guard (Stein 1998; Loshin 1997). The various commercial offerings are differentiated by the operating systems they support, the protocols they handle, the types of packet filters they offer, and their ease of administration.

APPLICATION CASE 11.2

E-Commerce Sites Top Hacker Hit List

"If your company operates a high-visibility electronic commerce site, that site probably is experiencing as many as five serious security attacks per month." Based on an analysis of the traffic of customers from May to September in 1997, NetSolve, a network management company out of Austin, Texas, determined that:

- Half the attacks originate from ISP addresses as opposed to independent addresses.

- All the attacks were against EC sites (rather than informational sites).
- Almost three-fourths of the attacks originated outside the United States.
- Internet Message Access Protocol attacks (they can modify internal files) and Smurf attacks were on the rise.

In spite of the attacks, most of the security precautions instituted by the sites disabled them before they did significant damage.

Source: Yasin (1997).

VIRTUAL PRIVATE NETWORKS

Suppose an enterprise wishes to provide mobile or remote workers with secure access to enterprise data that is normally accessed over a LAN. Some of this data resides in Web pages, but most is contained in standard files (like word documents) and legacy systems (like large relational databases). Traditionally, remote and mobile workers access this data through a bank of modems or a remote access server (RAS) that allows them to dial in over phone lines to the LAN. The chance of eavesdropping on the transmission is nil, but it is an expensive way to do business because of the long-distance phone charges that are incurred. A less expensive alternative is a **virtual private network (VPN).** A VPN combines encryption, authentication, and protocol tunneling to provide secure transport of private communications over the public Internet. It is as if the Internet becomes part of a larger enterprise WAN. In this way, transmission costs are drastically reduced because workers can access enterprise data by making a local call into an ISP rather than a long-distance call. The savings can be substantial if workers rely on ISPs that charge a flat monthly rate (e.g., $20) instead of connecting to the network over a $0.5 per minute 1-800 number (which is likely to cost over $100 per month per user). In addition to supporting mobile or remote workers, VPNs can also be used to support site-to-site connectivity. For example, branch offices can be connected to a corporate headquarters through tunnels that transport communications over the Internet. Similarly, a company can be connected to its suppliers and distributors by a VPN, thus providing a secure extranet (chapter 7). Again, the cost savings can be substantial, especially if the branch offices, suppliers, or distributors are located around the world.

The real challenge of a VPN is to ensure the confidentiality and integrity of the data transmitted over the Internet. This is where protocol tunneling comes into the picture. In protocol tunneling, data packets are first encrypted and then encapsulated into IP packets that can be transmitted across the Internet. The IP packets are decrypted by a special host or router at the destination address. Protocol tunneling also supports multiprotocol networking. Local area networks usually rely on protocols like NetWare's IPX protocol. To access the LAN via the Internet, the packets needed for LAN communications (say, IPX packets) need to be encapsulated into IP packets before being transmitted across the Internet. In this way, LAN packets can be delivered across the Internet in such a way that it appears to end users as if they were directly connected to the LAN. Protocol tunneling provides this form of encapsulation.

Various protocols can be used to carry out protocol tunneling (i.e., to encrypt and encapsulate the data being transmitted). At the moment there is no agreed-upon standard. Instead, there are competing protocols. Some of the protocols are aimed primarily at site-to-site VPNs. One of these protocols is IPv6 tunneling, which is based on the Authentication Header Protocol and the Encapsulating Security Protocol (AH/ESP). With AH/ESP, encryption and encapsulation are carried out on the fly by routers located at the various sites. Of course, the requirement is that the routers support the AH/ESP. Other protocols are used to support VPNs that provide employees, customers, and others with dial-up access by an ISP. One of these protocols is Microsoft's Point-to-Point Tunneling Protocol (PPTP), which has been submitted to the IETF as a proposed standard. This protocol is an extension of the Point-to-Point Protocol used by ISPs to provide dial-up Internet access and offers secure multiprotocol network support. It requires the enterprise to have Windows NT 4.0 on the server side but no special hardware or software on the end user's desktop. Instead, it is up to the ISP to support the protocol. Because PPTP is Windows based, other point-to-point protocols have been proposed as standards. One of these is L2TP, which has actually been proposed by both Cisco and Microsoft.

TABLE 11.4 VPN Products and Providers

Vendor	Product Name and Description
Aventail, Seattle (www.aventail.com)	VPN 2.5 implements a reverse Socks proxy gateway.
Data Fellows, San Jose (www.datafellows.com)	F-Secure VPN1.1 supports LAN-to-LAN VPNs.
Digital Equipment Corporation (www.altavista.software.digital.com)	AltaVista Tunnel97 supports tunneled LAN-to-LAN and client-to-LAN connections.
Extended Systems, Boise, Idaho (www.extendedsystems.com)	ExtendNET VPN product supports dial-up users.
IBM (www.ibm.com)	IBM eNetwork VPN series provides standards-based security, firewall, management, and directory services.
InfoExpress (www.infoexpress.com)	VTCP/Secure, is a software-only C/S solution that uses a proprietary protocol for tunneling.

Several vendors, including the firewall companies, offer products for creating and managing VPNs. Table 11.4 lists some of the available products.

Many telecom carriers now offer VPN services for Internet-based, B2B communications. These carriers use their own private network backbones to which they have added security features, intranet connectivity, and new dial-up capabilities for remote services. According to Forrester Research, VPN carrier service revenues were less than $40 million in 1997 but are expected to increase rapidly to reach $1.5 billion by 2000. At that time, 40 percent of all business Internet sales are expected to involve VPN services linking intranets. Major services and providers are listed in Table 11.5.

11.6 Selling on the Web

FUNCTIONAL REQUIREMENTS

The TCP/IP, Web browsers, commercial Web servers, encryption, and firewalls provide an open foundation for creating Web sites that can easily support marketing and service activities. While they provide an infrastructure for conducting business online,

TABLE 11.5 VPN Service Providers

Service Provider	Service
America Online, Inc (www.aol.com)	AOL Enterprise VPN service as part of its privatized AOL Enterprise online service for corporate customers.
Advanced Network Systems (www.ans.com)	Virtual Private Data Network (VPDN) provides a fully meshed, site-to-site WAN that furnishes a secure networking solution for intranets, extranets, and closed user groups.
AT&T (www.att.com)	WorldNet VPN service allows business users to create IP-based WANs within an AT&T Internet backbone.
UUNet (www.us.ww.net)	The world's largest ISP company offers Extralink TCP/IP backbone network.

Source: Szuprowicz (1998), pp. 183–86. Used by permission.

the technical requirements for fashioning an electronic storefront for selling products to consumers are much more stringent than those for nontransactional sites. An electronic storefront must support the same steps and tasks that a physical store must support. In particular, an electronic storefront needs to offer a buyer the ability to:

- discover, search for, and compare products for purchase;
- select a product to be purchased and negotiate or determine its total price;
- place an order for desired products;
- have their order confirmed, ensuring that the desired product is available;
- pay for the ordered products (usually through some form of credit);
- verify their credit and approve their purchase;
- have orders processed;
- verify that the product has been shipped;
- request postsales support or provide feedback to the seller.

In order to provide these capabilities, an electronic storefront must contain at least three interrelated systems (DeWire 1998):

- a merchant system or storefront that provides the merchant's catalog with products, prices, and promotions;
- a transaction system for processing orders and payments and other aspects of the transaction;
- a payment gateway that routes payments through existing financial systems primarily for the purpose of credit card authorization and settlement.

ELECTRONIC COMMERCE SOLUTIONS: OUTSOURCING VERSUS INSOURCING

Like traditional merchants, Web merchants have a number of options for creating and operating their electronic storefronts. The first question a prospective Web merchant must address is whether to contract with an outside firm to create and operate their electronic storefront or whether to build and run it in-house. The choice depends on factors such as the company's size, its previous experience with the Web and EC, and the capabilities of its internal IT staff.

Smaller or medium-sized companies with few IT staff and smaller budgets are best served by outside contractors. Outside contractors have also proven to be a good selection for large companies wanting to "experiment" with EC without a great deal of up-front investment, to protect their own internal networks, or to rely on experts to establish their sites over which they will later assume control. Some of the best-known B2C sites on the Web are run by third-party vendors including Eddie Bauer and 1-800-FLOWERS (Lowery 1998). There are three types of providers who offer services for creating and operating an electronic storefront.

Internet malls. There are over 3,000 malls on the Web (Maddox 1998). Like a real-world mall, an **Internet mall** consists of a single storefront entry to a collection of electronic storefronts. In contrast to earlier cybermalls, today's malls have a common look and feel. A well-run mall offers cross-selling from one store to another and provides a common payment structure where buyers can use a single credit card purchase to buy products from multiple stores. Theoretically, a mall has wider marketing reach than a stand-alone site and, as a consequence, generates more traffic. The downside is that income must be shared with the mall owner.

Internet malls come in a variety of shapes and sizes. There are regional malls like South Florida's (www.sf-mall.com), specialty malls like the Golf Mall (www.golf-mall.com), and general-purpose malls like Choice Mall (www.choicemall.com). Choice Mall is typical of a large mall, with over 1,500 stores covering 18 categories and

70 regional sites. It costs between $1,695 and $2,995 depending on the number of pages devoted to the store and has a $25 monthly fee for host and maintenance services. Maddox (1998) has a fairly extensive write-up on this and other Internet malls.

Internet Service Providers. In addition to providing Internet access to companies and individual users, a large number of ISPs offer host services for EC. For the most part, ISPs are focused on operating a secure transaction environment and not on store content. This means that merchants using the services of an ISP must still design their own pages. Again, this task can be outsourced to a third party. A listing of top site designers can be found at www.internetworld.com. More recently, some of the national ISPs like UUNet have begun offering more complete EC solutions.

Telecommunication companies. Increasingly, the large telecommunication companies have expanded their hosting services to include the full range of EC solutions. MCI, for instance, offers MCI Web Commerce for a rate of $500 per month. Web Commerce runs on Open Market and Microsoft Commerce Server technologies (which we discuss in this chapter). Similarly, AT&T provides of number of EC services including AT&T eCommerce Suite for $695 per month. Even though the telecoms service companies of all sizes, their major focus is on big companies who also use their long-distance services.

While there are a number of technical and marketing complexities associated with building and running an electronic storefront, most companies have opted to do it on their own. The development of an electronic storefront should be guided by a company's existing IT standards and practices. For example, those companies that are "Unix shops" are obviously inclined to employ Unix hardware, tools, and software to build their stores. Again, those companies who choose to create their own sites can take one of three approaches. A store can be built from scratch; it can be created from a packaged electronic catalog or merchant server solution; or it can be produced from a high-end, packaged EC suite.

Those companies with experienced IT staff can use standard components (e.g., a secure Web server), software languages (e.g., C++, Visual Basic, or Perl), and third-party APIs and subroutines to create and maintain an electronic storefront solely on their own. From a software standpoint, this alternative offers the greatest flexibility and is the least expensive. However, it can also result in a number of false starts and wasted experimentation. For this reason, even those companies with experienced staff are probably better off customizing one of the packaged solutions.

According to a Dataquest "Digital Commerce Software and Services Market Share" report (www.openmarket.com), six companies dominate the market for packaged EC solutions—Open Market (30 percent), Broadvision (8 percent), iCat (7 percent), Interworld (5 percent), Netscape (4 percent), and Microsoft (4 percent). These market leaders actually fall into two broad categories—packaged electronic catalog/merchant server solutions and complete EC suites. Both categories provide the following functions (Maddox 1998):

- electronic storefront setup
- product presentation
- order and purchase order processing
- payment processing
- support for third-party software such as shipping and tax calculation packages

What distinguishes the two is the amount of customization that is allowed and required and the number of server components that must be integrated in order to deliver the complete solution. Both categories are described below along with details about major products within each category.

ELECTRONIC CATALOGS AND MERCHANT SERVERS

Electronic catalogs are the virtual equivalents of traditional product catalogs. Like its paper counterpart, an electronic catalog contains written descriptions and photos of products along with information about various promotions, discounts, payment methods, and methods of delivery. Electronic catalog and **merchant server software** include features that make it simple and relatively inexpensive (usually less than $10,000) to set up a catalog operation where the pricing and product configuration are straightforward. Among the features commonly included with this category of software are:

- Templates or wizards for creating a storefront and catalog pages with pictures describing products for sale.
- Electronic shopping carts that enable consumers to gather items of interest until they are ready for checkout.
- Web-based order forms for making secure purchases (either through an SSL or a SET).
- A database for maintaining product descriptions and pricing, as well as customer orders.
- Integration with third-party software for calculating taxes and shipping costs and for handling distribution and fullfillment.

Figure 11.12 outlines the major components in an electronic catalog or merchant server system. As shown in Figure 11.12, a single server is used to handle product presentation, order processing, and payment processing (Treese and Stewart 1998). Likewise, in these systems a single database is used to store the catalog (i.e., product descriptions) and to handle the details of customer orders. The pages of the electronic catalog are created dynamically from the product descriptions contained in the catalog database. For those merchants with only a few products for sale, there is no need to

FIGURE 11.12 Merchant Server Architecture.

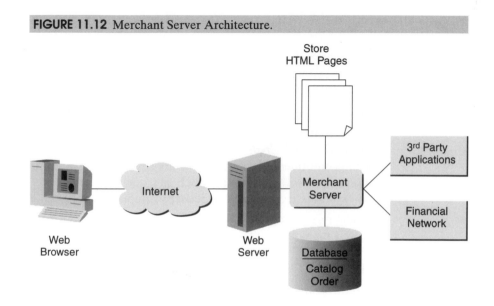

store the product descriptions in a database. Instead, the pages of the Web catalog can be created ahead of time.

Two of the best-known products in this category are iCat Corporation's Commerce Suite (www.icat.com) and Microsoft's Commerce Server (www.microsoft.com).

iCat's Suite comes in two editions—standard and professional. The standard edition, which costs $3,495 and runs on Windows NT, is designed for those merchants with smaller catalogs of products and with minimal need for customization. The standard edition includes:

- catalog templates
- shopping carts
- product searching
- cross-selling
- secure payment processing

The professional edition of the Suite, which costs $9,995 and runs on Unix, is aimed at merchants who need greater flexibility and customization. Toward this end, this edition provides:

- support for high-end databases
- integration with ISAPI (Microsoft's Information Server Application Programming Interface) and Netscape's NSAPI (Netscape Server Application Programming Interface)
- options for third-party plug-ins for searching, user tracking, sale pricing, discounting, and so on

Some of iCat's better-known customers are Nabisco, Volkswagen, Guess Inc., and the Kentucky Derby.

Microsoft's Commerce Server offering, whose cost starts at $4,600, is aimed at medium-sized to large companies wanting to develop either a B2C or B2B site. Commerce Server supports merchants with more extensive requirements and thus has a wider range of capabilities than iCat's offerings. Among the more important features of this product are:

- Commerce Sample Sites providing templates for complete applications;
- Microsoft's Wallet supporting a variety of digital currencies;
- Site Builder Wizard for stores with multilevel departments;
- Commerce Server Software Development Kit (SDK) for developing custom-order processing;
- order-processing pipeline for managing orders according to specified business rules;
- Microsoft's Wallet Software Development Kit (SDK) for supporting a variety of digital payment schemes;
- Promotion and Cross-selling Manager for administering a range of specialized promotions, discounts, and cross-selling opportunities;
- integration with Microsoft's Web site development (e.g., Visual InterDev) and administrative (e.g., NT Security Support) tools.

Office Depot, Barnes and Noble, 1-800-Flowers, and Eddie Bauer are some of the companies that rely on Microsoft's Commerce Server.

ELECTRONIC COMMERCE SUITES

Electronic commerce suites offer merchants greater flexibility, specialization, customization, and integration in supporting complete front- and back-office functional-

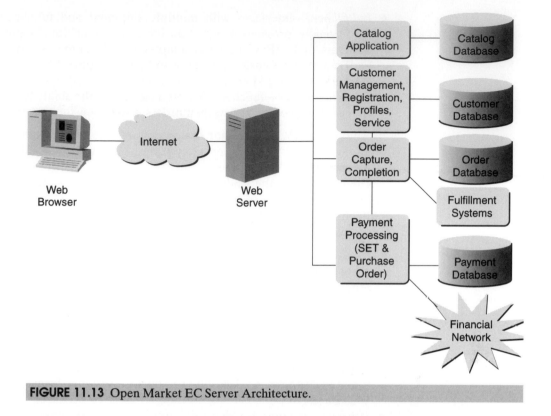

FIGURE 11.13 Open Market EC Server Architecture.

ity. In an EC suite, store functionality is distributed across a number of servers and databases instead of relying on a single server and database as is done in electronic catalog and merchant server systems. The architecture of Open Market's Transact system, shown in Figure 11.13, is indicative of the manner in which store operations are distributed in these high-end suites (Treese and Stewart 1998).

The discussion that follows describes the offerings of two of the market leaders in the EC suite software segment—Interworld (www.interworld.com) and Open Market (www.openmarket.com).

The main product from InterWorld Technology Ventures is Commerce Exchange, which starts at $75,000. Commerce Exchange offers an object-oriented, open, scalable architecture that supports four primary functions:

- *Catalog/product merchandising*—interactive catalog modules that support extensive personalization facilities including personalized product presentations; dynamic product pricing and personalized discounts and coupons; upselling and cross-selling pointing customers to alternative, complementary, or substitute products; product comparisons, alternatives, and recommendations based on buyer characteristics or past purchases; and buyer assistance for making product selections.
- *Order management*—order management modules that support capturing the information required to place an order (order entry); finalizing the details of the order including the payment, shipping, inventory, and taxation (order processing); billing and account management including definition of preferences such as billing addresses, ship-to addresses, credit card information, credit limits, and credit card verification (payment).

- *Fulfillment*—interfaces with multiple shipment and fulfillment solutions. Additionally, provides specific "Business Adapters" for shipping with either TanData or FedEx. The latter adapter was developed in conjunction with FedEx and offers customers access to FedEx shipment, ship estimation, ship alert, and tracking systems.
- *Customer service*—functions that offer customers the ability to verify, edit, and change their profiles; review their orders; and review their payment history.

Among InterWorld's major customers are American Eagle, Cendant Software, Comdisco, Digital Equipment Corporation (DEC), J&R Music and Computer Worlds, and Micro Warehouse.

Open Market is the leading market provider of EC suites. Their focus is on EC sites with high volumes of transactions. Their flagship product is OM-Transact, whose architecture is depicted in Figure 11.13. OM-Transact provides a compete set of end-to-end transaction services including:

- *Analysis and profiling*—analyze sales, buyer behavior, and buyer profiles in order to determine the effectiveness of advertisements, special offers, and other promotions.
- *Demand generation*—deliver digital offers and digital coupons to attract target customer groups.
- *Order management*—capture orders, validate payment and address information, and control processing of shipments, credits, and orders.
- *Fulfillment*—deliver physical goods, digital goods, and subscriptions with automated customer notification by enterprise systems, faxes, e-mail, or secure Web pages.
- *Payment*—support for real-time authorization, automatic settlement, subscription renewals, partial billing, and credit payments and for all types of payment mechanisms (purchase orders, credit cards, procurement cards, microtransactions, debit cards, smart cards, frequent buyer points, and other payment types).
- *Self-service*—provide customers with personalized Smart Statements™; secure access to complete shipping, payment, and billing information. Transact can even retrieve tracking information from a third-party shipping company.
- *Customer service*—support customer service representatives with a set of tools for analyzing and resolving customer issues.
- *Reporting*—provide an array of standard reports, as well as support for most popular reporting and analysis tools, so that you can easily stay on top of your growing Internet business.

Open Market products are not only used by individual merchants but also by a number of third-party providers of hosting services that specialize in EC transactions. Included in this latter group are AT&T's SecureBuy Service; BarclaySquare, a leading online mall run by Barclay's Bank in the United Kingdom; Internet Commerce Services Group (ICOMS), which supports companies like Kodak and Hasbro; Edmond's GOItaly, whose first customer is the Italian opera La Scala; and ECnet, a South African hosting service.

11.7 Chatting on the Web

For the most part businesses have ignored the potential economic payoff from online communications. Except for e-mail, the Internet and Web have been treated as a broadcast or narrowcast medium with information flowing in only one direction (either pulled by or pushed to the end user). More recently, businesses have begun to recognize that the Internet and Web offer the ability to engage customers in a dialogue and to create virtual communities where customers can also communicate with one another. After all, the Internet is primarily about establishing and reinforcing connections between people.

Online forums and **chat groups** are now being used for a variety of purposes in EC. Online forums are equalivalent to Usenet newsgroups (but with a better interface), and chat groups are similar to Internet Relay Chat (IRC). Elderbrock and Borwanker (1996) categorize the various uses of these forums and chat groups in the following way:

- *Communication centers*—businesses whose primary service is a virtual meeting place where communications can take place among the participants. Revenue is generated either through subscription fees or advertising revenues. One example is Match.Com (www.match.com), which is an online matchmaking service for professional single adults. Another is the WebChat Broadcasting System (www.wbs.com), which is organized into over 200 chat rooms where customers can chat in a text-based environment for an hourly fee.
- *Customer service*—a number of customer service sites now offer online support where customers can converse with help-line staff and other customers. Much of the discussion revolves around product questions, problems, and advice. Most online support centers are organized as forums rather than chat groups. There are some exceptions. Mercant (www.intersolv.com/csupport /index.asp), a software vendor supplying database and programming utilities, not only provides online forums but also "live cyber discussions" where customers can chat with product managers and outside experts.
- *Community discussion*—several EC sites provide forums and chat services with a marketing eye toward developing a community of loyal users, followers, and advocates. A good example of this strategy is the forums provided by many of the online financial investment firms (e.g., Motley Fool). Another example is the sports chat rooms and forums provided by sport news sites such as ESPNnet (www.espn.com).

Technically speaking, it is possible for a business to establish its own newsgroup or IRC server in order to provide an online forum or chat group. The problem is that these facilities require specialized clients, as well as servers, and lack seamless integration to the Web. Using CGI, a database gateway, or server-side scripting it is possible, but certainly not easy, to service an online forum. The "store-and-forward," asynchronous nature of a forum makes it possible to create a bulletin board where collections of messages about particular subjects can be stored in a database and, in response to user queries, be dynamically turned into HTML pages. Chat rooms are another story. Because of its stateless, connectionless nature, it is a very difficult task to create a Web-based chat facility supporting simultaneous communications among participants.

Because of the technical difficulties associated with implementing both online forums and chat groups, a number of software vendors are now providing packaged systems designed solely for these purposes. O'Reilly's WebBoard (www.oreilly.com/catalog/wboard3) is a conferencing system that supports multiple, threaded, subject-based forums. Another product that can be used for this purpose is Allaire Forums (www.allaire.com). Products that support real-time chat are slightly different. For the most part these products use a Web browser as a shell and rely on either a special plug-in, Java applet, or ActiveX control as the client interface. Instead of communicating with a Web server by HTTP, these clients talk to an IRC server over the IRC protocol. Ichat Inc. (www.ichat.com), for instance, offers a plug-in client along with a proprietary server that supports chat. Similarly, Microsoft has integrated a chat server with their Internet Information Server (IIS 4.) that can be accessed via an ActiveX control or a Java applet that they provide or any other IRC-compatible client. One chat product that relies solely on Web-based standards is WebChat from WBS, which utilizes the Perl programming language and CGI scripting.

11.8 Multimedia Delivery

In the early and mid-1990s executives like John Malone envisioned the Information Superhighway being delivered to the homes of consumers by cable connections in the form of "500 cable channels" providing media content and information on demand. During this time period a number of cable television companies conducted experimental programs by wiring selected communities with cable on demand. Their aim was to gauge consumer willingness to pay for these additional interactive services. Virtually all of these experimental programs were a resounding flop. One impact was a shake-up of the cable industry and concomitant decline in the valuation of cable stocks. More recently, the cable industry has begun to turn its attention away from delivering more television programming into homes toward offering an infrastructure for delivering a combination of audio, video, Web browsing, and Internet telephone services. This has resulted in a flurry of mergers, acquisitions, and investments among cable, telephone, computer, and Web companies, as the various conglomerates race to gain control of the wire into the consumer's home.

WEBCASTING

Rather than wait for a victor in the battle between these conglomerates, several Web companies like Real Networks (www.real.com) and Broadcast.Com (www.broadcast.com) are already delivering real-time Webcasts. **Webcasting** is a term used to describe Internet-based broadcasting of audio and video content. Webcasting is distinguished from standard Web content delivery because it provides a constant stream of information, can be presented live in addition to allowing on-demand listening and viewing, and offers the potential for two-way communication between the broadcaster and the listener or viewer. Webcasting encompasses a variety of content. Novak and Markiewicz (1998) provide a complete listing of the various types of Webcasts, which is summarized below:

- *Text streams*—text-only wordcasts and datacasts that are streamed to the end user's desktop in the form of banner ads or chat windows. Text streams are used, for example, to deliver constant news and stock price updates.
- *Ambient Webcasts*—video content that is captured from a Webcam and delivered as single-frame updates that are transmitted at periodic intervals (e.g., every few minutes). EarthCam (www.earthcam.com) provides a directory of Webcam sites. There are literally thousands of these sites throughout the world.
- *Streaming audio*—this is the Web equivalent of radio. The quality of the audio that is delivered ranges from voice quality to AM radio quality to FM radio quality to broadcast quality to near-CD quality. The quality of the audio that can be received by an end user depends on the communication speed at which their desktop is connected to the Internet (see the discussion about bandwidth below). Streaming audio is used to deliver everything

from talk radio to sports broadcasts to music previews to archived music and radio shows. The clear leader in streaming audio technology is Real Networks with its RealAudio technology. Among the content leaders is Broadcast.com, which provides an extensive listing of live audio Webcasts.

* ***Streaming video***—like streaming audio, streaming video offers a variety of content that varies in terms of speed and quality. Small-screen slide shows offer solid images delivered in a 200-pixel (you can think of a pixel as a small dot) window at a rate of about 1 frame every 2 seconds. In contrast, talking head videos offer a combination of video that is delivered at a rate of 1 to 10 frames per second in combination with low-quality audio. This can be used, for instance, to deliver videoconferences where high-quality images are not required and there is not much movement among participants. Next comes quarter screen animation. This provides 300×200 pixel images delivered at a range of 10 frames per second and combined with AM-radio-quality audio. Quarter screen animation can be used, for example, to deliver high-quality product demonstrations. Finally, at the high end of the video spectrum is full-motion, full screen video. Here, video is delivered in a 640×480 pixel window at rates of 10 to 30 frames per second. This video format is similar to digital satellite broadcasts and provides for CD-quality audio.

The popularity of Webcasting is burgeoning. According to survey data from Media Metrix Inc. (www.mediametrix.com), the number of homes who received some form of streaming audio or video in December 1997 was close to 10 million. A year later in December 1998, the number had exploded to 19 million. In order to receive a streaming audio or video Webcast, the end user's desktop needs to have a specialized player. Concomitantly, in order for a Web site to conduct a Webcast it needs a specialized server. The way a Webcast works is straightforward. Assuming that the end user has downloaded and installed the required player on his or her desktop, the end user first accesses a Web page with a link to a Webcast of interest. When the user clicks on that link, the Web server sends a special "metafile" to the user's browser. Among other things, the metafile contains the name of the type of Webcast player needed to listen to or view the Webcast, the location of the Webcast server, and the name of the Webcast. Upon receiving the metafile the user's browser deciphers the file and invokes the specified player. At this point, the player takes over, establishing a two-way communication between the player and the Webcast server. The server finally begins streaming the desired Webcast. All of this interaction takes place in a matter of seconds.

Real Networks (www.real.com), Liquid Audio (www.liquidaudio.com), Xingtech with its Streamworks technology (www.xingtech.com), Apple with its QuickTime system (quicktime.apple.com), and Microsoft with its NetShow software (www.microsoft.com/windows/windowsmedia) are some of the companies that offer both Webcast servers and players. Real Networks, Apple, and Microsoft offer general-purpose audio/video servers and players. In contrast, Liquid Audio focuses "on the needs of the music industry, providing labels and artists with software tools and technologies to enable the secure online preview and purchase of CD-quality music." Similarly, Xingtech specializes in servers and players aimed at full-motion, full-screen video/audio. Among these companies, Real Networks is the clear leader. Its Real Player has been downloaded by hundreds of thousands of users, and over 100,000 of its servers are currently in operation.

While the various servers can import various types of multimedia files, the streams that they produce are usually delivered in a proprietary format. For instance, until recently the Real Networks servers accepted Quicktime video files (MOV), Windows audio files (WAV), and Windows video files (AVI) as input but converted the files to their RM format before streaming. The latest versions of their servers now stream files natively over a network. This means that MPEG, AVI, WAV, VIVO, AIF, and other multimedia files can be dropped into the RealServer's content path and streamed without converting the files to RM.

For some Webcasts, like a major sporting event, the audience can number in the thousands. A standard Webcast server running as a unicast system can handle approximately 1,000 concurrent streams. Obviously, this is inadequate for larger events. This is where multicasting comes into play. The first multicast system was the Internet Multicast Backbone (MBONE). The MBONE was an experimental system that ran as a virtual tunneling network over the Internet and required specialized IP multicast packets and routers to deliver and handle the audio and video transmissions. Today, commercial Webcast servers handle multicasting by streaming a Webcast from a central server to other media servers that are distributed to different locations. With multicasting, when a listener or viewer clicks on a Webcast link they are automatically routed to the closest server.

BANDWIDTH REQUIREMENTS FOR STREAMING AUDIO AND VIDEO

In its current state the Internet and the Web are designed to deliver fixed file content, not real-time audio or video. When audio or video is delivered, it is usually in the form of small, downloaded files like midi, wave, and avi files that are played with an external multimedia program. While current Internet protocols (like IP) and the processing speed of the average consumer's home are impediments to delivering real-time audio and video, the biggest barrier is bandwidth.

Bandwidth refers to the speed with which content can be delivered. Most consumers connect to the Internet over the telephone through modems whose speeds range from 14.4 kbps to 56 kbps (kilobits per second). In some areas or at work, users have access to higher-speed connections. For instance, some home users connect to the internet over ISDN telephone lines. Here, the connection speed is 128 kbps. Recently, in some areas telephone companies began offering home users digital subscriber line (DSL) connections, which run at 1 to 1.5 mbps (megabits per second) where 1 mbps equals 1 million kbps. Likewise, some cable companies have begun offering cable connects in selected areas. Cable connections offer download over cable wires at speeds of 10 mbps but provide upload through the user's standard modem. The download speed of a cable modem is the connection speed that many people have at their place of employment. To appreciate the impact of the differences in speed, compare the time it takes to download a standard Web page with text and graphics (say around 400 kilobits) using a 56 kbps modem versus a cable modem. The 56 kbps modem takes about 7 seconds, while the cable modem takes about .04 seconds.

What do the various speeds mean for audio and video transmissions? Simply put, the modems used by many consumers are only equipped to handle low-quality transmissions. Table 11.6, which is based on the content types provided in Novak and Markiewicz (1998), summarizes the types of streaming content that can be handled by the various connections.

INTERNET TELEPHONES

In addition to providing audio and video content, the large cable and telephone companies also have their eye on Internet telephone service, although this service is now the purview of a handful of commercial vendors providing Internet telephone soft-

TABLE 11.6	Delivery Capabilities of Various Internet Connections by Streaming Content Type				
Content	*28 Kpbs Modem*	*56 Kbps Modem*	*ISDN Line 128 Kbps*	*DSL 1 Mbps*	*Cable 10 Mbps*
Text Stream	X	X	X	X	X
Ambient Webcam	X	X	X	X	X
Voice-Quality Audio	X	X	X	X	X
AM-Quality Audio	X	X	X	X	X
Talking Head Video/Audio		X	X	X	X
Quarter Screen Animation		X	X	X	X
Slide Show with Audio		X	X	X	X
FM-Quality Audio			X	X	X
Broadcast-Quality Audio			X	X	X
High-Quality Small-Screen Video				X	X
Near-CD Quality Audio				X	X
Full-Motion, Full-Screen Video				X	X

Note: X implies that it is capable of handling the transmission.

Widespread delivery of high-quality streaming audio and video to the general public will have to await broad distribution of DSL and cable connections.

Source: Novak and Markiewicz (1998).

ware. Internet phones are not real telephones—they are programs that let you talk with other people using the Internet. The main attraction of Internet telephones is cost. Depending on the type of Internet phone connection, the added cost to the end user (over and above the monthly fee paid to an ISP) is at best zero and at worst a substantially lower charge than a standard telephone call.

Internet phones come in three versions—PC-to-PC, PC-to-Phone, and Phone-to-Phone. With PC-to-PC Internet phone calls, the caller and recipient are both required to have the same Internet phone software on their computers. Each computer must be equipped with a (full duplex) sound card, speakers, a microphone, and an Internet connection. The Internet phone software runs outside of a browser and usually appears as a telephone. When a call is placed the audio is broken into digital packets and transmitted over the Internet to the recipient's computer (which can be identified by the user's e-mail address) where the packets are transformed back into audio. In order for the call to be successful, each of the participants must be online and be using the same Internet phone software. In contrast PC-to-Phone systems only require the caller to have the Internet phone software. The recipient answers the call with a regular telephone. In this case, the vendor providing the phone software has special Internet gateway computers located throughout the world. When the Internet phone user places a call, the software compresses the audio and turns it into packets that are shipped to the gateway computer closest to the recipient's location. When the packets reach the gateway computer they are reassembled into a voice signal that is transmitted through the public switch telephone network to the recipient. In this way the call is basically a local call rather than long distance. The last Internet phone configuration is Phone-to-Phone. Here, the caller and the recipient use a regular telephone. When the call is placed, the voice signal travels to a gateway computer located near the caller. Again, the gateway computer compresses the signal and converts it into packets. The packets are transmitted to another gateway computer located near the recipient. At this point, the packets are converted back into a voice signal, which is sent over the regular telephone lines to the recepient.

Three vendors dominate the Internet telephone marketplace. VocalTec (www. vocaltec.com) introduced the Internet telephone in 1995. Their Internet Phone product is in its fifth release and provides not only PC-to-PC and PC-to-Phone calls but also features supporting video transmissions, audio conferencing, white boarding, and text chat. The second vendor, International Discount Telecommunications Corporation (IDT), can be reached at (www.net2phone.com). They introduced their Net2Phone product back in 1996. Obviously, this product supports PC-to-Phone calls over IDT's Net2Phone gateways. The third vendor is Delta Three (www.deltathree.com). Delta Three specializes in PC-to-Phone and Phone-to-Phone services and has the largest Internet telephone infrastructure.

While market analysts predict that Internet telephone has a bright future, its market growth has not been anywhere near as spectacular as the growth in streaming audio and video. In large part, this is due to the uneven quality of Internet telephone transmissions. As some analysts have suggested, "The concept sounds wonderful, but the calls themselves often don't. And there are other gotchas. [With PC-to-PC Internet telephone] the other person must be online when you are and use the same Net phone software. And you'll have to install the software, configure it, and do a fair amount of troubleshooting just to get the sound up to an acceptable quality" (Bass 1997). Internet telephone has also been under considerable scrutiny by national governments and opposed by existing local and long-distance telephone carriers. They are concerned because, even though the Internet relies on the worldwide telephone infrastructure, Internet phone calls avoid the long-distance fees associated with regular telephone calls. Over the next five years these concerns are likely to change the economic playing field for Internet telephone.

APPLICATION CASE 11.3

V-Commerce: The Next Frontier?

Edify Corporation recently announced an agreement with Nuance Communications that will combine Nuance's voice-recognition software with Edify's self-service Electronic Workforce software. The combination will make it possible for companies to simultaneously create both Web-enabled and voice-enabled customer service applications. The latter applications fall under the heading of voice-commerce (v-commerce).

For instance, First American National Bank, in Nashville, Tennessee, created a system with Edify's new software that lets users access the same checking account information over the telephone as it does over the Web. A customer who dials up his or her account might be told, "You have three bills to pay. The first is Visa for $500." In the future, the customer will be able to command the Edify.

Will v-commerce become more ubiquitous than EC? Theoretically, it could become much bigger because there are nine times as many telephones as Web browsers. The potential size of the marketplace has not gone unnoticed. Edify is getting a whole new set of competitors. Other companies are now providing software for building v-commerce. Lernout and Hauspie (www.lhs.com) have made an agreement to include their RealSpeak human-sound-synthesized speech with GTE BBN speech-recognition technologies (www.bbn.com) to create interactive voice-recognition technologies. Similarly, in 1999 Conversational Computing (www.conversa.com) will deliver a commercial software product that enables conversing among Web sites.

11.9 Analyzing Web Visits

Both B2C and B2B Web sites require a thorough understanding of the usage patterns of their sites—the who, what, where, and when. Fortunately, every time a user accesses a Web server, the server logs the transaction in a special **access log file.** Access logs are text files. Each line of the file details an individual access. Regardless of the type of Web server, access logs use a common **log file** format. A typical entry appears as www.somewhere.com-[18/Aug/1998:12:00:00+0000] "GET/a.htm HTTP/1.0" 200 15000 where:

- www.somewhere.com is the name of the system making the request
- -[18/Aug/1998:12:00:00+0000] is the time of the request
- GET is the type of request and a.htm is the page requested
- 200 is a return code indicating an accepted request
- 15000 is the size of the file in bytes

Access logs can tell you which pages are most popular, which times are most popular, which geographical regions make the most requests, and other interesting tidbits that help site administrators maintain and refine their sites.

Because log files can grow quite voluminous, it is hard to analyze the accesses by hand. For this reason, most Web servers provide "free" software for analyzing access log files. There are also commercial products that provide more sophisticated log analyses. Included are products like:

- net.Analysis from net.Genesis (www.netgen.com)
- Insight from Accrue (www.accrue.com)
- WebTrends Log Analyzer from Web Trends Corporation (www.egsoftware. com)

11.10 Managerial Issues

As more and more industries move to the Web, the question for most companies is no longer "Will they move to the Web?" but "When will they move to the Web?" For those companies that are hesitant, there are several outsourcing services that make it possible to experiment with online marketing, selling, and customer service without committing extensive resources.

1. **It is the business issues that count.**   When one thinks of the Web, one immediately thinks of the technology. Some of the most successful sites on the Web rely on basic technologies—freeware Web servers, simple Web page design, and few bells and whistles. What makes them successful is not the technology but their understanding of how to meet the needs of their online customers.

2. **In-house or outsource.**   While many large-scale enterprises are capable of running their own publicly accessible Web sites for marketing purposes, Web sites for online selling involve complex integration, security, and performance issues. For those companies venturing into Web-based selling, a key issue is whether the site should be built in-house, thus providing more direct control, or outsourced to a more experienced provider. Outsourcing services, which allow companies to start small and evolve to full-featured functions, are available through many ISPs, telecommunication companies, Internet malls, and software vendors who offer merchant server and EC applications.

3. **Analyzing the data.** One advantage of online marketing and selling is that an automatic record is made of everyone who visits your Web site. The data that is collected can be invaluable in understanding these visitors and the steps that need to be taken to encourage first-time and repeat visitors. Not only do managers need to understand the types of data that can be gathered but also the software that is available for creating management reports from the data.

4. **Security.** While several technologies and techniques are available for securing an online business (almost to a greater degree than IT environments), incidents like the Melissa virus serve to remind us that Web-based businesses can be subject to attack by clever individuals. Even with simple marketing Web sites, it is paramount that management take every precaution to ensure the security of their sites and their communications with site visitors.

5. **Evolving Web.** The Web is still in its infancy. The underlying standards, protocols, and governance continue to undergo rapid change. Without a basic understanding of their overall direction, it will be difficult to determine which EC technologies will be flexible enough to accommodate the change.

Summary

The compilation of this chapter helps you in attaining the following learning objectives:

1. **Protocols underlying Internet client/server applications.** While there is substantial variation in the content of various EC sites, their underlying infrastructure is basically the same. At the core is a network of networks based on open protocols. The key protocols are the TCP and the IP defining the Internet's overall communication and address structure. Layered on top of TCP/IP are the protocols controlling the Internet's client/server applications. Among these, HTTP is central to the operation of the Web. New versions of these protocols (such as IPv6) are on the horizon. These newer protocols, along with lessons learned from experiments like Internet2, will help evolve the Internet and Web to the next generation.

2. **Functions and structures of Web browsers and servers.** Like other Internet applications, the Web is client/server based. Initially, the clients (called browsers) were aptly described as "thin." In their latest versions, the market-leading browsers from Microsoft and Netscape not only support the display of Web pages but also e-mail, Web page authoring, collaboration, and rich application programming. Similarly, Web servers, which are software programs, have become more complex, offering enhanced performance, security, and, in some cases, support for online selling and buying. Although there are large numbers of servers in the market, surveys indicate that the market is dominated by the freeware Apache server, Microsoft's IIS, and Netscape's Enterprise Server.

3. **Discuss the security requirements of Internet and EC applications and how these requirements are fulfilled by various hardware and software systems.** The four cornerstones of Internet and Web security are authenticity, privacy, integrity, and nonrepudiation. Public and private key encryption help ensure the confidentiality and privacy of messages on the Internet, while digital signatures and digital certificates help verify identities and limit repudiation. In addition to these technologies, enhanced protocols like SSL and SET are required to secure credit card and other economic transactions. Enterprises rely on firewalls to guard their internal networks against intruders while simultaneously allowing authorized users to access the network from the Internet and the Internet from the network.

4. **Describe the functional requirements for online selling and what specialized services and servers perform these functions.** Just like their physical counterparts, online stores must provide the means to search for and compare products, to select products, to place and confirm orders, to pay for products, to verify credit, to process orders, to verify shipments, and to provide postsales support. Electronic catalog and merchant server software allow businesses to create simple, straightforward electronic storefronts. For more complex operations, a number of vendors offer EC suites that support most stages of the supply and buying chains.

5. **Describe the business functions that Web chat can fulfill and list some of the commercially available systems that support chat.** Online forum and chat group technologies offer a variety of business opportunities. Chat groups involving customers and helpline staff are one way of offering enhanced customer service. Virtual meeting places can be created and fees charged for participation. Finally, marketing and sales Web sites can enhance customer loyalty by establishing chat rooms where customers can share information with one another. A handful of commercial vendors offer software packages that make the construction and maintenance of online forums and chat groups relatively painless and within the abilities of most companies.

6. **Understand the ways in which audio, video, and other multimedia content are being delivered over the Internet and to what business uses this content is being applied.** One of the fastest growing areas on the Web is Webcasting—real-time broadcasting of streaming audio and video. One of the leaders in this arena is Real Networks. Webcasting ranges from simple text streams; to periodic transmission of Webcam images; to low-quality audio and animation; to high-end CD-quality audio; and full-motion, full-screen video. The major barrier to widespread participation in Webcasts is bandwidth. Most consumers connect to the Internet using lower-speed modems (28 kbps to 56 kbps). Soon this will change as the cable television and telephone companies battle for the privilege of wiring homes with Internet connections whose speeds rival the Internet connection speeds that most workers enjoy at their work places.

Keywords

- Authenticity
- Access log file
- Bandwidth
- Bastion gateway
- Certificate authorities (CAs)
- Chat group
- Cryptography
- Digital certificate
- Digital envelop
- Digital signature
- Domain name
- Dual-homed gateway
- Electronic catalog
- Encryption
- Firewall
- HyperText Transport Protocol (HTTP)

- Integrity
- Internet mall
- Internet Protocol (IP)
- Internet Service Provider (ISP)
- Log file
- Merchant server software
- Multipurpose Internet Mail Extension (MIME)
- Network access point (NAP)
- Network service provider (NSP)
- Next Generation Internet Protocol (IPng)
- Nonrepudiation
- Packet
- Packet Filter
- Privacy
- Private key encryption

- Protocol
- Proxy
- Public key encryption
- Router
- Screen-host gateway
- Secure electronic transaction (SET)
- Secure socket layer (SSL)
- Stateless
- Transmission Control Protocol/ Internet Protocol (TCP/IP)
- Tunneling
- Universal Resource Locator (URL)
- Virtual private network (VPN)
- Webcasting

Questions for Review

1. Describe the physical structure of the Internet.
2. What is a protocol and which protocols handle Internet communications?
3. What is a domain name and how is one issued?
4. List the key client/server protocols for the Internet.
5. What are Internet2 and the Next Generation Internet and why are they important?
6. How does "statelessness" impact electronic shopping (see appendix B for additional information)?
7. List the primary functions of a Web server.
8. What are the "cornerstones" of Internet security?
9. How do private and public key encryption work?
10. What is the role of a firewall?
11. Outside of firewalls, what are some of the major technologies used to ensure Internet security?
12. What is a VPN and which technology is key to its operation?
13. List the functional requirements of selling on the Web.
14. What types of options are available for outsourcing the creation and maintenance of an online store?
15. What are the major differences between a merchant server and an EC suite?
16. Describe the key types of video and audio streaming.
17. How does bandwidth impact the widespread use of Webcasting?
18. What are some of the business uses of chat groups?
19. How do log files indicate who has visited a site and what they were looking at?

Questions for Discussion

1. How does the Internet survive without a governing body? Do you think centralized control will be required in the future?
2. Two businesses want the same domain name. How is the dispute currently solved? How will it be solved in the future?
3. Microsoft and Netscape continue to battle for dominance in the Web browser marketplace. In what ways is this beneficial or harmful for consumers? Who do you think will ultimately prevail and why?
4. A merchant has heard a number of stories about hackers breaking into company Web sites and is worried about taking his store online. Explain to the merchant how an online operation can be secured.
5. Someone signs an electronic contract and e-mails the contract to you. How can you prove who sent it?
6. Why is simplicity a key to success for an online store?
7. A large company with a number of products wants to start selling on the Web. Should they use a merchant server or an electronic suite? Assuming they elect to establish an electronic storefront, how would you determine whether the company should outsource the site or run it themselves?
8. In order to save money and employee time, a company decides to institute a telecommuting program. What Internet technology could be used to enable workers to dial up the company's internal network?
9. A computer hardware company that sells to other high-tech companies wants to jazz up their electronic catalog with Webcasting. What sorts of streaming audio and video might they try? In general, would this make sense for the company?
10. Now suppose a company that sells to home consumers wants to jazz up their electronic catalog with Webcasting. What sorts of streaming audio and video would you recommend to them?
11. Should Internet telephone users be required to pay for long-distance charges? Why or why not?

12. The cable television and telephone companies are battling to control the "wire into the consumer's home." Who has the best chance of winning? What do you think this means for the future convergence of audio, video, Web browsing, and telephones?
13. Describe how you can use chat groups to support and improve customer service?
14. In what ways do you think the log files at a Web site violate your privacy? Explain.

Internet Exercises

1. Visit the Web sites for the IETF (www.ietf.org) and the IANA (www.iana.org).
   - Based on the contents of these sites, what role does each play in the governance of the Internet?
   - What other governing bodies help regulate the Internet?

2. Several domain name disputes have arisen on the Internet. Search the Yahoo! site for some of the more interesting domain name controversies.
   - What is the general nature of these disputes?
   - Some of these disputes have resulted in court cases. What sort of law has been applied to these cases?

3. Internet experts claim that the Internet needs a new protocol (IPv6). Access playground.sun.com/pub/ipng/html/ipng-main.html. Based on information at this site, why is IPv6 needed?

4. Netcraft conducts regular surveys of the types of Web servers on the Internet. Access Netcraft's Web site.
   - Use their Explore facility to determine what type of server is being used either by your school or place of work
   - How is their survey conducted and what are some of the problems they encounter in doing the survey?
   - They also conduct a survey of SSL servers. What types of information does this survey provide and who might use the survey results?

5. VeriSign is a leading provider of "digital ids." Go to digitalid.verisign.com and read about digital ids. What functions does a digital id serve? If possible, apply for a 60-day trial id.

6. The World Wide Web (W3) organization provides an extensive FAQs document about Internet security. Link to www.w3.org/security/faq/www-security-faq.html. Based on this document:
   - What are the major categories of security risks associated with Web servers?
   - Which operating system is most vulnerable to attack? Why?
   - Which operating system is least vulnerable to attack? Why?

7. Access the Choice Mall Web site. While there, visit some of the online stores in the mall.
   - What are some of the benefits of online malls?
   - Do you think a shopper is better off using a mall or using a search site like AltaVista to locate a store providing a product of interest?
   - In what ways could Choice Mall improve the chance of having buyers make return visits?

8. Select an online storefront of your own choice. What functions does it provide to shoppers? In what ways does it make shopping easy? In what ways does it make shopping more enjoyable?

9. Open Market is the leading vendor of EC software. At their site they provide demonstrations illustrating the types of storefronts that they can create for shoppers. They also provide demonstrations of how their software is used to create a store.
   - Run either the Shopsite Merchant or Shopsite Pro demonstration to see how this is done.

- What sorts of features are provided by Shopsite?
- Does Shopsite support larger or smaller stores?
- What other products does Open Market offer for creating online stores? What types of stores do these products support?

10. Visit Broadcast.Com.

- What types of audio and video Webcasts do they offer?
- Some of the Webcasts involve radio broadcasts. What advantages are gained by listening to these broadcasts over the Internet, rather than listening directly on the radio?

11. Go to www.earthcam.com. Visit several of the Webcam sites listed at Earthcam's site.

- What is the overall quality of the images provided by a Webcam?
- Based on this observation, what are some of the business uses for these images?

12. You have been asked to set up an online forum for your company's customer service unit. You have heard of two products—O'Reilly's Webboard and Allaire's Forum. Visit their respective Web sites to determine the capabilities of each of the products. From this comparison, which of these products would you select and why?

13. Log files provide a number of details about visitors to a Web site. Select a commercial product (such as net.Analysis) that offers log files analysis. What types of information does the product provide, and how can this information be used to improve a Web site?

Team Exercises

1. Universities run extensive and secure Web sites. Prepare a joint report documenting the basic architecture of your university's or college's Web site, noting the various servers and their interconnections, the types of functions provided by these servers, and the technologies used to ensure secure access.

2. Select a series of Web sites catering to the same type of buyer. For instance, several Web sites offer CDs or computer hardware for sale. Divide the sites among team members and prepare an analysis of the different sorts of functions provided by the sites along with a comparison of the strong and weak points of each site from the buyer's perspective.

3. Several vendors offer products for creating online stores. The Web sites of each vendor usually list those online stores using their software. Assign one or more vendors to each team member. Visit the online stores using each vendor's software. Prepare a report comparing the similarities and differences among the sites. Do the sites take advantage of the functionality provided by the various products?

4. Analysts often suggest that the simpler the Web site the better. This leaves little room for using advanced multimedia technologies. Have team members survey several (say 10 to 15 each) sites to inventory the overall use of multimedia objects (animation, audio, video, and so forth). What are the primary uses of these objects? Select one of the simpler sites and suggest ways that multimedia might be usefully incorporated.

R E A L   W O R L D   C A S E

Internet Bookseller Realizes 440 Percent Internet Sales Growth

Soda Creek Press, located in Ukiah, California, specializes in providing publisher overstocks and out-of-print books at substantially reduced prices (up to 90 percent). In 1997, Soda Creek Press rented space in an e-mall run by a northern California ISP. Soda Creek Press was 1 of 100 shops in the mall. Actually, Soda Creek Press set up three stores in the mall to handle their three lines of business—bargain books, mystery books, and women's fiction. The mall itself was powered by a high-end Sun Microsystems server connected to the Internet through multiple high-speed lines.

By the end of 1997, Soda Creek Press expected their sites to produce 15 percent of their overall revenues. The gains were never realized. "Having experienced continuing frustration with the 'off-the-shelf' solution, they realized that they needed a customized application to provide services that would allow them to remain competitive." In September 1998 they switched ISPs to one in Tempe, Arizona. This company created a custom solution

for Soda Creek Press using Microsoft's Site Server, Commerce Edition. The new system, which was run by the ISP, provided customers with enhanced search, enhanced order processing, and improved customer service. The system proved to be faster, more scalable, and more reliable.

At the same time that the Web site was being reengineered, Soda Creek Press also undertook several new marketing initiatives. Included among the new programs were grassroots marketing, tie-in programs, and an aggressive partnering program.

The result of these changes was a 440 percent increase in sales during the 5-month time period from September 1, 1998, to January 31, 1999. During that same period, the total number of orders increased 410 percent.

As the CEO of Soda Creek Press put it, "The long term success of any e-commerce operation will be the offering of products at very attractive prices, excellent customer service with creative and aggressive niche marketing."

CASE QUESTIONS

1. Were Soda Creek's initial expectations of doing 15 percent of their business on the Web reasonable?
2. Soda Creek blamed the original "off-the-shelf" software (which was an EC suite that shall remain nameless). Do you think the software was the issue or were other factors just as important?
3. What sort of features does Microsoft's Internet Server, Commerce Edition provide?
4. Go to Soda Creek Press's Web site at www. lbookstreet.com. Given what you know about

other booksellers, is there anything unique about the site? Can you think of future enhancements for the site?
5. Do you think the increased sales and orders were primarily a function of the new technology or the new marketing? Explain.
6. The Web is well suited for niche markets. What are some of the ways for a small, relatively unknown business like Soda Creek Press to become better known on the Web?

References

R. Barrett, "Internet2; Can the Commercial Net Benefit," *Interactive Week* (August 4, 1998).

Steve Bass, "Internet Phones Take On Ma Bell," *PC World Online* (June 1997).

D. Blakenhorn, "Kiosks Boost Internet Interaction," *Advertising Age* (November 1997).

S. Danish and P. Gannon, *Database Driven Web Catalogs* (New York: McGraw-Hill, 1998).

J. Davis, "Mall Rats," *Business 2.0* (January 1999).

D. DeWire, *Thin Clients: Delivering Information over the Web* (New York: McGraw-Hill, 1998).

D. Elderbrock and N. Borwanker, *Building Successful Internet Businesses* (Foster City, CA: IDG Books, 1996).

S. Garfinkel and G. Spafford, *Practical Unix and Internet Security* (Cambridge, MA: O'Reilly and Associates, 1996).

D. Hakala and J. Richard, "A Domain by Any Other Name," *Boardwatch* (May 1996).

R. Handfield and E. Nichols, *Supply Chain Management* (Upper Saddle River, NJ: Prentice Hall, 1999).

D. Kosiur, *Understanding Electronic Commerce* (Redmond, WA: Microsoft Press, 1997).

P. Loshin, *Extranet Design and Implementation* (San Francisco: Sybex Network Press, 1997).

J. Lowery, *Netrepreneur* (Indianapolis, IN: Que, 1998).

K. Maddox, *Web Commerce* (New York: John Wiley & Sons, 1998).

D. Minoli and E. Minoli, *Web Commerce Technology Handbook* (New York: McGraw-Hill, 1998).

R. Mudry, *Serving the Web* (Scottsdale, AZ: Coriolis Group Books, 1995).

J. Novak and P. Markiewicz, *Guide to Producing Live Webcasts* (New York: John Wiley & Sons, 1998).

B. Pffafenberger, *Building a Strategic Internet* (Foster City, CA: IDG Books, 1998).

E. Schwarz, "V-commerce: The Next Frontier," *InfoWorld* (December 14, 1998).

L. Stein, *Web Security: A Step-by-Step Reference Guide* (Reading, MA: Addison-Wesley, 1998).

B. Szuprowicz, "Extranet and Intranet: E-commerce Business Strategies for the Future," Computer Technology Research Corp., 1998 (www.ctrcorp.com).

G. W. Treese and L. Stewart, *Designing Systems for Internet Commerce* (Reading, MA: Addison-Wesley, 1998).

R. Yasin, "E-Commerce Sites Top Hacker Hit List," *InternetWeek* (November 24, 1997).

CHAPTER 12

Economics, Global, and Other Issues in EC

Learning Objectives

Upon completion of this chapter, the reader will be able to:

- Identify the major impacts of Web-based economics.

- Describe the major components of Web-based economics.

- Analyze the impact of online markets on competition.

- Describe the impacts on industry structure and intermediation.

- Describe the role and impact of virtual communities.

- Evaluate the issues involved in global EC.

- Analyze the impact of EC on small businesses.

- Understand the research opportunities in EC.

- Describe the factors that will determine the future of EC.

12.1 Electronic Distribution of Music by N₂K

N₂K, a producer and retailer of high-quality music (now a part of CDNow), grew rapidly. In 1996 it merged with Telebase, which operated an Internet music store called Music Boulevard (www.musicblvd.com). The site provided content-rich access to a wide variety of information that music fans want, such as artist biographies, tour schedules, music samples, and reviews. The Internet store sells CDs, T-shirts, and other paraphernalia. Unfortunately, the revenues were unimpressive, about $85,000 in the first three months of its operation.

N₂K realized that a single Web site could not adequately address the needs of all music fans. Therefore, the company created genre-specific sites where each focused on the specific needs of an Internet community. The Internet is viewed as a network that provides new kinds of "spaces," a world of online communities, virtual chat rooms, and so on. As we discuss in this chapter, members of an **Internet community** share the same interests. They enter a Web site that is an interesting place to visit, a kind of virtual community center. Members create their own Web pages in the community and therefore can be targets for interactive advertisement. Starting with three sites—one for classical music (www.classicalinsites.com), one for jazz (www.jazzcentralstation.com), and one for rock music. N$_2$K focuses on the specific needs of the communities by providing them with what they really want. For example, classical music fans can listen to real-time audiocasts of classical performances, can be linked to other classical music sites, and much more. A message board and a chat room are also provided. Interestingly, N$_2$K's community sites do not push products. Rather, the focus is "to be able to respond to the instant gratification sale that naturally occurs through discourse and review." The classical music community, for example, seeks a refuge where members can meet to discuss issues and to learn.

The results were astonishing. By making connections with Internet community members, N$_2$K increased its sales dramatically. Furthermore, frequent visitors to the classical music site even flew to New York for a face-to-face dinner. The members have a high level of loyalty to the site, and this results in a substantial increase in sales. Being an online store, N$_2$K can keep a huge virtual inventory by having access to many distributors; yet, their inventory cost is minimal. Overall quarterly sales increased from \$85,000 to \$450,000, with the inception of the community sites, to \$3.6 million one year later. Additional community sites are being opened and dedicated to specific artists (such as www.davidbowie.com, and www.leonardbernstein.com). Moreover, N$_2$K is so well known that they have started to sell their own record label and products, which they sell both on the community sites and through traditional retail channels.

Despite the initial encouraging results, N$_2$K is facing strong competition from other online companies (such as K-Tel and Amazon.com, which sells CDs in addition to books). The competition intensifies when newcomers entered the market and some competitors also affiliate themselves with virtual communities. *Note*: In fall 1998, N$_2$K merged with one of its major competitors, CDNow (www.cdnow.com).

Source: Condensed from: E. Hall, "Music Retailer Finds Commerce in Communities," *InfoWorld*, February 2, 1998, and from L. Sherman, "N$_2$K: Discerning Ears Behind the Net Music," *Interactive Week*, July 20, 1998.

12.2 Marketplace vs. Marketspace

The N$_2$K case points to some interesting factors that are characteristics of EC:

1. N$_2$K utilizes the concept of virtual communities to increase revenue and profits.
2. The scope of advertisement has been changed from mass advertisement to a targeted one.
3. Competition intensifies due to new extranets, mostly "online only" competitors.
4. The company is basically an online company, using a new business model.

These factors are related to the economics of E.C. Schwartz (1997), who coined the term **Webonomics**, or Web economy. He claimed that Webonomics amount to new economic rules, new forms of currency, and new consumer behavior.

The N$_2$K case is only one example of some of the changes that are introduced by EC into our economic system. These changes are the subject of this concluding chapter. Other related topics that are discussed here are the concept of Internet communities such as N$_2$K, global EC, small companies, EC research directions, and the future of EC.

Before analyzing the economic aspects of EC, it will be useful to review the economic role of markets. Markets, according to Bakos (1998), play a central role in the economy, facilitating the exchange of information, goods, services, and payments. In the process they create economic value for buyers, sellers, market intermediaries, and for society at large.

Markets (electronic or otherwise) have three main functions, as shown in Table 12.1: matching buyers and sellers; facilitating the exchange of information, goods, services, and payments associated with market transactions; and providing an institutional infrastructure, such as a legal and regulatory framework that enables the efficient functioning of the market.

Recent years have seen a dramatic increase in the role of IT in markets (for example, Turban et al. 1999). Basically, IT was successful in increasing market efficiencies by expediting or improving the functions listed in Table 12.1. Furthermore, IT was able to significantly decrease the cost of executing these functions.

The emergence of electronic marketplaces, called marketspaces, especially those that are Internet based, changed several of the processes used in trading. These changes, which were driven by IT, resulted in even greater economic efficiencies. Electronic commerce leverages IT with increased effectiveness and lower distribution

---

TABLE 12.1   Functions of a Market

Matching Buyers and Sellers

- Determination of product offerings
  - Product features offered by sellers
  - Aggregation of different products
- Search (of buyers for sellers and of sellers for buyers)
  - Price and product information
  - Organizing bids and bartering
  - Matching seller offerings with buyer preferences
- Price discovery
  - Process and outcome in determination of prices
  - Enabling price comparisons

Facilitation of Transactions

- Logistics
  - Delivery of information, goods, or services to buyers
- Settlement
  - Transfer of payments to sellers
- Trust
  - Credit system, reputations, rating agencies like Consumer Reports and BBB. Special escrow and trust online agencies

Institutional Infrastructure

- Legal
  - Commercial code, contract law, dispute resolution, intellectual property protection
  - Export and import law
- Regulatory
  - Rules and regulations, monitoring, enforcement

Source: Based on Bakos (1998), p. 35.

costs, leading to more efficient, "friction-free" markets. An example of such efficiency can be seen in the Chemdex case at the end of this chapter.

Rayport and Sviokla (1994) noted that the process of doing business in the virtual world is completely different because instead of processing raw materials and distributing them, EC involves gathering, selecting, synthesizing, and distributing information. Therefore, the economics of EC, starting with supply and demand and ending with pricing and competition, are completely different. The new order of economics covers many topics, and it cannot be covered in one chapter (for detailed coverage see Choi et al., 1997). Therefore only selected topics are discussed here.

12.3 The Components of Digital Economics

Similar to a marketplace, in the **marketspace,** sellers and buyers exchange goods and services for money (or for other goods and services if bartering is used). Exchange of goods and services is a subset of economic activities (Hanappi and Rysavy, 1998). The marketspace includes actions that bring about a new distribution of goods and services. The expected utility of the entities pursuing this trade is rising. The major components and players of a marketspace are digital products, consumers, sellers, infrastructure companies, intermediaries, support services, and content creators. A brief description of each follows.

Digital products. One of the major differences between the marketplace and the marketspace is the possible digitization of products and services. In addition to digitization of software and music, it is possible to digitize dozens of other products and services, as shown in Table 12.2. Digital products have different cost curves than that of regular products. In digitization, most of the costs are fixed and the variable cost is very small. Therefore, profit will increase very rapidly as sales increases.

The consumers. The tens of millions of people worldwide that surf the Web are potential buyers of goods and services offered or advertised on the Net. The consumers are looking for bargains, customized items, collectors' items, entertainment, and more. They are in the driver's seat. They can search for detailed information, compare, bid, and sometimes negotiate.

The sellers. Hundreds of thousands of storefronts are available on the Net, advertising and/or offering millions of items. Every day it is possible to find new offerings of products and/or services.

The infrastructure companies. Thousands of companies provide the hardware and software necessary to support EC. Many companies that provide software also provide consulting services on how to set up a store on the Internet. Other companies offer hosting services for small sellers (for example, www.tpn.geis.com).

The intermediaries. Intermediaries of all kinds offer their services on the Web. The role of these intermediaries as seen throughout the book and, especially in chapter 5, is different from that of regular intermediaries. Intermediaries create the online market (such as the Chemdex case at the end of this chapter), they help in matching buyers and sellers, they provide for some infrastructure services, and they help customers and/or sellers to institute and consummate transactions.

The support services. Hundreds of support services are available, ranging from certification and trust, which assures security, to knowledge providers. These services are created by the need to address implementation issues.

Content creators. Hundreds of media-type companies create and perpetually update Web pages and sites. They do it for their own Web sites as well as for others. The quality of Web content is a major critical success factor in EC.

CHAPTER 12 *Economics, Global, and Other Issues in EC* **429**

TABLE 12.2 Examples of Digital Products

1. Information and entertainment products that are digitized:
   - Paper-based documents: books, newspapers, magazine journals, store coupons, marketing brochures, newsletters, research papers, and training materials
   - Product information: product specifications, catalogs, user manuals, sales training manuals
   - Graphics: photographs, postcards, calendars, maps, posters, x-rays
   - Audio: music recordings, speeches, lectures, industrial voice
   - Video: movies, television programs, video clips
   - Software: programs, games, development tools
2. Symbols, tokens, and concepts:
   - Tickets and reservations: airlines, hotels, concerts, sports events, transportation
   - Financial instruments: checks, electronic currencies, credit cards, securities, letters of credit
3. Processes and services:
   - Government services: forms, benefits, welfare payments, licenses
   - Electronic messaging: letters, faxes, telephone calls
   - Business-value-creation processes: ordering, bookkeeping, inventorying, contracting
   - Auctions, bidding, bartering
   - Remote education, telemedicine and other interactive services
   - Cybercafes, interactive entertainment, virtual communities

Source: Based on Choi et al. (1997), p. 64.

12.4 Competition in Marketspace

Competition in the traditional markets is going through a fundamental change as can be seen in the Amazon.com versus Barnes & Noble example (Application Case 12.1). Amazon's example demonstrates the following impacts on competition:

- *Lower buyers' search cost.* Electronic markets reduce the cost of searching for product information. This can significantly impact competition (Bakos 1997). Enabling customers to find cheaper (or better) products, forces sellers in turn to reduce prices and/or improve customer service. Companies that do just that can exploit the Internet to gain a considerably larger market share.
- *Speedy comparisons.* Not only can the customers find inexpensive products, they can find them quickly. The customer does not have to go to several bookstores. Using shopping search engines such as www.compare.com, customers can find what they want and compare prices. Companies that trade online and provide information to more search engines will benefit.
- *Differentiation.* Amazon.com provides customers with information that is not available in a physical bookstore such as communication with authors, almost real-time book reviews, and more. In fact, EC enables customization

of products and services. For example, Amazon will notify you by e-mail when new books on your favorite subject (or by your favorite author) are published.

Consumers like differentiation and are frequently willing to pay more for it. Differentiation reduces the substitutability between products. Also, price cutting (in differentiation) does not impact market shares very much.

- *Lower prices.* Amazon.com offers lower prices due to its lower cost (no physical facilities, minimum inventories, and so on). In some cases, prices are reduced by 40 percent.
- *Customer service.* Amazon.com provides superior customer service. As discussed in chapters 2, 4, and 6, such a service is an extremely important competitive factor.

Other competitive factors to consider are:

- The size of the firm may not be a significant competitive advantage.
- Geographical distance from the consumer may play an insignificant role.
- Some language barriers may be easily removed.
- Digital products lack normal wear and tear.

All in all, EC supports efficient markets and could result in almost perfect competition. In such markets, a commodity is produced when the consumer's willingness to pay equals the marginal cost of producing the commodity, and neither sellers nor buyers can influence supply or demand conditions individually.

In order to be in perfect competition it is necessary to:

1. Enable many buyers and sellers to enter the market at no entry cost (no barriers to entry).
2. Not allow the many buyers and sellers to individually influence the market.
3. Make certain products homogeneous (no product differentiation).
4. Supply buyers and sellers with perfect information about the products and the market participants and conditions.

APPLICATION CASE 12.1

Amazon.com versus Barnes & Noble

In the first three years of its existence, Amazon's sales grew very rapidly (for example, 800 percent in 1997 versus 1996). It took Barnes & Noble about one and a half years to react to Amazon's initiative by opening a competing online division. By that time Amazon was in full control of the market with a strong leadership position. While Amazon was still losing money in 1998, it controlled over 75 percent of all online book sales, and it established business partnerships with over 100,000 companies by midyear (*Interactive Week*, July 1998).

Barnes & Noble demonstrated initiative by adding to the B2C market, which Amazon controlled, B2B. Amazon.com, on the other hand, acquired several online companies in other countries and diversified its product line by adding CDs and other products. To increase its competitive edge, Barnes & Noble created a completely separate company to handle all its online activities including B2B.

The competition between the two companies will continue to increase in the future and new innovations and strategies are expected soon. In addition to lowering prices on many books by as much as 40 percent due to the lower distribution cost of online operations, customers enjoy a huge selection of easy-to-find books.

Electronic Commerce could provide, or come close to providing, these conditions. It is interesting to note how the ease of finding information benefits both buyers (finding information about products, vendors, prices, and so on) and sellers (finding information about the customers and their demands, about competitors, and the like).

Barnes & Noble, the world's largest bookstore, underestimated the impact of Amazon and did not respond for almost two years. This gave Amazon sufficient time to establish its name. The name Amazon.com is probably much more known worldwide than that of Barnes & Noble. The Amazon versus Barnes & Noble example illustrates that the nature of competition in business may be changing. Let us see how.

First, it is said that competition between companies is being replaced by competition between networks. The company with better networks, advertisement capabilities, and relationships with other Web companies (Amazon had over 120,000 business partners in 1999) has a strategic advantage.

Using Porter's competitive model (Figure 12.1), one can make the following observations regarding competitiveness:

- There will be many new entrants, some of which will be online exclusively (such as Amazon.com). There will also be many out-of-town and global new entrants.

FIGURE 12.1 Porter's Five Forces Model (including the major determinant of each force).

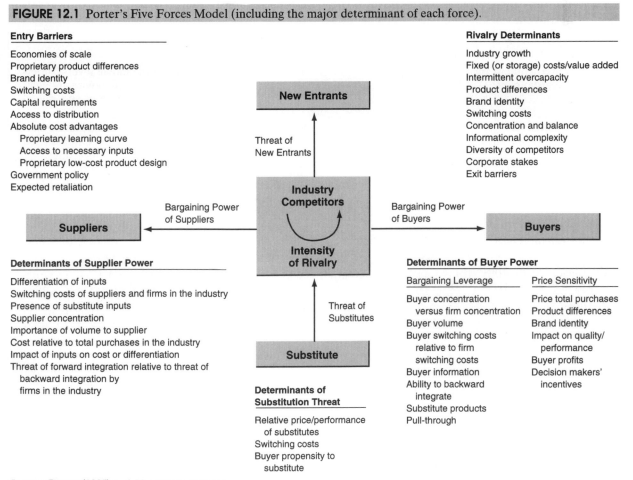

Source: Porter (1985) p. 6. Used by permission.

- The bargaining power of buyers is likely to increase due to the availability of more sellers and products and the availability of information and comparative analysis on the Web.
- There will be more substitute products and services ranging from digital products to innovative products/services that are Web based.
- The bargaining power of suppliers may decrease due to the increased number of suppliers, ease of conduct bidding (request for quotes), and the entry of small and foreign suppliers into the market.
- The number of industry competitors in one location will increase.

In other words, competition will intensify in the marketplace. The competition is not only between offline and online services but also among online services as shown in the case of books, music, and videos (Application Case 12.2).

APPLICATION CASE 12.2

Strong Competition in Selling Books, Music, and Videos

The success of Amazon.com and CDNow attracted dozens of online and offline vendors all hoping to make a fortune from EC. Each vendor claims some competitive advantage. Here are some examples:

Newcomers	*Competitive Advantage*
Big Star Entertainment Inc. (www.bigstar.com)	**Selection**: Big Star aims to be the movie lovers' superstore, offering more than 100,000 movies and television programs in VHS, laser disc, and digital videodisc (DVD) formats.
Borders Online Inc. (www.borders.com)	**Brand Name**: Banking on its name, distribution network, and retail know-how, Borders aims to sell many thousands book, music, and video titles.
K-Tel International Inc. (www.ktel.com)	**Brand Name**: K-Tel Express features more than 250,000 music titles, including the "Hooked On" series and compilations of greatest hits it sold primarily through its television ads.
Netflix Inc. (www.netflix.com)	**Specialty**: NetFlix wants to be the one-stop source for owners of DVD players. In addition to selling DVD titles, it offers one-week rentals.
3Dnet Inc.'s Orchid Music (www.orchid.buysafe.com)	**Price**: Part of a network of specialty retailers called BuySafe.com (www.buysafe.com), Orchid Music is a "loss leader" that offers more than 220,000 titles for "bargain-conscious" music buyers in the hopes of getting consumers to shop at the other BuySafe.com stores.
Total E (www.totale.com)	**Connections**: A spin-off of direct-mail marketing and music giant Columbia House Co., Total E hopes to cross-sell CDs, cassettes, videos, and, in coming months, CD-ROMs, books, and audio books to the 13 million Columbia House club members.
www.pawprintbooks.com	**Specialty**: A virtual bookstore for rare and out of print titles. Locates more than 1 million out-of-print titles and ships them.
Computerliteracy.com	**Niche Market**: Technical, computer-oriented books.

12.5 Some Issues in Digital Economy and Success Factors

There are several other issues related to the economics of EC. Most of them are discussed by Choi et al. (1997). Some examples follow:

- ● *Cost curves.* The total cost curves of many physical products and services are U-shaped (Figure 12.2a). First, as quantity increases the cost declines, but later the cost (average per product) increases due to the growth of the variable cost (especially administrative and marketing).

    With digital products (Figure 12.2 b), the variable cost per unit is very low (in most cases) and almost fixed regardless of the quantity. Therefore, cost per unit will decline as quantity increases due to the proration of the fixed component of the cost over more units.

- ● *Buying versus renting.* Just like with physical products, in EC one can rent, or a group can share, products. Availability of such options will influence both demand and prices.

- ● *Bundling products/services.* Bundling several products or services is especially common in software products that are digitized. Bundling is a useful price discrimination method and it is used extensively by vendors. In EC there are more opportunities for bundling and the pricing issue becomes critical. Bundling will be an even more important factor in the future when micropayment mechanisms will be economically feasible.

Here we will describe three other issues that have a major impact on the deployment of EC.

THE NEED FOR A CRITICAL MASS OF BUYERS AND SELLERS

A critical mass of buyers is needed for EC to survive. As indicated earlier, the fixed cost of deploying EC is high, sometimes very high. Without a large number of buyers, sellers will not make money. In 1999 the number of Internet users worldwide was estimated at the 250 million to 350 million range. This number is still small as compared with an estimated 1.3 billion televisions. This situation will change, especially when TV/PC integration becomes economically feasible.

So, should you wait a few years before starting EC? Definitely not. You must not be misled by the above macrostatistics. You should also look at the microlevel

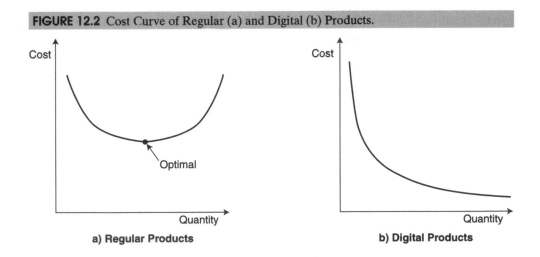

FIGURE 12.2 Cost Curve of Regular (a) and Digital (b) Products.

a) Regular Products

b) Digital Products

segmentation of the market you are trying to reach. For example, if your target market segment is not the average consumer but the highly educated ones, the percentage online may be much higher, therefore affording you a larger critical mass factor. The reason, for example, that PCs and PC-related equipment have been popular items for Internet sales is that most PC users have a much higher rate of Internet access than the rest. On the business side, if we take Intel, IBM, Cisco Systems, and Marshall Industries as prime examples, their primary customers have been Internet users longer than most other customers.

At the global level, a critical mass of EC-enabled nations is required. Canada, for example, has a goal to be recognized as an EC-friendly country to attract international investments and business to it. Hong Kong is developing a multibillion Cyberport, which will facilitate EC development and may position the country as a center for global EC in southeast Asia.

Finally, in addition to the issue of profitability, critical mass of both buyers and sellers is needed for markets to be truly efficient, where strong and fair competition can be developed.

QUALITY UNCERTAINTY AND QUALITY ASSURANCE

While price is becoming the major factor influencing many Web purchasers, quality is extremely important in many situations. When you buy a brand-name PC from Dell, IBM, or Compaq, you are fairly sure about the quality of the product or service you buy. When you buy from a not so well-known vendor, however, quality can become a major issue. The issue of quality is related to the issue of trust, which was discussed in chapter 3, and the issue of consumer protection, which was covered in chapter 10. In both places we described the idea of providing quality assurance by a trusted third-party intermediary. For example, TRUST-e and the BBB provide a testimonial seal for participating vendors. The BBB is known for its quality assurance system of physically testing products.

The problem of quality is frequently referred to as the **quality uncertainty**. Customers have a cognitive difficulty accepting products that they have never seen from a strange vendor. The BBB and TRUST-e seals can convince some customers but not all. Customers are not sure what they will get. Here are some possible solutions.

- *Provide free samples.* This is a clear signal that the vendor is confident about the quality. However, samples cost money. It is a sunk cost that needs to be recovered from future sales. Shareware-type software is based on this concept.
- *Return if you are not satisfied.* This policy is common in several countries and is used by most large retailers and manufacturers. This policy, which provides a guarantee or a full refund for dissatisfied customers, is facilitating EC. Such a policy, however, might not be feasible for digital products for several reasons.

First, many digital products such as information, knowledge, or educational material are fully consumed when they are viewed by consumers. After they are consumed, therefore, returning the products has little meaning. Unlike physical products, returning a digital product does not prevent the consumer from using the product in the future. Also, the vendor cannot resell the returned product.

Second, returning a product or refunding a purchase price may be impractical due to transaction costs. A microproduct—a small digital product costing a few cents or less—for example, must be transported twice over the network, so the cost for refund may exceed the price. Microproducts supported by micropayments, therefore, may not be sold with any quality guarantee or a refund. For further discussion of quality uncertainty see Choi et al. (1997).

PRICING ON THE INTERNET

Pricing products and services are very important in any economy, including the digital one. Pricing in many cases determines sale volume, market share, and product profitability. Several issues are related to pricing. A few are discussed next.

According to Bakos (1998), electronic marketplaces enable new types of **price discovery** to be employed in different markets. For example, some airlines auction last-minute unsold seats to the highest bidders, and Web-based auctions at Onsale.com have created markets for consumer goods that function like the financial markets. Intermediaries such as Priceline (www.priceline.com) allow buyers to specify product requirements and the amount they are willing to pay and then make corresponding offers to the participating sellers, reversing the traditional functioning of retail markets. Finally, intelligent agents such as Kasbah (http://ecommerce.media.mit.edu/kasbah) and Tête-à-Tête (http://ecommerce.media.mit.edu/tete-a-tete), can negotiate purchases on behalf of buyers and sellers, and may restructure the price discovery process in Internet marketplaces.

The ability to customize products, combined with the ability of sellers to access substantial information about prospective buyers, such as demographics, preferences, and past shopping behavior, is greatly improving sellers' ability to *price discriminate*—that is, to charge different prices for different buyers.

The new types of price discovery are changing the microstructure of consumer markets, the distribution channels, and the bargaining power of buyers and sellers (depending on the circumstances).

In a market with highly differentiated and customized products, prices tend to be determined by buyers' willingness to pay rather than by the cost of production. The market force behind this fact is the market power obtained by product differentiation. Thus, pricing is a matter of how valuable a product is to a buyer, not how much it costs to produce it. Suppose that a digital product can be produced at zero variable cost. Even then, prices can be set at the consumer's value. Therefore, its price will not be zero unless the product is truly valueless. Prices based on user values necessitate better information gathering about consumers' tastes (and income). The methods of collecting such information was discussed in chapter 3. The related issue of privacy was described in chapter 10.

Online vs. Offline Pricing

As described in chapters 2 and 5, many organizations operate both online and offline, offering the same products and services. For example, you can buy a book at Barnes & Noble's physical store or buy it at their online store. Your bank will offer you the same services online and offline and so will most stockbrokers. The question is how to price the online versus the offline products and services. This is an important strategic question. Some examples follow.

Pacific Brokerage Services (www.tradepbs.com) is a discount broker that was one of the early adopters of online trading. It offered almost 50 percent commission discount online ($15 versus $25 + $4 taxes). At the beginning they lost money due to lack of critical mass. Volume increased rapidly with time, however, and the strategy paid off; the company was bought by Dreyfus Brokerage Services, Inc. at a high profit to its owners.

In contrast, most banks do not offer any discounts for going online; some even charge additional (usually minimal) online fixed monthly service fees. Some banks, however, whose strategy is to aggressively go online, provide discounts. And what about retailers such as Toys "Я" Us and Wal-Mart? What about Disney Online or Tower Records? In most of these cases there is no clear strategy. Some products are offered online at a discount, others are not. Promotions are sometimes conducted online at different times from promotions offline. Futhermore, some retailers do not provide for any online discounts. Shoppers' convenience may play a major role in such a decision. If the vendors believe that the major reason the buyers come to the Web is convenience, they will not provide a discount. An example is Peapod Online. Grocery shoppers pay more at Peapod (www.peapod.com) than they pay in most supermarkets, and they pay additional delivery charges. Peapod's shoppers are looking primarily for convenience. This situation may change, though, when more online grocers and a critical mass of buyers join the marketspace. Netgrocer offers discounts, but they sell only nonperishable items.

CONTRIBUTORS TO ELECTRONIC MARKET SUCCESS

Based on an analysis of the EC examples previously discussed, it is apparent that EC will impact some industries more than others. The question then is what are some of the factors that determine this level of impact? Strader and Shaw (1997) have identified several factors that each fall within one of four categories: product, industry, seller, and consumer characteristics.

Product Characteristics

Digitizable products are particularly suited for electronic markets because they not only take advantage of the digitization of the market mechanism but also the distribution mechanism, resulting in very low transaction costs. It also enables the order fulfillment cycle time to be minimized.

The level of a product's price may also be an important determinant. The higher the product price, the greater the level of risk involved in the market transaction between buyers and sellers who are geographically separated and may have never dealt with each other before. Therefore, some of the most common items currently sold through electronic-markets in large quantities are low-priced items such as CDs and books.

Finally, computers, electronic products, consumer products, and even cars can be sold electronically because the consumer knows exactly what he or she is buying. This includes customized products such as PCs. The more standards and product information exist in an industry the better. The use of multimedia can dramatically facilitate product description.

Industry Characteristics

Electronic markets are most useful when they are able to directly match buyers and sellers. However, some industries require transaction brokers, so they may be affected less by electronic markets than are industries where no brokers are required. Stockbrokers, insurance agents, and travel agents may provide services that are still needed, but in some cases software may be able to replace the need for these brokers. This is particularly true as more intelligent systems that assist consumers become available.

Seller Characteristics

Electronic markets reduce search costs, enabling consumers to find sellers offering lower prices. In the long run this reduces profit margins for sellers that compete in electronic markets, although it may also increase the number of transactions that take place. If sellers in an industry are unwilling to participate in this environment, then the impact of electronic markets may be reduced. In highly competitive industries, with low barriers to entry, sellers may not have a choice. In oligopolistic situations, however, sellers may determine the success of electronic markets in an industry if they want to maintain an environment of lower-volume, higher-profit margin transactions.

Consumer Characteristics

Consumers can be classified as either impulse, patient, or analytical as discussed in chapter 3. Electronic markets may have little impact on industries where a sizable percentage of purchases are made by impulse buyers. For example, a high percentage of grocery store purchases are impulsive. Because electronic markets require a certain degree of effort on the part of the consumer, these markets are more conducive to consumers who do some comparisons and analysis before buying (the patient or analytical buyers). Analytical buyers can use the facilities available to analyze a wide range of information before deciding where to buy.

The determinants discussed provide a framework for estimating the impact of electronic markets on current or future industries. The more industry features (including product, industry, seller, and consumer characteristics) associated with higher electronic market impact, the greater the expected impact of electronic markets on that industry.

12.6   Impacts on Industry Structure, Intermediaries, and Others

It is apparent from the examples provided in this book that the diffusion of electronic markets in an industry has an impact on the structure of the value chain involved in supplying the products and/or services to the final consumers. Strader and Shaw (1997) compared the traditional market shown in Figure 12.3 (part a) with the electronic market (part b).

In a traditional market, customers search out information about the products available and their prices, quality, and features. This information comes from a wide range of sources including advertising, traveling to retail stores, and so forth. At some point, the consumers stop their search because they realize that further searching will probably not benefit them or that they have run out of time. Once the information gathered has been analyzed, the consumers decide if and where to buy the product. The product is then purchased at a store.

Electronic markets affect this consumer purchase process. The first phase in the transformation of the structure of an industry is the digitization of the market mechanism that reduces the search costs (money, time, and effort expended to gather product price, quality, and feature information) for consumers. Search also reduces the likelihood that sellers will be able to charge significantly higher prices than their competitors because the consumer is now aware of the competitors' prices. The result is that consumers can buy products for lower prices, intermediaries such as wholesalers are eliminated from the value chain, a new industry that provides access to electronic markets is created, and firms that produce products are able to maintain a profit margin comparable to the traditional markets.

The second phase in the transformation of the structure of an industry is the digitization of the product itself as well as its distribution. Digitized products involve a cost structure with increasing returns and low marginal reproduction costs. Increasing returns accrue when a business incurs large up-front expenditures to develop a new product/service, and the incremental cost of producing each new unit is minimal. Digitization also eliminates the need for sellers to maintain an inventory that must be physically shipped to the consumer. A digitized market can be especially efficient when electronic payment methods will become more widely used.

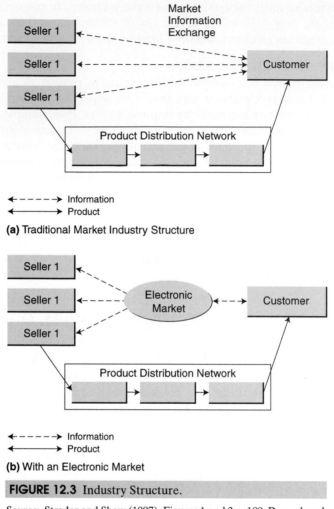

FIGURE 12.3 Industry Structure.

Source: Strader and Shaw (1997), Figures 1 and 2 p. 189. Reproduced with permission from Elsevier Science, Inc.

The electronic market and distribution network enables a wide range of seller and customer activities to converge into one place including marketing, order processing, distribution, payments, and even product development processes that could involve several separate firms. This makes these activities easier and more convenient while also reducing the costs involved. Beyond cost reduction, cycle time for order fulfillment is minimized, which may result in improved customer satisfaction. Digitized information can be distributed in minutes, while shipping a product generally takes days (or longer to some parts of the world). The characteristics of the phases in the transformation of industry structures enabled by EC are summarized in Table 12.3.

THE ROLES AND VALUE OF BROKERS IN E-MARKETS[1]

Producers and consumers interact directly in a marketplace: Producers provide information to customers, who select from among the available products. In general, producers set prices, but sometimes prices are negotiated. However, direct negotiations

---

[1]Condensed from Resnick et al. (1998).

	Traditional Market (example: retail store)	*Electronic Market (Phase 1)*	*Electronic Market and Distribution (Phase 2)*
TABLE 12.3 The Phases of Industry Structure Transformation Enabled by Electronic Markets			
Required industry characteristics	Transactions that do not require hierarchical governance	Accepted standards for describing the product through the electronic market	Description standards plus product that is feasibly digitized
Market digitized?	No	Yes	Yes
Product and distribution digitized?	No	No	Yes
Examples of intermediaries removed		Wholesalers and some forms of brokers (ones that simply gather and analyze information for consumers)	Phase 1 intermediaries plus firms in the physical distribution network
Examples of intermediaries added		Firms that provide access to the electronic market (ISPs or firms that operate electronic markets or electronic auctions) and possibly new forms of brokers (such as online better business bureaus)	Phase 1 intermediaries

Source: Strader and Shaw (1997). Reproduced with permission from Elsevier Science, Inc.

are sometimes undesirable or unfeasible. Fortunately, intermediaries, whether human or electronic, can address the following five important limitations of privately negotiated transactions.

Search Costs

It may be expensive for providers and consumers to find each other. In the bazaar of the information superhighway, for example, thousands of products are exchanged among millions of people. Brokers can maintain databases of customer preferences and reduce search costs by selectively routing information from providers to consumers and by matching customers with products and/or services. But producers may have trouble accurately gauging consumer demand for new products; many desirable items may never be produced simply because no one recognizes the demand for them. Brokers with access to customer preference data can predict demand. Large numbers of intermediaries already offer such services.

Lack of Privacy

Either the buyer or seller may wish to remain anonymous or at least to protect some information relevant to a trade. Brokers can relay messages and make pricing and allocation decisions without revealing the identity of one or both parties.

Incomplete Information

The buyer may need more information than the seller is able or willing to provide, such as information about product quality, competing products, or customer satisfaction. A broker can gather product information from sources other than the product provider, including independent evaluators and other customers. Examples are some travel agents online, stockbrokers, and real estate agencies.

Contracting Risk

A consumer may refuse to pay after receiving a product, or a producer may provide inferior products or give inadequate postpurchase service. Brokers have a number of tools to reduce risk. First, the broker can disseminate information about the behavior of providers and consumers. The threat of publicizing bad behavior or removing some seal of approval may encourage both producers and consumers to meet the broker's standard for fair dealing. Second, if publicity is insufficient, the broker may accept responsibility for the behavior of parties in transactions it arranges and act as a policeman on its own. Third, the broker can provide insurance against bad behavior. The credit card industry uses all three approaches just described to reduce providers' and consumers' exposure to risk. In the online auction area there are companies that act as "escrow agencies," as described in chapter 5.

Pricing Inefficiencies

By jockeying to secure a desirable price for a product, providers and consumers may miss opportunities for mutually desirable exchanges. This is particularly likely in negotiations over unique or custom products, such as houses, and markets for information products, and other public goods where free riding is a problem. Brokers can use pricing mechanisms that induce just the appropriate exchanges, for example, dealing with an imbalance of buy and sell orders in stock markets.

The Information Superhighway offers new opportunities for brokering services. First, brokers are especially valuable when the number of participants is enormous, as with the stock market, or when information products are exchanged. Second, many brokering services require information processing; electronic versions of these services can offer more sophisticated features at a lower cost than is possible with human labor. Finally, for delicate negotiations, a computer mediator may be more predictable, and hence more trustworthy, than a human. For example, suppose a mediator's role is to inform a buyer and a seller whether a deal should go through, without revealing either's reservation price to the other, since such a revelation would influence subsequent price negotiations. An independent auditor can verify that a software mediator will reveal only the information it is supposed to; a human mediator's fairness is less easily verified.

POTENTIAL WINNERS AND LOSERS IN EC

It is still unclear who will be the final winners and losers in EC. Some predict that many traditional brokers will soon become an "endangered species." Here are some potential winners and losers.

Winners

1. **Internet access providers.** America Online is clearly the winner, but several other companies will do well (for example, PSINet is a successful provider to the commercial market).
2. **Portal providers.** Many companies, including Yahoo and Lycos, offer portal services. These companies are expanding rapidly.
3. **Providers of diversified Internet services.** Yahoo, Lycos, Infoseek, and other early search engine providers are providing many related services, ranging from targeted advertisement to community hosting.
4. **EC software companies.** Starting from Netscape, IBM, Microsoft, and HP, there are scores of other winners in this area.
5. **Proprietary network owners.** Most EC networks will be open systems not owned by any one company. However, some large manufacturers or resellers (e.g., John Deere in farm equipment, W. W. Grainger in industrial supply distribution, or Baxter Healthcare in medical supplies) may have enough power to sustain proprietary systems at least for several years. With-

out regulatory action, these types of companies will be able to lower their selling costs, differentiate themselves from competitors without EC networks, attract new customers, and gain a significant strategic advantage.

6. **Midsize manufacturers.** Midsize manufacturers are squeezed between market leader dominance and smaller competitor flexibility. With an open EC network, midsize manufacturers will have greater access and exposure to customers. Small vendors will also gain access, but buyers will likely be skeptical about smaller vendors' support and financial and delivery capabilities. Exceptions are in niche markets and earlier players in EC that established a name, such as Amazon.com (section 12.9).

7. **Technology suppliers.** When EC networks revolutionize the distribution business, the demand for related software, services, and hardware will climb astronomically. Industry leaders such as Cisco will do very well.

8. **Advertisement and target marketing companies.** Starting with pioneers such as Broadvision and DoubleClick, there are scores of companies that are making their fortune in these rapidly expanding fields.

9. **A few large resellers.** With less need for customized support and the personal relationships it fosters, a few large resellers in each industry will use their economies of scale in logistics and automation to gobble up market shares. Some surprising companies may emerge in this large reseller arena. Express delivery companies such as FedEx or UPS are examples.

10. **Security, special infrastructure, and payment systems providers.** Dozens of companies are assuming leadership positions in the area of security, special infrastructures (such as VPN), encryption, payments and special Internet languages (Java, PERL, VRML, and so on).

11. **Online dedicated companies.** Companies such as E*TRADE, eBAY, eToys, and Amazon.com are establishing strong leadership roles in the online market.

12. **Conventional retailers that use online extensively.** Starting with Wal-Mart, Dell, and Cisco, there are hundreds of large corporations in manufacturing, retailing, banking, and services that have created successful online divisions, which provide them with strategic advantage.

13. **Market makers.** Companies that organize electronic markets such as Chemdex, GE Information Services, or Rowe.com will emerge by the dozens and replace traditional brokers and salespeople (see the losers).

14. **Others.** Dozens of other companies are growing rapidly by provided Internet and/or EC services. These range from Network Solutions Inc. (domain names) to @Home (Internet access over cable television).

Losers

1. **Most wholesalers, especially small ones.** There are almost half a million distributors in the United States alone; 98 percent of them have fewer than 100 employees. Technology has already reduced the need for local distributors that can provide rapid delivery and service. Electronic commerce will accelerate this trend.

2. **Brokers.** Brokers of all kinds will lose. Airlines are cutting commissions due to electronic ticketing, and many real estate, stock, insurance, and other brokers will lose their jobs.

3. **Salespeople.** Electronic commerce networks will dramatically alter the role of salespeople. Companies will increasingly rely on EC networks at the expense of product-focused salespeople. However, as EC networks provide

more pricing, product, and delivery data online, the surviving salespeople will be those that offer real, value-added consulting. They will help customers interpret, analyze, and prioritize the increased data available through EC networks. They will also help customers restructure their purchasing, stocking, and usage patterns.

4. **Nondifferentiated manufacturers.** Electronic commerce networks will expose to risk those companies that are neither low cost nor innovative. Over the last few years, increasing customer awareness and increasing availability of product and price information have already squeezed out many marginal suppliers. The ability of EC networks to highlight price and product information will accentuate this trend.

12.7 Virtual Communities

The N$_2$K opening vignette demonstrated an economic impact of **Internet communities.** With millions of members, such communities could have significant effects on markets. Many thousands of communities exist on the Net. On many Web sites, one can find some services for community members. For example, Recreational Equipment Inc. (www.recreational.com) uses its chat room to put wilderness experts in touch with shoppers. Several communities are independent and are growing rapidly. For instance, GeoCities (www.geocities.com) has grown to several million members in less than two years. Community members set up personal home pages on the site and advertisers buy ad space targeted to community members. In order to understand the economic impact of electronic communities, let us see what they really are.

THE INTERNET COMMUNITIES

Rheingold (1993) believes that the Web is being transformed into a social Web of communities. He thinks that every Web site should incorporate a place for people to chat. His popular Web site, http://www.minds.com, is an interesting place to visit, a kind of virtual community center. It is a place where discussions cover many controversial topics but mostly the impact of technology on life.

Electronic communities are also related to EC. For example, Champy et al. 1996 describe online, consumer-driven markets where most of the consumers' needs, ranging from finding a mortgage to job hunting, will be arranged from home. Electronic communities will eventually have a massive impact on almost every company that produces consumer goods and services, as was shown in the opening case. The electronic communities will change the nature of corporate strategy and the manner in which business is done.

Electronic communities are spreading quickly over the Internet. Armstrong and Hagel (1996) and Hagel and Armstrong (1997) recognize the following four types of electronic communities.

Communities of Transactions

These communities facilitate buying and selling. Members include buyers, sellers, intermediaries, and so on. In chapter 2, we provided examples such as Virtual Vineyards, which in addition to selling wines provides expert information on wines and a place for wine lovers to chat with each other. The GE/TPN network created an infrastructure for communities of traders to conduct bids or simply buy and sell (TPN-mart). Another example can be found at www.e-steel.com, which acts as a steel industry community center.

Communities of Interest

Here, people have the chance to interact with each other on a specific topic. For example, if you are interested in gardening, try www.gardenweb.com. The Motley Fool (www.fool.com) is a forum for individual investors. City411 provides comprehensive information about local communities where many topics such as entertainment, traffic, and weather reports are displayed. www.planetit.com is the community for the IT professionals.

Geocities' (www.geocities.com) several million members are organized into dozens of communities such as MotorCity (car lovers) and Nashville (country music). Members have a marketplace for buying and selling goods and services. One of the largest communities is the Web Chat Broadcasting System (www.wbs.net), which has several million members, mostly between 12 and 35 years of age, sharing Web-related interests. Infoseek purchased this community in April of 1998.

Communities of Relations

These communities are organized around certain life experiences. For example, the cancer forum on CompuServe contains information and exchange of opinions regarding cancer. Parent Soup is a favorite gathering spot for parents, seniors like to visit "SeniorNet," and Women's Wire is a well-known online community aimed at women, with regular celebrity chats and discussions.

Many communities are organized according to professional business interests. For example, plasticsnet.com is used by thousands of engineers in the plastics industry. A related extranet, www.commerx.com, provides a cybermarket for the industry.

Communities of Fantasy

Here, participants create imaginary environments. For example, AOL subscribers can pretend to be a medieval baron at the Red Dragon Inn. On ESPNet, participants can create competing teams and "play" with Michael Jordan. Related to this is a large number of games that thousands of people play simultaneously. In Aliens online you can win only if you join a team for $10 a month; in Politike you can plot with and against other players and Kingdom of Drakkar allows you to play various roles.

Interactive Week (May 11, 1998) provides the following suggestions on how to transform a community site into a commerce site:

1. Understand a particular niche industry, its information needs, and the step-by-step process by which it does the research needed to do business.
2. Build a site that provides that information, either through partnerships with existing publishers and information providers or by gathering it independently.
3. Set up the site to mirror the steps a user goes through in the information-gathering and decision-making process, for example, how a chip designer whittles down the list of possible chips that will fit a particular product.
4. Build a community that relies on the site for decision support.
5. Start selling products and services, such as sample chips to engineers, that fit into the decision-support process.

Forrester Research conducted a survey in 1998 that found the following expected payback by order of importance:

- customer loyalty increases,
- sales increase,
- customer participation and feedback increases,
- repeat traffic to site increases,
- new traffic to site increases.

Communities offer many services to their members. Typical services are message boards, including opinions and responses; and member activities, such as what is going on, site statistics, chat rooms, free e-mail service, and free Web page.

Electronic communities can create value in several ways as summarized in Figure 12.4. Members input useful information to the community in the form of comments, feedback, elaborating their attitudes and beliefs, and information needs that is retrieved and used by other members or by marketers. The community organizers may also put in their own content communities such as America Online, where members need to pay subscription fees.

Another possibility for value creation in electronic-communities arises from the fact that the community brings together consumers of specific demographics and interests. This presents opportunities for transacting business and communicating messages about products and services, which marketers and advertisers value and are willing to pay for. Marketers actually offer various discounts to members. In addition, electronic communities can attract advertising revenues from advertisers eager to communicate their messages to community members. (This is currently a significant source of revenue for electronic communities). Other opportunities arise from the marketing information that is generated within communities, which marketers and advertisers find valuable. Such information includes demographics and psychographics of members; their attitudes and beliefs about products, services, and issues; their behavior data with regard to business transactions within communities; and information on their interactions and interaction dynamics. Such information, which is collected from the chat

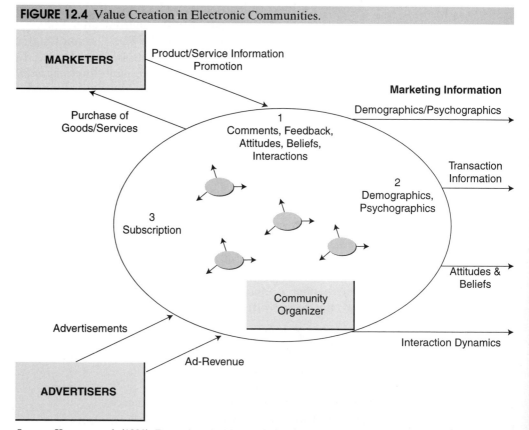

FIGURE 12.4 Value Creation in Electronic Communities.

Source: Kannan et al. (1998). Reproduced with permission from *Communications of the ACM.*

room, questionnaires, or e-mail communications, could be sold to marketers and advertisers if the members do not object.

Also, communities charge members content fees for downloading certain articles, music, or pictures. Finally, since community members create their own home pages, it is easy to learn about them and reach them for targeted advertisement and marketing. For a look at the ways companies can benefit by using communities to make connections with members and exploit opportunities, see the book *Net Again*, by Hagel and Armstrong (1997). A special report of *Business Week* (Hof et al. 1997) provides an overview of the field with coverage of the most interesting communities and their special terminology. Also see Kannan (1998).

12.8 Global Electronic Commerce

A global electronic marketplace has become the mantra of the free market and free traders. It means access to larger markets, mobility (to minimize taxes), and flexibility to employ workers and manufacture products anywhere using a worldwide telecommuting workforce. The potential for a global economy is certainly here, but artificial borders are being erected through local language preference, local regulations, access limitations, and so on.

While geographical market boundaries may be falling, global interest-based communities will spring up. These cybernations' interest or taste differences are as real as political boundaries. Online firms may gain access to these cybernations and to a specific segment of consumer groups on a worldwide scale.

Global electronic markets have existed for more than 20 years, mainly in support of B2B financial and other repetitive, standard transactions. Most well known are the EFT and EDI. However, these markets were supported by expensive private telecommunication lines and, therefore, were limited to medium and large corporations as well as to the nature of the transactions. The emergence of the Internet and the extranets resulted in an inexpensive and flexible infrastructure that can greatly facilitate global trade (Clinton and Gore 1997). The major advantage of EC is the ability to do business anytime and from anywhere and do it rapidly at a reasonable cost. Indeed, we have seen some incredible success stories in this area. For example:

- You can buy and sell stocks online in several countries using E*TRADE as your broker.
- Amazon.com sells books to individuals and organizations in over 150 countries.
- Small companies, such as www.wine.com, sell to hundreds of customers worldwide. Hothothot, for example, which has both a physical and online stores, reported its first international trade only after it went online. Within two years, global sales climbed to 25 percent of the offline sales.
- Major corporations, such as General Electric and Boeing Inc., reported an increasing number of out-of-the-country vendors participating in their electronic bids requests for quotes. The electronic bids resulted in a 10 percent to 15 percent cost reduction and an over 50 percent cycle time reduction.
- Many international corporations considerably increase their success in recruiting employees for foreign locations when online recruiting is utilized.

BARRIERS TO GLOBAL EC

There are many barriers to global EC. Some are similar to barriers of any EC (chapter 1) and are divided here into the following four categories.

Legal Issues

The U.S. and other major international organizations such as the European Commission, the United Nations Commission on International Trade Law (UNCITRAL), the OCED (chapter 10), and the World Trade Organization, are presently engaged in discussions pertaining to the development of domestic and global legal frameworks that will facilitate EC worldwide. Among these organizations there seems to be a consensus only to the extent that uncoordinated actions must be avoided and that an international policy of cooperation should be encouraged.

The challenge of an international policy accord is essentially how to secure the legal framework that will facilitate EC throughout the world without infringing on the freedom of governments to pursue their own objectives. Some of the legal issues involved are jurisdiction issues, export/import regulations and compliance, intellectual property (enforcement), cryptography (encryption) and security, contracts, notarized documents, authentication procedures, privacy protection, cross-border transactions (data protection), content control, and consumer protection. Most of these issues are generic and were discussed in chapter 10.

Market Access Issues

Market access issues, if not addressed, could impede the growth of global EC. Building a telecommunications infrastructure capable of accommodating all users and all types of data is a necessity. Companies starting EC need to evaluate bandwidth needs by analyzing the data required, time constraints, access demands, and user technology limitations. Monitoring and complying with technical standards developed will also minimize, if not eliminate, the possibility of incompatible technologies between the company and the user. The key issue for any company thinking about engaging in global EC is to keep abreast of the changing standards and laws associated with the Internet. Other issues include technical standards and electronic transmissions standards.

Financial Issues

Financial issues encompassing global EC include customs and taxation and electronic payment systems. It is difficult to administer tariffs for products ordered over the Internet and delivered the traditional way, surface or air. Many countries may want to add tariffs to the products, increasing the price to the consumer or business. All products delivered the traditional way will need to go through customs, which will lengthen the amount of time it takes for the customer to receive the merchandise. The timely delivery of goods is a key factor in a consumer's decision to order products over the Internet. The biggest time savings is reached in digitized products. Thus far, such purchases are not subject to sales tax and tariffs. This may have a large impact on the success of global EC. However, the tax freeze is for only until 2001 and its future is uncertain.

Another financial issue to consider is money exchange. All electronic payment systems will need to be able to exchange currency immediately. This is not all; for example, for some currencies the decimal points are more important than others are when converting (Andrews 1998). There are several other financial issues to consider when interacting in real time with other countries, particularly when credit cards are not used. (Credit card purchases generally take care of the currency exchange for you.) For example, the imposion of sales tax, and import/export charges. Also important is the integration of the EC transaction with the accounting/finance internal information system of the sellers.

Other Issues

Several other issues need to be considered in global EC, some of which are generic while others are unique. Representative issues are:

- identification of buyers and sellers,
- trust,
- security (for example, viruses),
- cultural diversity,
- international agreements (multilateral agreements),
- language and translation,
- purchasing in local currencies,
- role and policy of government.

Each of these topics can be discussed at length. Due to space limitations, we deal only with the last three issues.

Language and Translation

The language barrier between countries and regions presents an interesting and complicated challenge. Although English is widely accepted as the primary language of the Internet, an effective Web site in some cases may need to be specifically designed and targeted to the market that it is trying to reach. The primary problems with this level of language customization are cost and speed. It currently takes a human translator about a week to translate a medium Web site into just one language. The cost ranges from $10,000 to $500,000, depending on the complexity of the site and languages of translation. WorldPoint (www.worldpoint.com) presents a creative solution to these issues with their WorldPoint Passport multi-lingual software tool. www.freetranslation.com provide free translation in eight languages.

The WorldPoint Passport solution allows Web developers to create a Web site in one language and deploy it in several other languages. Cost of translation using the software is estimated at 24 cents per word of Chinese and 26 cents per word in French. In a 1999 demonstration of the software's power, WorldPoint translated Japan's primary telephone company's (NTT) Web site into 10 different Asian languages in only 3 days.

Purchasing in Different Currencies

A potential barrier to global commerce is the different currencies whose exchange rate may change every minute. A solution was provided in 1998 by WorldPay System (with PSINet). The software lets online sellers offer products in 126 different currencies and receive settlement payments in 16. Based on the SET protocol, the system provides real-time exchange rate information so buyers get the price of the products in their own currency. The concept is revolutionary. Today, many credit card issuers provide their customers with automatic currency exchange services for multiple currencies. However, buyers do not know how much they really paid until they receive a monthly statement, and many banks add steep service charges for such transactions. (For further details see *Internet World*, October 6, 1997.)

THE U.S. POLICY REGARDING GLOBAL EC

The U.S. policy on global EC per Clinton and Gore (1997) includes the following five principles:

1. *The private sector should lead.* The Internet should develop as a market-driven arena, not a regulated industry. Even where collective action is necessary, governments should encourage industry self-regulation and private sector leadership where possible.
2. *Governments should avoid undue restrictions on EC.* In general, parties should be able to enter into legitimate agreements to buy and sell products and ser-

vices across the Internet with minimal government involvement or intervention. Governments should refrain from imposing new and unnecessary regulations, bureaucratic procedures, or new taxes and tariffs on commercial activities that take place over the Internet.

3. ***Where government involvement is needed, its aim should be to support and enforce a predictable minimalist, consistent, and simple legal environment for commerce.*** Where government intervention is necessary, its role should be to ensure competition, protect intellectual property and privacy, prevent fraud, foster transparency, and facilitate dispute resolution, not to regulate.

4. ***Governments should recognize the unique qualities of the Internet.*** The genius and explosive success of the Internet can be attributed in part to its decentralized nature and to its traditions of bottom-up governance. We should not assume that the regulatory frameworks established over the past 60 years for telecommunications, radio, and television fit the Internet. Existing laws and regulations that may hinder EC should be reviewed and revised or eliminated to reflect the needs of the new electronic age.

5. ***Electronic commerce on the Internet should be facilitated on a global basis.*** The Internet is a global marketplace. The legal framework supporting commercial transactions should be consistent and predictable regardless of the jurisdiction in which a particular buyer and seller reside.

Another interesting issue in global EC is the opportunity for even the smallest businesses to go global with unprecedented low costs (for example, Application Case 12.3). The global marketspace erases national borders and gives even the smallest companies worldwide reach. For example, Seidman (1995) reported that a small company in Gilbert, Arizona, generated half of its international trade on the Web during its first year, and the international trade was growing at a rate of 50 percent per year. How small companies are doing in the marketspace is the topic of our next section.

APPLICATION CASE 12.3

Small Businesses and Global Trade

Cardiac Science (Irvine, California) has been trying to break into the international market for years. Today, 85 percent of the company's revenue is international and much of this is executed over a Web site (www.cardiacscience.com). The company makes cardiac medical devices, and in 1997, it shipped to 46 countries. The company answers inquiries within 24 hours, sending out product information to promising sales leads.

One of the issues to consider is that small businesses need a great deal of advice regarding doing global business. Here are some useful Web sites used by Cardiac:

- Universal Business Exchange (www.unibex.com) offers trade leads with the added capability of matching buyers and sellers automatically.
- Several government agencies provide online information for nominal fees (e.g., National Trade Data Bank, Economic Bulletin Board, and Globus; all are at www.stat-usa.gov.).

The Web business is not as simple as it sounds. Cardiac's CEO said that "crafting a solid export strategy takes a lot more commitment than putting up a snazzy Web site and waiting for the world to show up at our door. It's all about building relationships." The Internet is important for introductions, but you must follow it up properly.

12.9 Electronic Commerce in Small Companies

Some of the first companies to take advantage of EC on the Web were, in fact, small companies, some of which were start-ups. Prime examples are Virtual Vineyards, Hothothot, and Happy Puppy, cited earlier. In this section we explore both the advantages (opportunities) and the disadvantages and risks for small businesses in the Web economy. The following are the major advantages:

- Inexpensive source of information
- Inexpensive way of advertising
- Inexpensive way of conducting market research
- Inexpensive way to build (or rent) a storefront
- Lower transaction cost
- Niche market; specialty products (cigars, wines, sauces) are the best
- Image and public recognition can be accumulated fast
- Inexpensive way of providing catalogs
- Inexpensive way and opportunity to reach worldwide customers

The following is a list of risks and disadvantages for small businesses:

- Inability to use EDI, unless it is EDI/Internet
- Lack of resources to fully exploit the Web
- Lack of expertise in legal issues, advertisement, etc.
- Less risk tolerance than a large company
- Disadvantage when a commodity is the product (for example, CDs)
- No more personal contact, which is a strong point of a small business
- No advantage of being in a local community

There are basically two contradictory opinions regarding small companies. The first one is that EC is a blessing, the second is that the small companies will not survive for an extended period of time. Here are some of the arguments.

One attempt to explain the differences was rendered by King and Blanning (1997), who developed a matrix that classifies online companies into two categories: convivial niche and virtual storehouse. Convivial niches are mainly small companies (such as Virtual Vineyards) with low volumes of business (Table 12.4). The virtual

TABLE 12.4 Market Models		
Feature	*Convivial Niche*	*Virtual Storehouse*
Focus	Select variety Shopping experience	Extensive listings Convenience
Buyers	Upscale	High-tech
Price	Not an issue	Discounted, adaptable
Information	In-depth reviews Customer education	Comparisons Configuration Third-party reviews
Promotions	Samplers, Gifts Featured product testimonials	Time-based specials Offline ads
Feedback	Advice, forums	Customer support Demographic data
Size	Small	Large

Source: Based on King and Blanning (1997).

storehouse is characterized by large-volume, commodity-type products (like Amazon.com).

Small businesses have had online success mainly by selling specific product/services such as:

- Niche products, those with a low volume that are not carried by regular retail stores.
- Special books (for example, old, technical).
- International products, which are not easily available to consumers.
- Information. This category has a wide spectrum. GartnerGroup provides access to online research material that users can subscribe to. Yahoo provides search engines to indexed Internet information. Smaller companies may choose to provide specialized information such as home and gardening pages. Revenue sources could include home and garden retailers who place advertisements on the small business's Web page.

Many of the small businesses that have succeeded on the Internet have the following strategies in common:

- Capital investment must be small, to keep the companies' overhead and risk low.
- Inventory should be minimal or nonexistent.
- Electronic payments must be transmitted using secure means to reassure customers. Small businesses can work with vendors to provide this service.
- Payment methods must be flexible, to accommodate different levels of users. Some prefer to mail or fax in a form or talk to a live agent as opposed to transmitting a credit card number over the Internet.
- Logistical services must be quick and reliable. Small businesses have successfully subcontracted out their logistical services to FedEx, who are experts in the field.
- The Web site should be submitted to directory-based search engine services like Yahoo.
- Join an online service or mall, such as America Online or Viaweb's Viamall.
- Design a Web site that is functional and provides all needed services to consumers. In addition, Web sites should look professional enough to compete with larger competitors and be updated on a continual basis to maintain consumer interest.

Although there are many risks associated with EC, overall, the level of risk would be less for a small business when compared to opening brick-and-mortar businesses that require much more capital. In addition, many businesses that could not have survived outside of the Internet have been able to thrive due to the lower cost of entry.

SUPPORTING SMALL BUSINESSES

There are many ways in which support is provided to small businesses. For example, technical support is provided by IBM's services ($25 per month) (see www.businesscenter.lbm.com); Digital's virtual stores; and Microsoft's PWS. Even a government may support online commerce of small business as shown in Application Case 12.4.

To start an online business involves two major issues. The first one is how to start a business, which is a generic issue. The second one is how to open a business online. For tutorials on both topics see www.latimes.com/smallbiz.

Korean Government Helps Online Business

Most domestic software companies in Korea, especially small ones, do not have distribution channels of their own. Therefore, they pay almost a 40 percent commission to distributors pushing their products to end users. This is a major competitive disadvantage. To solve the problem the government established a software cybermall. The Internet shopping mall, which opened in 1998, provides demonstration products and the ability to buy and pay electronically. The mall is connected to the sites of many vendors. The process of buying in the mall is shown in the attached picture. Note that the software is downloaded rather than delivered physically.

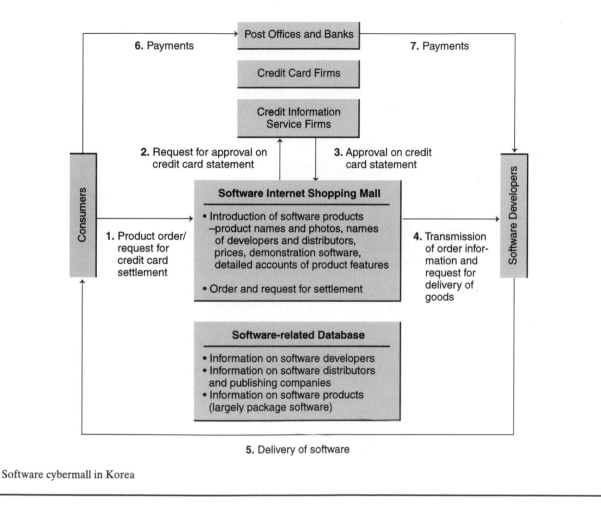

Software cybermall in Korea

12.10 Research in EC

The multidisciplinary nature of EC opens the door to a wide range of research, some of which can be done jointly by two or more disciplines. A simple way to classify EC research is to divide it into three categories: behavioral, technical, and managerial. Suggested representative research topics in each are provided by category.

BEHAVIORAL TOPICS

- Consumer behavior: cognitive processes, overcoming the limitations of remote control, and identifying impacts on people.
- Building consumers' behavioral profiles and identifying ways to utilize them.
- Seller's behavior and motivation: resistance to change and how to overcome it.
- Issue-oriented research.
    a. Why there is a slow adaptation of some applications and others are rapid.
    b. How will people accept/adjust EFT of government benefits?
- Internet usage pattern and willingness to buy.
- Mental model of consumer product search process, comparison process, and negotiation.
- How to build trust in the marketspace.

SUGGESTED TECHNICAL TOPICS

- Methods that help customers find what they want (such as using intelligent agents).
- Models for extranet design and management.
- Natural language processing and automatic language translation.
- Matching smart card technology with payment mechanisms.
- Integrating EC with existing corporate information systems, databases, and so on.
- Retrieval of information from an electronic industry directory.
- Establishing standards for international trade.
- Building a mobile Internet distribution command system (e.g., GPS).

SUGGESTED MANAGERIAL RESEARCH TYPES

- Advertisement: measuring the effectiveness, integration, and coordination with conventional advertisement.
- Applications: creating a methodology of finding EC business applications, analyzing the success or failure of applications (CSF) and configuring, distributing knowledge on the Internet.
- Strategy: defending strategic advantage (attack, defense) strategy for EC; initiating "Where to market" strategy; finding ways to integrate EC into organizations; developing methods of how to conduct "business intelligence"; and developing a methodology for conducting EC cost-benefit analysis.
- Impacts: identifying the organizational structure and organizational culture.
- Implementation: developing a framework for EC implementation activities like outsourcing, redesigning the role of intermediaries in EC, and developing methodologies for conducting consumer research.
- Others: building a framework for EC auditing, finding a methodology for pricing of online products/services, identifying solutions for distribution

channel conflict management, and studying the relationship between EC and BPR and EC and supply chain management.

Kimbrough and Lee (1997) raised the following questions regarding EC research:

1. What is possible and desirable with EC?
2. What are the operational and functional requirements for the applications of EC?
3. What does widespread realization of the possibilities for EC mean?

They also surveyed and summarized research issues, many of which related to EDI. Some of their suggested topic areas are open EC; electronic trade procedures; audit controls; automated trade procedures; protocols and contracts for intelligent negotiation agents; supporting management and decision making; optimizing using interface, interaction and customization; and multilingual electronic documents.

A framework for EC research is shown in Figure 12.5. The outcomes are basically consumers' buying attitudes and real purchasing. The influencing process variables are listed in the middle, and possible influential contextual variables are shown on the left.

FIGURE 12.5 A Framework for EC Research.

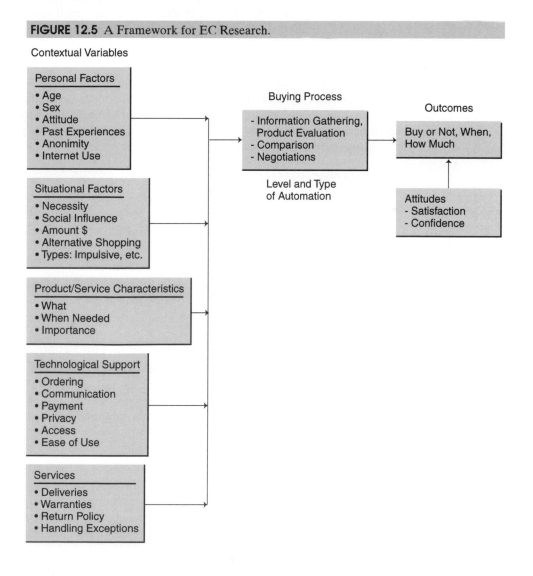

Many hypotheses can be formulated with this model and then tested empirically (journals such as the *International Journal of Electronic Commerce and the International Journal of Electronic Markets* publish such research results).

12.11   The Future of EC

Generally speaking, there is a consensus regarding the future of EC—it is bright. Differences exist as to the anticipated growth rate and the identification of industry segments that will grow the fastest. Such optimism about the future of EC is based on the following trends and observations.

INTERNET USAGE

The number of Internet users is increasing exponentially. With the integration of computers and television, cheaper PCs, increased availability of access kiosks, and increased publicity, there will be more and more Net surfers. As younger people grow, the usage will grow even further. There is no question that sooner or later there will be a billion people who surf the Net. By 1999 the number of worldwide Internet users was estimated to be over 250 million and the number of e-mail addresses over 400 million since many people have multiple addresses.

OPPORTUNITIES FOR BUYING

The number of products and services available on the Net is increasing rapidly with improved trading mechanisms, intermediary services, presentation in multiple languages, and sellers' willingness to give it a try. It is logical to expect significantly more purchasing opportunities. Several Web sites are reporting 15 percent to 25 percent monthly increases in sales.

PURCHASING INCENTIVES

The buyers' advantages described in chapter 1 are likely to increase. Prices will go down further, and the purchasing process will be streamlined. Many innovative options will be available, and electronic shopping may even become a social trend.

INCREASED SECURITY AND TRUST

One of the major inhibitors of B2C growth is the perception about poor security and privacy, and lack of trust. As time passes we expect significant improvements in all these areas.

EFFICIENT INFORMATION HANDLING

Much information will become accessible from anywhere, in real time. Using data warehouses and intelligent agents, companies can constantly learn about their customers, steering marketing and service activities accordingly. The notion of real-time marketing might not be so far away. This will facilitate the use of EC.

INNOVATIVE ORGANIZATIONS

Organizations are being restructured and reengineered with the help of IT (Turban et al. 1999 and Hammer and Stanton 1995). Using different types of empowered teams, some of which are virtual, organizations become innovative, flexible, and responsive. The trend for process reengineering is increasing and so is the organizational creativity. Innovative organizations will probably be more inclined to use EC.

VIRTUAL COMMUNITIES

Virtual communities of all kinds are spreading rapidly with some already reaching several million members. As seen in the opening case, virtual communities can enhance commercial activities online. Also, some communities are organized around professional areas of interest and can facilitate B2B commerce.

PAYMENT SYSTEMS

The ability to use e-cash cards and make micropayments is getting close to reality; when implemented on a large scale, many EC activities will flourish. As international standards become the norm, electronic payments will extend globally, facilitating global EC.

BUSINESS-TO-BUSINESS

Figures about the growth of B2B are being revised frequently. In some cases industry-type extranets are almost forcing everyone to participate. Business-to-business will continue to dominate the EC field (in terms of volume traded) for the intermediate future. There will be more sellers, more buyers, more services; the rapid growth will continue. The success of B2B (as well as B2C) will depend upon the success of integrating EC technology with business processes and with conventional information systems.

TECHNOLOGY TRENDS

The trend in EC technologies generally points toward significant cost reduction coupled with improvement in capabilities, ease of use, increased availability of software, ease of site development, and improved security and accessibility. Some specifics follow below.

- *Clients.*   PCs of all types are getting cheaper, smaller, and more capable. The concept of a network computer (NC), also known as a *thin client,* which moves processing and storage off the desktop and onto centrally located servers running Java-based software on UNIX (Windows on Microsoft's version), could bring the price of a PC to that of a television.

    Another major trend is the movement toward embedded clients. A client, in such a case, can be a car or a washing machine with an embedded microchip. In many cases, an expert system is embedded with rules that make the client "smarter" or more responsive to changes in the environment.

- *Servers.*   A major trend is to move to Windows NT as the enterprise operating system. Among NT's capabilities is providing clustering. Clustering servers can add processing power in much smaller increments than was previously possible. Clustering servers are very economical, resulting in cost reduction.

- *Networks.*   The use of EC frequently requires rich multimedia (such as color catalogs or providing samples of movies or music). A large bandwidth is required to accomplish this. Several broadband technologies (such as XDSL) will increase bandwidth manyfold. This could help in replacing expensive WANs or VANs by the inexpensive Internet. Security on the Internet can be enhanced by the use of VPNs.

    For countries without fiber-optic cables, wireless communication can save considerable installation time and money. In 1998, wireless access reached the T1 speed (about 1.5 mbps), with cost savings of over 80 percent. However, wireless networks may be too slow for some digitized products.

- *EC software and services.* The availability of all types of EC software will make it easier to establish stores on the Internet and to conduct all types of trades. Already hundreds of sites offer pages for inexpensive rent for a variety of activities ranging from conducting your own auctions and bids to selling in a foreign language. Other support services, such as escrow companies that support auctions and multiple types of certifications, are developing rapidly. Also, a large number of consultants are being trained to assist in specialty areas.

- *EC knowledge.* Being a new phenomenon, EC includes many uncertain and unknown aspects. However, as time passes the quantity and quality of related knowledge is increasing rapidly. The more we know about EC the more we can facilitate its expansion, which, in our opinion, is grossly underestimated.

- *Integration.* The forthcoming integration of the computer and the TV, and the computer and the telephone, including cellular phones, will increase accessibility to the Internet (e.g., see Silverman 1999).

Many people conclude (for example, Clinton and Gore 1997) that the impact of EC on our life will be as much as, and possibly more than, that of the Industrial Revolution. No other phenomenon since the Industrial Revolution has been classified in this category.

Summary

The compilation of this chapter helps you in attaining the following learning objectives:

1. **The major impacts of Web-based economics.** Everything will be different and the impacts are many. Marketing is changed to direct marketing, where intermediaries (if they survive) make the market or add special value. Competition is intensified and its nature changes. Customers pay less and get more, including superb customer service. Virtual communities play an increased role in the economy. Industry structure is changed and global trading accelerates. Even small companies get a big chance. Finally, certain markets are becoming very efficient.

2. **The major components of Web-based economics.** These are buyers, sellers, digital products and services, infrastructure companies, intermediaries, support services, and content creators. They all form marketspaces where transactions take place.

3. **The impact of the online market on competition.** The major impact is increased competition because more vendors enter the market and more information is available to both buyers and sellers. Small and foreign vendors, who previously competed in their local markets, are now operating globally. Some companies now sell at or even below cost, making profit from selling advertisement and e-mail lists. This intensifies competition even further. Companies offer larger differentiation and product customization. Finally, it becomes more difficult to sustain competitive advantage in many cases, which is visible in the marketspace and easy to duplicate.

4. **The impact on industry structure and intermediation.** Of the many impacts, most important are the reduction in distribution channels, reducing the information search cost (and time) of consumers, the digitization of products and their distribution, reduction of inventories, changing the role of partners

in the supply chain, and providing efficient market operations. Electronic intermediation is completely different from the physical one. Intermediaries will organize markets and provide value-added services ranging from acting as a trusted third-party intermediary to matching special customers' requirements with vendors' capabilities.

5. **The role and impact of virtual communities.** Virtual communities create new types of business—people with similar interests that are congregated in one Web site, a natural target for advertisers and marketers. Using chat rooms, members can exchange opinions about certain products and services. Of special interest are communities of transactions whose interest is the promotion of commerce buying and selling. The communities help to foster customer loyalty, increase sales of related vendors, and increase customers' feedback for improved service and business.

6. **Issues in global EC.** Going global with EC can be done quickly with a relatively small investment. However, in cases of some products/services and/or large volume, attention to certain issues must be paid. These include legal issues such as jurisdiction and contracts, intellectual property, government regulations regarding export/import, tariffs and taxation, payment mechanisms, Web site presentation, language translation, and currency conversion. The U.S. government policy is to make global trade free from restrictions simple, and without sales tax. There is little international agreement on such a policy as well as on the necessary payments and other standards.

7. **Small business in EC.** Depending on the circumstances, small companies have a tremendous chance to enter EC with little cost and expand rapidly, or they may be eliminated by larger online competitors. Being in a niche market provides the best chance for small business. Going after high-volume, commodity-type products (such as CDs, books, or computers) can be too risky for a small company.

8. **Research opportunities in EC.** There are hundreds of research topics in the new discipline. They can be categorized as behavioral (mainly of consumers), technological, and managerial.

9. **The future of EC.** Electronic commerce will continue to expand rapidly. To begin with, its infrastructure is becoming better and less expensive with time. Second, consumers will be more experienced and will try different products and services and also tell their friends about it. Security, privacy protection, and trust will be much higher, and more support services will simplify the transaction process. Legal issues will be clarified, and more and more products and services will be online at reduced prices.

Keywords

- Digital products (services)
- Economics of electronic commerce
- Global electronic commerce
- Internet (virtual) community
- Marketspace
- Micropayments
- Price discovery
- Quality uncertainty
- Webonomics

Questions for Review

1. Define marketspace and marketplace.
2. Define digitized products (services) and provide some examples.
3. List the five EC principles of the U.S. government.
4. List the major components of digital economies.
5. Define electronic communities.
6. List the major types of electronic communities.

7. List the major components of the behavioral research framework.
8. List the major drivers of global EC.
9. List the potential benefits and limitations of a small business online.
10. List the major factors that could facilitate EC in the future.
11. Describe the issue of uncertain quality and the possible solutions.

Questions for Discussion

1. Below are six statements regarding conditions that are necessary for success of an electronic market. For each, explain why you agree or disagree:
   a. The market should be fragmented on both the buying and selling side, with a lot of vendors and a lot of buyers and no overly dominant player on either side.
   b. The market should be technologically sophisticated, with an Internet-savvy customer base.
   c. The online service should be able to fully describe products on the Web so that buyers receive enough information to make purchases.
   d. The products being offered on the Web should not be a pure commodity; for a lively marketplace, vendors should be able to distinguish their offerings.
   e. If a certain market is already efficient, there is no sense moving it online.
   f. Trading stocks online becomes a commodity.
2. Compare and contrast competition in the traditional markets with competition in digital markets.
3. Compare a traditional market industry structure with an electronic market structure.
4. Discuss the relationship between virtual communities and doing business on the Internet.
5. How does behavioral EC research differ from behavioral IT research in general?
6. Relate price discovery to price discrimination. Provide an example in retailing and an example in services.

Internet Exercises

1. Enter www.opentrade.com and find the various ways that the services offered can facilitate the conduct of international trade over the Internet. Register with the site (free for 30 days) and open a home page. Create your letterhead and business cards. Prepare a report.
2. Use Porter's five-force model to analyze the impact of EC on the bookstore industry and on the airline industry. Find the impact on each force, then analyze the proposed defense strategies.
3. Use a currency conversion table (for example, try www.xe.net/currency/iso) to find out how much local currencies of Brazil, Canada, China, India, Sweden, and South Africa can be purchased with U.S. $100.
4. Competition between online companies is increasing rapidly. Prepare a report on the competition between www.ticketmaster.com, www.tickets.com and www.ticketslive.com (*Interactive Week*, July 27, 1998, to start). Identify market niches for each, strategies, and relationships to offline operations. Generalize to the entire entertainment ticketing industry.
5. Enter the Web site of an Internet community (www.Xoom.com, www.tripod.com, or www.geocities.com). Build a home page free of charge. You can add a chat room and a message board using the free tools provided.
6. Several professional-oriented communities are active on the Internet. For example, www.plasticsnet.com caters to plastic-related industries. Explore the site and identify the members' benefits.
7. Investigate the community services provided by Yahoo to its members (www.clubs.yahoo.com). List all the services available and assess their potential commercial benefits to Yahoo.

8. Conduct research on small businesses and their use of the Internet for EC. Visit sites such as www.sbwebsites.com, www.success.com, and www.uschamber.org.

Team Assignment

1. Assign a team to find the latest information on global EC issues. Each member researches one area (legal, financial, and so on). Have the team make a report.
2. Each team member is assigned to an area of fierce online competition: books, computers and their parts, CDs, toys, auctions, and stock trading. Find some evidence for competition in the area, at least one case each of offline versus online and online versus online competition. Identify common threads. Submit a report.
3. Read the story about Marshall Industries at www.simnet.org/public/programs/ capital/97paper/paper1.html. Prepare a report on all the economic implications derived from this case. Concentrate on the following issues: changes in the value chains, the competitive strategy, the role of the intermediaries, and the roles of the CEO and CIO.
4. Two competing industry-type extranets operate in the steel market (www.metal-site.net and www.e-steel.com). Enter both sites and compare the two. Look at the structure of the market they make, at the services, and so on. Is there a need for two such market makers? If only one will survive, which one? Why?

R E A L   W O R L D   C A S E S

Chemdex Brings Efficiencies to Chemical Market

Research chemicals are used by over 300,000 laboratory scientists across the United States and many more in other countries. There are over 250,000 specialty bioscience products produced by more than 2,000 manufacturers, most of which are very small. Overall, more than $1 billion of chemicals are traded every year, and the market is growing rapidly.

Until 1998, the market centered on paper-based catalogs with Sigma-Aldrich Corporation acting as a distributor to about 15 percent of the market, consolidating several hundred printed catalogs in the paper-based market. Buyers had to search through many paper catalogs, some of which were not current, and had to use distributors who charged up to 40 percent commission; yet, buyers frequently missed the best suppliers. Sellers were unable to reach all potential buyers and were subject to the mercy of the distributors. The market was very inefficient, with prices often varying 40 percent on similar items from different vendors. Comparison shopping was hard to do, and customers (mostly very small) were scattered and costly to reach.

Chemdex (www.chemdex.com) changed the situation by creating an extranet to connect the buyers and sellers. The company aggregated the vendors' catalogs into a Web-accessible database and created a commerce site searchable by product and category. Buyers can find what they need, compare prices, get detailed product information, and place an order. Chemdex collects a 5 percent to 12 percent commission from the sales versus 40 percent charged by traditional distributors.

The Chemdex Web market completed its Beta testing in mid-1998 and has grown very rapidly since then. By March 1999, Chemdex was offering over 150,000 products from 160 vendors, with thousands of additional products and 20 vendors joining each month.

Buyers were impressed. Ken Kilgore from the Department of Pharmacology at the University of Michigan, said: "It's long overdue, it's user friendly, it's a basic system, and my technicians can use the system in minutes instead of searching hours." He also seemed encouraged by the prospect that the consolidation of chemical information might help to standardize an industry in which reagents tend to differ qualitatively.

Small vendors were especially happy. Dako Corp., for example, claims that its products, which sell very well among clinical pathologists, are little known among biotech researchers who use similar products. The company hopes that Chemdex will help by placing Dako products alongside those of better-known competitors. In 1999 Chemdex won the best B2B EC site award (see *Internet Week*, April 19, 1999). ■

Source: Condensed from *Interactive Week* (January 26, 1998), p. 42, and from *The Scientist* (July 6, 1998), p. 17.

CASE QUESTIONS

1. What market inefficiencies are corrected by Chemdex and how?
2. Do traditional distributors have any chance to survive?
3. What incentives exist for large vendors to join?
4. Are there any disadvantages to the system?
5. A large buyer said, "I can get better prices because of volume purchasing." Should such a buyer join Chemdex? Why or why not?

New Entrants to the Dutch Flower Market

The Dutch auction flower market is the largest in the world, attracting 11,000 sellers from dozens of countries such as Thailand, Israel, and East Africa; 3,500 varieties of flowers are sold in 120 auction groups to about 5,000 buyers. The auctions are semiautomated; buyers and sellers must come to one location, where the flowers are shown to the buyers. The auctioneer of each flower variety uses a clock with a large hand, which he starts at a high price and drops until a buyer stops the clock by pushing an ordering button. Using an intercom, the quantity ordered is clarified; then, the clock hand is reset at the starting price level for the next batch of flowers. The process continues until all the flowers are sold.

In September 1994, the Dutch growers (DFA), who own the auction organization, decided to ban foreign growers from participating during the summer months in order to protect the Dutch growers against low prices from abroad. By March 1995, some foreign growers, together with some local buyers, created a competing auction place called the Tele Flower Auction (TFA), an electronic auction that enables its initiators to penetrate the Dutch flower market. Here is how it works.

In the TFA, buyers can bid on flowers via their PCs at designated times, from any location connected to the private network. The process is similar to the traditional one, and the auction clock is shown on the PC screen. The buyers can stop the clock by pushing the space bar. The auctioneer then converses with the buyers by telephone, a sale is concluded, and the clock is reset. The flowers are not physically visible to the buyers; however, a large amount of relevant information is available online. For example, the buyers are alerted to a specific auction, in real time, when their item of interest is auctioned.

Initial results indicated that buyers and growers were enthusiastic. While prices are about the same as in the regular auctions, the process is much quicker and the after-sale delivery is much faster than in other markets (less than half an hour). A major issue could be the quality of the flowers, since the buyers cannot see them. But the quality is actually better since there is less handling (no need to bring the flowers to an auction site), and the growers stand behind their products. As a result, there is enough trust so that everyone is happy.

The TFA has gained considerable market share at the expense of existing organizations and is a real new-entrant success story. Using IT, the new entrant quickly built a competitive advantage. This advantage impressed the DFA, but it took more than a year to cancel the import restrictions and implement their own electronic clearinghouse for flowers. However, the TFA continues its own auctions. ■

Source: E. van Heck et al., "New Entrants and the Role of IT—Case Study: The Tele Flower Auction in the Netherlands," *Proceedings of the 30th Hawaiian International Conference on Systems Sciences*, Hawaii, January 1997. See also, A. Kambil and E. van Heck, "Reengineer the Dutch Flower Auctions," *Information Systems Research*, March 1998 and van Heck and Ribbers in *Electronic Markets* 7 (4:1997).

CASE QUESTIONS

1. Why was the TFA successful?
2. How can the TFA sustain its success while competitors are copying its new concept?
3. The cancellation of the import restrictions is not working too well for the Dutch growers associations (DFA). Why?
4. Can this concept be extended to the Internet? If so, how can real-time auctions be implemented?

References

W. Andrews, "Global Commerce Forces Web Merchants to Find Ways to Handle Many Currencies," *Internet World* (February 23, 1998).

A. G. Armstrong and J. Hagel, "The Real Value of Online Communities," *Harvard Business Review* (May/June, 1996).

Y. Bakos, "The Emerging Role of Electronic Marketplaces on the Internet," *Communications of the ACM* (August 1998).

———, "Reducing Buyers' Search Costs: Implications for Electronic Marketplaces," *Management Sciences* (December 1997).

———, "A Strategic Analysis of Electronic Marketplaces," *MIS Quarterly* 15 (3:1991).

R. Benjamin and R. Wigand, "Electronic Markets and Virtual Value Chains on the Information Superhighway," *Sloan Management Journal* 36 (2:1995).

J. Champy, R. Buday, and N. Nohria, "The Rise of the Electronic Community," *InformationWeek* (June 10, 1996).

S. Y. Choi, D. O. Stahl, and W. B. Whinston, *The Economics of Electronic Commerce* (Indianapolis, Macmillan Technical Pub., 1997).

W. Clinton, and A. Gore, "A Framework for Global Electronic Commerce," 1997 (www.iitf.nist.gov/eleccomm/ecomm.htm).

M. Dickerson, "Going Global by Going Online," *Los Angeles Times* (February 11, 1998).

L. Eaton, "Slow Transition in Investing as Market Meets Internet," *The New York Times: CybertTimes* (November 11, 1996).

K. Frieswick, "Challenging channels," *CFO* (February 1999).

A. Gupta, ed., "The Economics of Electronic Commerce," *Decision Support Systems* 24 (1–2: 1998).

J. Hagel and A. G. Armstrong, *Net Gain* (Boston: Harvard Business School Press, 1997).

M. Hammer and S. A. Stanton, *The Reengineering Revolution: A Handbook* (New York: HarperCollins, 1995).

G. Hanappi and E. Rysavy, "Economic Foundations of Electronic Commerce," *Proceedings International Conference on Electronic Commerce* (Seoul, Korea, April 1998), www.icec.net.

S. Jarvenpaa and P. A. Todd, "Consumer Reactions to Electronic Shopping on the World Wide Web," *International Journal of Electronic Commerce* 1 (2:1997).

R. Kalakota and A. B. Whinston, *Frontiers of Electronic Commerce* (Reading, MA: Addison-Wesley Publishing Co., 1996).

P. K. Kannan et al., "Marketing Information on the I-Way," *Communication of the ACM* (March 1998).

S. D. Kimbrough and D. M. Lee, "Formal Aspects of Electronic Commerce: Research Issues and Challenges," *International Journal of Electronic Commerce* (Summer 1997).

D. King and R. Blanning "Electronic Commerce—A Tutorial," presented at HICSS, Hawaii (January 1997).

D. M. Lamberton, ed., *The Economics of Communication and Information* (Ghcftenham, U.K.: Pub. Ltd., 1996).

G. E. Lee, "Do Electronic Marketplaces Lower the Price of Goods?" *Communication of the ACM* (January 1998).

W. C. Lisse, "The Economics of Information and the Internet," *Competitive Intelligence Review* 9 (4:1998).

J. R. Oliver, "Artificial Agents Learn Policies for Multiissue Negotiations," *International Journal of Electronic Commerce* (Summer 1997).

S. Poon and P. M. C. Swatman, "An Exploratory Study of Small Business Internet Commerce Issues," *Information and Management* 35 (1999).

H. H. Preston and U. Flohr, "Internationalizing Code from the Start Minimizes and Leads to Big Payoffs," *Byte* (March 1997).

J. F. Rayport and J. J. Sviokla, "Managing in the Marketspace," *Harvard Business Review* (November/December 1994).

P. Resnick et al., "Roles for Electronic Brokers," http://ccs.mit.edu/ccswp179.html. 1998. Also, see in G. W. Brock (ed.), *Toward a Competitive Telecommunication Industry* (Mahwah, NJ: Lawrence Arlbaam Assoc., 1995).

H. Rheingold, *The Virtual Community: Homesteading on the Electronic Frontier* (Reading, MA: Addison-Wesley Publishing Co., 1993).

E. I. Schwartz, *Webonomics* (New York: Broadway Books, 1997).

V. Swass, "Structure and Macro-Level Impacts of Electronic Commerce," in K. E. Kendall (Ed.) *Emerging Information Technologies,* Thousand Oaks, Ca: Sage Pub., 1999.

S. Silverman, "Just Say Nokia Wired" (September 1999).

T. J. Strader, and H. J. Shaw, "Characteristics of Electronic Markets," *Decision Support Systems* 21 (1997).

E. Turban et al., *Information Technology for Management* (New York: John Wiley & Sons, 1999).

D. Upton and A. McAfee, "The Virtual Factory," *Harvard Business Review* (July/August 1996).

H. Wang et al., "Consumer Privacy About Internet Marketing," *Communication of the ACM* (March 1998).

J. Ware et al., *The Search for Digital Excellence* (New York: McGraw-Hill [with CommerceNet Press], 1998).

Appendix A

Creating Web Pages

For the most part, the contents of a Web site consist of a series of pages. Some of these pages are "static," created ahead of time (like a word document or a text file), and stored at the site. Anyone who accesses a static Web page is going to see the same thing. Other pages delivered by a Web site are "dynamic." This means that the contents of the page are created by a computer program that is run every time the page is accessed. Thus, the contents can vary from one user to the next or from one time to the next. Regardless of whether a Web page is static or dynamic, that language used to create the page is the same. This language is called the **HyperText Markup Language,** or **HTML** for short. This appendix discusses HTML basics and examines how static Web pages are created. In contrast, Appendix B examines various scripting languages and programming interfaces that are used to create dynamic pages and to add higher levels of interactivity than those provided by standard HTML. This appendix also examines other markup languages including the **Virtual Reality Model Language** (VRML) for creating three-dimensional (3D) worlds and the **Extensible Markup Language** (XML), standard that may eventually supplant HTML.

A.1 HYPERTEXT MARKUP LANGUAGE (HTML)

When Tim Berners-Lee first conceived of the World Wide Web in 1989, he was searching for a formal language that could be used to create and hyper-link text documents in a distributed network. A colleague, Anders Berglund, advised him to use an "SGML-like" syntax. At the time, SGML (Standard Graphic Markup Language) was a well-established but highly complicated markup language used for managing complex documents. Berners-Lee knew that SGML was too complex for the average researcher to use. What he took from SGML was its use of "markup" tags. The end result was a highly simplified markup language that he called the HyperText Markup Language (HTML).

Simple Example

For virtually every page on the Web, there is an underlying text (ASCII) file containing markup tags describing the structure and content of the page. When you view a particular page, you are seeing your browser's rendering or interpretation of those tags. For instance, consider the sample Web page shown in Figure A.1. This is the home page (starting page) on a Web site (www.premiumselect.com) for a hypothetical merchant called Premium Selections. Throughout this appendix, this simple site will serve to illustrate various features of HTML and Web page construction. This particular home page links readers to three other static pages—one containing selections from the wine shop, another containing selections from the cheese shop, and a third that enables consumers to review the wines and cheeses they have placed in their electronic shopping cart and to purchase those selections. The HTML text file underlying this home page is shown in Figure A.2. Like other static Web pages, this page consists of a series of tags. Most, but not all, tags come in pairs. For example, in Figure A.2 the pair "⟨H1⟩ . . . ⟨/H1⟩" are tags indicating that the enclosed text is to be treated as a "number 1 headline." If you want to see the HTML tags underlying any particular page on the Web, access the page, click the "View" menu at the top of the browser, then select either "Source" under the View menu for Microsoft's Internet Explorer or "Page Source" for Netscape's Navigator. At that point a window will appear containing the HTML code for the page.

Before we look in detail at the syntax and use of particular HTML tags, let us briefly review those shown in Figure A.2.

1. The ⟨HTML⟩ . . . ⟨/HTML⟩ tags that surround the other tags on the page basically tell the browser that this is a Web page.
2. The "head" (⟨HEAD⟩ . . . ⟨/HEAD⟩) is the first component of the page. The head contains a "title" (⟨TITLE⟩{title text} ⟨/TITLE⟩). The text of the title is dis-

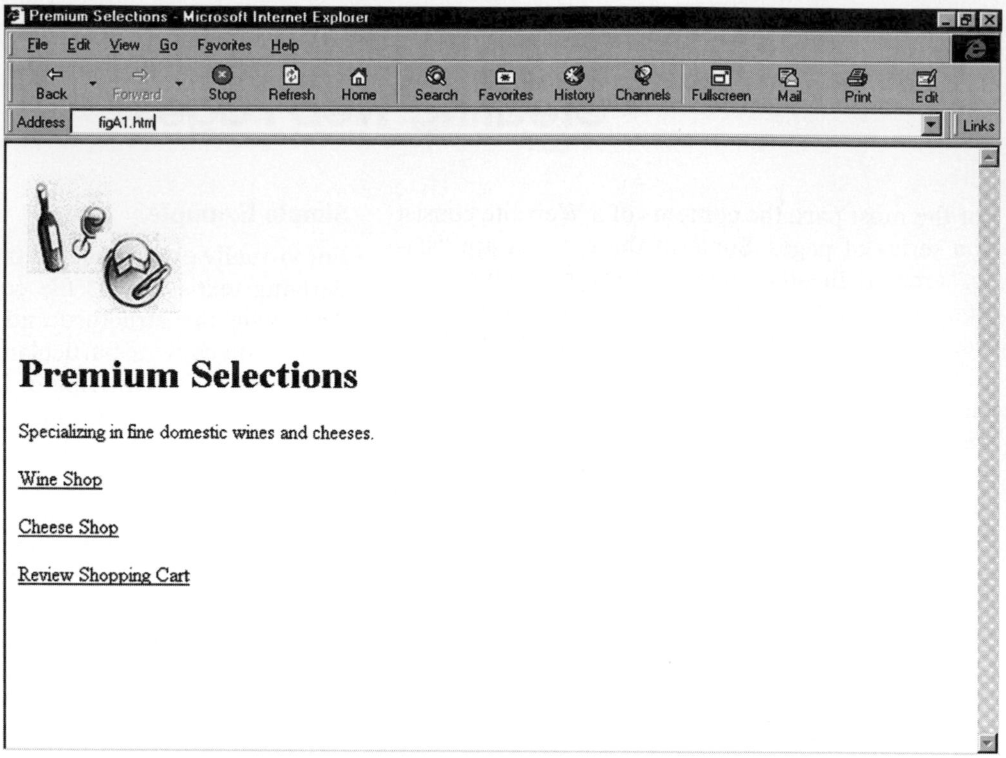

FIGURE A.1 Home Page for Premium Solutions.

played on the title bar at the top of the browser. In this case the words "Premium Selections" will appear on the title bar.

3. The second major component of the page is its body (⟨BODY⟩...⟨/BODY⟩). In this example the body tag specifies various color parameters on the page. Included among these parameters are the page's background color (BGCOLOR = "white"), the color of its text (TEXT = "black"), and the color of the hypertext links (LINK = "black") on the page. The body of the page is where you find the real contents—in this case a company logo, some headline text, some descriptive text, and three hypertext links pointing to other pages at the site.

4. At the top of the page is an image of the company's logo. The image is specified by an "⟨IMG⟩" tag. Like the body tag, the image tag usually contains a series of parameters delimiting various features of the image. Here there is only one parameter—the "source" of the image or,

more specifically, the name of the image file (SRC = "www.premiumselect.com/companylogo.gif").

5. The logo is followed by a headline specified by a headline tag "⟨H1⟩{headline text}⟨/H1⟩". Headlines come in various sizes from H1 to H6. The number determines the size and style of the font used to display the headline text. The smaller the number, the larger the font. The browser determines the specific font that is used with a particular number.

6. After the headline comes simple descriptive text ("Specializing in fine domestic wines and cheeses"). Since there is no tag associated with the text, it will be displayed as is (again, with the font determined by the browser).

7. Next is a series of three hypertext links each specified with an "anchor" tag "⟨A⟩{some text or an image}⟨/A⟩." Each of the anchor tags has a hypertext reference ("HREF") that designates the page that will be returned when a user clicks the

```
⟨HTML⟩

⟨HEAD⟩
⟨TITLE⟩Premium Selections⟨/TITLE⟩
⟨/HEAD⟩

⟨BODY BGCOLOR="white" TEXT="black" LINK="black"⟩

⟨P⟩
⟨IMG SRC="premium.gif"⟩
⟨/P⟩

⟨H1⟩Premium Selections⟨/H1⟩

Specializing in fine domestic wines and cheeses.

⟨P⟩
⟨A HREF="wines.htm"⟩Wine Shop⟨/A⟩
⟨/P⟩

⟨P⟩
⟨A HREF="cheeses.htm"⟩Cheese Shop⟨/A⟩
⟨/P⟩

⟨P⟩
⟨A HREF="shoppingcart.exe"⟩Review Shopping Cart⟨/A⟩
⟨/P⟩

⟨/BODY⟩
⟨/HTML⟩
```

FIGURE A.2 Sample Web Page.

anchor. For instance, when the user clicks on the first anchor ⟨A HREF="www.premiumselect.com/wines.htm"⟩Wine Shop⟨/A⟩, the page "wines.htm" will be retrieved. Anchors appear on a page in the form of text or an image. In this example the anchors are text. How is the text of an anchor distinguished from regular text? There are two ways. First, the text of an anchor is underlined and often has a different color than regular text. Second, when the mouse cursor is over an anchor, the shape of the cursor usually changes from an arrow to a hand.

8. Finally, there are a series of paragraph tags "⟨P⟩...⟨/P⟩" surrounding the image tag and anchor tags. These paragraph tags simply serve to add line spacing around the image and anchor text. If they were not there, everything would run together.

At this point, you might want to experiment a little bit with this example. To do this, activate a simple text editor (like Microsoft's Notepad). Type in the text that appears in Figure A.2. However, leave out the "IMG" tag and the paragraph tags surrounding the image. Name the file something like "myfile.htm" and save it to a subdirectory on your machine (*Note*: If you are using Notepad, the first time you save the file you will have to save it as a File Type of "All Files" rather than as a File Type of "Text Document"). After you save the file, *do not close the text editor*. Now, open your Web browser. Once it is open, click on the "File" menu at the top of the browser, then select "Open" from the File menu. A file selection dialogue box will appear. Find the file you saved and open it. If you have not made any mistakes, you should see something similar to Figure A.1 but without the logo. Now we are ready for some experimentation. Go back to the text editor and try some of the changes noted below:

1. Change BGCOLOR from "white" to "blue," the TEXT from "black" to "white," and LINK from "black" to "yellow." Save the file but do not close the ed-

itor. Now return to your browser. In the browser, click on the "View" menu and select "Refresh" from this menu. At this point you should see the colors change.

2. Change the headline tags from a "number 1 headline" (⟨H1⟩...⟨/H1⟩) to a "number 2 headline" (⟨H2⟩...⟨/H2⟩). Save the file but do not close the editor. Now return to your browser. In the browser, click on the "View" menu and select "Refresh" from this menu. At this point you should see a change in the font size of the headline.

3. Remove the paragraph tags surrounding the anchor tags. Save the file but do not close the editor. Now return to your browser. In the browser, click on the "View" menu and select "Refresh" from this menu. At this point, you should see all the anchor tags appearing on a single line.

In the remainder of the appendix you will be exposed to a variety of other tags that can be used to create both simple and complex pages.

Overview of HTML Tags

The original version of HTML (version 1.0) consisted of a small set of tags that made it possible to create primitive Web pages consisting of basic text and images. Compared to the features offered by existing word processors (like Microsoft Word), the tags in HTML 1.0 made it difficult, if not impossible, to:

- control font sizes and styles,
- place text and images at specific points on a page,
- display data and text in tables,
- create forms for entering data that could be sent to a Web server for processing.

The fact that the initial version of HTML lacked these capabilities did little to deter the growth of the Web. In fact, the combination of HTML 1.0 and the early Web browsers, like Mosaic, resulted in a graphical user interface (GUI) that spurred tremendous growth in the Web. The simple standards made it easy for Web authors to create pages and for Web readers to access those pages. With growth came increased demands from Web authors for new tags that addressed the limitations in HTML 1.0. Over a three- to four-year period, HTML went through rapid changes, moving from

version 2.0 to version 3.2 and then, in 1998, to version 4.0. The HTML standards are still undergoing changes today.

In this short appendix there is no way to do justice to the myriad of tags in HTML 4.0 and the variety of methods and techniques used to create the sophisticated pages found across the Web. If you are interested in understanding the current HTML standard, then you should look at a book like Graham (1998). If your interest is in Web site design, then books like LeMay and Tyler (1998) fit the bill. Since it is also possible to list the HTML source behind any Web page, another way to learn about design ideas and the use of various tags is to browse the Web and view the source for pages that look interesting. If you decide to utilize someone else's source on your own pages, you need to be careful about what you use. Certain images, text, and general designs are trademarked and copyrighted.

While HTML 4.0 makes it possible to create very sophisticated Web pages, it is important to note that many of the most successful sites rely on a handful of tags and very simple designs. In this way the pages can be quickly downloaded over even the slowest modems and viewed in virtually any Web browser. Table A.1 lists some of the basic tags used with many of today's sites. This collection of tags can be used to create sites like Yahoo!, Amazon.com, and the Virtual Vineyards and UPS sites discussed in chapter 11, to name just a few. Rather than detailing each of the individual tags in Table A.1, the discussion that follows looks at the use of anchors, images, tables, frames, and forms.

Linking One Page to Another with Anchor Tags

Anchor tags provide the hypertext links that enable users to "surf" the Web from one site or one page to another. On a Web page, an anchor appears in the form of either underlined text or an image (which sometimes is denoted with a border around it). In either case, when the mouse cursor moves over another the mouse cursor changes shape, indicating that a click will retrieve the linked page. The syntax of an anchor tag is ⟨A HREF="{url}"⟩{anchor text or image}⟨/A⟩, where "url" represents the Web address of a linked Web page or another location on the same Web page. For example, in Figure A.2 the anchor tag ⟨A HREF="www.premiumselect.com/wines.htm"⟩Wine Shop⟨/A⟩ is displayed on the page as the underlined text "*Wine Shop.*" When this anchor is clicked, a request will be sent to the Web

TABLE A.1 Basic HTML Tags	
Type	*HTML Tags*
Text Formatting	⟨B⟩bold⟨/B⟩
	⟨EM⟩emphasis⟨/EM⟩
	⟨H#⟩header1⟨/H#⟩where # is 1–6
	⟨FONT⟩—text font
Positions, Paragraphs, Spacing	⟨CENTER⟩centered content⟨/CENTER⟩
	⟨BR⟩—line break
	⟨P⟩paragraph⟨/P⟩
	⟨DIV⟩divided content⟨/DIV⟩
	⟨SPAN⟩span of content⟨/SPAN⟩
Tables	⟨TABLE⟩table content⟨/TABLE⟩
	⟨TR⟩table row⟨/TR⟩
	⟨TH⟩table header⟨/TH⟩
	⟨TD⟩table data⟨/TD⟩
Lists	⟨UL⟩unorder list⟨/UL⟩
	⟨OL⟩ordered list⟨/OL⟩
	⟨LI⟩list item⟨/LI⟩
Form	⟨FORM⟩form content⟨/FORM⟩
	⟨INPUT⟩—iput area
	⟨TEXT⟩—text input box
	⟨TEXT AREA⟩—multiline text input
	⟨SELECT⟩list of selections⟨/SELECT⟩
Document	⟨HTML⟩html document⟨/HTML⟩
	⟨HEAD⟩doc head⟨/HEAD⟩
	⟨BODY⟩doc body⟨/BODY⟩
	⟨TITLE⟩doc title⟨/TITLE⟩
Graphics	⟨IMG⟩—graphic image
	⟨HR⟩—horizontal rule/line
Linking and Anchor	⟨A HREF⟩anchor content⟨/A⟩

server "www.premimumselect.com" to retrieve the HTML page "wines.htm."

Anchors can also be used to tell a Web server to run a program. At an EC site the program might be used to collect marketing data from a potential consumer and store it in a database for later use, display a particular catalog page depending on a consumer's query, or process a consumer's purchase order. Usually a program will require some input information in order to run. For instance, to process a purchase order, the program will need the buyer's name, address, credit card number, items and quantities being purchased, and so on. This information can be specified with the anchor tag or collected from a Web form. Once a program is run, the program will dynamically produce a response in the form of an HTML page that will be returned by the Web server.

In order to run a program, the syntax of the anchor needs to look like this: ⟨A HREF="{server _name/subdirectory/program_name}"⟩{anchor text or image}⟨/A⟩. For example, in Figure A.2, when the following anchor is clicked, ⟨A HREF="www. premiumselect.com/shoppingcart.exe"⟩Review Shopping Cart⟨/A⟩, the "www.premiumselect.com" Web server will run a program called "shoppingcart.exe" that will show a potential buyer the purchases that he or she has selected up to that point in time.

Adding Images to a Page

One of the major attractions of the Web is the integration of text and images. The Web would be a rather unexciting place if it were simply "hypertext" rather than "hypermedia." In an HTML page, images serve a variety of functions such as:

- embellishing the aesthetics of a page,
- enhancing the information and data contained in the page,
- serving as buttons or icons linking one page to another,
- focusing or attracting attention to particular areas of a page (e.g., an animated advertisement).

As noted in our earlier example, images are incorporated in a page with the IMG tag whose syntax is: ⟨IMG SRC="image file" {image parameters}⟩, where the "image file" is the name of the image file and "{image parameters}" represents a list of potential parameters specifying things like the image's width, height, alignment, and so on.

A wide variety of image "formats" are supported on the Web. The two most popular formats are GIF (.gif files) and JPEG (.jpg files). JPEG is used when higher-quality images are required. A variant of the GIF format is the "animated" GIF. An animated GIF file contains a series of pictures or graphics that are displayed in a designated order and with a specified timing (almost like the "cells" in an animated cartoon). Animated GIFS have become the standard image format for creating the banner ads that appear on a number of pages (i.e., these are the simple animated images that are ubiquitous throughout the Web).

To use an image as a hypertext button or icon linking one page to another, the image tag needs to be embedded between an anchor tag. As an example, consider Figure A.3 and its associated HTML file shown in Figure A.4. Again, there are three anchors on the page. Each of the anchors is denoted with image and text. For example, the first anchor, which links to the Wine Shop, has an image (⟨IMG SRC="wines.gif" BORDER=0 ALIGN=bottom⟩ followed by some text ("Wine Shop"). In this case the image has two additional parameters. The first says that the image should be displayed without a border (BORDER=0). The other option is BORDER=1. The second parameter (ALIGN=middle) says that the middle of the image should be lined up with the text. Some other options are ALIGN=top or ALIGN=middle.

The reason for using both text and images is that a picture is not always "worth a thousand words." Often, it is very hard for a user to determine the meaning of an anchor solely from an image. Imagine, for instance, that the words "Review Shopping Cart Contents" did not accompany the shopping cart image. Do you think a user could determine the meaning of the anchor solely from the image?

FIGURE A.3 Images as Anchors for Hypertext Linking.

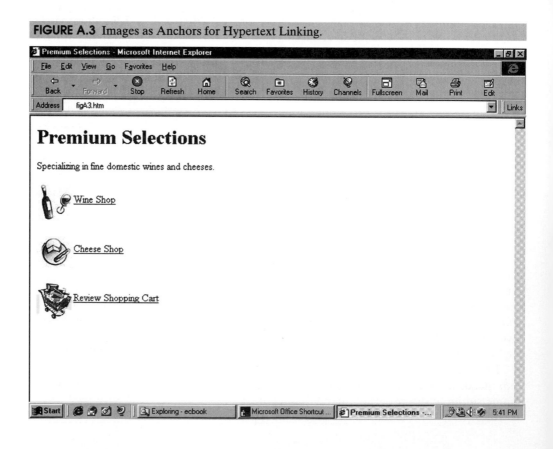

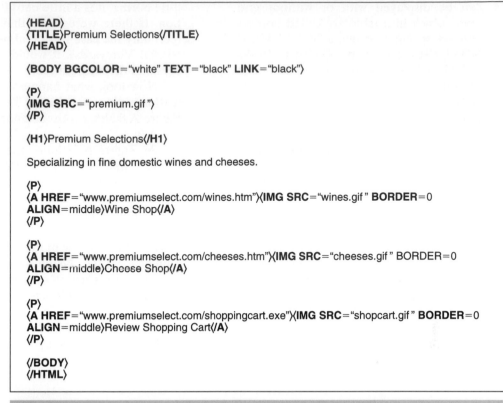

```
⟨HEAD⟩
⟨TITLE⟩Premium Selections⟨/TITLE⟩
⟨/HEAD⟩

⟨BODY BGCOLOR="white" TEXT="black" LINK="black"⟩

⟨P⟩
⟨IMG SRC="premium.gif "⟩
⟨/P⟩

⟨H1⟩Premium Selections⟨/H1⟩

Specializing in fine domestic wines and cheeses.

⟨P⟩
⟨A HREF="www.premiumselect.com/wines.htm"⟩⟨IMG SRC="wines.gif " BORDER=0
ALIGN=middle)Wine Shop⟨/A⟩
⟨/P⟩

⟨P⟩
⟨A HREF="www.premiumselect.com/cheeses.htm"⟩⟨IMG SRC="cheeses.gif " BORDER=0
ALIGN=middle)Cheese Shop⟨/A⟩
⟨/P⟩

⟨P⟩
⟨A HREF="www.premiumselect.com/shoppingcart.exe"⟩⟨IMG SRC="shopcart.gif " BORDER=0
ALIGN=middle)Review Shopping Cart⟨/A⟩
⟨/P⟩

⟨/BODY⟩
⟨/HTML⟩
```

FIGURE A.4 HTML Tags for Image Anchors.

Displaying Data and Controlling Page Layout with Tables

In HTML, tables are used for two purposes—to display numbers and text in tabular form and to control the layout of various sections and components on a page. Figure A.5 outlines the basic structure of an HTML table.

To understand the rudiments of HTML tables (Figure A.5), you need to know that HTML tables (⟨TABLE⟩. . .⟨/TABLE⟩):

1. consist of three basic elements—headers (⟨TH⟩. . .⟨/TH⟩), rows (⟨TR⟩. . .⟨/TR⟩), and cells (⟨TD⟩. . .⟨/TD⟩);
2. are laid out row by row starting with the row of column headers at the top of a table;
3. have headers and cells that can contain virtually anything including text, images, anchors, other tables, or some combination of these;

FIGURE A.5 Elements of an HTML Table

Table begin ⟨TABLE⟩

Table Row Begin ⟨TR⟩	Column Header ⟨TH⟩...⟨/TH⟩	Column Header ⟨TH⟩...⟨/TH⟩	...	Column Header ⟨TH⟩. . .⟨/TH⟩	Table Row End ⟨/TR⟩
Table Row Begin ⟨TR⟩	Row Header ⟨TH⟩...⟨/TH⟩	Cell ⟨TD⟩...⟨/TD⟩	...	Cell ⟨TD⟩. . .⟨/TD⟩	Table Row End ⟨/TR⟩
...	...	...	...	...	...
Table Row ⟨TR⟩	Row Header ⟨TH⟩. . .⟨/TH⟩	Cell ⟨TD⟩. . .⟨/TD⟩	...	Cell ⟨TD⟩. . .⟨/TD⟩	Table Row End ⟨/TR⟩

Table End ⟨/TABLE⟩

4. can be displayed with or without grid lines, which in a table are called borders and are specified as being "on" ⟨TABLE BORDER=1⟩ or "off" ⟨TABLE BORDER=0⟩. If you think of a page as a table of cells where the borders between the cells are turned off, then you begin to see how tables can be used to control the layout of a page by simply putting text and images within particular cells of the table.

Tables can get very complicated because tables can contain other tables and because rows and columns can span one another. In this discussion we stick with the basics. To illustrate the basics, first examine the page shown in Figure A.6. This is the wine shop page for the Premium Select site. The associated HTML file is shown in Figure A.7. There are no tables on this page. Instead, a whole series of paragraph tags (⟨P⟩...⟨/P⟩) and break tags (⟨BR⟩) are interspersed throughout the page to control its layout. Besides the fact that the look of the page is a little boring, it is a little hard to follow the information. If there were more than a handful of wines (certainly the case for a real on-line wine store like Virtual Vineyards), it would really be hard to understand the information.

Now look what happens when the same information is placed in a table. The results are shown in Figure A.8 along with the underlying HTML in Figure A.9.

As Figure A.9 shows, the table is specified between the ⟨TABLE BORDER=1 CELLPADDING=5⟩ and ⟨/TABLE⟩ tags. The table is displayed with grid lines because the BORDER=1. The headers and cells of the table have a little extra space because CELLPADDING=5 has been added. The first row of the table consists of the column headers (i.e., Name, Description, Price–$USD, and Shopping Cart). Next comes the row of data for the Merlot wine. This is followed by the row of data for the Chardonnay wine.

Even though the HTML 4.0 provides specific mechanisms for placing components at particular

FIGURE A.6 Displaying Text and Data without HTML Tables.

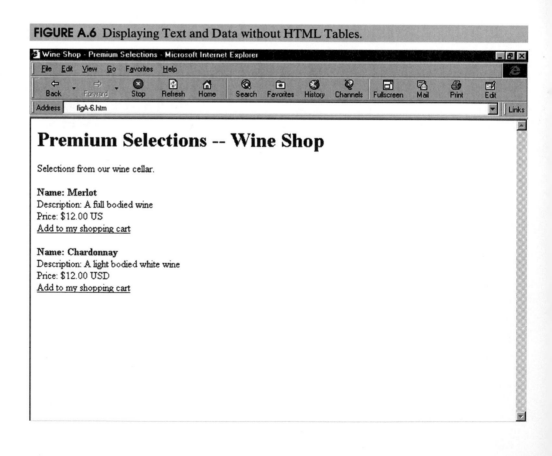

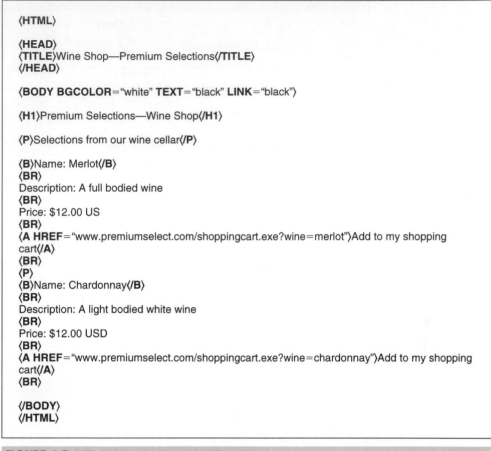

```
⟨HTML⟩

⟨HEAD⟩
⟨TITLE⟩Wine Shop—Premium Selections⟨/TITLE⟩
⟨/HEAD⟩

⟨BODY BGCOLOR="white" TEXT="black" LINK="black"⟩

⟨H1⟩Premium Selections—Wine Shop⟨/H1⟩

⟨P⟩Selections from our wine cellar⟨/P⟩

⟨B⟩Name: Merlot⟨/B⟩
⟨BR⟩
Description: A full bodied wine
⟨BR⟩
Price: $12.00 US
⟨BR⟩
⟨A HREF="www.premiumselect.com/shoppingcart.exe?wine=merlot"⟩Add to my shopping
cart⟨/A⟩
⟨BR⟩
⟨P⟩
⟨B⟩Name: Chardonnay⟨/B⟩
⟨BR⟩
Description: A light bodied white wine
⟨BR⟩
Price: $12.00 USD
⟨BR⟩
⟨A HREF="www.premiumselect.com/shoppingcart.exe?wine=chardonnay"⟩Add to my shopping
cart⟨/A⟩
⟨BR⟩

⟨/BODY⟩
⟨/HTML⟩
```

FIGURE A.7 HTML Tags for Data and Text Display.

locations on a page, HTML tables still remain the popular method for controlling the placement of various objects on a Web page, including images.

Controlling Navigation with Frames

Frames divide an HTML page into a series of well-defined, independent segments much like the pancs in a window. On many of those Web pages with frames, one of the frames (typically on the left side or top of the page) is often used as a menu or table of contents for navigating from one page in the Web site to the next. One of the other frames displays the contents of the page selected from the menu.

As an illustration, consider the page shown in Figure A.10 and the accompanying code shown in Figure A.11.

When the page displayed in Figure A.10 is first opened, an index frame is displayed on the left, while the view frame is displayed on the right. The contents of the index frame come from a page labeled "index.htm," while the contents of the view frame come from a page labeled "start.htm." When a user clicks on one of the selections in the index frame (say, "Wine Shop"), the associated Web page (here "wines.htm") is displayed in the view frame.

Some of the more interesting pages on the Web use frames. Unfortunately, if you try to view the HTML source for these pages, you will encounter a problem. The only thing that will be displayed is the HTML code used to specify the frames, not their content. For instance, if you tried to use your browser to look at the source for the page in Figure A.10, then you would see the source in Figure A.11. You could not, for example, see the source for either "index.htm" or "start.htm," which are the pages that are actually shown in the frames.

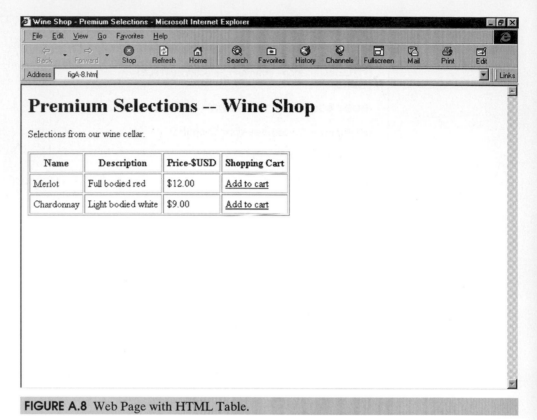

FIGURE A.8 Web Page with HTML Table.

In the past the use of frames was controversial because they were not supported by all of the browsers. Today this is no longer the case. They are used extensively throughout the Web.

Sending Information to the Web: Universal Resource Locators versus Forms

How does a Web browser send information to a Web server? One way is by attaching "key-value" pairs to the end of a URL in an anchor tag. For example, reconsider the listing in Figure A.8. Here the user can add a wine to his or her shopping cart by clicking on the words "Add to Cart." How does the Web server at the Web site "www.premiumselect. com" know that the user has selected the Merlot or the Chardonnay? Look carefully at the underlying anchor tags:

⟨A HREF="www.premiumselect.com/shop-pingcart.exe?wine=merlot"⟩Add to Cart⟨/A⟩

⟨A HREF="www.premiumselect.com/shop-pingcart.exe?wine=chardonnay"⟩Add to Cart⟨/A⟩

When the user clicks on either of the anchors, a request is sent to the Web server to run a program called "shoppingcart.exe." A key-value pair (i.e., wine=merlot or wine=chardonnay) is attached to the request after the "?" mark so that the program knows the type of wine to add to the cart.

Passing parameters as key-value pairs attached to a URL works fine when there is a small set of parameters and the specific values for those parameters are known in advance. However, most of the time there are a number of parameters and their values are not known in advance. For instance, in the above example suppose we want to give the user the option to specify the number of bottles to add to the cart. This is where HTML FORMs come into play. The page shown in Figure A.12 provides users with a form that allows them to designate the number of bottles of merlot they want to purchase. The HTML underlying this form is displayed in Figure A.13. The various elements in the form are contained between the beginning ⟨FORM⟩ tag and the associated ending ⟨/FORM⟩ tag. There are three el-

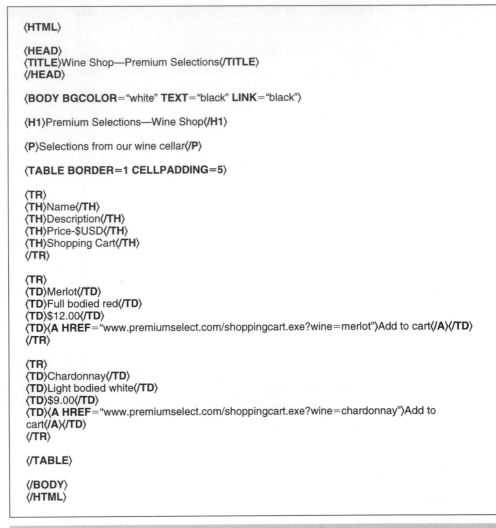

```
⟨HTML⟩

⟨HEAD⟩
⟨TITLE⟩Wine Shop—Premium Selections⟨/TITLE⟩
⟨/HEAD⟩

⟨BODY BGCOLOR="white" TEXT="black" LINK="black"⟩

⟨H1⟩Premium Selections—Wine Shop⟨/H1⟩

⟨P⟩Selections from our wine cellar⟨/P⟩

⟨TABLE BORDER=1 CELLPADDING=5⟩

⟨TR⟩
⟨TH⟩Name⟨/TH⟩
⟨TH⟩Description⟨/TH⟩
⟨TH⟩Price-$USD⟨/TH⟩
⟨TH⟩Shopping Cart⟨/TH⟩
⟨/TR⟩

⟨TR⟩
⟨TD⟩Merlot⟨/TD⟩
⟨TD⟩Full bodied red⟨/TD⟩
⟨TD⟩$12.00⟨/TD⟩
⟨TD⟩⟨A HREF="www.premiumselect.com/shoppingcart.exe?wine=merlot")Add to cart⟨/A⟩⟨/TD⟩
⟨/TR⟩

⟨TR⟩
⟨TD⟩Chardonnay⟨/TD⟩
⟨TD⟩Light bodied white⟨/TD⟩
⟨TD⟩$9.00⟨/TD⟩
⟨TD⟩⟨A HREF="www.premiumselect.com/shoppingcart.exe?wine=chardonnay")Add to cart⟨/A⟩⟨/TD⟩
⟨/TR⟩

⟨/TABLE⟩

⟨/BODY⟩
⟨/HTML⟩
```

FIGURE A.9 HTML Tags for Tabular Display of Text and Data.

ements in this form. First there are the "INPUT TYPE=TEXT" fields, where the user types in the number of bottles of each type of wine to be purchased. Next there is a "SUBMIT" button (i.e., INPUT TYPE=SUBMIT). If the user types in "2" for the number of bottles of Merlot, when he or she clicks the "SUBMIT" button the key-value pairs "quantity_merlot=2" and quantity_chardonnay=0" will be sent to the "www.premiumselect.com" server, which is designated in the "ACTION" field of the FORM tag.

Again, there are a wide variety of form elements including "radio buttons," "check boxes," "selection lists," "text input fields," "submit buttons," "regular buttons," "images," "textareas," "password input boxes," and "reset buttons." A detailed discussion of these elements is beyond the scope of this appendix. Readers are referred to Graham (1998) for a complete discussion.

A.2 HTML EDITORS

With HTML 1.0 and 2.0 it was easy to create Web pages with a basic text editor (like Microsoft's Notepad), manually typing in the content as well as the appropriate tags. Although many Web designers

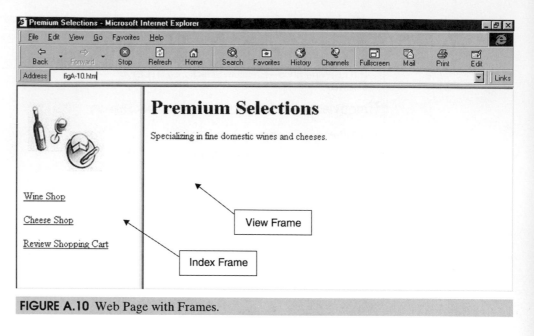

FIGURE A.10 Web Page with Frames.

still rely on these simple tools, a larger number employ specialized HTML editors to create pages. The editors are of two sorts: Web-authoring tools that provide WYSIWYG ("What You See Is What You Get"), graphical layout control and automatically generated underlying HTML and specialized text editors that still require the use of tags but alleviate the problem of remembering the various tags and their syntax. Microsoft's Front Page, Symantec's Visual Page, and NetObjects' Fusion are examples of authoring tools. Homesite from Allaire, Hot Dog Pro from Sausage Software, and Hot Metal Pro from SoftQuad are specialized editors. While the authoring tools make it easier to create aesthetically pleasing pages, designers still need to understand HTML in order to maintain, modify, and edit existing pages, especially given the differences that exist in the way the two main browsers display HTML pages.

A.3 CASCADING STYLE SHEETS AND DYNAMIC HTML

Today, many of the tags in HTML 4.0 deal with graphic presentation. This is primarily the result of competition between Netscape and Microsoft, as

FIGURE A.11 HTML Tags for Frames.

```
⟨HTML⟩

⟨HEAD⟩
⟨TITLE⟩Premium Selections⟨/TITLE⟩
⟨/HEAD⟩

⟨FRAMESET COLS="25%, *"⟩
    ⟨FRAME SRC="index.htm" NAME=index⟩
    ⟨FRAME SRC="start.htm" NAME=view⟩
⟨/FRAMESET⟩

⟨/HTML⟩
```

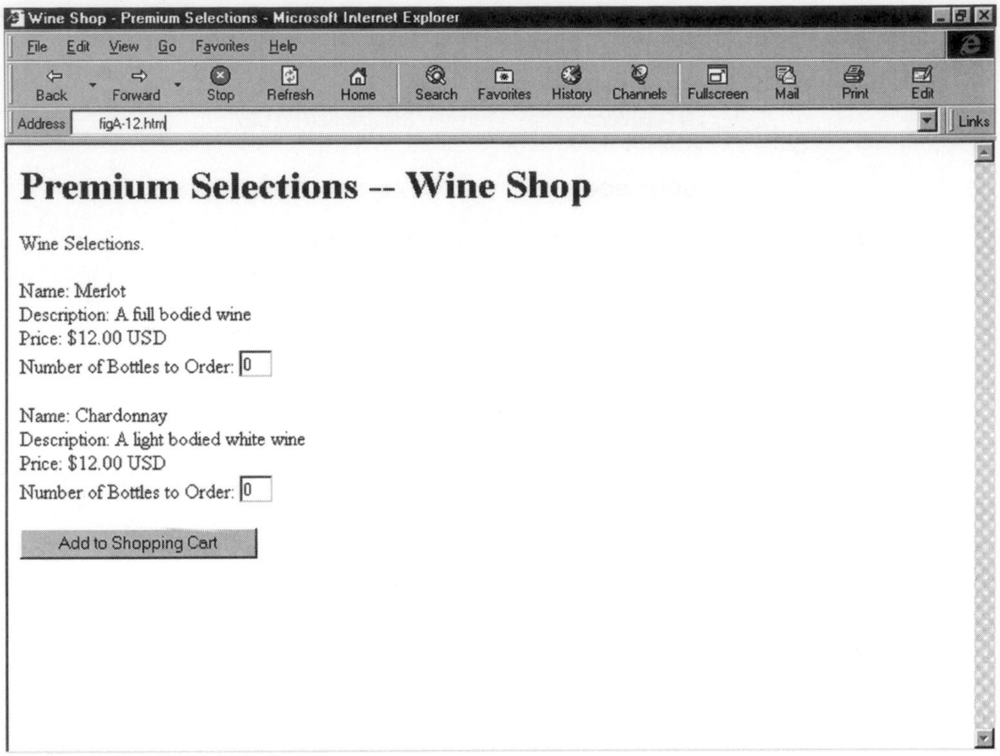

FIGURE A.12 Web Page with Forms.

they have both vied for browser superiority, and the need for Web site designers to control the quality of the layout and visual aesthetics of their Web pages. Toward this end, both companies have established a set of proprietary tags that go by the name of "dynamic HTML" (DHTML). At the moment, neither set of tags has been adopted as a standard. Instead, the World Wide Web Consortium (W3C) has ratified a new set of "style" standards—Cascading Style Sheets (CSS1 and CSS2)—that give designers enhanced control over the "look and feel" of their pages. Cascading Style Sheets enable Web designers to establish a template of styles and then to apply those styles throughout a document, application, or entire site.

As an example of the way that styles might be used, consider Figure A.14, which defines a style for the body and "number1 headers" for the home page of the Premium Selections site. Styles are usually defined in the "head" of a page and are denoted by the ⟨STYLE⟩...⟨/STYLE⟩ tags. In this case there

are two styles that are defined. The first states that the "BACKGROUND" color of the "BODY" will be white. The second says that all H1 headlines will use a 24-point font (FONT-SIZE: 24) and will be italicized (FNT-WEIGHT: ITALIC). The page that results from these styles is essentially the same as the one shown in Figure A.1.

In practice, styles are usually placed in a separate file that is linked to a page rather than physically embedding the styles within a page. In this way a set of styles can be applied to more than one page or document, much like the style templates shared among word documents. For a good discussion of Cascading Style Sheets, see Boumphey (1998).

A.4 VIRTUAL REALITY MODELING LANGUAGE (VRML)

Virtual reality is a term that usually refers to computer-generated or -enhanced 3D environments that can be manipulated by the end user. High-end

```
⟨HTML⟩

⟨HEAD⟩
⟨TITLE⟩Wine Shop—Premium Selections⟨/TITLE⟩
⟨/HEAD⟩

⟨BODY BGCOLOR="white" TEXT="black" LINK="black"⟩

⟨H1⟩Premium Selections—Wine Shop⟨/H1⟩

⟨P⟩Wine Selections.⟨/P⟩

⟨FORM ACTION="www.premium.select" METHOD=POST⟩

Name: Merlot⟨BR⟩
Description: A full bodied wine⟨BR⟩
Price: $12.00 USD⟨BR⟩
Number of Bottles to Order:
⟨INPUT TYPE=TEXT SIZE=2NAME=quantity_merlot VALUE="0"⟩
⟨P⟩

Name: Chardonnay⟨BR⟩
Description: A light bodied white wine⟨BR⟩
Price: $12.00 USD⟨BR⟩
Number of Bottles to Order:
⟨INPUT TYPE=TEXT SIZE=2 NAME=quantity_chardonnay VALUE="0"⟩
⟨P⟩

⟨INPUT TYPE=SUBMIT VALUE="Add to Shopping Cart"⟩
⟨/P⟩

⟨/FORM⟩

⟨/BODY⟩
⟨/HTML⟩
```

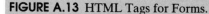

FIGURE A.13 HTML Tags for Forms.

virtual reality requires the use of specialized equipment (like goggles and gloves) that immerses the end user in a 3D world. The Internet version of virtual reality involves documents created with a markup language called the Virtual Reality Modeling Language (VRML, pronounced like "vermil").

Like HTML, VRML files are text files containing special tags that define 3D scenes from more primitive objects (such as cubes, cones, cylinders, and the like). Virtual Reality Modeling Language has the ability to link virtual scenes or worlds together by turning various objects into anchors or links. For example, the VRML file shown in Figure A.15 defines a scene with a wall that contains a door, which in turn contains a door panel and a doorknob. The doorknob has been defined as an anchor that when clicked leads the user to a technology chat room.

There are a variety of VRML editors that enable Web designers with minimal graphic training to create fairly complex scenes depicting furniture, people, virtual rooms, buildings, outdoor scenery, cities, 3D graphics, and the like that can be linked to other VRML files or HTML pages. The scene displayed in Figure A.16 is a rendering of the page defined in Figure A.15 and illustrates the 3D quality of VRML pages.

Unlike regular GIF or JPEG images, when a VRML file is encountered by a browser, it is displayed within the browser in a special VRML viewer (e.g., Cosmo 2.0). The special viewer provides the ability to navigate through the scene in a 3D fashion,

```
⟨HTML⟩

⟨HEAD⟩

⟨TITLE⟩Premium Selections⟨/TITLE⟩

⟨STYLE⟩
BODY {BACKGROUND:white}
H1 {FONT-SIZE:24 pt; FONT-WEIGHT:italic}
⟨/STYLE⟩

⟨/HEAD⟩

⟨BODY⟩

⟨P⟩
⟨IMG SRC="premium.gif "⟩
⟨/P⟩

⟨H1⟩Premium Selections⟨/H1⟩

Specializing in fine domestic wines and cheeses.

⟨P⟩
⟨A HREF="wines.htm"⟩Wine Shop⟨/A⟩
⟨/P⟩

⟨P⟩
⟨A HREF="cheeses.htm"⟩Cheese Shop⟨/A⟩
⟨/P⟩

⟨P⟩
⟨A HREF="shoppingcart.exe"⟩Review Shopping Cart⟨/A⟩
⟨/P⟩

⟨/BODY⟩
⟨/HTML⟩
```

FIGURE A.14 HTML Tags for Embedded Styles.

moving over, under, and around the objects. VRML also has the capability to animate a scene changing the location and shape of objects in response to user or system actions.

From the point of EC, VRML is still in its infancy. Few EC sites use the technology, even though there are a number of potential applications including 3D:

- advertisements,
- storerooms and showcases,
- chat rooms with animated figures representing the participants,
- adventure games,
- animated charts and graphs,
- city guides and travelogues.

In the future, there may be more widespread use when the VRML viewers become faster and easier for consumers to use. For an extensive discussion of VRML, see Ames et al. (1996).

A.5 THE COMING OF XML AND XSL

The Web is a fast-moving environment, especially from a software standpoint. Today's standards are next year's legacies. The following table summarizes some of the new "standards" and shifting emphasis that has taken place over the last year.

Function	Last Year	This Year
Creating Content	HTML 3.2	HTML 4.0 Dynamic HTML—DHTML Cascading Style Sheets—CSS Level 1–2
Distributing Content	HTTP 1.0	HTTP 1.1
Enhancing Interactivity	Java 1.1 ActiveX JavaScript VBScript	Java 1.2 JavaBeans JavaScript VBScript DHTML and Document Object Model (DOM)
Delivering Dynamic Content	CGI Database Gateways	CGI Database Gateways Server-Side Scripting Active Server Pages

FIGURE A.15 Sample VRML Defining a Door.

```
#VRML V2.0 utf8

Group {
  children [

#Draw the door
    Anchor {
    Description "Doorway to Chat Room"
    url ["skyline.gif "]
    Shape {
        appearance Appearance {material Material {diffuseColor 0.6 0.55 0.4}}
        geometry Box {size 7.0 12.0 .25 }
      }

    }
# Draw door panel
    Shape {
        appearance Appearance{material Material {diffuseColor 0.3 0.2 0.0}}
        geometry Box {size 3.0 7.01 0.33} }

#Draw door knob
    Transform {
        translation 1.1 -0.25 0.325
        children [
            Anchor {
              url ["techchat.htm"]
              children [
              Shape {
              appearance Appearance {
                material Material {diffuseColor 0.6 0.6 0.0}}
              geometry Sphere {radius 0.2}
                }}}]}

#Put name on door
    Transform {
        translation -1.0 2.25 0.5
        children Shape {
          appearance Appearance{material Material {diffuseColor 1.0 0.0 0.0}}
        geometry Text {
            string ["Doorway","to","TechChat"]
            fontStyle FontStyle {
                family "SANS" style "BOLD"justify "CENTER" size 0.6} } } }
    ]}
```

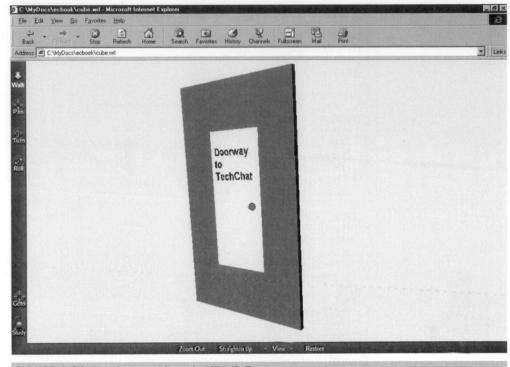

FIGURE A.16 Rendering of Sample VRML Page.

Next year is not likely to be any different. Looming on the horizon is a new standard that promises to dramatically change the way in which Web content is created, stored, and delivered. The standard is called XML. The problem with HTML is that it is a hodgepodge of tags that deal with document structure, content, and display. This fact makes it difficult for Web designers and Webmasters to create and maintain the myraid of pages found at most EC Web sites. This fact also makes it difficult for software robots and software agents to either index or find specific content on the Web.

To help understand the difficulties, look at the code displayed in Figure A.17 (remember that Web designers and software robots work with code and not the actual display). Now answer a couple of questions. First, "What do these figures represent?" You probably guessed stock prices. Second, "What was the closing price for Microsoft stock (MSFT) on this particular date?" You can certainly determine this, but it requires effort. The problem is that HTML mixes up display with content and provides few clues to the meaning of the content.

Now look at the code in Figure A.18 and try to answer the questions again. This is a no-brainer.

The code in Figure A.18 is XML, which is a markup language that focuses on describing the content of the data as opposed to the structure of the document or display. In XML there are no fixed tags. Instead, the Web designer or author is free to create his or her own tags, which is why the markup language is called extensible. The manner in which the tags are used in an XML document is defined in a file called the Document Type Definition (DTD). A DTD is basically a set of grammar rules that dictate the makeup of the tags' particular document. Used primarily for purposes of determining the validity of an XML document, DTDs are optional. If you are really interested in understanding DTDs refer to Boumphey (1998).

An open question is: "How does a browser display an XML?" The answer is that XML has an accompanying markup language that defines the style for displaying an XML document. This markup language is called XSL (for Extensible Style Language). Like a Cascading Style Sheet, an XSL document provides a set of rules for displaying XML tags. A very simple XSL document is shown in Figure A.19. Again, we will not dwell on the specifics of the file. The resulting Web page is shown in Figure A.20.

```
<HTML>
<HEAD>
<TITLE>Sample Table</TITLE>
</HEAD>
<BODY>

<H1>PRICES FOR 8/20/98</H1>

<TABLE>
  <TR>
  <TH>Ticker</TH>
  <TH>Hi</TH>
  <TH>Low</TH>
  <TH>Close</TH>
  <TH>Volume</TH>
</TR>
<TR>
  <TD>MSFT</TD>
  <TD>123</TD>
  <TD>118</TD>
  <TD>120</TD>
  <TD>1000000</TD>
</TR>
<TR>
  <TD>XYZ</TD>
  <TD>80</TD>
  <TD>78</TD>
  <TD>78</TD>
  <TD>100000</TD>
</TR>
</TABLE>

</BODY>
</HTML>
```

FIGURE A.17 Mystery Table.

FIGURE A.18 Sample XML Code for Stock Prices.

```
<STOCK REPORT ID="101">
 <DATE>8/20/98</DATE>
 <STOCKS>
  <STOCK>
   <TICKER>MSFT</TICKER>
   <HI>123</HI>
   <LOW>118</LOW>
   <CLOSE>120</CLOSE>
   <VOLUME>1000000</VOLUME>
  </STOCK>
  <STOCK>
   <TICKER>XYZ</TICKER>
   <HI>80</HI>
   <LOW>78</LOW>
   <CLOSE>78</CLOSE>
   <VOLUME>100000</VOLUME>
  </STOCK>
 </STOCKS>
</STOCK REPORT>
```

```
〈XSL〉
〈RULE〉
 〈TARGET-ELEMENT TYPE="date"〉
  〈DIV FONT-STYLE="bold"
    〈CHILDREN/〉
  〈/DIV〉
 〈/RULE〉
 〈RULE〉
 〈TARGET-ELEMENT TYPE="date"〉
  〈DIV FONT-STYLE="italic"
    〈CHILDREN/〉
  〈/DIV〉
 〈/RULE〉
〈/XSL〉
```

FIGURE A.19 Sample XSL Rules for Displaying XML Stock Report.

While XML is a child of the Web, its primary focus is not on the browser. Extensible Markup Language is display-device independent, and its documents can be used with any display device (browsers, printers, PDAs, cell phones, and so on). Documents composed of XML can also be more easily understood and manipulated by other soft-ware programs. Today, the files accessed by software programs are stored in either ASCII or some proprietary binary format. Many of the problems associated with both formats are alleviated by XML and it is easier for programs to interchange data. Recognizing this fact, several task forces and consortiums have begun defining industry-specific and

FIGURE A.20 Sample Output from XSL Rules.

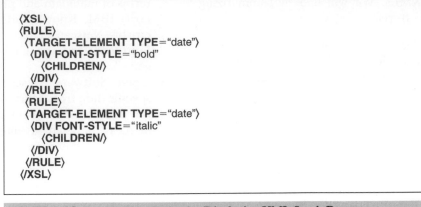

task-specific XMLs. We will end by summarizing some of these efforts.

- Channel Definition Format (CDF)—an XML specification proposed by Microsoft and PointCast for defining Web broadcast channels for automatically "pushing" content to the browser rather than having the content "pulled" by the end user.
- Open Financial Exchange (OFX)—an XML specification proposed by Microsoft, Intuit, and Checkfree for exchanging financial transaction documents.
- Open Trading Protocol (OTP)—an XML standard proposed by a 30-company consortium for handling remote electronic purchases regardless of the payment mechanism.
- Web Interface Definition Language (WIDL)—an XML metadata syntax proposed by webMethods that defines Application Programming Interfaces (APIs) to Web data and services.
- Resource Description Framework (RDF)—an XML specification governing the interoperability of applications in terms of metadata and proposed by DVL, Grif, IBM, KnowledgeCite, LANL, Microsoft, Netscape, Nokia, OCLC, Reuters, SoftQuad, and the University of Michigan.
- Open Software Description—an XML specification from Marimba and Microsoft for describing software package components to be used in automated software distribution environments.

An extensive description of these and other efforts can be found in Cover (1998).

References

A. Ames, D. Nadeau, and J. Moreland, *VRML 2.0 Sourcebook* (New York: John Wiley & Sons, 1996).

F. Boumphey, *Professional Style Sheets for HTML and XML* (New York: Wrox Press, 1998).

R. Cover, *XML Reference Page*, www.oasis-open.org/cover/xml.html (December 1998).

I. Graham, *HTML 4.0 Sourcebook* (New York: John Wiley & Sons, 1998).

L. LeMay and D. Tyler, *Sam's Teach Yourself Web Publishing with HTML 4 in 21 Days* (Indianapolis, IN: Sams.net Publishing, 1998).

Appendix B

Web Programming: Adding Desktop Interactivity and Dynamic Data Access

Originally, the Web was designed to deliver static Web pages from a Web server connected somewhere on the Internet to a Web browser sitting on a user's desktop computer. Basically, all a user could do was click on a hot spot or hypertext link to retrieve a new page, read it, then go on to the next page. The Web was not designed to support EC sites, especially B2C sites. In its original state there was no way to create pages that would allow consumers to easily determine what products were for sale, to select products as they moved from page to page (i.e., an electronic shopping cart), to place an order, or to verify an order. Similarly, there was no simple way to integrate a Web server with a database system containing product, pricing, and promotional data with transactional systems for processing orders and with payment systems for handling credit card purchases and settlements. Over time, these limitations have been addressed. First, "forms" were added to HTML (Appendix A discusses HTML forms). Forms provided a way to produce Web pages from which a consumer could select, order, and pay for products. Second, special programming and scripting languages (like Java and JavaScript) were created. These newer languages allowed application developers to produce interactive Web pages whose functionality emulated the rich functionality of standard windows-based applications. Finally, a standard application programming interface (API) called the common gateway interface (CGI) was introduced. Generally speaking, an API provides a way for one software program to communicate with another, whereas CGI provides a way for software developers and application programmers to integrate Web servers with various back-end programs and data sources. Because of CGI's inefficiencies, newer APIs and special database gateway programs were also introduced. As a result of these changes, the Web is now well suited for the dynamic world of EC.

This appendix briefly looks at the issues of end-user interactivity and dynamic data access. The first sections focus on Java and JavaScript, which are special programming languages that can be used to create Web pages with rich graphical user interfaces (GUIs). The remaining sections examine various methods—CGI programming, specialized APIs, database gateways, and server-side scripting—for integrating a Web server with back-end programs, especially relational databases.

B.1 DESKTOP INTERACTIVITY AND PROCESSING

Most of us are familiar with various applications running on Microsoft Windows. One of the hallmarks of a Window's application is the GUI (i.e., its look and feel) and the (on-screen) interactivity it provides. To regular Windows users, scrolling, clicking, double-clicking, dragging and dropping, entering data, and similar actions are almost second nature. In Windows these actions are handled by the desktop computer on which the application resides. So, for instance, if a user of Microsoft Excel enters a formula and hits the "Enter" key, then the desktop computer calculates the result, which is displayed immediately in the Excel spreadsheet. Even with a client/server application where processing is distributed between a desktop computer and a back-end server, the desktop still handles the user's actions. Initially, the type of interactivity found in a Window's application was missing from the Web. The earliest Web pages were built solely with HTML (described in detail in Appendix A). Until forms were added to HTML, the only actions supported by HTML were clicking (on a hypertext link to access a new page). What forms added was data entry along with a series of new elements (like radio buttons, check boxes, and drop-down selection lists). Yet, even with these the only thing a user could do was click. In the same vein, there was no way for the browser (i.e., the user's desktop) to process the user's actions. All the processing had to occur on a Web server. While this is fine for some applications, there are a number of applications that are better served with the types of interactions supported by

Windows. This is where Java and the scripting languages such as JavaScript come into play. Java and JavaScript provide the means to create applications that support the types of user interactions found in Windows. They also make it possible for processing to be distributed between the desktop and the server.

Java

Java had its roots in work done at the beginning of the 1990s by a developer named James Gosling at Sun Microsystems. This original work focused on developing software and networks for consumer devices (like VCRs, Personal Digital Assistants, toasters, and so forth). The result of this work was a programming language called Oak. Recognizing the growing import of the Internet, the developers at Sun Microsystems turned their attention from consumer devices to making Oak a premier programming language for the Web. In 1995, Oak was renamed Java. In that same year a number of software and hardware vendors licensed Java from Sun, including IBM, Netscape, Microsoft, and Symantec.

Java is language similar to C++ and can be used to produce stand-alone applications or applets. An applet is a Java program that is written for and runs in a Web browser. As a programming language, it is well suited to Web development because of its native support for Internet communications.

If Java were simply a programming language, then it would not have generated much interest outside the programming community. After all, how many of us are excited or know much about C++, even though it is the development language used in most commercial software products. What makes Java interesting to industry observers is that it also has a run-time environment called a virtual machine (VM). Any computer that has a Java VM can run a Java program. Both Netscape and Microsoft's browsers have Java VMs built in. Unlike Java, other programming languages require developers to write and then compile their programs on the machine on which the program is to be run. Compilation refers to the process of converting the human readable form of a program into binary or machine code that can be run by a specific computer. So, for example, if a developer wants his or her program to run on a PC and a Unix computer, then he or she must write and compile the program on both machines. Even if it is the same type of computer (say a PC), the pro-

gram must be written for and compiled on each generation of the machine. Of course, you can see that standard program languages are ill-suited for the Web because of the large variety of computers that are attached to the Web. In contrast, Java is a "write once, run anywhere" (WORA) programming language. That is, a programmer writes a Java program and compiles it. Unlike other language compilers that turn a program into machine-specific code, the Java compiler produces an intermediate form of code (called byte code) that is not machine specific. When Java byte code is sent to a Web browser, it is executed on the fly by the Java VM. Where does the Java VM reside? It comes with a Web browser.

Special APPLET tags are used to incorporate applets within an HTML page. The page shown in Figure B.1 comes from the GM site. This particular page uses a Java applet that enables potential buyers to select a vehicle that matches their lifestyle. The same could have been provided with a form. However, the interactivity would not have been the same.

The code behind part of this page is shown in Figure B.2. The applet is defined by an ⟨APPLET⟩ ...⟨/APPLET⟩ tag. The CODE parameter in this tag specifies a file containing all the Java code to be downloaded from the Web server. Technically, this code is called a class. The WIDTH and HEIGHT parameters of the APPLET tag define a rectangular region in which the applet will be displayed on the Web page.

When a Web browser accesses a page with an APPLET tag, it begins by rendering the page. During this process, it sees the APPLET tag and knows to: (1) reserve a display space within the page and (2) request the Web server to send the Java applet code. Once the applet arrives, the browser's Java VM begins executing the applet code.

Any interaction that takes place between the user and an applet is handled by the VM. It is as if there were a separate program running within the page. One advantage of having the VM in control is that it can enforce security, providing a "sandbox" that limits the applet's access to system resources. For the most part, applets do not have access to any system resources. For instance, they cannot read or write files to the desktop disk. This is why it is difficult for a hacker to write an applet that plays havoc with a user's system. There are also drawbacks to this control, however. In earlier versions, applets

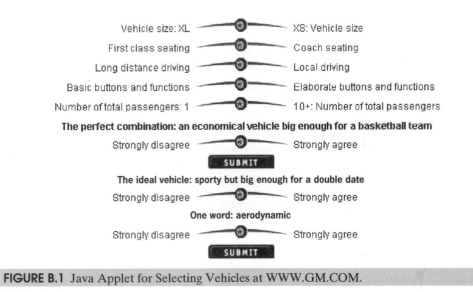

FIGURE B.1 Java Applet for Selecting Vehicles at WWW.GM.COM.

could not print because printing is a system resource. This constraint has recently been eliminated. The fact that an applet cannot read or write to disk means that an end user cannot store interim work or the results of any analysis. This sort of functionality is crucial for those users that do not have constant access to the Web server (like mobile executives).

Today, few EC applications employ Java applets. Extranet applications are one place where they show some signs of promise. IBM, for instance, is developing many of their B2B applications in Java. There are a couple of reasons why the use of Java in EC applications has been constrained. First, most users' Internet connections are still fairly slow.

This makes downloading anything but trivial applets a painstaking process. In the same vein, when an applet arrives, the speed with which it executes still does not compare with programs developed with standard programming languages. Both factors contributed, for example, to the rapid demise of Corel Inc.'s attempt to deliver a Java version of their suite of office applications. Finally, the notion of WORA is more hype than reality (a current joke rephrases it "write once, debug everywhere"). Just as there are substantial differences between the two major browsers, there are major differences among the Java VMs provided by the different vendors. Recent testing of the various VMs by *Java World* (1998) show that for the second year in a row Mi-

```
To find out, drag the marker to the point on the scale ⟨BR⟩ that best represents your lifestyle and vehicle preferences.
⟨P⟩
⟨APPLET ARCHIVE=Quest.zip CODE=Quest.class WIDTH=600 HEIGHT=250⟩
⟨PARAM NAME="submit" VALUE="submit.gif "⟩
⟨PARAM NAME="arch" VALUE="arch.gif "⟩
⟨PARAM NAME="wheel" VALUE="wheel.gif "⟩
⟨PARAM NAME="vtype" VALUE="utility"⟩
⟨PARAM NAME="num" VALUE="6"⟩
⟨PARAM NAME="q3" VALUE="Long distance driving"⟩
⟨PARAM NAME="a3" VALUE="Local driving"⟩
⟨PARAM NAME="h3" VALUE="GB"⟩
⟨PARAM NAME="Q2" VALUE="FIRST CLASS SEATING"⟩
⟨PARAM NAME="a2" VALUE="Coach seating"⟩
⟨PARAM NAME="h2" VALUE="DC7"⟩
⟨PARAM NAME="q1" VALUE="Vehicle size: XL"⟩
⟨PARAM NAME="a1" VALUE="XS: Vehicle size"⟩
⟨PARAM NAME="h1" VALUE="DC3"⟩
⟨PARAM NAME="q4" VALUE="Basic buttons and functions"⟩
⟨PARAM NAME="a4" VALUE="Elaborate buttons and functions"⟩
⟨PARAM NAME="h4" VALUE="DC2"⟩
⟨PARAM NAME="q5" VALUE="Number of total passengers: 1"⟩
⟨PARAM NAME="a5" VALUE="10+: Number of total passengers"⟩
⟨PARAM NAME="h5" VALUE="PCAP"⟩
⟨PARAM NAME="a6" VALUE="Strongly agree"⟩
⟨PARAM NAME="q6" VALUE="Strongly disagree"⟩
⟨PARAM NAME="h6" VALUE="PV12"⟩
⟨PARAM NAME="t6" VALUE="The perfect combination: an economical vehicle big enough for a basketball team"⟩
⟨PARAM NAME="url" VALUE="cgi-bin/vchooser.cgi"⟩
⟨PARAM NAME="pad" VALUE="1"⟩
Please visit the ⟨A HREF="utility_1.html"⟩non-Java version⟨/A⟩ of this applet.
⟨/APPLET⟩
⟨html⟩
```

FIGURE B.2 Java Applet Tags for Selecting Vehicles at WWW.GM.COM.

crosoft's Java VM was the most efficient and compatible VM (running all of the test applets), even more so than the VM developed by Sun Microsystems, the originators of Java.

JavaScript and the Document Object Model (DOM)

Java applets are not the only way to add interactivity to Web pages. Interactivity can also be provided through JavaScript. The name JavaScript is the property of Netscape. Microsoft's version of the language is called JScript. JavaScript has been standardized by the European Computer Manfacturers Association. The name of the standard is ECMAScript. As usual, neither of the browsers currently supports the standard.

JavaScript, often confused with Java, is not a lightweight version of Java. The two languages have different capabilities and are used for different purposes. JavaScript can control the objects, content, and interactions within the browser. It cannot draw graphics or directly access the network. Java has no control over the browser but can obviously do graphics and networking. JavaScript can interact with and control Java applets within a Web page but the reverse is not true.

To program in JavaScript, you simply write the JavaScript programming statements and functions directly in the Web page, interspersed with the HTML statements. When a Web browser receives a Web page containing JavaScript, it automatically knows to execute the program. The listing in Figure B.3 exemplifies how JavaScript is embedded among the HTML statements on a Web page. The page shown in Figure B.4 is what results when the code is executed.

In Figure B.3 the JavaScript program is contained between the ⟨SCRIPT⟩ tags. Without going into specific details, when the user clicks the SUBMIT button, the function "onClick" is executed. The function checks to see "if" the "value" of the "Name" input field in this particular form is empty.

```
〈html〉
〈head〉
〈title〉JavaScript Validation〈/title〉
〈/head〉

〈script language="javascript"〉

function valcheck(){
  if (document.forms[0].elements[0].value==""){
    alert("Please enter a name")
  }
}

〈/script〉

〈body bgcolor="#FFFFFF"〉

〈h2〉JavaScript Validation〈/h2〉

〈form method="POST"〉
〈p〉Name: 〈input type="text" size="32" name="T1"〉〈/p〉
〈p〉〈input type="button" name="B1" value="Submit" onClick="valcheck()"〉〈/p〉
〈/form〉

〈/body〉
〈/html〉
```

FIGURE B.3 JavaScript Validating User Input.

If it is empty, then an alert window pops up the message, "Please enter a user name." Otherwise, the form is submitted.

When JavaScript was first introduced, one of its major purposes was to validate user input (just like the above example). Today, it is widely used at EC sites to enhance the dynamic character of Web pages and to accomplish a variety of tasks including the sorts of examples described below (Flanagan, 1998).

Like everything else on the Web, JavaScript has gone through a number of changes. Today, JavaScript is intimately tied to the set of elements that can be contained in a Web page. These elements include the text and all the other components of a page like the HTML tables, images, buttons, forms, and so forth. The collection of possible Web page elements is called the DOM. For each of these elements in the DOM, there is a well-defined set of user actions that the element can recognize—in pro-

FIGURE B.4 Java Form with Validated Input.

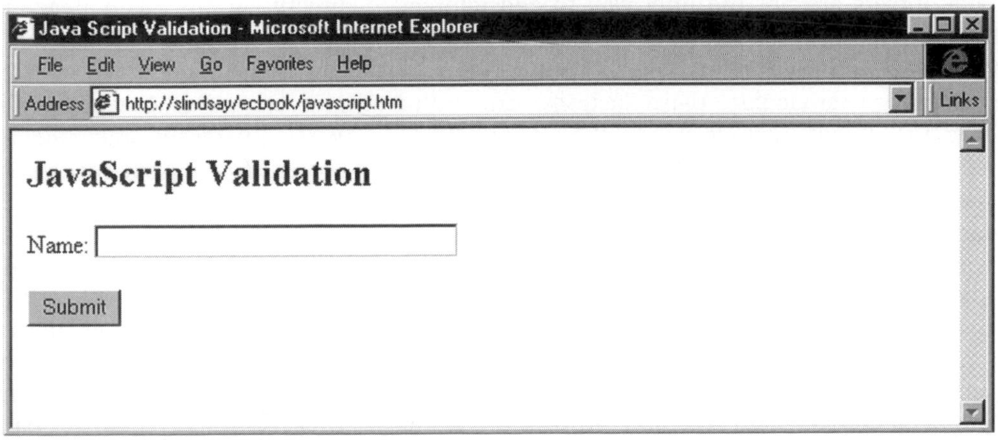

TABLE B.1   Functions of JavaScript

Function	Example
Client-side form validation	Ensuring that there are no blank input fields, that numbers are numbers and text fields are text, that the length of a field (like a ticker) is the correct length, and that numeric input values fall within a given range.
Client-side calculations	As users input or select specific values, new calculations can be computed and immediately displayed on the page. Examples include mortgage calculations, currency conversion, or calculating the price of a product based on the features selected by a user.
Client-side lookup databases	JavaScript provides associative data arrays that enable values to be looked up on the basis of keys. For instance, given a company name, an associate array could provide the stock ticker (e.g., StockTicker ("Comshare")="CSRE"). Simple databases can be embedded in JavaScript, providing lookup tables that can assist end users with data input.
Client-side image maps	Image maps are large graphics that are divided into areas where each area provides a different response when clicked by an end user. For instance, an image map might represent the states in the United States. When the user clicks on a particular state, a specified Web page is retrieved. In a client-side image map, each of the areas can be associated with particular JavaScript functions, making it possible to carry out a variety of client-side actions besides simply retrieving a page.
Providing interactive feedback	As the user moves the mouse across various objects, help messages can be displayed on the status bar at the bottom of the browser window.
Personalizing a document before it is displayed	If the Script code is contained in the ⟨HEAD⟩ of a document, the code is executed before the document is displayed. In this way personalized documents can be created based on the date, data contained in cookies, and so on.
Manipulating Java applets or ActiveX objects within a page	JavaScript can be used along with various input objects (like buttons) to control applets or ActiveX objects contained on the same page. For instance, there might be a applet displaying a graph and a series of buttons linked to script that enable a user to select the type of graph, background color, and so on.

gramming vernacular these actions are called "events." Events include things like mouse actions, keyboard entry, and changes in the state of a document (e.g., loading a document is a state). The collection of events is called an "event model." Taken together, the DOM and event model determine how a scripting language like JavaScript can be used to manipulate a Web page.

Initially, the number of elements in the DOM was small. Slowly but surely, the DOM has evolved into a comprehensive collection of elements. At the moment, a DOM standard has been proposed to the W3C. Currently, Microsoft's Internet Explorer 4.0 comes close to supporting the proposed standard, while Netscape's Navigator 4.0 does not. Both companies have pledged to support the standard that emerges from the W3C in the 5.0 versions of their browsers. Even though neither browser completely supports the proposed standard, Web page authors and designers now have the tools to create highly interactive Web pages without having to resort to Java. Both Goodman (1998) and Isaacs (1997) provide excellent discussions of the DOM, the event model, and their relationship to JavaScript.

A Word about ActiveX and VBScript

When Java and JavaScript first appeared, Microsoft saw them as a direct threat to their control of the desktop marketplace. With these languages software vendors could create desktop and front-office applications (like word processing, spreadsheets, and the like) that could be stored on any Web server (not just Microsoft's Internet Information Server), downloaded to any Web browser (not just Microsoft's Internet Explorer), and run on any computer (not just a PC with Microsoft Windows or NT). Clearly, widespread adoption of Java and JavaScript applications could reduce Microsoft's market share, although that has not happened so far. One of the things that Microsoft did in response was to introduce their own proprietary components and scripting language called ActiveX components and VBScript (Visual Basic Script), respectively. While both are designed for the Web, they only work with Microsoft's Internet Explorer.

Like Java applets, ActiveX components are stored on a Web server. When a user of Internet Explorer downloads a Web page referencing an ActiveX component, the browser retrieves the component and executes it. Unlike Java, ActiveX does not run in a "sandbox." ActiveX components can access system resources, e.g., reading from and writing to files on the desktop.

All of Microsoft's office applications—Word, Excel, Access, PowerPoint, and others—come with a scripting language called Visual Basic for Applications (VBA), which can be used to write everything from simple macros for automating various manual processes to full-blown custom applications built on top of one of the desktop applications. You can think of VBScript as VBA for Internet Explorer. VBScript works the same way as JavaScript and has the same capabilities. This means that VBScript programs, intertwined with the HTML on a Web page, can control the elements of the DOM and their associated events. In fact, both VBScript and JavaScript can be included on the same Web page. Of course, it requires Internet Explorer to run the page. If the page were accessed with Netscape's Navigator, the VBScript would be ignored and the JavaScript would be run, even though the page would not make much sense.

Although Microsoft actively promotes ActiveX and VBScript, they continue to hedge their bets. Microsoft is one of the leading vendors of Java development tools (Visual J++) and also supports their own version of JavaScript (called JScript).

B.2 DELIVERING DYNAMIC CONTENT

Most EC sites on the Web provide some level of personalization, interactivity, and data access. In this case, static pages that are constructed ahead of time and stored on a server just do not work. With a static page every user sees the same content. Imagine, for instance, a Web site like Yahoo! that provides stock quotes that are updated every 15 minutes. There is no practical way for a site like this to "grab" the price/volume data for every stock and then generate new static pages (including tables and charts) every 15 minutes. Obviously, what are used are other external programs running on the Web server (or some other server) that generate "dynamic" Web pages on the fly in response to individual user requests. In this case, when an individual user requests an update on a particular stock (say, Microsoft, whose ticker is MSFT), the external program receives the request, grabs the new stock quote (in real time), and then generates a Web page with the updated information. How this is actually accomplished is detailed below.

Common Gateway Interface (CGI) Programming

The standard way in which dynamic Web pages are generated is diagrammed in Figure B.5. The key element in the process is CGI. From a technical standpoint, CGI is a set of standard methods and routines used to write a stand-alone software program that knows how to receive requests from a Web server and return data to the server. In other words, CGI is a standard protocol used to converse with a Web server. A program that has this capability is called a CGI program. These programs can be written in a wide variety of programming languages. On Unix the "Perl" programming language is often used. On Windows 95/98 or Windows NT, Visual Basic or C/C++ are frequently used.

To illustrate the basics of CGI programming, consider the simple example shown in Figure B.6. Here the user can obtain the current stock price (within the last 15 minutes) for either Microsoft or Netscape by clicking on the company name. Behind each name is a URL. In this case, the URL refers to

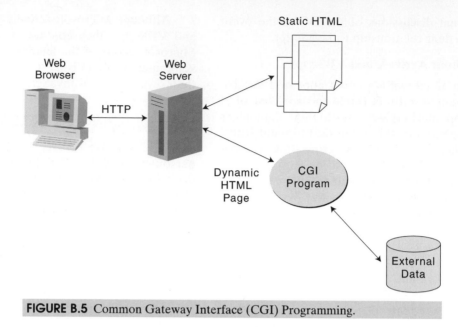

FIGURE B.5 Common Gateway Interface (CGI) Programming.

a program rather than a static document. For instance, the URL associated with the Microsoft selection is: "www.stocknews.com/cgi-bin/stock.exe?ticker=MS FT". Based on this URL, the Web server that receives the request is "www.stocknews.com." Upon receipt, the server knows that it needs to invoke a CGI program called "stock.exe" rather than retrieve a particular Web document. When it invokes the program, it passes the program the information after the "?" mark. The information after the "?" mark is called a "query string." The query string specifies various parameters and values that the CGI pro-

gram will use during execution. In this case, the query string specifies the stock ticker whose current price is sought. Once the program determines the associated price, it will return the results to the Web server in the form of an HTML page. In turn, the server will return the page to the user's browser in exactly the same fashion that it would return any other page.

In most real-world applications, HTML forms are used instead of URLs with query strings. The details of how this is done are well beyond the scope of this appendix. For those readers who are inter-

FIGURE B.6 Accessing Stock Prices through URL.

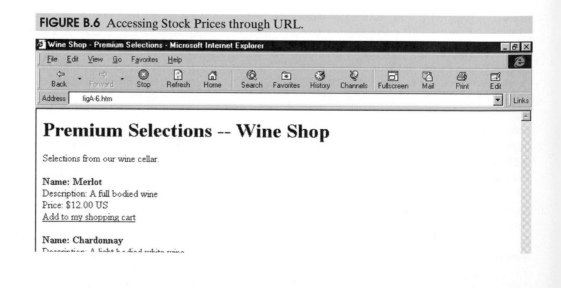

ested in the details of CGI programming see Gundavaram (1998).

Alternative APIs

While CGI programs are widely used, they suffer from some significant technical limitations, especially at Web sites where there is a lot of traffic. Common gateway interface programs are either separate executable programs or interpreted scripts. When a Web server invokes a CGI program, an individual copy of the program is brought into memory. After the program has run, the executable program is unloaded from memory. If the server receives another request while the first program is still running, then it will invoke a second instance. The number of copies in memory will depend on the number of requests the server is trying to service. At a large site, the number of copies could run in the thousands. Obviously, the frequent loading and unloading of a large number of copies is very inefficient, not to mention the fact that the performance of the server will degrade substantially as the number of requests increases.

In response, other gateway architectures and APIs have been developed to overcome the limitations of CGI programming. Two of the better-known APIs are Netscape's NSAPI (Netscape Server API) and Microsoft's ISAPI (Internet Server API). The difference between these APIs and CGI is that the server only invokes a single instance of the program and a technique known as "multithreading" is used to handle individual requests (each request is now a thread instead of the entire program). The overall result is increased efficiency and substantially improved performance.

Database Gateways

Relational databases are an integral part of most EC sites. A couple of years ago, CGI programs were the primary method used to update and access the data within relational databases. This required programmers to write special code to construct and issue SQL statements on the fly in order to handle data entries and queries made by end users. Since that time, a number of database vendors (like Oracle and Microsoft), as well as third-party software vendors, have produced specialized "database gateways" that eliminate the need for creating a customized CGI program. While there are differences among the various products, they all work in essentially the same fashion.

A simple example, that relies on Microsoft's Internet Database Connector (IDC), serves to illustrate how the various database gateways work. Suppose a consumer wants to obtain information about those dealers in his or her area who have used cars (say, Hondas) on hand. The Web page shown in Figure B.7 allows a user to select from one of two models and to specify the desired region. Again, behind each selection is a URL. For instance, if the user selects Honda Accords in the North, then the underlying URL is "www.autosite.com/usedcars. idc?model=accord&region=north". In this case, when the Web server (www.autosite.com) receives

FIGURE B.7 Sample Web Database Connection.

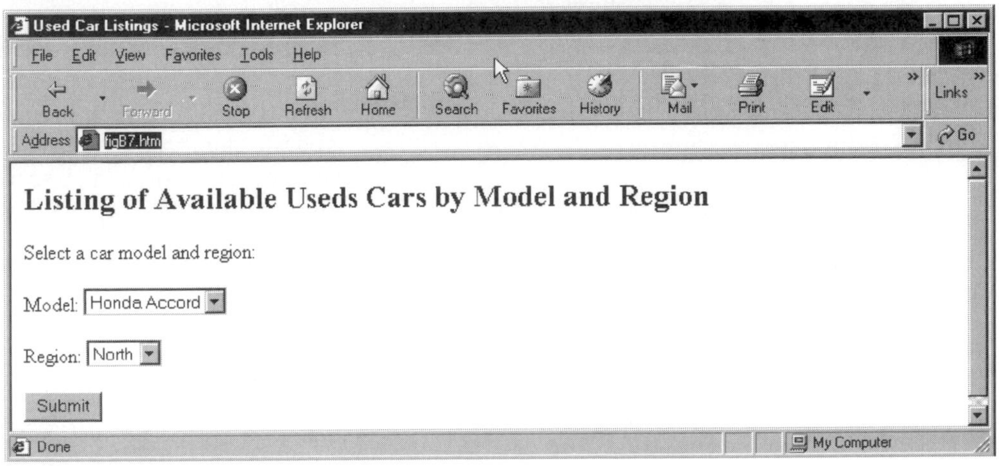

the user's request, it sees the ".idc" extension and knows that it needs to run the Microsoft database gateway program.

The gateway program uses the other information in the URL to respond to the user's request. In the case of the Microsoft gateway, this information provides two things—the name of an ".idc" file ("usedcars.idc") that is used as a query template and a set of database fields and values that will be used to fill in the template (i.e., model=accord and region=north). In this instance, the idc file might appear as follows:

```
Datasource: Used Cars
Username: Guest
Template: usedcar.idc
SQLStatement:
+SELECT region, dealerName, dealerAddress
+FROM usedcars
+WHERE model=%model% AND region=
%region%
```

This file specifies the name of the database to be queried, the user's name, a template file to be used in generating a response to the user's request, and the SQL statement to be executed. Within the SQL statement are various query parameters that are filled in with the values passed in the URL (i.e., %model% will be replaced with "accord" and %region% will be replaced with "north").

Once the query is run by the gateway program, the results are used to fill in the template response file ("usedcar.htx"). The sample file might look like this:

```
⟨HTML⟩
⟨HEAD⟩
⟨TITLE⟩Used Car Listings⟨/TITLE⟩
⟨HEAD⟩
⟨BODY⟩
The following dealers offer Honda Accords in
the North:
⟨TABLE⟩
⟨TR⟩⟨TH⟩DealerName⟨/TH⟩⟨TH⟩Dealer-
Address⟨/TH⟩⟨TR⟩
⟨%begindetail%⟩
⟨TR⟩⟨TD⟩dealcrName⟨/TD⟩⟨TD⟩dealerAddress
⟨/TD⟩⟨TR⟩
⟨%enddetail%⟩
⟨/TABLE⟩
⟨/BODY⟩
⟨HTML⟩
```

In this file the "%begindetail%" and "%enddetail%" tags indicate that the associated table is to be filled in with all the values returned by the database query.

Again, the details behind these gateway programs are beyond the scope of this appendix. Interested readers are referred to Keyes (1998).

Server-Side Scripting

In addition to specialized database gateways, both Netscape and Microsoft have added support for server-side scripting in their Web server products. Netscape supports a scripting language called server-side JavaScript (not to be confused with Java), while Microsoft supports both JavaScript and VBScript in its Active Server Page (ASP) technology. For those sites that utilize either Netscape's or Microsoft's servers (of which there are a substantial number) server-side scripting represents an alternative to CGI programming.

Server-side scripting works much the same way that template files operate in a database gateway program, that is, specialized tags and variables are used to embed the scripting code directly within the HTML code. Whenever an HTML page containing the intermingled script and HTML code is accessed, the server first executes the script code within the page and then sends the resulting page back to the browser. In this way the contents of the HTML page are dynamically generated (just as they are in CGI programming).

Server-side scripting gives the programmer, application builder, or Webmaster direct scripting access to a wide variety of objects. Server-side scripts can read and write files on the server. They also have direct access (with virtually no programming) to the information provided in a Web form. Finally, they provide the means to perform relational (SQL) database updates and queries. Because they support database queries, they preclude the need to have a separate database gateway. In fact, for those shops running Microsoft's Web server (IIS), IDC has been almost completely replaced by ASP.

Maintaining State: Cookies, Hidden Fields, and Other Tricks

In any dynamic application, one of the key issues faced by a Web developer is "state" maintenance. In a standard client/server application, when the user logs on to the system a connection is created between the desktop client and the back-end server (often a database program). The connection between the client and server remains open until the user explicitly logs off. During this time, the server keeps track of who is connected and which clients have issued which requests. There is no need for the programmer to develop any code for this purpose. The system handles it automatically. On the Web, things are entirely different. As noted earlier, in its native form the Web is "stateless." Each time a request is fulfilled, the connection between a client and server is broken. The next time the server gets a request it has no memory of the fact that a particular user might have just been connected.

"Statelessness" comes into play in a variety of situations. At most subscription sites, users receive personalized pages and personalized editions. As the user navigates from page to page, how does a Web server keep track of which user should receive which page if there is no state information identifying the user? At a multiuser game site, how does a server maintain scores for the individual players if there is no state information identifying the players? At other types of sites, end users are required to fill out multipage forms. For instance, at the GM site, where users issue queries to determine whether a dealer has a particular car in stock, users are led through a series of forms in order to specify the make, model, and location of interest. As the user moves from form to form, how does the server carry the information forward from previous forms if it has no memory of which users selected which makes, models, or locations? You get the picture. Except in the most trivial cases, virtually all client/server applications (Web or otherwise) require "state" information.

Almost from the Web's beginning, Web programmers and developers recognized the problem. In response they devised a variety of methods to track users from one page to the next and to make information on previous pages available on subsequent pages. Three methods are used quite frequently (often in combination with one another). They include:

- *QueryStrings/URLs*—for those situations where an application needs to track users, one simple way is to assign each user an ID. The ID is assigned when the user first accesses the site. From that point on, the user's ID is appended to every URL that

appears on each page that is returned to the user (usually in the form of a query string). For instance, try visiting Amazon.com, a well-known online bookstore. When you first access the site, you are assigned an ID. This ID is then tacked on to the end of the anchor URLs on the page. You can see how it works by simply moving your cursor over all the hypertext links on the page and watching the Browser address bar as you do it. You will see your assigned ID at the end of every URL. This method can be used to append any sort of information. In a shopping cart application, the query string might have all the products the consumer has selected (e.g., "userID=UID001&product1=Shirt09&product2=Tie01"). However, because there are limits on the number of characters in a query string, the method is primarily used when only a small amount of data is to be passed back and forth between the browser and server.

- *Hidden Fields*—a hidden field is a special INPUT tag that looks and acts like a standard INPUT tag in an HTML form. The difference is that the user does not see it. Hidden fields are generated dynamically by the server in response to the end user's actions. Again, in the case of a shopping cart application, hidden fields might be used to store the user ID along with the products he or she has selected. The following shows what the hidden fields might look like in this sort of application:

⟨FORM NAME="cart" METHOD=POST ACTION="www.anystore.com/cgi-bin/shoppingbasket.exe⟩
⟨INPUT TYPE=HIDDEN NAME="ID" VALUE="S001"⟩
⟨INPUT TYPE=HIDDEN NAME="PROD1" VALUE="SHIRT001"⟩
⟨INPUT TYPE=HIDDEN NAME="PROD2" VALUE="SHIRT002"⟩

. . .
rest of form tags
. . .
⟨INPUT TYPE=SUBMIT VALUE="Submit"⟩
⟨/FORM⟩

Here, the shopper would never see the hidden fields. Instead, the user is only shown those fields and objects (e.g., check boxes, radio buttons, and so forth) that are used to obtain more input.

• *Cookies*—a cookie is a small data file created by a Web server, sent to the browser in the HTTP header of the returned Web page, and stored on the client desktop by the Web browser. The use of cookies is controversial. A lot of end users do not like the idea of a Web server being able to write anything to their hard disk that has the potential of doing damage to their computer. For this reason, both of the major browsers give end users the option of turning off the cookie feature. This is why cookies are not a good choice for maintaining state in a B2C application because there is no assurance that the consumer will have the cookie feature turned on. However, cookies can be used with intranet and extranet applications where

Webmasters have more control and can dictate (to a large extent) whether employees should turn the feature on or off.

Of the three techniques, hidden fields are probably the best choice for transferring data from one page to another or recalling user preferences or state variables when a user leaves a page and returns.

References

D. Flanagan and D. Shafer, *JavaScript: The Definitive Guide* (Sebastopol, CA: O'Reilley, 1998).

D. Goodman, *Dynamic HTML: The Definitive Reference* (Sebastopol, CA: O'Reilley, 1998).

S. Gundavaram and A. Oram, *CGI Programming on the World Wide Web* (Sebastopol, CA: O'Reilley, 1998).

S. Isaacs, *Inside Dynamic Html* (Redmond, WA: Microsoft Press, 1997).

J. Keyes, *Datacasting: How to Stream Databases over the Internet* (New York: McGraw-Hill, 1998).

J. Neffenger, "Which Java Scales Best?" *Java World* (August 1998).

Appendix C

Software Agents

For the past 10 years or more, software agents—also known as intelligent agents, knowbots, softbots, or bots for short—have been the subject of a great deal of speculation and marketing hype. This sort of hype has been fueled by "computer science fiction"—personified images of agents reminiscent of the robot HAL in Stanley Kubrick's movie *2001* or the personal assistant Phil in Apple Computer's video *The Knowledge Navigator*. As various chapters in the book demonstrate, software agents have come to play an increasingly important role in EC—providing assistance with Web search, helping consumers comparison shop, and automatically notifying users of recent events (like new job openings). This appendix is provided for those readers who want to learn a little more about the general features and operation of software robots in a networked world like the Web.

C.1 WHY SOFTWARE AGENTS FOR EC, ESPECIALLY NOW?

For years pundits heralded the coming of the networked society or global village. They imagined an interconnected web of networks linking virtually every computer and database on the planet, a web that science fiction writer William Gibson dubbed the matrix. Few of these pundits envisioned the problems that such an interconnected network would wrought. One exception was Alvin Toffler, who warned in *Future Shock* (1970) of the impending flood, not of water but of information. He predicted that people would be so inundated with data that they would become paralyzed and unable to choose between options. Whether they have become paralyzed and unable to choose is an open question. There is no doubt, however, that today's world of networked computers—intranets, Internet, and extranets—has opened the floodgates.

Information Overload

Consider some simple facts:

- Enterprises like Verifone and Sun Microsystems report that employees receive on average over 100 e-mail messages a day. For Sun, that is a million and a quarter messages a day.
- Regardless of the metric used (i.e., growth in the number of networks, hosts, users, or traffic), the Internet is growing at least 10 percent per month. The content of the Web grows by an estimated 170,000 pages daily.
- Surveys of data warehouse projects reveal that a number of the larger retail and telecommunications companies (like Wal-Mart and MCI) have multiple terabyte databases. Based on estimates from the Aberdeen Group, the "average data warehouse can be expected to grow six- to sevenfold every 18 months."

As Paul Saffo, a director at the Institute of the Future, reminds us, we have clearly succeeded in the first half of the information revolution — "access and volume." We have provided end users with "point-and-click" applications that enable them to browse and navigate through gigabytes and terabytes of data to their heart's content.

Unfortunately, end users are often overwhelmed. They spend most of their time navigating and sorting through the data, spending little time interpreting, and even less time actually doing something about what they find. The end result is that much of the data we gather goes unused. For example, according to the Gartner Group:

- The amount of data collected by large enterprises doubles every year.
- Knowledge workers can analyze only about 5 percent of the data.
- Most of their efforts are spent trying to discover important patterns in the data (60 percent or more), a much smaller percentage is spent determining what those patterns mean (20 percent or more), and very little time (10 percent or less) is spent actually doing something about the patterns.
- Information overload reduces their deci-

sion-making capabilities by 50 percent.

What is the solution to the problem of data overload? In Saffo's terms, "How do we bring end users the second half of the information revolution, reducing the flood of data to a meaningful trickle?"

Delegate, Do Not Navigate

As far back as 1986, Alan Kay, one of the inventors of Windows-based computing, recognized the problems associated with point-and-click navigation of very large data repositories and the potential utility of "agent-based" systems for addressing information overload. More recently, Nicholas Negroponte, director of MIT's Media Lab, echoed the same theme in his acclaimed book *Being Digital*. Negroponte said:

> Future human computer interface will be rooted in delegation, not the vernacular of direct manipulation—pull down, pop-up, click—and mouse interfaces. "Ease of use" has been such a compelling goal that we sometimes forget that many people don't want to use the machine at all. They want to get something done. What we call "agent-based interfaces" will emerge as the dominant means by which computers and people will talk to one another.

Value of Software Agents in a Networked World

A major value of employing software agents with intranet, Internet, and extranet applications is that they are able to assist in locating and filtering all the data. They save time by making decisions about what is relevant to the user. They are able to sort through the network and the various databases effortlessly and with unswerving attention to detail to extract the best data. They are not limited to hard (quantitative) data but can also be useful in obtaining soft data about new trends that may cause unanticipated changes (and opportunities) in local or even global markets. With an agent at work, the competent user's decision-making ability is enhanced with information rather than paralyzed by too much input. Agents are artificial intelligence's answer to a need created by internetworked computers.

Information access and navigation are today's major applications of software agents in the intranet, Internet, and extranet worlds, but there are other reasons why this technology is expected to grow rapidly:

- *Mundane personal activity.* In a fast-paced society, time-strapped people need new ways to minimize the time spent on routine personal tasks such as shopping for groceries or travel planning, so that they can devote more time to professional activities.
- *Search and retrieval.* It is not possible to directly manipulate a distributed database system in an EC setting with millions of data objects. Users will have to relegate the task of searching and cost comparison to agents. These agents will perform the tedious, time-consuming, and repetitive tasks of searching databases, retrieving and filtering information, and delivering it back to the user.
- *Repetitive office activity.* There is a pressing need to automate tasks performed by administrative and clerical personnel in functions such as sales or customer support to reduce labor costs and increase office productivity. Today, labor costs are estimated to be as much as 60 percent of the total cost of information delivery.
- *Decision support.* There is a need for increased support for tasks performed by knowledge workers, especially in the decision-making area. Timely and knowledgeable decisions made by these professionals greatly increase their effectiveness and the success of their businesses in the marketplace.
- *Domain experts.* It is advisable to model costly expertise and make it widely available. Examples of expert software agents could be models of real-world agents such as translators, lawyers, diplomats, union negotiators, stockbrokers, and even clergy.

To date the list of tasks to which commercially available agents and research prototypes have applied includes advising, alerting, broadcasting, browsing, critiquing, distributing, enlisting, empowering, explaining, filtering, guiding, identifying, matching, monitoring, navigating, negotiating, organizing, presenting, querying, reminding, reporting, retrieving, scheduling, searching, securing, soliciting, sorting, storing, suggesting, summarizing, teaching, translating, and watching.

Overall, software agents make the networked world less forbidding, save time by reducing the effort required to locate and retrieve data, and improve productivity by off-loading a variety of mundane, tedious, and mindless tasks.

C.2 BRIEF HISTORY OF INTELLIGENT AGENTS

The concept of software agency is surprisingly old. Over 50 years ago, Vannebar Bush envisioned a machine called the Memex that enabled users to navigate through oceans of data and information. In the 1950s, John McCarthy conceived the Advice Taker, a software robot living and working in a computer network of information utilities (much like today's Internet). When given a task by a human user, the software robot could take the necessary steps or ask advice from the user when it got stuck. The futuristic prototypes of intelligent personal agents, such as Apple Computer's Phil or Microsoft's Bob, perform complicated tasks for their users following the same functions laid out by McCarthy in his Advice Taker. While modern approaches to software agency can trace their roots to these earlier visions, current research started in the mid-1980s and has been influenced by work done in a number of fields including artificial intelligence (e.g., reasoning theory and artificial life), software engineering (e.g., object-oriented programming and distributed processing), and human-computer interaction (e.g., user modeling and cognitive engineering).

C.3 DEFINITIONS

Outside the realm of computers, the term agent is well defined. It derives from the concept of agency, referring to employing someone (like a theatrical agent) to act on your behalf. An agent represents a person and interacts with others to accomplish a predefined task. In the computer realm, things are not so simple. There are almost as many definitions for the term software agent as there are people employing it. Here are some examples:

- An agent is anything that can be viewed as perceiving its environment through sensors and acting on that environment through effectors (Russell and Norvig 1995, p. 33).
- Autonomous agents are computational systems that inhabit some complex dynamic environment sense and act autonomously in this environment, and by doing so realize a set of goals or tasks for which they are designed (Maes 1995, p. 108).
- An agent is a persistent software entity dedicated to a specific purpose. Persistent distinguishes agents from subroutines; agents have their own ideas about how to accomplish tasks or their own agenda. Special purpose distinguishes them from the entire multifunction applications; agents are typically much smaller (Smith et al. 1994).
- An intelligent agent is software that assists people and acts on their behalf. Intelligent agents work by allowing people to delegate work that they could have done to the agent software. Agents can, just as assistants can, automate repetitive tasks, remember things you forgot, intelligently summarize complex data, learn from you, and even make recommendations to you (Gilbert 1997, p.1).
- A piece of software that performs a given task using information gleaned from its environment to act in a suitable manner so as to complete the task successfully. The software should be able to adapt itself based on changes occurring in its environment, so that a change in circumstances will still yield the intended result (Hermans 1996, p. 14).
- Intelligent agents continuously perform three functions: perception of dynamic conditions in the environment, action to affect conditions in the environment, and reasoning to interpret perceptions, solve problems, draw inferences, and determine actions (Hayes-Roth 1995).

Besides differing definitions, individual researchers have also invented a variety of synonyms in order to promote their particular brand of software agency. Included among the alternatives are intelligent agent, software robot, knowbot (knowledge-based robot), softbot (intelligent software robot), taskbot (tasked-based robot), autonomous agent, personal assistant, and digital proxy. The different terms can be confusing, although they do serve a purpose. Not only do they capture our attention—a term like knowbot is certainly more engaging than a term like agent—but they also connote the character of the various agents—the roles they play (like tasks) and the features they possesses (like intelligence).

C.4 CHARACTERISTICS OF SOFTWARE AGENTS: THE ESSENTIALS

Although there is no commonly accepted definition for the term software agent, there are several possible traits or abilities that people think of when they discuss software agents. Four of these traits—autonomy, temporal continuity, reactivity, and goal driven—are essential to distinguish agents from other types of software objects, programs, or systems. Software agents possessing only these traits are often labeled "simple" or "weak." Virtually all commercially available software agents are of this sort. Besides these essential traits, a software agent may also possess additional traits such as adaptability, mobility, sociability, and personality. Typically, these latter traits are found in more advanced research prototypes. In this section, we will consider the essential traits. The other traits will be covered in later sections.

Autonomy

As Maes (1995) points out, regular computer programs only respond to direct manipulation. In contrast, a software agent senses its environment and acts autonomously upon it. A software agent can initiate communication, monitor events, and perform tasks without the direct intervention of humans or others.

Temporal Continuity

A software agent is a program to which a user assigns a goal or task. The whole idea is that once a task or goal has been delegated, it is up to the agent to work tirelessly in pursuit of the goal. Unlike regular computer programs that terminate when processing is complete, an agent continues to run—either actively in the foreground or sleeping in the background—monitoring system events that trigger its actions. You can think of this attribute as "set and forget."

Reactivity

A software agent responds in a timely fashion to changes in its environment. This characteristic is crucial for delegation and automation. The general principle on which software agents operate is

"When X happens, do Y" where "X" is some system or network event that the agent continually monitors (Gilbert 1997).

Goal Driven

A software agent does more than simply respond to changes in its environment. An agent can accept high-level requests specifying the goals of a human user (or another agent) and decide how and where to satisfy the requests. In some cases, an agent can modify the goals or establish goals of their own.

C.5 SIMPLE SOFTWARE AGENTS: HOW DO THEY WORK?

Figure C.1 depicts the operation of a "simple" software agent possessing the essential traits described above. The operation of a simple agent is best understood in the context of an example. A good example is an e-mail agent. Virtually all PC-based or Internet-based e-mail packages provide end users with the ability to create agents that scan incoming and outgoing e-mail messages and carry out some predefined action based on the content of the message. Let us see how these agents operate.

Automating a Single Set of Tasks Within a Single Application

Simple agents work within the context of a single application and focus on a single set of tasks with a circumscribed set of outcomes. Much of the work done by these agents automates simple repetitive tasks that could be performed by a person, if that person had the time, the inclination, or was available to do so. This is certainly the case with e-mail agents.

Electronic-mail agents operate within the confines of an e-mail package. Their sole purpose in life is to scan incoming and outgoing messages, looking for various keywords that have been designated by the end user, and performing one or more of a handful of possible operations like deleting the message, forwarding the message, or storing the message within a given folder. Clearly, these are all things that could be performed by the end users. Yet, agents have their advantages. They never sleep (unless the application or the system is shut down). They are always available, even when the end user is away from their desk. They are never bored, and they never miss a word. Some executives, managers, and knowledge workers receive more than 100 to

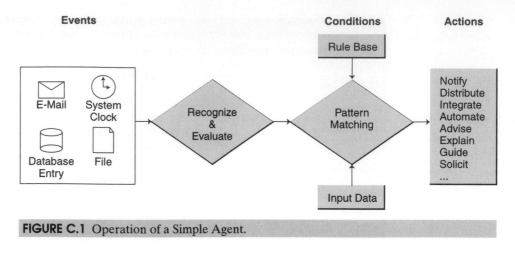

FIGURE C.1 Operation of a Simple Agent.

200 messages a day. Reviewing these messages can be a tedious, time-consuming, and error-prone task. Automating the review with an e-mail agent can off-load some of the review process and "administrivia."

The goals of a simple software agent are explicitly specified by an end user. This is done by either creating a set of "if/then/else" rules or a script that predefines the actions to be taken by the agent when certain conditions arise. The actions are invoked by the agent without end-user intervention.

In the case of an e-mail agent, the goals usually come in the form of if/then rules. Users do not actually input if/then statements. Instead, the end user fills in a form or dialogue box, and the rules are generated from the entries. The entry screen shown in Figure C.2 comes from the "Out-of-Office" agent provided with Microsoft's Exchange and Outlook e-mail packages. Here, the end user specifies both a set of keywords for one or more of the fields in an e-mail message—in this instance, the end user has entered "John Smith" in the "From" field—and an action to be taken by the agent if the specified keywords appear in the designated fields—in this case the message is to be "Forwarded" to "Sarah Jones." When the end user clicks "OK," the underlying if/then rule is automatically generated. For Figure C.2 the rule would read something like, "When the 'out-of-the-office switch is on, *if* a message arrives that has the exact words 'John Smith' in the 'From' field, *then* 'Forward' the message to 'Sarah Jones.'"

Once a set of goals has been established, the agent fades into the background out of sight from the end user, waiting for some system event to occur. The event might be a mouse click or keystroke, the passage of time (measured by the system's internal clock), the arrival of a message flowing across a communication port, a modification to a database, or the deletion or saving of a file in a particular directory. When an event of interest occurs, the agent performs its designated tasks according to the goals that have been specified. With e-mail agents, the events of interest are the arrival or sending of e-mail messages at or from the end user's desktop.

Given that an event of interest has occurred, the agent begins its logical processing. The processing algorithms used by an agent differ from one application to the next. However, the processing usually involves pattern matching of a single item (like a document) against each of the if/then rules that have been established by the end user. If an item satisfies a particular rule, the action specified in the "then" part of the rule is executed. In the case of an e-mail agent, the agent simply compares an incoming or outgoing message against all of the end user's if/then rules. If a message satisfies the conditions specified in the "if" part of the rule, the actions designated in the "then" part are carried out by the agent.

C.6 LEARNING AGENTS

Software agents are called "intelligent" if they have the capacity to adapt or modify their behavior; that is, to learn. Simple software agents, like e-mail agents, lack this capacity. If a simple software agent has any intelligence at all, it is found in the subroutines or methods that the agent uses to do pattern

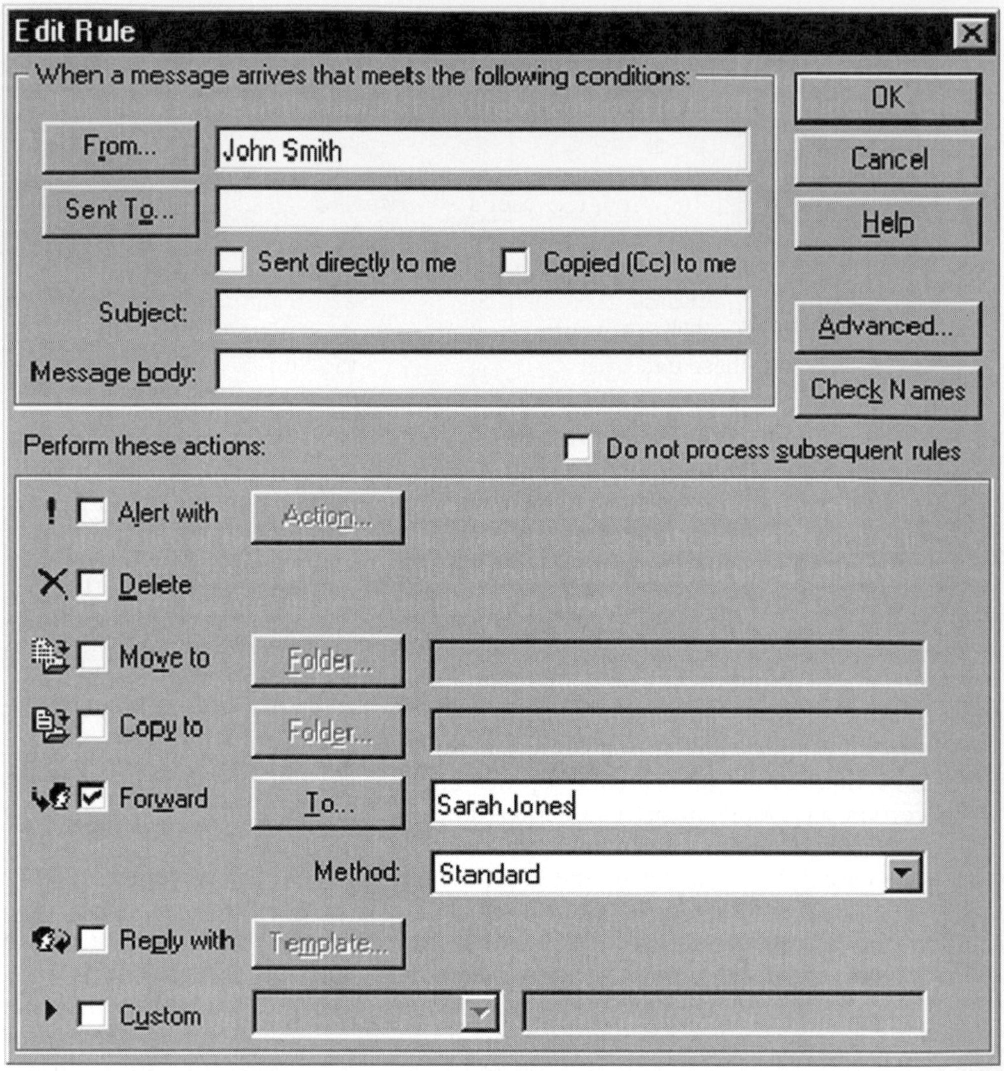

FIGURE C.2 Out-of-Office Agent in Microsoft Mail.

matching. However, these subroutines or methods are built in to the program and cannot be modified by the agent. At present, few, if any, commercially available agents have the ability to learn. There are, however, research prototypes with this capability.

A number of these prototypes have been developed by Pattie Maes and her colleagues at the MIT Media Lab. They have created a series of "user interface" agents employing machine learning techniques and inspired by the metaphor of a "personal assistant." In Maes's (1994) words:

Initially, a personal assistant is not very

familiar with the habits and preferences of his or her employer and may not even be very helpful. The assistant needs some time to become familiar with the particular work methods of the employer and organization at hand. However, with every experience the assistant learns, either by watching how the employer performs tasks, by receiving instructions from the employer, or by learning from other more experienced assistants within the organization. Gradually, more tasks that were initially performed directly by the employer can be taken care of by the assistant.

As Maes suggests, there are four ways for an interface agent to modify its behavior:

1. *"Look over the shoulder" of the user.* An agent can continually monitor the user's interactions with the computer. By keeping track of the user's actions over an extended period of time, the agent can discern regularities or recurrent patterns and offer to automate these patterns.
2. *Direct and indirect user feedback.* The user can provide the agent with negative feedback either in a direct or indirect fashion. Directly, the user can tell the agent not to repeat a particular action. Indirectly, the uscr can neglect the advice offered by an agent and take a different course of action.
3. *Learn from examples given by the user.* The user can train the agent by providing it with hypothetical examples of events and actions that indicate how the agent should behave in similar situations.
4. *Ask the agents of other users.* If an agent encounters a situation for which it has no recommended plan of action, it can ask other agents what actions they would recommend for that situation.

Learning Agents: An Example

The major difference between the operation of an intelligent learning agent and the workings of a simple software agent is found in the ways in which the if/then rules are created. With a learning agent the onus of creating and managing rules rests on the shoulders of the agent, not the shoulders of the end user. To understand the difference let us compare the operation of an intelligent e-mail agent with its simpler counterpart discussed in Figure C.3.

Maxim (Maes 1994) is an intelligent e-mail agent that operates on top of the Eudora e-mail system. This prototype relies on a form of learning known as case-based reasoning. Maxim continually monitors what the user does routinely with e-mail and memorizes the "situation-action" pairs. These pairs are stored in memory as examples. The situations are described in terms of fields and keywords in the message (i.e., the "From," "To," and "Cc" lists, the keywords in the "Subject" field, and so on),

while the actions are those actions performed by the user with respect to the message (e.g., the order in which the user reads it, whether the user deleted or stored it, and so on). When a new situation occurs, the agent analyzes its features based on its stored cases and suggests an action to the user (such as read, delete, forward, or archive).

The agent measures the confidence or fit of a suggested action to a situation. Two levels of confidence are used to determine what the agent actually does with its suggestion. If the confidence is above the "do-it" threshold, the agent automatically executes the suggestion. If the confidence is above the "tell-me" threshold, the agent will offer a suggestion and wait for input from the user. The screen shot in Figure C.3 displays a series of messages along with those suggestions that exceed the tell-me threshold.

Value of Learning Agents

Learning agents address the problem of end-user competence. With simple software agents, the end uscr is required to:

- recognize when an agent should be used,
- create the agent,
- specify the rules to be used by the agent,
- modify or edit the rules to account for changing interests and work patterns.

While learning agents remove all these impediments, they are not a total panacea. Learning agents like Maxim operate on the assumptions that the application involves a substantial amount of repetition and that the repetition varies considerably from one end user to another. Without these assumptions there is no way to build the requisite levels of confidence, nor is there any need to learn the underlying rules if a general set of rules can be applied to all users. Additionally, critics argue that most people do not want "intelligent" agents "looking over their shoulders" (Greif 1994). They contend that simple software agents that require end users to fill out forms are easy to use and provide enough utility for the average end user.

C.7 KEEPING UP WITH AND WATCHING OUT FOR THE FUTURE

Only a few years ago, discussions about software agents were always qualified with the phrase: "In the future software agents will ...." Well, the future is finally here. The Web has proven to be a fer-

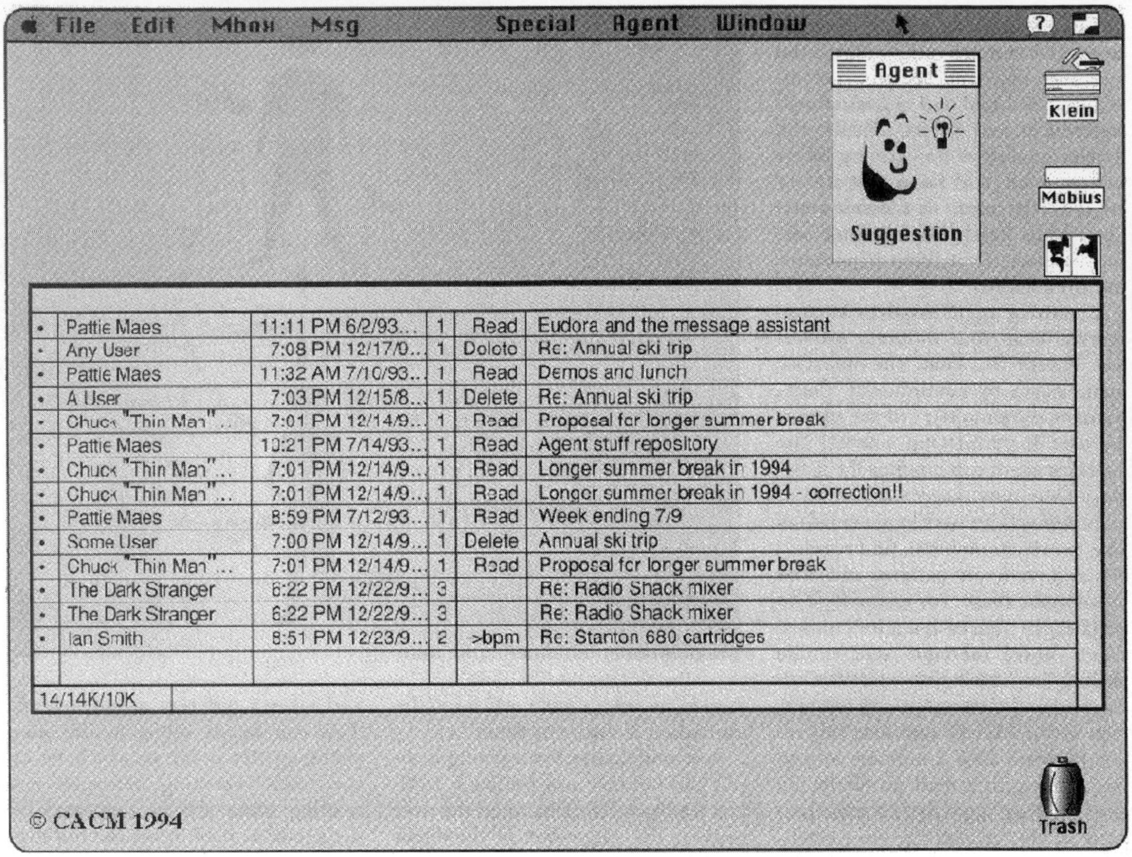

FIGURE C.3 Maxim E-Mail Learning Agent.

tile ground for practical applications of software agents. Auction watchers, comparison shoppers, personal Web spiders, newshounds, site recommenders, and portfolio assistants are some of the agents operating in today's world of EC. It does not stop there, however. If anything, the pace at which existing and experimental agent technologies are being applied to the virtual world has quickened. A good place to monitor new applications of software agents and to keep an eye on both their near-term and long-term future is the Bot Spot Web site (www.botspot.com). The Bot Spot offers a compendium of existing commercial applications and products, as well as pointers to ongoing research sites (academic and commercial). One of the key research sites to watch is MIT's Software Agent Group (agents.www.media.mit.edu/groups/agents). A number of MIT's research projects (like Firefly) have made their way to the Web.

Commercial applications of software agents raise a number of issues about personal privacy. Take, for instance, a software agent that recommends new CDs that you might want to buy. To do this, the agent builds a personal profile of you, collecting demographic information and information about the types of music you like and the CDs that you have purchased. Based on this information, it compares your profile to the profiles of others. It then generates recommendations by finding the profiles of people like you and seeing what they have purchased but you have not. In other words, "birds of a feather" should like the same things. Commercial agents of all sorts are not only privy to your personal profile but also to your personal actions. As you move about the Web under the guidance of an agent, the agent has the potential of knowing where you have been and where you are likely to go. The question becomes, "Whose information is it?" Fortunately, commercial suppliers of agent technology are at least aware of the issues. For instance, Firefly (www.firefly.net), which was one of the early companies trying to bring "recommendation" agents to the Web, has proposed a series of standards like "P3P" (the Platform for Privacy Preferences), which makes individual control and informed consent the key operating principles of software agents. The standards are currently being considered by W3C and the Internet community at large. Only time will tell how effective these standards will be.

References

D. Gilbert, *Intelligent Agents: The Right Information at the Right Time* (IBM white paper, IBM Corporation, Research Triangle Park, NC, May 1997), http://www.networking.ibm.com/iag/iagwp1.html.

I. Greif, "Desktop Agents in Group-Enabled Products," *Communication of the ACM*, 38 (7: July 1994).

B. Hayes-Roth, "An Architecture for Adaptive Intelligent Agents," *Artificial Intelligence: Special Issue on Agents and Interactivity*, 72 (1 & 2: January 1995).

A. Kay, "Computer Software," *Scientific American*, 251 (September 1984).

P. Maes, "Agents that Reduce Work and Information Overload," *Communication of the ACM*, 38 (7: July 1994).

———, "Artificial Intelligence Meets Entertainment: Life-like Autonomous Agents," *Communication of the ACM*, 38 (11: 1995).

N. Negroponte, *Being Digital* (New York: Alfred Knopf, 1995).

J. Russell and P. Norvig, *Artificial Intelligence: A Modern Approach* (Englewood Cliffs, NJ: Prentice Hall, 1995).

D. C. Smith et al., "Kidsim: Programming Agents without a Programming Language," *Communication of the ACM,* 38 (7: July, 1994).

A. Toffler, *Future Shock* (New York: Random House, 1970).

Glossary

Access log file a text file consisting of entries recording each time a Web server is accessed. The contents of an access log adhere to the common log file format standards.

Acquirer a financial institution that establishes an account for merchants and acquires the vouchers of authorized sales slips.

Ad views (also page views or impressions) the number of times an ad is seen by users. Exposure to an ad.

Advertisement dissemination of information in order to influence buyers to buy.

Agent-based services services that are provided by agents such as real estate agents, stock or insurance brokers, or job-finding agents.

Analytical buyers consumers who do substantial research before making a decision to purchase products or services.

Associated ad display strategy the appearance of an ad as a result of a request made for related information.

Authentication a method to verify the buyer's identity before payments are authorized.

Authenticity one of the cornerstones of secure Internet communications, referring to the fact that the sender (either client or server) of a message is who they claim to be.

Bandwidth the speed with which content can be delivered across a network.

Banner a graphic display on a Web page used for advertisement. A banner ad is linked to an advertiser's Web page.

Banner exchange a market where companies can trade or exchange placement of banner ads on each other's Web sites.

Bastion gateway in a dual-homed gateway firewall, this special server connects a private internal network to the outside Internet.

Biometric controls security controls that involve unique physical or behavioral characteristics of an individual (e.g., fingerprints).

Business-to-business EC (B2B) electronic trading where both the buyers and the sellers are organizations.

Business-to-consumer EC a situation where a business is selling online to an individual consumer.

Call center a help desk where customers can communicate by telephone, fax, and e-mail.

Certificate a document that is issued by a trusted third party, certificate authority, to identify the holder.

Certifying authorities trusted third-party companies that issue digital certificates. Individuals use these certificates to verify their identity and to distribute their public keys.

Chat group a real-time online forum for discussing issues of public and personal interest.

Clicks (or ad clicks) every time a visitor clicks on an advertising banner to access the advertiser's Web site, it is counted as a "click" or "click-through."

Clickwrap contracts a contract to use software in exchange for payment derived entirely over the Internet.

Code of ethics a set of ethical behavioral rules developed by an organization or a professional society.

Competitive intelligence information that is useful for analyzing a company's strategic position in the industry. Information about the competitors and their actions.

Competitive strategy a strategy of a company aimed at increasing its competitiveness. It can be offensive or defensive.

Consumer behavior the process by which consumers make decisions to purchase goods and services.

Cookie a web server sends a program, to be stored on the user's hard drive, called a "cookie" frequently without a disclosure or the user's content. The information stored will surface when the user's browser again crosses a specific server.

Cooperative strategy strategic alliance or joint venture strategy with a competitor(s) in an industry.

CPM cost-per-thousand impressions. The cost of delivering an impression to 1,000 people (or homes).

Critical success factors (CSF) the indispensable business, technology, and human factors that would help achieve the desired level of an organization's goal.

Cryptography the process of encrypting and decrypting messages. There are four components involved in the process: (1) plaintext—the message to be encrypted; (2) ciphertext—the encrypted message; (3) encryption algorithm or formula used to encrypt the message; (4) key—secret key used to encrypt and decrypt the cipertext.

Customer loyalty the degree of a customer staying with a specific vendor or brand.

Customer service a series of activities designed to enhance the level of customer satisfaction before, during, and after a purchase.

Customer value the difference between the benefits that a customer is receiving from the acquired products and services and the effort and cost that the customer has to invest to get the product.

Customer-oriented marketplace electronic marketplace, which customers like big companies open to invite bidding.

Cyberbanking (electronic banking) conducting banking from home. It includes many activities ranging from paying bills to securing a loan.

Cycle time the processing time of a business process from beginning to end. Also known as **time-to-market**.

Debit card a card that is used instead of cash in shopping. The buyer's account is instantly debited. It is necessary to get authorization for each transaction.

Decryption the process of recovering encrypted messages.

Defensive strategy strategy that either raises the structural barriers or lowers the inducement for attack.

Deterrence-base trust trust that is related to the threat of punishment.

Digital certificate a digital file issued to an individual or company by a certifying authority that contains the individual's or company's public encryption key and verifies the individual's or company's identity.

Digital envelope the secret key encrypted by the receiver's public key, which is necessary to open prior to decrypting messages encrypted by a secret key.

Digital products digital products that are transformed to information that can be expressed digitally. Music, software, movies, and magazines can be digitized and delivered electronically to buyers.

Digital signature a phrase (like John J. Jones) that is encrypted with a sender's private key and attached like a signature to an encrypted message to ensure that the sender is who he (or she) claims to be. The recipient uses the sender's public key to decrypt the signature.

Direct marketing marketing without intermediaries between the sellers and the buyers.

Disintermediation removing the layers of intermediaries between sellers and buyers.

Distance learning learning off-campus, from home or other places.

Domain name the name used to reference a computer on the Internet like www.abc.com. The name is divided into segments with the top-level domain on the right, the designation of the specific computer on the left, and the subdomain in between the two.

Dual-homed gateway a basic type of firewall in which a bastion gateway server is used to connect a private internal network to the outside. The gateway has two network cards so that communications reaching one card are not directly relayed to the other. The communications between the networks are controlled by special software programs called proxies.

Economics of electronic commerce see Webonomics.

Edutainment combining education and entertainment online.

Electronic auctions auctions conducted online. Initially on private networks, now on the Internet.

Electronic broker (e-broker) electronic intermediary who only introduces the commercial sites and is not responsible for the order fulfillment and guarantee (versus electronic distributor).

Electronic cash (e-cash) cash in an electronic form, usually stored on a smart card and/or in a software called digital wallet.

Electronic catalogs presentation of information about products (services) that traditionally were in paper catalogs. However, electronic catalogs can include multimedia, such as voice and video clips.

Electronic chat an arrangement where participants exchange messages in real time.

Electronic check (e-check) a check in an electronic form, deliverable through the network.

Electronic commerce business transactions that take place by telecommunication networks. A process of buying and selling products, services, and information over computer networks.

Electronic communities Internet communities of people who share the same interest and gather to share information, chat, and collaborate online.

Electronic credit card a credit card used on the network.

Electronic data interchange (EDI) computer-to-computer direct transfer of standard business documents (such as purchase orders).

Electronic distributor electronic intermediary who fulfills the order and arranges for a guarantee. The electronic storefront and malls belong to this category (versus electronic broker).

Electronic fund transfer (EFT) transferring money from one account to others.

Electronic markets a place where buyers and sellers negotiate, submit bids, agree on orders, and if appropriate finish the transactions electronically.

Electronic shopping cart a virtual shopping cart that enables consumers to collect items as they browse an online sales site until they are ready to purchase the items.

Electronic shopping mall (e-mall) a set of independent electronic stores who share an electronic marketing environment such as servers, software, and payment systems.

Electronic store (e-store) a unit of electronic distributor under one management.

Electronic surveillance tracking peoples' activities online (e.g., monitoring e-mail or Web visits).

Electronic (or digital) wallet a software that can store (or retrieve) electronic cash and certificates.

Encryption a process of making messages indecipherable except by those who have an authorized decryption key.

Enterprise resource planning (ERP) an integrated software package for the business.

Ethics a branch of philosophy that deals with what is considered to be right or wrong.

Extranet a network that links the intranets of business partners using the virtually private network on the Internet.

Fare tracker the act of an intelligent agent that monitors fares on certain airline routes and notifies the user periodically on special fares.

Firewall a network node consisting of both hardware and software that isolates a private network from public networks. There are two basic types of firewalls: dual-homed gateways and screen-host gateways.

Full cybermarketing synonym of pure cybermarketing.

Generalized electronic store a store/broker who handles a wide variety of categories of items (versus specialized electronic store).

Global electronic commerce electronic commerce where the buyer(s) is in a different country from the seller. The buyer imports the product (service) from another country.

Hedonic consumers consumers who carry out a shopping activity because it is fun.

Hit Web speak for any request for data from a Web page or file.

HyperText Transport Protocol (HTTP) a lightweight, stateless protocol that Web browsers and Web servers use to communicate with one another.

Identification-based trust trust that is based on empathy and common values with the other trading partner's desire and intentions.

Impressions see *ad views*

Impulsive buyer consumers who purchase products quickly without analysis or much thinking.

Indirect marketing the products and services are sold through third-party distributors (versus direct marketing).

Industry and competitive analysis monitoring, evaluating, and disseminating information from the external and internal environments.

Influencer a person whose advice or views carry some weight in making a final buying decision in consumer purchase decision making.

Information privacy privacy issues related to the use of IT, such as invasion of privacy.

Initiator a person who first suggests or thinks of the idea of buying a particular product or service in consumer purchase decision making.

Integrity one of the cornerstones of secure Internet communications, referring to the fact that the contents of a message have not modified (intentionally or accidentally) during its transmission.

Intellectual property the right of individual (organizations) to receive royalties for copyrighted or patented original work.

Interactive advertisement any advertisement that requires or allows the viewer/consumer to take some action.

Interactive marketing the consumer interacts with the online sellers, e.g., requesting more information, by sending an e-mail or clicking on a link and answering a questionnaire.

Intermediary the third party between sellers and buyers, such as retailing or distributors.

Internet self-regulated network connecting millions of computer networks around the globe.

Internet community a group of people with similar interests who are organized on a Web site where they can chat and collaborate.

Internet mall like a real-world mall, this electronic counterpart consists of a single entry to a collection of electronic storefronts. In contrast to earlier efforts, today's Internet malls have a common look and feel. See electronic shopping mall.

Internet Protocol (IP) in order for one computer to send a request or a response to another computer on the Internet, the request or response must be divided into packets that are labeled with the addresses of the sending and receiving computers. Internet Protocol formats the packets and assigns addresses.

Internet service provider (ISP) private companies supplying local and regional connections to the Internet and providing individuals and businesses with Internet access for a fee.

Internet II see *Next generation Internet*.

Internet-based EDI the EDI that runs on the Internet usually using the Web environment.

Interorganizational information system (IOS) a system that allows information flow between two (or more) business partners.

Intrabusiness EC application of EC methods inside one organization, usually on its intranet, creating a paperless environment. Activities range from internal customer service to selling products to employees.

Intranet a corporate LAN or WAN that functions with Internet technologies behind the company's firewall.

IP Security Protocol a popular tunneling protocol developed by the Internet Engineering Task Force.

Joint venture a cooperative business activity formed by multiple separate organizations for a strategic purpose.

Just-in-time delivery delivering the ordered items at a designated time. This is seriously needed by business buyers who have to run just-in-time manufacturing.

Keyword banners banners that appear when a predetermined word is queried from a search engine.

Knowledge-based trust trust that is grounded in the knowledge of the other trading partner.

Localization the process of adapting media products to a local situation, for example, translating to another language. It considers local culture, language, and other factors.

Market research effort to find useful information that describes the relationship between consumers, products, marketing methods, and marketers through experiments, information search, and processing.

Market segmentation the process of dividing a consumer market into a logical group for marketing research decision making, advertisement, and sales activities.

Marketspace an electronic marketplace (see Electronic markets).

Mass customization producing large numbers (mass) of customized items.

Merchant server packaged software systems designed to help companies establish and run an electronic storefront on a single server (computer). The software usually provides templates for creating an electronic product catalog, setting up electronic shopping carts, handling secure payments, and processing customer orders.

Metatag a metatag gives a spider (search engine) specific information, such as keywords or site summaries.

Micropayment payment of a very small amount.

Microproducts products or services whose price is small, and so is the profit margin. These require electronic micropayments to be traded economically.

Multipurpose Internet Mail Extension (MIME) a header found at the top of all documents returned by a Web server that describes the contents of the document (e.g., a Web page, a multimedia object, or a document produced by an external program).

Network access point (NAP) intermediate network exchange points connecting Internet service providers (ISPs) to the Internet backbone.

Network service provider (NSP) one of the private companies maintaining and servicing the Internet's high-speed backbones. Included among the companies are MCI, Sprint, UUNET/MIS, PSINet, and BBN Planet.

Next generation Internet a U.S. government initiative supporting the creation of a high-speed network, interconnecting various research facilities across the country.

Nonrepudiation one of the cornerstones of secure Internet communications, referring to the fact that the sender of a message cannot deny that they actually sent the message.

Offensive strategy various direct attack strategies on competitors such as frontal assault or flanking maneuver strategy.

One-to-one marketing relationship marketing that treats each customer in a unique way to fit the customer's need and other characteristics.

Online banking see cyberbanking.

Online catalogs see electronic catalogs.

Online market research market research that utilizes the Internet to get more efficient responses.

Online publishing dissemination of newspapers, magazines, and other publishable material on the Internet (intranets). Also, dissemination of material specially prepared for the Web.

Online stock trading buying and selling stocks by giving the order on a PC, usually on a broker's form. Confirmation is done by mail or by e-mail.

Organizational buyer buyers who purchase products and services for organizations.

Organizational mission the purpose for the organization's existence.

Packet in order for one computer to communicate with another over the Internet, the communications or message must be broken down into smaller units called packets. Each packet contains both data and a header specifying the addresses of the sending and receiving computers.

Packet filter rules used by a firewall to accept or reject incoming (network communication) packets based on source and destination IP addresses, source and destination port numbers, and packet type. These rules can also be used to reject any packet from the outside that claims to come from an address inside the network.

Partial cybermarketing a strategy of selling products and services both by the traditional distribution channels and the Internet.

Passive pull strategy sending targeted information to customers either on request or as a result of knowing something about the customers.

Patient buyer consumers who purchase products after planning, analyzing, and comparing.

Pointcasting the delivery of *customized* information using push technology (in contrast to information broadcast to everyone).

Price discovery ability to get discounts through auctions, bids, and other Internet-based searches.

Price discrimination charging different prices from different buyers for the same product (service).

Privacy the right to be left alone and the right to be free of unreasonable personal intrusions.

Privacy policies (codes) organizational policies and rules designed to protect the privacy of employees and customers.

Private key encryption also called a symmetrical key encryption. With this type of encryption, the same encryption key is used to both encrypt and decrypt a message, and the key is agreed upon and shared by both the sender and receiver.

Proactive strategic posture toward cybermarketing a strategy that the company's main distribution channel is the Internet and internal management is focused to effectuate the benefit of cybermarketing (in contrast with reactive strategic posture).

Protocol a set of rules that determines how two computers communicate with one another over a network.

Protocol tunneling technique allowing secure communications across the Internet to an enterprise's internal LAN. With tunneling, the data packets are first encrypted and then encapsulated into IP packets that can be transmitted across the Internet. The IP packets are decrypted by a special host or router at the destination address.

Proxy a special software program that runs on a firewall gateway server, intercepts the communications sent across the Internet, and repackages it so that it can be sent to a secure internal network.

Public key the key that is open to all authorized senders for secure encryption of messages to be sent to the receiver who holds the counterpart private key.

Public key encryption also known as an asymmetrical key encryption. With this type of encryption, a pair of encryption keys are used—a public key and a private key. The public key is made available to anyone who wants to send an encrypted message to the holder of the private key. The only way to decrypt the message is with the private key. In this way messages can be sent without agreeing on the keys in advance.

Purchasing channel different ways products and services are delivered to consumers.

Purchasing decision-making model a process composed of need identifications stage, information search stage, alternative evaluation stage, purchase and delivery stage, and after-purchase evaluation stage.

Purchasing types purchasing behavior that classifies buyers as impulsive, patient, and analytical.

Pure cybermarketing a strategy of selling products and services only through the Internet (versus partial marketing).

Push technology automatically delivered information to a viewer who specifies some requirements. Push technology compiles information from several sources. It is contrasted with pull technology where the user actively searches for information (e.g., by using a search engine).

Quality uncertainty buying from an unknown vendor, or buying unknown brands or products, makes the buyer uncertain about the quality of the product/service provided.

Random banners banners that appear at random, not as a result of the viewer's action.

Reach the number of people or households that are exposed to an advertisement at least once over a specified period of time.

Reactive strategic posture toward cybermarketing a strategy that leaves the traditional distribution methods as the company's main distribution channels resulting in no management style unchanged even though the company has opened on-line distribution channels.

Reintermediation 1) Redefining the role of traditional intermediaries. They provide value-added services that cannot be provided online; 2) Establishing new electronic intermediaries in place of disintermediated traditional intermediaries.

Relationship marketing the overt attempt of exchange partners to build a long-term relationship and association in marketing.

Return on investment a ratio of resources required versus benefits generated. It measures the success of an investment.

ROI see return on investment.

Router special computers whose primary task is to guide the transmission of data packets across the Internet. Routers have updatable maps of the networks on the Internet that enables the routers to determine the paths for the data packets.

Screened-host gateway special firewall architecture with a network router that controls access to a bastion gateway server and ensures that all inbound Internet traffic must pass through the bastion gateway.

Secret key the key that should be kept secret by its owner for encryption and decryption.

Secure electronic transaction (SET) a set of cryptographic protocols jointly developed by Visa, Mastercard, Netscape, and Microsoft and designed to provide secure Web credit card transactions for both consumers and merchants.

Secure socket layer (SSL) a special communication protocol used by Web browsers and servers to encrypt all communications online. This protocol makes secure Web transmissions transparent to end users.

Software piracy copying software without paying for it or without getting permission from the owner.

Spamming sending an unwanted advertisement to users. Analogous to "junk mail."

Specialized electronic store a store/broker who handles a focused category of items (versus generalized electronic store).

Splash screen a multimedia effect designed to capture the user's attention for a short time.

Stateless a property of the Web's HyperText Transport Protocol (HTTP) referring to the fact that every request made by a Web browser for a particular Web document opens a new connection on a Web server that is immediately closed after the document is returned. This means that the server cannot maintain state information about successive requests from the same browser.

Stored-value card a card that stores money value in numbers, like transportation and phone cards.

Strategic alliance partnership of multiple corporations to achieve strategically significant objectives that are mutually beneficial.

Strategic planning planning for a set of managerial decisions and actions that determine the long-term performance of an organization.

Strategy formulation developing long-range plans to effectively manage environmental opportunities and threats in light of corporate strengths and weaknesses.

Strategy reassessment review and monitoring of a strategy after its implementation to evaluate its effectiveness and to decide whether any changes are needed for the future.

Supplier-oriented marketplace electronic marketplace where the supplying companies are passively waiting for customers.

Supply chain management management of all the activities along the supply chain; from suppliers to internal logistics within a company and to distribution to customers. This includes ordering, monitoring, billing, and so on.

SWOT strengths, weaknesses, opportunities, and threats.

Teleweb a call center that adds Web channels and portallike self-service.

Time stamp a cryptographically unforgeable digital attestation that a document was in existence at a particular time.

Transmission Control Protocol (TCP) part of the combined TCP/IP protocol, TCP ensures that two computers can communicate with one another in a reliable fashion. Each TCP communication must be acknowledged as received. If the communication is

not acknowledged in a reasonable time, then the sending computer must retransmit the data.

Trust the psychological status of involved partners who are willing to pursue further interactions to achieve a planned goal.

Tunneling protocol a protocol for secured data transmission across the Internet by authenticating and encrypting all IP packets. See protocol tunneling.

Uniform Resource Locator (URL) the addressing scheme used to locate documents on the Web. The complete syntax for a Web address is: "access-method://server-name[:port]/directory/file". An example of a complete address is "http://www.mycompany.com:80/default.htm," while a shortened address relying on default settings might be "www.mycompany.com."

Utilitarian consumers consumers who carry out a shopping activity to achieve a goal or complete a task.

Value chain a series of activities a company performs to achieve its goal by adding additional values when each activity proceeds from one stage to the next one.

Value-added networks (VANs) networks that add communication services to existing common carriers.

Value-chain partnership a strong and close alliance in which a company forms a long-term arrangement with a key supplier or distributor for a mutual advantage.

Virtual community see Internet community.

Virtual corporation a partnership of two or more companies who create a new organization whose partners are in different locations. The corporation can be temporary or permanent.

Virtual private network (VPN) a special combination of encryption, authentication, and protocol tunneling technologies that provide secure transport of private communications over the public Internet. Most enterprises rely on third-party companies to host their VPNs.

Virtual realtors a real estate agency that interacts with its customers electronically, usually for prepurchasing activities.

Visit a visit is a sequence of requests made by one user to enter a site. Once a visitor stops making requests from a site for a given period of time, called a timeout, the next hit by this visitor is considered a new visit.

Watermarks invisible unobstructive marks embedded in source data that can be traced to discover illegal copying of digital material.

Web content design planning and deciding what to put in the Web applications.

Web hosting the placement of the Web site on a certain server and providing the necessary infrastructure for its operation.

Web team a group of people recruited from different functional areas to accomplish a Web project.

Webcasting Internet-based broadcasting of audio and video content. It is distinguished from standard Web content delivery because it provides a constant stream of information, can be presented live in addition to allowing on-demand listening and viewing, and offers the potential for two-way communication between the broadcaster and the listener or viewer.

Webonomics Web economy. The economic environment and rules of EC.

Index